WEAPON

WEAPON

A VISUAL HISTORY OF ARMS AND ARMOR

LONDON, NEW YORK, MELBOURNE,
MUNICH AND DELHI

SENIOR ART EDITORS Sunita Gahir, Sharon Spencer
ART EDITORS Paul Drislane, Michael Duffy
DESIGNERS Philip Fitzgerald, Tim Lane, Peter Radcliffe
DTP DESIGNERS John Goldsmid, Sharon McGoldrick

SENIOR EDITOR Paula Regan
PROJECT EDITORS May Corfield, Tarda Davison-Aitkins,
Nicola Hodgson, Cathy Marriott,
Steve Setford, Andrew Szudek
US EDITOR Jenny Siklos

PICTURE RESEARCHER Sarah Smithies
DK PICTURE LIBRARIAN Romaine Werblow

PHOTOGRAPHY Gary Ombler
ILLUSTRATIONS KJA-artists.com

PRODUCTION CONTROLLER Elizabeth Warman

MANAGING ART EDITOR Karen Self
ART DIRECTOR Bryn Walls
MANAGING EDITOR Debra Wolter
PUBLISHER Jonathan Metcalf

CONSULTANTS AT THE ROYAL ARMOURIES
Philip Abbott, Head of Library Services
Ian Bottomley, Senior Curator of Arms and Armour
Mark Murray Flutter, Senior Curator of Firearms
Thom Richardson, Keeper of Armour
Bob Woosnam Savage, Senior Curator of Edged Weapons
Peter Smithhurst, Keeper of Weapons

First American Edition, 2006
DK Publishing
375 Hudson Street, New York, New York 10014

A Penguin company

Copyright © 2006 Dorling Kindersley Limited
Foreword © 2006 Richard Holmes

2 4 6 8 10 9 7 5 3 1

Library of Congress Cataloging-in-Publication Data

Weapon. -- 1st American ed.
p. cm.
Includes index.
ISBN-13: 978-0-7566-2210-7
ISBN-10: 0-7566-2210-7
1. Military weapons--History.
U800.W37 2006
623.4--dc22
2006016165

ISBN-13: 978-0-7566-2210-7
ISBN-10: 0-7566-2210-7

Color reproduction by GRB, Italy
Printed and bound in China by Hung Hing

Discover more at
www.dk.com

Foreword   6
Introduction   8

THE ANCIENT WORLD
(3000 BCE–1000 CE)   24

The First Weapons   30
Mesopotamian Weapons and Armor   32
Ancient Egyptian Weapons and Armor   34
Ancient Greek Weapons and Armor   40
GREAT WARRIORS: Greek Hoplite   42
Ancient Roman Weapons and Armor   44
GREAT WARRIORS: Roman Legionary   46
Bronze- and Iron-Age
   Weapons and Armor   48
Anglo-Saxon and Frankish
   Weapons and Armor   50
Viking Weapons and Armor   52

THE MIDDLE AGES
(1000–1500)   56

European Swords   62
Japanese and Chinese Swords   66
European Daggers   68
European Staff Weapons   72
Asian Staff Weapons   74
GREAT WARRIORS: Mongol Warrior   76
Longbows and Crossbows   78
WEAPON SHOWCASE: Crossbow   80
Aztec Weapons and Shields   82
European Helms and Basinets   86
European Jousting Helms,
   Barbutes, and Sallets   88

GREAT WARRIORS: Medieval Knight   90
European Mail Armor   92
European Plate Armor   94

THE EARLY MODERN
WORLD (1500–1775)   96

Two-handed Swords   102
European Infantry and Cavalry Swords   104
GREAT WARRIORS: Landsknecht   108
European Rapiers   110
European Smallswords   112
European Hunting Swords   116
WEAPON SHOWCASE: Hunting Trousse   118
Japanese Samurai Swords   120
WEAPON SHOWCASE: Wakazashi Sword   124
GREAT WARRIORS: Samurai   126
Indian and Sri Lankan Swords   128
European Daggers   130
Asian Daggers   134
European One-Handed Staff Weapons   136
European Two-Handed Staff Weapons   140
Indian and Sri Lankan Staff Weapons   142
European Crossbows   144
Asian Bows   146
Matchlock and Flintlock Long Guns   148
WEAPON SHOWCASE: Matchlock Musket   150
European Hunting Guns 1600–1700   152
European Hunting Guns From 1700   154
Asian Matchlocks   156
Combination Weapons   158
European Pistols 1500–1700   160
European Pistols 1700–1775   162

CONTENTS

European Tournament Armor 166
European Tournament Helmets 168
Asian Armor and Helmets 170
Samurai Armor 172

THE REVOLUTIONARY WORLD (1775–1900) 174

European Swords 180
Amcrican Civil War Swords 184
Ottoman Empire Swords 186
Chinese and Tibetan Swords 188
Indian Swords 190
Indian and Nepalese Daggers 192
European and American Bayonets 194
Indian Staff Weapons 196
African Edged Weapons 198
GREAT WARRIORS: Zulu Warrior 200
Oceanian Clubs and Daggers 202
North American Knives and Clubs 204
North American Hunting Bows 208
Australian Boomerangs and Shields 210
Flintlock Pistols From 1775 212
Flintlock Pistols To 1850 214
Percussion Cap Pistols 216
American Percussion Cap Revolvers 218
GREAT WARRIORS:
   US Civil War Infantryman 220
British Percussion Cap Revolvers 222
Brass Cartridge Pistols 224
WEAPON SHOWCASE: Colt Navy Pistols 226
Self-Loading Pistols 228
Flintlock Muskets and Rifles 232

WEAPON SHOWCASE: Baker Rifle 234
Percussion Cap Muskets and Rifles 236
WEAPON SHOWCASE: Le Page Sport Gun 238
Percussion Cap Breech Loaders 240
GREAT WARRIORS: British Redcoat 242
Sport Guns 244
Ottoman Empire Firearms 246
Single-Shot Breech-Loading Rifles 248
WEAPON SHOWCASE:
   Enfield Rifle-Musket 250
Manually Loaded Repeater Rifles
   1855–1880 252
Manually Loaded Repeater Rifles
   1881–1891 256
Manually Loaded Repeater Rifles
   1892–1898 258
Indian Firearms 260
Asian Firearms 262
Multi-Shot Firearms 264
Ammunition Pre-1900 266
Indian Armor and Shields 268
African Shields 270
Oceanian Shields 272

THE MODERN WORLD (1900–2006) 274

African Edged Weapons 280
Bayonets and Knives 1914–1945 284
GREAT WARRIORS:
   French WWI Infantryman 288
Self-Loading Pistols 1900–1920 290
Self-Loading Pistols 1920–1950 292

Self-Loading Pistols From 1950 294
Revolvers 1900–1950 296
Revolvers From 1950 298
Manually Loaded Repeater Rifles 300
GREAT WARRIORS:
   Red Army Infantryman 302
Self-Loading Rifles 1914–1950 304
WEAPON SHOWCASE: AK47 306
Self-Loading Rifles 1950–2006 308
WEAPON SHOWCASE: SA80 310
Sport Guns 312
Shotguns 314
Sniper Rifles 1914–1985 318
Sniper Rifles 1985–2006 320
Recoil-Operated Machine Guns 322
Gas-Operated Machine Guns 324
WEAPON SHOWCASE: MG43 326
Light Machine Guns 1914–1945 328
Light Machine Guns Since 1945 330
Submachine Guns 1920–1945 332
WEAPON SHOWCASE: MP5 334
Submachine Guns Since 1945 336
Ammunition Since 1900 338
Man-Portable Anti-Tank Weapons 340
Rifle-Mounted Grenade Launchers 342
Stand-alone Grenade Launchers 344
GREAT WARRIORS: US Navy SEAL 346
Improvised Guns 1950–1980 348
Helmets From 1900 350

Index 354
Acknowledgments 360

FOREWORD

Joining the Board of Trustees of the Royal Armouries in 2005 spun my life full circle. As a Cambridge undergraduate I spent a summer working at the Armouries, then located in the Tower of London. Had my career taken a different turn, I might easily have become a curator rather than a military historian. In one sense the two paths are not that divergent, for military history is never far from the battlefield: it is hard to think of men in battle without considering the weapons they use.

Warfare is older than civilization—in fact it is older than the human race itself, as clues from our hominid ancestors show—and weapons are the tools of the soldier's trade. The following pages reveal the importance of weapons, showing how they grew quickly from primitive implements used for hunting wild animals, and soon took on the characteristics that were to define them for thousands of years. First there were percussion weapons, used to strike an opponent directly, beginning with the club and proceeding through axes to swords, daggers and thrusting-spears. There were also missile weapons, propelled from a distance, starting with the sharpened stick—hurled as a javelin—and developing into throwing spears, arrows, and crossbow bolts. Gunpowder weapons, which made their presence felt from the 15th century, did not immediately replace percussion or missile weapons. In the 17th century musketeers were protected by pikemen, and Napoleonic cavalry plied swords in close-quarter combat. Even at the beginning of the 21st century the bayonet, descendent of the edged weapons of yesteryear, is still part of the infantry soldier's equipment.

The huge chronological and geographical spread of this book reveals illuminating similarities between weapons in entirely different cultures and periods. The appearance of firearms was not immediately decisive, and historians argue whether the period of change spanning the first half of the 17th century was rapid and thorough enough to

constitute a "military revolution." However, their impact was certainly profound. Fortresses built to withstand siege-engines crumbled before artillery, and in this respect the fall of Constantinople in 1453 was a landmark. So too were battles like Pavia in 1525, when infantry armed with muskets repulsed armored horsemen. Firearms were essential to the advent of mass armies, for they became subject to mass production. Their development has been rapid: little more than a century and a half separates the muzzle-loading flintlock musket—short-ranged, inaccurate, and unreliable—from the modern assault rifle.

But weapons are more than the soldier's tools, and leafing through the pages you will be amazed at the ingenuity and creativity that weaponry induces for hunting, self-defence, and law-enforcement. Some weapons had religious or magical connotations and others, like the pair of swords worn by the Japanese samurai or the smallsword at the hip of the 18th century European gentleman, were badges of status, and reflections of wealth too. There has been a long connection between the right to carry weapons and social position, and some societies, such as the city-states of ancient Greece, saw a direct connection between civic rights and bearing arms.

It is impossible to consider arms without reflecting on armor too, and this book also illustrates how armor has striven to do more than safeguard its wearers. It is often intended to impress or terrify as well as advertise its wearer's wealth or status: the horned helmet of the bronze-age warrior and the mempo face-guard of the samurai have much in common. The past century has witnessed its rediscovery, and the contemporary soldier, with his Kevlar helmet and body armor, has a silhouette which is both ancient and modern.

It has been a real pleasure to have been involved in this project, which embodies the scholarship of the Royal Armories' curatorial staff and provides a showcase for the Armories' world-class collection.

RICHARD HOLMES

BOWS, ARROWS, AND SPEARS

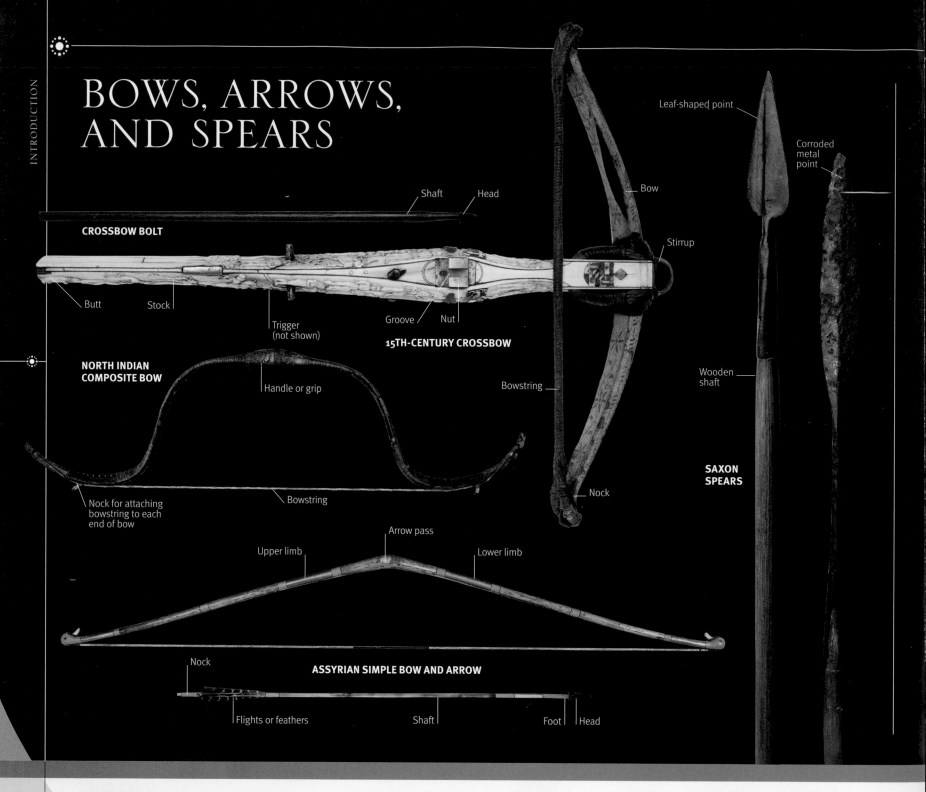

CROSSBOW BOLT

Shaft

Head

Butt

Stock

Trigger (not shown)

Groove

Nut

15TH-CENTURY CROSSBOW

Bow

Stirrup

Leaf-shaped point

Corroded metal point

NORTH INDIAN COMPOSITE BOW

Handle or grip

Bowstring

Wooden shaft

Nock for attaching bowstring to each end of bow

Bowstring

Nock

SAXON SPEARS

Arrow pass

Upper limb

Lower limb

Nock

ASSYRIAN SIMPLE BOW AND ARROW

Flights or feathers

Shaft

Foot

Head

PROJECTILE weapons, such as bows and spears, allow the exercise of force at a distance, and the evident utility of this in hunting led to their use from the very earliest times. The simplest form is the throwing spear, a pole with a pointed end. The principal disadvantage is that once thrown, the weapon is lost and might indeed be hurled back by an enemy. The Roman *pilum* solved this by having an iron shank that bent on contact, rendering further use impossible.

Simple bows are made up of a shaft of wood with a drawstring attached at both ends. In this form, they are easy to construct and operate, and saw use throughout the Ancient World. The composite bow, made of several pieces of wood glued together, its core strengthened with bone and sinew, has greater elasticity, and

therefore a greater range. In the hands of nomadic peoples such as the Mongols, it could devastate infantry formations that would be picked off at a distance. From the 13th century, the English made extensive use of the longbow, a simple bow up to 6½ ft (2 m) long made of yew. It combined range and rapidity of fire, and proved key to victory against the Scots at Falkirk (1298) and the French at Crécy (1346) and Agincourt (1415).

THE CROSSBOW

The crossbow is a form of mechanical bow shooting wooden or metal bolts with a stock that enables it to be kept loaded

without a string being held taut by hand. First attested in Han China (206 BCE–220 CE), they were widely used in medieval Europe from the crusades onward. As time went on, the mechanism to reload (or span) the crossbow became increasingly complex, including the use of foot-operated levers and the cranequin. Such devices allowed the crossbow to be made more powerful, but meant it was slower to reload. By the late 16th century, it had almost disappeared from the battlefield.

JAPANESE ARROW
Japanese samurai used a variety of arrowheads. This type of bifurcated arrowhead, known as a *kurimata*, could inflict multiple wounds and was used for hunting as well as in battle.

AXES AND CLUBS

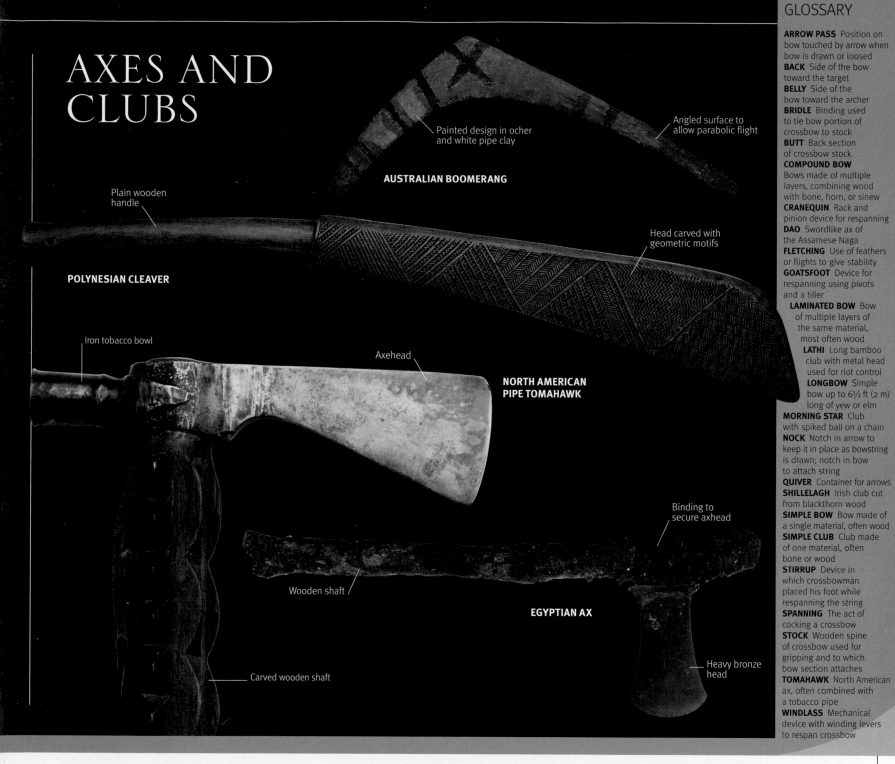

Painted design in ocher and white pipe clay

Angled surface to allow parabolic flight

AUSTRALIAN BOOMERANG

Plain wooden handle

Head carved with geometric motifs

POLYNESIAN CLEAVER

Iron tobacco bowl

Axehead

NORTH AMERICAN PIPE TOMAHAWK

Binding to secure axhead

Wooden shaft

EGYPTIAN AX

Carved wooden shaft

Heavy bronze head

ROCKS and sharpened stones would have been the most primitive form of weaponry. When these were mounted on a stick the result —a club or ax—immediately gave greater range and increased the force, through leverage, of the blow. Clubs could deliver crushing blows to armored opponents, while even a glancing strike from an ax could lead to massive bleeding.

Simple clubs appeared very early, but their effectiveness is proved by their appearance in such diverse forms as the Zulu's *knobkerrie* club, whalebone clubs from the Arctic regions of the Americas, and highly decorated wooden clubs from New Zealand. In the Pacific, such clubs were the most widespread weapon before European colonization. Composite clubs, with a head bound or socketed to a shaft, often added spikes or flanges, with a corresponding increase

in lethality. In Australia, throwing clubs, or boomerangs, were developed, some curved in such a way that their flight carried back to the thrower should they miss their target.

FORGING AHEAD

Hand axes were first used about 1.5 million years ago and were probably used as scrapers. Bronze-headed axes appeared in the Near East in the 3rd millennium BCE and became commonplace as far apart as Egypt and Scandinavia. The invention of iron and steel made the forging of sharper heads with thinner blades more practical. Although the Romans did not make extensive use of the ax, some of their

barbarian opponents employed them, such as the Frankish throwing ax (or *francisca*). The Vikings used a large two-handed battle ax as a principal weapon, and some forms persisted into the Middle Ages in modified form as halberds. In societies that retained a strong hunting tradition, however, axes remained in common use, from the North American tomahawk to the *dao*, a hybrid sword ax, of the Assamese Naga people.

ELITE CLUB

Although wooden clubs were used for fighting in South Africa, this beautifully produced example, with the ball at its end carved into 19 segments, is as likely to have been a prestige object belonging to a notable.

SWORDS AND DAGGERS

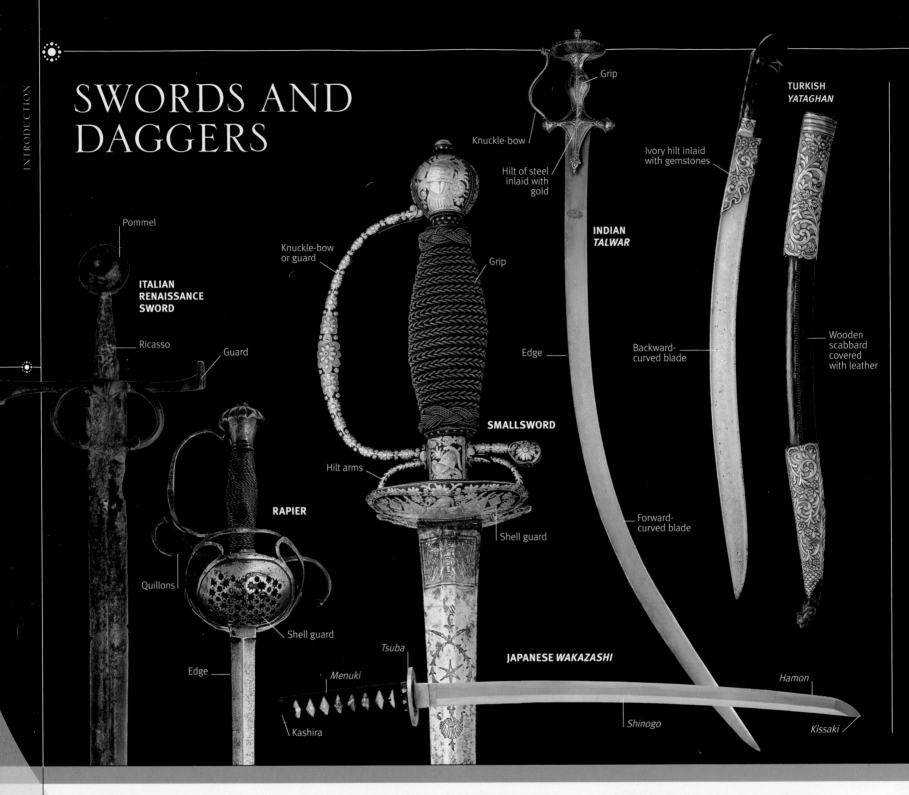

Pommel

ITALIAN RENAISSANCE SWORD

Ricasso

Guard

Knuckle-bow or guard

Hilt arms

RAPIER

Quillons

Shell guard

Edge

Menuki

Tsuba

Kashira

Grip

Knuckle-bow

Hilt of steel inlaid with gold

Grip

INDIAN *TALWAR*

Edge

SMALLSWORD

Shell guard

JAPANESE *WAKAZASHI*

TURKISH *YATAGHAN*

Ivory hilt inlaid with gemstones

Wooden scabbard covered with leather

Backward-curved blade

Forward-curved blade

Shinogo

Hamon

Kissaki

THE sword is one of the most widespread of weapons. In essence a long knife with a grip, its greater length and variations in the blade's shape and areas of sharpness mean it can be adapted for cutting or thrusting. The earliest blades were constructed of flint or obsidian, and it was not until the invention of bronze around the 3rd millennium BCE that swords really came into their own, with blades of increased strength and durability. Minoan and Mycenaean short swords (c.1400 BCE) lack sophisticated grips, but already flanges

CUP-HILT RAPIER

Hilts, such as the cup-shaped hilt on this rapier, became common in the 17th century. On other examples the quillons sweep down to deflect an opponent's stroke.

between the grip and hilt had been designed to protect the wearer's hand. By 900 BCE, with the invention of iron, and subsequently pattern-welding to blend the parts of the blade into a stronger and flexible whole, swords became more lethal.

SWORDS

The Greek hoplite's sword, however, was still a secondary weapon and it was not until the advent of the Roman legionaries' short *gladius hispaniensis*, designed for an upward stabbing stroke at close quarters, that swordplay in its own right became a part of infantry tactics.

By the Middle Ages in Europe, the carrying of a sword became the mark of a military elite. At first they tended to be broad-bladed for cutting and delivering crushing blows against mail armor. With the appearance of plate armor from the 14th century, swords tended to become narrower, more adapted to thrusting at vulnerable joints between the plates. They ultimately developed into the rapiers of the 16th and 17th centuries. Hilts became ever more elaborate, often with cups and baskets of metal bars to protect the bearer's hands.

Outside Europe, the sword reached the apogee of its development in 14th-century Japan.

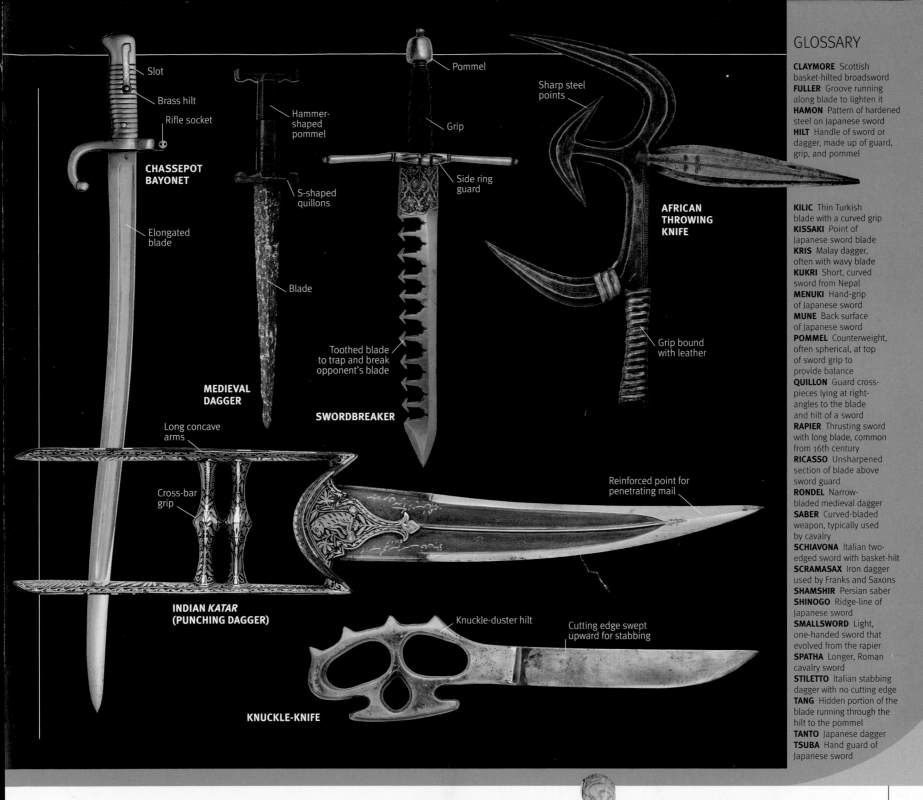

Slot

Brass hilt

Rifle socket

CHASSEPOT BAYONET

Elongated blade

Hammer-shaped pommel

S-shaped quillons

Blade

MEDIEVAL DAGGER

Pommel

Grip

Side ring guard

Toothed blade to trap and break opponent's blade

SWORDBREAKER

Sharp steel points

AFRICAN THROWING KNIFE

Grip bound with leather

Long concave arms

Cross-bar grip

INDIAN *KATAR* (PUNCHING DAGGER)

Reinforced point for penetrating mail

Knuckle-duster hilt

Cutting edge swept upward for stabbing

KNUCKLE-KNIFE

The *katana* long sword of the Japanese samurai was both a badge of rank and, with its layered folded steel blade, a lethally effective blade. The Islamic world, too, had a long history of swordmaking, with Damascus long acting as a center for sword manufacture and trade. The Ottoman Empire, with its emphasis on cavalry, produced many fine types, such as the curved *kilij* and *yataghan* sabers: from Mughal India came the *talwar*, with its characteristic disc-shape pommel.

CEREMONIAL SWORDS

The advent of hand-held firearms, however, rendered the sword—as many other close-quarters arms—almost redundant. In Western armies, the sword survived longest as a combat weapon in the cavalry, where a downward stroke at the gallop with a curved saber could inflict severe wounds. But by the 20th century, the sword was largely a ceremonial weapon, confined to the dress uniforms of officers.

DAGGERS

Daggers were some of the earliest weapons, an evolution of a cutting knife for use in combat. Because of the relative shortness of their blades—from 6 to 19½ in (15 to 50 cm)—daggers are principally a close-quarters weapon, used for thrusting or stabbing.

In Africa, however, throwing knives evolved, with a variety of points designed to pierce at whatever angle they struck the target. Some daggers, such as the Indian *katar*, had reinforced blades and enhanced gripping surfaces to allow the penetration of mail armor. In the 17th century, as fencing techniques became more elaborate, the dagger emerged, wielded in the other hand from the sword to allow parrying and close-in stabbing under the opponent's guard. Occasionally, daggers with toothed edges were used that could catch and break an enemy's weapon. From the 17th century, the dagger gave rise to the bayonet—essentially a dagger attached to a firearm should hand-to-hand combat occur.

The dagger continues to find use among warriors who are liable to find themselves in close contact with the enemy, such as those in the special forces.

MACHETE

A South American weapon with a characteristic curved blade that can be used both for cutting through undergrowth and hacking at enemies. This lightweight palm-wood example is from Ecuador.

STAFF WEAPONS

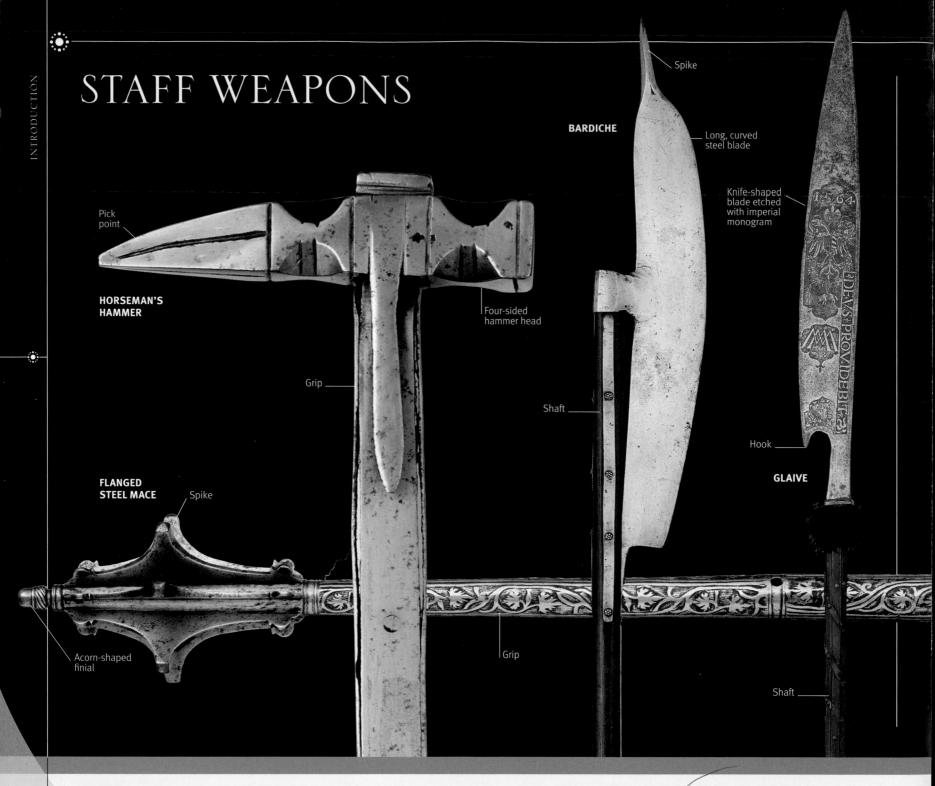

HORSEMAN'S HAMMER

Pick point

Grip

FLANGED STEEL MACE

Spike

Acorn-shaped finial

BARDICHE

Spike

Long, curved steel blade

Four-sided hammer head

Shaft

Grip

Knife-shaped blade etched with imperial monogram

GLAIVE

Hook

Shaft

THE attaching of a blade or club to a long, commonly wooden, shaft to create a staff weapon gave foot soldiers some means to attack cavalry, or at least to keep them at bay. The greatest variety of types were seen in the later Middle Ages and Renaissance in Europe, just at the time social changes pitted infantry militias from Switzerland, the Netherlands, and Italy against armies of mounted knights.

Yet in origin, they are far more ancient than this. The principal weapon of the Greek hoplite in the 6th century BCE was a spear used in a phalanx formation as a thrusting weapon to create an almost impenetrable metal hedgehog. Alexander the Great's Macedonians in the

4th century BCE employed an extended—almost 20 ft (6 m) long—pike (or *sarissa*), but thereafter long-shafted staff weapons largely fell out of favor until the 13th century.

CRUSHING WEAPONS

Among those staff weapons used primarily for close-quarters fighting was the mace, which came to be a symbol of authority in some countries. The Egyptian ruler is seen wielding one on the Palette of Narmer (c.3000 BCE), while in late medieval Europe, the mace became associated with civic and royal power. Its military use was as a crushing weapon that could break bones even when they were shielded by armor.

Steel flanges were often used to focus the force of the blow and to inflict even more severe injuries upon oponents.

Many of the staff weapons that appeared from the 14th century onward had their origins in the modification of agricultural implements. The bill, for example, which had a sharp edge on the inside of the blade, is a modified scythe, while the military fork or trident is an adaptation of the farmer's pitch fork.

JOUSTING LANCE
Tournament lances such as this, with a tapering wooden shaft, were designed to shatter on impact with armor or a shield. If the point, or fragments of the wood, penetrated the neck or helmet, the injuries caused could be fatal.

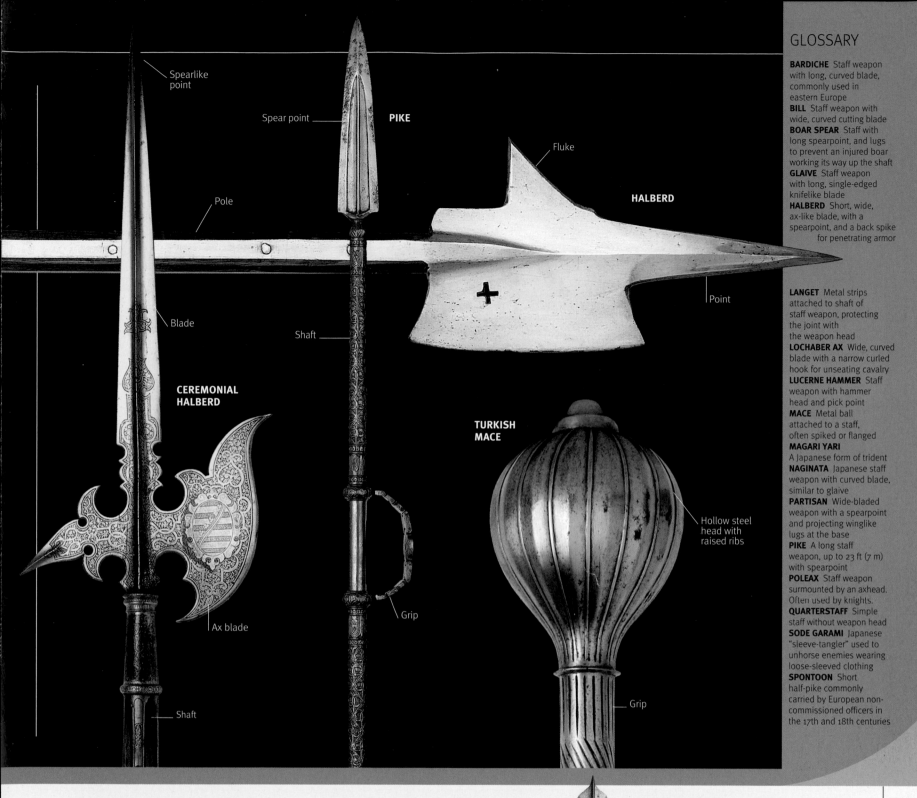

Spearlike point

Spear point

PIKE

Pole

Fluke

HALBERD

Blade

Shaft

CEREMONIAL HALBERD

Point

TURKISH MACE

Hollow steel head with raised ribs

Ax blade

Grip

Shaft

Grip

GLOSSARY

BARDICHE Staff weapon with long, curved blade, commonly used in eastern Europe
BILL Staff weapon with wide, curved cutting blade
BOAR SPEAR Staff with long spearpoint, and lugs to prevent an injured boar working its way up the shaft
GLAIVE Staff weapon with long, single-edged knifelike blade
HALBERD Short, wide, ax-like blade, with a spearpoint, and a back spike for penetrating armor

LANGET Metal strips attached to shaft of staff weapon, protecting the joint with the weapon head
LOCHABER AX Wide, curved blade with a narrow curled hook for unseating cavalry
LUCERNE HAMMER Staff weapon with hammer head and pick point
MACE Metal ball attached to a staff, often spiked or flanged
MAGARI YARI A Japanese form of trident
NAGINATA Japanese staff weapon with curved blade, similar to glaive
PARTISAN Wide-bladed weapon with a spearpoint and projecting winglike lugs at the base
PIKE A long staff weapon, up to 23 ft (7 m) with spearpoint
POLEAX Staff weapon surmounted by an axhead. Often used by knights.
QUARTERSTAFF Simple staff without weapon head
SODE GARAMI Japanese "sleeve-tangler" used to unhorse enemies wearing loose-sleeved clothing
SPONTOON Short half-pike commonly carried by European non-commissioned officers in the 17th and 18th centuries

The pike, a simple variant of the ancient form, became the most widespread staff weapon, having earlier fallen out of favor. Wielded in dense formation by infantrymen, most notably the Swiss, and in mixed formations, such as the Spanish *tercio*, as a defensive shield behind which musketeers could fire, it would prove to be a useful multipurpose weapon. The pike showed its effectiveness in battles such as Courtrai (1302) where Flemish militiamen armed with long spears and wooden clubs (or *goedendags*) disrupted a charge by French knights and then hacked them to pieces.

LATER STAFF WEAPONS

The addition of an axhead to a pike point, along with a spike on the back of the head, created a halberd, a versatile weapon that— shorter than a pike—could be used for thrusting, hooking cavalrymen from horses, or clubbing. A common type of staff weapon in eastern Europe was the bardiche, which had a long cutting edge similar to an ax, but lacked the pointed end of the halberd.

Particularly in use among cavalrymen was the war-hammer—with a hammer head on one side of the shaft-head and a picklike blade on the other. The hammer was used to stun opponents, the pick to penetrate armor to finish them off.

The increasing importance of firearms, however, meant fewer infantrymen were equipped with staff weapons. Increasingly they became badges of office for non-commissioned officers, lingering on into the 18th and 19th century as the spontoon.

Yet just at this time, staff weapons in the form of the lance gained wider use in cavalry formations. Having their origins in the jousting weapons of medieval knights, lances were reintroduced in Napoleonic times as a shock weapon for units of Uhlans. As late as World War I, lances were still carried by the cavalry of some armies, but by then, both staff weapons and cavalry itself were relics of a past era.

GERMAN PARTISAN
Almost the last type of staff weapon to survive was the partisan. Decorative versions, such as this late-17th century German example, were used as badges of office by sergeants and other non-commissioned officers.

13

FIREARMS

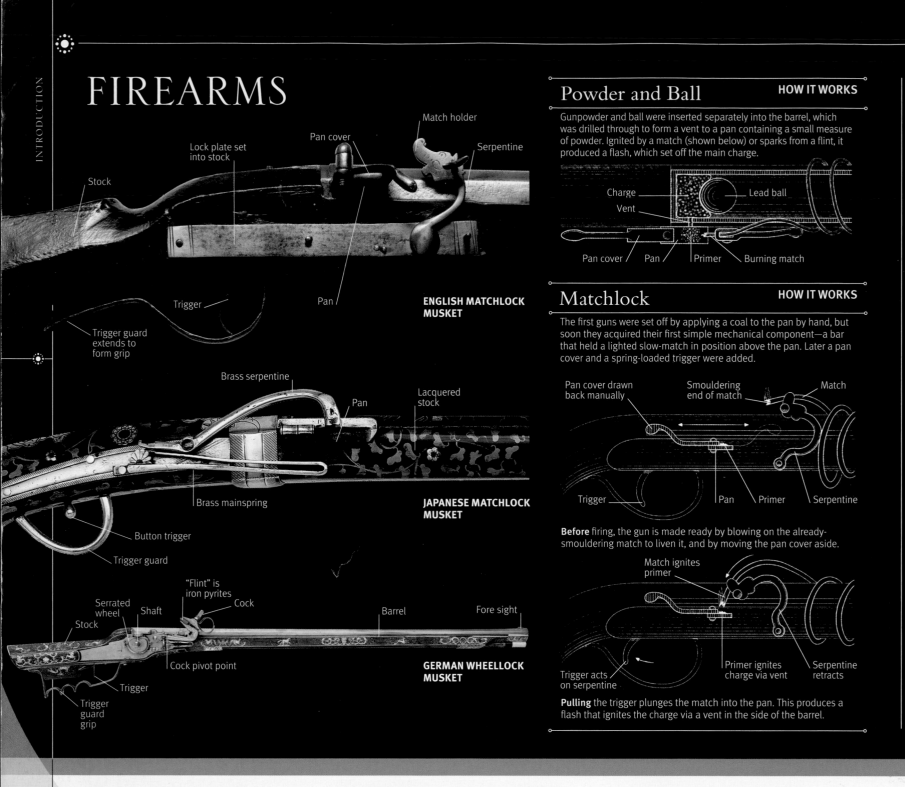

Match holder

Pan cover

Lock plate set into stock

Serpentine

Stock

Trigger

Pan

ENGLISH MATCHLOCK MUSKET

Trigger guard extends to form grip

Brass serpentine

Pan

Lacquered stock

Brass mainspring

JAPANESE MATCHLOCK MUSKET

Button trigger

Trigger guard

"Flint" is iron pyrites

Cock

Serrated wheel

Shaft

Barrel

Fore sight

Stock

Cock pivot point

GERMAN WHEELLOCK MUSKET

Trigger

Trigger guard grip

Powder and Ball

HOW IT WORKS

Gunpowder and ball were inserted separately into the barrel, which was drilled through to form a vent to a pan containing a small measure of powder. Ignited by a match (shown below) or sparks from a flint, it produced a flash, which set off the main charge.

Charge

Lead ball

Vent

Pan cover

Pan

Primer

Burning match

Matchlock

HOW IT WORKS

The first guns were set off by applying a coal to the pan by hand, but soon they acquired their first simple mechanical component—a bar that held a lighted slow-match in position above the pan. Later a pan cover and a spring-loaded trigger were added.

Pan cover drawn back manually

Smouldering end of match

Match

Trigger

Pan

Primer

Serpentine

Before firing, the gun is made ready by blowing on the already-smouldering match to liven it, and by moving the pan cover aside.

Match ignites primer

Trigger acts on serpentine

Primer ignites charge via vent

Serpentine retracts

Pulling the trigger plunges the match into the pan. This produces a flash that ignites the charge via a vent in the side of the barrel.

THERE is no certainty as to where gunpowder was invented; China, India, The Middle East, and Europe all have their supporters. As to when, most agree that it took place sometime during the 13th century, though it may have been earlier. We can be a little more precise about the invention of the gun, however. This took place prior to 1326, for two separate contemporary manuscripts tell us so, and from that date onward, references to guns become more frequent. The earliest known example of a gun was found in the ruins of the castle of Monte Varino, in Italy, which was destroyed in 1341. The gun was a simple tube, closed at one end and drilled through near that end to allow the charge of powder inside to be ignited with a glowing wire or coal. It was fitted with a pole at the breech, and probably required two men to fire it.

MATCHLOCKS

The first improvement to this simple design, which created the matchlock, saw the addition of a serpentine (so-called because it was S-shaped and resembled a snake) which held a length of string (or "slow-match"), treated with saltpeter to keep it alight. The serpentine was pivoted around its center; pulling back on its lower arm pushed its upper arm forward, touching the glowing end of the string into the priming powder. The latter lay in a pan outside the barrel, but was connected to the main charge of powder and ball by a touch-hole. The chief advantage of this design was that one man could use it on his own. A trigger was added later, to act upon the serpentine

by way of a connecting sear, along with a spring that held the match off the pan until positive pressure was applied to the trigger. A version was also produced in which the spring worked the other way (when the sear was released, it propelled the match forward)—but the impact often extinguished the match.

WHEELLOCK PISTOL
Known as the wheellock, the first attempt to detonate the charge mechanically used a wheel, wound against a spring and released by the trigger. Iron pyrites held to the wheel gave off sparks, which lit the priming.

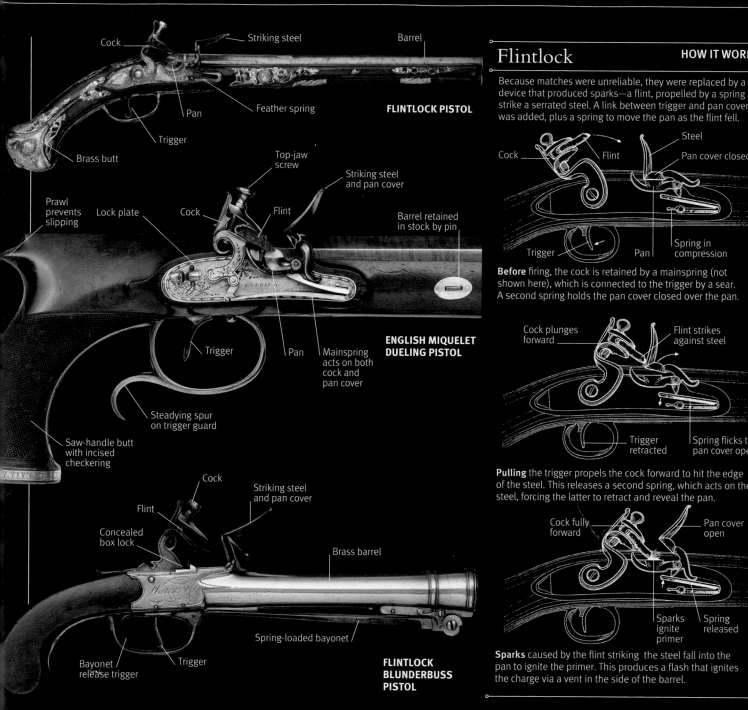

FLINTLOCK PISTOL
Cock — Striking steel — Barrel
Pan — Feather spring
Trigger
Brass butt

ENGLISH MIQUELET DUELING PISTOL
Prawl prevents slipping — Lock plate — Cock — Top-jaw screw — Flint — Striking steel and pan cover — Barrel retained in stock by pin
Trigger — Pan — Mainspring acts on both cock and pan cover
Steadying spur on trigger guard
Saw-handle butt with incised checkering

FLINTLOCK BLUNDERBUSS PISTOL
Cock — Striking steel and pan cover — Flint — Concealed box lock — Brass barrel
Bayonet release trigger — Trigger — Spring-loaded bayonet

Flintlock

HOW IT WORKS

Because matches were unreliable, they were replaced by a device that produced sparks—a flint, propelled by a spring to strike a serrated steel. A link between trigger and pan cover was added, plus a spring to move the pan as the flint fell.

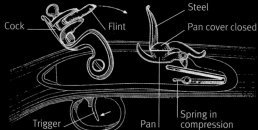

Cock — Flint — Steel — Pan cover closed
Trigger — Pan — Spring in compression

Before firing, the cock is retained by a mainspring (not shown here), which is connected to the trigger by a sear. A second spring holds the pan cover closed over the pan.

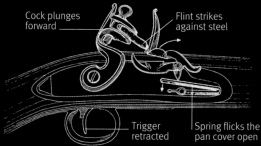

Cock plunges forward — Flint strikes against steel
Trigger retracted — Spring flicks the pan cover open

Pulling the trigger propels the cock forward to hit the edge of the steel. This releases a second spring, which acts on the steel, forcing the latter to retract and reveal the pan.

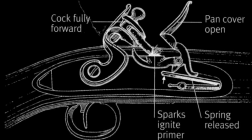

Cock fully forward — Pan cover open
Sparks ignite primer — Spring released

Sparks caused by the flint striking the steel fall into the pan to ignite the primer. This produces a flash that ignites the charge via a vent in the side of the barrel.

Despite various improvements, however, the matchlock remained a cumbersome and unpredictable device. Far more reliable was the wheellock, invented around 1500, which used a wheel turned by a coiled spring to strike sparks from pyrites into the pan. Though complicated, it made it possible for the gun to be used one-handed and for it to be held ready for use.

FLINTLOCKS

The next step was to find a simpler way of creating sparks. This was achieved by using a spring-loaded flint (which lasted longer than pyrites) and bringing it into contact with a suitably-shaped serrated steel,

striking sparks from it in the process. The first such lock was known in English as a snaphance, or snaphaunce, a corruption of a Dutch phrase, *schnapp hahn*, "pecking hen," which described the action of what became known as the cock.

The snaphance originated in northern Europe, but at around the same time, a very similar device was coming into use in Italy. It had shortcomings, notably the way the pan cover was displaced by an awkward linkage to the trigger, but these were overcome in Spain about halfway through the 16th century by the simple expedient of extending the foot of the steel to become the pancover, and flicking it out of the way

at the vital moment by means of the exposed mainspring, creating the miquelet lock.

About 60 years later, a French gunmaker, Marin le Bourgeois, combined the one-piece steel and pan cover of the miquelet lock with the internal mainspring of the snaphance to produce the first true flintlock. Later improvements were minor, and saw the addition of roller bearings and strengthening bridles.

HADLEY FLINTLOCK SPORT GUN, 1770
The flintlock was perfected by about 1750, having acquired roller bearings to act on the springs and bridles to hold the components in perfect alignment. This shotgun is an example of the flintlock in its heyday.

FIREARMS

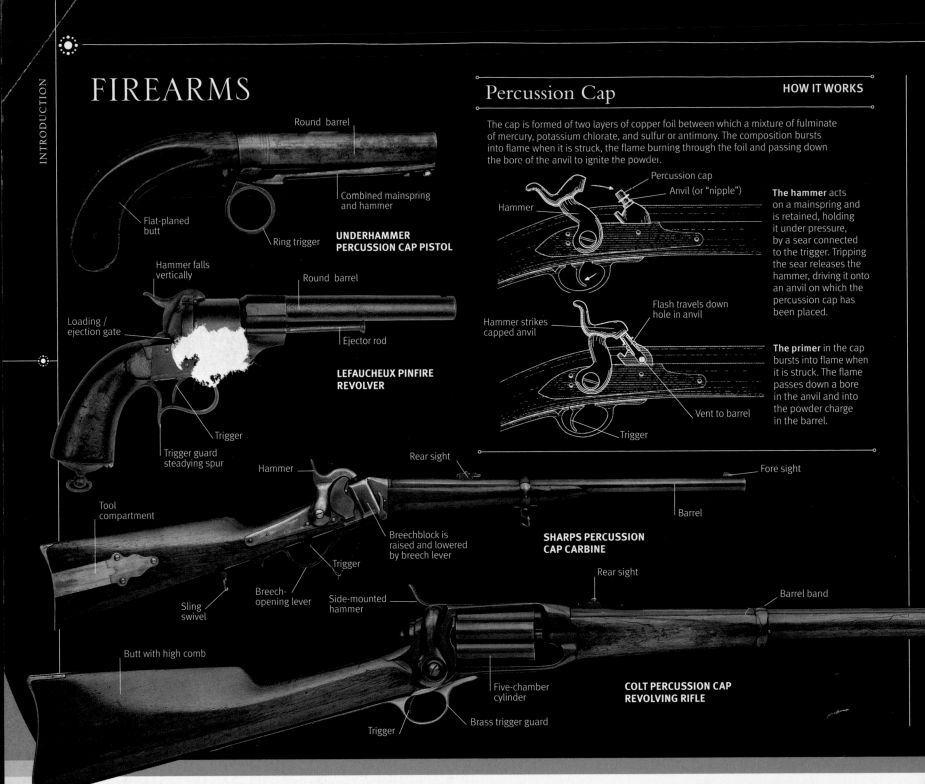

Round barrel

Combined mainspring and hammer

Flat-planed butt

Ring trigger

UNDERHAMMER PERCUSSION CAP PISTOL

Hammer falls vertically

Round barrel

Loading / ejection gate

Ejector rod

LEFAUCHEUX PINFIRE REVOLVER

Trigger

Trigger guard steadying spur

Hammer

Rear sight

Fore sight

Tool compartment

Barrel

Breechblock is raised and lowered by breech lever

SHARPS PERCUSSION CAP CARBINE

Trigger

Breech-opening lever

Side-mounted hammer

Rear sight

Barrel band

Sling swivel

Butt with high comb

COLT PERCUSSION CAP REVOLVING RIFLE

Five-chamber cylinder

Brass trigger guard

Trigger

Percussion Cap

HOW IT WORKS

The cap is formed of two layers of copper foil between which a mixture of fulminate of mercury, potassium chlorate, and sulfur or antimony. The composition bursts into flame when it is struck, the flame burning through the foil and passing down the bore of the anvil to ignite the powder.

Percussion cap

Anvil (or "nipple")

Hammer

The hammer acts on a mainspring and is retained, holding it under pressure, by a sear connected to the trigger. Tripping the sear releases the hammer, driving it onto an anvil on which the percussion cap has been placed.

Flash travels down hole in anvil

Hammer strikes capped anvil

The primer in the cap bursts into flame when it is struck. The flame passes down a bore in the anvil and into the powder charge in the barrel.

Vent to barrel

Trigger

PERCUSSION CAPS

Even in its most efficient form, the flintlock had its drawbacks. Chief among these were the need for the flint to be kept in precisely the right shape and place, and for the touch-hole to be kept clear of residue. There was also a delay between the cock falling and the gun firing. Fulminating salts, which exploded on impact, had been known for over a century, but they were still too volatile to be a practical substitute for flint. Then, in 1800, Edward Howard synthesized fulminate of mercury, which was relatively docile. The Reverend Alexander Forsyth (a keen wildfowler) combined it with potassium chlorate and used the new priming to detonate gunpowder. It was another 20 years before a reliable system of delivering fulminate primer to the breech, in the shape of percussion caps, was developed, but when it was (probably by British-born artist Joshua Shaw, working in the US in 1822), it rendered all other ignition systems obsolete.

REVOLVERS

The first firearms produced to exploit the new development were conversions of existing weapons (single-shot muzzle-loading pistols and rifles), but they were soon joined by multiple-barreled pistols, known as pepperboxes, in which a group of barrels was mounted on an axial rod which was turned, complete with charge and percussion cap, to present a fresh barrel to the hammer. And then, in 1836, a young American named Samuel Colt patented the cylinder revolver, and began producing both pistols and rifles in this form. Colt's guns could fire six shots in a few seconds, but they were still slow to load, even though the loading process had become easier with the invention of the waterproof cartridge, which contained both charge and projectile and didn't have to be introduced via the muzzle.

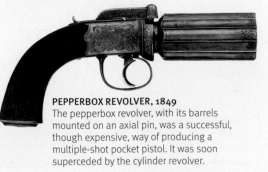

PEPPERBOX REVOLVER, 1849
The pepperbox revolver, with its barrels mounted on an axial pin, was a successful, though expensive, way of producing a multiple-shot pocket pistol. It was soon superceded by the cylinder revolver.

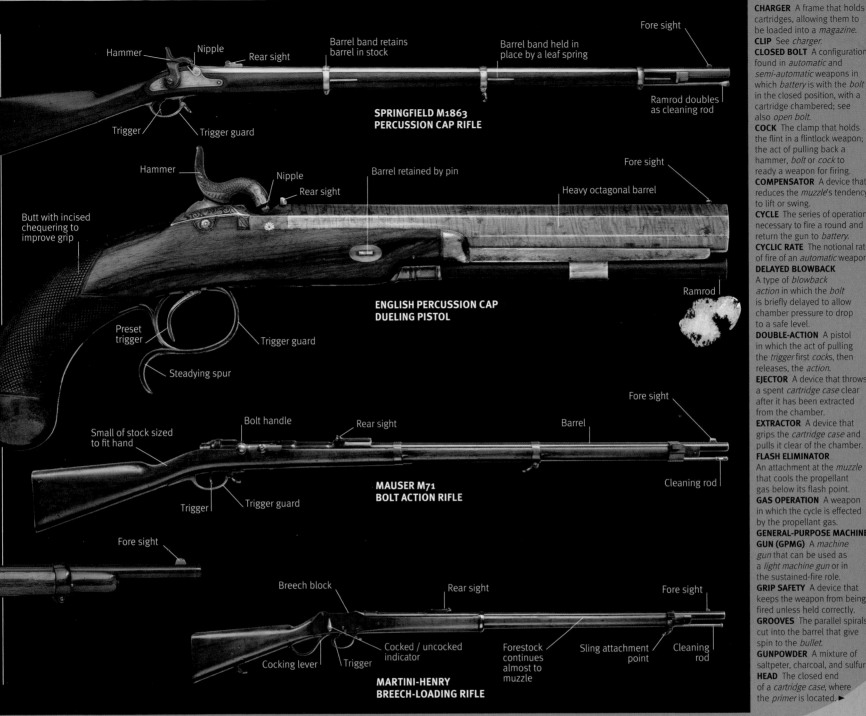

Hammer
Nipple
Rear sight
Barrel band retains barrel in stock
Barrel band held in place by a leaf spring
Fore sight
Ramrod doubles as cleaning rod
Trigger
Trigger guard

SPRINGFIELD M1863 PERCUSSION CAP RIFLE

Hammer
Nipple
Rear sight
Barrel retained by pin
Fore sight
Heavy octagonal barrel
Butt with incised chequering to improve grip
Preset trigger
Trigger guard
Steadying spur
Ramrod

ENGLISH PERCUSSION CAP DUELING PISTOL

Small of stock sized to fit hand
Bolt handle
Rear sight
Barrel
Fore sight
Trigger
Trigger guard
Cleaning rod

MAUSER M71 BOLT ACTION RIFLE

Fore sight
Breech block
Rear sight
Fore sight
Cocking lever
Trigger
Cocked / uncocked indicator
Forestock continues almost to muzzle
Sling attachment point
Cleaning rod

MARTINI-HENRY BREECH-LOADING RIFLE

CHARGER A frame that holds cartridges, allowing them to be loaded into a *magazine*.
CLIP See *charger*.
CLOSED BOLT A configuration found in *automatic* and *semi-automatic* weapons in which *battery* is with the *bolt* in the closed position, with a cartridge chambered; see also *open bolt*.
COCK The clamp that holds the flint in a flintlock weapon; the act of pulling back a hammer, *bolt* or *cock* to ready a weapon for firing.
COMPENSATOR A device that reduces the *muzzle*'s tendency to lift or swing.
CYCLE The series of operations necessary to fire a round and return the gun to *battery*.
CYCLIC RATE The notional rate of fire of an *automatic* weapon.
DELAYED BLOWBACK A type of *blowback action* in which the *bolt* is briefly delayed to allow chamber pressure to drop to a safe level.
DOUBLE-ACTION A pistol in which the act of pulling the *trigger* first *cock*s, then releases, the *action*.
EJECTOR A device that throws a spent *cartridge case* clear after it has been extracted from the chamber.
EXTRACTOR A device that grips the *cartridge case* and pulls it clear of the chamber.
FLASH ELIMINATOR An attachment at the *muzzle* that cools the propellant gas below its flash point.
GAS OPERATION A weapon in which the cycle is effected by the propellant gas.
GENERAL-PURPOSE MACHINE GUN (GPMG) A *machine gun* that can be used as a *light machine gun* or in the sustained-fire role.
GRIP SAFETY A device that keeps the weapon from being fired unless held correctly.
GROOVES The parallel spirals cut into the barrel that give spin to the *bullet*.
GUNPOWDER A mixture of saltpeter, charcoal, and sulfur.
HEAD The closed end of a *cartridge case*, where the *primer* is located. ►

Colt enjoyed a monopoly until 1857, but by the 1850s gunmakers on both sides of the Atlantic had begun to consider afresh the thorny problem of how to load a gun at the breech and then to make a gas-tight seal there—a process called obturation.

BRASS CARTRIDGES

Already, by about 1840, Parisian gunmaker Louis Flobert had produced the first brass cartridges—tiny affairs (used for indoor target practice) in which the propellant was fulminate. Flobert showed his cartridges at the Great Exhibition in London in 1851, and thus to every gunmaker of note in the world. One of these, Daniel Wesson, took the idea further, and combined fulminate primer, contained in the rim of a brass case, with gunpowder and a bullet;

the unitary brass cartridge was born. This new type of cartridge solved two problems at once. It combined all the elements of a gun's ammunition into one package, and it guaranteed perfect obturation, since the brass casing itself formed the seal at the breech. Rim-fire cartridges were imperfect and soon disappeared in all but the smallest calibers, but more robust center-fire cartridges were available by 1866, and soon the world's armies were clamoring for them. Just as the first percussion weapons had been converted flintlocks, so the first martial breech-loaders were converted muzzle-loaders, but these were stop-gap measures,

and it was only a few years before the first purpose-designed breech-loaders, such as the Martini-Henry and the Mauser M71, were being issued.

THE GATLING GUN, 1875
Richard Gatling produced his first workable hand-cranked multiple-barrel machine gun in 1862. Cartridges were introduced from a top-mounted hopper into the open breech of the barrel in the twelve o'clock position. The breech closed on its way down to six o'clock, where that barrel was fired, and opened again on its way back up.

FIREARMS

WINCHESTER 1866 UNDERLEVER RIFLE

- Fore sight
- Barrel
- Barrel band
- Rear sight
- Exposed hammer
- Ring to hang rifle on saddle
- Tubular magazine
- Trigger
- Trigger guard extends to form cocking lever

COLT SINGLE-ACTION ARMY REVOLVER

- Hammer notched to act as rear sight
- Hinged loading/ejection gate
- Six-chamber fluted cylinder
- Spring-loaded ejector rod
- Barrel
- Blade fore sight
- Trigger
- Hard rubber grip
- Lanyard ring

REMINGTON DOUBLE DERRINGER PISTOL

- Hammer
- Barrel hinge
- Over-and-under barrels
- Fore sight
- Stud trigger

SMITH & WESSON MILITARY AND POLICE REVOLVER

- Blade fore sight
- Six-chamber cylinder
- Cylinder locking slot
- Hammer
- Cylinder release catch
- Ejector rod
- Cylinder gate pin
- Trigger
- Lanyard ring

LEE-ENFIELD NO 4 BOLT ACTION RIFLE

- Rear sight
- Bolt
- Forestock extends almost to the muzzle
- Protected fore sight
- Bolt handle
- Trigger
- Magazine release catch
- Detachable magazine
- Studded muzzle
- Sling swivel

REPEATER FIREARMS

At the other end of the scale, Wesson and his partner Horace Smith, who had worked for Winchester, had turned their attention to designing a revolver to take brass cartridges, but had discovered that a patent already existed for the "bored-through" cylinder that they needed to utilize. Fortunately, they were able to acquire it, in return for a royalty of 15 cents for every gun they produced, and in 1857, as soon as they were free to exploit Colt's patent, they unveiled the first effective cartridge revolver. Colt was then frustrated by patent protection in his turn, and it was only in 1873, 11 years after his death, that his company was able to bring out another world-beater: the Single-Action Army revolver, widely known as the Peacemaker. Elsewhere, others were attempting to exploit the

self-contained nature of the brass cartridge to produce other types of repeating firearm. Two were notably successful early on: Christopher Spencer and Benjamin Tyler Henry, both of whom produced tubular magazine repeater rifles in 1860 (Spencer's had its magazine in the butt; Henry's was below the barrel). Both were imperfect, however, for they could only handle low-powered ammunition, and this did not satisfy military requirements. The US Army, therefore, clung to its single-shot breech-loaders, but in Europe, thanks largely to the Mauser brothers' success with the M/71, attention swung to designing

rifles with rotating bolts. Spencer's and Henry's guns had another weakness, too: their tubular magazines. The problem lay in the fact that the tip of the bullet was lodged against the primer of the cartridge ahead of it, and in certain circumstances could work as a firing pin, with catastrophic results.

SPRINGFIELD M1903
The US Army kept single-shot breech-loaders until 1892, when it adopted a bolt-action magazine rifle, the Norwegian Krag. In 1903 it replaced the Krag with a modified Mauser type rifle from the Springfield Armory.

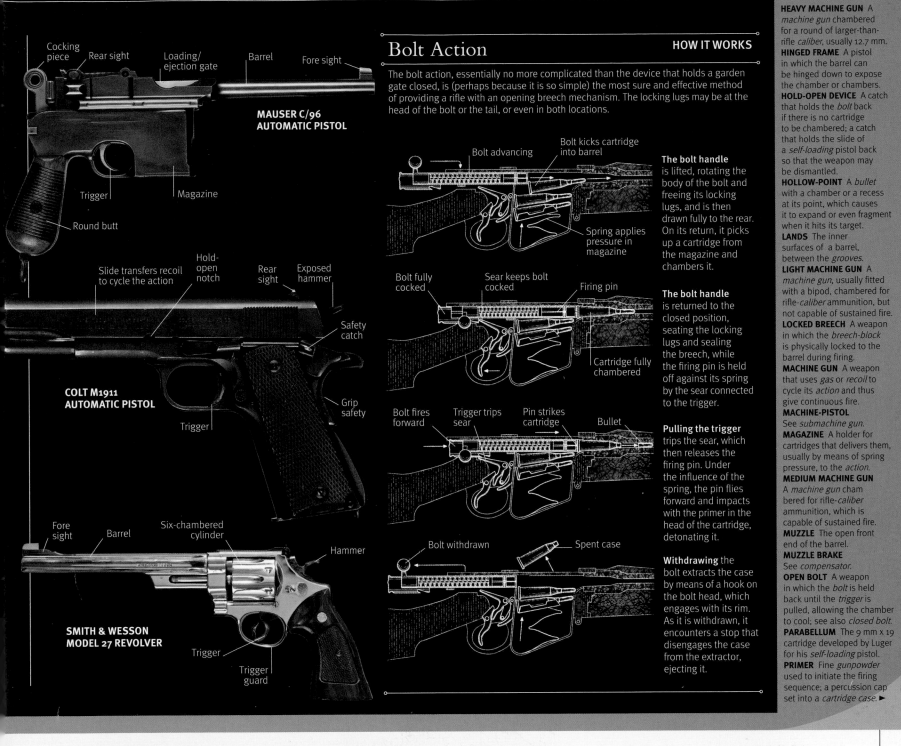

Cocking piece — **Rear sight** — **Loading/ejection gate** — **Barrel** — **Fore sight**

MAUSER C/96 AUTOMATIC PISTOL

Trigger — **Magazine**

Round butt

Slide transfers recoil to cycle the action — **Hold-open notch** — **Rear sight** — **Exposed hammer**

COLT M1911 AUTOMATIC PISTOL

Trigger

Safety catch

Grip safety

Fore sight — **Barrel** — **Six-chambered cylinder**

Hammer

SMITH & WESSON MODEL 27 REVOLVER

Trigger

Trigger guard

Bolt Action

The bolt action, essentially no more complicated than the device that holds a garden gate closed, is (perhaps because it is so simple) the most sure and effective method of providing a rifle with an opening breech mechanism. The locking lugs may be at the head of the bolt or the tail, or even in both locations.

Bolt advancing — **Bolt kicks cartridge into barrel**

The bolt handle is lifted, rotating the body of the bolt and freeing its locking lugs, and is then drawn fully to the rear. On its return, it picks up a cartridge from the magazine and chambers it.

Spring applies pressure in magazine

Bolt fully cocked — **Sear keeps bolt cocked** — **Firing pin**

The bolt handle is returned to the closed position, seating the locking lugs and sealing the breech, while the firing pin is held off against its spring by the sear connected to the trigger.

Cartridge fully chambered

Bolt fires forward — **Trigger trips sear** — **Pin strikes cartridge** — **Bullet**

Pulling the trigger trips the sear, which then releases the firing pin. Under the influence of the spring, the pin flies forward and impacts with the primer in the head of the cartridge, detonating it.

Bolt withdrawn — **Spent case**

Withdrawing the bolt extracts the case by means of a hook on the bolt head, which engages with its rim. As it is withdrawn, it encounters a stop that disengages the case from the extractor, ejecting it.

HEAVY MACHINE GUN A *machine gun* chambered for a round of larger-than-rifle *caliber*, usually 12.7 mm.
HINGED FRAME A pistol in which the barrel can be hinged down to expose the chamber or chambers.
HOLD-OPEN DEVICE A catch that holds the *bolt* back if there is no cartridge to be chambered; a catch that holds the slide of a *self-loading* pistol back so that the weapon may be dismantled.
HOLLOW-POINT A *bullet* with a chamber or a recess at its point, which causes it to expand or even fragment when it hits its target.
LANDS The inner surfaces of a barrel, between the *grooves*.
LIGHT MACHINE GUN A *machine gun*, usually fitted with a bipod, chambered for rifle-*caliber* ammunition, but not capable of sustained fire.
LOCKED BREECH A weapon in which the *breech-block* is physically locked to the barrel during firing.
MACHINE GUN A weapon that uses *gas* or *recoil* to cycle its *action* and thus give continuous fire.
MACHINE-PISTOL See *submachine gun*.
MAGAZINE A holder for cartridges that delivers them, usually by means of spring pressure, to the *action*.
MEDIUM MACHINE GUN A *machine gun* chambered for rifle-*caliber* ammunition, which is capable of sustained fire.
MUZZLE The open front end of the barrel.
MUZZLE BRAKE See *compensator*.
OPEN BOLT A weapon in which the *bolt* is held back until the *trigger* is pulled, allowing the chamber to cool; see also *closed bolt*.
PARABELLUM The 9 mm x 19 cartridge developed by Luger for his *self-loading* pistol.
PRIMER Fine *gunpowder* used to initiate the firing sequence; a percussion cap set into a *cartridge case*. ►

Some European gunmakers used tubular magazines in bolt-action rifles, but they were soon discredited, and box magazines took their place.

SELF-LOADING FIREARMS

Mauser was the dominant force in military rifle design during the latter part of the 19th century, and went on to capture much of the global market for heavy-caliber sport rifles, too. Most other designers simply copied Mauser's work, and only in the United Kingdom, at the Royal Ordnance Factory at Enfield, was a markedly different type of bolt-action rifle, the work of an American of Scottish birth, James Paris Lee, produced in very significant numbers (though designs by other Europeans, notably the Austro-German Ferdinand von Mannlicher and the Swiss Schmidt were adopted by smaller armies).

Elsewhere in Germany, driven by Prussian militarism, increasing numbers of companies were entering the field of armaments manufacture. One, Ludwig Loewe, which had started life as a manufacturer of sewing machines, was to obtain a license to make Maxim's machine guns, and prospered as Deutsche Waffen und Muntitionsfabrik (DWM), swallowing up Mauser in the process.

It was at DWM that the first workable self-loading pistol, the Borchardt C/93, was produced. The company also made most of the Mauser C/96s, and it was while working for DWM that Georg Luger produced his masterpiece, the P'08.

The latter part of the century saw the emergence of another singular force in gunmaking: John Moses Browning, a Mormon

from Ogden, Utah. Having worked for Winchester, where he produced the first pump- and self-loading shotguns, he then began an alliance with Fabrique National of Herstal, near Liège, in Belgium, and produced designs for machine guns and self-loading pistols, which were to be among the best in the world.

BERGMANN M18/1
The unwieldiness of the first generation of rapid-fire pistols lead to the creation of the submachine gun. One of the first of these was the Bergmann M18/1, made in 1918.

FIREARMS

Rear sight
Ammunition belt feedway
Fore sight
Rifle-type butt
Pistol grip
Trigger
Water jacket
Muzzle compensator
Integral bipod

**MG08/15
RECOIL-OPERATED
MACHINE GUN**

Rear sight
Drum magazine
Barrel shroud acts as radiator
Cooling fins
Trigger
Grip

**LEWIS
GAS-OPERATED
MACHINE GUN**

Muzzle compensator
Optical sight
Box magazine
Butt contains gun action
Trigger

**FN P90
GAS-OPERATED
SUBMACHINE GUN**

Every action, Isaac Newton's Third Law of Motion tells us, has an equal and opposite reaction. The action produced in a firearm propels the bullet down the barrel and on toward its target, and the reaction, known as the recoil, drives the gun into the shoulder or hand of the firer. Hiram Maxim was the first to realize that this reaction could be employed to cycle the gun's mechanism, and produced his machine guns on that principle.

Cocking handle **Direction of force** **Sear retains bolt** **Barrel spring**
Mainspring **Firing pin** **One of several lugs**

The cocking handle is drawn back against the mainspring. As it returns to battery, it strips a round from the magazine and chambers it, while the lugs that lock it in place are forced into their recesses.

Spring released by trigger **Pin strikes cartridge** **Bolt jumps forward, chambering cartridge**

During the cocking process, the firing pin is held off by the sear connected to the trigger. Pulling the trigger releases the sear, allowing the pin to fly forward and impact with the primer, detonating it.

Trigger retracted **Bullet fires from cartridge**

By the time the projectile has left the muzzle, the recoil is working on the bolt to overcome the mechanism which is holding the locking lugs in place.

Direction of force **Ejected shell**
Spring will propel bolt forward **Recoil throws bolt to rear** **Next cartridge for chamber**

When the locking mechanism has been overcome, the bolt is free to travel to the rear, extracting the empty case and chambering a fresh one.

MACHINE GUNS

An American, Hiram Stevens Maxim, built his first machine gun in London in 1883. It used the weapon's recoil to extract the fired case and chamber another, cocking the action in the process. If the trigger was held down, the process repeated until the ammunition supply was exhausted (or the gun jammed, which was more likely in the early days). It took some years for the real meaning of his invention to sink in, but when it did, it changed the very nature of warfare.

Maxim's patents had expired by the outbreak of World War I, and already there were competing designs in production. But inasmuch as three of the six major combatants—Britain, Germany, and Russia (and one of the minor: the Ottoman Empire, which was armed by Germany)—relied on Maxim designs, they can fairly be said to have

dominated that conflict. Indeed, Britain and what was by then the Soviet Union, were still relying on Maxims (the former in the shape of the Vickers) throughout World War II. The French Army fielded a machine gun of its own, the gas-operated, air-cooled Hotchkiss, which had gone into production in 1893. It was considerably simpler than the Maxim, but tended to overheat—a problem from which the water-cooled gun never suffered, so long as a supply of coolant was available.

Heavy machine guns like the Maxim and the Hotchkiss, and the Austro-Hungarian Skoda and Schwarzlose, and the American Browning (the denomination refers not to the ammunition for which they were chambered, which was rifle-caliber, but to their ability to maintain heavy sustained fire) were not the only

automatic weapons found on the battlefields of World War I. Lighter, more portable weapons such as the Lewis and the lightened Maxim, known as the MG08/15, chambered for the same rounds, but which could accompany infantrymen in the assault, were also present.

DESERT EAGLE, 1983

The Israeli Desert Eagle was the first self-loading pistol capable of handling the heaviest, most powerful Magnum pistol ammunition, thanks to its gas-operated, locked-breech design.

Rear sight

Cocking handle

Barrel stocked close to muzzle

Fore sight

Trigger

Intergral box magazine

Bayonet attachment lug

MI GARAND GAS-OPERATED RIFLE

Cocking handle

Carrying handle protects rear sight

Plastic forestock

Trigger

Grip

Detachable magazine

M16A2 GAS-OPERATED ASSAULT RIFLE

Variable-magnification telescopic sight

Cocking handle

Detachable box magazine

Folded bipod

Flash hider

Safety catch

Trigger

WALTHER WA2000 GAS-OPERATED SNIPER RIFLE

Gas

HOW IT WORKS

As an alternative to harnessing the force of the gun's recoil, it is possible to use some of the energy produced by the sudden production of a relatively large volume of gas that propels the bullet down the barrel. Some of that gas can be tapped off after the bullet has passed, and employed to unlock the gun's action and drive the breech-block or bolt to the rear, cycling it.

Spring

Bolt

Piston

Gas cylinder

Barrel

Sear retains bolt

Ammunition belt

Trigger releases bolt

Bullet fires from cartridge

Direction of force

Firing pin strikes cartridge

Direction of force

Bolt fully retracted

Ejected shell

Gas pushes on piston

Next cartridge for chamber

Gas bleeds off into cylinder

The bolt is drawn back against the mainspring. As it returns to battery, it strips a round from the magazine and chambers it.

On pressing the trigger, the bolt flies forward and detonates the charge in the cartridge.

The bolt is attached to a piston in a cylinder running parallel to the barrel. At its head is a vent into the barrel. As the projectile passes the vent, propellant gas is bled off, forcing the piston back. As the bolt travels to the rear, the spent cartridge case is ejected. If the trigger remains depressed, the cycle continues.

Toward the end of World War I, the rifle-caliber machine guns were joined by a much smaller automatic weapon, chambered for pistol ammunition and designed to put automatic firepower into the hands of the individual infantryman. The Bergmann MP18/I played only a very minor role, but it was to be a prophetic one. By the time war broke out in Europe again, the submachine gun had become ubiquitous. That, however, is not to say that its role has ever been completely understood in anything but close-quarters combat. Indeed many, even now, would maintain that its best feature is the shock it can generate, especially in a confined space, for such a weapon, capable of firing up to 1200 rounds per minute, is virtually impossible to control if the trigger is held down for any length of time. It is significant

that perhaps the best of the genre in modern times, Heckler & Koch's MP5, is available shorn of its rapid-fire setting. The police officers (and many of the soldiers) who carry such weapons do so not for their firepower, but for the increase in accuracy they offer over a pistol, thanks to their longer barrels, and for the greater capacity of their magazines.

Submachine guns have never been seen as replacements for the infantryman's assault rifle. Indeed, thanks to the drastic modifications the assault rifle has undergone, there is now more reason than ever to suggest that the submachine gun will soon join the pistol in having no effective military role beyond self-defense. More than any other man-portable weapon,

the assault rifle (much-reduced in weight and length, thanks to the introduction of "bullpup" designs, which have the mechanism housed within the shoulder stock, and chambered for much lighter ammunition) has changed to accommodate the nature of the task facing the soldier who carries it.

PROJECTOR, INFANTRY, ANTI-TANK, 1942
The British Army's PIAT of World War II vintage was perhaps one of the most bizarre weapons of the 20th century, yet despite its simplicity, it was capable of disabling even heavy tanks at up to a hundred yards, and could also function as a mortar and "bunker buster."

ARMOR AND HELMETS

GERMAN GOTHIC

Sallet

Visor

Bevor

Besagew

Breastplate

Spaulder

Rerebrace

Coulter

Gauntlet

Cuisse

Poleyn

Greave

Leather shoes

VIKING

Leather neck strip

Mail shirt

MUGHAL

Riveted mail cloak

Reinforced scalloped plates

Large protective plates

JAPANESE SAMURAI

Helmet crest

Kabuto (Helmet)

Mempo (Face mask)

Kote (Armored sleeves)

Do (Cuirass)

Kasazuri (Tasset)

Haidate (Skirt guard)

Suneate (Shin guards)

THE most ancient form of armor was probably made of animal hides, followed by leather or cotton. As metal technology progressed, bronze, and then iron armor appeared. Greek hoplites from the 7th century BCE wore a bronze helmet, a bell-shaped corselet of leather or bronze, and bronze greaves for the shins.

During the early empire, the Romans developed banded-iron armor (called *lorica segmentata*), with reinforced sections across the shoulder, that allowed for more flexible movement. Later Roman infantry tended to be less heavily armored, although their cavalry (or cataphracts) wore a coat of heavy mail.

Mail then remained the dominant form of armor in western Europe until the 15th century.

Steppe nomads, such as the Turks and Mongols, wore both scale and *lamellar* armor, the latter constructed of individual pieces (or *lames*) laced together in horizontal rows (rather than being sewn on). The arrangement of protective plates thus formed could become quite elaborate, reaching the summit of its development in the *O-Yoroi* armor of Japanese samurai. Their hardened leather

BADGE OF RANK
The gorget was among the last pieces of armor to be worn on the battlefield. By the 18th century, a reduced version had become a badge marking out officers.

plates coated in lacquer to give strength equal to steel also provided greater flexibility and lightness.

TECHNOLOGICAL IMPROVEMENTS
By the 15th century, the danger from improved weapons including the longbow, crossbow, and firearms meant that chain armor, well adapted for deflecting sword blows, became more vulnerable. Small plates or discs of steel had already been added to armor to protect the most vulnerable areas, and these now evolved into entire suits of toughened steel.

Gradually, from the 16th century, armor was reduced to save weight—and expense—for foot soldiers. For the cavalry, however, back- and breastplates (or cuirasses) survived into the 19th century, and in ceremonial form even later. With the development in the 20th century

Helmet bowl

Reinforced ridge

Cheek guard

VIKING

Eye holes

"Frog-shaped" visor

Ridge shape to deflect lances

JOUSTING HELM

Metal top knot

Cone-shaped headpiece

Nosepiece

Felt ear flaps contain iron plates

KOREAN

Chin strap

Stirnpanzer (additional steel plate)

Stud

Attaching strap

Peak

GERMAN WORLD WAR I

Outer steel shell

Inner padded lining

US M1 HELMET

GLOSSARY

ARMET Bowl-shaped helmet with cheek plates meeting at the chin, attached by hinges
ARMING CAP Quilted cap worn under a helmet
AVENTAIL Skirt of mail to defend neck
BANDENHELM Germanic helmet held together by central band or ridge
BARD Armor designed for a horse
BASINET Conical or globular skull, often without visor
BESAGEW Small discs laced to the shoulder to defend armpit
BEVOR Cupped chin defense
CHAPEAU DE FER Simple metal domed helmet
COOLUS HELMET Late republican/early imperial Roman helmet with basin shape
CORINTHIAN HELMET Classic Greek hoplite helmet
CUISSE Armor for the thigh
DO Japanese cuirass
GAUNTLET Hand armor of small plates attached to leather
GORGET Neck armor, often fixed to the plate with a latch or pin
GREAT HELM Large helmet enclosing entire skull and neck
GREAVE Plate to defend lower leg
HAIDATE Skirtlike guard to protect groin
HAUBERK A mail shirt
KABUTO Japanese helmet
KOTE Armored sleeves in samurai armor
MEMPO Ornamented face mask in Japanese armor
POLEYN Knee defense, often articulated and with projecting wings
REREBRACE Tubular defense for upper arm
SABATON Foot armor of articulated plates ending in toe-cap worn over leather shoes
SALLET Helmet with flared tail and visor
SPANGENHELM Germanic helmet of segmented construction
TOP Indian Mughal helmet with mail veil
VAMBRACE Tubular defense for forearm

of lightweight materials such as Kevlar, which could impede bullets, body armor made a return to the battlefield in the form of ballistic jackets.

HELMETS

After the fall of Rome, the techniques for creating helmets from a single sheet of iron disappeared. Segmented helmets such as the Bandhelm, popular among the Vikings, replaced them, with a band holding the two parts of the bowl of the helmet together.

Such early medieval European helmets did not protect the whole face, and just as body armor became heavier, so did head protection, leading to the evolution by the 12th century of "Great Helms" that covered the whole face and neck. Again, these proved too heavy and impractical and lighter versions, such as basinets,

appeared by the later Middle Ages.

Turkish and Mongol helmets often took a peaked form, a version in metal of the steppe nomads' felt cap, while the Japanese samurai wore elaborate helmets of lacquered leather, with a *mempo* for additional protection. With the increased use in firearms, helmets began to disappear until improved designs, which could defend against bullets and shrapnel led to a renaissance in helmets, from World War I "tin-pot" helmets, to the reinforced Kevlar helmets of the modern infantryman.

SAMURAI HELMET
Japanese samurai helmets came in a wide variety of styles. This Hineno *zunari bachi* is a "head-shaped" version, with a helmet bowl of simplified construction, lacquered in red, with its frontal plate finished in gold lacquer.

THE ANCIENT WORLD

THE FIRST WARRIORS
This rock painting from Algeria shows one of the earliest images of warfare, as ranks of warriors armed with hunting bows confront each other.

The earliest weapons—the bow, spear, club, and ax—had their origins in hunting, but it was in warfare—the competition for resources conducted by violent means—that they were honed and perfected as killing tools. Although the basic design of these weapons, and the materials used to make them, remained largely unchanged throughout the ancient period, from stone to copper, bronze and then iron, their efficacy (and the organization of those who wielded them) increased.

IN PREHISTORIC TIMES there were no armies as such, merely *ad hoc* bands of warriors armed with stone weapons for raids on neighboring groups. But, as Neolithic agricultural settlements coalesced into villages and then, from the 4th millennium BCE, into towns and cities with organized ruling and priestly classes, the means and weapons for waging war increased correspondingly in sophistication and effectiveness.

Agriculture implied the concentration of greater resources in a fixed position, and the need to defend food, manpower, and minerals gave rise to the first walled city, Jericho, and fortified villages such as Çatal Hüyük in modern Turkey. It was in the fertile river valleys of Egypt, India, and, more particularly, in the Sumerian culture of Mesopotamia that this process reached its fruition, with the growth of the earliest armies from around 3000 BCE.

The Sumerians inhabited many city-states, existing in an almost continuous state of warfare fueled by competition for the bounty of the "land between the two rivers." The

"Royal Standard of Ur," excavated from one of the most successful of these city-states, carries the earliest depiction of an organized armed force, led by its *lugal* or king. It consists of a mixture of light infantry bearing javelins and battle axes (but no shields) and helmeted heavy infantry wielding a mass of longer spears. The Sumerian chariots were cumbersome affairs with solid wheels drawn by four ass-like creatures—hardly practical vehicles for warfare. A commemorative tablet known as the Stele of Vultures shows that by c.2450 BCE, the Sumerians were fighting in a tight formation of helmeted spearmen, which prefigured the phalanx—the mainstay of infantry warfare for over 2,000 years.

The Sumerian cities were eventually overcome by Sargon of Agade (c.2300 BCE), who built the world's earliest empire, campaigning with an army that was the first to exploit mixed arms, combining light troops with heavier infantry and archers. Although warfare continued to plague the region, the pace of technological change was relatively slow, mainly consisting of refinements of existing weaponry. One example of this is in the improved molding that allowed the Mesopotamian battle ax to become double-bladed, inflicting appalling slashing and gouging wounds, and leading, in turn, to the increased use of metal helmets.

TECHNOLOGICAL INNOVATIONS
A series of cultural and technological developments in the 2nd millennium BCE changed the face of warfare and allowed states to project their power ever further, garner more resources, and repeat the process until they came up against a stronger foe. One of these developments was the widespread domestication of the horse. At the same time, the perfection of bent-wood techniques, allowed spokes to be used on chariot wheels. Along with the development of a practical composite bow that allowed rapid fire from these new chariots, these developments helped New Kingdom Egypt—which though long politically united, had remained very

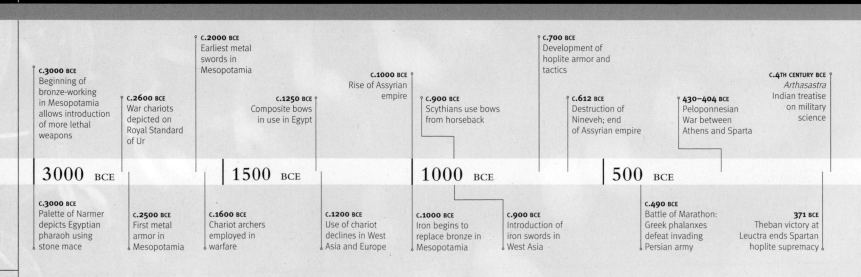

c.3000 BCE
Beginning of bronze-working in Mesopotamia allows introduction of more lethal weapons

c.2600 BCE
War chariots depicted on Royal Standard of Ur

c.2000 BCE
Earliest metal swords in Mesopotamia

c.1250 BCE
Composite bows in use in Egypt

c.1000 BCE
Rise of Assyrian empire

c.900 BCE
Scythians use bows from horseback

c.700 BCE
Development of hoplite armor and tactics

c.612 BCE
Destruction of Nineveh; end of Assyrian empire

430–404 BCE
Peloponnesian War between Athens and Sparta

c.4TH CENTURY BCE
Arthasastra
Indian treatise on military science

3000 BCE | **1500 BCE** | **1000 BCE** | **500 BCE**

c.3000 BCE
Palette of Narmer depicts Egyptian pharaoh using stone mace

c.2500 BCE
First metal armor in Mesopotamia

c.1600 BCE
Chariot archers employed in warfare

c.1200 BCE
Use of chariot declines in West Asia and Europe

c.1000 BCE
Iron begins to replace bronze in Mesopotamia

c.900 BCE
Introduction of iron swords in West Asia

c.490 BCE
Battle of Marathon: Greek phalanxes defeat invading Persian army

371 BCE
Theban victory at Leuctra ends Spartan hoplite supremacy

conservative in its use of military technology —to launch a devastating series of campaigns in the Middle East. The chariots' principle task was to disrupt opposing infantry and cut them down as they fled. Chariots rarely engaged each other directly, as at Kadesh (c.1275 BCE), the earliest well-documented battle, where the army of Pharaoh Rameses II fought a draw with the Hittites, who had become Egypt's principal rival.

The discovery in around 1200 BCE of hot-hammering and quenching iron in water to give stronger and longer-lasting blades added a new element of lethality to warfare, and also helped the spread of longer stabbing and slashing swords to supplant the daggers and axes, which had hitherto been the most common bladed weapons.

THE FIRST STANDING ARMY

It was the Assyrians who were the first to really exploit this development. Employing the earliest standing army—as many as 100,000 strong according to one text—and exploiting their military prowess and reputation for ruthless extermination of those who opposed them, they carved out an enormous empire encompassing most of Mesopotamia. The Assyrians possessed a well-defined chain of command, with specialist units of cavalry, armed with iron-tipped spears, slingers, and bowmen, whose massed fire could be devastating to an enemy, and which led to an increased use in armor, such as knee-length scale tunics. They also developed extensive expertise in siege warfare, and in the taking of Lachish (701 BCE) deployed siege engines that were not surpassed until Roman times. The Assyrian state under kings such as Tiglath-Pileser III (745–27 BCE) was capable of fighting sustained campaigns and defending a large area with mobile chariot forces. In the end, however, the multinational nature of its empire was to prove its undoing, as its resources became overstretched and a series of revolts caused its rapid collapse in c.612 BCE. The Persians, too, built a multiethnic empire from the mid-6th century BCE, but on a magnified scale, stretching from the borders of India to the Aegean. At the heart of their army was an elite corps of "Immortals," fighting with short spear and bow from behind a shield-wall. As the Persian domain expanded, light cavalry from Media, light infantry from the mountain regions, and even a camel-corps from the Middle East were added. Ironically, despite this well-balanced combination, the Persians were eventually defeated by an apparently tactically inflexible force, the Greek hoplite army.

Greece was ill-suited to cavalry, its generally mountainous terrain was better for to small-scale infantry warfare. Emerging by 800 BCE from the dark age of heroic warfare depicted in the epic poems of Homer, the Greek city-states relied on massed ranks of infantry soldiers, or hoplites.

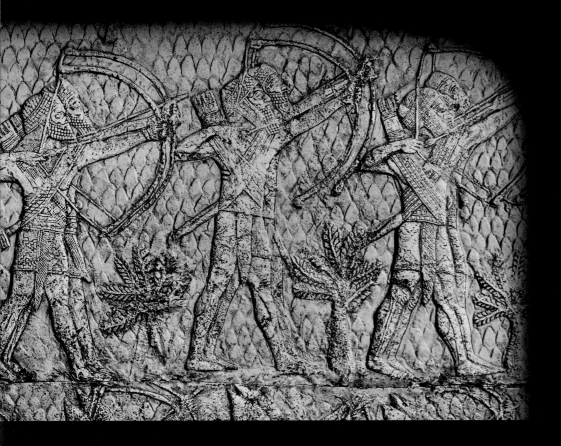

ASSYRIAN SIEGE
Archers formed a key component in an Assyrian army whose sophistication enabled it to fight pitched battles, send chariot forces across large distances, and deploy complex siege engines against any city that dared oppose it.

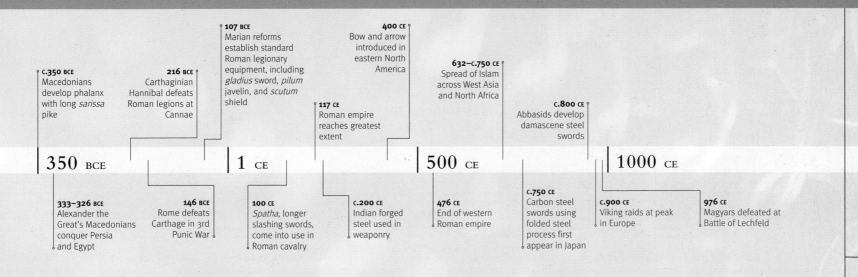

C.350 BCE
Macedonians develop phalanx with long *sarissa* pike

216 BCE
Carthaginian Hannibal defeats Roman legions at Cannae

107 BCE
Marian reforms establish standard Roman legionary equipment, including *gladius* sword, *pilum* javelin, and *scutum* shield

117 CE
Roman empire reaches greatest extent

400 CE
Bow and arrow introduced in eastern North America

632–c.750 CE
Spread of Islam across West Asia and North Africa

c.800 CE
Abbasids develop damascene steel swords

350 BCE   **1 CE**   **500 CE**   **1000 CE**

333–326 BCE
Alexander the Great's Macedonians conquer Persia and Egypt

146 BCE
Rome defeats Carthage in 3rd Punic War

100 CE
Spatha, longer slashing swords, come into use in Roman cavalry

c.200 CE
Indian forged steel used in weaponry

476 CE
End of western Roman empire

c.750 CE
Carbon steel swords using folded steel process first appear in Japan

c.900 CE
Viking raids at peak in Europe

976 CE
Magyars defeated at Battle of Lechfeld

Wielding a large shield held by a central hand-grip that protected only the left-side of the body, hoplites were dependent on their neighbor to shield their unguarded right side. Deployed in a phalanx, eight to twelve men deep, wielding long spears and protected by bronze helmets that left only the eyes and mouth exposed, the hoplites presented a shield and spear wall that opponents found very difficult to penetrate. The earliest depiction of such a phalanx occurred in around 670 BCE. By the time of the Persian invasion in 490 BCE, the development of this style of warfare, which depended on the cohesion of the soldiers within it, and their momentum as a mass, had been perfected by the Spartans, who possessed a full-time army trained in basic drills and able to conduct maneuvers such as facing an enemy coming from two directions. At Marathon (490 BCE) and Plataea (479 BCE), the Persians crumbled in the face of a hoplite charge, unable to counter with their cavalry, and undermined by their inferior discipline and cohesion.

THE ARMY OF ALEXANDER THE GREAT

By the 4th century BCE, it was a very different Greek army that took the fight to the Persians. The Macedonian army of Alexander the Great resolved the fundamental weakness of the hoplite force—its lack of a mounted striking arm. Alexander's "Companions," an elite cavalry unit, was trained to fight in a wedge-shaped formation ideal for penetrating other cavalry formations and disrupting infantry shield-walls. Added to this were the foot-companions, who fought on foot in a phalanx formation and were armed with the *sarissa*, a pike around 19½ ft (6 m) long. The *sarissa* of the foremost rank would project around 13 ft (4 m) in front of the phalanx, that of the second rank 6½ ft (2 m) and so on, creating an obstacle to deter all but the most determined assailant and which could also deflect missiles.

The weight of the *sarissa* was such that the members of the phalanx wore just light leather corselets and *greaves* and carried only daggers as sidearms. In battle, the Companions would generally punch a hole in the enemy line, which the *sarissa* phalanx would exploit. The tactical genius of Alexander, who used oblique formations, feints, and envelopments to devastating effect, combined with the tactical flexibility that the mixed cavalry-infantry army of Macedonia permitted, enabled him to defeat the numerically superior Persians at Issus (333 BCE) and Gaugamela (331 BCE) and take over their empire wholesale. What they won through military cohesion, the Macedonian successors of Alexander lost through political fractiousness, and by the 1st century BCE, the successor states in Asia and Africa were much weakened, while a manpower crisis in Greece meant traditional hoplite armies were increasingly difficult to sustain.

THE RISE OF ROME

It was into this arena that the new Mediterranean power of Rome encroached, backed up by a military force of unparalleled efficiency —the legion. Rome overcame its enemies, in part by its capacity to keep large armies constantly in the field (as many as 13 legions by 190 BCE). The Romans could survive even such a devastating defeat as the Carthaginian Hannibal inflicted on them at Cannae in 216 BCE—but their enemies had no such luxury. The organization of the legions developed over time, but by the early 1st century CE, had reached their full development (*see box*). It was above all the professionalism of the legionaries —who each served for 25 years—and the Roman Empire's superior logistics, enabling it to equip, train, and transport large armies, that helped it to annex a huge area of Europe, North Africa, and West Asia and hold it for over four centuries.

The Romans excelled in pitched battle and sought to force such confrontations whenever possible. Against more mobile foes, or

THE ROMAN ARMY

The Roman Empire's survival for over 400 years is a tribute to its ability to modify its military organization to face changing strategic needs. Under Marius in the late 2nd century BCE, extensive reforms created the classic Roman legion, with standardized equipment supplied by the state, the cohort of around 100 men as the tactical unit, and a legion strength of about 4–5,000 men. Legionaries bore the short *gladius* (sword), the *pilum* (heavy throwing spear) —designed to break on impact —— the oval *scutum* (shield), and, from the 1st century CE, generally *lorica segmentata* (armor). The legions were supported by auxiliary troops, with more varied equipment, and specialists such as mounted archers and slingers. Under the later empire, legion sizes became much smaller—as little as 1,000—while the role of the cavalry and units recruited from Germanic tribes increased.

CARVED TABLET

EGYPTIAN SPEARHEAD

This spearhead, discovered wrapped in a linen binding, is typical of the weapons carried by Pharaonic armies from the Old Kingdom right up until military changes during the New Kingdom brought chariot-borne archers to the fore.

opponents who had no cities or fixed centers to defend, however, the Roman way of war faltered. When defending long, fixed frontiers the legions could not cover all possible points of attack. Long vulnerable to mounted horse archers, such as the Parthians who overwhelmed Crassus at Carrhae in 53 BCE, the Romans also found it increasingly difficult to absorb the sapping pillage and run tactics of the German warrior federations that evolved from the 3rd century. The late empire, from the time of Gallienus (260–68 CE), came to depend more on a mobile field force (the *comitatenses*), with an enhanced heavy cavalry arm, wielding longer *spatha* swords. With their suits of mail, and sometimes carrying lances, these armored soldiers began to resemble the knights of early medieval times. At the same time, the frontier troops (*limitanei*), starved of resources and motivation, became increasingly unable to withstand the successive waves of Goths, Vandals, Huns, and other barbarian invaders.

AFTER THE ROMANS

When the Roman Empire in the West finally collapsed in 476 CE, the Germanic successor states inherited many of its legal and administrative systems. The most powerful of these, the Frankish kingdom, was able to project its power beyond the Rhine, into Italy and even northern Spain in the late 8th century under Charlemagne. Fighting in mailed byrnies (leather jackets) and armed with long swords and axes, the Frankish army's superior arms and organization, along with its use of auxiliaries from conquered nations such as the Saxons and Carinthians, made it invulnerable to everything save the political division and dynastic squabbling that fragmented the kingdom in the 9th century.

The break-up of the Frankish Empire came just as Europe and Byzantium—the remnant of the Roman Empire in the East—faced fresh military challenges. From the north came the Vikings, at first small groups of ship-borne raiders preying on lightly-defended coastal territories, and then larger forces carried inland on ponies or by portage along rivers to bring devastation as far afield as Anglo-Saxon Wessex, Paris, Kievan Rus, and Constantinople. Fighting with double-edged swords 28½–32 in (70–80 cm) in length, light spears for throwing and heavier ones for thrusting, and long-handled broad-bladed battle axes, the Vikings inspired terror in Europe for over 250 years.

Out of the Middle East, meanwhile, came another military force, which was to endure far longer. From the 630s, Arab armies, united under the banner of the new religion of Islam, swept through the peninsula and then outward to overwhelm the tired autocracies of Byzantium and Persia. The Islamic victory was not achieved at first through any superior technology—although the Arab armies' use of the camel for transportation doubtless assisted them in the desert terrain of many of their victories—but through the cohesive inspiration of ideology. When the new religion spread to the Turkic horse archers of the Central Asian steppes by the 9th century, the combination threatened for a time to be unstoppable.

TERRACOTTA WARRIOR
The terracotta army, buried in the tomb of Emperor Huang Di, who unified China c.220 BCE, is testament to the variety and sophistication of Chinese armies of the time.

THE ANCIENT WORLD

THE FIRST WEAPONS

THE ABILITY OF HUMAN BEINGS to manufacture tools was an early step toward gaining mastery over their environment. Among the first tools to appear were simple hand blades and axes made from hard rock; they would have been used to kill and dismember animals, but they also had the potential to be employed against other humans. The distinction between hunting and military weaponry necessarily remained blurred for many millennia. With the invention of the handle or shaft, and the development of projectile weapons—the spear and, above all, the bow and arrow—a revolution in hunting and fighting was underway.

PALEOLITHIC BLADES

To be able to cut was of prime importance for early man, and these blades—dating back to about 40,000 BCE—would have been used to dismember animals that had been killed by paleolithic hunters. Such blades were capable of severing sinew, and separating the skin from the animal's flesh.

DATE	c.40,000 BCE
ORIGIN	UNKNOWN
LENGTH	4 IN (10 CM)

Area held by hand

Serrated teeth for sawing

Narrowed point

Rough cutting edge

HAND AX

A key tool of the paleolithic age, the hand ax was shaped to provide both a cutting edge and a point. Although hand axes were essentially domestic tools, they were capable of inflicting savage wounds against both animals and people. Their cutting ability made them highly prized implements.

DATE	c.250,000–70,000 BCE
ORIGIN	UNKNOWN
LENGTH	6 IN (15 CM)

Fine cutting edge

Sharp broad point

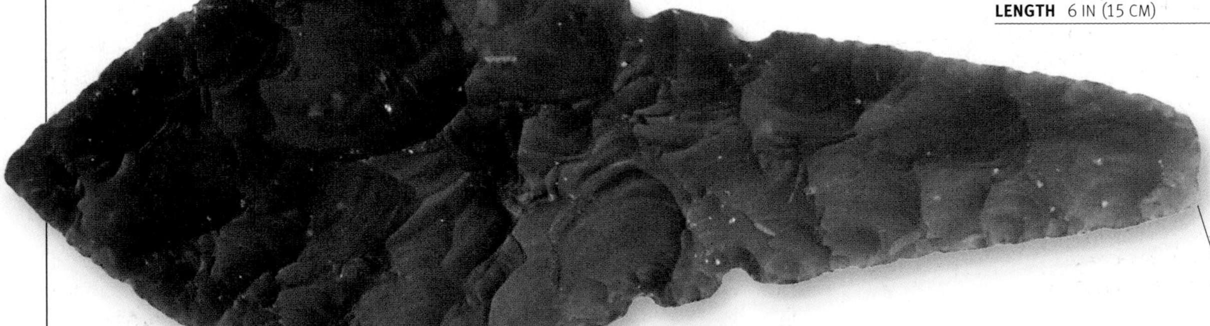

FLINT DAGGER HEAD

A development of the hand ax, this dagger is fashioned from flint, a hard rock readily available in areas of chalk downland and capable of taking a sharp edge. A piece of flint would be repeatedly struck by a stone hammer, knocking off small flakes of flint until a fine edge remained.

DATE	c.2000 BCE
ORIGIN	UNKNOWN
LENGTH	6 IN (15 CM)

SERRATED FLINT KNIFE

A development of the simple flint dagger is the serrated knife shown here. The knife's teeth make possible a sawing action, and this provided the paleolithic hunter with an opportunity of cutting through harder objects such as bone, gristle, and—during the Ice Age—frozen meat.

DATE	2,500,000–10,000 BCE
ORIGIN	UNKNOWN
LENGTH	8 IN (20 CM)

Antler horn sleeve

Wooden shaft

Stone ax head

Sinew or leather binding

Flint blade

Leather binding

FLINT HAND DAGGER

By lashing the flint blade to a wooden shaft with a binding of sinew or leather strips, the simple hand dagger was transformed into a deadly weapon of war. The addition of the shaft enabled the Stone-Age fighter to plunge the blade into his opponent with the full force of his arm.

DATE	2,500,000–10,000 BCE
ORIGIN	UNKNOWN
LENGTH	12 IN (30 CM)

EARLY ADZE

The stone head of the adze is inserted into a sleeve made from antler-horn, which is then bound to the wooden shaft by strips of leather. The adze is primarily a domestic or agricultural tool, but it does not take too much imagination to see this as a forerunner to the battle ax.

DATE	8000–4000 BCE
ORIGIN	UNKNOWN
LENGTH	8 IN (20 CM)

Cutting edge

Originally attached to shaft

Leather strips binding axhead to shaft

Smooth stone axhead

SMALL CLOVIS POINT

In 1932 this Ice-Age spearhead was unearthed in Clovis, New Mexico, along with other weapon points. The broad blade of this spearhead could inflict severe wounds. The binding of the spearhead to a long wooden shaft gave the fighter an opportunity to throw it at his opponent with great force, from a relatively safe distance.

DATE	c.10,000 BCE
ORIGIN	US
LENGTH	4 IN (10 CM)

STONE AXHEAD

A dual-purpose tool, the stone ax could have been used for clearing vegetation, but would have been capable of smashing in a human skull. The addition of a wooden handle provided greater reach and power. This axhead was dredged from the Thames River in London.

DATE	4000–2000 BCE
ORIGIN	ENGLAND
LENGTH	8 IN (20 CM)

Reproduction wooden handle

Triangular point

Tang to attach arrowhead to shaft

Reproduction wooden handle

FLINT ARROWHEADS

The bow was a leap forward in weapon technology, enabling the archer to fire from a distance with power and accuracy. Made from flint, these arrowheads have barbs that would embed themselves deep inside the victim, ensuring that any attempt to remove them would be difficult.

DATE	c.2700–1800 BCE
ORIGIN	UNKNOWN
LENGTH	2 IN (5 CM)

MESOPOTAMIAN WEAPONS AND ARMOR

ORGANIZED WARFARE ORIGINATED in the Sumerian city states of southern Mesopotamia in around 3000 BCE. Armor was made from leather, copper, and bronze, and the chief weapons were the bow and spear. Mobility was provided by chariots, at first four-wheeled vehicles drawn by asses, but improved to become light, horse-drawn, two-wheeled platforms for archers and spearmen. Improvements in city fortification led to developments in siege warfare techniques, such as the use of battering rams and scaling towers.

CEREMONIAL DAGGER

Excavated from the burial site of the Sumerian Queen Pu-Abi in around 2500 BCE, this ceremonial dagger is of the highest quality—a suitable weapon for a monarch to carry on her journey to the afterlife. The blade and scabbard are made from gold, while the hilt is constructed from lapis lazuli finished with gold decoration.

DATE	c.2500 BCE
ORIGIN	SUMERIA
LENGTH	9½–12 IN (20–30 CM)

Blue lapis lazuli hilt

Diadem

Intricate geometric design

Gold scabbard

Double-edged blade

Hair-effect decoration

Hole for attaching lining

Cheek guards to protect side of face

HELMET OF MESKALAM-DUG

Made from an alloy of gold and silver, this ceremonial helmet was found in the Sumerian city of Ur and dates back to the third millennium BCE. Known as a wig helmet, the decoration mimics the hairstyle worn by Sumerian kings of the period.

DATE	c.2500 BCE
ORIGIN	SUMERIA
LENGTH	8½ IN (22 CM)

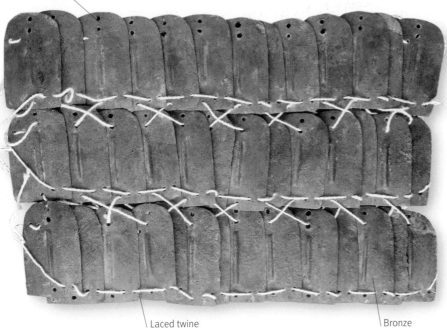

Holes for twine

Laced twine

Bronze plates

ASSYRIAN SCALE ARMOR

Constructed from bronze, this early example of *lamellar* armor—where small plates are laced together—was worn by an Assyrian warrior. Such armor was popular in the Middle East until the end of the Middle Ages.

DATE	1800–620 BCE
ORIGIN	ASSYRIA
LENGTH	EACH PLATE: 2 IN (5 CM)

ASSYRIAN WARFARE

Assyrian warriors, here depicted on a relief carving, in the Battle of Til-Tuba c.650 BCE. Some men are well protected with armor and large shields, and the two main Assyrian weapons, spear and bow, are clearly in evidence.

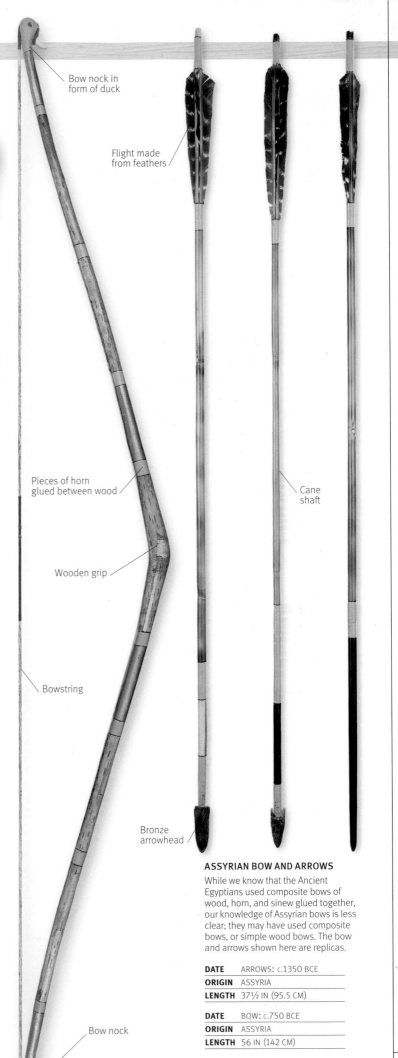

Bow nock in form of duck

Flight made from feathers

Pieces of horn glued between wood

Cane shaft

Wooden grip

Bowstring

Bronze arrowhead

Bow nock

ASSYRIAN BOW AND ARROWS

While we know that the Ancient Egyptians used composite bows of wood, horn, and sinew glued together, our knowledge of Assyrian bows is less clear; they may have used composite bows, or simple wood bows. The bow and arrows shown here are replicas.

DATE	ARROWS: c.1350 BCE
ORIGIN	ASSYRIA
LENGTH	37½ IN (95.5 CM)

DATE	BOW: c.750 BCE
ORIGIN	ASSYRIA
LENGTH	56 IN (142 CM)

◄ 32–33 MESOPOTAMIAN WEAPONS AND ARMOR ► 40–41 ANCIENT GREEK WEAPONS AND ARMOR ► 44–45 ANCIENT ROMAN WEAPONS AND ARMOR

ANCIENT EGYPTIAN WEAPONS AND ARMOR

FROM APPROXIMATELY 3000–1500 BCE the Egyptian army fought mainly on foot, its soldiers protected by large wooden shields and armed with bows, spears, and axes. The long struggle with the people of Hyksos, who came to rule parts of Egypt in the second millennium BCE, brought about a change in weapon technology. Helmets, armor, and swords became more common, and chariots provided highly mobile archery platforms.

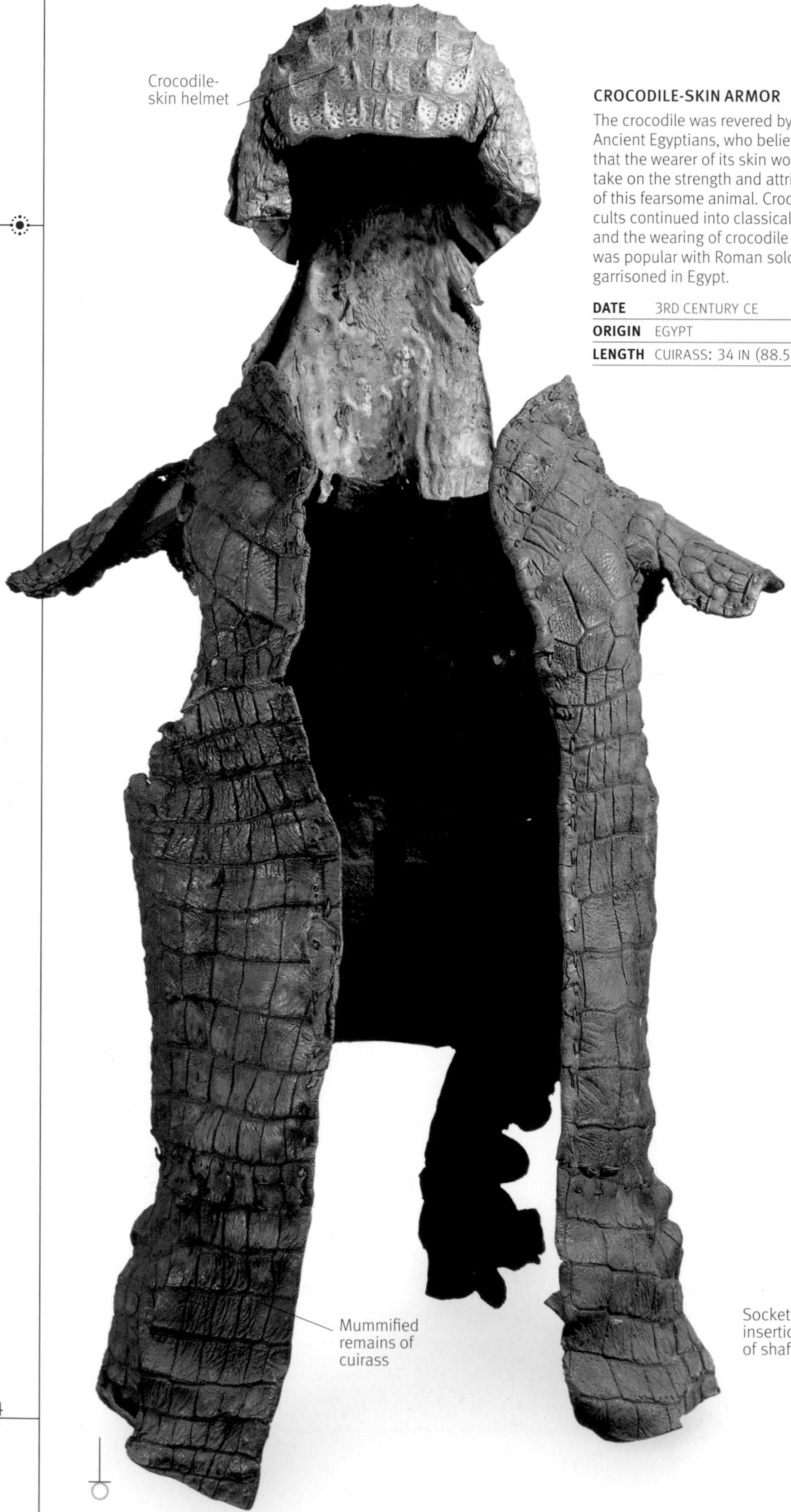

Crocodile-skin helmet
Mummified remains of cuirass

CROCODILE-SKIN ARMOR

The crocodile was revered by the Ancient Egyptians, who believed that the wearer of its skin would take on the strength and attributes of this fearsome animal. Crocodile cults continued into classical times, and the wearing of crocodile armor was popular with Roman soldiers garrisoned in Egypt.

DATE	3RD CENTURY CE
ORIGIN	EGYPT
LENGTH	CUIRASS: 34 IN (88.5 CM)

Attachment holes
1912
6-8
40
Thin, curved, scalloped ax blade

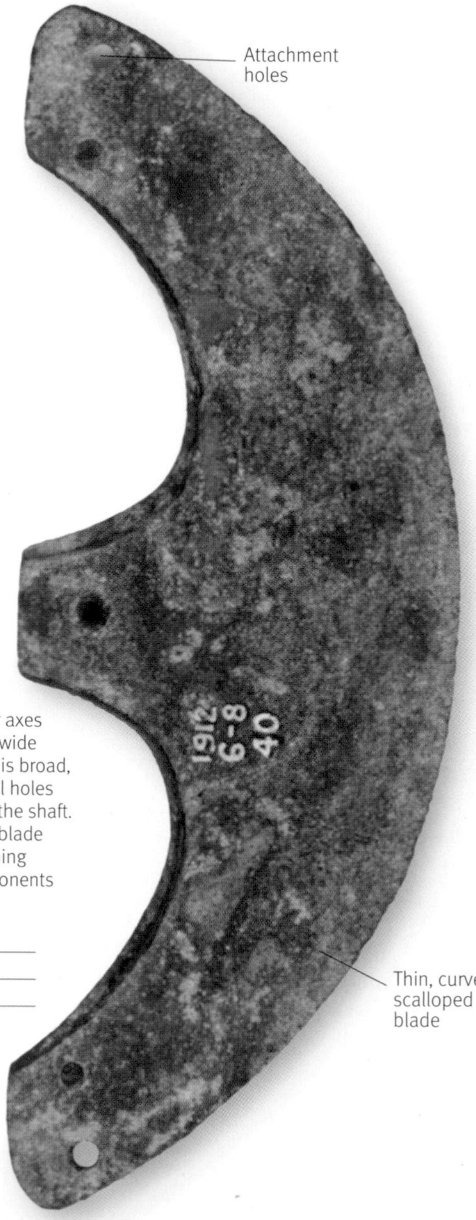

BRONZE AXHEAD

The Egyptian enthusiasm for axes led to the development of a wide variety of axhead shapes. This broad, scalloped example has small holes where the head is bound to the shaft. The distinctive shape of the blade makes possible a wide slashing action, effective against opponents wearing little or no armor.

DATE	2200–1640 BCE
ORIGIN	EGYPT
LENGTH	6 IN (17.1 CM)

BRONZE SPEARHEAD

This spearhead is typical of those carried by Egyptian infantrymen, whose main weapon was the spear. Made from bronze, it was covered in fine linen cloth, whose weave is apparent in this view. This weapon would have been used mainly for thrusting, not thrown as a javelin.

DATE	c.2000 BCE
ORIGIN	EGYPT
LENGTH	10 IN (25 CM)

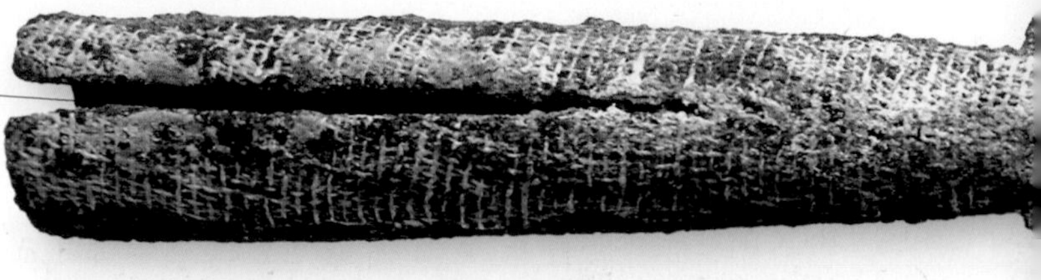

Socket for insertion of shaft

FLINT ARROWHEAD

The Egyptians were early exponents of the bow, and it formed the most effective element within their armory. The first composite bow was portrayed on a victory monument as early as 2800 BCE. Early arrowheads were made from flint, subsequently to be replaced by bronze.

Tang

Triangular arrowhead designed to kill victim outright

DATE	5500–3100 BCE
ORIGIN	EGYPT
LENGTH	2 IN (6.1 CM)

BRONZE HEAD

Used either to arm a thin spear or an arrow, this bronze head is notable for its pronounced barbs. Although expensive to produce, bronze arrowheads were widely used by the Egyptians, who fitted them to shafts made from the long reeds growing along the Nile River.

Pronounced barb

Broad head

DATE	1500–1070 BCE
ORIGIN	EGYPT
LENGTH	2 IN (7 CM)

Shield made from gilded wood

Khepesh (sickle-shaped sword)

"LION KING" SHIELD

Tutankhamen guarded by falcon god Horus

One of the eight ceremonial shields discovered in the annex to Tutankhamun's tomb, it depicts the king in the guise of a lion scattering his enemies before him. This is one of a number of depictions showing Tutankhamun adopting a martial pose. Simple wooden versions of this type of shield would have been carried by Egyptian foot soldiers.

DATE	1333–1323 BCE
ORIGIN	EGYPT
LENGTH	33 IN (85 CM)

Intricate openwork wood carving

"SMITING A LION" CEREMONIAL SHIELD

The discovery of the tomb of Tutankhamun (who reigned c.1336–1327 BCE) provided a mass of information on Egyptian life, including the weapons and tools of the period. This ceremonial shield shows the king slaying a lion while armed with an unusual type of sword called a *khepesh*.

DATE	1333–1323 BCE
ORIGIN	EGYPT
LENGTH	33 IN (85 CM)

Pattern of original fine Egyptian linen

Leaf-shaped spearpoint

3000 BCE—1000 CE

◄ **32–33** MESOPOTAMIAN WEAPONS AND ARMOR   ► **40–41** ANCIENT GREEK WEAPONS AND ARMOR   ► **44–45** ANCIENT ROMAN WEAPONS AND ARMOR

ANCIENT EGYPTIAN WEAPONS AND ARMOR

Detailing influenced by
Middle Eastern design

Wide, double-edged
metal blade

SHORT SWORD

Until the New Kingdom (c.1539–1075 BCE) the sword had not been highly regarded by the Egyptians, but military encounters with warlike peoples from the Middle East encouraged the development of edged weapons capable of penetrating armor. This broad-bladed short sword has a gold gilt handle, almost certainly that of a member of the Egyptian royal family.

DATE	1539–1075 BCE
ORIGIN	EGYPT
LENGTH	12½ IN (32.3 CM)

Gold gilt handle

Wooden shaft

Decorated
gold handle

Double-edged
iron blade

A PHARAOH'S DAGGER

Belonging to Tutankhamen, this gold-handled dagger has an iron blade rare in this period. The Egyptians had no direct access to iron ore and were dependent on supplies from the Middle East—often under the control of their enemies—which consequently made the production of iron weapons a difficult business.

DATE	c.1370–1352 BCE
ORIGIN	EGYPT
LENGTH	16¼ IN (41.1 CM)

Mushroom-shaped pommel

Wooden shaft

LONG SWORD

Featuring a large, mushroom-shaped pommel, this sword has a copper blade, while the handle is covered in gilded gold. Although copper was readily available in Egypt, it lacked the strength of bronze and iron, and the blade could not be made to take a sharp edge.

DATE	1539–1075 BCE
ORIGIN	EGYPT
LENGTH	16 IN (40.6 CM)

Gold gilt handle

Double-edged
copper blade

BATTLE AX

Wooden shaft

This heavy bronze axhead is inserted into a wooden shaft and then bound securely in place. Such axes would have been capable of penetrating leather, and light bronze armor.

Axhead inserted into groove in shaft

DATE	1630–1520 BCE
ORIGIN	EGYPT
LENGTH	16¼ IN (41.1 CM)

Bronze axhead

Original binding

Open metalwork axhead

Intricate warrior -on-horseback design

CEREMONIAL AX

The ax (and the mace) were weapons that had strong associations with power and prestige, and ceremonial versions were carried by Egyptian rulers. Typically, a scene showing the triumph of the Pharaoh would be engraved on the axhead, although in this instance, a warrior is depicted on horseback in an open metalwork design.

DATE	1539–1075 BCE
ORIGIN	EGYPT
LENGTH	17 IN (43.5 CM)

REPLICA BATTLE AX

This modern reconstruction of an Egyptian battle ax shows the axhead in place within a wooden shaft. This is the type of weapon that would have been used by the ordinary Egyptian foot soldier, and was a response to the increased use of armor by Egypt's enemies during the middle of the second millennium BCE.

DATE	20TH CENTURY
ORIGIN	EGYPT
LENGTH	16½ IN (42 CM)

Leather strip binding to lash axhead to shaft

Cutting edge of blade

TUTANKHAMUN
Egyptian King Tutankhamun
(r.1332–1322 BCE) shoots arrows
at retreating enemies from his chariot.
Evidence that bows and arrows were among
the most common weapons of this period is found in
tomb paintings, on coffins, and from excavated finds. These
weapons would have been used alongside axes and short swords.

3000 BCE—1000 CE

◄ 34–37 ANCIENT EGYPTIAN WEAPONS AND ARMOR ► 42–43 GREAT WARRIORS: GREEK HOPLITE ► 44–45 ANCIENT ROMAN WEAPONS AND ARMOR

THE ANCIENT WORLD

ANCIENT GREEK WEAPONS AND ARMOR

WARFARE IN CLASSICAL GREECE was centered around the hoplite, a heavily equipped foot soldier armed with a spear and sword, and protected by a large round shield, bronze helmet, bronze or leather cuirass, and greaves. Hoplites fought closely together, forming a wall of shields in a phalanx that maximized their protection while enabling them to use their spear. The hoplite phalanx was supported by light infantry armed with bows and sling shots.

Spearpoint

HOPLITE SPEAR BUTT

Made from bronze, this spear butt's main purpose was to act as a counterweight to the head at the other end of the spear, although if the spearhead broke off in battle, the butt could be used as a weapon. A thick bronze ring secured the butt to the spear.

DATE	4TH CENTURY CE
ORIGIN	MACEDONIA
LENGTH	15 IN (38 CM)

Ridges to align with body muscles

Socket for spear shaft

Wide leaf-shaped spear blade

Two plates joined at side by leather strap

Indentation for bronze securing ring

GREEK SPEARHEAD

The spear was the hoplite's principal weapon, his short iron sword only being used if his spear was broken during fighting. This spearhead is wide-bladed and made from iron, and the missing shaft would have been fashioned from strong wood such as ash.

DATE	6–5TH CENTURIES BCE
ORIGIN	GREECE
LENGTH	12¼ IN (31 CM)

Open side areas most vulnerable sections

BRONZE CUIRASS

This muscled cuirass consists of a breast- and backplate joined together by hooks and straps. It would have been worn by a senior officer and would have been made to measure. The ordinary hoplite wore a more simple cuirass made either from bronze or from stiffened leather.

DATE	5TH CENTURY BCE
ORIGIN	ITALY
LENGTH	19½ IN (50 CM)

CORINTHIAN HELMET

An early example of perhaps the most famous Greek helmet, this Corinthian design follows the shape of the skull, and extends downward toward the shoulders and neck, leaving a narrow face opening with space for the eyes between a nasal.

DATE	c.650 BCE
ORIGIN	GREECE
WEIGHT	3½ LB (1.54 KG)

Nasal between two eye sights

Helmet made from a single piece of bronze

BRONZE GREAVES

The hoplite's large shield protected the lower abdomen and thighs, but to protect his knees and shins, he wore a pair of bronze greaves. The greaves shown here are sufficiently light and flexible that they could be "clipped on" over the soldier's calves without the need for leather straps.

DATE	6TH CENTURY BCE
ORIGIN	GREECE
LENGTH	19 IN (48 CM)

Shaped to fit leg muscles

Ridge decoration

CORINTHIAN HELMET

The hoplite wearing his Corinthian helmet would have been a frightening sight to any opponent: a pair of glaring eyes behind stylized cutouts in the helmet face. A large horsehair crest was typically attached to the crown of the helmet to make the soldier look more impressive, as well as providing a means of identification in the thick of battle.

DATE	6–5TH CENTURIES BCE
ORIGIN	GREECE
WEIGHT	3½–3¾ LB (1.5–1.75 KG)

Long nosepiece

Cheek guards

Almond-shaped eye sights

CORINTHIAN HELMET

The Corinthian helmet provided good protection against all but the heaviest blows, but it was undeniably heavy, and it restricted sight and hearing while fighting. Toward the end of the 5th century, lighter designs became more popular.

DATE	6–5TH CENTURIES BCE
ORIGIN	GREECE
WEIGHT	3½–3¾ LB (1.5–1.75 KG)

Long, pronounced cheek guards

ATTIC HELMET

Based on the Chalcidian helmet —which had evolved from the Corinthian—the Attic helmet provided better all-round vision and hearing, even if protection was reduced. Although named after the region around Athens, the Attic helmet proved most popular in the Greek city states in southern Italy.

DATE	5TH CENTURY BCE
ORIGIN	GREECE
WEIGHT	3½–3¾ LB (1.5–1.75 KG)

Hinged cheek flaps could be raised when out of battle

Ceremonial or religious figure

GREEK HOPLITE

CORINTHIAN HAMMERED BRONZE HELMET

FROM THE 7TH TO THE 4TH century BCE, the city states of Ancient Greece had citizen armies built around heavy infantry known as hoplites. Fighting at close quarters in tight formation, they proved more than a match for Persian invaders at Marathon and Plataea, and fought one another in the internecine Peloponnesian Wars. After the decline of the city states, Greek infantry served in the all-conquering army of Alexander the Great and as mercenaries fighting for Middle Eastern powers.

CITIZEN SOLDIERS

The hoplite of the city-state era was an amateur, part-time soldier. Military service was both a duty and a privilege of his status as a citizen of Athens, Sparta, or Thebes. The hoplite was obliged to present himself for service equipped with armor, shield, sword, and spear when the state required.

Only well-off citizens could afford the panoply of armor and other equipment, so hoplites were of necessity a social elite. They fought banded together in a tight formation known as a phalanx, while lightly armed infantry from the lower classes swarmed around their flanks armed with missile weapons. The best trained and disciplined of the city-state armies was that of Sparta. Its citizens were dedicated to military life from the age of seven and young men lived in barracks, away from their wives, to encourage male bonding. In general, though, as one would expect of a citizens' militia, hoplites were not rigorously trained. Physical fitness through competitive games was considered a better preparation for war than drill or strict discipline.

Their effectiveness as fighters was largely consequent upon the high morale of free men battling for their own city and for their reputation in the eyes of their fellow citizens. This gave them the resolve to prevail in face-to-face, close-quarters combat.

HOPLITE ARMOR
A fully armored hoplite wore a helmet, cuirass, and greaves, all made of bronze. Polished until it shone, armor provided an impressive visual display of status as well as practical protection.

Bronze helmet with cheek guards

Cuirass molding idealizes warrior's muscles

Two cuirass plates held together at sides with leather straps

Bronze greaves protect legs exposed below shield

HOPLITE AND CHARIOT
Chariots are frequently represented in Ancient Greek art, because they feature prominently in the story of the Trojan Wars as narrated in Homer's *Iliad*. By the city-state period, the Greeks no longer used chariots, although their enemies, the Persians, certainly did.

HOPLITES ENTERING BATTLE
As hoplites enter combat, the stabbing spear is wielded overarm while the large round shield is worn hooked over the left forearm. The need for greaves to protect the lower leg, exposed beneath the level of the shield, is evident. The horsehair crests on the helmets were probably for visual effect. Showing the hoplites without clothing aside from their armor is only an artistic convention.

"GO NEAR, STRIKE WITH A LONG SPEAR OR A SWORD AT CLOSE RANGE, AND KILL A MAN. SET FOOT AGAINST FOOT, PRESS SHIELD AGAINST SHIELD, FLING CREST AGAINST CREST..."

SPARTAN POET TYRTAEUS, 7TH CENTURY BCE

TOOLS OF COMBAT

SPEARHEAD

SPEAR-BUTT SPIKE

CORINTHIAN HELMET

PHALANX FORMATION

Greek hoplites fought standing shoulder to shoulder in a phalanx, confronting the enemy with a wall of shields. Since each man's safety depended on his neighbor standing firm, it was a style of warfare in which group bonding was at a premium. When two phalanxes met, charging in opposite directions, there was a mighty clash of shield on shield. The hoplites stabbed with their spears and pushed with their shields until one of the formations broke and fled.

HOPLITE PHALANX

ANCIENT ROMAN WEAPONS AND ARMOR

THE ROMAN ARMY was the finest fighting machine of the Ancient World. Its troops were highly disciplined, well trained, and generally well led. The Roman legionary was also well equipped for whatever task was demanded of him. Archers and javelin-throwing light troops would disrupt the enemy, but the main battle was invariably fought by the heavy foot soldier: protected by a large rectangular shield, he fought in close formation to overwhelm the enemy with his short sword.

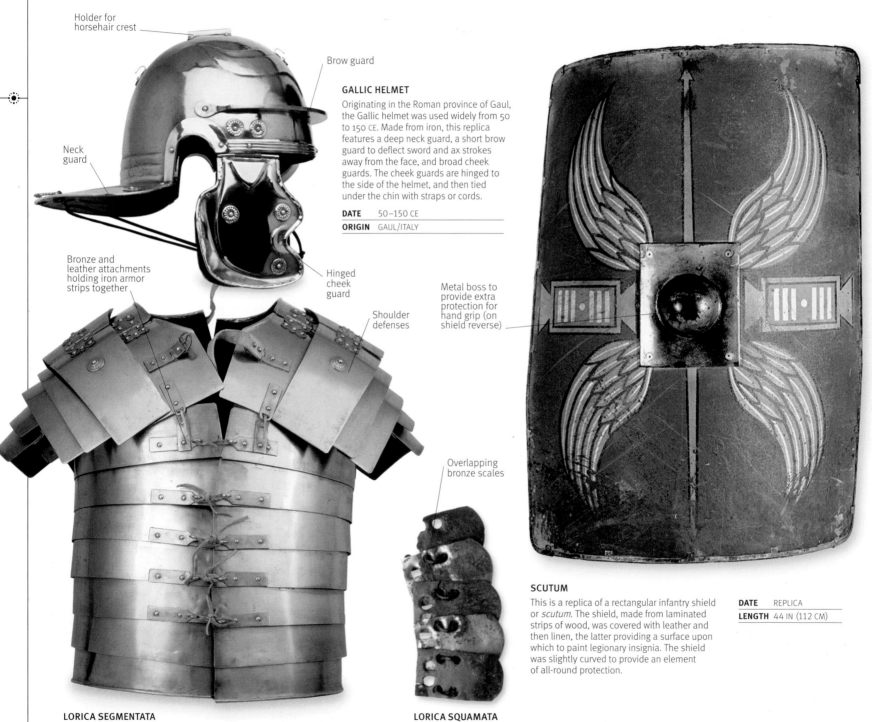

Holder for horsehair crest

Brow guard

Neck guard

Bronze and leather attachments holding iron armor strips together

Hinged cheek guard

Shoulder defenses

Metal boss to provide extra protection for hand grip (on shield reverse)

Overlapping bronze scales

GALLIC HELMET

Originating in the Roman province of Gaul, the Gallic helmet was used widely from 50 to 150 CE. Made from iron, this replica features a deep neck guard, a short brow guard to deflect sword and ax strokes away from the face, and broad cheek guards. The cheek guards are hinged to the side of the helmet, and then tied under the chin with straps or cords.

DATE	50–150 CE
ORIGIN	GAUL/ITALY

SCUTUM

This is a replica of a rectangular infantry shield or *scutum*. The shield, made from laminated strips of wood, was covered with leather and then linen, the latter providing a surface upon which to paint legionary insignia. The shield was slightly curved to provide an element of all-round protection.

DATE	REPLICA
LENGTH	44 IN (112 CM)

LORICA SEGMENTATA

Made of iron strips, this reproduction *lorica segmentata*—a combination of cuirass and shoulder defense—was worn from early in the 1st century CE to the 3rd century CE. This armor gave the Roman legionary a reasonable degree of protection and mobility.

DATE	1–3RD CENTURIES CE
ORIGIN	ROMAN EMPIRE

LORICA SQUAMATA

Another type of cuirass was the squamata. This was made of overlapping bronze or iron scales attached to hide or strong cloth. The scales, joined to each other with metal wires, were usually positioned in horizontal rows.

GLADIUS AND SCABBARD

While spears were important in softening up the enemy, the key Roman weapon was the short sword or *gladius*, which the legionary used to stab his opponent. Decorated in gold and silver, this magnificent ceremonial *gladius* was probably presented to a favored officer by the Emperor Tiberius.

DATE	c.15 CE
ORIGIN	ROME
LENGTH	22½ IN (57.5 CM)

LANCEA

PILUM

Long iron point

Traces of wood from scabbard adhering to steel blade

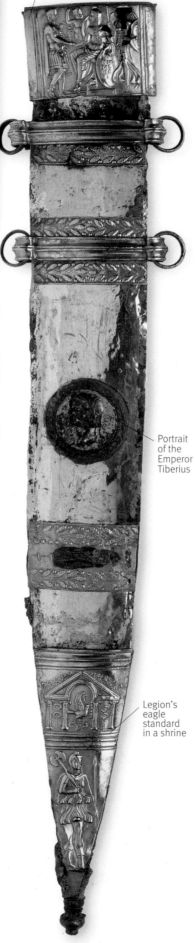

Rusted and corroded steel sword blade

Long shaft made of ash

Gold decoration showing Tiberius presenting his victories to stepfather Emperor Augustus

Portrait of the Emperor Tiberius

Legion's eagle standard in a shrine

LANCEA AND PILUM

There are three main types of Roman spear: the heavy thrusting spear (*hasta*), the light thrusting spear (*lancea*), and the weighted javelin (*pilum*). This replica *pilum* has a long iron spearhead intended to pierce shields or armor; it was also designed to bend or break off on impact to prevent the enemy from throwing it back.

Horsehair crest

Simple circular design

MONTEFORTINO HELMET

This replica helmet design dates back to 200 BCE, and was based on that used by the Romans' Celtic opponents. Like the similar Coolus helmet, it was made from bronze, and produced in vast numbers for Roman legionaries until the mid-1st century CE.

DATE	2ND BCE—1ST CE
ORIGIN	ITALY

Holder for horsehair plume

Long cheek guards

Deep neck guard

GALLIC HELMET

This replica Roman Gallic-style helmet proved effective for the Roman Army: it provided good protection for the head and shoulders and allowed the legionary good visibility and the ability to hear commands.

Scenes of gladiatorial combat

Shallow visor

Protective grates over eyes

Full face protection

GLADIATOR'S HELMET

The *provocator* (or challenger) gladiator was equipped with a helmet based on the Roman legionary's Gallic pattern, but with the addition of a full-face visor with two round eye holes covered with protective grates.

DATE	1ST BCE—3RD CE
ORIGIN	ROME

ROMAN LEGIONARY

ROMAN INFANTRY SHIELD

THE ROMAN ARMY of the 1st century CE held together an empire stretching from Britain to North Africa, and from Spain to the Middle East. The majority of the soldiers of the Roman legions were armored infantry. Stationed in fortresses, forts, and camps around the empire, the legionaries acted as police, administrators, construction workers, and engineers, and carried out duties that ranged from patrols to full-scale wars.

PROFESSIONAL SOLDIERS

The Roman legionary was a professional soldier engaged for 20 years active service plus five years lighter duties as a "veteran." Legionaries were recruited from Roman citizens, mostly volunteers from the poorer classes. They were organized into centuries of 80 men, led by a centurion. Six centuries made a cohort and ten cohorts a legion. The system encouraged group loyalty at every level.

Rigorous training and daily drill made the legionary a disciplined, hardened fighting man. He was trained to march 20 miles (322 km) in five hours and to fight with absolute ruthlessness. Drawn up for battle, legionaries waited until the enemy was almost upon them before throwing their *pilum* (spear), then attacking with the *gladius* (short sword). Punishments for lapses of discipline were brutal—a man who slept on guard was clubbed to death by his colleagues. On retirement, the legionary received a plot of land or a lump-sum payment in recognition of his service.

TRAJAN'S COLUMN
In a scene from the Dacian Wars (101–106 AD), as depicted on Trajan's Column in Rome, Roman soldiers fight back against a Dacian assault on the walls of their fort, while a column of legionaries with a mounted officer arrives to rescue them. Erected to commemorate the emperor Trajan's campaigns, the column provides a visual record of Roman military life.

LEGIONARY DRESS
When the Roman Empire was at its height, legionaries wore simple bronze helmets and segmented armor (*lorica segmentata*). Under the armor, they had a belted tunic and, on their feet, sturdy metal-studded sandals. The ability of the Roman state to equip all its soldiers with armor and helmets contrasted with the Empire's "barbarian" enemies.

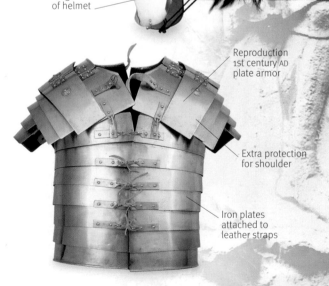

Horsehair crest may have indicated rank

Reproduction 1st century BCE bronze Montefortina-style helmet

Cheek pieces hinged to side of helmet

Reproduction 1st century AD plate armor

Extra protection for shoulder

Iron plates attached to leather straps

HADRIAN'S WALL

EXCAVATED VINDOLANDA FORT RUINS AT HADRIAN'S WALL

Roman legionaries could be classified as combat engineers, for construction work was as much a part of their duties as fighting. Hadrian's Wall, which stretches across 73 miles (118 km) of northern England, was built by legionaries in the early 2nd century. Marking the northern limit of the Empire, the wall and its forts were manned by the legions for over 250 years.

"THE ROMANS INSTILL INTO THEIR SOLDIERS FORTITUDE, NOT ONLY OF BODY, BUT ALSO OF SOUL."

CONTEMPORARY JEWISH HISTORIAN JOSEPHUS, THE JEWISH WAR

ROMAN AUXILIARIES
Two Roman auxiliaries offer the severed heads of their enemies to the emperor, behind the backs of a rank of legionaries. Whereas all legionaries were Roman citizens, the auxiliaries were non-citizens. They can be distinguished by their oval shields and mail body armor. The auxiliary legions had lower status but were often made to bear the brunt of the fighting.

TOOLS OF COMBAT

ORIGINAL SCABBARD

SWORD BLADE

GLADIUS: SHORT SWORD

HASTA AND PILUM: THROWING SPEARS

GLADIUS SCABBARD

3000 BCE—1000 CE

◄ 40–41 ANCIENT GREEK WEAPONS AND ARMOR   ◄ 44–45 ANCIENT ROMAN WEAPONS AND ARMOR   ► 50–51 ANGLO-SAXON AND FRANKISH WEAPONS AND ARMOR

THE ANCIENT WORLD

BRONZE- AND IRON-AGE WEAPONS AND ARMOR

THE CELTS WERE great warriors: in 390 BCE they crushed the army of the Roman Republic and sacked Rome itself. They were known as swordsmen, heavy infantry who repeatedly charged their enemies. Most fought on foot with little armor other than a helmet and shield. The nobles fought from horseback or, particularly in Britain, chariots. The Celts are famed for their decorative and metalworking skills.

Horns were often symbols of gods in the Ancient World

BRONZE HELMET

The only horned Iron-Age helmet to be found in Europe, this piece is made from bronze sheets riveted together. Dredged from the Thames River in London, it is almost certainly a parade helmet, not being strong enough to wear in battle.

DATE	250–50 BCE
ORIGIN	BRITAIN
HEIGHT	9.5 IN (24 CM)

Decorative bronze metalwork on hilt

Carefully worked bronze rivets

Iron blade

CELTIC DAGGER

The breathtaking art of the Celts is displayed on the hilt of this dagger. As with so many pieces of arms and armor that have survived, it has probably done so because it was used for funerary or display purposes. Knives and daggers were working tools, but this is so beautiful and intricate that it may not have been designed for everyday use.

Celtic La Tène-style decoration

Estimated to fit head size 22½ in (56 cm)

Originally highly polished and shiny

| DATE | UNKNOWN |
| ORIGIN | BRITAIN |

One-piece casting

The edges were hammered repeatedly

Wood, bone, or horn plates

BRONZE LEAF-SHAPED SWORD

Until iron working started around 600 BCE, bronze dominated weapon manufacture. This leaf-shaped sword is typical in size and shape of Bronze-Age swords, with a double-edged blade. Bronze is hard to sharpen and keep sharp, so this blade represents significant metalworking skills.

DATE	c.1000 BCE
ORIGIN	BRITAIN
LENGTH	22¾ IN (57.9 CM)

GERMANIC BRONZE SWORD

Bronze-Age one-piece, leaf-shaped swords were designed for slashing and were often more effective than a spear or longer thrusting sword. This suited the method of fighting the Celts preferred.

Engraved ornamentation on pommel

Hilt originally wrapped in leather

Extended unsharpened ricasso

DATE	1000 BCE
ORIGIN	GERMANY
LENGTH	25¾ IN (66.5 CM)

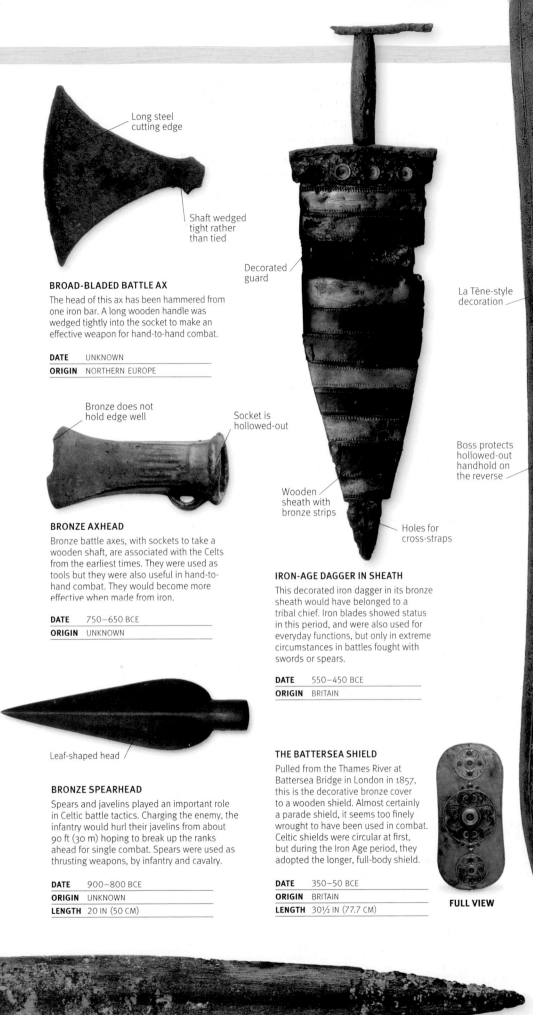

BROAD-BLADED BATTLE AX

Long steel cutting edge

Shaft wedged tight rather than tied

The head of this ax has been hammered from one iron bar. A long wooden handle was wedged tightly into the socket to make an effective weapon for hand-to-hand combat.

DATE	UNKNOWN
ORIGIN	NORTHERN EUROPE

BRONZE AXHEAD

Bronze does not hold edge well

Bronze battle axes, with sockets to take a wooden shaft, are associated with the Celts from the earliest times. They were used as tools but they were also useful in hand-to-hand combat. They would become more effective when made from iron.

DATE	750–650 BCE
ORIGIN	UNKNOWN

IRON-AGE DAGGER IN SHEATH

Decorated guard

Socket is hollowed-out

Wooden sheath with bronze strips

Holes for cross-straps

This decorated iron dagger in its bronze sheath would have belonged to a tribal chief. Iron blades showed status in this period, and were also used for everyday functions, but only in extreme circumstances in battles fought with swords or spears.

DATE	550–450 BCE
ORIGIN	BRITAIN

BRONZE SPEARHEAD

Leaf-shaped head

Spears and javelins played an important role in Celtic battle tactics. Charging the enemy, the infantry would hurl their javelins from about 90 ft (30 m) hoping to break up the ranks ahead for single combat. Spears were used as thrusting weapons, by infantry and cavalry.

DATE	900–800 BCE
ORIGIN	UNKNOWN
LENGTH	20 IN (50 CM)

THE BATTERSEA SHIELD

Pulled from the Thames River at Battersea Bridge in London in 1857, this is the decorative bronze cover to a wooden shield. Almost certainly a parade shield, it seems too finely wrought to have been used in combat. Celtic shields were circular at first, but during the Iron Age period, they adopted the longer, full-body shield.

DATE	350–50 BCE
ORIGIN	BRITAIN
LENGTH	30½ IN (77.7 CM)

FULL VIEW

La Tène-style decoration

Boss protects hollowed-out handhold on the reverse

Shield has 27 studs of red glass

3000 BCE—1000 CE

◄ 40–41 ANCIENT GREEK WEAPONS AND ARMOR   ◄ 44–45 ANCIENT ROMAN WEAPONS AND ARMOR   ◄ 48–49 BRONZE- AND IRON-AGE WEAPONS AND ARMOR

THE ANCIENT WORLD

ANGLO-SAXON AND FRANKISH WEAPONS AND ARMOR

THE MASS OF ANGLO-SAXON and Frankish warriors were infantryman, who carried a shield and a dagger (a *seax*), often wore a helmet, and fought with spears, axes, and the single-bladed heavy weapon called variously the *scamasax*, *scramasax*, or long *seax*. The nobility and their retinues of professional soldiers had more sophisticated armor and weaponry: chain mail; *spangenhelm* helmets with neck and face protection; *angons* (throwing spears similar to the Roman *pilum*); and, of course, swords.

False, unsharpened edge

Grip made of wood or bone wrapped in leather

Blades are always single-edged

BLADE OF A SEAX

Swords were extremely expensive weapons, so most people carried a blade that doubled as a fighting dagger and a working tool. Called the *sax* or *seax* (the root of the name "Saxon"), examples have been found from the 5th century onward.

DATE	900–1000 CE
ORIGIN	NORTHERN EUROPE
WEIGHT	2 OZ (0.06 KG)
LENGTH	9¾ IN (24.76CM)

SCAMASAX

The *scamasax* or *scramasax* is a long *seax*—the length of a sword—with a lower, curved, sharpened edge, and no pommel. Crude, easier to manufacture than a sword, and more like machetes, they were effective weapons that would see service until the 15th century, providing those who could not afford a sword with a long blade.

Long grip for wielding with both hands

Tough single-edged blade

DATE	900–1000 CE
ORIGIN	NORTHERN EUROPE
WEIGHT	2 OZ (0.06 KG)
LENGTH	7½ IN (19 CM)

Leaf-shaped spearhead

SHORT SAXON SPEAR

The main weapon of this period was the spear, carried equally by a lord, his retinue, professional fighters, and the mass of troops. There were two types, those used for hand-to-hand combat and those thrown before contact with the enemy, which tend to be lighter and, in the case of the Frankish *angon*, much like the Roman *pilum*.

Socket hammered tight to shaft and riveted

DATE	400–500 CE
ORIGIN	NORTHERN EUROPE
LENGTH	8½ IN (21.5 CM)

Long spears were used by, or against, cavalry

Grip made of wood or bone covered with leather

Typical, slightly tapering, double-edged blade

Wooden
curved
shaft

FRANCISCA THROWING AX

The throwing ax was popular
with the Germanic warriors who
fought against Rome in its later
years. It was used in a similar
way to the javelin—thrown before
contact with the enemy to create
gaps in their battle lines.

Iron head
angled
from the
shaft

DATE	400–500 CE
ORIGIN	EUROPE
WEIGHT	15 OZ (0.43 KG)
LENGTH	6¼ IN (16.5 CM)

Plates held
together with
reinforced bands

NORTHERN EUROPEAN AXHEAD

Axes were popular weapons because
they doubled as tools and were
cheap to make. The technique was
very simple. A strip of iron was folded
in half around a mandrel, creating a
socket. Between the two halves, the
cutting edge of harder iron or steel
was fire-welded in place. A wooden
shaft of suitable length was then
wedged into the socket.

DATE	900–1000 CE
ORIGIN	NORTHERN EUROPE
WEIGHT	17½ OZ (0.50 KG)
LENGTH	8¾ IN (22 CM)

Elongated
lower edge
gives the name
"bearded" axe

LONG SAXON SPEAR

The use of spears is portrayed in the Anglo-Saxon poem
about the Battle of Maldon in 991 CE. Eorl Byrhtnoth
throws two javelins, killing two men, before he himself
is wounded by a thrown Viking spear. Only then does he
draw his sword. Thrusting spears were longer, with larger
heads such as this example, attached to the shaft with
a split socket and rivet.

DATE	400–500 CE
ORIGIN	NORTHERN EUROPE
LENGTH	19 IN (48 CM)

Long head

FRANKISH SPANGENHELM

As with mail and armor,
helmets were taken from the
dead on the battlefield and
are rarely found in burials.
However, a sufficient number
of these *spangenhelm*
survived. The style originated
in the Middle East and spread
to Western Europe by the 3rd
century CE.

DATE	500–600 CE
ORIGIN	WESTERN EUROPE

Tip less sharp
than many
seaxes or
scamasaxes

Cheek
guard

SAXON SWORD

Swords were expensive and time-consuming
to manufacture by pattern welding. They
were only used in Saxon society by people
of high rank or professional warriors, and
were objects of great veneration.

DATE	500–600 CE
ORIGIN	NORTHERN EUROPE

VIKING WEAPONS AND ARMOR

THE SEAFARING SCANDINAVIANS known as Norsemen or Vikings have a special place in European history. From the British Isles to the Varangian Guard in Kievan Rus, they came to symbolize the quintessential Dark-Age warrior. Striking from the sea in their longboats, they plundered the coasts of Europe before colonizing and settling possibly as far afield as Novia Scotia. They were well armed, in particular with swords and axes, but also with spears, javelins, and bows. They carried round shields and most wore helmets; many wore mail as well.

MAIL SHIRT WITH DAGGED POINTS

Initially worn only by the rich and powerful, mail shirts, called *brynja* or *hringserle*, became more common in the 11th and 12th centuries.

DATE	900–1000 CE
ORIGIN	UNKNOWN

Rings were riveted, flame-welded, or with overlapping unriveted ends

Early mail was jerkin (thigh) length but later mid-calf

IRON AXHEAD

This ax has a convex blade with a hardened edge welded on separately, and a flattened ovoid socket. It would have had a wooden handle.

DATE	900–1000 CE
ORIGIN	NORTHERN EUROPE
WEIGHT	UNKNOWN
LENGTH	8¾ IN (22 CM)

Hardened iron or steel to carry a better edge

Blade curves downward and inward

Decoration continues over socket

Bound around edge with leather or iron

Brightly painted, often with crosses once Christianity was adopted

Projections around socket stop axhead from shearing

FULL VIEW

PAINTED WOODEN SHIELD

The shield was an important part of the Viking's battlefield armory. Made from wood, they were covered in leather. This example is a replica.

DATE	900–1000 CE
ORIGIN	NORTHERN EUROPE
WEIGHT	UNKNOWN
DIAMETER	30–40 IN (70–100 CM)

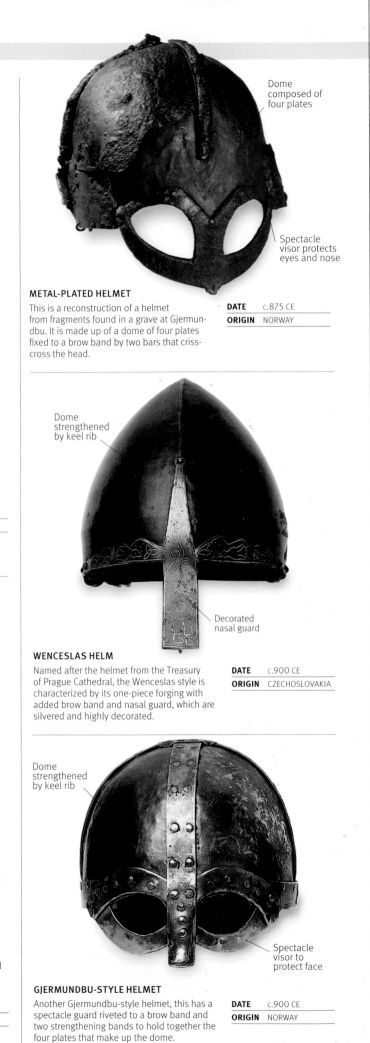

SWEDISH HELMET

Discovered in a grave at Vendel in Sweden, this conical helmet is similar to the Gjermundbu find with its spectacle visor. Most Viking warriors possessed helmets, but few would have been as ornate as this.

DATE	800–900 CE
ORIGIN	SWEDEN

Shaped plates make up dome

Animal decoration

Nasal offers nose protection

ENGRAVED IRON AXHEAD

This beautifully decorated axhead was found in Mammen in Jutland, and is the name for this style of ornamentation.

DATE	c.970 CE
ORIGIN	DENMARK
LENGTH	6½ IN (16.5 CM)

Silver wire ornamentation

IRON AX

This is one of three forms of Viking ax, the bearded ax whose elongated lower edge and slanting blade favored downward blows.

DATE	c.900 CE
ORIGIN	UNKNOWN

Broad, crescent-shaped blade

Cutting edge made of hardened steel

Long handle to allow two-handed blow

METAL-PLATED HELMET

This is a reconstruction of a helmet from fragments found in a grave at Gjermundbu. It is made up of a dome of four plates fixed to a brow band by two bars that crisscross the head.

DATE	c.875 CE
ORIGIN	NORWAY

Dome composed of four plates

Spectacle visor protects eyes and nose

WENCESLAS HELM

Named after the helmet from the Treasury of Prague Cathedral, the Wenceslas style is characterized by its one-piece forging with added brow band and nasal guard, which are silvered and highly decorated.

DATE	c.900 CE
ORIGIN	CZECHOSLOVAKIA

Dome strengthened by keel rib

Decorated nasal guard

GJERMUNDBU-STYLE HELMET

Another Gjermundbu-style helmet, this has a spectacle guard riveted to a brow band and two strengthening bands to hold together the four plates that make up the dome.

DATE	c.900 CE
ORIGIN	NORWAY

Dome strengthened by keel rib

Spectacle visor to protect face

VIKING WEAPONS
AND ARMOR

FULL VIEW

Guard formed of large
boat-shaped plate

Two-edged
pattern-welded blade

8TH–9TH CENTURY VIKING SWORD

This iron sword is typical of Viking weapons,
being straight-sided and about 35½ in
(90 cm) long. It has a two-piece pommel
and guard, both of which are decorated
with an interlace pattern in brass inlay.
The blade is inlaid in iron on one face
with a figure-of-eight mark.

DATE	900–1000
ORIGIN	UNKNOWN
LENGTH	35½ IN (90 CM)

Straight guard

Typical iron
double-edged
blade

Large
decorated
pommel

DOUBLE-EDGED SWORD

There were many variations in Viking swords,
mainly in the form of the pommel, guard, and hilt.
Most blades were double-edged with a rounded
tip because they were used for big, slashing
blows delivered to miss a shield or defensive
parry, which could severely damage the blade.

DATE	800–1100
ORIGIN	DENMARK
LENGTH	90CM (35½IN)

Hilt decorated with
geometric patterns
of silver and brass

Rounded
pommel

Pattern-welded
blade

EMBELLISHED DOUBLE-EDGED SWORD

Many Viking swords such as this one were
pattern-welded for extra strength. This ancient
process involves introducing carbon into the red-
hot iron and making a number of rods. These are
twisted and forged together with rods containing
less carbon, producing a patterned appearance.

DATE	700–800
ORIGIN	DENMARK
LENGTH	35½ IN (90 CM)

LATE VIKING SWORD

This broad, straight, two-edged blade retains
traces of an inlaid inscription, now indecipherable,
and a scroll-design pommel; the grip is missing.
The sword is more tapered than earlier versions.

DATE	900–1150
ORIGIN	SCANDINAVIA
LENGTH	35½ IN (90 CM)

VIKING SWORD BLADE

This later Viking sword blade is much corroded,
as are so many found on archaeological sites.
Their wooden scabbards and hilts have almost
always completely rotted away, making
interpretation of runic inscriptions very difficult.

DATE	900–1000
ORIGIN	UNKNOWN
LENGTH	80–100CM (c.31–39IN)

Hilt
arrangement

Blade
strengthened
by rib

Longer blade
used for
thrusting

WINGED SPEARHEAD

This lugged or "winged" spearhead, of
a type used for war and hunting, has a
corroded iron head, leaf-shaped blade of
flattened diamond-section—now curved
out of true by heat or burial—and a tapered
iron socket. The wings can catch and lock
an opponent's weapon in hand-to-hand
combat, stop a blade from sliding down
the spear toward the user's hands, and
can hook a shield out of the way.

DATE   700–800
ORIGIN   NORTHERN EUROPE
LENGTH   18 IN (47 CM)

LOZENGE-SHAPED SPEARHEAD

Throwing spears were important Viking
weapons, and their use is recorded in the sagas,
including stories of those who could throw two
at once. Olaf Tryggvasson was said to be able
to do this from each hand at the same time.

DATE   600–1000
ORIGIN   NORTHERN EUROPE
LENGTH   14¼ IN (36.6 CM)

Many thrusting
spears have wings
on either side

Rounded
pommel

Pommel top held
in place by rivets

Decoration on
hilt also serves
to provide grip

Vikings often
decorated
sword hilts in
gold or silver

VIKING SWORD HILT

This sword hilt has a characteristic Viking rounded
pommel – it is probably made from copper and
decorated with inlaid geometric designs in silver. The
sword is too finely crafted to have been used in battle
and would have been carried by a chieftain to show
his status or used in ceremonies.

DATE   c.700–1050
ORIGIN   NORTHERN EUROPE

Fuller to
lighten blade

Thick, square-section,
downward-pointing quillons

Semi-circular pommel

Later blades taper
more toward the point

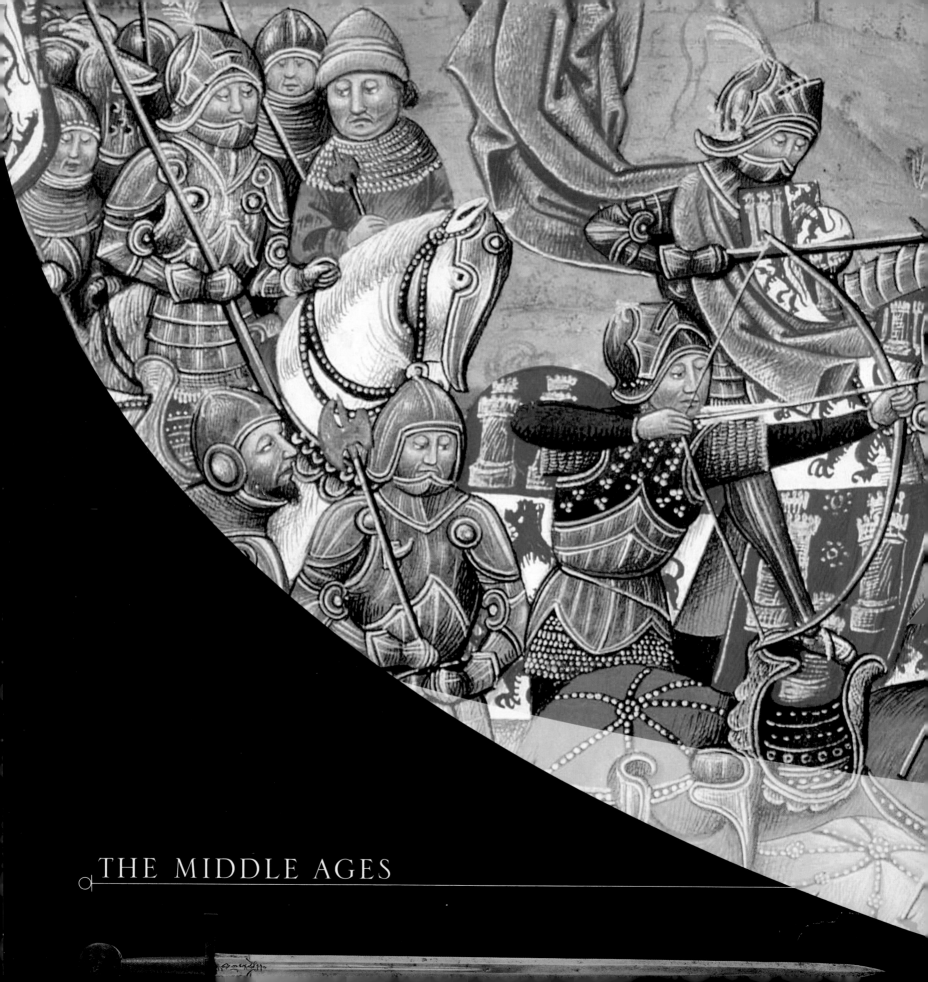

THE MIDDLE AGES

Many of the weapons, tactics, and forms of social organization popularly held to be characteristic of the Middle Ages had, in fact, been prefigured in late antiquity. Heavy cavalry, the holding of land in exchange for military service, religious warfare, and the struggle of urban cultures against incursions by mounted nomads were themselves new phenomena. What altered at the end of the medieval period was the growth in the capacity of states to maintain a centralized administration and the appearance of gunpowder weapons—powerful indicators of changes to come.

FROM 955 CE, when the heavy cavalry of Otto I of Germany crushed the lighter mounted Magyars at the Battle of Lechfeld, Europe experienced a period of comparative peace. Yet, it was also a time of political fragmentation, as, most notably in France and Germany, the centralized kingdoms of the 9th century gave way to a constellation of smaller states often no larger or more enduring than the ability of a local warlord to enforce his will. As the capacity of royal courts to organize large armed bodies declined, a system of feudalism arose to fill the breach (see box page 60).

THE EMERGENCE OF MOUNTED ARMIES

The core of feudal armies was formed by mounted men-at-arms—not all of them knights. The ability to fight on horseback—as opposed to merely arriving by horse on the battlefield or engaging with the enemy at bow-shot distance—had been hugely enhanced in the 8th century with the arrival in Europe of the stirrup, which gave a mounted warrior a much more stable platform from which to employ swords or spears. The characteristic dress of such 11th- and 12th-century fighters is summed up in the 1181 Assize of Arms of Henry II of England, which declared "let every holder of a knight's fee have a hauberk [coat of mail], a helmet, a shield and a lance."

Such armies were expensive to maintain and inflexible, and as the obligatory period of service was so short, campaigns could not be long. This, and the need to avoid casualties among the hard-to-replace heavy cavalry, meant that the raid or *chevauchée* came to be the standard form of warfare. Pitched battles were relatively rare, although those large-scale battles that did occur, such as the defeat of the

NORMAN ATTACK
William of Normandy's mail-clad army assault the Breton town of Dinan, defended by a motte-and-bailey fortification, in the style the Normans would import into England.

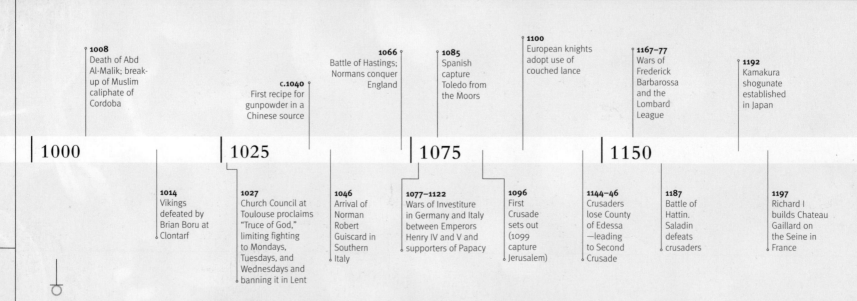

1008
Death of Abd Al-Malik; break-up of Muslim caliphate of Cordoba

c.1040
First recipe for gunpowder in a Chinese source

1066
Battle of Hastings; Normans conquer England

1085
Spanish capture Toledo from the Moors

1100
European knights adopt use of couched lance

1167–77
Wars of Frederick Barbarossa and the Lombard League

1192
Kamakura shogunate established in Japan

1000   **1025**   **1075**   **1150**

1014
Vikings defeated by Brian Boru at Clontarf

1027
Church Council at Toulouse proclaims "Truce of God," limiting fighting to Mondays, Tuesdays, and Wednesdays and banning it in Lent

1046
Arrival of Norman Robert Guiscard in Southern Italy

1077–1122
Wars of Investiture in Germany and Italy between Emperors Henry IV and V and supporters of Papacy

1096
First Crusade sets out (1099 capture Jerusalem)

1144–46
Crusaders lose County of Edessa —leading to Second Crusade

1187
Battle of Hattin. Saladin defeats crusaders

1197
Richard I builds Chateau Gaillard on the Seine in France

English king Harold II by the Norman Duke William at Hastings in 1066, were all the more decisive for it.

William's army is depicted on the Bayeux Tapestry clothed in mail and sporting conical helms. A large portion of the Norman army was, in fact, composed of archers, with shortbows or mechanical crossbows. At Hastings, massed volleys of arrows, combined with hit-and-run cavalry attacks, overcame the English shield wall manned by Harold's *huscarls*, warriors of undoubted effectiveness wielding two-headed axes, but who lacked the mobility to counter the Norman tactics.

CASTLE BUILDING

The establishment of Norman rule across England was accompanied by a program of castle building. The rapid spread of such fortifications controlled by local magnates, rather than the royal courts, became a defining feature of the political landscape of western Europe. In England, these were at first of the motte-and-bailey type with a fortified wooden tower constructed on an earth mound. By the 13th century, they had become more sophisticated affairs of stone, with concentric rings of defenses and rounded towers to guard against undermining. Castles such as Harlech in Wales or Chateau Gaillard in France could be defended by relatively small numbers of trained troops and, if well provisioned, withstand quite extensive sieges. Wars came to center on the reduction of such strongholds by storming, diplomacy, or—most often—by waiting for hunger or disease to strike down the defenders; in 1138 King David of Scotland captured Wark Castle by allowing the garrison to go free and even providing them with horses to replace their own, which they had been forced to eat.

THE CRUSADES

Further refinements in military architecture, such as the use of castellation, were imported from the Middle East during the time of the Crusades. The Muslim armies of the Levant were composed mostly of lightly armed mounted archers, who used their maneuverability and elusiveness to deft effect in wearing down and picking off the more cumbersome Crusader knights. Western armor had by this time become heavier, with the mail coat reaching down to the knee, and long kite-shaped shields intended to provide maximum protection on horseback. Armed with couched lances, a massed charge by the crusader knights, as at Arsuf in 1191, could be devastating, but equally, as when Saladin wore down the Christian army through heat and thirst at Hattin in 1187, such a heavily armored force could rapidly become ineffective if denied supply and shelter.

One solution to over-reliance on an expensive and inflexible mounted arm was to increase the role of footsoldiers. In truth, knights often did fight on foot—at Dorylaeum in 1097 during the First Crusade, one half of

MONGOL WARRIORS
Genghis Khan's Mongol cavalry were almost unstoppable on open terrain, even against other mounted opponents such as the Tartars.

the crusading army dismounted and fought as infantry. But states came increasingly to rely on pure footsoldiers, first in a supporting role, and then as a principal element in their armies. This was particularly marked from the 13th century as the economic power of towns grew and their capacity to provide soldiers burgeoned. In 1340, Bruges was able to raise 7,000 men from its population of 35,000. Armed with weapons such as polearms, which required less training than the equipage of a knight, the later medieval infantry relied on solidarity and massed formations, very much in the spirit of the Macedonian phalanx.

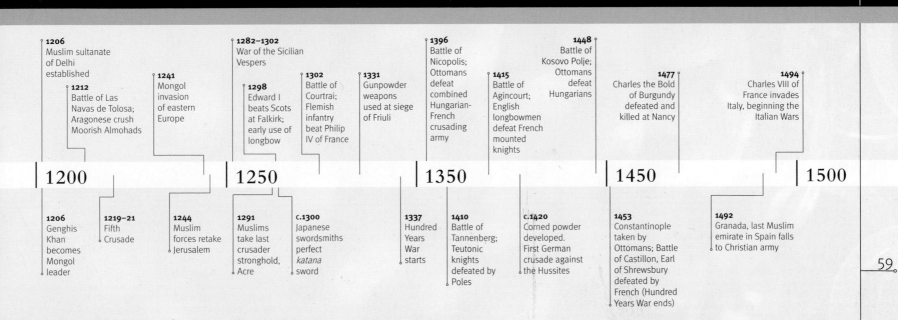

1206 Muslim sultanate of Delhi established

1212 Battle of Las Navas de Tolosa; Aragonese crush Moorish Almohads

1241 Mongol invasion of eastern Europe

1282–1302 War of the Sicilian Vespers

1298 Edward I beats Scots at Falkirk; early use of longbow

1302 Battle of Courtrai; Flemish infantry beat Philip IV of France

1331 Gunpowder weapons used at siege of Friuli

1396 Battle of Nicopolis; Ottomans defeat combined Hungarian-French crusading army

1415 Battle of Agincourt; English longbowmen defeat French mounted knights

1448 Battle of Kosovo Polje; Ottomans defeat Hungarians

1477 Charles the Bold of Burgundy defeated and killed at Nancy

1494 Charles VIII of France invades Italy, beginning the Italian Wars

1200 **1250** **1350** **1450** **1500**

1206 Genghis Khan becomes Mongol leader

1219–21 Fifth Crusade

1244 Muslim forces retake Jerusalem

1291 Muslims take last crusader stronghold, Acre

c.1300 Japanese swordsmiths perfect *katana* sword

1337 Hundred Years War starts

1410 Battle of Tannenberg; Teutonic knights defeated by Poles

c.1420 Corned powder developed. First German crusade against the Hussites

1453 Constantinople taken by Ottomans; Battle of Castillon, Earl of Shrewsbury defeated by French (Hundred Years War ends)

1492 Granada, last Muslim emirate in Spain falls to Christian army

FEUDALISM

"Feudalism" is a modern term to describe the complex system of land tenure and military obligation that characterized medieval Europe. In its classic form, feudalism meant that each man had an overlord (or liege) and provided him with services—most often military—in exchange for the holding of land (the fief). It was ideally adapted to a situation where rulers needed to supply land to maintain a military elite for the realm's defense, but fared less well as towns grew in importance and sovereigns could buy the services of soldiers (including mercenaries) outside the system of feudal obligations.

AN OATH OF FEALTY

A defining moment came in 1302 at Courtrai, when a force of Flemish burghers, armed with pikes and spears, routed an army of French knights as it stumbled through a muddy, broken terrain of ditches and trench traps.

THE CROSSBOW AND THE LONGBOW

The infantry did not rely solely on static defensive weapons such as pikes, or close-quarter bludgeons such as clubs. An increase in the effectiveness of missile technology brought crossbows and, most particularly, longbows to prominence on the battlefield. The crossbow was already well-established in Europe by 1139 when the Lateran Council sought—in vain —to ban its use against Christians because of the terrible wounds it inflicted. The crossbow bolt's penetrative power and the fact that to use it required little expertise, meant its use became extremely widespread. The English, however, favored the longbow, which required great strength—both in its construction and from the archer—but whose rate of fire was roughly four times that of a crossbow. Although first used to real effect at Falkirk against the Scots in 1297, the longbowmen played a key role during the Hundred Years War in defeating the French at Poitiers in 1356 and Agincourt in 1415. In both cases, however, the French army also fell victim to a persistent tendency to favor the heavy cavalry charge, even when the terrain slowed and channeled their progress to make them especially vulnerable to arrow-fire.

One response to this weakness was to increase the protective capacity of the knight's armor yet further. In the 14th century, open helmets were replaced with closed "great helms" and the following century saw the gradual introduction of full plate armor, which became increasingly elaborate and beautifully worked. Although fluting of the metal and the molding of the pieces to the physique of the wearer meant they were not as impossibly heavy as they seemed, such suits of armor were almost luxury items, affordable only by the aristocracy. While they might protect and mark out commanders, they were a further indication that armies composed largely of mounted knights were on the verge of obsolesence.

THE MONGOLS

In the mid-13th century, another group of light cavalry again showed the power of massed horse archers. The Mongols emerged from central Asia, overwhelming first northern China—which they took in 1234—then Persia and the Muslim states of the Levant, before sweeping down on Russia and eastern Europe in the 1240s. Relying on light,

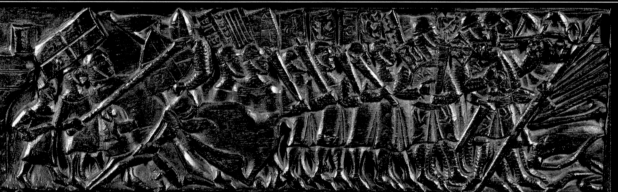

COURTRAI CHEST
A scene from the Battle of Courtrai (1302), where Flemish communal infantry held firm against a French cavalry charge. It became known as the "Battle of the Golden Spurs" due to the number of spurs collected from the defeated French knights on the field.

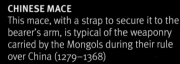

CHINESE MACE
This mace, with a strap to secure it to the bearer's arm, is typical of the weaponry carried by the Mongols during their rule over China (1279–1368)

mounted bowmen who could travel long distances rapidly, even in adverse conditions, the Mongols were able to bring opponents to battle on their own terms. They employed tactics of surprise and terror to such effect that many towns simply surrendered to them rather than risk the wholesale slaughter of their citizenry. In April 1241, within a few days, they simply crushed two European armies of Poles and Hungarians that dared to face them. Only the capricious nature of the Mongol dynastic succession saved western Europe from utter devastation.

EARLY FIREARMS

During their Chinese campaigns, the Mongols would, for the first time, have faced a new type of weaponry—firearms. The earliest recipe for gunpowder comes from the *Wujing Zongjao* (c.1040), while the Chinese may have used "fire-lances" against the nomadic Jurchen in 1132. The Mongols themselves used primitive gunpowder weapons in their abortive invasions of Japan in 1274 and 1281, but it was their successors, the Ming, who first exploited them, justifying the name by which

gunpowder came to be known in Europe— "Chinese salt." The Ming, indeed, had a military school by the early 1400s specifically tasked with instructing soldiers in the use of firearms, and also employed dragoons— mounted handgunners.

Although cannons were used by the English at Crécy in 1346, it was only at the very end of the period that firearms really began to play a significant role. This was most notable in siege warfare, where the problems of transporting the massive cannons was less pressing than in battlefield use. The huge bombards used by the Ottomans against Constantinople in 1453 heralded a brief age in which strong fortifications were no longer a reliable protection for defending forces. It was not, however, until the introduction of iron balls, which meant cannons could be smaller, and corned powder (around 1420), which gave them more power, that field artillery became a possibility. The victory of the French at Castillon in 1453, when Jean Bureau's cannons raked the English army and forced its flight, was perhaps the first example of a victory won through its use.

The first handguns had appeared in the early 1400s—by 1421 John the Fearless of Burgundy was said to have 4,000 in his army. Yet it was not until the introduction, from around 1450, of matchlock arquebuses, which were possible —just—to reload in combat, that the handgun began to find a place on the battlefield. Even so, the late 15th century was very much a time of transition: as late as 1494, half the French army that invaded Italy was composed of heavy cavalry, while, in contrast, the Swiss mercenaries who defeated the Burgundians at Nancy in 1477 were composed of a combined force of pikemen mixed with handgunners. The Burgundians could not penetrate the Swiss phalanx, leaving them vulnerable to volleys of fire from the handgunners.

By the early 16th century, the idea of military obligation in return for land had faded in western Europe and, elsewhere, states, such as those of the Ming and the Ottoman Turks were consolidating to such an extent that central resources were once again equal to deploying larger armies and keeping them in the field for extended periods. The world lay on the verge of a military revolution.

RENAISSANCE BATTLE
Serried ranks of heavily armored lance-wielding knights from Florence and Siena fought at the Battle of San Romano in 1432—a style of warfare soon to be rendered obsolete.

EUROPEAN SWORDS

IN MEDIEVAL EUROPE the sword was the most highly regarded of weapons. It was not only a magnificent weapon of war—often handed down through the generations—but had evolved into a symbol of status and prestige; a man became a knight by the dubbing of a sword on his shoulders. Early medieval swords were heavy cutting weapons that were used to hack their way through mail. The development of high-quality plate armor encouraged the introduction of sharply pointed thrusting swords, whose blades became progressively longer.

Round pommel

Straight cross-guard

Double-edged cutting blade

Heavily corroded blade

CRUSADER SWORD

This type of sword—with its broad blade, simple cross-guard, and pommel—became popular during the Crusades, and spread throughout Europe. The heavy cutting blade would have been devastating against lightly armed opponents.

DATE	12TH CENTURY
ORIGIN	WESTERN EUROPE
WEIGHT	2 LB (1.27 KG)
LENGTH	38 IN (96.5 CM)

Large wheel pommel

Wooden grip bound with cord

Ricasso: part of blade close to hilt left unsharpened

Arabic inscription

FULL VIEW

Curved finger guard

ITALIAN SWORD

Probably Italian in origin, the Arabic inscription on this sword's ricasso—a part of the blade close to the hilt—states that it was given to the Arsenal of Alexandria by an Egyptian Sultan in 1432. The long ricasso enabled the swordsman to hook his forefinger over the cross-guard and grip the blade, thereby providing better control.

DATE	c.1400
ORIGIN	ITALY
WEIGHT	1 LB (0.76 KG)
LENGTH	41 IN (104 CM)

Droplike terminals

"Scent-stopper" form pommel

Remains of wooden grip survive

Rose-window pattern

Circular cross-section, straight cross-guard

Traces of gilding

Straight two-edged blade

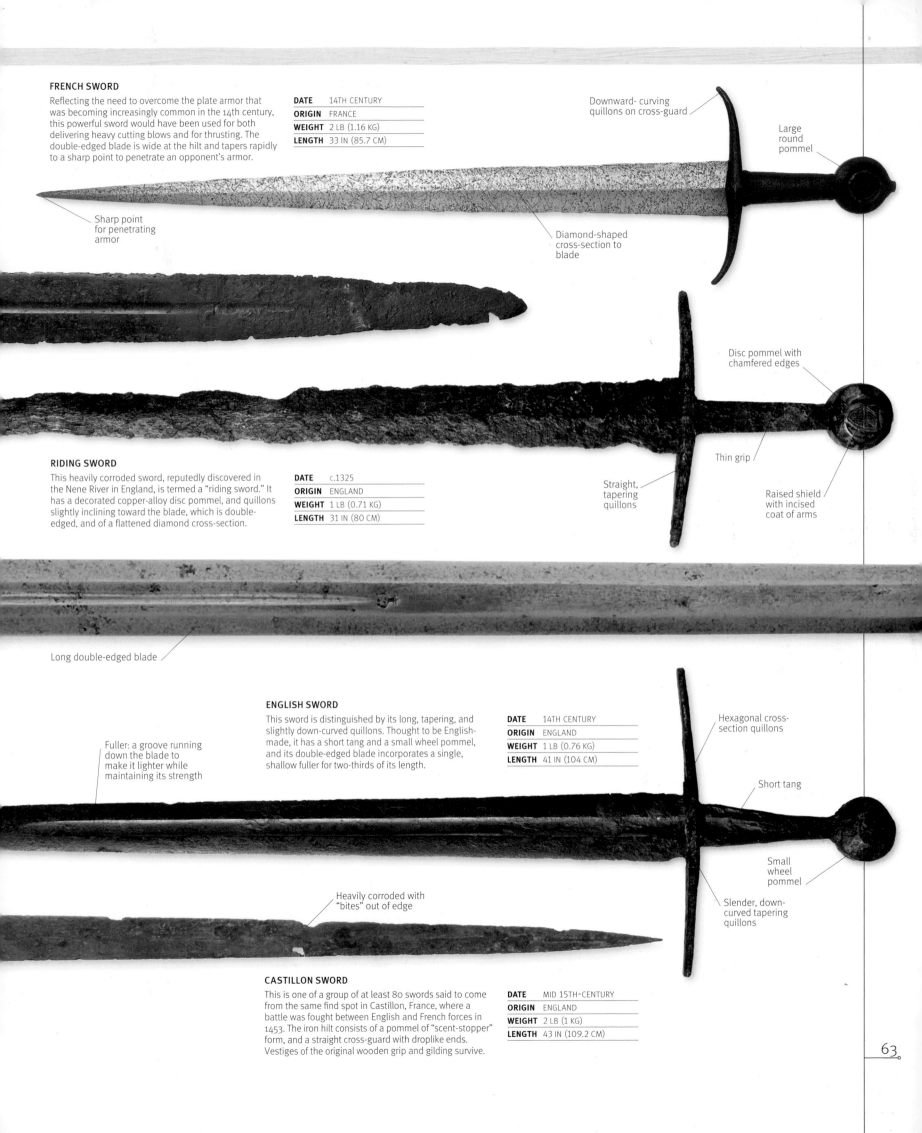

FRENCH SWORD

Reflecting the need to overcome the plate armor that was becoming increasingly common in the 14th century, this powerful sword would have been used for both delivering heavy cutting blows and for thrusting. The double-edged blade is wide at the hilt and tapers rapidly to a sharp point to penetrate an opponent's armor.

DATE	14TH CENTURY
ORIGIN	FRANCE
WEIGHT	2 LB (1.16 KG)
LENGTH	33 IN (85.7 CM)

Downward- curving quillons on cross-guard

Large round pommel

Sharp point for penetrating armor

Diamond-shaped cross-section to blade

RIDING SWORD

This heavily corroded sword, reputedly discovered in the Nene River in England, is termed a "riding sword." It has a decorated copper-alloy disc pommel, and quillons slightly inclining toward the blade, which is double-edged, and of a flattened diamond cross-section.

DATE	c.1325
ORIGIN	ENGLAND
WEIGHT	1 LB (0.71 KG)
LENGTH	31 IN (80 CM)

Disc pommel with chamfered edges

Thin grip

Straight, tapering quillons

Raised shield with incised coat of arms

Long double-edged blade

ENGLISH SWORD

This sword is distinguished by its long, tapering, and slightly down-curved quillons. Thought to be English-made, it has a short tang and a small wheel pommel, and its double-edged blade incorporates a single, shallow fuller for two-thirds of its length.

DATE	14TH CENTURY
ORIGIN	ENGLAND
WEIGHT	1 LB (0.76 KG)
LENGTH	41 IN (104 CM)

Hexagonal cross-section quillons

Short tang

Fuller: a groove running down the blade to make it lighter while maintaining its strength

Small wheel pommel

Slender, down-curved tapering quillons

Heavily corroded with "bites" out of edge

CASTILLON SWORD

This is one of a group of at least 80 swords said to come from the same find spot in Castillon, France, where a battle was fought between English and French forces in 1453. The iron hilt consists of a pommel of "scent-stopper" form, and a straight cross-guard with droplike ends. Vestiges of the original wooden grip and gilding survive.

DATE	MID 15TH-CENTURY
ORIGIN	ENGLAND
WEIGHT	2 LB (1 KG)
LENGTH	43 IN (109.2 CM)

1000—1500

▶ **102–103** TWO-HANDED SWORDS ▶ **104–105** EUROPEAN INFANTRY AND CAVALRY SWORDS ▶ **180–183** EUROPEAN SWORDS 1775–1900

EUROPEAN SWORDS

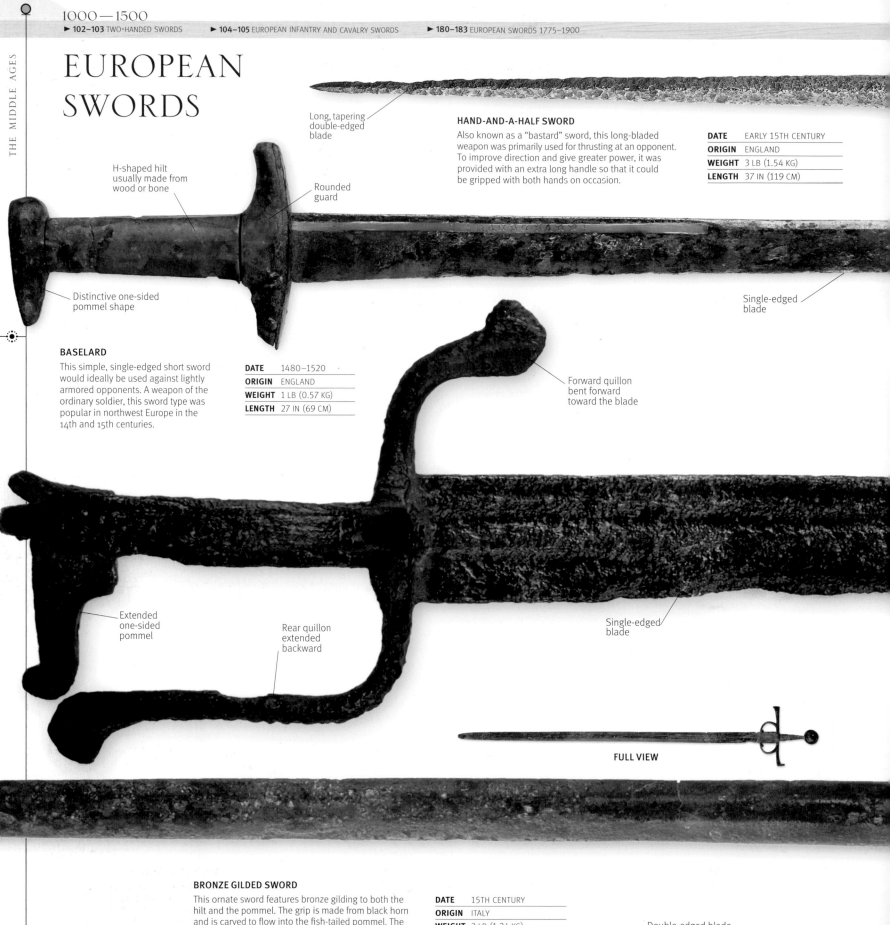

Long, tapering double-edged blade

H-shaped hilt usually made from wood or bone

Rounded guard

Distinctive one-sided pommel shape

HAND-AND-A-HALF SWORD

Also known as a "bastard" sword, this long-bladed weapon was primarily used for thrusting at an opponent. To improve direction and give greater power, it was provided with an extra long handle so that it could be gripped with both hands on occasion.

DATE	EARLY 15TH CENTURY
ORIGIN	ENGLAND
WEIGHT	3 LB (1.54 KG)
LENGTH	37 IN (119 CM)

Single-edged blade

BASELARD

This simple, single-edged short sword would ideally be used against lightly armored opponents. A weapon of the ordinary soldier, this sword type was popular in northwest Europe in the 14th and 15th centuries.

DATE	1480–1520
ORIGIN	ENGLAND
WEIGHT	1 LB (0.57 KG)
LENGTH	27 IN (69 CM)

Forward quillon bent forward toward the blade

Extended one-sided pommel

Rear quillon extended backward

Single-edged blade

FULL VIEW

BRONZE GILDED SWORD

This ornate sword features bronze gilding to both the hilt and the pommel. The grip is made from black horn and is carved to flow into the fish-tailed pommel. The four-sided, double-edged blade is in remarkably good condition and tapers to a sharp fine point.

DATE	15TH CENTURY
ORIGIN	ITALY
WEIGHT	3 LB (1.34 KG)
LENGTH	34 IN (88.3 CM)

Double-edged blade

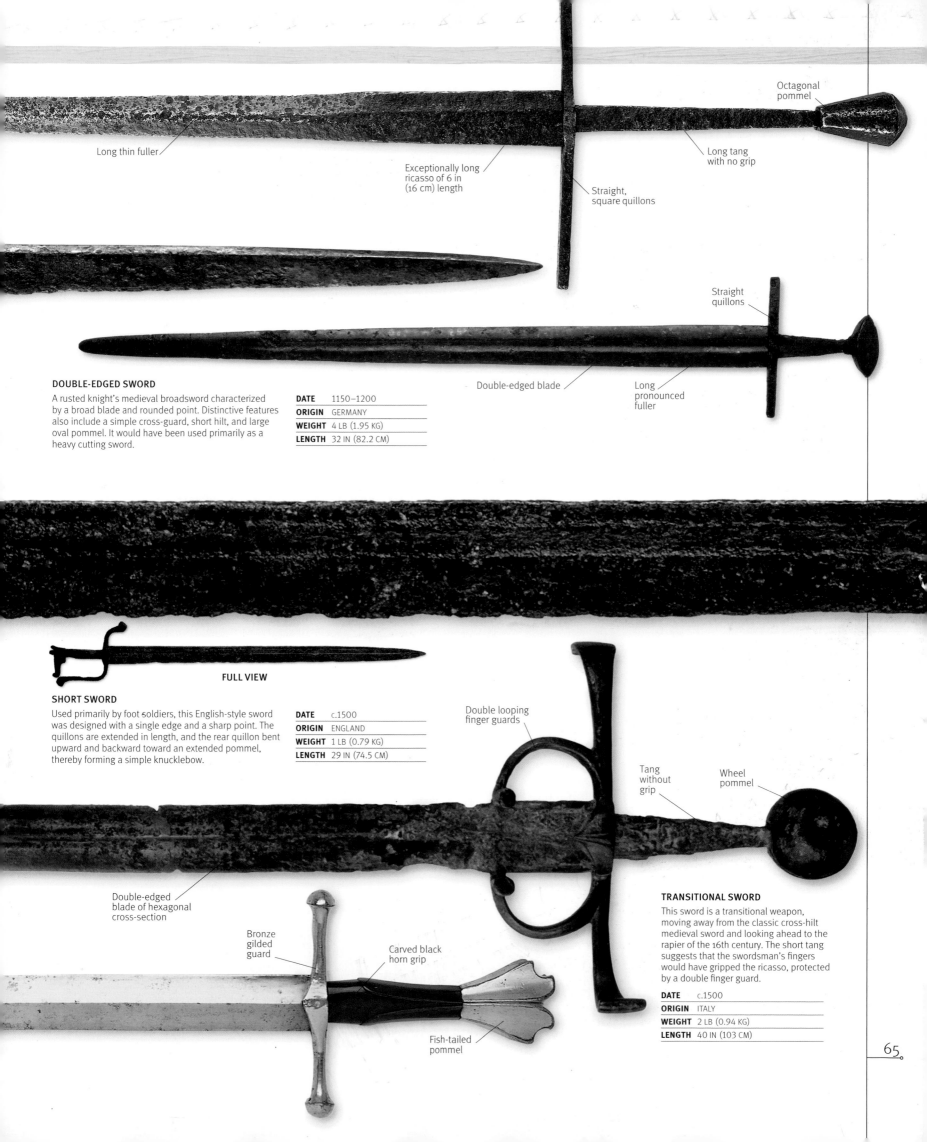

DOUBLE-EDGED SWORD

A rusted knight's medieval broadsword characterized by a broad blade and rounded point. Distinctive features also include a simple cross-guard, short hilt, and large oval pommel. It would have been used primarily as a heavy cutting sword.

DATE	1150–1200
ORIGIN	GERMANY
WEIGHT	4 LB (1.95 KG)
LENGTH	32 IN (82.2 CM)

Octagonal pommel

Long tang with no grip

Straight, square quillons

Exceptionally long ricasso of 6 in (16 cm) length

Long thin fuller

Straight quillons

Double-edged blade

Long pronounced fuller

FULL VIEW

SHORT SWORD

Used primarily by foot soldiers, this English-style sword was designed with a single edge and a sharp point. The quillons are extended in length, and the rear quillon bent upward and backward toward an extended pommel, thereby forming a simple knucklebow.

DATE	c.1500
ORIGIN	ENGLAND
WEIGHT	1 LB (0.79 KG)
LENGTH	29 IN (74.5 CM)

Double looping finger guards

Tang without grip

Wheel pommel

Double-edged blade of hexagonal cross-section

Bronze gilded guard

Carved black horn grip

Fish-tailed pommel

TRANSITIONAL SWORD

This sword is a transitional weapon, moving away from the classic cross-hilt medieval sword and looking ahead to the rapier of the 16th century. The short tang suggests that the swordsman's fingers would have gripped the ricasso, protected by a double finger guard.

DATE	c.1500
ORIGIN	ITALY
WEIGHT	2 LB (0.94 KG)
LENGTH	40 IN (103 CM)

JAPANESE AND CHINESE SWORDS

THE SWORDS USED by Japanese samurai warriors were among the finest cutting weapons ever made. Japanese swordsmiths were elite craftsmen who used a process of smelting, forging, folding, and hammering to create curved blades that were immensely hard, but not brittle. Only the steel of the sharp cutting edge was water-quenched to full hardness. The softer back of the blade (the *mune*) was used to block blows—the samurai carried no shield. Chinese swords, sometimes straight rather than curved, had little of the almost mystical prestige of their Japanese equivalents.

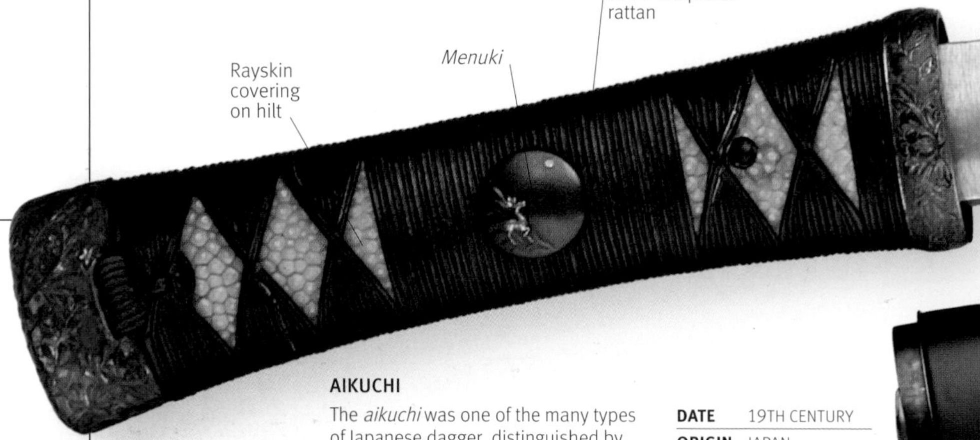

Black lacquered rattan

Menuki

Rayskin covering on hilt

AIKUCHI

The *aikuchi* was one of the many types of Japanese dagger, distinguished by having no hand guard (*tsuba*). It was often carried by ageing samurai in semi-retirement. This *aikuchi*, shown with its scabbard, is a 19th-century reproduction of a medieval weapon.

DATE	19TH CENTURY
ORIGIN	JAPAN
WEIGHT	¼ LB (0.28 KG)
LENGTH	22 IN (c.55 CM)

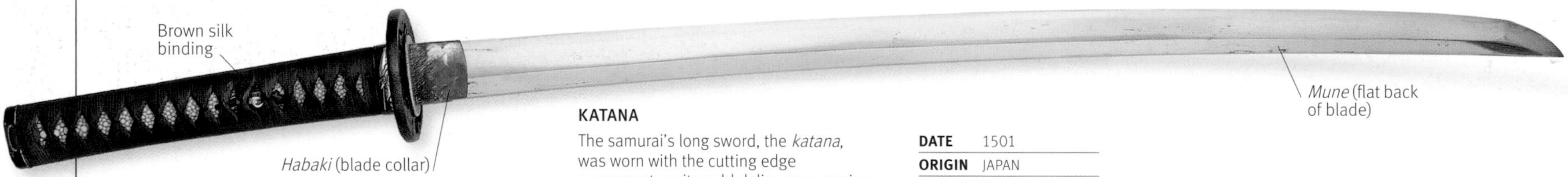

Sageo (cord) fastened scabbard to belt

Brown silk binding

Habaki (blade collar)

KATANA

The samurai's long sword, the *katana*, was worn with the cutting edge uppermost, so it could deliver a sweeping cut in a single movement. This *katana* is signed by swordsmith Kunitoshi.

Mune (flat back of blade)

DATE	1501
ORIGIN	JAPAN
WEIGHT	1½ LB (0.66 KG)
LENGTH	36¾ IN (94 CM)

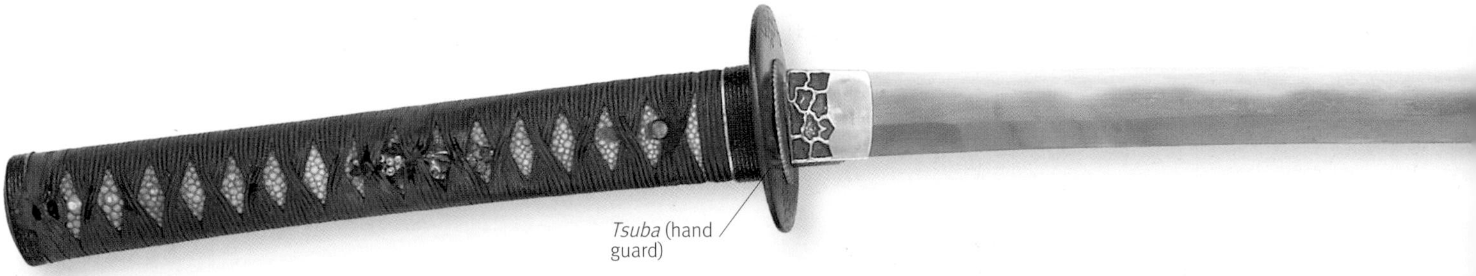

Tsuba (hand guard)

Kashira (pommel)

Wooden hilt covered with ray- or sharkskin, then wrapped in braid

Sageo (cord) of gilded Dutch leather

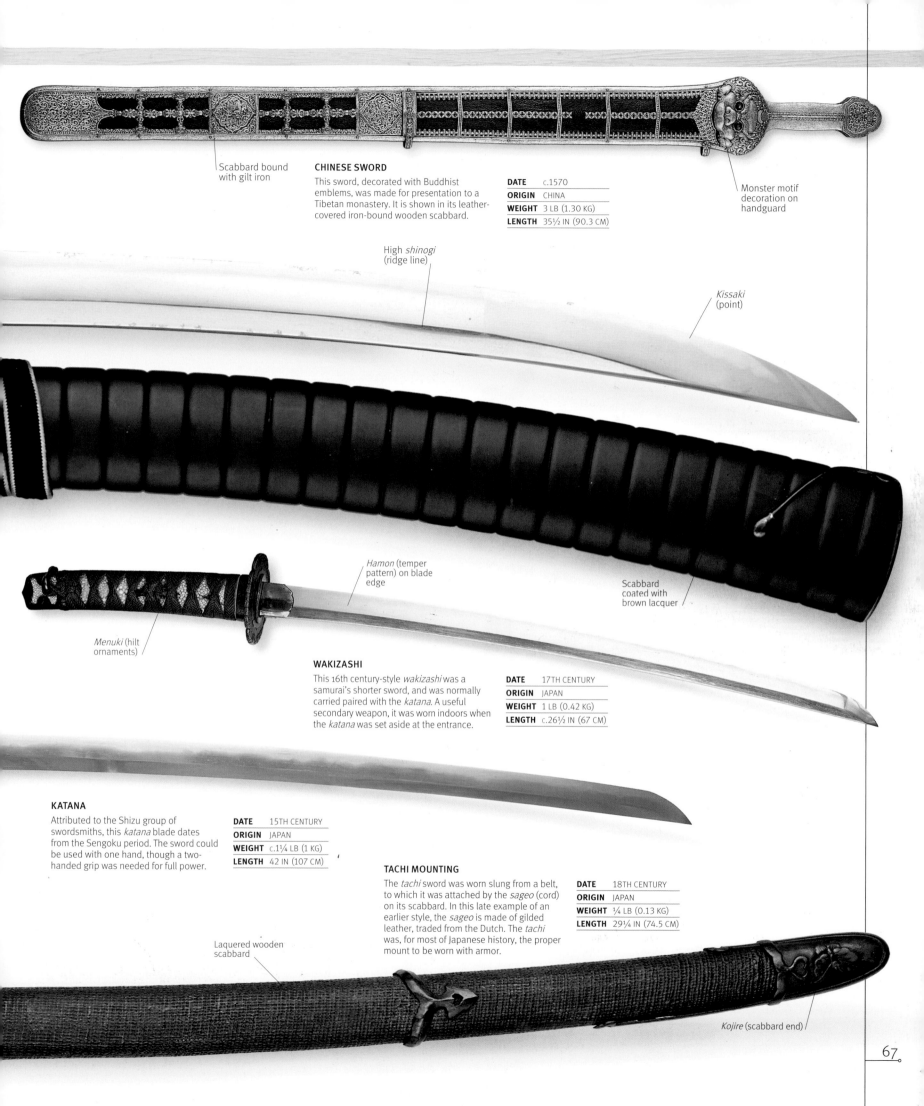

CHINESE SWORD

This sword, decorated with Buddhist emblems, was made for presentation to a Tibetan monastery. It is shown in its leather-covered iron-bound wooden scabbard.

DATE	c.1570
ORIGIN	CHINA
WEIGHT	3 LB (1.30 KG)
LENGTH	35½ IN (90.3 CM)

Scabbard bound with gilt iron

Monster motif decoration on handguard

High *shinogi* (ridge line)

Kissaki (point)

Hamon (temper pattern) on blade edge

Scabbard coated with brown lacquer

Menuki (hilt ornaments)

WAKIZASHI

This 16th century-style *wakizashi* was a samurai's shorter sword, and was normally carried paired with the *katana*. A useful secondary weapon, it was worn indoors when the *katana* was set aside at the entrance.

DATE	17TH CENTURY
ORIGIN	JAPAN
WEIGHT	1 LB (0.42 KG)
LENGTH	c.26½ IN (67 CM)

KATANA

Attributed to the Shizu group of swordsmiths, this *katana* blade dates from the Sengoku period. The sword could be used with one hand, though a two-handed grip was needed for full power.

DATE	15TH CENTURY
ORIGIN	JAPAN
WEIGHT	c.1¼ LB (1 KG)
LENGTH	42 IN (107 CM)

TACHI MOUNTING

The *tachi* sword was worn slung from a belt, to which it was attached by the *sageo* (cord) on its scabbard. In this late example of an earlier style, the *sageo* is made of gilded leather, traded from the Dutch. The *tachi* was, for most of Japanese history, the proper mount to be worn with armor.

DATE	18TH CENTURY
ORIGIN	JAPAN
WEIGHT	¼ LB (0.13 KG)
LENGTH	29¼ IN (74.5 CM)

Laquered wooden scabbard

Kojire (scabbard end)

EUROPEAN DAGGERS

THE VAST ARRAY of medieval dagger types was used mainly for thrusting at an opponent: for self-defense, assassinations, and for close-combat fighting where a sword would be too cumbersome. Traditionally, daggers were considered a weapon of the low-born, but, during the 14th century, men-at-arms and knights began to carry them, the weapon normally being worn at the right hip.

Pommel curls backward around rivet

Tang tapering toward blade

Scrolling quillons

Double-edged blade with rectangular cross-section

QUILLON DAGGER

So named because it resembles a scaled-down version of a sword, with prominent quillons that curve down toward the blade. This example has an unusual pommel—mirroring the quillons—that is curled around a rivet. Sword daggers were typically carried by men of high rank, especially when not wearing armor.

DATE	14TH CENTURY
ORIGIN	ENGLAND
WEIGHT	0.2 LB (0.1 KG)
LENGTH	12 IN (31 CM)

Inlaid geometric design

Inlaid brass mark in center of ricasso

QUILLON DAGGER

This example of a sword dagger has a distinctive brass pommel and quillons with an inlaid geometric design. The blade has a short ricasso with a mark inlaid in brass at the center, and the original grip is missing from the tang.

DATE	c.1400
ORIGIN	ENGLAND
WEIGHT	0.3 LB (0.1 KG)
LENGTH	11 IN (27.94 CM)

Heavy faceted blade

S-shaped quillons

Single-edged blade

Hammerhead projection from pommel

QUILLON DAGGER

A good example of the more basic and widely used daggers of the late Middle Ages, crudely constructed for the ordinary fighting man. This dagger's unusual features are its hammer-head pommel and the horizontally S-shaped quillons of the guard.

DATE	15TH CENTURY
ORIGIN	ENGLAND
WEIGHT	0.6 LB (0.29 KG)
LENGTH	15 IN (40 CM)

BASELARD

The name possibly derives from the Swiss city of Basel, and the baselard (or basilard) was in use throughout western Europe in the 14th and 15th centuries. This example has a reconstructed H-shaped hilt—made of bone—combined with the original broad blade that tapers to a sharp point.

DATE:	15TH CENTURY
ORIGIN:	EUROPE
WEIGHT	0.3 LB (0.14 KG)
LENGTH	12 IN (30.5 CM)

QUILLON DAGGER

This English dagger is distinguished by brass quillons, a crown-shaped brass pommel, and an unusual scalloped grip highlighted with pins. The heavy, single-edged blade—triangular in shape with a spearpoint—could have been used for both thrusting and cutting.

DATE	16TH CENTURY
ORIGIN	ENGLAND
WEIGHT	0.6 LB (0.26 KG)
LENGTH	13 IN (34.5 CM)

Symmetrical brass quillons

Hand grip made from scalloped bone or close-grained wood

Crown-shaped brass pommel

Brass pin

Single-edged blade with triangular cross-section

Lower rondel with wooden hilt

Round pommel fitted with conical metal cap

Lozenge-section blade

RONDEL DAGGER

The rondel dagger is distinguished by its round, disclike guard and pommel. It was also known as a *dague à rouelles* and was a popular dagger with the gentry and aristocracy. In this example, the tang runs directly through the hand grip and attaches to the pommel.

DATE	15TH CENTURY
ORIGIN	ENGLAND
WEIGHT	0.5 LB (0.23 KG)
LENGTH	13 IN (35 CM)

Hilts often carved from wood, horn, or ivory

BALLOCK DAGGER

Also euphemistically known as a "kidney dagger," this weapon was named after the distinctive shape of its guard, with two rounded lobes. The ballock dagger was used throughout Europe, although it was most popular in England and the Low Countries, and equipped soldiers of all ranks.

DATE	c.1500
ORIGIN	ENGLAND
WEIGHT	0.4 LB (0.17 KG)
LENGTH	13 IN (34.9 CM)

Circular grip flaring out toward the pommel

Distinctive rounded hand guard

Quillons formed by two bone plaques

Heavily patinated, double-edged blade

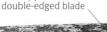

Brass strip

BATTLE OF HATTIN
Using crossbows, arrows, swords, and staff weapons, as well as the heat of the desert, Saladin and his army defeated the Christian crusaders in 1187 at the Horns of Hattin, near Lake Tiberias in northern Palestine. The loss of this battle was a disaster that led to the destruction of the Kingdom of Jerusalem.

EUROPEAN STAFF WEAPONS

THE LONG, TWO-HANDED staff weapons of the Middle Ages were used primarily by infantrymen as a defense against the usually invincible armored knight. At the battle of Courtrai in 1302, a rag-tag army of Flemish peasants and townspeople defeated a force of armored French cavalry using long, axlike weapons, a forerunner of the halberd. Cavalry were also armed with pole arms, although these were single-handed weapons such as the war hammer and mace. They could be wielded on horseback and were capable of causing severe injuries to even the best-protected men.

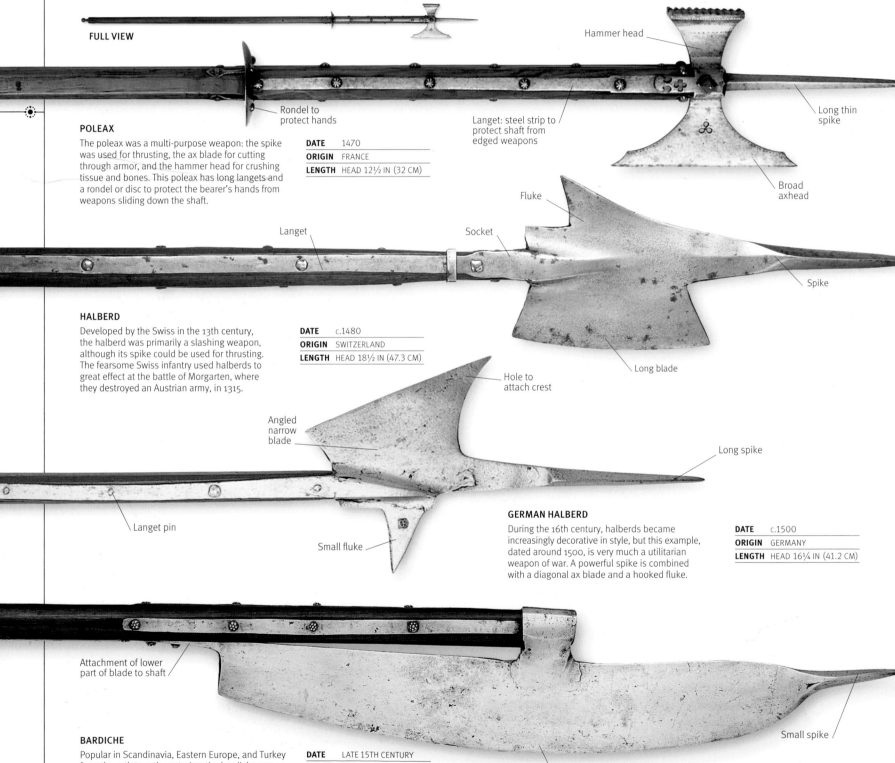

FULL VIEW

Hammer head

Long thin spike

Rondel to protect hands

Langet: steel strip to protect shaft from edged weapons

Broad axhead

POLEAX

The poleax was a multi-purpose weapon: the spike was used for thrusting, the ax blade for cutting through armor, and the hammer head for crushing tissue and bones. This poleax has long langets and a rondel or disc to protect the bearer's hands from weapons sliding down the shaft.

DATE	1470
ORIGIN	FRANCE
LENGTH	HEAD 12½ IN (32 CM)

Fluke

Langet

Socket

Spike

HALBERD

Developed by the Swiss in the 13th century, the halberd was primarily a slashing weapon, although its spike could be used for thrusting. The fearsome Swiss infantry used halberds to great effect at the battle of Morgarten, where they destroyed an Austrian army, in 1315.

DATE	c.1480
ORIGIN	SWITZERLAND
LENGTH	HEAD 18½ IN (47.3 CM)

Long blade

Hole to attach crest

Angled narrow blade

Long spike

Langet pin

Small fluke

GERMAN HALBERD

During the 16th century, halberds became increasingly decorative in style, but this example, dated around 1500, is very much a utilitarian weapon of war. A powerful spike is combined with a diagonal ax blade and a hooked fluke.

DATE	c.1500
ORIGIN	GERMANY
LENGTH	HEAD 16¼ IN (41.2 CM)

Attachment of lower part of blade to shaft

Small spike

BARDICHE

Popular in Scandinavia, Eastern Europe, and Turkey from the 15th to 17th centuries, the bardiche was a form of poleax. A particular feature of the weapon was the attachment of the lower end of the axhead to the wooden shaft.

DATE	LATE 15TH CENTURY
ORIGIN	RUSSIA
LENGTH	HEAD 30¼ IN (77 CM)

Long curved blade

WAR HAMMER

The single-handed war hammer typically comprised a blunt hammer head or set of claws at the front with a sharp pick at the back. The war hammer became increasingly popular during the Hundred Years War (1337–1453), although it had been in use since the 13th century.

DATE LATE 15TH CENTURY
ORIGIN ITALY
LENGTH 27¼ IN (69.5 CM)

Leaf-shaped spike

Pick for piercing armor

Richly etched gilt decoration

Hammer head to stun opponent

Engraved geometric design on blade

Socket for shaft

ENGRAVED AXHEAD

Favored weapons of the Vikings, axes continued to be used by warriors in the Middle Ages, often thrown with deadly accuracy. The Bayeux Tapestry shows several instances of foot soldiers using axes, both single- and double-handed.

DATE MEDIEVAL
ORIGIN GERMANY

BRONZE MACE

The mace was a clublike weapon usually made entirely of metal, or, at least, with a metal head. This example consists of a circular bronze head—with vertical ridges or flanges—and a thick wooden shaft. Like the war hammer, maces were popular with cavalrymen.

DATE 14TH CENTURY
ORIGIN EUROPE
LENGTH 3¼ IN (8 CM)

Wooden shaft with langets

Short curved spikes

MACE HEAD

Cast from a copper alloy, this mace head was originally thought to have dated back to the Bronze Age, but is now believed to come from the 12th-13th centuries. The hollow-socketed head features several short spikes.

DATE 12–13TH CENTURIES
ORIGIN EUROPE
LENGTH HEAD 3¼ IN (8 CM)

Fine tapering point

LANCE HEAD

The lance was a defining weapon of the medieval knight, and used the momentum of the knight's horse to deadly effect. A typical lance was 169 in (430 cm) in length, the shaft made from a wood such as ash, and fitted with a small iron or steel head.

DATE MEDIEVAL
ORIGIN EUROPE
LENGTH 7½ IN (19 CM)

Bronze head with vertical flanges

LONG-HANDLED AX

In the 11th century, axes were used by the English Saxons and Scandinavian warriors, but during the next two centuries, the ax became common throughout continental Europe. This long-handled ax would have been used with both hands.

DATE 13TH CENTURY
ORIGIN EUROPE

Circular curved blade

Circular socket to attach ax blade to top of shaft

Pronounced spike

Wooden shaft

SHORT AX

Although heavily rusted, the highly curved blade of this single-handed ax is clearly visible. Instead of the shaft being inserted into a socket on the axhead, here a tanglike projection is forced into the shaft. Another distinctive feature is the long spike at the back of the head.

DATE 14TH CENTURY
ORIGIN EUROPE

Extended tang to attach axhead to shaft

Gilt ax butt with scrolls

73

THE MIDDLE AGES

1000—1500

◄ 72–73 EUROPEAN STAFF WEAPONS   ► 136–137 EUROPEAN ONE-HANDED STAFF WEAPONS   ► 140–141 EUROPEAN TWO-HANDED STAFF WEAPONS   ► 142–143 INDIAN AND SRI LANKAN STAFF WEAPONS

ASIAN STAFF WEAPONS

MEDIEVAL ASIAN ARMIES deployed a wide range of staff weapons, including maces and long-handled battle axes, and weapons with blades or pointed heads. Staff weapons generally evolved from agricultural implements or from simple clubs, but they could be highly effective in face-to-face combat. Although gradually rendered obsolete by the gunpowder revolution, many such weapons remained in use, virtually unaltered, in some Asian armies into the 18th and even 19th centuries.

Tang—to be fitted to shaft

Holes for pegs to fix tang to shaft

Grip

MUGHAL MACE

This 16th century-style mace is in essence little more than a curved solid iron bar, but it could undoubtedly deliver a powerful blow if energetically wielded. Maces of this kind were used by Mughal soldiers during the conquest of India in the 1500s. They are recognizable in many miniature paintings that represent the Mughals at war.

DATE	18TH CENTURY
ORIGIN	INDIA
WEIGHT	3 LB (1.5 KG)
LENGTH	30 IN (77.5 CM)

Central grip

Protective knucklebow

DECORATED IRON MACE

This splendid mace dates from the period of Chinese history in which the rule of the Mongol invaders was overthrown and the native Ming dynasty took power. The elaborate decoration suggests that it would have served a warrior of high status, possibly a member of the Mongol elite fighting on horseback.

DATE	14TH CENTURY
ORIGIN	CHINA OR MONGOLIA
WEIGHT	2 LB (1.17KG)
LENGTH	15 IN (40 CM)

Elaborately decorated iron mace head

Handguard

Metal shaft

CURVED BLADE BATTLE AX

In Asia as in medieval Europe, the battle ax became a weapon of choice for aristocratic cavalrymen to use when fighting dismounted. No helmet or armor could offer sure protection against the powerful blow such an ax could deliver. The spikes radiating around the axhead could do damage as well as the blade.

DATE	17TH CENTURY
ORIGIN	INDIA
WEIGHT	2 LB (1 KG)
LENGTH	17 IN (44 CM)

Grip

Ornate curved blade

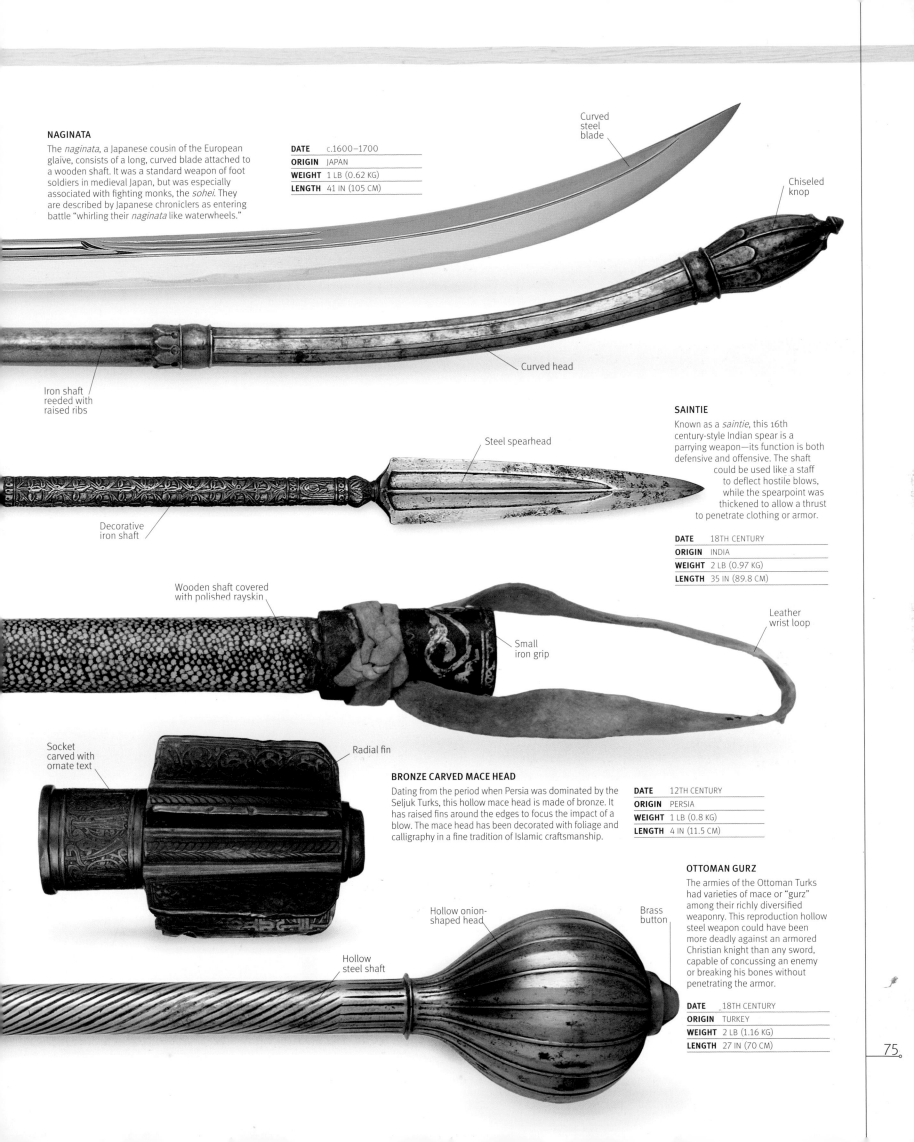

NAGINATA

The *naginata*, a Japanese cousin of the European glaive, consists of a long, curved blade attached to a wooden shaft. It was a standard weapon of foot soldiers in medieval Japan, but was especially associated with fighting monks, the *sohei*. They are described by Japanese chroniclers as entering battle "whirling their *naginata* like waterwheels."

DATE	c.1600–1700
ORIGIN	JAPAN
WEIGHT	1 LB (0.62 KG)
LENGTH	41 IN (105 CM)

Curved steel blade

Chiseled knop

Curved head

Iron shaft reeded with raised ribs

SAINTIE

Known as a *saintie*, this 16th century-style Indian spear is a parrying weapon—its function is both defensive and offensive. The shaft could be used like a staff to deflect hostile blows, while the spearpoint was thickened to allow a thrust to penetrate clothing or armor.

DATE	18TH CENTURY
ORIGIN	INDIA
WEIGHT	2 LB (0.97 KG)
LENGTH	35 IN (89.8 CM)

Steel spearhead

Decorative iron shaft

Wooden shaft covered with polished rayskin

Leather wrist loop

Small iron grip

BRONZE CARVED MACE HEAD

Dating from the period when Persia was dominated by the Seljuk Turks, this hollow mace head is made of bronze. It has raised fins around the edges to focus the impact of a blow. The mace head has been decorated with foliage and calligraphy in a fine tradition of Islamic craftsmanship.

DATE	12TH CENTURY
ORIGIN	PERSIA
WEIGHT	1 LB (0.8 KG)
LENGTH	4 IN (11.5 CM)

Socket carved with ornate text

Radial fin

OTTOMAN GURZ

The armies of the Ottoman Turks had varieties of mace or "gurz" among their richly diversified weaponry. This reproduction hollow steel weapon could have been more deadly against an armored Christian knight than any sword, capable of concussing an enemy or breaking his bones without penetrating the armor.

DATE	18TH CENTURY
ORIGIN	TURKEY
WEIGHT	2 LB (1.16 KG)
LENGTH	27 IN (70 CM)

Hollow onion-shaped head

Brass button

Hollow steel shaft

MONGOL WARRIOR

IN THE 13TH CENTURY, the Mongol horsemen of the Asian steppe were the world's most effective fighting men. Under the leadership of Genghis Khan and his successors, they created an empire that stretched from China and Korea to the eastern edge of Europe. Totally without humane sentiment, the Mongols had a well-earned reputation for massacre, using terror systematically to weaken the resolve of their enemies. But the foundation of their success lay in traditional military qualities: rapidity of movement, disciplined battlefield maneuver, and the ruthless pursuit of decisive victory.

HARDY HORSEMEN

Every Mongol tribesman was a warrior. From early childhood he learned to fire an arrow and ride a horse, the two essential skills of steppe warfare. The harsh life of the Asian steppe taught toughness and endurance, while the disciplined mass maneuvers required for an effective war of movement were learned on tribal hunting expeditions.

Organized into army groups 10,000 strong, the Mongol horsemen swept across Eurasia at a speed of up to 60 miles (100 km) a day. Each man had a string of horses, so he could change mount when necessary. The horses were also a mobile source of food—warriors drank their milk and their blood. Advancing in columns preceded by scouts, the Mongols sought to destroy enemy armies.

Most of the horsemen were archers, using their composite bows in hit-and-run warfare familiar to all steppe nomads—closing in to release their volleys of arrows, fleeing before the enemy could engage them, and ambushing any foe foolish enough to pursue them. After the archers had done their work, the Mongols' elite fighters, armed with lances, maces, and swords, would close in to finish off the already decimated enemy. Over time, the Mongol armies adapted to siege warfare and even naval operations, exploiting the skills of conquered peoples, Muslim and Chinese. But their political skills were never equal to the task of retaining the power won by their military prowess.

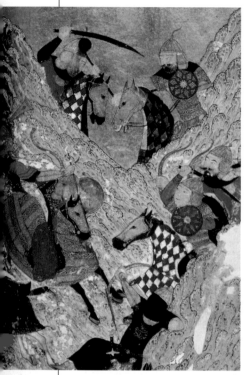

MOUNTAIN WARFARE
Mongol warriors fighting the Chinese in steep mountain terrain. Both sides carry typically Mongol recurved bows and round shields.

WARRIOR ARMOR
Most Mongol warriors fought as light horsemen, wearing leather body armor and, if possible, a silk undershirt—allegedly offering protection against an arrow shot. Their minority of heavy cavalry, however, were sometimes equipped with Chinese-style metal armor. Made of overlapping plates, usually sown onto a backing garment, this is a replica of a mongol armor that was flexible and offered good protection in close combat.

Rounded helmet designed to deflect blows

Plate protection for neck

Scale armor made of overlapping steel plates

Leather backing garment

Powerful composite bow

Straight double-edged sword

Bowcase suspended by strap from the shoulder

Quiver for arrows

WAR LEADER

PORTRAIT OF GENGHIS KHAN

Born around 1162, Genghis Khan was a chief's son in one of the many warring nomadic tribes that inhabited the Mongolian steppe. An aggressive warrior and a skilled diplomat, by 1206 he had united the tribes under his rule. He led them in campaigns against the Chinese Empire to the east and the empire of Khwarazam in central Asia. Genghis died in 1227, but his sons and grandsons continued his work of empire building.

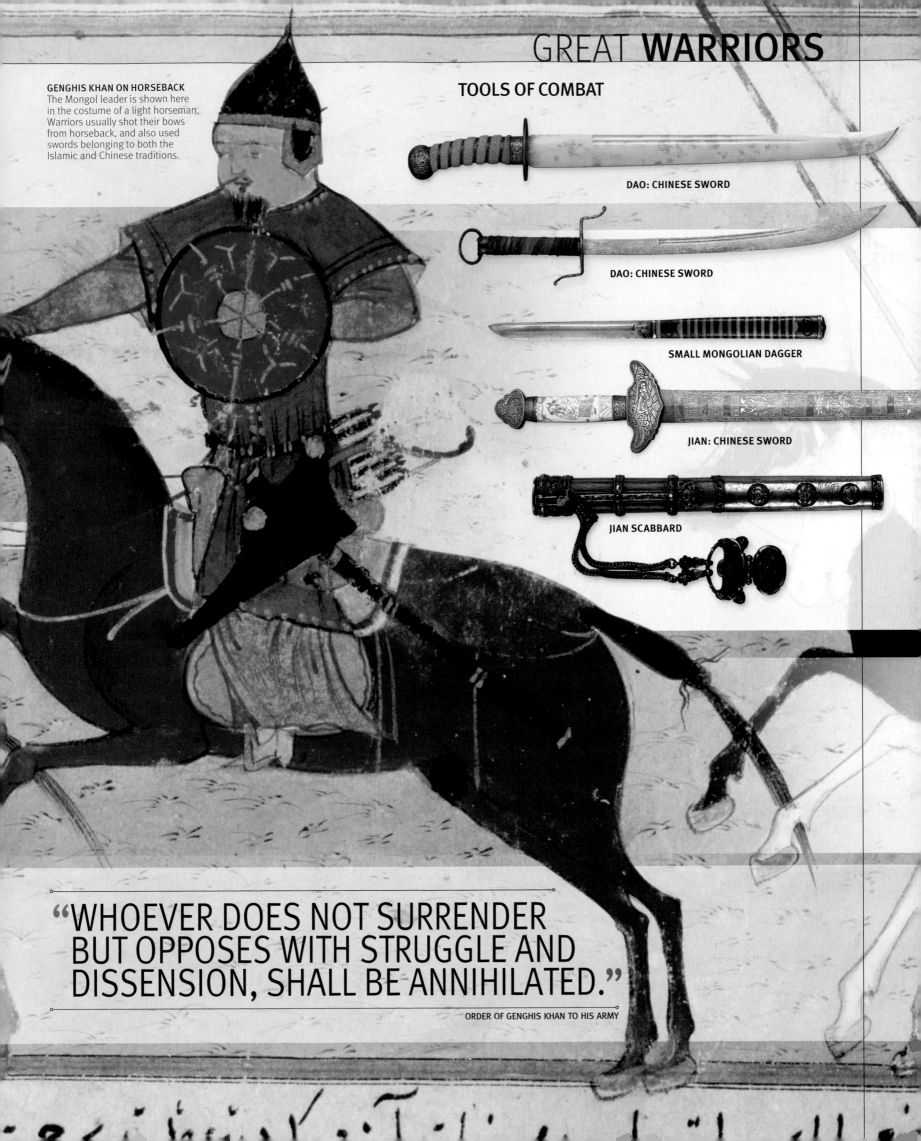

GENGHIS KHAN ON HORSEBACK
The Mongol leader is shown here in the costume of a light horseman. Warriors usually shot their bows from horseback, and also used swords belonging to both the Islamic and Chinese traditions.

TOOLS OF COMBAT

DAO: CHINESE SWORD

DAO: CHINESE SWORD

SMALL MONGOLIAN DAGGER

JIAN: CHINESE SWORD

JIAN SCABBARD

"WHOEVER DOES NOT SURRENDER BUT OPPOSES WITH STRUGGLE AND DISSENSION, SHALL BE ANNIHILATED."

ORDER OF GENGHIS KHAN TO HIS ARMY

THE MIDDLE AGES

LONGBOWS AND CROSSBOWS

INVENTED IN CHINA, the crossbow came into widespread use in Europe from the 12th century. Fired from the shoulder, it was both powerful and accurate, effective against armored knights and in siege warfare. The longbow was developed in Wales and was used in the English Army from the 13th to the 16th century. It is given credit for victories at Crécy, Poitiers, and Agincourt. Capable of ten times the rate of fire of crossbows, longbows were typically shot in unaimed volleys, decimating an advancing enemy with sheer volume of arrows.

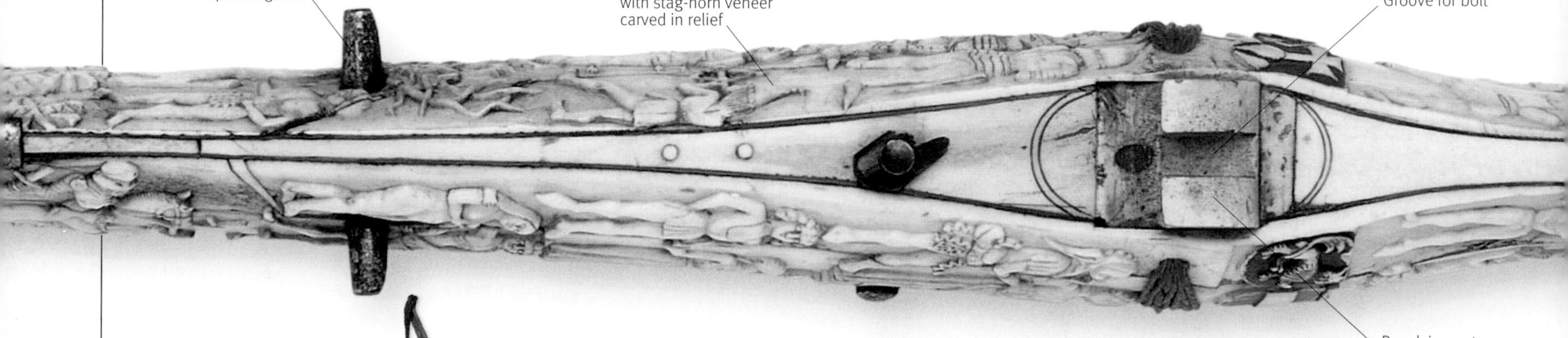

Steel pin to engage mechanism for spanning bow

Wooden stock or tiller with stag-horn veneer carved in relief

Groove for bolt

Revolving nut released by trigger below

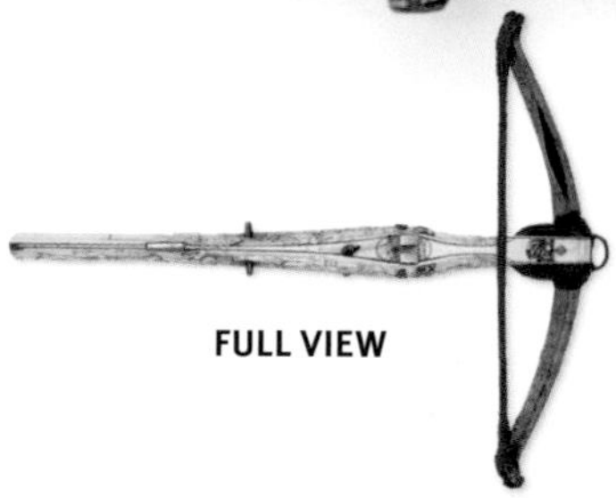

HUNTING CROSSBOW

The crossbow was an effective weapon for hunting because the hunter could carry the bow spanned and loaded with a bolt, ready to shoot.

FULL VIEW

DATE	c.1460
ORIGIN	EUROPE
WEIGHT	9½ LB (4.4 KG)
LENGTH	28¼ IN (72 CM)

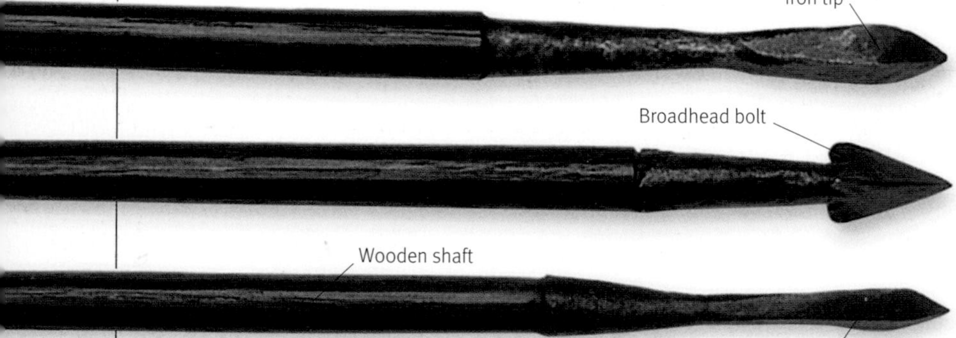

Iron tip

Broadhead bolt

Wooden shaft

Bodkin arrowhead

CROSSBOW BOLTS

Bolts, or quarrels, shorter and thicker than longbow arrows, had different tips, depending on the effect required. Broadhead bolts, with wide barbed heads, were used primarily for hunting. Against armor, a crossbowman used bolts with chisel-shaped bodkin heads. The tip of the bolt served as a sight when aiming.

DATE	c.1500
ORIGIN	GERMANY
LENGTH	TOP: 14½ IN (37 CM)

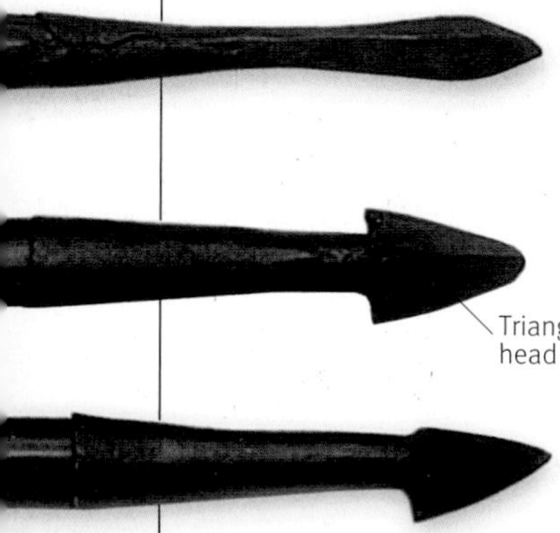

Cord bowstring

Steel pin

Wooden tiller

Nut

Triangular head

GERMAN CROSSBOW

A crossbow such as this, with a composite lath of horn, sinew, and wood, required the use of a spanning lever. At one end, this hooked onto the steel pins on the tiller, and at the other, clawed over the bowstring. Operating the lever drew back the string to hook over the nut. The bowman then placed a bolt in the groove. When he pressed the trigger, the nut turned, releasing the string and loosing the bolt.

DATE	c.1500
ORIGIN	GERMANY
WEIGHT	6½ LB (2.98 KG)
LENGTH	28¼ IN (71.7 CM)

CROSSBOW BOLTS

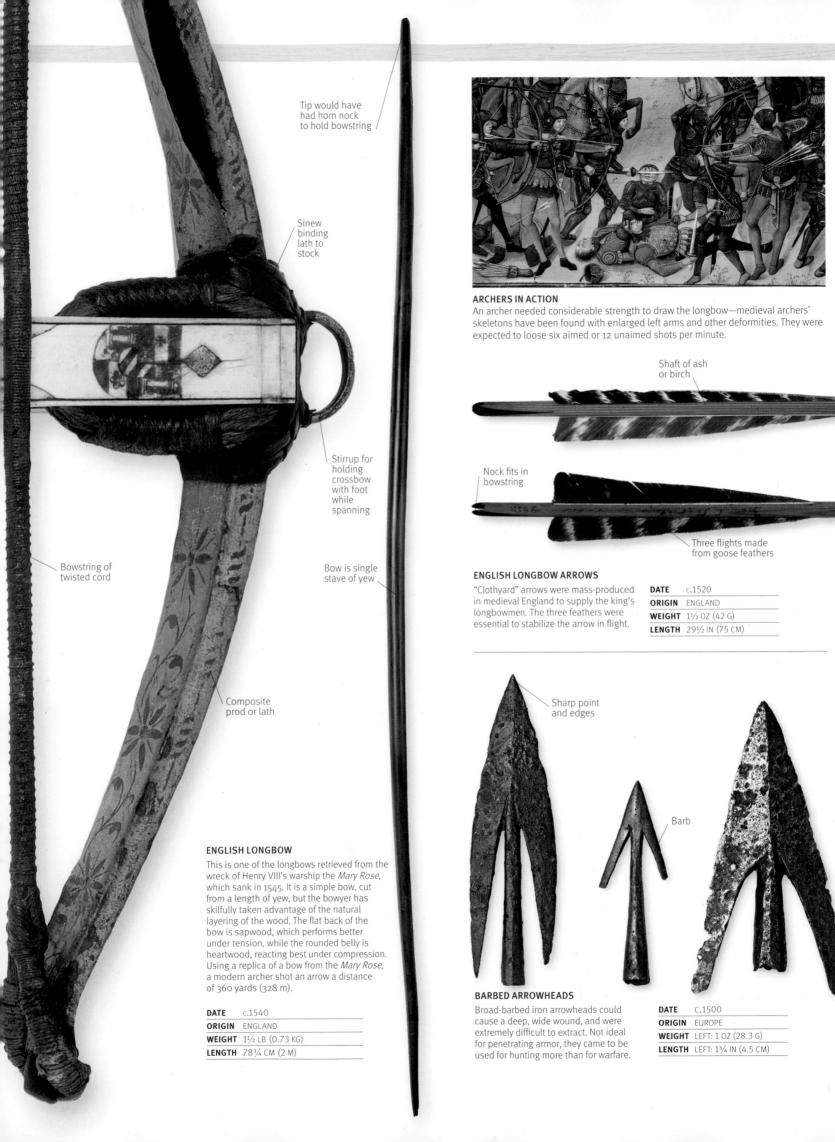

Tip would have had horn nock to hold bowstring

Sinew binding lath to stock

Stirrup for holding crossbow with foot while spanning

Bowstring of twisted cord

Bow is single stave of yew

Composite prod or lath

ARCHERS IN ACTION

An archer needed considerable strength to draw the longbow—medieval archers' skeletons have been found with enlarged left arms and other deformities. They were expected to loose six aimed or 12 unaimed shots per minute.

Shaft of ash or birch

Nock fits in bowstring

Three flights made from goose feathers

ENGLISH LONGBOW ARROWS

"Clothyard" arrows were mass-produced in medieval England to supply the king's longbowmen. The three feathers were essential to stabilize the arrow in flight.

DATE	c.1520
ORIGIN	ENGLAND
WEIGHT	1½ OZ (42 G)
LENGTH	29½ IN (75 CM)

Sharp point and edges

Barb

ENGLISH LONGBOW

This is one of the longbows retrieved from the wreck of Henry VIII's warship the *Mary Rose*, which sank in 1545. It is a simple bow, cut from a length of yew, but the bowyer has skilfully taken advantage of the natural layering of the wood. The flat back of the bow is sapwood, which performs better under tension, while the rounded belly is heartwood, reacting best under compression. Using a replica of a bow from the *Mary Rose*, a modern archer shot an arrow a distance of 360 yards (328 m).

DATE	c.1540
ORIGIN	ENGLAND
WEIGHT	1½ LB (0.73 KG)
LENGTH	78¾ CM (2 M)

BARBED ARROWHEADS

Broad-barbed iron arrowheads could cause a deep, wide wound, and were extremely difficult to extract. Not ideal for penetrating armor, they came to be used for hunting more than for warfare.

DATE	c.1500
ORIGIN	EUROPE
WEIGHT	LEFT: 1 OZ (28.3 G)
LENGTH	LEFT: 1¾ IN (4.5 CM)

CROSSBOW

THIS TYPICAL LATE MEDIEVAL European hunting bow could shoot a bolt roughly 328 yards (300 m). Its composite lath (or bow), made of layers of wood, sinew, and horn, had far too high a draw-weight to be spanned by unaided muscle power. Using the rack-and-pinion device known as a cranequin (also called a cric or rack), the archer pulled the bowstring back to the nut, where it was hooked until released by pressing the long trigger under the crossbow tiller. When shooting, the huntsman rested the butt of the crossbow on his shoulder, looking along the tiller and using the tip of the bolt as his sight.

Flights

Wooden shaft

CROSSBOW BOLT

Bolts were typically twice as heavy as other arrows. The flights were of wood or paper, and only two were used, because a third would snag on the nut.

Steel pin

Rotating nut

CROSSBOW

This German crossbow, with its handsome bone veneer, would have belonged to a wealthy individual who enjoyed hunting as a leisure pursuit. It was spanned using the small cranequin shown below.

DATE	c.1500
ORIGIN	GERMANY
WEIGHT	6½ LB (2.98 KG)
LENGTH	28 IN (71 CM)
SPAN	26 IN (66 CM)

Hexagonal wheel case

Cord loop hooks onto tiller pins

CRANEQUIN

The cranequin was first introduced in Europe in the late 14th century. One of its advantages was that it could be employed on horseback. It was an expensive device and worked slowly—two considerations that made it less suitable for warfare than for use by wealthy huntsmen.

Preparing The Crossbow

To use a cranequin, the archer first anchored it to the crossbow by looping the cord over the steel pins on the tiller. The claws at the front end of the toothed rack lay over the bowstring. By turning the lever, the archer rotated geared cogwheels engaged with the teeth of the rack, thus drawing the bowstring and bending the bow. When the string was hooked over the nut, the archer removed the cranequin, laid a bolt in the groove, and was ready to shoot.

HOW IT WORKS

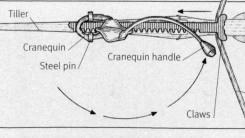

Tiller

Cranequin

Steel pin

Cranequin handle

Claws

Bowstring

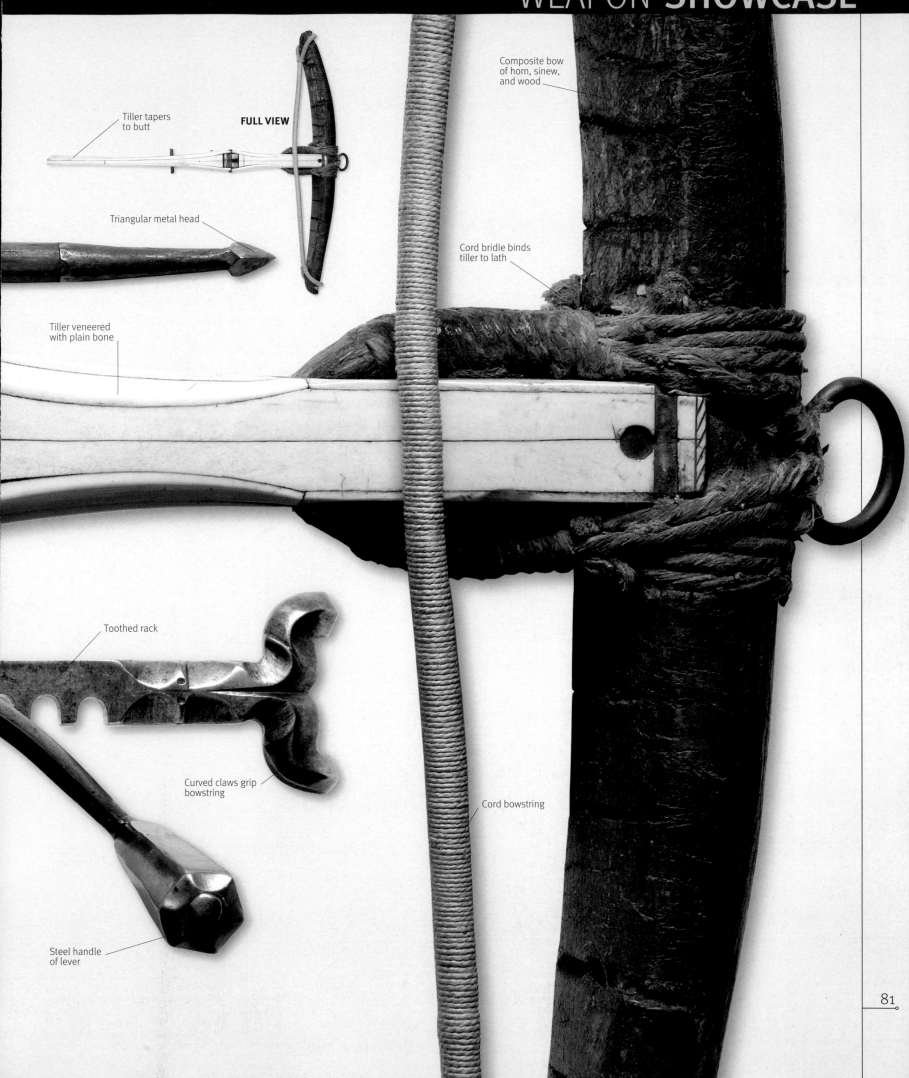

Tiller tapers to butt

FULL VIEW

Triangular metal head

Composite bow of horn, sinew, and wood

Cord bridle binds tiller to lath

Tiller veneered with plain bone

Toothed rack

Curved claws grip bowstring

Cord bowstring

Steel handle of lever

1000–1500

► 202–203 OCEANIAN CLUBS AND DAGGERS   ► 204–205 NORTH AMERICAN KNIVES AND CLUBS   ► 270–271 AFRICAN SHIELDS   ► 272–273 OCEANIAN SHIELDS

THE MIDDLE AGES

AZTEC WEAPONS AND SHIELDS

WARFARE IN THE AZTEC EMPIRE, which covered much of what is now Mexico, was driven by the need for a regular supply of prisoners for human sacrifice. Although the Aztecs had bows, slings, and throwing spears, they preferred to use close-quarters cutting weapons to disable an enemy, often by a blow to the legs. Ultimately, the "stone-age" Aztec weaponry proved no match for the steel and gunpowder of the Spanish invaders who conquered the region in the 16th century.

OBSIDIAN KNIFE

The Aztecs referred to human sacrifice as "the flowered death by the obsidian knife." Obsidian, a volcanic glass, provided a razor-sharp blade that Aztec priests used to cut out the hearts of sacrificial victims. After the heart had been ritually burned, the corpse was dismembered.

DATE	c.1500
ORIGIN	AZTEC EMPIRE
LENGTH	11¾ IN (30 CM)

Eyes made of shell and obsidian or haematite

Teeth shaped from shell

Serrated edge

Knives were sometimes decorated to resemble the face of the god to whom sacrificial hearts were offered

DECORATED FLINT KNIFE

This decorated flint knife was found in the Great Temple, which stood in the center of the Aztec capital, Tenochtitlan. More than 20,000 victims may have been sacrificed at the dedication of the Temple in 1487.

DATE	c.1500
ORIGIN	AZTEC EMPIRE
LENGTH	11¾ IN (30 CM)

FLINT KNIVES

Practical and easy to make by flaking, flint knives like these two examples had a wide range of uses in Aztec society. Aztec priests often used them to carry out human sacrifice in preference to obsidian knives because obsidian, although sharper than flint, was extremely brittle.

DATE	c.1500
ORIGIN	AZTEC EMPIRE
LENGTH	11¾ IN (30 CM)

Head and shaft are made of wood

Obsidian blade set in grooves along edge of club

ORNATE CHALCEDONY KNIFE

The handle of this sacrificial knife represents an eagle warrior, one of a prestigious order of Aztec fighting men. The knife blade is chalcedony, a type of quartz.

DATE	c.1500
ORIGIN	AZTEC EMPIRE
LENGTH	12½ IN (31.7 CM)

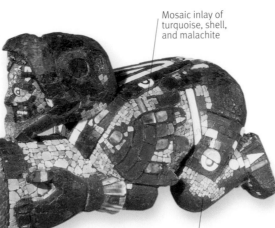

Mosaic inlay of turquoise, shell, and malachite

Wooden handle carved into shape of crouching figure

Stone blade made of chalcedony

Jaguar skin covering

Decorative feather bands

Stone flake

FULL VIEW

THROWING SPEAR

The Aztec's stone-edged spears were often launched by a throwing stick, or *atlatl*. This made them powerful weapons capable of causing severe injury—even to a fully armored Spanish soldier.

DATE	c.1500
ORIGIN	AZTEC EMPIRE

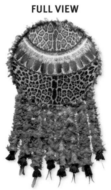

FULL VIEW

CHIMALLI (SHIELD)

An Aztec warrior's round shield, or *chimalli*, was highly decorated, partly to intimidate the enemy. The shield had a wooden or bamboo frame covered in feathers and skin. Shields were made by featherworkers, who also produced fans and headdresses.

DATE	c.1500
ORIGIN	AZTEC EMPIRE

ENEMY CAPTURE

This image from a Mexican codex shows an Aztec warrior taking an enemy fighter prisoner. The warrior carries a *chimalli* shield and wears a cumbersome feather-covered frame on his back, which marks him out as of officer status. The more captives a warrior took, the higher his status grew.

MAQUAHUITL (CLUB)

The principal close-quarters weapon was a wooden club with obsidian blades. Known as a *maquahuitl*, it was wielded like a sword, delivering a razor-sharp cut that could sever a horse's head.

DATE	c.1500
ORIGIN	AZTEC EMPIRE
LENGTH	29½ IN (75 CM)

Feather tassels

SPANISH CONQUESTS
The war in Mexico between
the Aztecs and the plate-armor-
clad Spanish conquistadors in the 16th
century was fought with the shields and axes
of a society that did not have steel, on one side, and
the steel spears and swords of the Spanish on the other.

1000—1500

► 88–89 EUROPEAN JOUSTING HELMS, BARBUTES, AND SALLETS   ► 168–169 EUROPEAN TOURNAMENT HELMETS   ► 350–351 HELMETS FROM 1900

THE MIDDLE AGES

EUROPEAN HELMS AND BASINETS

THE SPANGENHELM WITH NASAL that had been worn by the Normans was replaced at the end of the 12th century with a rounder helmet, which eventually covered the entire face, and evolved into the great helm. Although providing good protection, the great helm was cumbersome, making it hard for the wearer to turn and see clearly. During the 14th century, it was largely relegated to a tournament role, being superseded by the basinet, a helmet that provided a good compromise between protection, mobility, and visibility.

Holes for vervelles

GREAT BASINET

The origins of the basinet helmet go back to the metal skull cap worn inside a mail coif and under a great helm. In the case of the basinet, the skull cap extended to protect the side and back of the head. This basinet has no visor, but the holes for the vervelles that secured the mail aventail are visible.

DATE	c.1370
ORIGIN	NORTHERN ITALY
WEIGHT	6¾ LB (3 KG)

Pointed crown

Rounded skull

GREAT HELM

This great helm is constructed from three plates of steel, with a pointed crown and skull to deflect blows. The vision slits, or "sights" are formed between the skull and side plates, and the lower part of the helm is pierced by numerous ventilation holes called breaths.

DATE	c.1350
ORIGIN	ENGLAND
WEIGHT	5½ LB (2.5 KG)

Cross-shaped openings for toggle-ended chain to secure helm to breastplate

Iron plates, originally covered in gilt copper sheet

Triangular plates riveted together

SEGMENTED HELM

This segmented helm dates back to the 11th century and is constructed from four triangular iron plates, originally covered in gilt copper sheet, and joined by copper rivets.

DATE	11TH CENTURY
ORIGIN	POLAND
WEIGHT	6¾ LB (3 KG)

Copper rivets with silver-bound heads

Vervelle

"Ogival" skull (like pointed arch)

Hinge and pivot

Removable pin to allow visor to be taken off

GREAT BASINET

This skull from a great basinet shows how the helmet sides extend further down than was the case with a standard basinet. Over time the mail aventail was replaced by a bevor and gorget plates. This helmet comes from the Yorkshire tomb of Sir John Melsa in the UK.

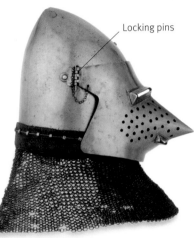

Ovoid, medially ridged form

Flared sides

DATE	LATE 14TH CENTURY
ORIGIN	UK
WEIGHT	6¾ LB (3.06 KG)

HOUNSKULL BASINET

The distinctive pointed visors found on many basinet helmets were nicknamed "hounskulls," an English corruption of the German *hundsgugel* ("dog head"). The whole visor could easily be removed by withdrawing the locking pins—shown here tethered by a chain.

Locking pins

DATE	1350–1400
ORIGIN	ITALY
WEIGHT	15½ LB (7 KG)

Narow sights

Rows of breathing holes (or "breaths")

Conical visor

Brass borders decorated with "wriggled" cable pattern

Mail aventail

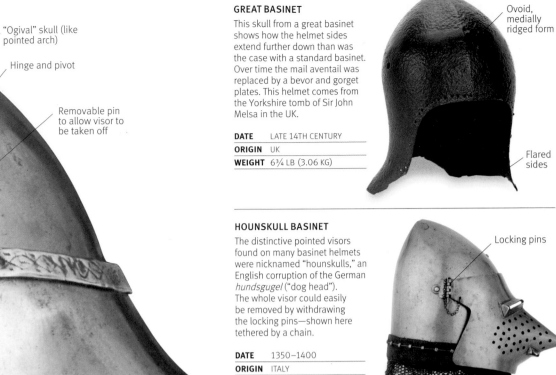

BASINET AND AVENTAIL

This hounskull basinet with an ogival skull is typical of that worn by knights throughout Europe in the middle-to-late 14th century. The mail collar or aventail has a leather band on the upper edge with holes that fit onto the brass vervelles that border the helmet's rim. A small hole has been drilled into each vervelle, through which a piece of string is drawn, attaching the vervelle to the basinet.

FULL VIEW

DATE	1350–1400
ORIGIN	NORTHERN ITALY
WEIGHT	15¾ LB (7.12 KG)

THE MIDDLE AGES

EUROPEAN JOUSTING HELMS, BARBUTES, AND SALLETS

THE GREAT HELM—relegated to the jousting field in the mid-14th century —evolved into the frog-mouthed helmet, a piece of armor ideally suited to jousting. During the 15th century the basinet was superseded by a range of newer designs, of which the sallet was the most popular. Toward the end of the century, northern Italy and southern Germany began to take a lead in armor development that other countries followed. Italian armor was rounded in style, while the German or Gothic style featured decoration in the form of radiating patterns of lines and ridges over the entire harness of armor.

Rounded skull

Rivet to join metal plates together

FROG-MOUTHED HELM

The frog-mouthed helm provided the jousting knight with basic straight-ahead vision and maximum protection at the point of impact. He would lean his head forward at the commencement of the charge to look out of the vision slit or sight, but the moment before the lances clashed he would swiftly lift his head up to deny his opponent any opportunity to thrust his lance into the sight.

DATE	EARLY 15TH CENTURY
ORIGIN	ENGLAND
WEIGHT	22 LB (10 KG)

Helmet collar

JOUSTING HELM

The frog-mouthed jousting helm would sit squarely on the knight's cuirass, and, in the case of this example, have steel attachments to lock it firmly to breast- and backplates. The forward part of the helmet was specifically designed to deflect the opponent's lance.

DATE	c.1480
ORIGIN	SOUTHERN GERMANY
WEIGHT	22½ LB (10.2 KG)

Sight or
vision slit

JOUSTING HELM

The construction of a frog-
mouthed jousting helm is fairly
straightforward because it
consists of just two pieces of
steel: the first sits on the skull
while the second is wrapped
around the whole head, coming
to a rounded point at the front
of the face. A series of prominent
rivets join the edges together.

DATE	15TH CENTURY
ORIGIN	EUROPE
WEIGHT	16¼ LB (7.4 KG)

BARBUTE

The barbute (or barbuta) is a
close-fitting, shoulder-length
helmet, and many have a
T-shaped opening for the face.
This example also has a nasal,
and because of its similarity to
the helmets of classical Greece,
it is known as a "Corinthian"
barbute. The helmet was usually
worn by infantry and was in use
throughout the 15th century.

DATE	c.1445
ORIGIN	ITALY
WEIGHT	5¾ LB (2.67 KG)

SHORT-TAILED SALLET

Originating in Italy, the sallet was
a helmet adopted by all classes
of fighting men in 15th-century
Europe, worn either with or
without a visor. This visorless
helmet is closely shaped to the
head and has a tail considerably
shorter than most other sallets.

DATE	c.1440
ORIGIN	NORTHERN ITALY
WEIGHT	3¼ LB (1.48 KG)

Tail of sallet
helmet to
protect neck

Frog-mouthed
sight

LONG-TAILED SALLET

This helmet is fairly typical of
German sallets toward the end of
the 15th century, featuring a long
sweeping tail to protect the neck,
as well as a visor with a single
sight. For knights and men-at-
arms, sallets would normally be
worn with a bevor to protect the
throat, chin, and lower face.

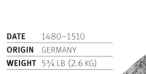

DATE	1480–1510
ORIGIN	GERMANY
WEIGHT	5¾ LB (2.6 KG)

Visor with
single sight

Flame pattern on skull

PAINTED SALLET

It was not uncommon for
sallets to be covered in cloth or
leather, or have heraldic designs
painted on them. This sallet has
numerous pairs of small holes to
attach a fabric covering, and is
painted with a checkered design
in red, white, and green, on the
visor and lower part.

DATE	1490
ORIGIN	GERMANY
WEIGHT	5 LB (2.2 KG)

Visor with
double sights

Geometric design
with star and
portcullis motifs

IRON QUILLON DAGGER

MEDIEVAL KNIGHT

THE ARMORED KNIGHT was the elite fighting man of medieval Europe. With his horse, armor, lance, and sword, he was both a costly warrior and a figure with high cultural and social prestige. Although warfare rarely lived up to the ideal of mounted nobles clashing in chivalrous combat, knights were highly skilled soldiers who adapted well to the constantly evolving challenges of the medieval battlefield.

WITH SWORD AND LANCE

Medieval society expected any young male of social standing to seek glory in war. Training was taken very seriously. Boys served first as pages and then as squires in the household of a knight who ensured their education in horsemanship and the use of the sword and lance. After graduation to knighthood, training continued through tournaments that honed fighting skills, and through more or less constant warfare. If there was no fighting to be had close to home, knights would seek it out, traveling to the edges of the Christian world to fight the "infidels." The classic form of knightly combat was the charge with couched lance on horseback. But knights were also effective on foot, wielding swords, maces, or battle-axes. The code of chivalry to which knights subscribed expressed a Christian ethic of warfare, but in practice the plundering, skirmishing, and sieges of medieval warfare left little place for idealism. In the relatively rare pitched battles, knights were sometimes routed by disciplined foot soldiers or bowmen, but they remained a dominant force into the 16th century.

TEMPLARS

In the 12th century, knights of the Christian kingdoms in Palestine formed military monastic orders such as the Knights Templar. Obeying austere religious rules, these fighting monks became elite forces dedicated to the struggle against Islam. Named after the Temple in Jerusalem where they had their headquarters, the Templars accumulated wealth that attracted the envy of kings. The order was condemned for alleged heresy and suppressed in 1312.

TEMPLAR KNIGHT READY FOR BATTLE

PLATE ARMOUR

The full steel plate armor worn by knights in the 15th century offered excellent protection. The helmet was curved to deflect the impact of a mace blow, and slashing sword strokes would have no effect. The knight was only vulnerable to steel crossbows and firearms. This "Gothic" armor, with its elaborate decorative detail, was made in Germany.

TOOLS OF COMBAT

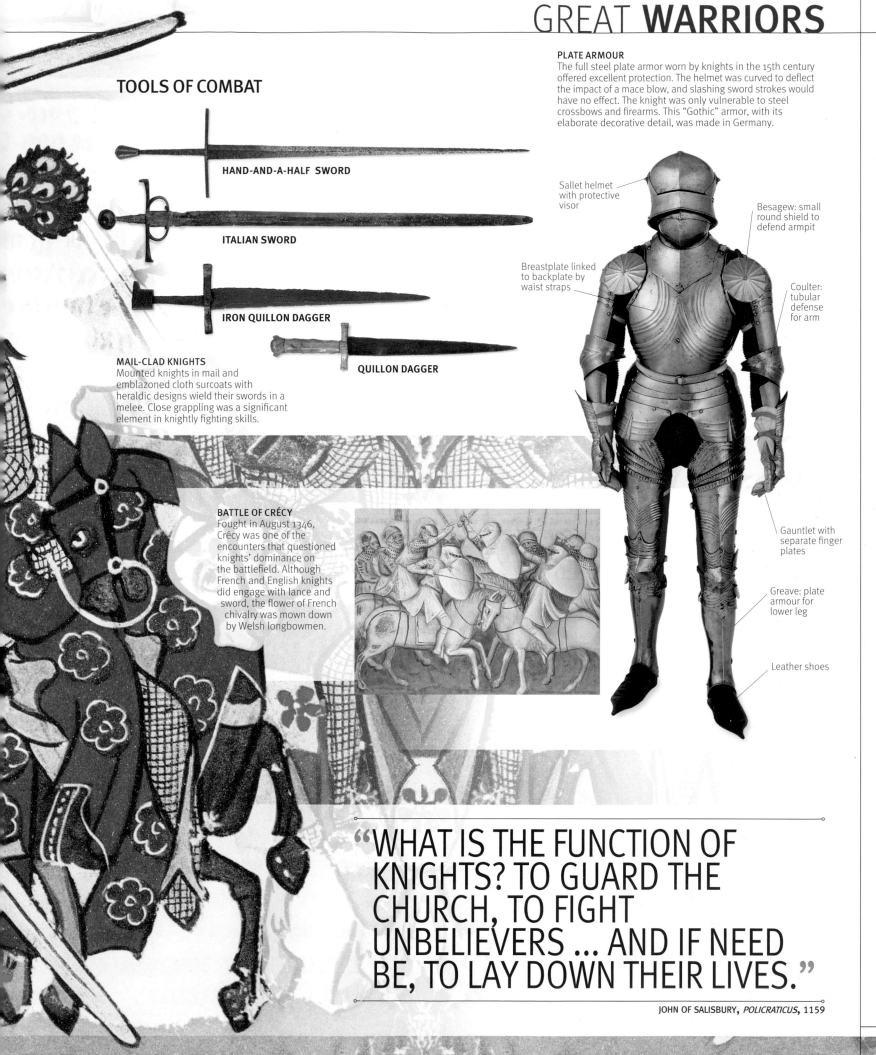

HAND-AND-A-HALF SWORD

ITALIAN SWORD

IRON QUILLON DAGGER

QUILLON DAGGER

MAIL-CLAD KNIGHTS
Mounted knights in mail and emblazoned cloth surcoats with heraldic designs wield their swords in a melee. Close grappling was a significant element in knightly fighting skills.

BATTLE OF CRÉCY
Fought in August 1346, Crécy was one of the encounters that questioned knights' dominance on the battlefield. Although French and English knights did engage with lance and sword, the flower of French chivalry was mown down by Welsh longbowmen.

Sallet helmet with protective visor

Besagew: small round shield to defend armpit

Breastplate linked to backplate by waist straps

Coulter: tubular defense for arm

Gauntlet with separate finger plates

Greave: plate armour for lower leg

Leather shoes

"WHAT IS THE FUNCTION OF KNIGHTS? TO GUARD THE CHURCH, TO FIGHT UNBELIEVERS ... AND IF NEED BE, TO LAY DOWN THEIR LIVES."

JOHN OF SALISBURY, *POLICRATICUS,* 1159

EUROPEAN MAIL ARMOR

MAIL ARMOR—the linking together of small iron or steel rings to form a mesh—dates back as far as the 5th century BCE. By the time of the Norman Conquest of England in 1066, three-quarter length mail armor was common among knights and, by the 13th century, it was being worn from head to toe. Construction was a slow and laborious process, and as many as 30,000 separate links were required for a single shirt of mail.

Anglo Saxon-style square neck

MAIL HAUBERK

The hauberk or byrnie—a knee-length shirt of mail—was the central item of armor for 11th- and 12th-century knights and men-at-arms. To guard against blunt trauma blows to the body, the knight would wear a padded garment called a gambeson underneath his hauberk.

DATE 20TH-CENTURY REPLICA
ORIGIN EUROPE

FULL VIEW

MAIL COIF

Although some suits of mail armor included an integral hood with the hauberk, others had a separate hood, or coif, to be worn under a plate helmet. Mail was usually constructed from wrought iron, although mild steel was used on occasion.

DATE 20TH-CENTURY REPLICA
ORIGIN EUROPE

Horseman's slit to allow freedom of movement while on horseback

Mail flap to be drawn across face while in combat

Short sleeves for mobility

Welded iron rings

MAIL SHIRT

This mail shirt—called a "haubergeon"—has been made in the Asian style. All the rings have been welded together, whereas in the west, the common practice was for mail to be made of alternate lines of welded and riveted rings.

DATE 20TH-CENTURY REPLICA
ORIGIN EUROPE

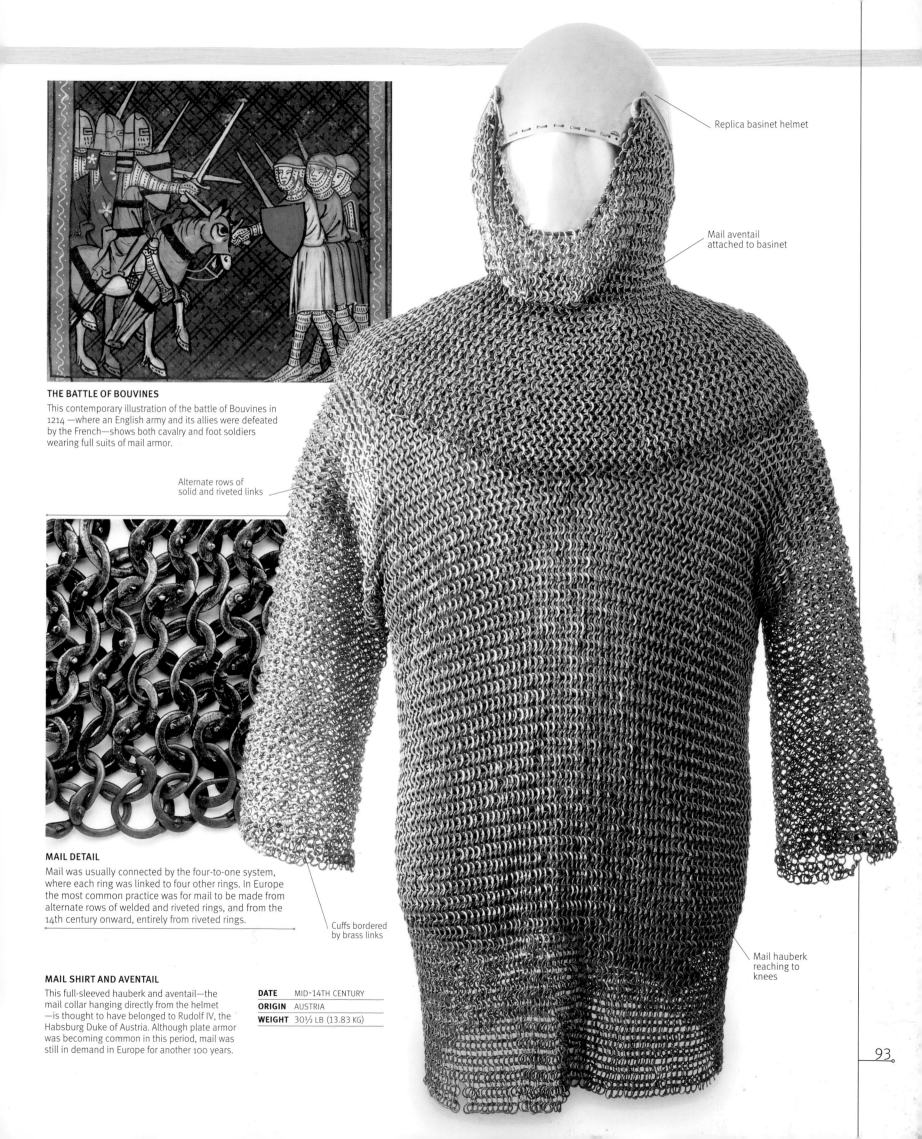

THE BATTLE OF BOUVINES

This contemporary illustration of the battle of Bouvines in 1214 —where an English army and its allies were defeated by the French—shows both cavalry and foot soldiers wearing full suits of mail armor.

Alternate rows of
solid and riveted links

MAIL DETAIL

Mail was usually connected by the four-to-one system, where each ring was linked to four other rings. In Europe the most common practice was for mail to be made from alternate rows of welded and riveted rings, and from the 14th century onward, entirely from riveted rings.

Cuffs bordered
by brass links

MAIL SHIRT AND AVENTAIL

This full-sleeved hauberk and aventail—the mail collar hanging directly from the helmet —is thought to have belonged to Rudolf IV, the Habsburg Duke of Austria. Although plate armor was becoming common in this period, mail was still in demand in Europe for another 100 years.

DATE	MID-14TH CENTURY
ORIGIN	AUSTRIA
WEIGHT	30½ LB (13.83 KG)

Replica basinet helmet

Mail aventail
attached to basinet

Mail hauberk
reaching to
knees

EUROPEAN PLATE ARMOR

DURING THE 14TH CENTURY mail armor was increasingly supplemented by plate armor, which was surprisingly flexible and provided its wearer with a good deal of mobility. By the middle of the 15th century, knights were equipped with complete suits of plate armor with mail relegated to covering exposed areas behind the armor joints. During the late 15th and early 16th centuries, plate armor reached its apogee, and the main elements are revealed in this breakdown of a mid-16th-century Italian suit of armor.

ITALIAN ARMOR

The close helm tightly encloses the entire head. Its pivoted visor is divided into two parts: the visor proper and the upper bevor. The cuirass, covering the torso, consists of a breastplate linked to a backplate (not shown) by leather straps. Extending from the breastplate are skirts and tassets to guard the abdomen and upper thighs. Neck, arm, and leg defenses complete the head-to-toe protection.

DATE	MID-16TH CENTURY
ORIGIN	ITALY

Longitudinal comb

Eye slit in visor

Lifting peg to raise visor

Breathing vents

Upper bevor in raised position

Hinge and pivot

CLOSE HELM

Lower bevor

Hook to attach upper and lower bevors

Gorget plates to overlap gorget

Gorget—to protect neck and join helmet to cuirass

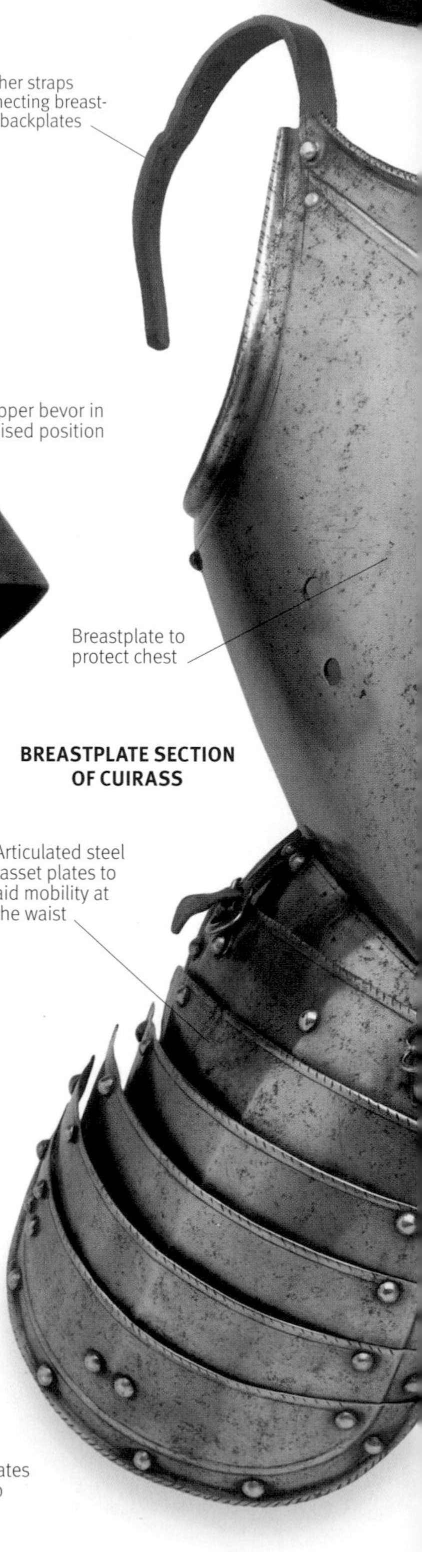

Leather straps connecting breast- and backplates

Breastplate to protect chest

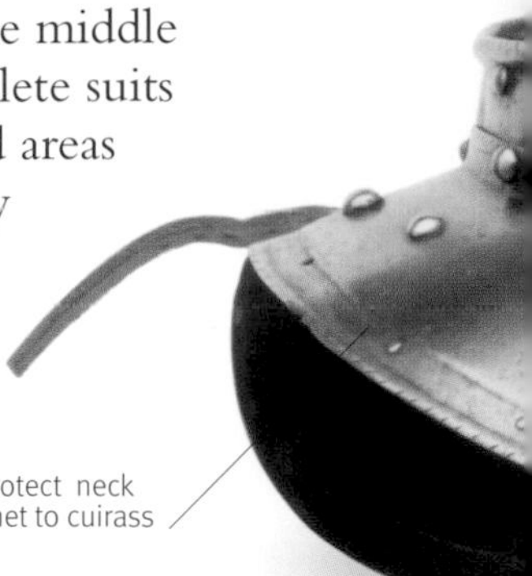

BREASTPLATE SECTION OF CUIRASS

Articulated steel tasset plates to aid mobility at the waist

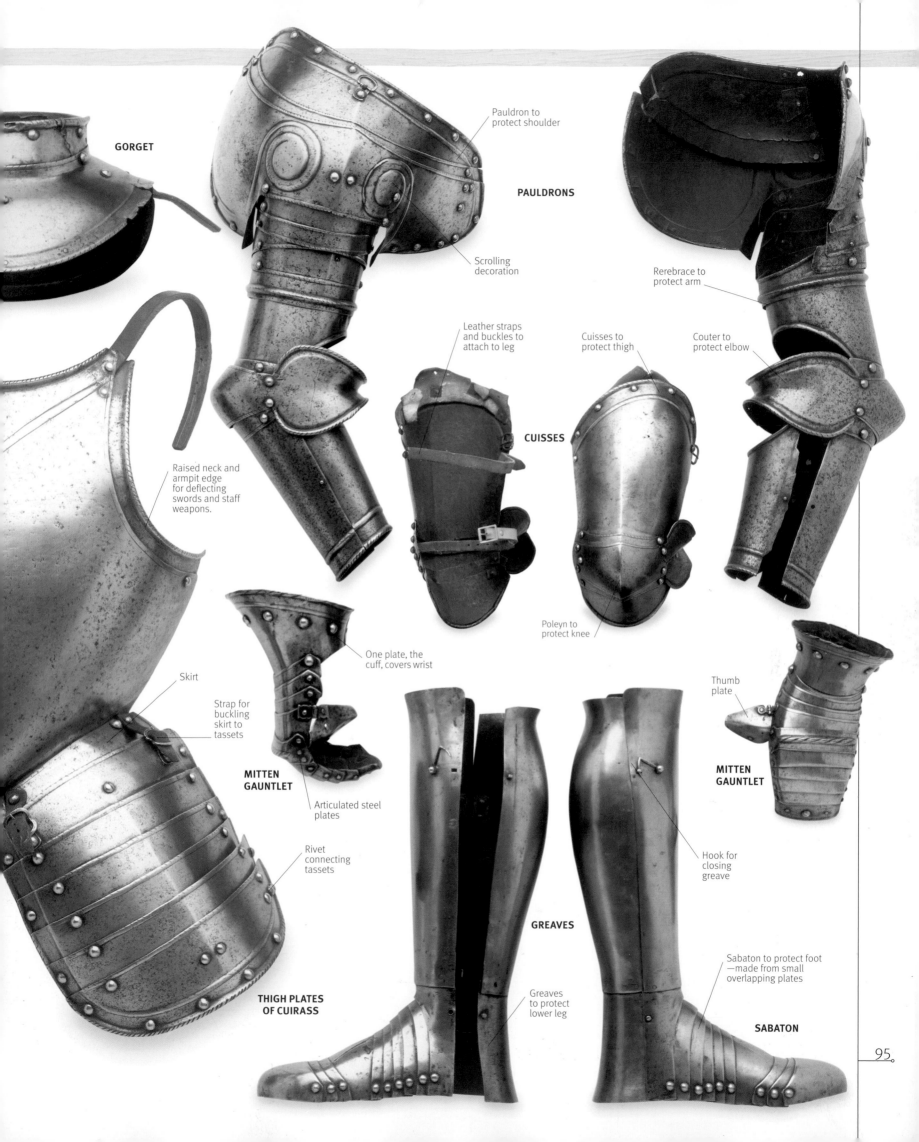

GORGET

Pauldron to protect shoulder

PAULDRONS

Scrolling decoration

Rerebrace to protect arm

Leather straps and buckles to attach to leg

Cuisses to protect thigh

Couter to protect elbow

Raised neck and armpit edge for deflecting swords and staff weapons.

CUISSES

Poleyn to protect knee

One plate, the cuff, covers wrist

Thumb plate

Skirt

Strap for buckling skirt to tassets

MITTEN GAUNTLET

MITTEN GAUNTLET

Articulated steel plates

Rivet connecting tassets

Hook for closing greave

THIGH PLATES OF CUIRASS

GREAVES

Greaves to protect lower leg

Sabaton to protect foot —made from small overlapping plates

SABATON

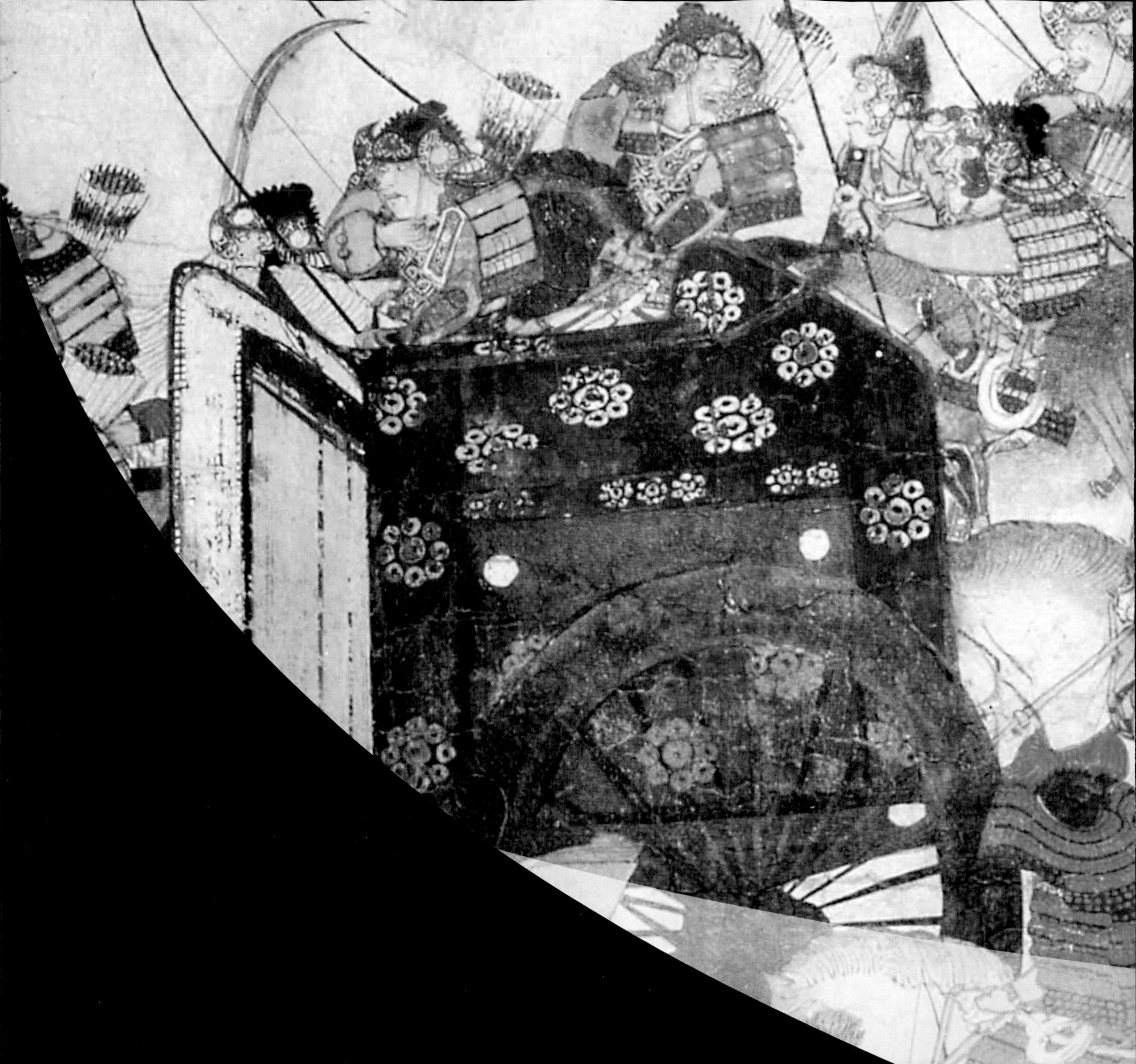

THE EARLY MODERN WORLD

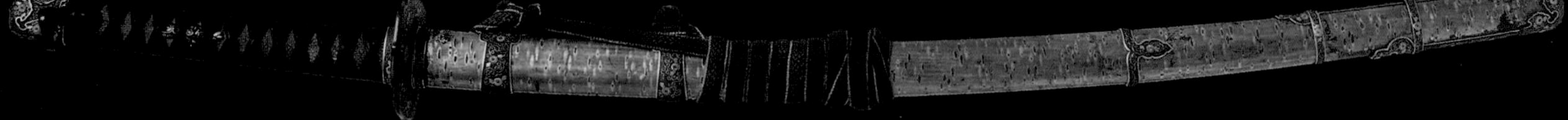

The 16th and 17th centuries saw the rapid spread of firearms, both within and outside Europe, and the modification of military and political strategy to cope with the effects of the new technology. A world in which elites were not born to military service, but rather trained and drilled to it, coupled with a generalized growth in the capacity of states both to raise taxes and—to a lesser extent —to direct their expenditure effectively, meant that armies, as well as the weapons they deployed, became ever more lethal.

BY THE EARLY 16TH CENTURY, artillery had clearly demonstrated its effectiveness. This was underlined by developments such as the introduction of the trunnion—horizontally projecting lugs that allowed guns to be elevated or depressed more effectively. For a short period, the late medieval propensity to skulk behind powerful fortifications and for campaigns to focus on sieges and raids was replaced by a phase during which armies, aware that they could no longer defend fixed points, were much more willing to risk pitched battles.

SIEGE WARFARE

The Italian Wars (1494–1509) saw the first large-scale demonstrations of the potency of field artillery and firearms on the battlefield. At Cerignola (1503), the Spanish fought from shelter behind a trench and earth parapet, subjecting the French cavalry to withering fire. At the battle of Ravenna (1512), the combat opened with a two-hour artillery duel, the first of these ever to be recorded. This era of open warfare, however, was soon replaced by a long period in which sieges became once more the dominant feature in campaigns. The spread of *trace italienne* fortifications (*see box page 100*) meant that sieges became prolonged and costly affairs and the benefits to a defending army of remaining safe within city walls more obvious.

The arquebus was a primitive firearm that was widely used from the 15th–17th centuries. Around the 1520s a new weapon appeared— the musket. Weighing up to 20 lb (9 kg)—much heavier than the arquebus—it required a forked rest to allow its bearer to fire, but did have the advantage of delivering a ball with much greater force. The musket's unwieldiness meant it was most effective in sieges. The advent of gunpowder weapons did not, at a stroke, make infantry stalwarts such as the pike obsolete. Swiss pike formations were a common feature of early 16th century battles, and their aggressive tactics, such as charging entrenched arquebusiers at Novara (1513), made them

OPEN FIGHTING
At Pavia (1525), the combat was decided by imperial arquebusiers and pikemen fighting in the open, unshielded by entrenchment; the French Army was decimated and their king, Francois I, was captured by Charles V, the Holy Roman Emperor.

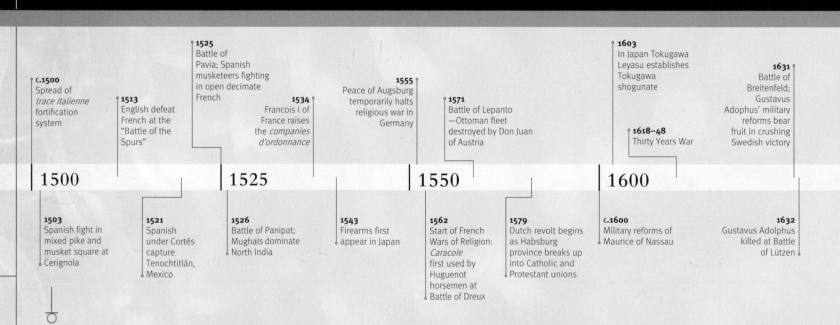

c.1500 Spread of *trace italienne* fortification system

1513 English defeat French at the "Battle of the Spurs"

1525 Battle of Pavia; Spanish musketeers fighting in open decimate French

1534 Francois I of France raises the *companies d'ordonnance*

1555 Peace of Augsburg temporarily halts religious war in Germany

1571 Battle of Lepanto —Ottoman fleet destroyed by Don Juan of Austria

1603 In Japan Tokugawa Ieyasu establishes Tokugawa shogunate

1618–48 Thirty Years War

1631 Battle of Breitenfeld; Gustavus Adophus' military reforms bear fruit in crushing Swedish victory

1500　　　　**1525**　　　　**1550**　　　　**1600**

1503 Spanish fight in mixed pike and musket square at Cerignola

1521 Spanish under Cortés capture Tenochtitlán, Mexico

1526 Battle of Panipat; Mughals dominate North India

1543 Firearms first appear in Japan

1562 Start of French Wars of Religion: *Caracole* first used by Huguenot horsemen at Battle of Dreux

1579 Dutch revolt begins as Habsburg province breaks up into Catholic and Protestant unions

c.1600 Military reforms of Maurice of Nassau

1632 Gustavus Adolphus killed at Battle of Lützen

rightly feared. The proportions of pikemen in armies steadily declined, however, to as little as one in five by the mid-17th century.

The retention of the pike was one aspect of a self-conscious tendency in European armies for military theorists (as much as Renaissance architects) to draw on ancient classical models, such as the spear-wielding Greek hoplites or the disciplined ranks of the Roman army, for their own campaigns. In 1534 Francois I of France established seven *companies d'ordonnance*, each 6,000-strong, modeled on the Roman legions, while Italian theorists promoted a standard infantry company of 256, drawn up in a 16 by 16 square.

EUROPE'S GROWING ARMIES

The Italian poet Fulvio Testi wrote in the 1640s, "This is the century of the soldier," in reference both to the increased bloodiness of battles—at Ceresole in 1544, some 7,000 of the 25,000 combatants perished—and to the sheer size of armies. That of Charles the Bold of Burgundy had been regarded as large in the 1470s at 15,000, a number dwarfed by Philip II of Spain's 86,000-strong army in the Netherlands a century later. The huge expense of refortifying towns and raising ever-larger armies put enormous strain on the leading powers in Europe.

European wars had, until the late 15th century, been fought principally for dynastic reasons, but the Protestant Reformation in the early 16th century added a religious and ideological dimension to warfare. By the 1560s, both France and the Netherlands had descended into religious civil war. The French Wars of Religion ended in 1589, but the revolt of the Netherlands was more protracted—ending only in 1648—and saw the resources of the Habsburgs under Charles V and then Philip II stretched to the limit. It also became the crucible of significant developments in military strategy.

The use of firepower brought about a change in battlefield formation as it was most effectively delivered in a line of battle, rather than a traditional block. Throughout the 16th and 17th centuries, the ranks of armies thinned out and their lines extended. Fighting in line formation, however, required greater discipline —especially as opposing armies often opened fire at a range of only 164 ft (50 m). The Dutch Protestant leader Maurice of Nassau began to introduce his troops to "exercises" in the 1590s, drilling them and instructing them in basic maneuvers. His brother William Louis pioneered a system whereby consecutive rows of musketeers fired in turn, then retired to reload, allowing for continuous fire.

THE OLD WORLD MEETS THE NEW WORLD

The 16th century saw the first really successful projection of European power overseas. In the Americas, the Spanish confronted the Inca and Aztec empires, neither of which had developed iron. Wooden clubs and stone axes could not penetrate Spanish cuirasses, and only the Aztecs' copper-tipped arrow made

SPANISH SQUARES
The Spanish were among the first to mingle pikemen and arquebusiers into a mixed square known as a *tercio*, several of which are shown here in combat during the Eighty Years War (1568–1648) against the Dutch.

much impact against their enemies. At the siege of Cuzco in 1536, 190 Spanish soldiers defeated up to 200,000 Inca warriors armed largely with stones. The Spanish benefited from divisions among their enemies as much as from their technology. In Mexico they harnessed the antipathy of the Tlaxcala toward the Aztecs to obtain intelligence, while in Peru they exploited a civil war between two rival claimants to the Inca throne. Yet indigenous peoples learned fast. In North America the Massachussetts Indians were manufacturing shot by the 1670s, so that, whereas in earlier encounters there were few European casualties, in King Philip's War in 1675–76 there were 3,000 English wounded.

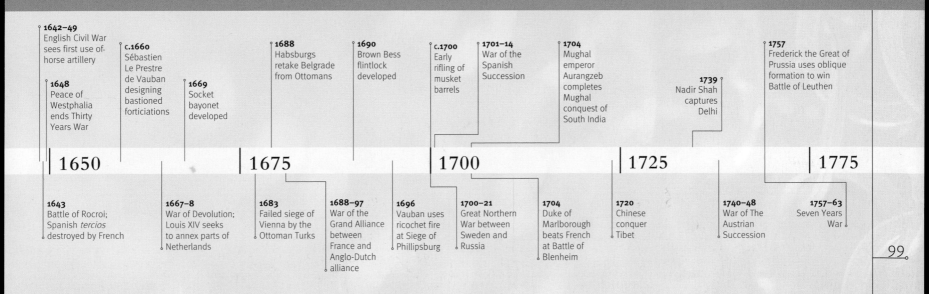

1642–49
English Civil War sees first use of horse artillery

1648
Peace of Westphalia ends Thirty Years War

c.1660
Sébastien Le Prestre de Vauban designing bastioned forticiations

1669
Socket bayonet developed

1688
Habsburgs retake Belgrade from Ottomans

1690
Brown Bess flintlock developed

c.1700
Early rifling of musket barrels

1701–14
War of the Spanish Succession

1704
Mughal emperor Aurangzeb completes Mughal conquest of South India

1739
Nadir Shah captures Delhi

1757
Frederick the Great of Prussia uses oblique formation to win Battle of Leuthen

1650   1675   1700   1725   1775

1643
Battle of Rocroi; Spanish *tercios* destroyed by French

1667–8
War of Devolution; Louis XIV seeks to annex parts of Netherlands

1683
Failed siege of Vienna by the Ottoman Turks

1688–97
War of the Grand Alliance between France and Anglo-Dutch alliance

1696
Vauban uses ricochet fire at Siege of Phillipsburg

1700–21
Great Northern War between Sweden and Russia

1704
Duke of Marlborough beats French at Battle of Blenheim

1720
Chinese conquer Tibet

1740–48
War of The Austrian Succession

1757–63
Seven Years War

MUSKET DRILL
The musket was a complex weapon, requiring as many as 20 separate movements to ensure correct firing. Drill manuals illustrating the correct positions, such as this mid-17th century Dutch version, became an essential military accoutrement.

FORTIFICATION

The development of new siege artillery led to a search for improved forms of military architecture. The solution was polygonal and angled bastions, which, when manned by arquebusiers, created interlocking fields of fire and a killing zone for attackers. From its origins in Italy, the new type of fortification became known as the *trace italienne*. New levels of sophistication were reached in the late 17th century by the French engineer Vauban, whose employment of concentric rings of outworks and exploitation of topography to maximize defensive firepower made fortresses such as Lille forbidding obstacles for besieging forces.

MODEL OF VAUBAN-STYLE FORTIFICATION

THE DEVELOPMENT OF GUNPOWDER

Against the Asian powers of Ottoman Turkey, Mughal India, Tokugawa Japan, and Ming and Qing China, military in-roads by Europeans were relatively minor. Until their defeat at the second siege of Vienna (1683), the Ottomans pressed hard, engaging in constant small-scale warfare with the Austrian Habsburgs. The janissary infantry corps that had brought the Turks such great successes in the 16th century were beginning to atrophy as a military power, but they still possessed a light cavalry arm unmatched in Europe.

Although the Chinese had developed gunpowder earlier, Europe had opened up a technological lead by the 16th century. The Chinese then acquired Portuguese cannons in the 1520s, but were not content with merely aping the foreign technology. During the 16th century, they developed a "continuous bullet gun," a primitive form of machine gun. A military manual of 1598 set out the precise measurement of gun barrels to tiny fractions of inches, while Chinese guns were stamped with serial numbers, indicating tight central control on production.

In Japan, the Onin Wars of 1467–76 had set in train a period of political fragmentation when local warlords, the *daimyo,* built up independent domains. Japan acquired firearms in 1542—from Portuguese passengers on a pirate ship that blew off course—and they spread rapidly. Units of musketeers (*teppotai*) played a crucial role in the unification of Japan under Oda Nobunaga, who captured the royal capital of Kyoto in 1568 and conquered most of Japan before his death in 1582.

Battles in Japan at this time became more similar to the pitched encounters of European armies than the challenge and counter-challenge of elite samurai warriors that characterized earlier warfare there. Japanese armies showed considerable technical and tactical ingenuity; at Osaka in 1576, Nobunaga had seven ships constructed, shielded by armed plates, which were armed with canons and muskets, creating a very early version of an ironclad; while at Nagashina in 1575, Nobunaga's musketeers fired in ranks in rotation, some years before the practice became established in Europe. Yet the final unification of Japan under the Tokugawa after 1600 meant that military conflict, and with it the impetus for technical development, declined. Already in 1588, the "Sword-hunt Edict" had ordered the confiscation of all weapons held in private hands, including firearms, contributing to a demilitarization that would leave it ill-equipped to face western intruders in the 19th century.

THE THIRTY YEARS WAR

The Thirty Years War (1618–48), a complex struggle, that pitted the Catholic Habsburgs against a shifting coalition of mostly

Protestant foes, saw a further evolution in the sophistication of armies and tactics. Increasingly armies wore uniforms, or at least some identifying colour – the Habsburgs favoured red, while their French enemies wore blue. The Swedish army under Gustavus Adophus took the reforms further than most. Gustavus effectively introduced conscription with his 1620 "Ordinance of Military Personnel", while a War Board was established to supervise military administration. The fruit of these

INDIAN BLADE
This 18th-century dagger, with a hilt in the form of a dragon, is known as a *bichiwa* or "kiss of the scorpion." Shivaji, the 17th-century Indian guerrilla leader, used such a concealed blade to assassinate his opponent Afzal Khan.

improvements came in a string of spectacular Swedish battlefield successes. At Breitenfeld (1631) a Swedish army formed up in six ranks faced a Habsburg army drawn up in "squares" 30 deep and 50 wide and won a crushing victory, killing almost 8,000 of their opponents.

Throughout the Thirty Years War, states had been forced to rely on mercenaries for manpower. Military entrepreneurs had flourished, such as Albrecht von Wallenstein, who was able to offer the services of a force numbering 25,000-strong. But after the Peace of Westphalia (1648), countries increasingly established standing armies, which were not disbanded at the end of a campaign. France's army reached 125,000 by 1659 (and around 400,000 by 1690), while even the tiny German state of Jülich-Berg maintained a permanent fighting force of 5,000.

By now, wars cost huge sums to fight; between 1679 and 1725, the Russian armed forces cost 60 percent of total revenue in peacetime, and nearly all of it in wartime. In Louis XIV's France, the construction of a barrier of fortresses across the northeastern Frontier, many designed by Vauban (*see box*) was ruinously expensive—that at Ath took six years and five million livres to build. Campaigns once more centered on sieges —during the Nine Years War (1688–97) the French sought to push their frontier eastward, but the siege of just one fortress, Philippsburg, took two months.

USE OF THE MUSKET AND BAYONET
The late 17th century saw the final demise of the pike, and its replacement by the bayonet. The plug bayonet, which blocked the muzzle of the musket and needed to be removed for firing, did not catch on. However, in 1669 the socket bayonet was developed, which created no such impediment. By 1689 it was becoming standard issue for French infantry. The latter 17th century also saw the development of the flintlock musket, lighter than the matchlock and with double the rate of fire.

The introduction of pre-packaged cartridges, with the gunpowder charge already measured out, also increased the rate of fire (they became general issue in the French army by 1738).

THE BEGINNINGS OF GLOBAL WARFARE
For a time in the 17th century, armies had employed a cavalry tactic, known as "caracole," where the cavalry, armed with wheellock pistols, would trot into range, let off a volley and then retreat. But the combination of flintlock and socket bayonet made the mounted arm especially vulnerable, and by the late 18th century, they made up only 16 percent of the French army, principally used against other cavalry or in pursuit of already broken infantry.

Toward the end of the period, however, the cavalry underwent a revival, as they largely abandoned their firearms and relied instead on the shock of rapid and decisive charges —the English general Marlborough's cavalry squadrons played a key role in his victory at Blenheim (1704) during the Spanish War of Succession.

Prussia under Frederick the Great (1740–86) built up Europe's most effective military force, founded on discipline and constant practice. Innovative tactics such as the oblique attack set a standard for other countries—the Russian Infantry Code of 1755 was firmly based on the Prussian model. During the Seven Years War (1756–63), the Prussians and their British allies faced a coalition of France, Austria, and Russia, intent on putting a stop to Prussian dominance of central Europe. This war is most notable, however, for being the first truly global conflict, as French and British rivalry played itself out across North America and the Indian subcontinent. From 1720 the Prussians had iron ramrods for their muskets, and could let off as many as three rounds a minute, fired on the move—a relatively new tactic—delivering Frederick successes such as Leuthen (1757), where some Prussian musketeers let off up to 180 rounds each.

As the 18th century progressed, field artillery became an increasingly vital component of armies. The French artillery train in Flanders in 1748 had no fewer than 150 cannon drawn by almost 3,000 horses. From 1739, barrels were cast in a single piece and then bored, allowing finer tolerances and more powerful pieces at a given size. With the establishment of gunnery schools, such as the French Royal Corps of Artillery in 1679, artillery officers were often some of the best trained in European armies. It is fitting, therefore, that it was to be a French artillery officer, Napoleon Bonaparte, who would finally bring an end to the ancient regime of the absolute monarchs and revolutionize warfare.

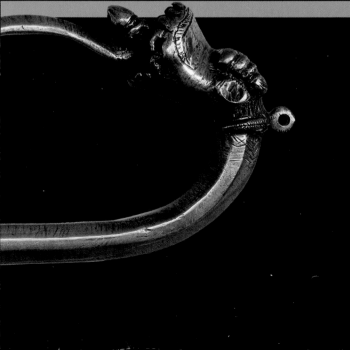

JAPANESE FIREARMS
At Nagashino in 1575, Oda Nobunaga's ranks of arquebusiers fired rotating volleys to decimate the charge of his opponent Takeda Katsuyori. Those of Takeda's horsemen who reached Oda's lines were held off by pikes, in an echo of European tactics of the era.

THE EARLY MODERN WORLD

TWO-HANDED SWORDS

DURING THE MIDDLE AGES, most infantry swords were relatively light and easy to wield, but by the late 15th century, a distinctive group of larger weapons grew in popularity, particularly in Germany. These two-handed (*doppelhänder*—double-hander or *beidenhände* —both-hander) swords were specialist weapons. The Landsknecht mercenaries who used them were called *doppelsöldner* and received double pay; but they earned it. They were expected to hack their way into enemy pike units. The impressive but clumsy weapons were also used for ceremonial duties and executions.

Spherical pommel

Double-edged blade shorter than German equivalent

HIGHLAND SWORD

The Scots developed their own tradition of "hand-and-a-half" weapons, derived from earlier medieval Scottish and Irish longswords. This Highland sword (*Claidheamh dà làimh*) has a blade just over 3 ft (1 m) long, and was shorter and lighter than German *doppelhänder* weapons. The forward-sloping quillons ending in quatrefoils were a common feature.

DATE	c.1550
ORIGIN	SCOTLAND
WEIGHT	5¾ LB (2.61 KG)
LENGTH	58¾ IN (1.5 M)

Flame or wave form of blade added for show

Grip bound in leather and pierced with metal studs

Forward-curving quillons terminate in curls

PARADE SWORD

In 16th- and early 17th-century Germany, particularly ornate two-handed swords such as this example were used on ceremonial occasions. These *paratschwerter* (parade swords, also called "bearing swords") were longer and heavier than battlefield weapons, and often so ornate that they were of little use as offensive weapons. The flame form of the blade (*flammenschwert*) was impressive, but made little difference to its cutting qualities.

DATE	c.1580
ORIGIN	GERMANY
WEIGHT	7¼ LB (3.3 KG)
LENGTH	63 IN (1.6 M)

Scottish style of hilt

German blade

LOWLAND SWORD

Outwardly this sword is typical of the weapons used by German Landsknecht mercenaries on European battlefields during the early and mid-16th century. However, in this particular example, the blade is surmounted by a hilt produced in Scotland, and it is of typical Scottish design.

DATE	c.1570
ORIGIN	SCOTLAND
WEIGHT	6½ LB (2.95 KG)
LENGTH	58½ IN (1.48 M)

Parrying lugs reflect those on battlefield swords

Only one edge of the two sharpened

Good grip to help balance weight

TWO-HANDED SWORD

This *doppelhänder* sword was designed as a battlefield weapon, and is of a type used by the German Landsknecht. The sword has a blunt tip because it was designed to hack through enemy units rather than to pierce its victims.

DATE	c.1550
ORIGIN	GERMANY
WEIGHT	7 LB (3.18 KG)
LENGTH	55 IN (1.4 M)

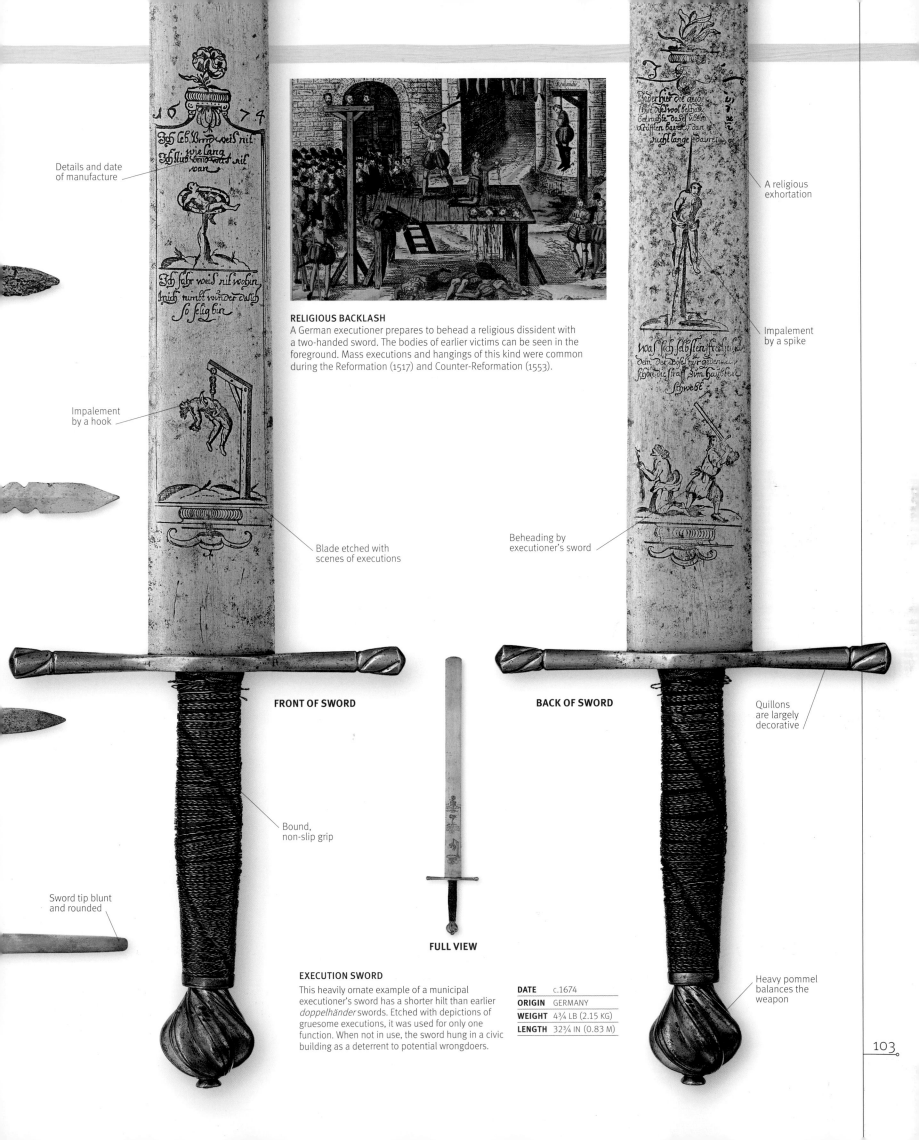

Details and date
of manufacture

Impalement
by a hook

Blade etched with
scenes of executions

RELIGIOUS BACKLASH
A German executioner prepares to behead a religious dissident with
a two-handed sword. The bodies of earlier victims can be seen in the
foreground. Mass executions and hangings of this kind were common
during the Reformation (1517) and Counter-Reformation (1553).

A religious
exhortation

Impalement
by a spike

Beheading by
executioner's sword

FRONT OF SWORD

BACK OF SWORD

Quillons
are largely
decorative

Bound,
non-slip grip

Sword tip blunt
and rounded

FULL VIEW

EXECUTION SWORD

This heavily ornate example of a municipal
executioner's sword has a shorter hilt than earlier
doppelhänder swords. Etched with depictions of
gruesome executions, it was used for only one
function. When not in use, the sword hung in a civic
building as a deterrent to potential wrongdoers.

Heavy pommel
balances the
weapon

DATE	c.1674
ORIGIN	GERMANY
WEIGHT	4¾ LB (2.15 KG)
LENGTH	32¾ IN (0.83 M)

103

THE EARLY MODERN WORLD

EUROPEAN INFANTRY AND CAVALRY SWORDS

WHILE THE MILITARY REVOLUTION that followed on the heels of the Renaissance meant that firepower was becoming increasingly important, the *arme blanche* (cold steel) still remained a battle-winning weapon, particularly for cavalry. Most infantry swords from the 16th century onward tended to be used as thrusting weapons, but cavalry still needed to slash downward at infantry, so they favored larger, double-edged swords that could be used equally well against mounted and dismounted opponents. However, standardized military sword patterns now emphasized style as much as practicality. They were more elegant, but probably no less deadly.

Religious icons often decorate the blades of Renaissance weapons

Simple wooden grip allows single- or double-handed grip

Curves on quillons could trap an opponent's blade

INFANTRY SWORD

In contrast to the other swords on this page, this highly decorated but simply designed sword offered little protection to the swordsman, but it could be wielded using one or two hands.

DATE	c.1500
ORIGIN	SWITZERLAND
WEIGHT	2 LB (0.91 KG)
LENGTH	35¼ IN (90 CM)

Blade was made a century after the hilt

Silver-encrusted hilt

FULL VIEW

BASKET-HILTED SWORD

This broadsword consists of an early 17th century German blade produced in Solingen attached to an English basket hilt dating from over a century before the blade was cast.

DATE	c.1540
ORIGIN	ENGLAND
WEIGHT	3 LB (1.36 KG)
LENGTH	41¼ IN (1.04 M)

Ornate scrollwork of guard reflects contemporary aesthetics

Single fuller imparts greater strength to blade

Maker's mark

CAVALRY SWORD

By the mid-18th century, cavalry swords had developed into two types: light, curved blades for light cavalry, and longer, heavier, straight blades for heavy cavalry. This example is typical of those used by European heavy cavalry for over a century. The single fuller (the groove along the back of the blade) meant that the blade was single-edged.

DATE	1750
ORIGIN	ENGLAND
WEIGHT	3 LB (1.36 KG)
LENGTH	39½ IN (1 M)

FULL VIEW

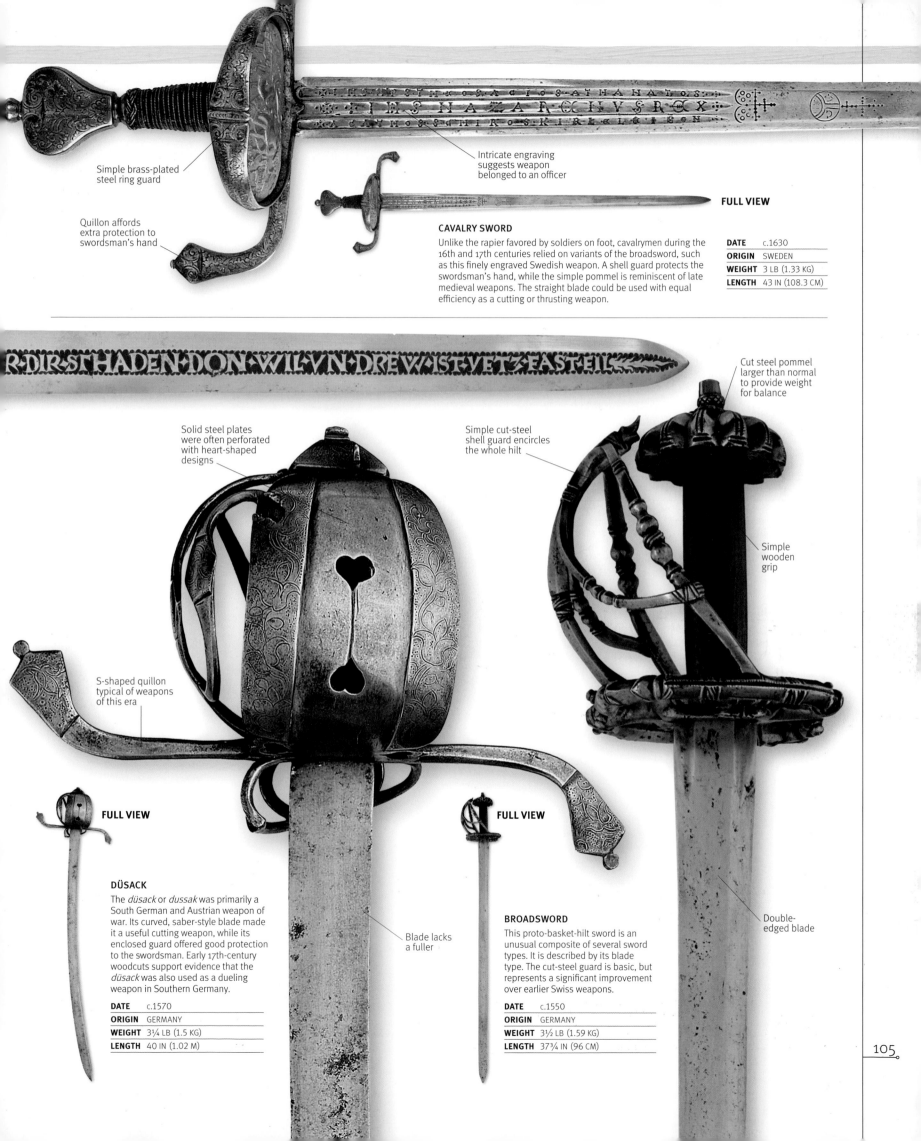

Simple brass-plated steel ring guard

Quillon affords extra protection to swordsman's hand

Intricate engraving suggests weapon belonged to an officer

FULL VIEW

CAVALRY SWORD

Unlike the rapier favored by soldiers on foot, cavalrymen during the 16th and 17th centuries relied on variants of the broadsword, such as this finely engraved Swedish weapon. A shell guard protects the swordsman's hand, while the simple pommel is reminiscent of late medieval weapons. The straight blade could be used with equal efficiency as a cutting or thrusting weapon.

DATE	c.1630
ORIGIN	SWEDEN
WEIGHT	3 LB (1.33 KG)
LENGTH	43 IN (108.3 CM)

Cut steel pommel larger than normal to provide weight for balance

Solid steel plates were often perforated with heart-shaped designs

Simple cut-steel shell guard encircles the whole hilt

Simple wooden grip

S-shaped quillon typical of weapons of this era

Simple wooden grip

Double-edged blade

FULL VIEW

FULL VIEW

Blade lacks a fuller

DÜSACK

The *düsack* or *dussak* was primarily a South German and Austrian weapon of war. Its curved, saber-style blade made it a useful cutting weapon, while its enclosed guard offered good protection to the swordsman. Early 17th-century woodcuts support evidence that the *düsack* was also used as a dueling weapon in Southern Germany.

DATE	c.1570
ORIGIN	GERMANY
WEIGHT	3¼ LB (1.5 KG)
LENGTH	40 IN (1.02 M)

BROADSWORD

This proto-basket-hilt sword is an unusual composite of several sword types. It is described by its blade type. The cut-steel guard is basic, but represents a significant improvement over earlier Swiss weapons.

DATE	c.1550
ORIGIN	GERMANY
WEIGHT	3½ LB (1.59 KG)
LENGTH	37¾ IN (96 CM)

EUROPEAN INFANTRY AND CAVALRY SWORDS

DESTINY'S CHARGE
With sword in hand, King Gustavus Adolphus of Sweden led a cavalry charge against his protestant German foes during the Battle of Lützen (1632). He outpaced his bodyguard and found himself surrounded by enemy horsemen, who cut the Swedish king down without mercy.

Pommel decorated with intricate inlaid brass scrollwork

Basket guard provides excellent protection

Inside of the basket lined with felt-covered leather

Wide double-sided blade good for cutting and thrusting

Pommel cast in the form of a cat's head

Wooden grip bound with thin silver wire

High-quality silverwork indicates this was possibly an officer's weapon

Quillon has probably been straightened

Double-edged blade inscribed with the slogan *In Mene* ("in mind")

FULL VIEW

BROADSWORD

Although basket-hilted swords were used throughout Europe from the mid-16th century, they are most closely associated with the 18th-century Scottish Highlander. Most of these were made in the lowlands, principally in Glasgow and Stirling, although many of the blades were imported from Germany. The characteristically Scottish basket-hilt guard was designed to protect the swordsman's hand.

DATE	c.1750
ORIGIN	SCOTLAND
WEIGHT	3 LB (1.36 KG)
LENGTH	35¾ IN (91 CM)

FULL VIEW

SCHIAVONA SWORD

This more delicate, characteristically Venetian example of a broadsword is known as a *schiavona*, meaning Slavonic. Schiavonas have a distinctive form of basket hilt, and almost always feature a pommel designed to resemble the head of a cat, an allusion to agility and stealth. They were primarily used by Dalmatian troops in the service of the Venetian Republic.

DATE	c.1780
ORIGIN	ITALY
WEIGHT	2¼ LB (1.02 KG)
LENGTH	41½ IN (1.05 M)

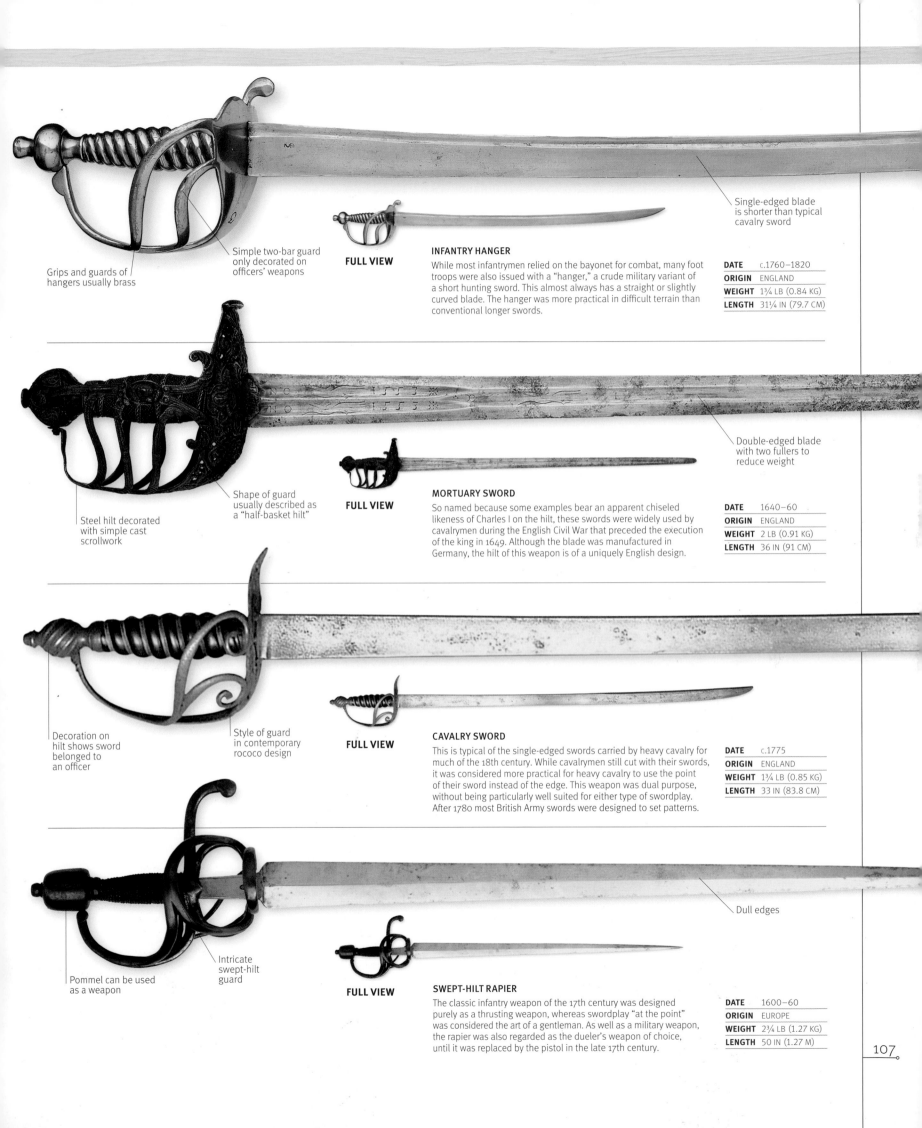

Grips and guards of
hangers usually brass

Simple two-bar guard
only decorated on
officers' weapons

FULL VIEW

INFANTRY HANGER

While most infantrymen relied on the bayonet for combat, many foot
troops were also issued with a "hanger," a crude military variant of
a short hunting sword. This almost always has a straight or slightly
curved blade. The hanger was more practical in difficult terrain than
conventional longer swords.

Single-edged blade
is shorter than typical
cavalry sword

DATE	c.1760–1820
ORIGIN	ENGLAND
WEIGHT	1¾ LB (0.84 KG)
LENGTH	31¼ IN (79.7 CM)

Shape of guard
usually described as
a "half-basket hilt"

Steel hilt decorated
with simple cast
scrollwork

FULL VIEW

MORTUARY SWORD

So named because some examples bear an apparent chiseled
likeness of Charles I on the hilt, these swords were widely used by
cavalrymen during the English Civil War that preceded the execution
of the king in 1649. Although the blade was manufactured in
Germany, the hilt of this weapon is of a uniquely English design.

Double-edged blade
with two fullers to
reduce weight

DATE	1640–60
ORIGIN	ENGLAND
WEIGHT	2 LB (0.91 KG)
LENGTH	36 IN (91 CM)

Decoration on
hilt shows sword
belonged to
an officer

Style of guard
in contemporary
rococo design

FULL VIEW

CAVALRY SWORD

This is typical of the single-edged swords carried by heavy cavalry for
much of the 18th century. While cavalrymen still cut with their swords,
it was considered more practical for heavy cavalry to use the point
of their sword instead of the edge. This weapon was dual purpose,
without being particularly well suited for either type of swordplay.
After 1780 most British Army swords were designed to set patterns.

DATE	c.1775
ORIGIN	ENGLAND
WEIGHT	1¾ LB (0.85 KG)
LENGTH	33 IN (83.8 CM)

Pommel can be used
as a weapon

Intricate
swept-hilt
guard

FULL VIEW

SWEPT-HILT RAPIER

The classic infantry weapon of the 17th century was designed
purely as a thrusting weapon, whereas swordplay "at the point"
was considered the art of a gentleman. As well as a military weapon,
the rapier was also regarded as the dueler's weapon of choice,
until it was replaced by the pistol in the late 17th century.

Dull edges

DATE	1600–60
ORIGIN	EUROPE
WEIGHT	2¾ LB (1.27 KG)
LENGTH	50 IN (1.27 M)

LANDSKNECHT

16TH-CENTURY GERMAN BROADSWORD

THE GARISHLY DRESSED, swaggering mercenary bands known as the Landsknecht were founded in 1486 by Holy Roman Emperor Maximilian I, who wanted his own infantry force to match the Swiss pikemen who had been victorious at the battles of Murten and Nancy in 1476–77. Officially, the Landsknecht were bound to serve the emperor, but the lure of pay and plunder soon led many of them to seek alternative employers. Feared and admired, they were a ubiquitous presence on European battlefields in the first half of the 16th century.

MERCENARY FIGHTERS

Individual mercenary captains were contracted to recruit, train, and organize regiments about 4,000 strong. The majority of recruits came from German-speaking areas, although some hailed from as far afield as Scotland. They were tempted by pay of four guilders a month, a good income for the time, but they had to supply their own equipment. Only the better off could afford full armor or an arquebus. The weapon of the majority was the pike,

15 or 20 ft (5 or 6 m) long, and costing around one guilder. The core of the Landsknecht battlefield formation was a phalanx of pikemen, supported by skirmishers armed with crossbows and arquebuses and, in the van, the regiment's best soldiers armed with two-handed swords. On the battlefield, the Landsknecht were disciplined and courageous but, when their wages were not paid, they gained a reputation for mutiny and plundering.

MOUNTED CAPTAIN
Distinguishable by the fineness of his clothes, a Landsknecht captain was a private entrepreneur, who employed his men and then sold their services to kings at a handsome profit.

Halberd

Broad, flat, beret-style hat decorated with tall feathers

Pike

Captain's bodyguard

Slash and puff clothing

BATTLE OF PAVIA
At Pavia in 1525, the Landsknecht Black Band, employed by French King François I, fought to the last man while the rest of the French forces fled the field.

THE SACK OF ROME

In 1527, the Landsknecht and other imperial forces of Charles V, Holy Roman Emperor, occupied Rome. As Lutherans, the Landsknecht hated the Catholic Church. One Landsknecht recorded: "We put over 6,000 men to the sword, seized all that we could find in the churches, burned down a great part of the city …". The occupation lasted nine months, with the mercenaries refusing to leave until they had been paid arrears of wages.

IMPERIAL FORCES ENTERING ROME

> " **WE WERE 1,800 GERMANS AND WERE ATTACKED BY 15,000 SWEDISH PEASANTS … WE STRUCK MOST OF THEM DEAD.** "

LANDSKNECHT PAUL DOLSTEIN, ON FIGHTING FOR THE KING OF DENMARK, JULY 1502

TOOLS OF COMBAT

PIKE

HALBERD

PARADE SWORD

TWO-HANDED SWORD

DOUBLE-PAY MEN
These Landsknecht *doppelsöldener*, or "double-pay men," earned their extra wages fighting in the front line. Wielding their two-handed swords, they assailed the ranks of enemy pikemen, opening up gaps in their formation. The bizarre outfits that the Landsknecht wore—extravagantly puffed and slashed, with assorted headgear—expressed an arrogant spirit that made them of doubtful loyalty to their employers, and a much-feared menace to civilians.

109

EUROPEAN RAPIERS

IN THE 16TH CENTURY, the rapier became the weapon of a gentleman; a symbol that he was a man of substance and status, and that he knew how to use his sword. The term is derived from the 15th-century Spanish term *espada ropera* (sword of the robes) meaning the weapon of a gentleman. By 1500 the rapier was used throughout Europe, and it would remain the premier gentleman's sword until the late 17th century. While it was certainly used on the battlefield, it is more readily associated with court, dueling, and fashion, hence the tendency toward delicate, intricate designs.

Decorated
steel grip

Pierced and chiseled
metalwork

Rompepuntus

Steel hilt

Cup provides excellent
protection for hand

Maker's name
inscribed on blade

Large spherical pommel

Single bar protects
knuckles

Grip ornately
bound in wire

Bars act as a guard

Blade inscribed with
religious invocations

CUP-HILT RAPIER

In Spain, and those parts of Italy under Spanish influence, the guard of the rapier became fully enclosed, producing the "cup-hilt" guard form shown here. The Romepuntus is used to trap opponents' blades.

DATE	c.1650
ORIGIN	SPAIN
WEIGHT	2¼ LB (1.02 KG)
LENGTH	37¾ IN (96 CM)

SWEPT-HILT RAPIER

This classic form of rapier guard is known as a swept-hilt, because the bars sweep up in a graceful curve from the ricasso to the pommel. Despite its apparent lack of protection, this style of rapier remained in fashion until the early 17th century, largely because of its elegant appearance.

DATE	EARLY 17TH CENTURY
ORIGIN	ITALY
WEIGHT	2¼ LB (1.02 KG)
LENGTH	53½ IN (1.36 M)

Pommel in the form of an urn

Pair of symmetrically pierced shell guards

Diamond-section twisting blade

PAPPENHEIM-HILT RAPIER

This style of rapier was popularized by Count Pappenheim, an imperial general of the Thirty Years War (1618–48). The design was soon copied throughout Europe as its two pierced shell guards provided good protection for the swordsman. The Pappenheim variant was designed for military use.

DATE	1630
ORIGIN	GERMAN
WEIGHT	2¾ LB (1.25 KG)
LENGTH	54¾ IN (139 CM)

Shell-shaped lenticular pommel

Straight double-edged blade

Early form of rapier hilt

EARLY RAPIER

The first rapiers were clumsy weapons compared to the elegant designs that followed them, more akin to contemporary military swords than weapons designed primarily for civilian wear. This example shows some reworking, which may suggest that the blade is a replacement. However, the guard itself has something of the elegance of later swept-hilt designs.

DATE	1520–30
ORIGIN	ITALY
WEIGHT	2¾ LB (1.21 KG)
LENGTH	44 IN (111.5 CM)

Hilt designed to provide added protection

Thickened blade

Swept hilt of chiselled iron

SWEPT-HILT RAPIER

Another variant of a swept-hilt rapier design, this weapon might be less elegant than its counterpart on the left, but its small, perforated shell guards offered better protection. In this example the grip is bound in woven wire. It suggests this rapier was made as a dress sword rather than for military use.

DATE	1590
ORIGIN	ENGLAND
WEIGHT	3 LB (1.39 KG)
LENGTH	50½ IN (128 CM)

Plain cup-hilt

Simple ricasso

Shallow diamond-section blade

Square-section blade

Circular stop-rib riveted to cup

CUP-HILT RAPIER

Unlike other rapiers, this later weapon was designed as a fencing piece rather than as a weapon that denoted gentlemanly status. It has an extremely narrow diamond-section blade, and a simple, unadorned cup and hilt.

DATE	c.1680
ORIGIN	ITALIAN
WEIGHT	2 LB (0.9 KG)
LENGTH	47 IN (119.8 CM)

EUROPEAN SMALLSWORDS

A DEVELOPMENT OF THE RAPIER, the smallsword came into general use in Western Europe toward the end of the 17th century. It was a civilian weapon: an essential item of dress for any gentleman that also acted as a dueling sword. Intended solely for thrusting, the smallsword typically had a stiff triangular blade, without sharpened edges, which in the hands of a skilful swordsman was a deadly fencing weapon. Although simple in overall design—the handguard consisting of a small cup, and finger and knuckle guards—many smallswords were magnificently decorated, reflecting the status of their owners.

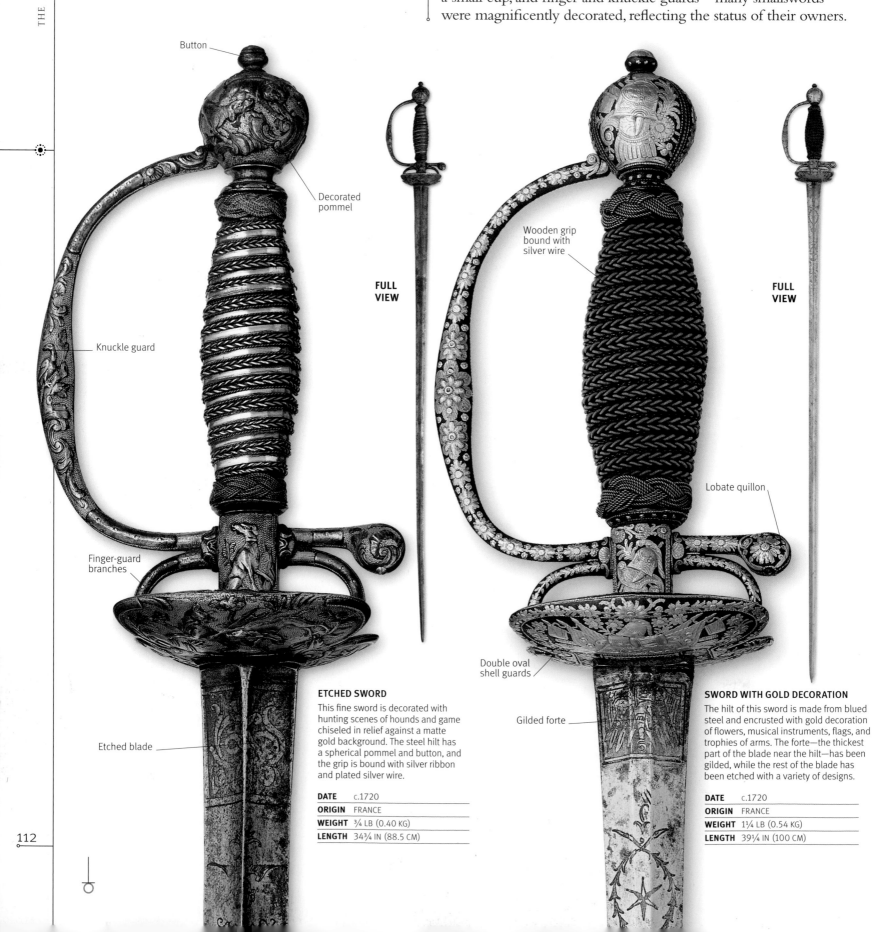

Button

Decorated pommel

Knuckle guard

Finger-guard branches

Etched blade

FULL VIEW

Wooden grip bound with silver wire

FULL VIEW

Lobate quillon

Double oval shell guards

Gilded forte

ETCHED SWORD

This fine sword is decorated with hunting scenes of hounds and game chiseled in relief against a matte gold background. The steel hilt has a spherical pommel and button, and the grip is bound with silver ribbon and plated silver wire.

DATE	c.1720
ORIGIN	FRANCE
WEIGHT	¾ LB (0.40 KG)
LENGTH	34¾ IN (88.5 CM)

SWORD WITH GOLD DECORATION

The hilt of this sword is made from blued steel and encrusted with gold decoration of flowers, musical instruments, flags, and trophies of arms. The forte—the thickest part of the blade near the hilt—has been gilded, while the rest of the blade has been etched with a variety of designs.

DATE	c.1720
ORIGIN	FRANCE
WEIGHT	1¼ LB (0.54 KG)
LENGTH	39¼ IN (100 CM)

Wide colichemarde forte

Acorn button

Double oval shell guards

FULL VIEW

COLICHEMARDE-TYPE SWORD

The silver hilt of this sword is chiseled with musical trophies and the grip is bound with silver foil and wire. The hollow triangular section of the blade is of a colichemarde type where the forte is particularly wide. The strengthened forte was used for parrying an opponent's sword, leaving the blade light at the point to increase speed and control.

DATE	c.1756
ORIGIN	ENGLAND
WEIGHT	1 LB (0.45 KG)
LENGTH	39¼ IN (99.5 CM)

Straight quillons

Urn-shaped pommel

Wire knuckle guard

Dished oval guard

Blued blade

FULL VIEW

SWORD WITH WIRE KNUCKLE GUARD

This sword's distinguishing features are the urn-shaped pommel, a knuckle guard of cut-steel beads strung on wire, and a dished oval guard decorated with pierced triangles in three rows. The blade is blued for much of its length with gold decoration.

DATE	c.1825
ORIGIN	ENGLAND
WEIGHT	1 LB (0.45 KG)
LENGTH	39 IN (99 CM)

Blued and gilded forte

Double oval shell guards

Spherical pommel

FULL VIEW

SWORD WITH GILDED GRIP

The spherical pommel and gilded grip of this smallsword are complemented by a lobate quillon and two symmetrical shell guards. The forte of the blade is blued with gold embellishments.

DATE	c.1770
ORIGIN	FRANCE
WEIGHT	15 OZ (0.43 KG)
LENGTH	15½ IN (39.5 CM)

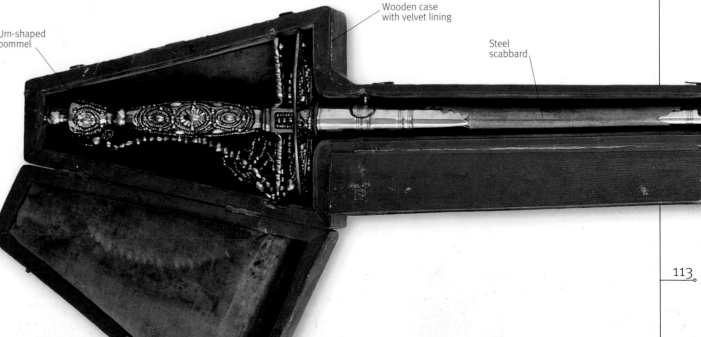

Urn-shaped pommel

Wooden case with velvet lining

Steel scabbard

CASED SWORD

Boxed within a sword case, this British smallsword has an urn-shaped pommel, a faceted steel grip, and a knuckle guard of cut-steel beads on wire. Below the straight quillons is a dished oval guard. The blade is encased within a scabbard.

DATE	c.1825
ORIGIN	ENGLAND
WEIGHT	1 LB (0.45 KG)
WEIGHT	39 IN (99 CM)

BATTLE OF MARIGNANO
French King François I
fought a close battle against
Swiss pikemen in September 1515
at Marignano, modern-day Melegnano
near Milan. The King and his army of Landsknecht
mercenaries are depicted here in a relief on the King's tomb.

EUROPEAN HUNTING SWORDS

DURING THE 16TH century specialist hunting swords came into widespread use among Europe's aristocracy. The swords were short in length, and often had a slightly curved, single-edged blade. For the most part, hunting swords were used to finish off an animal wounded by a spear or shot, although in the case of boar swords they might act as the primary weapon. In many instances, hunting swords were elaborately decorated and often featured engraved scenes of the chase. During the 18th century the hanger type of hunting sword acted as a model for the ordinary soldier's fighting sword.

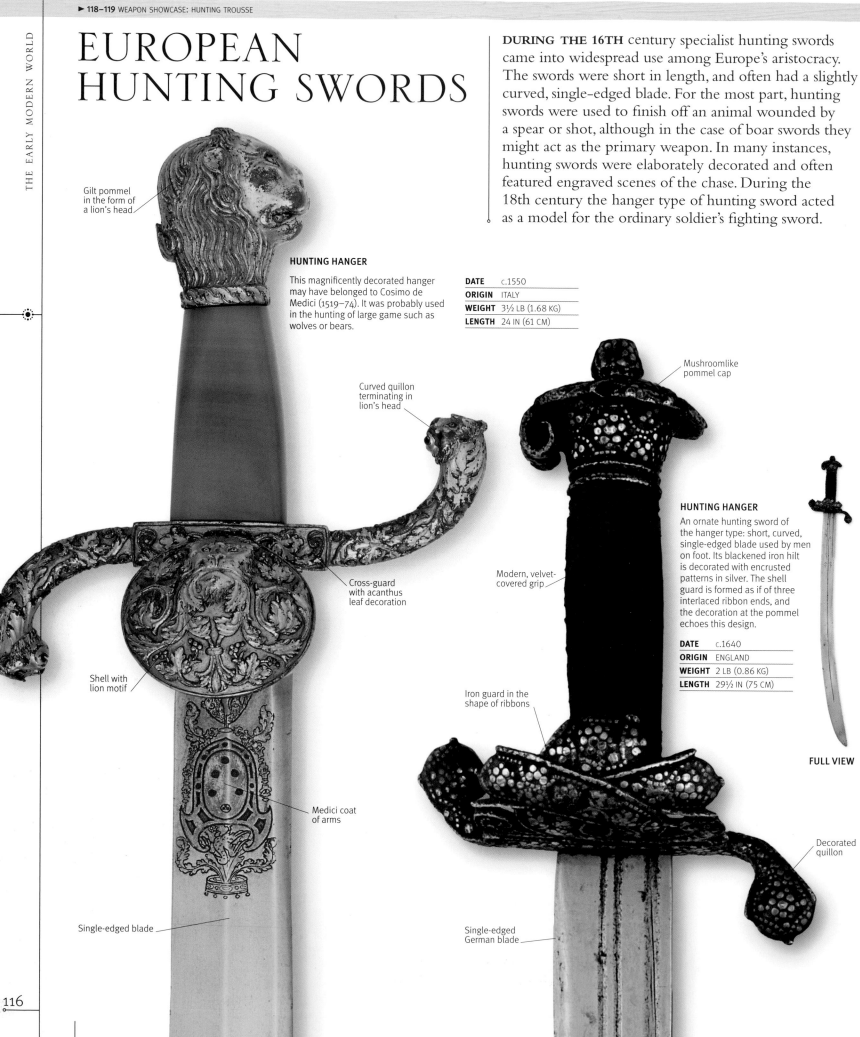

Gilt pommel
in the form of
a lion's head

HUNTING HANGER

This magnificently decorated hanger may have belonged to Cosimo de Medici (1519–74). It was probably used in the hunting of large game such as wolves or bears.

DATE	c.1550
ORIGIN	ITALY
WEIGHT	3½ LB (1.68 KG)
LENGTH	24 IN (61 CM)

Curved quillon
terminating in
lion's head

Cross-guard
with acanthus
leaf decoration

Shell with
lion motif

Medici coat
of arms

Single-edged blade

Mushroomlike
pommel cap

HUNTING HANGER

An ornate hunting sword of the hanger type: short, curved, single-edged blade used by men on foot. Its blackened iron hilt is decorated with encrusted patterns in silver. The shell guard is formed as if of three interlaced ribbon ends, and the decoration at the pommel echoes this design.

DATE	c.1640
ORIGIN	ENGLAND
WEIGHT	2 LB (0.86 KG)
LENGTH	29½ IN (75 CM)

Modern, velvet-
covered grip

Iron guard in the
shape of ribbons

Decorated
quillon

Single-edged
German blade

FULL VIEW

Heavy stiff
blade

See detail

Spear
point

Transverse bar

FULL VIEW

Pommel

Two-handed grip

Cross-guard with
long, straight
quillons

BOAR SWORD

Boars were one of the more popular
animals for the serious hunter, not
least because they could fight back
and had dangerous tusks. Boars were
traditionally hunted with spears, but
in the late 15th century a specialist
sword came into use, featuring a
stiff blade with a transverse bar.

DATE	c.1550
ORIGIN	EUROPE
WEIGHT	4¼ LB (1.98 KG)
LENGTH	51½ IN (131 CM)

TRANSVERSE BAR

A transverse piece of
metal was inserted
toward the end of the
blade to prevent the
charging boar from
running up the blade
and goring the hunter.
The boar was a ferocious
and fast-charging animal,
and in its death throes
would continue to force
its way up a conventional
spear or sword.

Quillon with
flattened
mushroom-
shaped terminal

Decorated
cap pommel

Sharpened
"false edge"

FULL VIEW

Knuckle guard
with central knob

HUNTING HANGER

This hanger has a single-edged curved blade
with a "false edge" (in fact, a sharpened
edge) for the last 4 in (10 cm) on the upper,
otherwise blunt side of the blade. The steel
hilt has a cap pommel, a wooden grip and
two shell guards, encrusted in silver dots
within a trellis pattern.

DATE	c.1650
ORIGIN	ENGLAND (HILT) GERMANY (BLADE)
WEIGHT	1½ LB (0.73 KG)
LENGTH	28½ IN (72.5 CM)

Maker's mark of Johannis Meigen

Piqué-decorated
cow horn hilt

Double fullers on
each face of the forte

Double-edged
blade with
hatchet point

FULL VIEW

HUNTING HANGER

Manufactured in England, but using a
German blade, the hilt of this sword is made
from cow horn and features a cruciform hilt
and "beak"-shaped pommel. The piqué
decoration takes the form of an inlay of
white metal studs (either silver or pewter)
and stag horn and ebony roundels.

DATE	1647
ORIGIN	ENGLAND (HILT) GERMANY (BLADE)
WEIGHT	2LB (0.86KG)
LENGTH	31 IN (78¾ CM)

Single-edged,
pointed blade

Pommel

Bone grip,
stained green

Cast-brass guard
with recurved
quillons and
rococo design

STRAIGHT HANGER

This short hunting sword from the late
18th century is of a more decorative than
functional design. The brass guard and
pommel are complemented by a straight,
finely engraved, single-edged blade.

FULL VIEW

DATE	c.1780
ORIGIN	FRANCE
WEIGHT	2LB (0.86KG)
LENGTH	29½ IN (75 CM)

HUNTING TROUSSE

HUNTING IN THE MEDIEVAL and Renaissance period was seen both as a means of putting meat on the table and as training for war. Preparatory to setting out on the chase, the huntsman would assemble a trousse; a set of carving and eating tools contained within a sheath. This would typically contain miniature saws, small cleavers, and carving knives that were used for killing, skinning, jointing, serving, and finally eating the animal. The German hunting tradition produced many fine examples of hunting weapons; the sword and cleaver displayed here are a matched set that would have been used by a Saxon huntsman in the late 17th century.

HUNTING SWORD

Relatively long for a hunting sword, this weapon features an interesting guard that comprises straight quillons combined with S-shaped quillons, the lower one forming a simple knuckle guard. All four are decorated with leaf-shaped finials.

DATE	1662
ORIGIN	GERMANY
WEIGHT	12LB (2.2KG)
LENGTH	35.2IN (90CM)

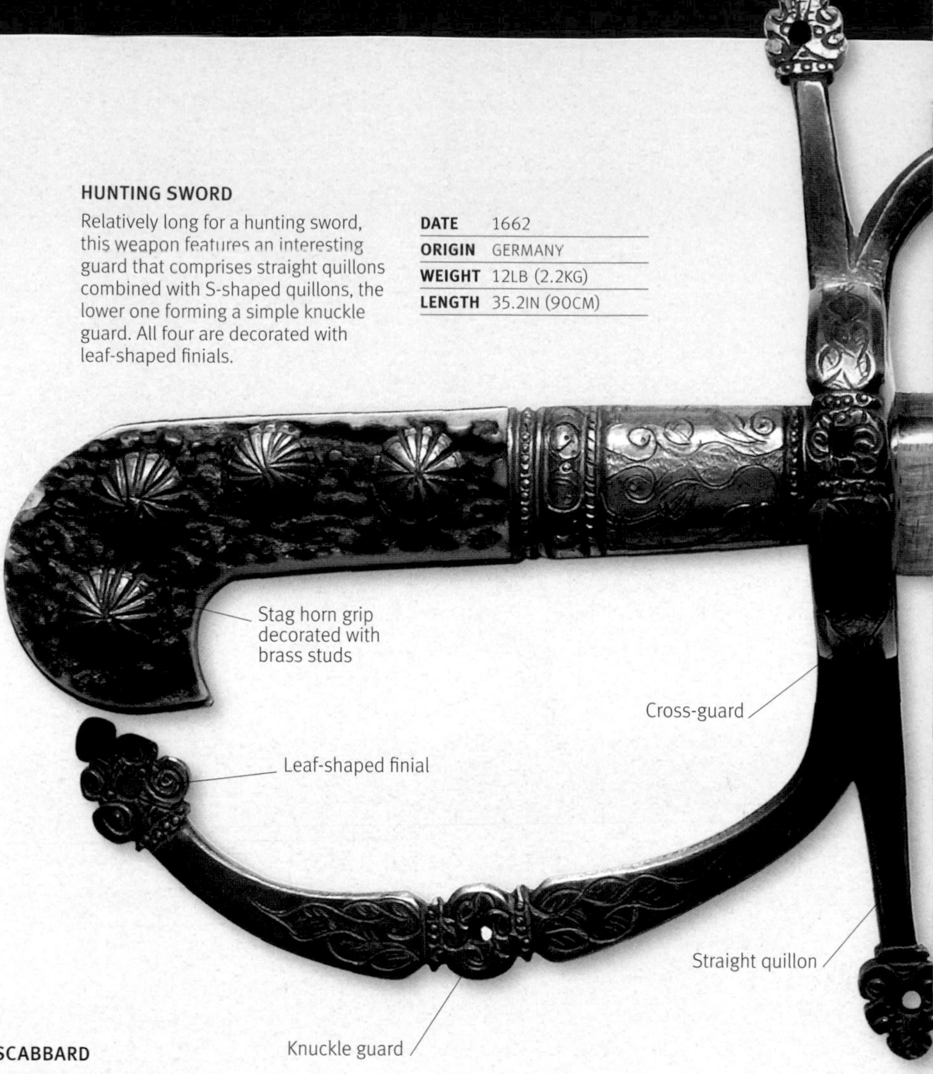

Stag horn grip decorated with brass studs

Cross-guard

Leaf-shaped finial

Straight quillon

Knuckle guard

TROUSSE SCABBARD

Made of leather to hold the thick-bladed cleaver, this scabbard also contains five meat-trimming utensils, including a carving knife (below).

Initials refer to the owner John-George II

HUNTING CLEAVER

While the sword delivered the *coup de grace* to the wounded animal, the cleaver was used to dismember the carcass. This sharp, heavy blade would have little trouble in cutting through animal joints, including those from larger beasts such as boar and deer.

DATE	c.1662
ORIGIN	GERMANY
WEIGHT	2¼LB (1KG)
LENGTH	18IN (46CM)

Guard

CARVING KNIFE

Maker's mark

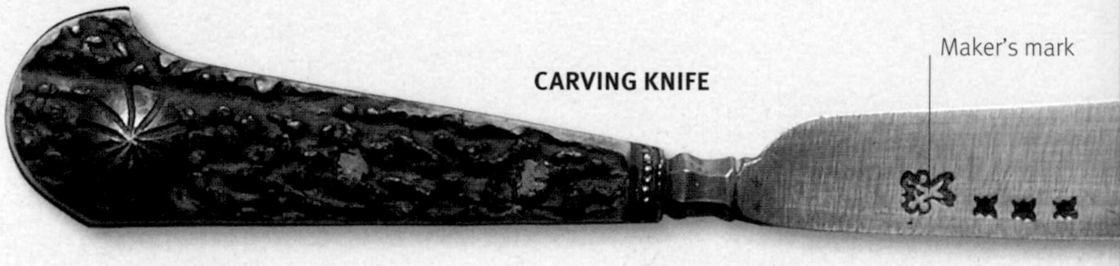

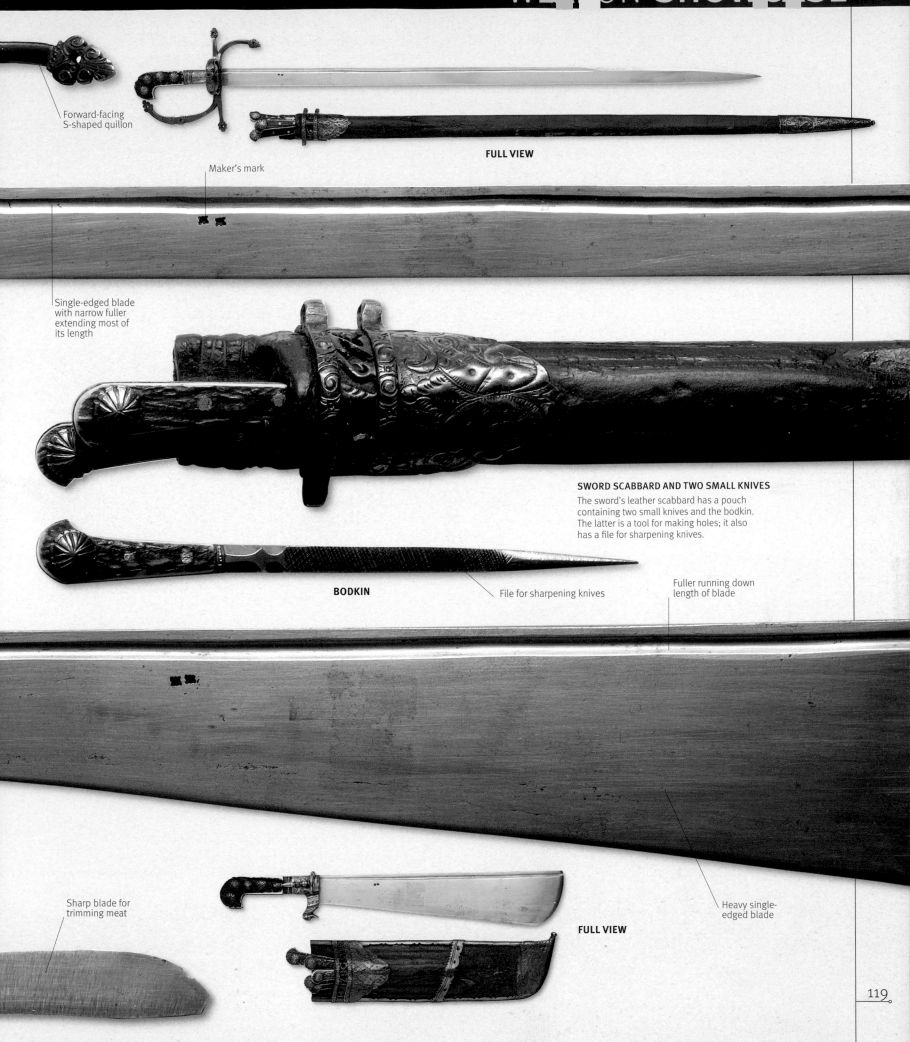

Forward-facing
S-shaped quillon

FULL VIEW

Maker's mark

Single-edged blade
with narrow fuller
extending most of
its length

SWORD SCABBARD AND TWO SMALL KNIVES
The sword's leather scabbard has a pouch
containing two small knives and the bodkin.
The latter is a tool for making holes; it also
has a file for sharpening knives.

BODKIN

File for sharpening knives

Fuller running down
length of blade

Sharp blade for
trimming meat

FULL VIEW

Heavy single-
edged blade

1500—1775

◀ **66–67** JAPANESE AND CHINESE SWORDS   ▶ **124–125** WEAPON SHOWCASE: WAKAZASHI SWORD   ▶ **126–127** GREAT WARRIORS: SAMURAI

THE EARLY MODERN WORLD

JAPANESE SAMURAI SWORDS

JAPANESE SWORD BLADES are considered among the finest ever made. Their success was due to the combination of a hard cutting edge with a softer, resilient core and back. After a complex process creating a soft core enfolded in hard outer layers of steel, the swordsmith covered the blade in clay, leaving only a thin layer over what was to become the cutting edge. During quenching the edge cools rapidly, becoming very hard, while the back cools more slowly, and softens. The mountings for blades developed their own aesthetic finesse. For example, in the 15th century, the manufacture of *tsuba* (guards) became a separate profession, and these are now collectors' items in their own right.

Shinogi (blade ridge)

Yokote—sharp, hard area of blade

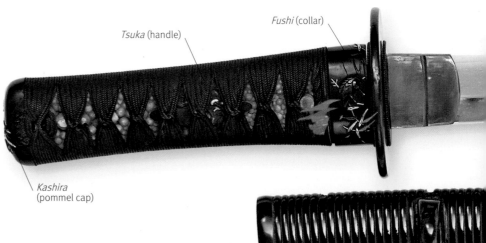

Tsuka (handle)

Fushi (collar)

Kashira (pommel cap)

Ridged decoration on scabbard

SAMURAI RULER
This print, entitled *Shizu Peak Moon*, shows the great Japanese warlord Toyotomi Hideyoshi (1536–98) blowing his war trumpet at dawn before the famous victory over Shibata Katsuie at Shizugatake in 1583, which made him undisputed ruler of Japan. Hideyoshi has a *tachi* and a *tanto* tied into his belt or *obi*.

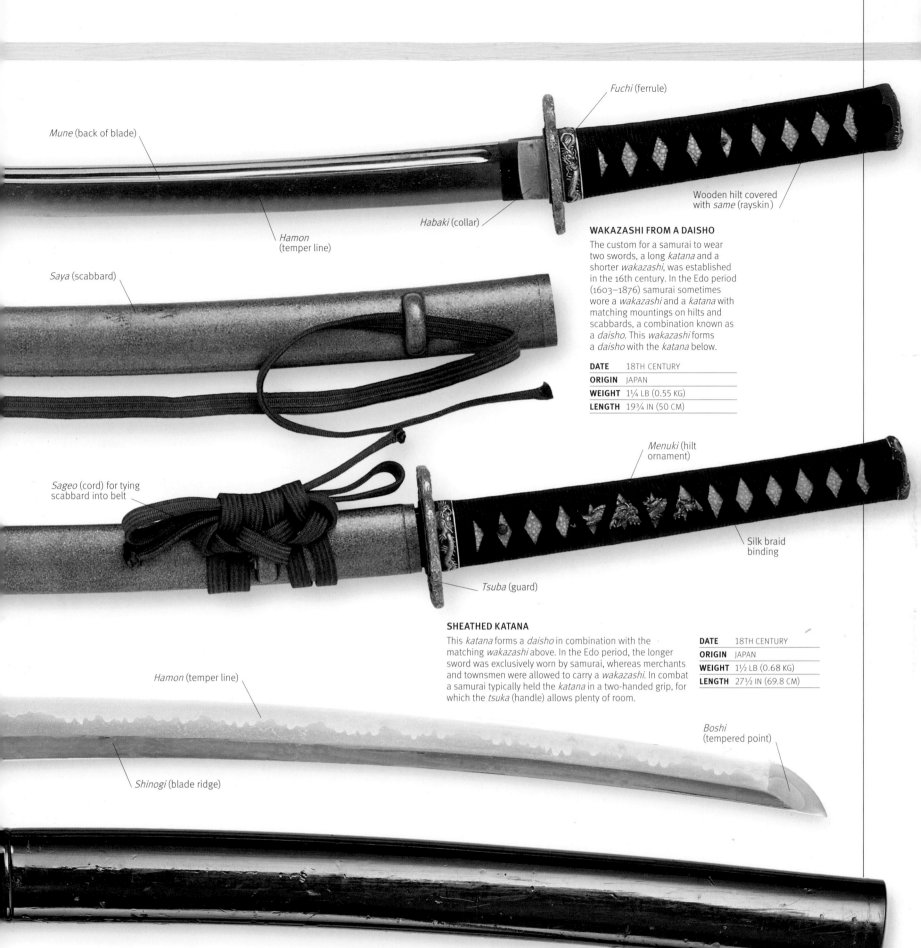

Mune (back of blade)

Fuchi (ferrule)

Hamon (temper line)

Habaki (collar)

Wooden hilt covered with *same* (rayskin)

Saya (scabbard)

WAKAZASHI FROM A DAISHO

The custom for a samurai to wear two swords, a long *katana* and a shorter *wakazashi*, was established in the 16th century. In the Edo period (1603–1876) samurai sometimes wore a *wakazashi* and a *katana* with matching mountings on hilts and scabbards, a combination known as a *daisho*. This *wakazashi* forms a *daisho* with the *katana* below.

DATE	18TH CENTURY
ORIGIN	JAPAN
WEIGHT	1¼ LB (0.55 KG)
LENGTH	19¾ IN (50 CM)

Menuki (hilt ornament)

Sageo (cord) for tying scabbard into belt

Silk braid binding

Tsuba (guard)

SHEATHED KATANA

This *katana* forms a *daisho* in combination with the matching *wakazashi* above. In the Edo period, the longer sword was exclusively worn by samurai, whereas merchants and townsmen were allowed to carry a *wakazashi*. In combat a samurai typically held the *katana* in a two-handed grip, for which the *tsuka* (handle) allows plenty of room.

DATE	18TH CENTURY
ORIGIN	JAPAN
WEIGHT	1½ LB (0.68 KG)
LENGTH	27½ IN (69.8 CM)

Hamon (temper line)

Boshi (tempered point)

Shinogi (blade ridge)

WAKAZASHI SWORD AND SCABBARD

A *wakazashi* is a sword with a blade 30–60 cm (12–24 in) long. Japanese blades are also differentiated by details of shape and by their *hamon*—the line left between the areas of the blade covered and uncovered during the tempering process. There are various patterns of *hamon*, some associated with specific swordsmiths. This blade was made by Seshu ju Nagatsuna.

DATE	c.17TH CENTURY
ORIGIN	JAPAN
WEIGHT	2 LB (0.97 KG)
LENGTH	18½ IN (46.8 CM)

JAPANESE SAMURAI SWORDS

Mekugi joins hilt to tang of blade

WAKAZASHI AND SCABBARD

The *wakazashi* was a samurai's constant companion, worn from waking until sleeping, and even kept nearby during the night. As well as serving as an additional fighting sword to the *katana* and as, in effect, a side-arm, it was often the weapon used by samurai to perform ritual suicide (*seppuku*).

DATE	17TH CENTURY
ORIGIN	JAPAN
WEIGHT	1 LB (0.42 KG)
LENGTH	19 IN (48.5 CM)

Pocket for *katagana*

Kashira (pommel)

Silk braid

TACHI IN GOLD SCABBARD

The blade of a *tachi* was traditionally over 24 in (60 cm) in length, although shorter than the *nodachi* field sword, which was worn slung over a samurai's shoulder. *Tachi* hilts were fitted with a traditionally shaped *kashira* that wrapped around the end.

DATE	LATE 18TH CENTURY
ORIGIN	JAPAN
WEIGHT	1½ LB (0.68 KG)
LENGTH	28¼ IN (71.75 CM)

Menuki (hilt ornament)

Rayskin

Ornate lacquered scabbard

Sageo (cord)

ORNATE WAKAZASHI

This is a lavishly mounted reproduction *wakazashi*. The real thing would almost certainly have been worn on ceremonial occasions as a display of status. The sides of the scabbard carry the *katagana* (knife) and *kogai* (hair-arranging implement) associated with the *wakazashi*.

DATE	20TH CENTURY
ORIGIN	JAPAN
WEIGHT	1 LB (0.42 KG)
LENGTH	20 IN (c.50 CM)

THE EARLY MODERN WORLD

Kissaki (point)

Semegane
(scabbard ring)

Sageo (cord)

Black lacquered scabbard

Gold-lacquered
saya (scabbard)

GUNTO IN SCABBARD

During the period of militarism in the 1930s, the
Japanese adopted a style of sword for army officers
based on the traditional *tachi*. Most were fitted with
a mass-produced blade, but the mount is capable
of being fitted to a traditional blade.

DATE	1933
ORIGIN	JAPAN
WEIGHT	1½ LB (0.72 KG)
LENGTH	27 IN (68.9 CM)

Shirasaya
(storage
scabbard)

Sayajira
(scabbard tip)

Kogatana (knife)
in pocket on side
of scabbard

Habaki (collar)

Hole in guard
for knife to
pass through

THE EARLY MODERN WORLD

WAKAZASHI SWORD

THE HILT AND GUARD of this Japanese short sword, or *wakazashi*, are of a style popular in the Edo period (1603–1876). It might have been worn by a samurai when in civilian dress, as an accompaniment to his long sword (*katana*), or on its own by rich merchants or townsmen. When indoors, a samurai would leave the long sword on a rack by the door, but would still wear the *wakazashi*. The mounting (hilt and guard) was a separate item to the blade. A well-off individual might have several mountings for a single blade, choosing the most suitable style for a given occasion. A lavish mounting was a visible symbol of the wearer's wealth.

SUNAGI
When it was not fitted on a blade, the mounting of the sword would be assembled on a wooden copy of a blade and tang called a *sunagi*. Separated from its mounting, the blade was stored in a wooden scabbard with a plain wood grip called a *shirasaya*.

DATE	17TH CENTURY
ORIGIN	JAPAN
BLADE WEIGHT	1 LB (0.49 KG)
BLADE LENGTH	21 IN (53.4 CM)

MEKUGI
The *mekugi* was a small peg that passed through a hole in the hilt and a corresponding hole in the tang of the blade. It thus fixed the hilt to the tang. The *mekugi* was usually made of bamboo, but occasionally of horn or ivory.

BLADE
The blade was the heart of the sword. Making its hard, sharp edge and softer, resilient core and back was a complex, skilled operation. The tang was often marked with the swordsmith's signature; this blade is signed by Tadahiro of Hizen province on Kyushu island.

Hamachi (edge notch)

Nakago (tang)

Hole for *mekugi*

Munemachi (back notch)

Kashira (pommel)   Rayskin   *Menuki* (hilt ornament)

TSUKA
The hilt, or *tsuka*, was made of magnolia wood. It was grooved on the inside to fit exactly the tapering shape of the tang. The rayskin covering was valuable, hence perhaps the lozenge openings in the silk braid that allow it to be seen. The *menuki* ornaments have the practical function of helping to fill the hand gripping the sword.

Silk braid

Hole for *mekugi*   *Fuchi* (collar)

HABAKI
The *habaki*, a part of the blade rather than the mounting, slid over the tang and butted against the blade notches.

TSUBA AND SEPPA
The metal guard, or *tsuba*, had a central hole for the tang, flanked by holes for the *kogatana* and *kogai*. Copper spacers (*seppa*) fitted on each side of the guard. *Tsuba* were decorated with gold or silver inlay.

Tsuba (handguard)

Hole for *tang*

Seppa (spacer)

Hole for *kogaana*

Hole for *kogai*

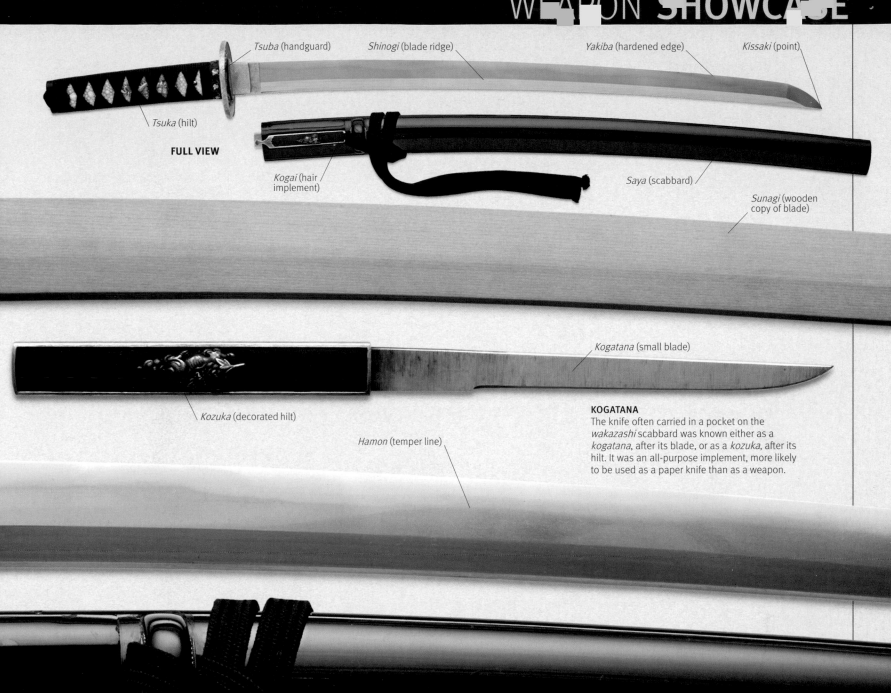

Tsuba (handguard) *Shinogi* (blade ridge) *Yakiba* (hardened edge) *Kissaki* (point)

Tsuka (hilt)

FULL VIEW

Kogai (hair implement)

Saya (scabbard)

Sunagi (wooden copy of blade)

Kogatana (small blade)

Kozuka (decorated hilt)

Hamon (temper line)

KOGATANA
The knife often carried in a pocket on the *wakazashi* scabbard was known either as a *kogatana*, after its blade, or as a *kozuka*, after its hilt. It was an all-purpose implement, more likely to be used as a paper knife than as a weapon.

SAYA
Like the hilt, the *saya* (scabbard) was made of magnolia wood. It was lacquered to protect it from the weather. The *sageo*, a length of strong braid, attached the scabbard to the owner's belt. Pockets on opposite faces of the scabbard held a small knife (*kogatana*) and an implement known as a *kogai*.

Sageo (cord for tying scabbard to belt)

Ear cleaner

Handle decoration matches *kozuka*

Thin end inserted into hair

KOGAI
The *kogai*, often slipped into a pocket on the *wakazashi* scabbard, was primarily an implement employed in arranging a samurai's hair. A knob on the end of the handle was used to clean out earwax.

125

**THE LONG SWORD
(KATANA)**

SAMURAI

ORIGINALLY FIGHTING in the service of the emperor or nobles, by the 12th century, the samurai had emerged as a warrior elite, dominating Japanese society. The shogunate, established in 1185, made the samurai rulers of Japan, with the emperor as a figurehead. Centuries of civil war took place between samurai clans and *daimyo* (warlords) until pacification under the Tokugawa shogunate in the 1600s reduced the clans to redundancy—a military elite with no wars to fight.

EVOLVING WARRIORS

The early samurai were, above all, archers. It was not until the 13th century that the sword gained ascendancy over the bow as a samurai weapon. Early samurai warfare was often individualistic and ritualized. When battle lines were drawn, leading warriors would challenge prominent enemies to combat with long, florid speeches, and then gallop forward shooting arrows. It was warfare largely conditioned by the fact that, with the exception of two brief Mongol landings in 1274 and 1281, the medieval samurai fought only one another. Along with ritualized combat went ritualized death, as the tradition developed of defeated samurai committing *seppuku* (ritual suicide) by *hara-kiri* (the belly-cut). The concept of an honorable death was given higher value than victory in battle.

In the Sengoku period, from the 1460s to 1615, samurai warfare became more practical, organized, and varied. As constant warfare raged between the *daimyo*, the samurai fought in large armies on foot or in the saddle, supported by disciplined bodies of infantry, the *ashigaru*, drawn from the common people. The samurai completely abandoned the bow, which became an *ashigaru* weapon, relying on their swords and long spears.

DOOMED ARCHER
Minamoto Yoshihira flourishes his bow, the prime weapon of the early samurai. Yoshihira was captured and executed by the rival Taira clan after being on the losing side in the Heiji Incident in 1160.

MINAMOTO YORIMASA

Minamoto Yorimasa is credited with establishing the pattern for samurai ritual suicide. He was a veteran in his 70s when, in 1180, he led the Minamoto clan against the Taira at the outset of the Gempei Wars. Defeated at the battle of Uji, Yorimasa retreated to a temple, where he wrote an elegant poem on the back of a fan before cutting open his abdomen with a dagger.

**MINAMOTO
YORIMASA IN
FORMAL DRESS**

SAMURAI ARMOUR

This samurai armour is in the *o-yoroi* (great armour) style that predominated from the 12th to the 14th century. Japanese armour is always designed to impress as well as protect.

Kuwagata (horned crest)

Fukigayeshi (side guards)

Mempo (ornamental face mask)

Sode (shoulder guard)

Laquered iron scales laced with silk and leather

Suneate (shin guards)

Style of boots reflected samurai's rank

ELITE FORCES

The samurai completely abandoned the bow, which became an *ashigaru* weapon, relying instead on their swords and long spears. Their battlefield dominance was challenged by the introduction of firearms—the great general Oda Nobunaga equipped his *ashigaru* with arquebuses to devastating effect at the battle of Nagashino in 1575. But the samurai remained elite forces and their professionalization in the Sengoku period did not preclude personal duels and legendary feats of individual swordplay. Many of these were attributed to *ronin*, wandering masterless samurai whose instruction manual *The Book of Five Rings* helped pass on the mystique of samurai swordsmanship to later generations.

After the definitive victory of the Tokugawa clan established a durable peace, the samurai remained a privileged class with the exclusive right to bear arms. It was at this time that the principles of samurai behavior were formalized into the chivalric *bushido* code, stressing loyalty as the supreme virtue and sacrificial death as the highest fulfilment of life. The samurai class was formally abolished in 1876 after the Meiji Restoration.

CLAN BATTLE
Armies of the Minamoto and Taira clans clash with swords in one of the battles of the Gempei Wars (1180–85), the conflict that established the Minamoto shogunate.

"IT IS NOT THE WAY OF THE WARRIOR TO BE SHAMED AND AVOID DEATH... I WILL HOLD OFF THE FORCES OF THE ENTIRE COUNTRY HERE AND DIE A RESPLENDENT DEATH."

SAMURAI TORII MOTOTADA, AT THE SIEGE OF FUSHIMI CASTLE, 1600

TOOLS OF COMBAT

TACHI SWORD AND SCABBARD

WAKAZASHI DAGGER AND SHEATH

LATE SAMURAI SPEAR

THE EARLY MODERN WORLD

INDIAN AND SRI LANKAN SWORDS

THE ESTABLISHMENT OF THE Mughal Empire in northern India in the 16th century brought with it the fine curved swords found through most of the Islamic world. These *talwars* and *shamshirs* were superb cutting instruments that achieved near-perfection of form and function. Although many Hindu princes adopted the *talwar*, the traditional straight-bladed Hindu *khanda* continued to be made. By the 18th century, many sword blades were being imported from Europe, where manufacturers produced to Indian designs.

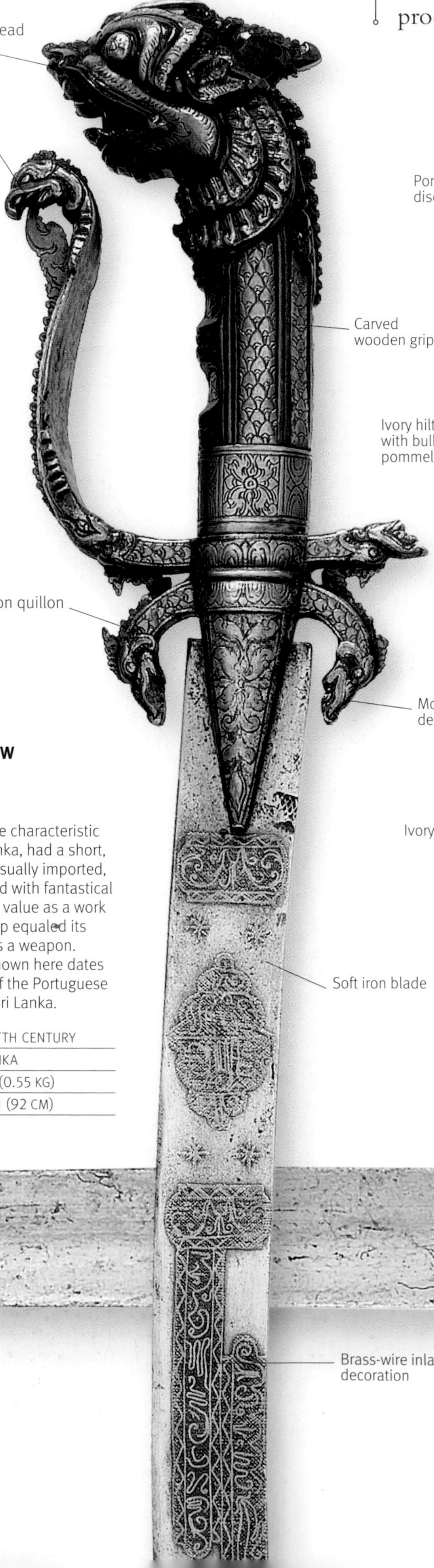

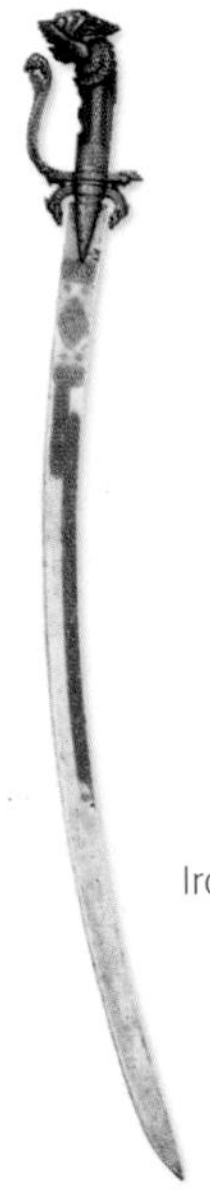

Dragon's head pommel

Knuckle guard

Carved wooden grip

Iron quillon

FULL VIEW

KASTANE

The *kastane*, the characteristic sword of Sri Lanka, had a short, curved blade, usually imported, and a hilt carved with fantastical decorations. Its value as a work of craftsmanship equaled its effectiveness as a weapon. The example shown here dates from the time of the Portuguese occupation of Sri Lanka.

DATE	HILT: 17TH CENTURY
ORIGIN	SRI LANKA
WEIGHT	1¼ LB (0.55 KG)
LENGTH	36¼ IN (92 CM)

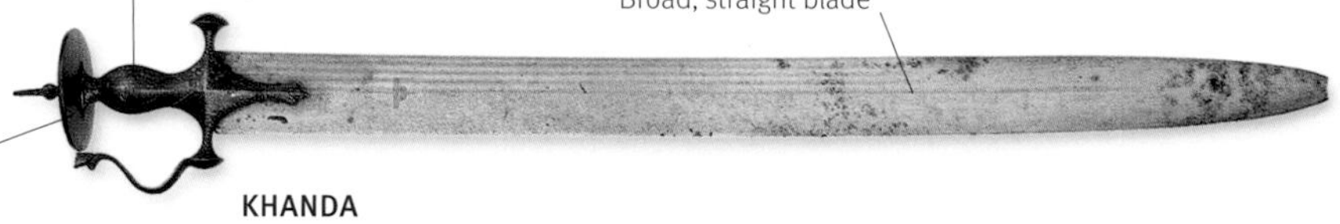

Soft iron blade

Brass-wire inlay decoration

Indo-Muslim hilt design

Pommel disc

Broad, straight blade

KHANDA

The straight *khanda* is the traditional sword of Hindu India. This example, made under the influence of the Mughal Empire, has a hilt that is of Indo-Muslim design. Its decoration includes the repeated image of an eagle.

DATE	1632–33
ORIGIN	MUGHAL INDIA
WEIGHT	2¾ LB (1.25 KG)
LENGTH	35 IN (89 CM)

Quillons end in petaled domes

Langet

Curved, tapered steel blade

Ivory hilt with bulbous pommel

Monster head decoration

TALWAR

The *talwar*, of Persian origin, was the quintessential sword of Mughal India. Many were works of outstanding craftsmanship. This *talwar* has a more shallowly curved blade than those produced later in the Mughal period.

DATE	EARLY 17TH CENTURY
ORIGIN	MUGHAL INDIA
WEIGHT	2¼ LB (1.04 KG)
LENGTH	37¾ IN (95.7 CM)

Short, straight quillon

Ivory grip

Deeply curved blade

SHAMSHIR

The *shamshir* is the sword known to Europeans as the scimitar. It was introduced to India in the 16th century from Persia. This example is typical of Persian production, with its deeply curved, single-edged, tapering blade. In combat, it was superbly suited to slashing, but less effective for thrusting.

DATE	EARLY 19TH CENTURY
ORIGIN	LUCKNOW, INDIA
WEIGHT	2 LB (0.86 KG)
LENGTH	36½ IN (93 CM)

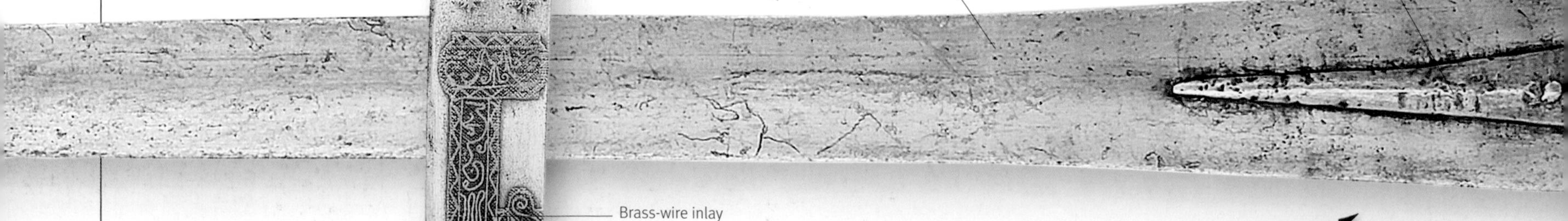

Double-edged blade

Langet riveted to blade strengthens attachment to hilt

FULL VIEW

AYUDHA KATTI

Indigenous to Mysore, Kurg, and the Malabar coast, the *ayudha katti* developed from an implement used to cut through dense undergrowth. Its blade, like that of the Turkish *yataghan* and northern Indian *sosun pattah*, is related to the Ancient Greek *kopis* blade.

DATE	18TH CENTURY
ORIGIN	KURG, INDIA
WEIGHT	2½ LB (1.15 KG)
LENGTH	23½ IN (59.5 CM)

Broad, forward-curving blade

Elliptical pommel plate

Hilt made of horn

Flat pommel with bent finial

Blade widens toward the tip

Hand guard padded with red velvet

TALWAR

This sword was in use in Mysore, southern India, at the time of the wars between the British East India Company and Mysore's ruler, Tipu Sultan. The deeply curved blade is in a traditional Indian style.

DATE	LATE 18TH CENTURY
ORIGIN	MYSORE, INDIA
WEIGHT	3 LB (1.38 KG)
LENGTH	34¾ IN (88.3 CM)

Short quillon with large knop

Knucklebow ends in an animal head finial

Wooden scabbard covered with red velvet

TALWAR

Probably made in Lahore, in what is now Pakistan, this *talwar* with a Persian blade bears a bilingual inscription in Hindi and Urdu inside the knucklebow. The hilt is decorated with *koftgari*—steel inlaid with gold—which was a form of ornamentation found on many Indian swords.

DATE	1801–02
ORIGIN	LAHORE, INDIA
WEIGHT	2 LB (0.91 KG)
LENGTH	23½ IN (59.5 CM)

Iron guard welded to langets

Rounded knop with brass cap

Ribbed iron grip

MALIBAR COAST SWORD

This straight, double-edged sword from southern India has a ribbed iron grip, and a U-shaped guard and pommel-plate. The blade broadens where it is riveted to langets on each face.

DATE	18TH CENTURY
ORIGIN	MALIBAR, INDIA
WEIGHT	1½ LB (0.65 KG)
LENGTH	36¾ IN (83 CM)

129

EUROPEAN DAGGERS

THE DAGGER'S PRIME ROLE as a weapon of self-defense continued into the 16th and 17th centuries, although some new variants evolved, including the left-hand, or *maingauche* dagger. As its name suggests, this dagger was held in the left hand and complemented a sword or rapier held in the right. The left-hand dagger parried thrusts and cuts from the opponent's blade, and acted as an offensive weapon in its own right. The bayonet, another modification of the dagger, continues in use to this day.

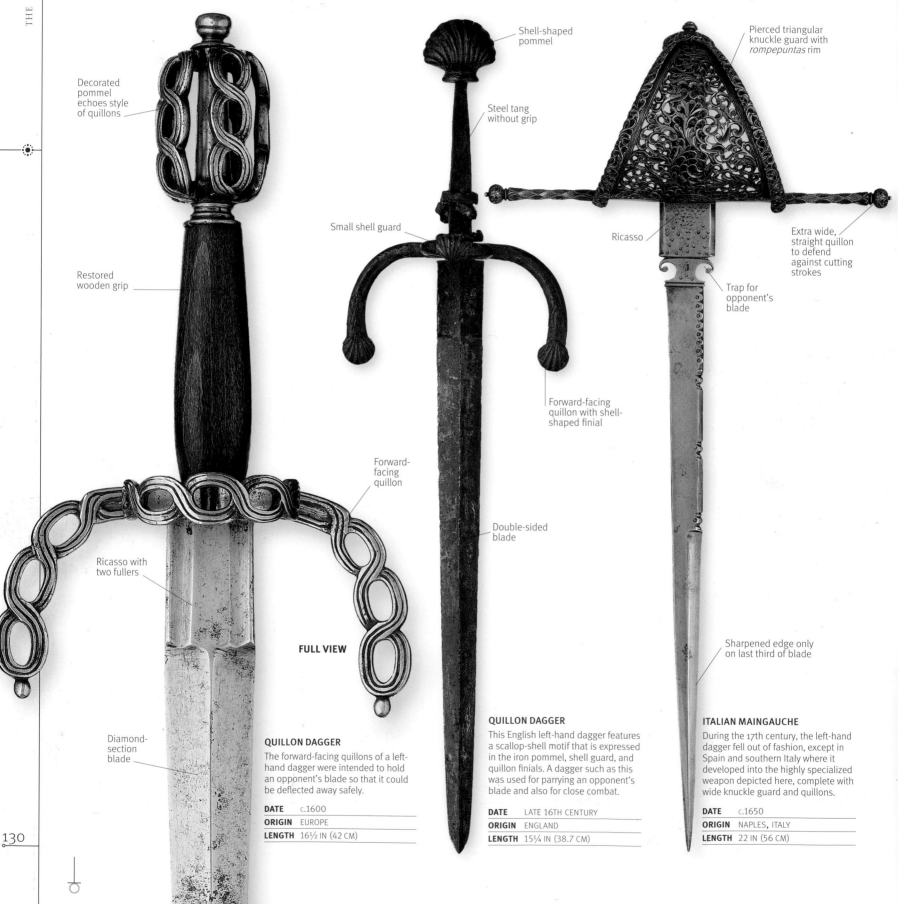

Decorated pommel echoes style of quillons

Restored wooden grip

Forward-facing quillon

Ricasso with two fullers

Diamond-section blade

FULL VIEW

Shell-shaped pommel

Steel tang without grip

Small shell guard

Forward-facing quillon with shell-shaped finial

Double-sided blade

Pierced triangular knuckle guard with *rompepuntas* rim

Ricasso

Extra wide, straight quillon to defend against cutting strokes

Trap for opponent's blade

Sharpened edge only on last third of blade

QUILLON DAGGER

The forward-facing quillons of a left-hand dagger were intended to hold an opponent's blade so that it could be deflected away safely.

DATE	c.1600
ORIGIN	EUROPE
LENGTH	16½ IN (42 CM)

QUILLON DAGGER

This English left-hand dagger features a scallop-shell motif that is expressed in the iron pommel, shell guard, and quillon finials. A dagger such as this was used for parrying an opponent's blade and also for close combat.

DATE	LATE 16TH CENTURY
ORIGIN	ENGLAND
LENGTH	15¼ IN (38.7 CM)

ITALIAN MAINGAUCHE

During the 17th century, the left-hand dagger fell out of fashion, except in Spain and southern Italy where it developed into the highly specialized weapon depicted here, complete with wide knuckle guard and quillons.

DATE	c.1650
ORIGIN	NAPLES, ITALY
LENGTH	22 IN (56 CM)

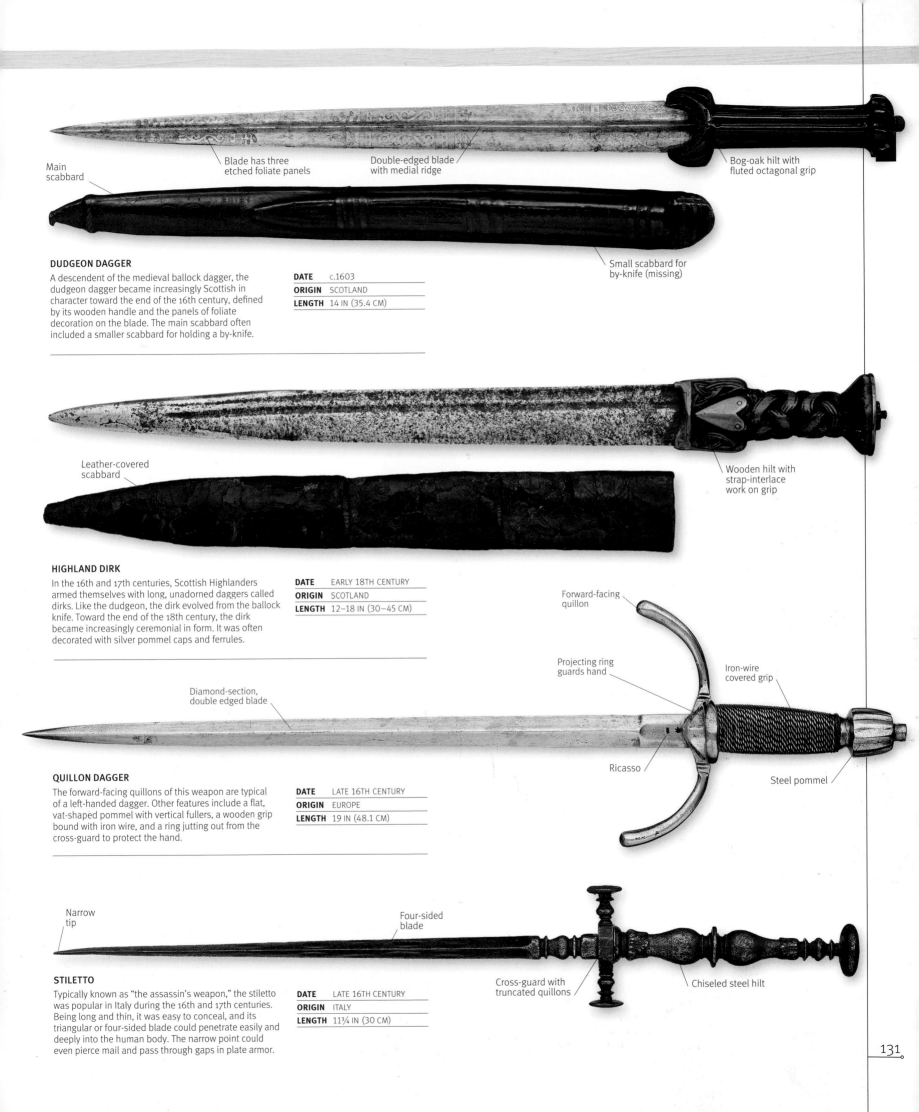

DUDGEON DAGGER

A descendent of the medieval ballock dagger, the dudgeon dagger became increasingly Scottish in character toward the end of the 16th century, defined by its wooden handle and the panels of foliate decoration on the blade. The main scabbard often included a smaller scabbard for holding a by-knife.

DATE	c.1603
ORIGIN	SCOTLAND
LENGTH	14 IN (35.4 CM)

Main scabbard

Blade has three etched foliate panels

Double-edged blade with medial ridge

Bog-oak hilt with fluted octagonal grip

Small scabbard for by-knife (missing)

HIGHLAND DIRK

In the 16th and 17th centuries, Scottish Highlanders armed themselves with long, unadorned daggers called dirks. Like the dudgeon, the dirk evolved from the ballock knife. Toward the end of the 18th century, the dirk became increasingly ceremonial in form. It was often decorated with silver pommel caps and ferrules.

DATE	EARLY 18TH CENTURY
ORIGIN	SCOTLAND
LENGTH	12–18 IN (30–45 CM)

Leather-covered scabbard

Wooden hilt with strap-interlace work on grip

QUILLON DAGGER

The forward-facing quillons of this weapon are typical of a left-handed dagger. Other features include a flat, vat-shaped pommel with vertical fullers, a wooden grip bound with iron wire, and a ring jutting out from the cross-guard to protect the hand.

DATE	LATE 16TH CENTURY
ORIGIN	EUROPE
LENGTH	19 IN (48.1 CM)

Forward-facing quillon

Projecting ring guards hand

Iron-wire covered grip

Diamond-section, double edged blade

Ricasso

Steel pommel

STILETTO

Typically known as "the assassin's weapon," the stiletto was popular in Italy during the 16th and 17th centuries. Being long and thin, it was easy to conceal, and its triangular or four-sided blade could penetrate easily and deeply into the human body. The narrow point could even pierce mail and pass through gaps in plate armor.

DATE	LATE 16TH CENTURY
ORIGIN	ITALY
LENGTH	11¾ IN (30 CM)

Narrow tip

Four-sided blade

Cross-guard with truncated quillons

Chiseled steel hilt

EUROPEAN DAGGERS

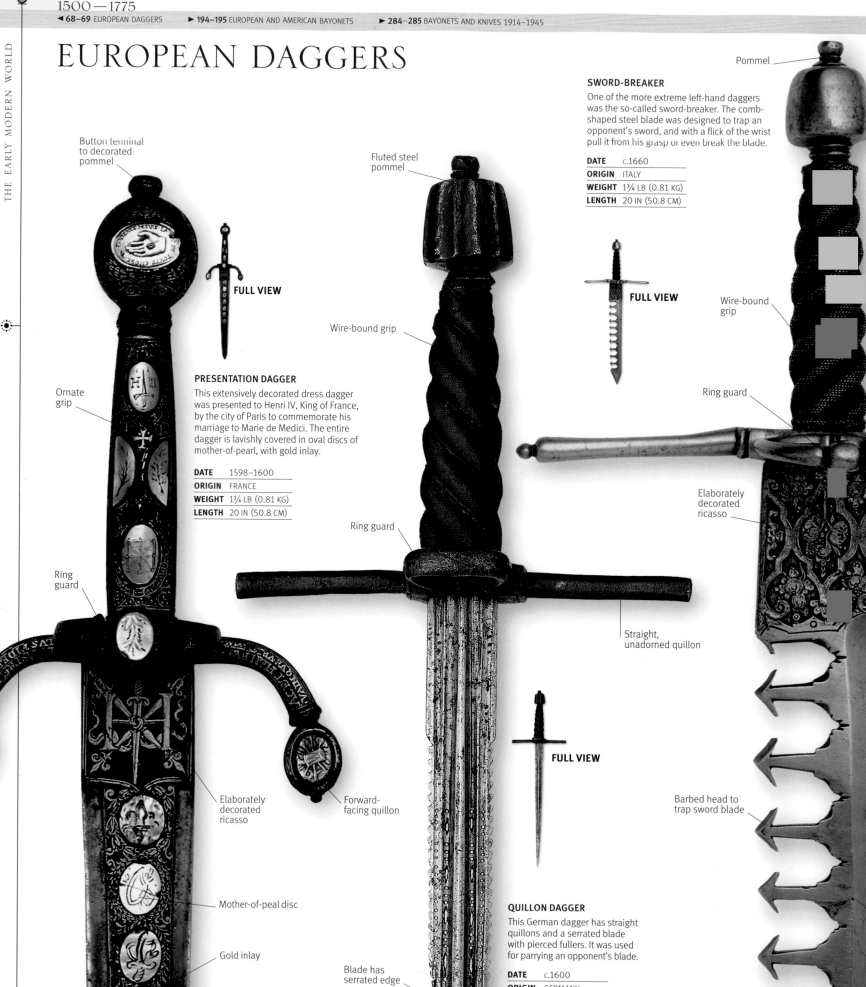

Pommel

Button terminal
to decorated
pommel

Ornate
grip

Ring
guard

Elaborately
decorated
ricasso

Forward-
facing quillon

Mother-of-peal disc

Gold inlay

Blade edge is
unadorned

FULL VIEW

PRESENTATION DAGGER

This extensively decorated dress dagger
was presented to Henri IV, King of France,
by the city of Paris to commemorate his
marriage to Marie de Medici. The entire
dagger is lavishly covered in oval discs of
mother-of-pearl, with gold inlay.

DATE	1598–1600
ORIGIN	FRANCE
WEIGHT	1¾ LB (0.81 KG)
LENGTH	20 IN (50.8 CM)

Fluted steel
pommel

Wire-bound grip

Ring guard

Blade has
serrated edge

FULL VIEW

QUILLON DAGGER

This German dagger has straight
quillons and a serrated blade
with pierced fullers. It was used
for parrying an opponent's blade.

DATE	c.1600
ORIGIN	GERMANY
WEIGHT	19½ IN (50 CM)
LENGTH	1½LB (0.75KG)

SWORD-BREAKER

One of the more extreme left-hand daggers
was the so-called sword-breaker. The comb-
shaped steel blade was designed to trap an
opponent's sword, and with a flick of the wrist
pull it from his grasp or even break the blade.

DATE	c.1660
ORIGIN	ITALY
WEIGHT	1¾ LB (0.81 KG)
LENGTH	20 IN (50.8 CM)

FULL VIEW

Wire-bound
grip

Ring guard

Elaborately
decorated
ricasso

Straight,
unadorned quillon

Barbed head to
trap sword blade

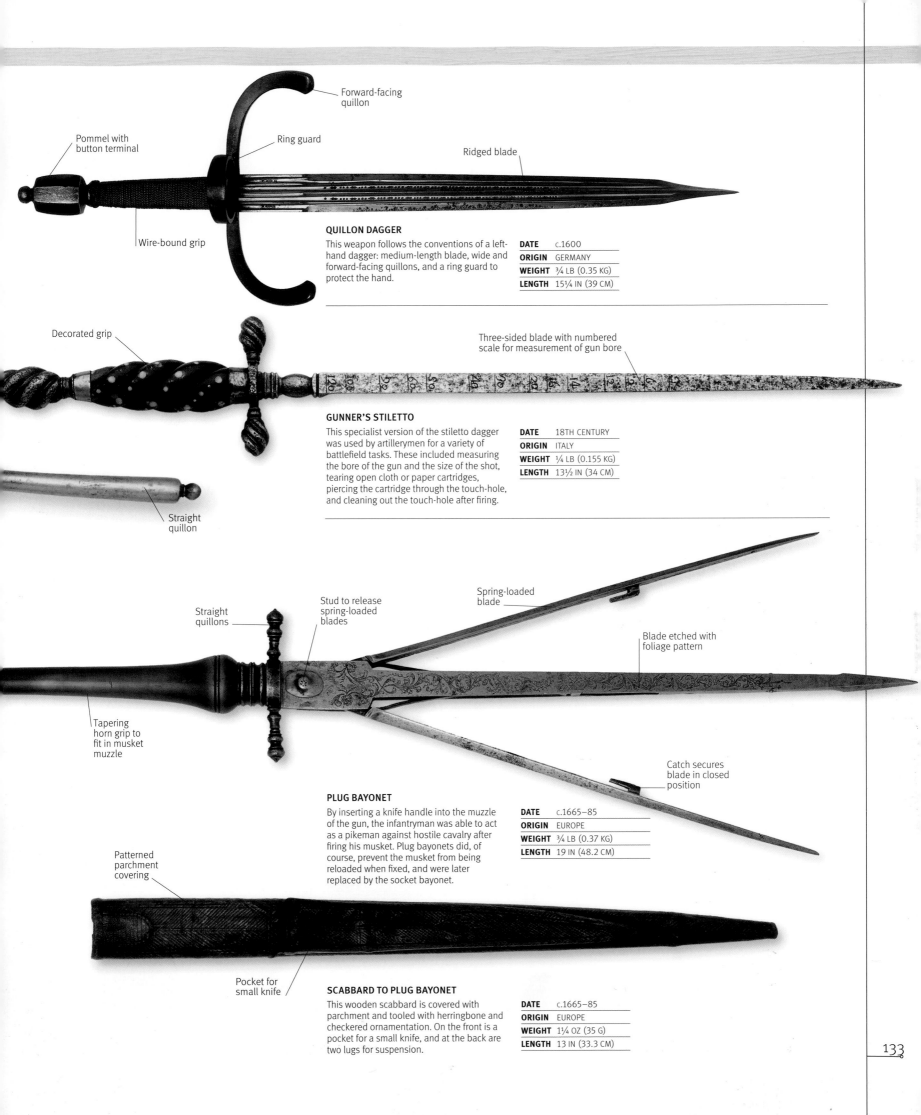

Forward-facing quillon

Pommel with button terminal

Ring guard

Ridged blade

Wire-bound grip

QUILLON DAGGER

This weapon follows the conventions of a left-hand dagger: medium-length blade, wide and forward-facing quillons, and a ring guard to protect the hand.

DATE	c.1600
ORIGIN	GERMANY
WEIGHT	¾ LB (0.35 KG)
LENGTH	15¼ IN (39 CM)

Decorated grip

Three-sided blade with numbered scale for measurement of gun bore

Straight quillon

GUNNER'S STILETTO

This specialist version of the stiletto dagger was used by artillerymen for a variety of battlefield tasks. These included measuring the bore of the gun and the size of the shot, tearing open cloth or paper cartridges, piercing the cartridge through the touch-hole, and cleaning out the touch-hole after firing.

DATE	18TH CENTURY
ORIGIN	ITALY
WEIGHT	¼ LB (0.155 KG)
LENGTH	13½ IN (34 CM)

Straight quillons

Stud to release spring-loaded blades

Spring-loaded blade

Blade etched with foliage pattern

Tapering horn grip to fit in musket muzzle

Catch secures blade in closed position

PLUG BAYONET

By inserting a knife handle into the muzzle of the gun, the infantryman was able to act as a pikeman against hostile cavalry after firing his musket. Plug bayonets did, of course, prevent the musket from being reloaded when fixed, and were later replaced by the socket bayonet.

DATE	c.1665–85
ORIGIN	EUROPE
WEIGHT	¾ LB (0.37 KG)
LENGTH	19 IN (48.2 CM)

Patterned parchment covering

Pocket for small knife

SCABBARD TO PLUG BAYONET

This wooden scabbard is covered with parchment and tooled with herringbone and checkered ornamentation. On the front is a pocket for a small knife, and at the back are two lugs for suspension.

DATE	c.1665–85
ORIGIN	EUROPE
WEIGHT	1¼ OZ (35 G)
LENGTH	13 IN (33.3 CM)

THE EARLY MODERN WORLD

ASIAN DAGGERS

FROM THE 16TH TO THE EARLY 18TH CENTURIES, when most of India was ruled by the Mughal Empire, the daggers of the Indian subcontinent were notable for their high-quality metalwork, ornamentation, and distinctive forms. Some daggers, such as the *kard*, were Islamic imports; others, including the *katar*, had specifically Indian roots. Daggers were worn by Indian princes and nobles for self-defense, for hunting, and for display. In combat, they were essential close-quarters weapons, capable of piercing the mail armor worn by Indian warriors.

Watered steel blade

Ivory grip with beaked pommel

Molded finial

Gilt brass chape

Velvet-covered scabbard

INDIAN KARD

Of Persian origin, the straight-bladed, single-edged *kard* was in use across much of the Islamic world by the 18th century, from Ottoman Turkey to Mughal India. It was mostly used as a stabbing weapon. This example bears the name of its maker, Mohammed Baqir.

DATE	1710–11
ORIGIN	INDIA
WEIGHT	¾ LB (0.34 KG)
LENGTH	15¼ IN (38.5 CM)

Sunken panel with chiseled figures

Dual cross-grip

Velvet-covered wood scabbard

Reinforced blade point

Gilded chape

INDIAN KATAR

To use this north Indian dagger, the warrior grasped the cross-grips, making a fist, so that the sidebars of the hilt lay on either side of his hand and forearm. With the blade horizontal, he then stabbed with a punching motion. The *katar's* form changed little over hundreds of years; this example is from the 19th century.

DATE	EARLY 19TH CENTURY
ORIGIN	INDIA
WEIGHT	1¼ LB (0.57 KG)
LENGTH	16¾ IN (42.1 CM)

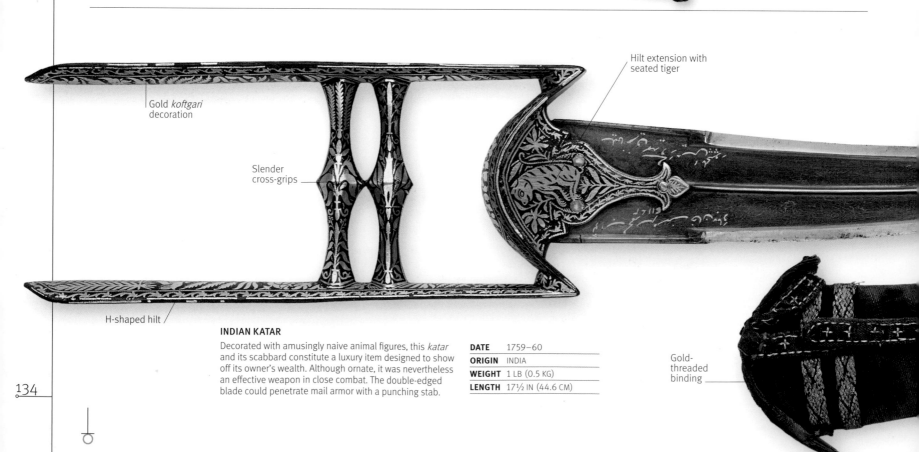

Gold *koftgari* decoration

Hilt extension with seated tiger

Slender cross-grips

H-shaped hilt

Gold-threaded binding

INDIAN KATAR

Decorated with amusingly naive animal figures, this *katar* and its scabbard constitute a luxury item designed to show off its owner's wealth. Although ornate, it was nevertheless an effective weapon in close combat. The double-edged blade could penetrate mail armor with a punching stab.

DATE	1759–60
ORIGIN	INDIA
WEIGHT	1 LB (0.5 KG)
LENGTH	17½ IN (44.6 CM)

SRI LANKAN PIHA KAETTA

The broad-bladed, single-edged knife known as a *piha kaetta* is native to the island of Sri Lanka. Many were produced by the royal workshops. With lavish use of silver on both knife and scabbard, this fine example probably belonged to a courtier, noble, or high-ranking official.

DATE	18TH CENTURY
ORIGIN	SRI LANKA
WEIGHT	½ LB (0.25 KG)
LENGTH	14¼ IN (36.5 CM)

Carved horn handle
Silver bands
Inlaid panel on back of blade
Clipped point
Silver filigree band
Sheet-silver scabbard covering

BHUTANESE DAGGER

This straight-bladed dagger originated from the remote Himalayan kingdom of Bhutan, which has borders with Nepal and India. The hilt is chiseled with various Chinese symbols of good luck on a background of tendrils. The wooden scabbard has a border and chape of gilded iron.

DATE	18TH CENTURY
ORIGIN	BHUTAN
WEIGHT	¾ LB (0.35 KG)
LENGTH	17 IN (43.4 CM)

Tapering, single-edged blade
Iron grip with gold and silver inlay
Silver mount
Scabbard bound with layers of paper and red velvet

INDIAN BICH'HWA

Named after an Indian word for scorpion, and derived from the shape of an animal horn, the *bich'hwa* was a small but deadly dagger. In this example, the iron hilt, decorated in silver *koftgari* (form), is in the form of a flattened loop, attached to the blade by two rivets. The recurved blade is reinforced at the point to increase its penetration.

DATE	18TH CENTURY
ORIGIN	INDIA
WEIGHT	½ LB (0.21 KG)
LENGTH	10¾ IN (27.2 CM)

Loop-shaped hilt
Recurved blade
Rosette on knuckle guard
Reinforced point

Thickened, mail-piercing blade tip
Chape decorated with image of parrot in foliage
Scabbard covering of mauve velvet

INDIAN BICH'HWA

This *bich'hwa* has a cast-brass hilt decorated with a fanciful monster's head. The knucklebow is designed so that the beast appears to be eating its own tail. The narrow, double-curved blade has a low medial ridge on both sides. The crudely cut marks on the quillon block may be letters.

DATE	18TH CENTURY
ORIGIN	INDIA
WEIGHT	½ LB (0.24 KG)
LENGTH	11¾ IN (29.6 CM)

Grip terminates with monster-head decoration
Brass knucklebow
Narrow octagonal grip
Quillon block
Medial ridge on blade

FULL VIEW

135

EUROPEAN ONE-HANDED STAFF WEAPONS

SINGLE-HANDED STAFF weapons were primarily used by horsemen; their role was to fracture plate armor or do internal damage to an opponent. These were simple, brutal weapons, although the pick of the war hammer was useful in penetrating gaps in armor. Despite their clublike nature, many were carried by men of high birth and, as a result, were finely crafted with elaborate decoration.

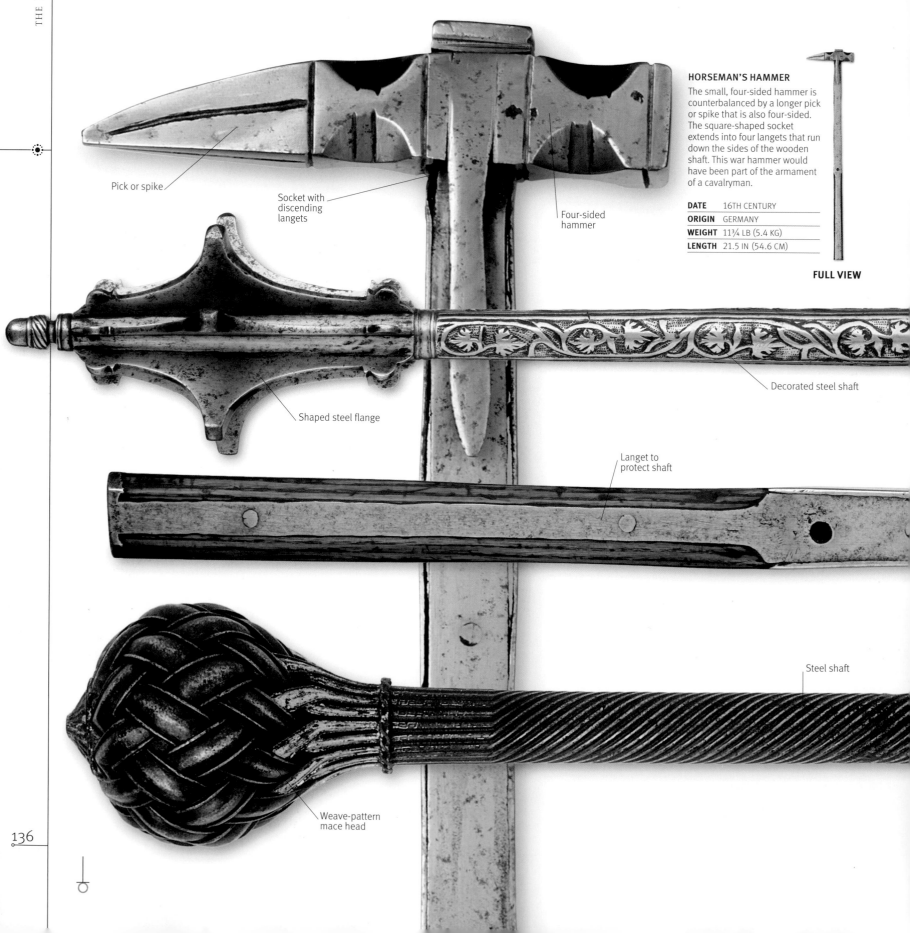

Pick or spike

Socket with discending langets

Four-sided hammer

HORSEMAN'S HAMMER

The small, four-sided hammer is counterbalanced by a longer pick or spike that is also four-sided. The square-shaped socket extends into four langets that run down the sides of the wooden shaft. This war hammer would have been part of the armament of a cavalryman.

DATE	16TH CENTURY
ORIGIN	GERMANY
WEIGHT	11¾ LB (5.4 KG)
LENGTH	21.5 IN (54.6 CM)

FULL VIEW

Shaped steel flange

Decorated steel shaft

Langet to protect shaft

Steel shaft

Weave-pattern mace head

MACE WITH FLANGED HEAD

From the late 15th century onward, most maces were made entirely from steel, with the head constructed from a number of flanges—seven was a common number—shaped with complex inundations and projections. Each flange would be brazed around a central tubular core.

Shaft with black grip

Steel finial

Flange brazed to central core

DATE	16TH CENTURY
ORIGIN	EUROPE
WEIGHT	3½ LB (1.56 KG)
LENGTH	24¾ IN (63 CM)

MACE WITH CONICAL FINIAL

Made from steel, this mace has a conical finial fitted above seven flanges, each of which is drawn to a concave-sided point. The shaft is decorated with scrolling vine foliage in shallow relief. The flanged mace was the most common type of mace in use during the 16th century.

Shaft bearing foliate decoration

Conical finial

DATE	16TH CENTURY
ORIGIN	EUROPE
WEIGHT	1.56KG (3½LB)
LENGTH	60CM (23IN)

DECORATED MACE

This flanged mace is decorated with a foliate pattern along the length of the shaft and is topped by an upper finial (or terminal) in the shape of an acorn. The hole visible halfway along the steel shaft is for a wrist loop, especially important for mounted soldiers, so that if the mace fell out of the hand, it could easily be retrieved.

Wrist-loop hole

DATE	16TH CENTURY
ORIGIN	EUROPE
WEIGHT	3½ LB (1.56 KG)
LENGTH	25 IN (63 CM)

HORSEMAN'S HAMMER

Popular with cavalrymen for smashing armor plate, war hammers were also used by those fighting on foot in tournaments. During the 16th century, the pick was increased in size and the hammer correspondingly reduced, suggesting greater primacy for the pick in combat.

DATE	16TH CENTURY
ORIGIN	EUROPE
WEIGHT	1¾ LB (0.82 KG)
LENGTH	8½ IN (21.5 CM)

Steel pick

Truncated, four-sided hammer

MACE WITH INTERLACE HEAD

This unusual mace from Egypt features an interlace design on a bulbous head and is signed, in gold, by its maker. Maces increasingly became ceremonial objects in the 16th and 17th centuries—the British House of Commons continues to use a mace as a symbol of its authority.

DATE	15TH CENTURY
ORIGIN	EGYPT
WEIGHT	3½ LB (1.56 KG)
LENGTH	c.23½ IN (60 CM)

BATTLE OF PAVIA
The Habsburg defeat of
France at the Battle of Pavia in
1525, is commemorated here in this
contemporary tapestry. It was a battle
in which the Imperial pikemen and
arquebusiers of the Italian army proved effective
against the advance of the armored French knights.

EUROPEAN TWO-HANDED STAFF WEAPONS

STAFF WEAPONS, ESPECIALLY when combined with bows, had proved highly effective against cavalry during the Middle Ages. In the 16th century, they continued to be the foot soldier's most effective weapon, although the bow was superseded by the musket. Swiss mercenaries popularized the halberd, which, in the hands of a strong man, was capable of smashing through plate armor: as was the poleax, the weapon favored by armored knights when fighting on foot. By the early 17th century, these weapons were being replaced by the pike, and used in a ceremonial capacity.

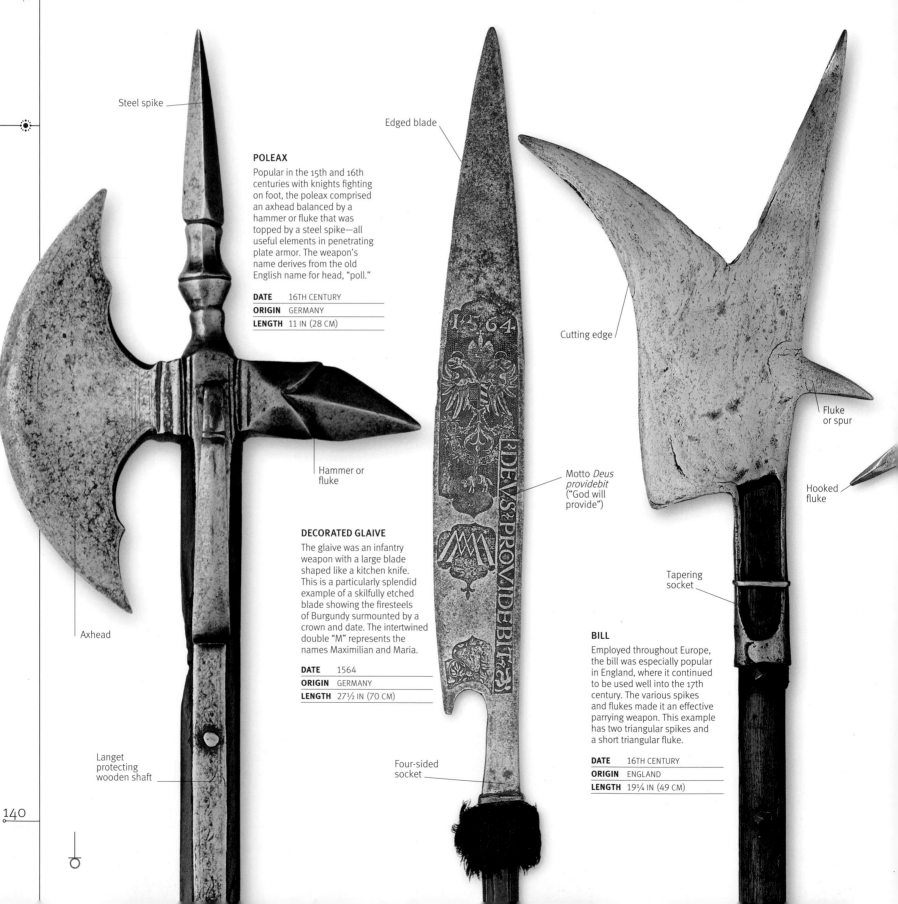

Steel spike

Edged blade

POLEAX

Popular in the 15th and 16th centuries with knights fighting on foot, the poleax comprised an axhead balanced by a hammer or fluke that was topped by a steel spike—all useful elements in penetrating plate armor. The weapon's name derives from the old English name for head, "poll."

DATE	16TH CENTURY
ORIGIN	GERMANY
LENGTH	11 IN (28 CM)

Cutting edge

Fluke or spur

Hammer or fluke

Axhead

DECORATED GLAIVE

The glaive was an infantry weapon with a large blade shaped like a kitchen knife. This is a particularly splendid example of a skilfully etched blade showing the firesteels of Burgundy surmounted by a crown and date. The intertwined double "M" represents the names Maximilian and Maria.

DATE	1564
ORIGIN	GERMANY
LENGTH	27½ IN (70 CM)

Motto *Deus providebit* ("God will provide")

Hooked fluke

Tapering socket

BILL

Employed throughout Europe, the bill was especially popular in England, where it continued to be used well into the 17th century. The various spikes and flukes made it an effective parrying weapon. This example has two triangular spikes and a short triangular fluke.

DATE	16TH CENTURY
ORIGIN	ENGLAND
LENGTH	19¼ IN (49 CM)

Langet protecting wooden shaft

Four-sided socket

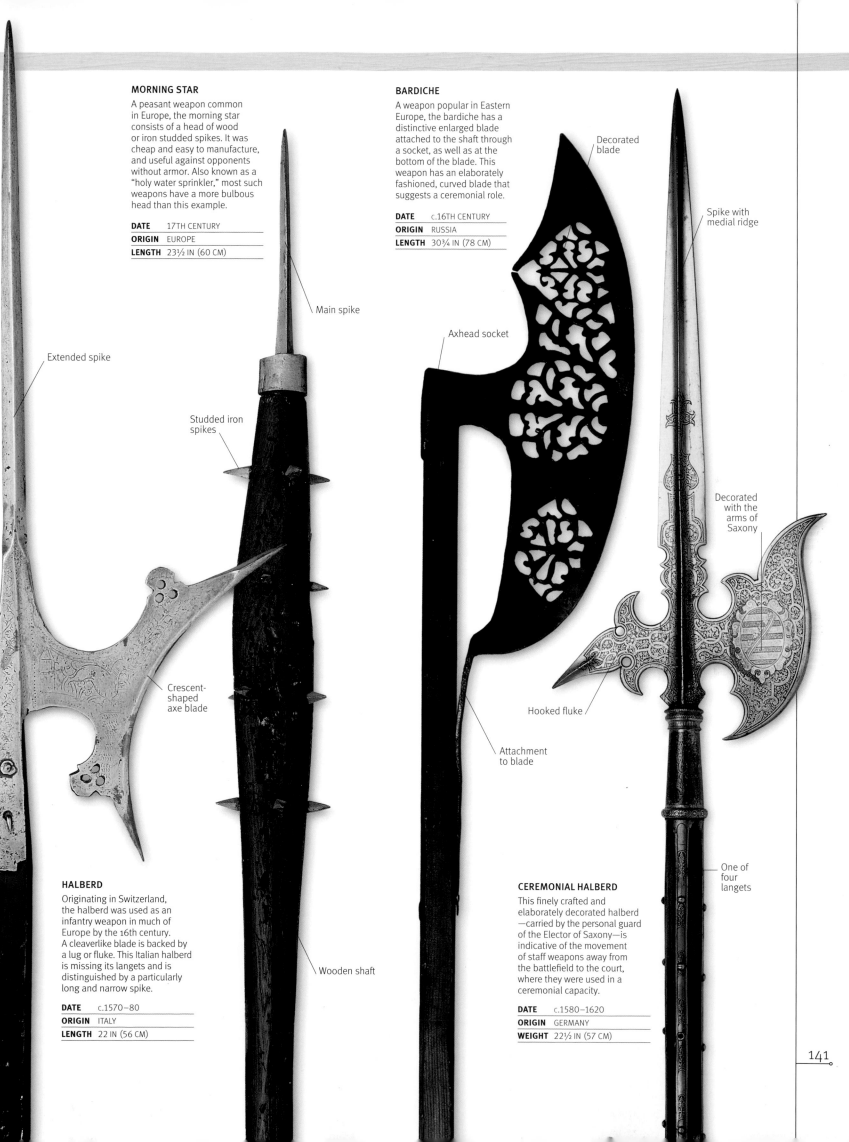

MORNING STAR

A peasant weapon common in Europe, the morning star consists of a head of wood or iron studded spikes. It was cheap and easy to manufacture, and useful against opponents without armor. Also known as a "holy water sprinkler," most such weapons have a more bulbous head than this example.

DATE	17TH CENTURY
ORIGIN	EUROPE
LENGTH	23½ IN (60 CM)

Main spike

Extended spike

Studded iron spikes

Crescent-shaped axe blade

HALBERD

Originating in Switzerland, the halberd was used as an infantry weapon in much of Europe by the 16th century. A cleaverlike blade is backed by a lug or fluke. This Italian halberd is missing its langets and is distinguished by a particularly long and narrow spike.

DATE	c.1570–80
ORIGIN	ITALY
LENGTH	22 IN (56 CM)

Wooden shaft

BARDICHE

A weapon popular in Eastern Europe, the bardiche has a distinctive enlarged blade attached to the shaft through a socket, as well as at the bottom of the blade. This weapon has an elaborately fashioned, curved blade that suggests a ceremonial role.

DATE	c.16TH CENTURY
ORIGIN	RUSSIA
LENGTH	30¾ IN (78 CM)

Decorated blade

Axhead socket

Attachment to blade

Spike with medial ridge

Decorated with the arms of Saxony

Hooked fluke

CEREMONIAL HALBERD

This finely crafted and elaborately decorated halberd —carried by the personal guard of the Elector of Saxony—is indicative of the movement of staff weapons away from the battlefield to the court, where they were used in a ceremonial capacity.

DATE	c.1580–1620
ORIGIN	GERMANY
WEIGHT	22½ IN (57 CM)

One of four langets

141

1500—1775

◀ 72–73 EUROPEAN STAFF WEAPONS   ◀ 74–75 ASIAN STAFF WEAPONS   ◀ 136–137 EUROPEAN ONE-HANDED STAFF WEAPONS   ▶ 196–197 INDIAN STAFF WEAPONS

INDIAN AND SRI LANKAN STAFF WEAPONS

UNTIL THE 17TH CENTURY, the development of staff weapons in the Indian subcontinent was broadly similar to their evolution in Europe, although local Hindu traditions and the influence of Muslim invaders guaranteed that there were notable differences in design and decoration. Despite the adoption of Western-style firearms by Indian rulers, maces and axes remained in active use with Indian armies long after they had become obsolete in Europe, largely because Indian warriors continued to wear armor.

Tubular iron shaft

Knop is unscrewed to remove concealed knife from shaft

Shaft and blade have sheet-silver decoration

Rounded flange ends in bird-head design

Iron shaft

Dish pommel with fluted knop

Sword-like "basket" hilt

Iron shaft

Hand guard

Rattan grip

TABAR

The saddle ax, or *tabar*, was a standard weapon of Indian armies. This example is from Sind, in what is now Pakistan. The curved cutting edge concentrated the weight of a blow at a narrow point of impact. Unscrewing the knop at the base of the weapon revealed a slim knife, 21¼ in (54 cm) long, concealed inside the hollow shaft.

DATE	18TH CENTURY
ORIGIN	SIND, INDIA
WEIGHT	2¾ LB (1.29 KG)
LENGTH	28 IN (71.3 CM)

CHILD'S MACE

With less than a tenth of the weight of a full-sized weapon and around a third of the length, this miniature mace was designed for use by a child. It may have been employed for early military training. The head has eight rounded flanges, and is topped by a small, ribbed knop.

DATE	18TH CENTURY
ORIGIN	NORTHERN INDIA
WEIGHT	½ LB (0.22 KG)
LENGTH	13 IN (32.8 CM)

FLANGED MACE

This mace, or *gorz*, has a knuckle guard in the "Hindu basket" style, as often seen on *khanda* swords. The eight spiral flanges on the head are sharpened to a cutting edge. The flanges focused the impact of a blow from this heavy weapon, making it effective even against armor.

DATE	18TH CENTURY
ORIGIN	RAJASTHAN, INDIA
WEIGHT	5½ LB (2.55 KG)
LENGTH	33¼ IN (84.2 CM)

SPIKED MACE

This mace resembles a more refined version of the "morning star" maces of 16th-century Europe. The grip of the spikes prevented curved armor from deflecting blows. With its fine decoration, this weapon was designed as much to show its owner's wealth and status as it was for combat.

DATE	EARLY 18TH CENTURY
ORIGIN	DELHI, INDIA
WEIGHT	5½ LB (2.5 KG)
LENGTH	33½ IN (85 CM)

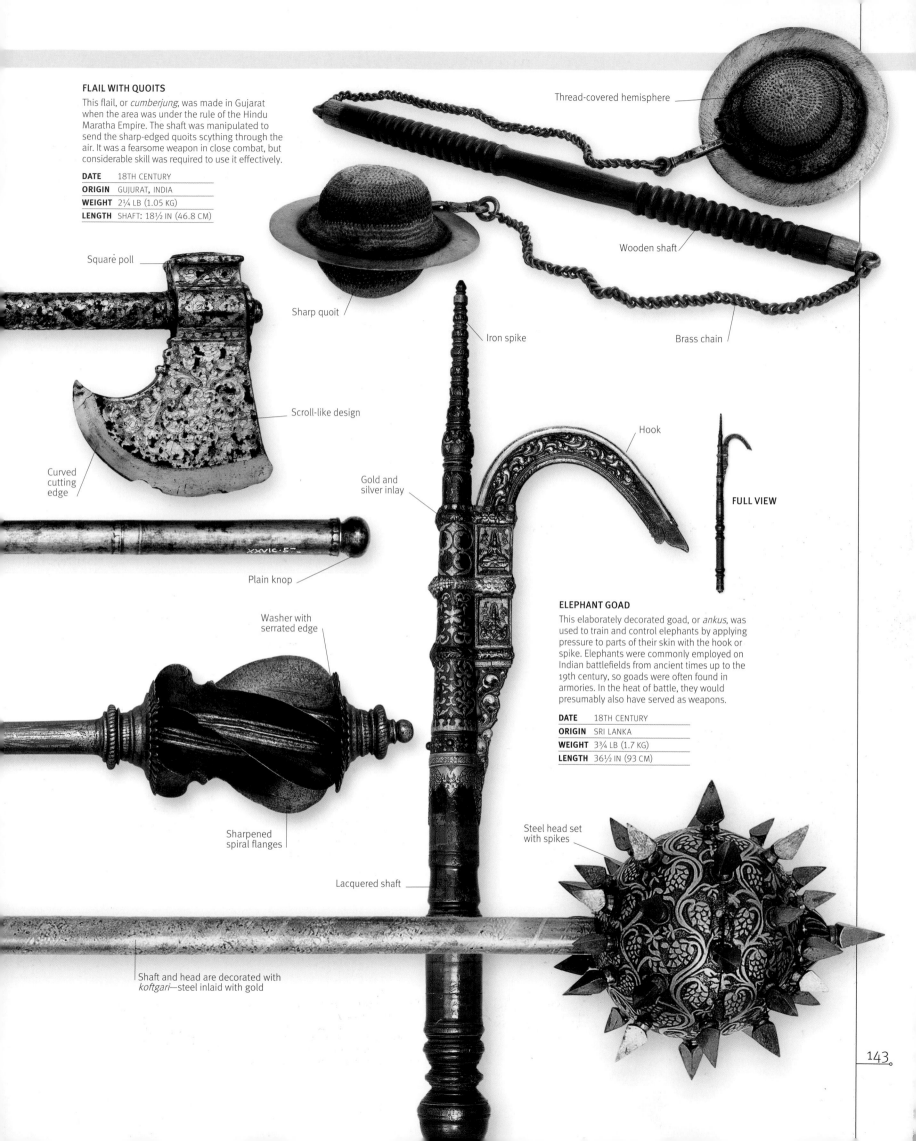

FLAIL WITH QUOITS

This flail, or *cumberjung*, was made in Gujarat when the area was under the rule of the Hindu Maratha Empire. The shaft was manipulated to send the sharp-edged quoits scything through the air. It was a fearsome weapon in close combat, but considerable skill was required to use it effectively.

DATE	18TH CENTURY
ORIGIN	GUJURAT, INDIA
WEIGHT	2¼ LB (1.05 KG)
LENGTH	SHAFT: 18½ IN (46.8 CM)

Thread-covered hemisphere

Wooden shaft

Brass chain

Square poll

Sharp quoit

Iron spike

Scroll-like design

Curved cutting edge

Hook

Gold and silver inlay

FULL VIEW

Plain knop

ELEPHANT GOAD

This elaborately decorated goad, or *ankus*, was used to train and control elephants by applying pressure to parts of their skin with the hook or spike. Elephants were commonly employed on Indian battlefields from ancient times up to the 19th century, so goads were often found in armories. In the heat of battle, they would presumably also have served as weapons.

DATE	18TH CENTURY
ORIGIN	SRI LANKA
WEIGHT	3¾ LB (1.7 KG)
LENGTH	36½ IN (93 CM)

Washer with serrated edge

Sharpened spiral flanges

Steel head set with spikes

Lacquered shaft

Shaft and head are decorated with *koftgari*—steel inlaid with gold

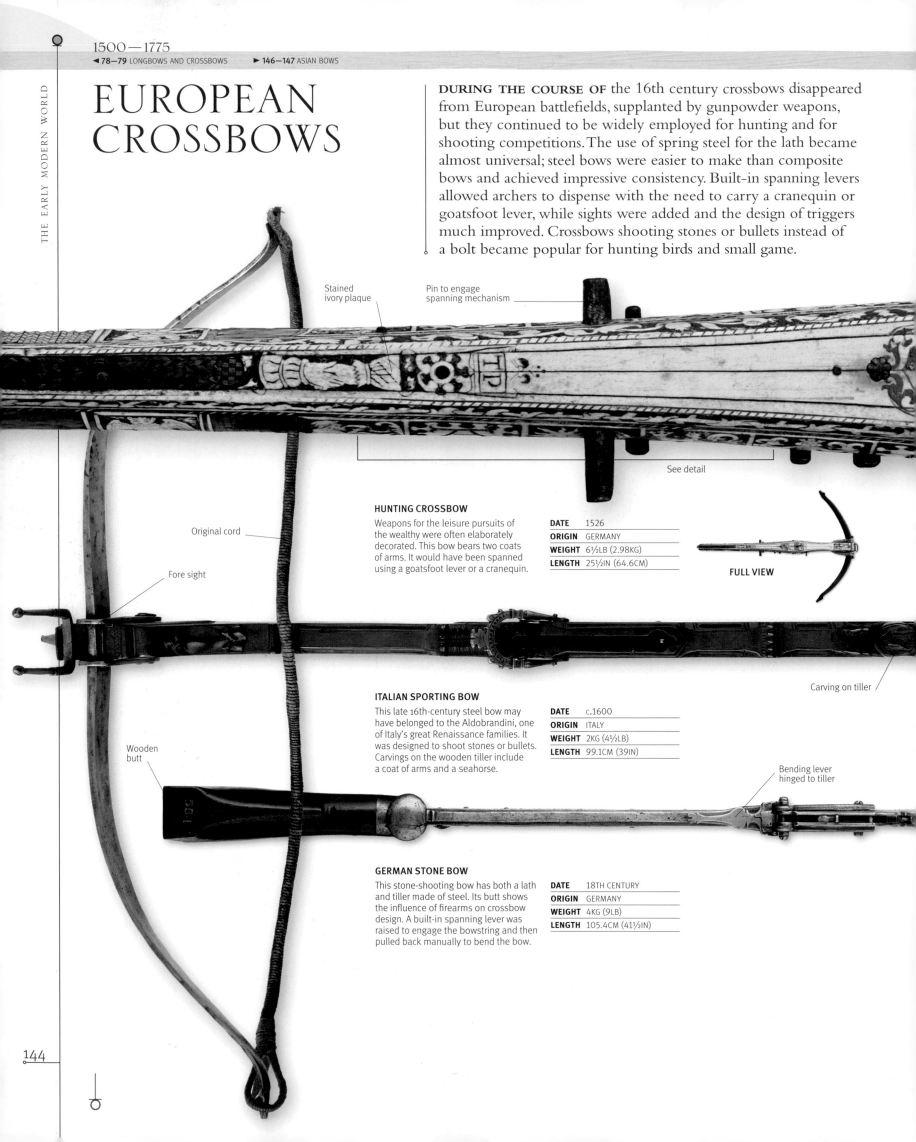

THE EARLY MODERN WORLD

EUROPEAN CROSSBOWS

DURING THE COURSE OF the 16th century crossbows disappeared from European battlefields, supplanted by gunpowder weapons, but they continued to be widely employed for hunting and for shooting competitions. The use of spring steel for the lath became almost universal; steel bows were easier to make than composite bows and achieved impressive consistency. Built-in spanning levers allowed archers to dispense with the need to carry a cranequin or goatsfoot lever, while sights were added and the design of triggers much improved. Crossbows shooting stones or bullets instead of a bolt became popular for hunting birds and small game.

Stained
ivory plaque

Pin to engage
spanning mechanism

See detail

HUNTING CROSSBOW

Weapons for the leisure pursuits of
the wealthy were often elaborately
decorated. This bow bears two coats
of arms. It would have been spanned
using a goatsfoot lever or a cranequin.

DATE	1526
ORIGIN	GERMANY
WEIGHT	6½LB (2.98KG)
LENGTH	25½IN (64.6CM)

FULL VIEW

Original cord

Fore sight

Carving on tiller

ITALIAN SPORTING BOW

This late 16th-century steel bow may
have belonged to the Aldobrandini, one
of Italy's great Renaissance families. It
was designed to shoot stones or bullets.
Carvings on the wooden tiller include
a coat of arms and a seahorse.

DATE	c.1600
ORIGIN	ITALY
WEIGHT	2KG (4½LB)
LENGTH	99.1CM (39IN)

Wooden
butt

Bending lever
hinged to tiller

GERMAN STONE BOW

This stone-shooting bow has both a lath
and tiller made of steel. Its butt shows
the influence of firearms on crossbow
design. A built-in spanning lever was
raised to engage the bowstring and then
pulled back manually to bend the bow.

DATE	18TH CENTURY
ORIGIN	GERMANY
WEIGHT	4KG (9LB)
LENGTH	105.4CM (41½IN)

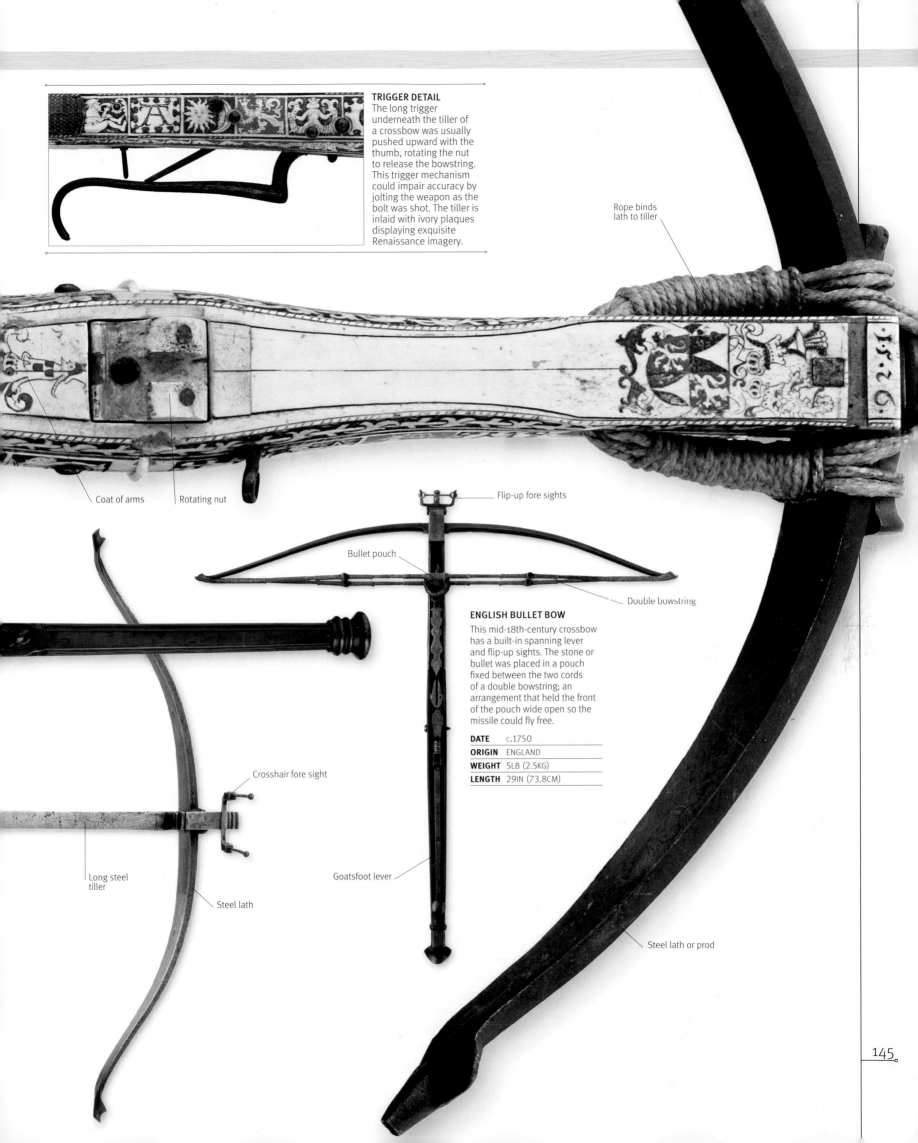

TRIGGER DETAIL
The long trigger underneath the tiller of a crossbow was usually pushed upward with the thumb, rotating the nut to release the bowstring. This trigger mechanism could impair accuracy by jolting the weapon as the bolt was shot. The tiller is inlaid with ivory plaques displaying exquisite Renaissance imagery.

Rope binds lath to tiller

Coat of arms

Rotating nut

Flip-up fore sights

Bullet pouch

Double bowstring

ENGLISH BULLET BOW
This mid-18th-century crossbow has a built-in spanning lever and flip-up sights. The stone or bullet was placed in a pouch fixed between the two cords of a double bowstring; an arrangement that held the front of the pouch wide open so the missile could fly free.

DATE	c.1750
ORIGIN	ENGLAND
WEIGHT	5LB (2.5KG)
LENGTH	29IN (73.8CM)

Crosshair fore sight

Long steel tiller

Steel lath

Goatsfoot lever

Steel lath or prod

THE EARLY MODERN WORLD

ASIAN BOWS

OFTEN SHOT FROM HORSEBACK, bows were central to Asian warfare. Although the Chinese were the inventors of the crossbow, laminated and composite bows predominated. Laminated bows were made from several layers of wood glued together. In composite bows, the layers were of different materials, usually horn, wood, and sinew. The strips of horn formed the belly of the bow, closest to the archer, with sinew used for the back and a wooden core sandwiched between the two. By exploiting the contrasting properties of these materials, bows of relatively small size achieved remarkable strength and power.

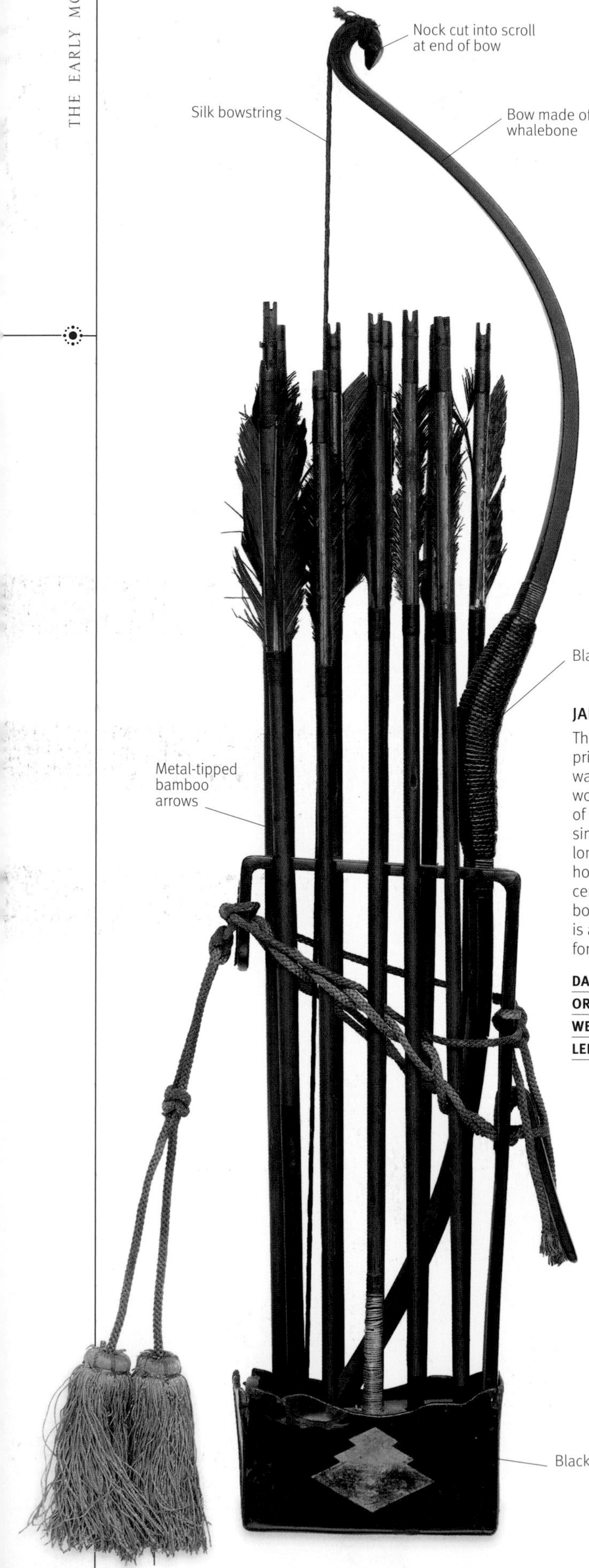

Nock cut into scroll at end of bow

Silk bowstring

Bow made of whalebone

Bow covered in birch bark

Back of bow

Grip

Belly of bow

String bridge

String bridge

Ear

Nock of horn

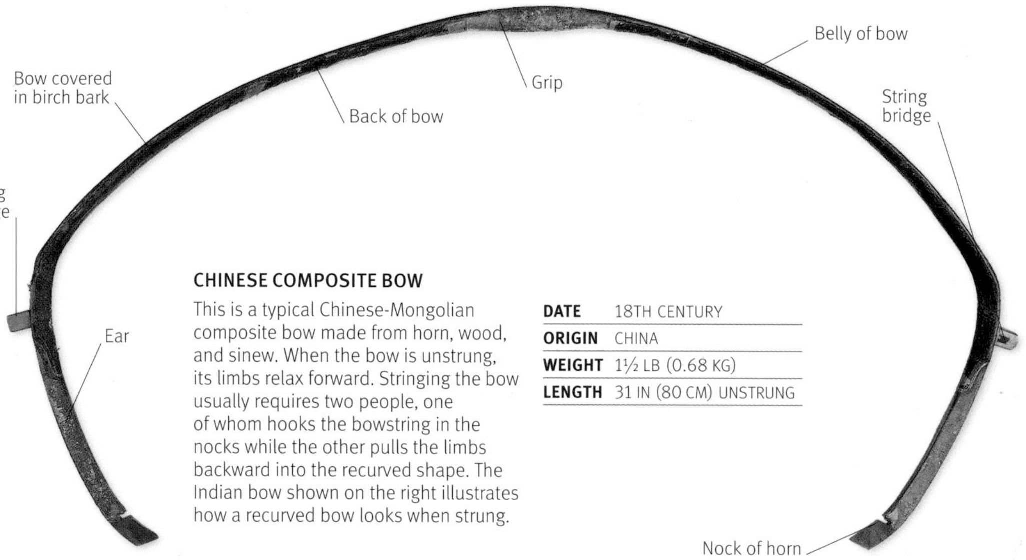

CHINESE COMPOSITE BOW

This is a typical Chinese-Mongolian composite bow made from horn, wood, and sinew. When the bow is unstrung, its limbs relax forward. Stringing the bow usually requires two people, one of whom hooks the bowstring in the nocks while the other pulls the limbs backward into the recurved shape. The Indian bow shown on the right illustrates how a recurved bow looks when strung.

DATE	18TH CENTURY
ORIGIN	CHINA
WEIGHT	1½ LB (0.68 KG)
LENGTH	31 IN (80 CM) UNSTRUNG

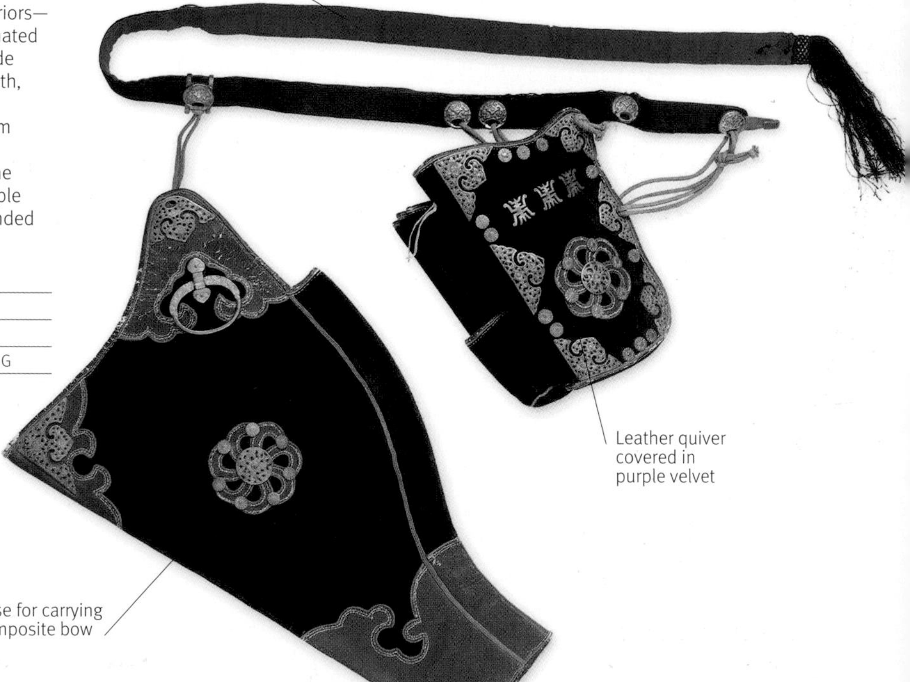

Black-cord grip

JAPANESE PALANQUIN BOW

The Japanese bow—the original prime weapon of samurai warriors—was typically made from laminated wood, but this example is made of whalebone. Despite its length, similar to that of an English longbow, it was often shot from horseback. The grip was not central, but placed closer to the bottom of the bow. This example is a small palanquin bow intended for ceremonial use.

DATE	18TH CENTURY
ORIGIN	JAPAN
WEIGHT	¼ LB (0.15 KG)
LENGTH	24¾ IN (63 CM) STRUNG

Metal-tipped bamboo arrows

Both bowcase and quiver hang from a silk belt

Leather quiver covered in purple velvet

Case for carrying composite bow

Black lacquered box

CHINESE BOWCASE AND QUIVER

This bowcase (*gongdai*) and quiver (*jiantong*) are made from leather covered with purple velvet, with added decorative leather shapes cut out on top. The bowcase is shaped to hold a composite bow. Folded layers of thick red felt inside the quiver would have helped to retain the arrows.

DATE	19TH CENTURY
ORIGIN	CHINA
WEIGHT	CASE 1½ LB (0.64 KG)
LENGTH	20¾ IN (53 CM)

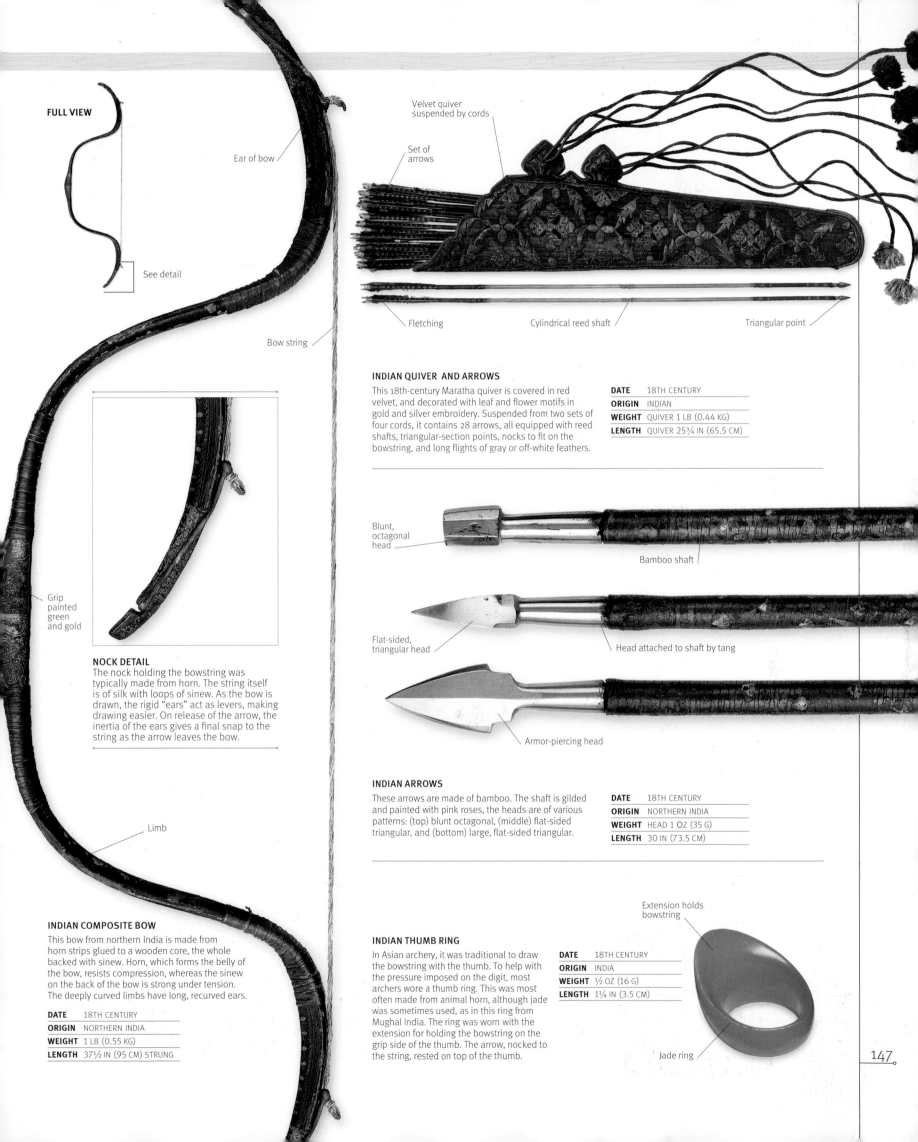

FULL VIEW

Ear of bow

See detail

Bow string

Grip painted green and gold

NOCK DETAIL
The nock holding the bowstring was typically made from horn. The string itself is of silk with loops of sinew. As the bow is drawn, the rigid "ears" act as levers, making drawing easier. On release of the arrow, the inertia of the ears gives a final snap to the string as the arrow leaves the bow.

Limb

INDIAN COMPOSITE BOW

This bow from northern India is made from horn strips glued to a wooden core, the whole backed with sinew. Horn, which forms the belly of the bow, resists compression, whereas the sinew on the back of the bow is strong under tension. The deeply curved limbs have long, recurved ears.

DATE	18TH CENTURY
ORIGIN	NORTHERN INDIA
WEIGHT	1 LB (0.55 KG)
LENGTH	37½ IN (95 CM) STRUNG

Velvet quiver suspended by cords

Set of arrows

Fletching

Cylindrical reed shaft

Triangular point

INDIAN QUIVER AND ARROWS

This 18th-century Maratha quiver is covered in red velvet, and decorated with leaf and flower motifs in gold and silver embroidery. Suspended from two sets of four cords, it contains 28 arrows, all equipped with reed shafts, triangular-section points, nocks to fit on the bowstring, and long flights of gray or off-white feathers.

DATE	18TH CENTURY
ORIGIN	INDIAN
WEIGHT	QUIVER 1 LB (0.44 KG)
LENGTH	QUIVER 25¾ IN (65.5 CM)

Blunt, octagonal head

Bamboo shaft

Flat-sided, triangular head

Head attached to shaft by tang

Armor-piercing head

INDIAN ARROWS

These arrows are made of bamboo. The shaft is gilded and painted with pink roses, the heads are of various patterns: (top) blunt octagonal, (middle) flat-sided triangular, and (bottom) large, flat-sided triangular.

DATE	18TH CENTURY
ORIGIN	NORTHERN INDIA
WEIGHT	HEAD 1 OZ (35 G)
LENGTH	30 IN (73.5 CM)

Extension holds bowstring

INDIAN THUMB RING

In Asian archery, it was traditional to draw the bowstring with the thumb. To help with the pressure imposed on the digit, most archers wore a thumb ring. This was most often made from animal horn, although jade was sometimes used, as in this ring from Mughal India. The ring was worn with the extension for holding the bowstring on the grip side of the thumb. The arrow, nocked to the string, rested on top of the thumb.

DATE	18TH CENTURY
ORIGIN	INDIA
WEIGHT	½ OZ (16 G)
LENGTH	1¼ IN (3.5 CM)

Jade ring

147

1500—1775

► 150–151 WEAPON SHOWCASE: MATCHLOCK MUSKET   ► 152–153 EUROPEAN HUNTING GUNS 1600–1700   ► 154–155 EUROPEAN HUNTING GUNS FROM 1700

THE EARLY MODERN WORLD

MATCHLOCK AND FLINTLOCK LONG GUNS

THE MATCHLOCK WAS AN EARLY firing mechanism, or "lock," for hand-held guns. Pulling the trigger plunged a smouldering match into a pan containing a tiny gunpowder charge, or primer. The primer ignited, sending a flash through a small touch hole in the barrel wall to set off the main charge. The matchlock was far simpler than the wheellock, its contemporary, which ignited the primer with sparks struck from a piece of iron pyrites by a spinning wheel. Only with the development of the flintlock, which produced sparks by striking a flint against a steel plate, did the matchlock begin to decline in popularity.

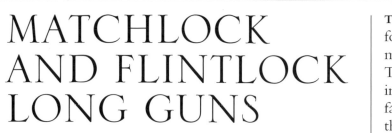

Striking steel attached to pan cover

Comb of stock puts shoulder in line of recoil

Cock holds flint between metal jaws

Barrel band is cut to act as rear sight

Blade fore sight

Lock plate stamped with name of armory

Small of stock sized to fit in hand

PRUSSIAN RIFLED FLINTLOCK CARBINE

King Frederick William I of Prussia, who came to the throne in 1713, raised a standing army that amounted to four percent of the country's adult male population. He established a state arsenal at Potsdam and among its early products were carbines like this, which were manufactured from 1722 to 1774. Ten men in each squadron of cuirassiers were issued with rifled weapons.

DATE	1722
ORIGIN	GERMANY
WEIGHT	7½ LB (3.37 KG)
BARREL	37 IN (94 CM)
CALIBER	15-BORE

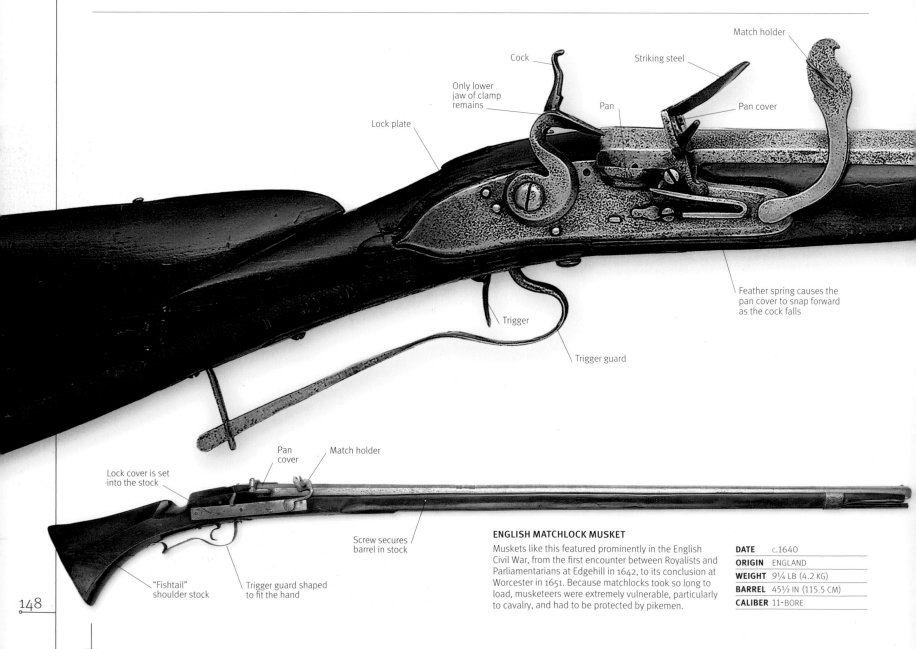

Match holder

Cock

Striking steel

Only lower jaw of clamp remains

Pan

Pan cover

Lock plate

Feather spring causes the pan cover to snap forward as the cock falls

Trigger

Trigger guard

Pan cover

Match holder

Lock cover is set into the stock

Screw secures barrel in stock

"Fishtail" shoulder stock

Trigger guard shaped to fit the hand

ENGLISH MATCHLOCK MUSKET

Muskets like this featured prominently in the English Civil War, from the first encounter between Royalists and Parliamentarians at Edgehill in 1642, to its conclusion at Worcester in 1651. Because matchlocks took so long to load, musketeers were extremely vulnerable, particularly to cavalry, and had to be protected by pikemen.

DATE	c.1640
ORIGIN	ENGLAND
WEIGHT	9¼ LB (4.2 KG)
BARREL	45½ IN (115.5 CM)
CALIBER	11-BORE

BRITISH MATCHLOCK

By the end of their period of dominance, the best matchlocks had acquired a simple sophistication, at least in their finish. They had also become much lighter, and thus were considerably easier to handle. A high-quality piece such as this would have been a prime contender for conversion into a snaphaunce or flintlock, had it not been preserved in a collection.

Pan cover

Match holder

Lock plate

Barrel is octagonal for first third of length, then round

Small of stock fits in hand

DATE	17TH CENTURY
ORIGIN	ENGLAND
WEIGHT	10½ LB (4.73 KG)
BARREL	46 IN (117.2 CM)
CALIBER	18 MM

LONG LAND-PATTERN FLINTLOCK MUSKET

This modified version of the original Land-Pattern Musket, or "Brown Bess," was issued in 1742. It had a new trigger guard, a more pronounced comb to the stock, and a bridle linking the flashpan with the screw that secured the combined striker and pan cover. This example by Tippin is a "sealed pattern," meaning that it was retained in the Tower of London Armory as a model for other gunmakers producing this type of musket.

Butt is bound with brass

Lock plate stamped with maker's name

Cock

Striking steel

Ramrod pipe

Sling swivel

Feather spring

Forestock sized to fit in the hand

DATE	1742
ORIGIN	ENGLAND
WEIGHT	10¼ LB (4.7 KG)
BARREL	46 IN (116.8 CM)
CALIBER	10-BORE

Rear sight

Ramrod pipe

FULL VIEW

DUTCH COMBINATION LONG GUN

This unusual musket is fitted with both a flintlock and a matchlock mechanism. The matchlock pan is part of the top of the striking steel. The flintlock is operated by the trigger guard, while the operation of the matchlock is by means of the trigger.

DATE	17TH CENTURY
ORIGIN	NETHERLANDS
WEIGHT	15 LB (6.8 KG)
BARREL	46 IN (117 CM)
CALIBER	0.9 IN

LIGHT DRAGOON FLINTLOCK CARBINE

During the Seven Years War, which spanned Europe, Asia, and America, the British Army's dragoons—cavalry armed with sabers—were issued this carbine. It was a scaled-down version of the Long Land-Pattern Musket, with a shorter barrel and in a smaller caliber. In form, although not in size, all the carbine's components are identical with those of the musket.

Stock has a high comb

Cock

Striking steel and pan cover

Ramrod pipe

Butt is bound with brass

Lock plate

Feather spring

Forestock fits in hand

Barrel-retaining pin

Small of stock is gripped in hand

Ramrod

DATE	1756
ORIGIN	BRITAIN
WEIGHT	7¼ LB (3.3 KG)
BARREL	36 IN (91.4 CM)
CALIBER	15-BORE

MATCHLOCK MUSKET

THE INVENTION OF THE MATCHLOCK *hackenbüsche*, or "arquebus," can not be dated precisely, but evidence points to it having taken place sometime around 1475, probably in Germany. Technically, matchlocks were superceded with the invention of the wheellock in the 16th century, but they continued to be employed until the end of the 17th century, largely due to their simplicity.

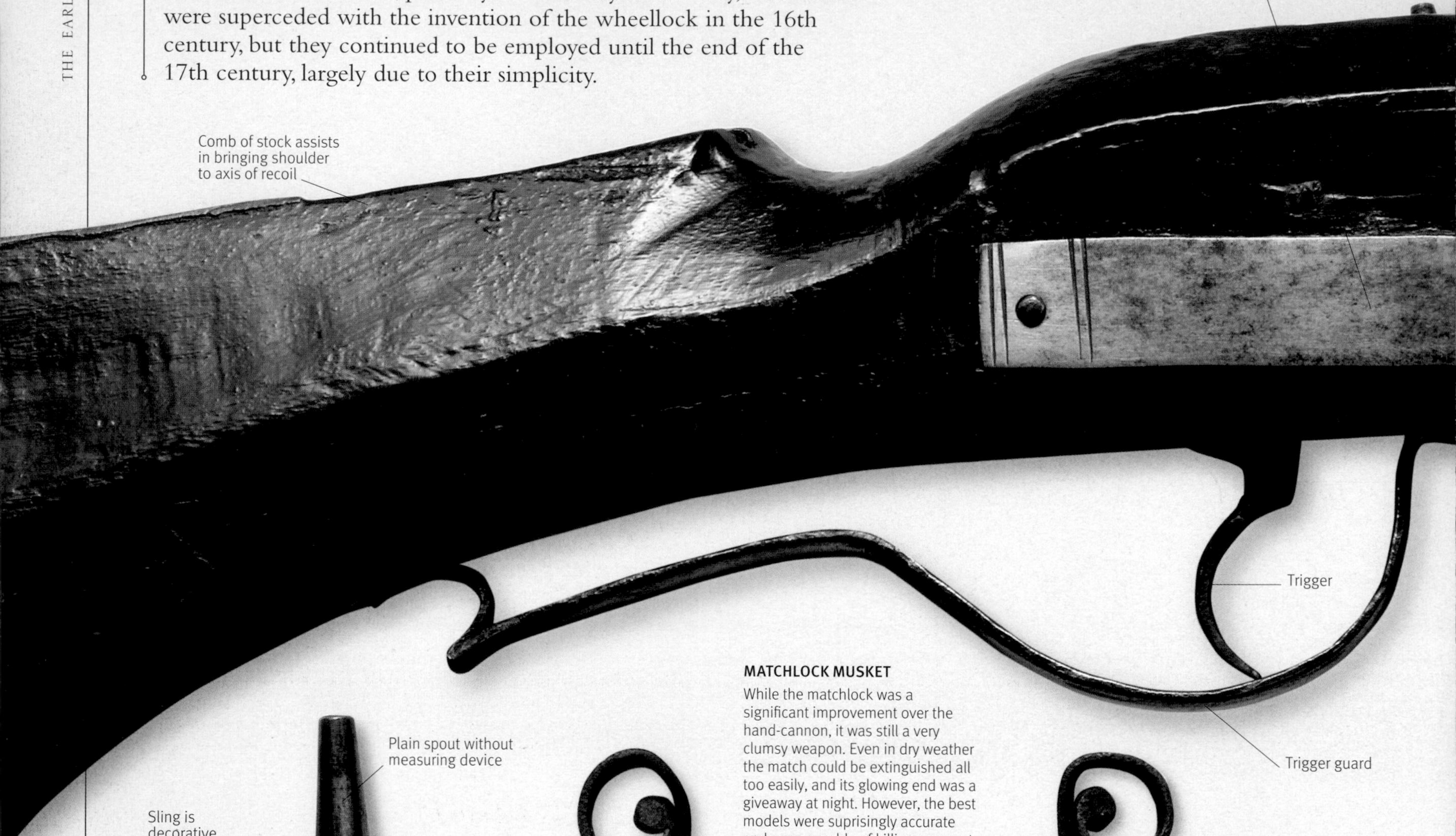

Iron lock cover

Comb of stock assists in bringing shoulder to axis of recoil

Trigger

Trigger guard

Plain spout without measuring device

Sling is decorative as well as functional

MATCHLOCK MUSKET

While the matchlock was a significant improvement over the hand-cannon, it was still a very clumsy weapon. Even in dry weather the match could be extinguished all too easily, and its glowing end was a giveaway at night. However, the best models were suprisingly accurate and were capable of killing a man at a hundred yards or more.

DATE	MID-17TH CENTURY
ORIGIN	UK
WEIGHT	13¼LB (6.05KG)
BARREL	49½IN (125¾CM)
CALIBER	.75IN

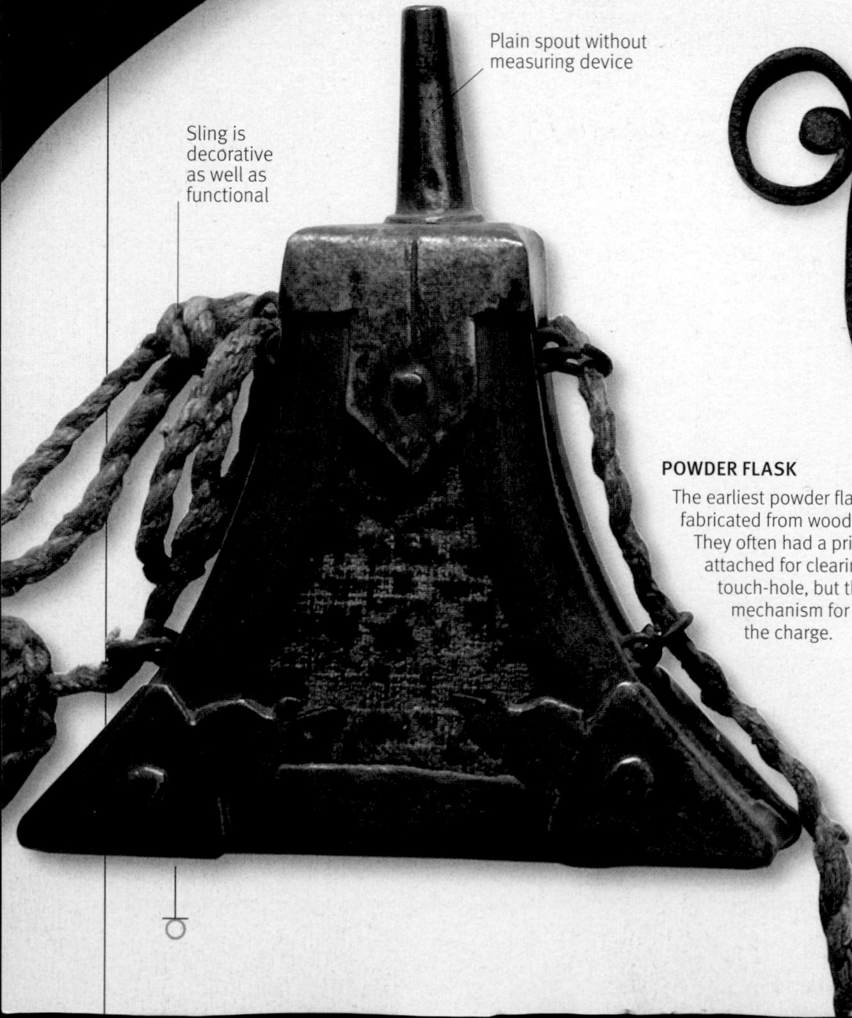

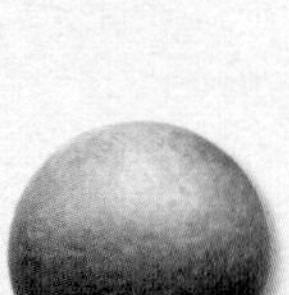

LEAD BALL

It was not until about 1600 that lead, with its low melting point and high specific gravity, became the universal material for bullets. Earlier, with armor still commonplace, iron balls had often been used.

POWDER FLASK

The earliest powder flasks were fabricated from wood or leather. They often had a pricker attached for clearing the gun's touch-hole, but there was no mechanism for measuring the charge.

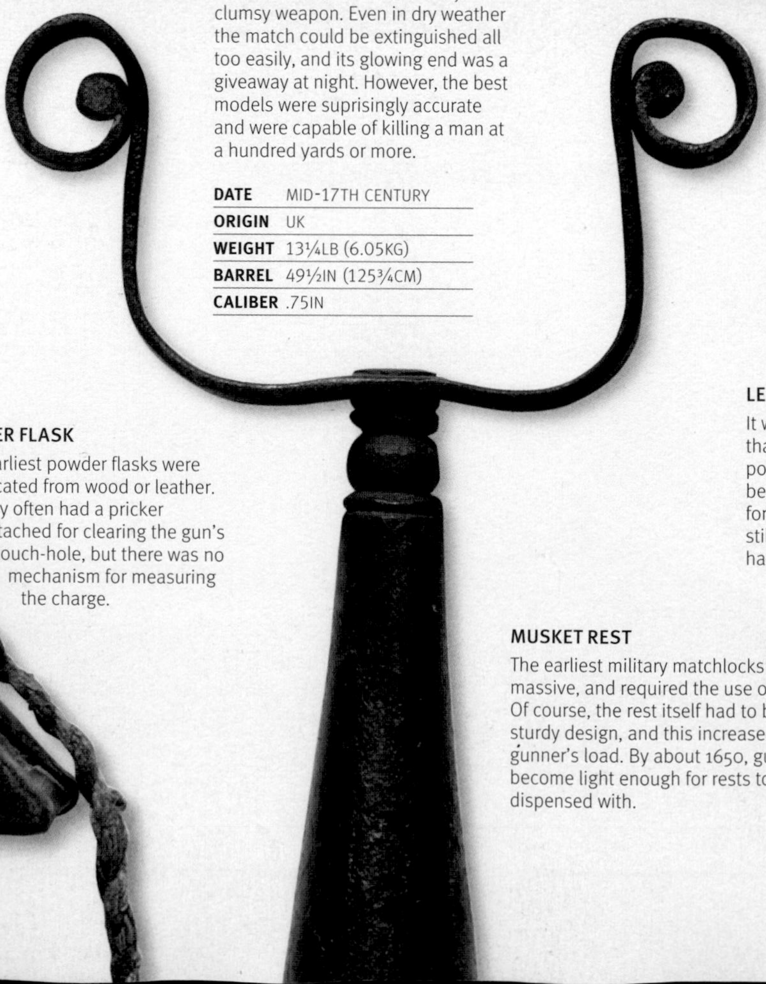

MUSKET REST

The earliest military matchlocks were massive, and required the use of a rest. Of course, the rest itself had to be of sturdy design, and this increased the gunner's load. By about 1650, guns had become light enough for rests to be dispensed with.

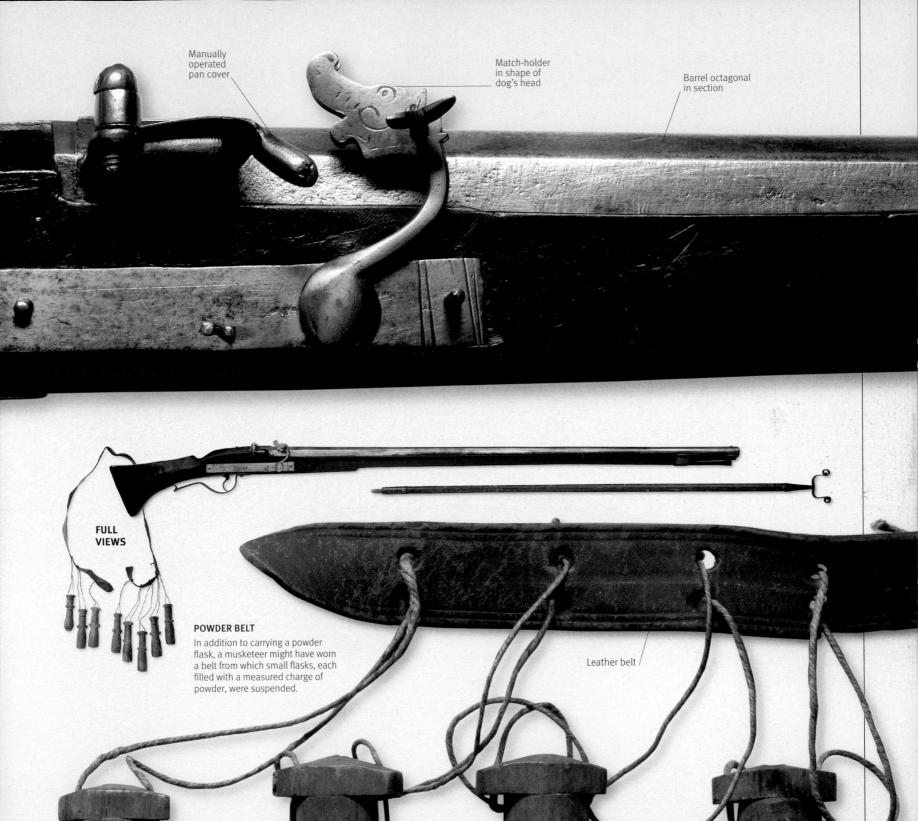

Manually operated pan cover

Match-holder in shape of dog's head

Barrel octagonal in section

FULL VIEWS

POWDER BELT
In addition to carrying a powder flask, a musketeer might have worn a belt from which small flasks, each filled with a measured charge of powder, were suspended.

Leather belt

Flask is carved from wood

151

EUROPEAN HUNTING GUNS 1600–1700

HUNTING, BOTH FOR SPORT and for the pot, became far more predictable with the introduction of firearms, and by the early 17th century, the wheellock had become commonplace within the ranks of the landed gentry. Rifled wheellocks from this period were useful against even small game such as rabbits, but were slow to load and needed to be stripped for cleaning after around 30 rounds had been fired.

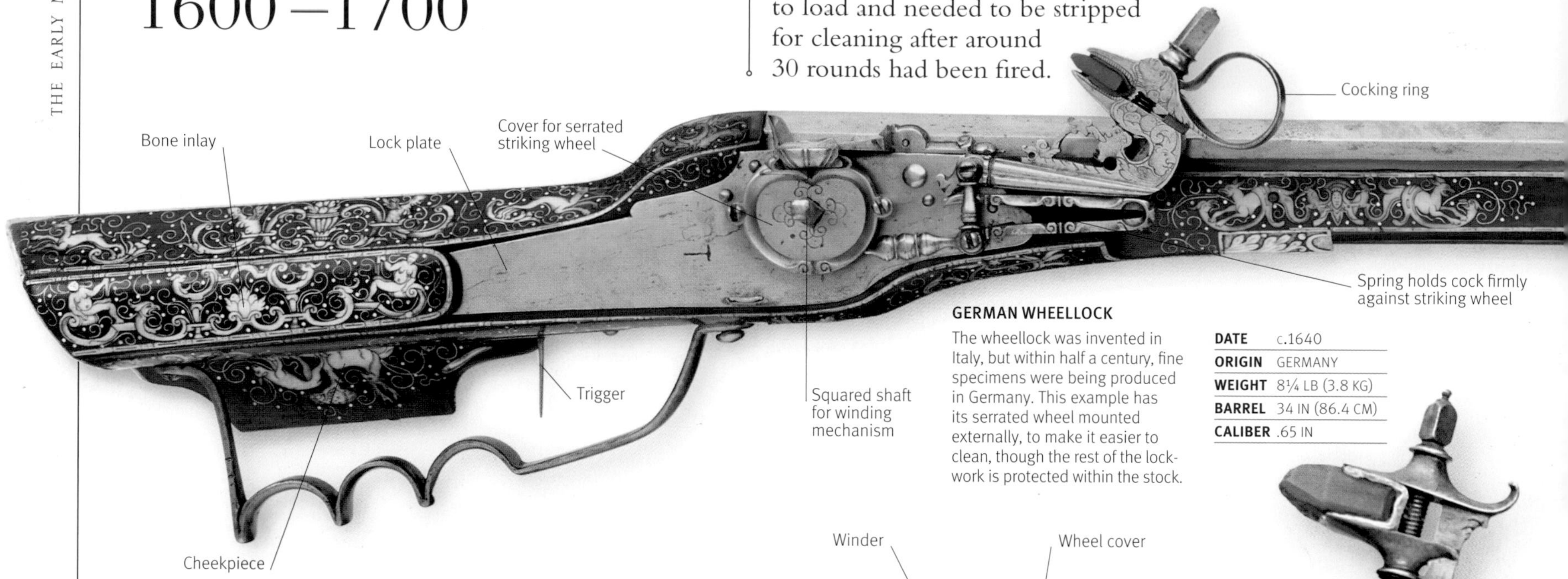

Cocking ring

Bone inlay

Lock plate

Cover for serrated striking wheel

Spring holds cock firmly against striking wheel

GERMAN WHEELLOCK

The wheellock was invented in Italy, but within half a century, fine specimens were being produced in Germany. This example has its serrated wheel mounted externally, to make it easier to clean, though the rest of the lock-work is protected within the stock.

DATE	c.1640
ORIGIN	GERMANY
WEIGHT	8¼ LB (3.8 KG)
BARREL	34 IN (86.4 CM)
CALIBER	.65 IN

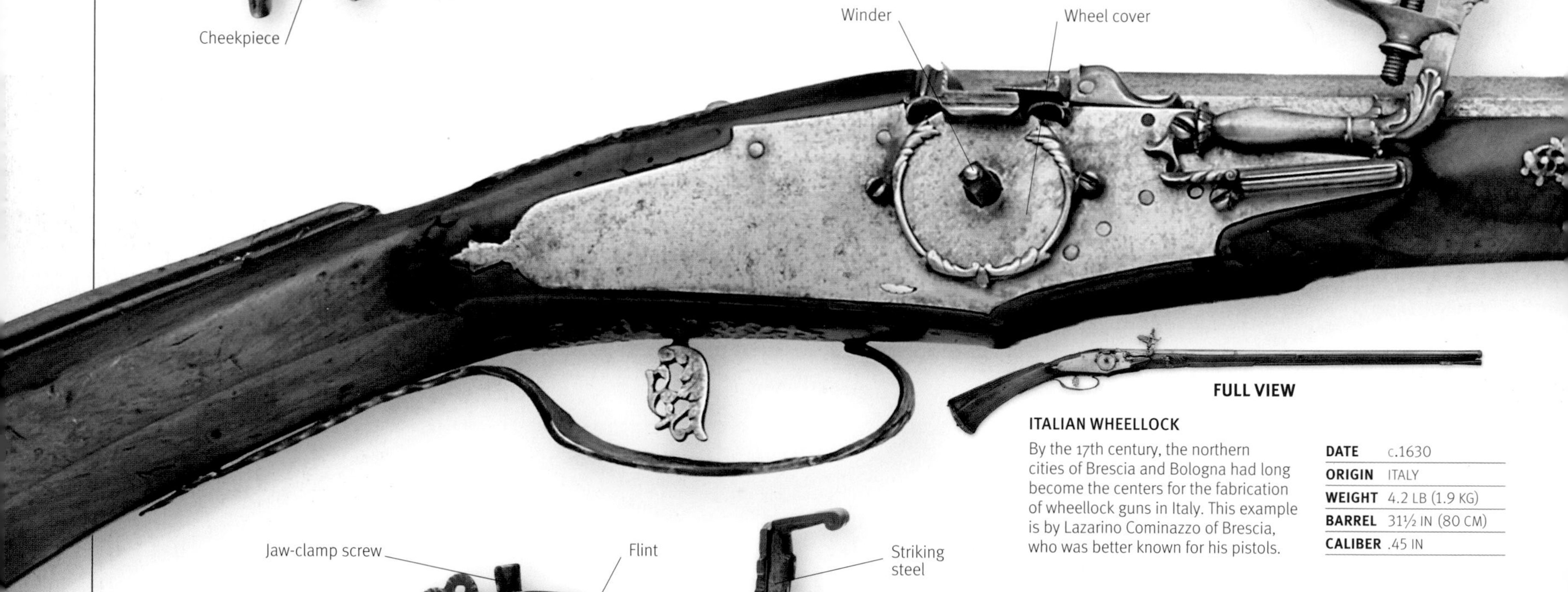

Trigger

Squared shaft for winding mechanism

Cheekpiece

Winder

Wheel cover

FULL VIEW

ITALIAN WHEELLOCK

By the 17th century, the northern cities of Brescia and Bologna had long become the centers for the fabrication of wheellock guns in Italy. This example is by Lazarino Cominazzo of Brescia, who was better known for his pistols.

DATE	c.1630
ORIGIN	ITALY
WEIGHT	4.2 LB (1.9 KG)
BARREL	31½ IN (80 CM)
CALIBER	.45 IN

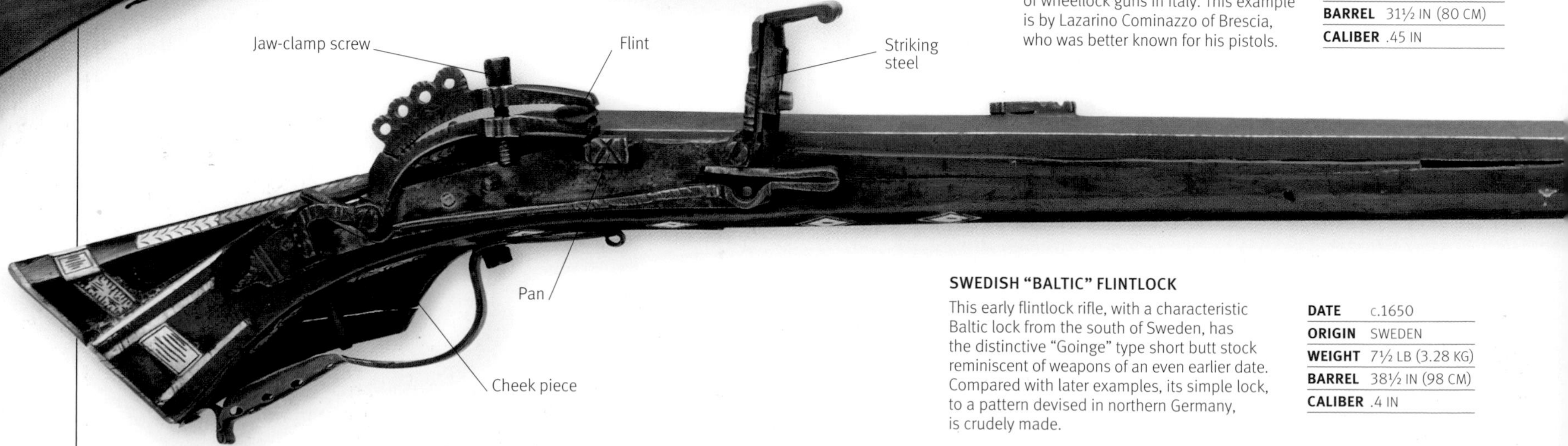

Jaw-clamp screw

Flint

Striking steel

Pan

Cheek piece

SWEDISH "BALTIC" FLINTLOCK

This early flintlock rifle, with a characteristic Baltic lock from the south of Sweden, has the distinctive "Goinge" type short butt stock reminiscent of weapons of an even earlier date. Compared with later examples, its simple lock, to a pattern devised in northern Germany, is crudely made.

DATE	c.1650
ORIGIN	SWEDEN
WEIGHT	7½ LB (3.28 KG)
BARREL	38½ IN (98 CM)
CALIBER	.4 IN

ITALIAN REPEATING FLINTLOCK

Italian gunmaker Michele Lorenzoni lived in Florence from 1683–1733, and invented an early form of repeating breech-loading flintlock. Paired magazines, one for powder and the other for shot, were located in the butt stock, and the breech block was rotated for charging by means of a lever on the left side of the gun.

DATE	c.1690
ORIGIN	ITALY
WEIGHT	8½ LB (3.95 KG)
BARREL	35 IN (89 CM)
CALIBER	.53 IN

Lock plate
Steel
Powder and shot magazines in butt stock
Revolving breech

GERMAN WHEELLOCK

Wheellocks exist in three basic forms: fully enclosed; with the wheel exposed but with the rest of the lock enclosed; and with the entire mechanism exposed. The latter form, known as a "Tschinke," from where it was devised, is more easily damaged but easier to clean and maintain. This example was made in Silesia, and its stock is inlaid with horn and mother-of-pearl.

DATE	c.1630
ORIGIN	GERMANY
WEIGHT	7¼ LB (3.4 KG)
BARREL	37 IN (94 CM)
CALIBER	.33 IN

Decorative inlays
Cock
Aperture rear sight
Exposed matchlock mechanism
Trigger

Barrel fixing pin

SCOTTISH SNAPHAUNCE

The name snaphaunce derives from the Dutch *schnapp-hahn*, meaning "pecking hen," which it was thought to resemble. It was the first attempt to simplify the wheellock's method of striking sparks from a piece of iron pyrites. This superb example is attributed to Alison of Dundee, and was a gift from James to Louis XIII of France.

DATE	1614
ORIGIN	SCOTLAND
WEIGHT	4¼ LB (2 KG)
BARREL	38 IN (96.5 CM)
CALIBER	.45 IN

Brass lock plate
Cock
Striking steel
Brass butt plate
Pan and touch-hole
Trigger guard

ENGLISH FLINTLOCK

Andrew Dolep was a Dutch gunmaker who settled in London and set up shop near Charing Cross. He produced this magnificent flintlock—its walnut stock extensively inlaid with silver wire—toward the end of his career. Dolep is credited with the design of the "Brown Bess" musket, which this gun resembles.

DATE	1690
ORIGIN	ENGLAND
WEIGHT	7 LB (3.2 KG)
BARREL	96½ CM (38 IN)
CALIBER	.75 IN

Striking steel
Fore stock
Fore sight
Pan and touch-hole
Ramrod thimble
Silver-wire inlay

THE EARLY MODERN WORLD

EUROPEAN HUNTING GUNS FROM 1700

THE GAP THAT HAD EXISTED between English gunmakers and their counterparts in Europe had largely disappeared by the start of the 18th century. The flintlock now predominated, except in southern Europe, where the more primitive miqulet lock was still widely used. While we see a more austere style, the remaining ornamentation became more sophisticated, with minimal ornate inlaying and emphasis placed on the natural qualities of the wood.

Striking steel

Barrel band

FLINTLOCK SPORT GUN

This full-stocked sport gun, attributed to John Shaw, shows considerable similarity to a military firearm of the same period. However, the attention that has been paid to the selection of the wood for its stock immediately sets it apart, as does the care that has been lavished on its finishing.

DATE	1700
ORIGIN	ENGLAND
WEIGHT	10½ LB (4.8 KG)
BARREL	55 IN (139.5 CM)
CALIBER	.75 IN

Cock

Striking steel

Small of the butt

Trigger

RUSSIAN FLINTLOCK

This beautifully decorated smooth-bore flintlock gun was made by Ivan Permjakov, one of the most accomplished Russian gunmakers. Although it was clearly intended as a sport gun, rather than a military weapon, it is believed to have been recovered from the field after the battle of the Alma River, which took place in 1854, during the Crimean War.

DATE	1770
ORIGIN	RUSSIA
WEIGHT	5 LB (2.2 KG)
BARREL	35 IN (89.8 CM)
CALIBER	.35 IN

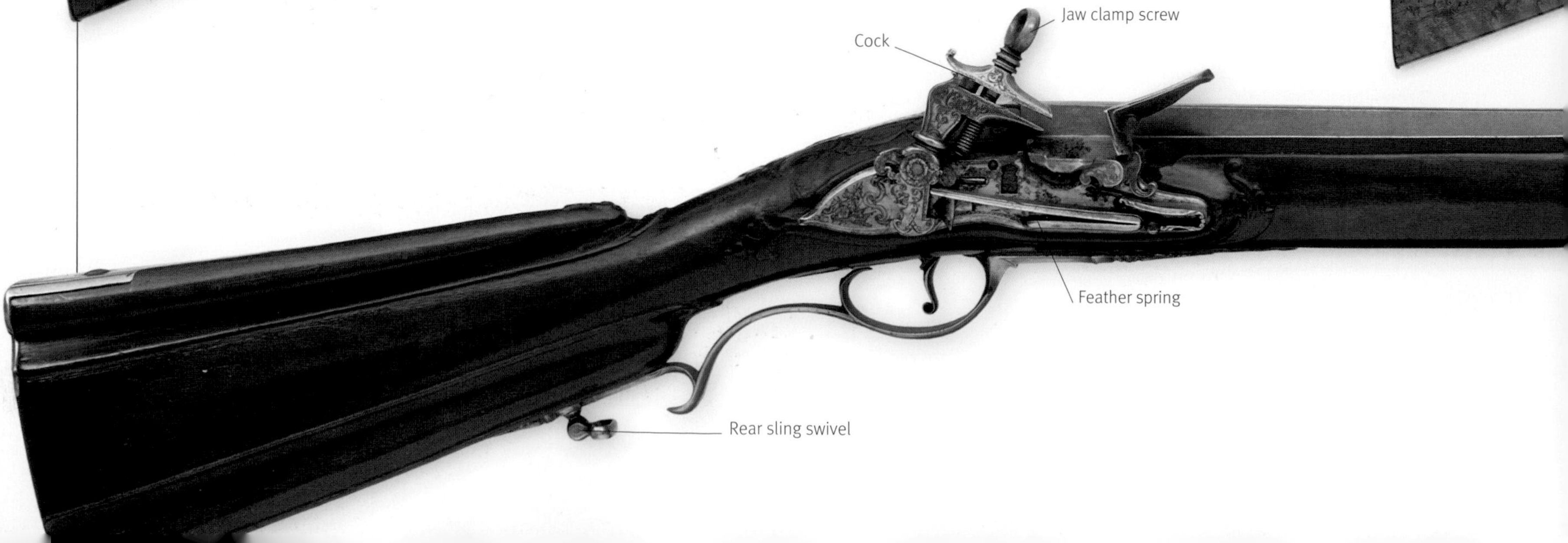

Jaw clamp screw

Cock

Feather spring

Rear sling swivel

Cock

Striking steel

Ornate pierced brass barrel band

Lock plate

ENGLISH FLINTLOCK SPORT GUN

The gunmaker Benjamin Griffin worked in fashionable Bond Street in London from 1735 to 1770, and was joined in 1750 by his son Joseph. Both father and son were renowned for their excellent pistols and long guns, many of which were graced with ornate engraving to the metal parts, decorative brasswork, and silver-wire inlay.

DATE	1760
ORIGIN	ENGLAND
WEIGHT	6¼ LB (2.84 KG)
BARREL	36 IN (91.4 CM)
CALIBER	.68 IN

Ramrod thimble

Ramrod

Jaw clamp screw

Gold-plated pan

Abbreviated forestock

Lock cover

Trigger for firing the left barrel

Trigger for firing the right barrel

DOUBLE-BARRELED FLINTLOCK SHOTGUN

This side-by-side double-barreled flintlock shotgun, attributed to Hadley, is typical of high-class fowling pieces of the latter part of the 18th century. Not only is its short stock silver mounted, but both its pans and its touch-holes are gold-plated to fend off corrosion.

DATE	C.1770
ORIGIN	ENGLAND
WEIGHT	5½ LB (2.55 KG)
BARREL	35½ IN (90.2 CM)
CALIBER	.6 IN

Fore sight

Ramrod retaining thimble

Figured walnut stock

Right trigger

Abbreviated forestock

Left trigger

SCOTTISH DOUBLE-BARRELED FLINTLOCK

By the beginning of the 19th century, the design of sport guns had already begun to diverge from that of military weapons, with shortened stocks becoming commonplace. This double-barreled piece is thought to have been made by Morris of Perth for Sir David Montcrieffe, a celebrated sportsman.

DATE	1819
ORIGIN	SCOTLAND
WEIGHT	7½ LB (3.4 KG)
BARREL	30 IN (76 CM)
CALIBER	.68 IN

Barrel band

Gilded decorative banding

Forward sling swivel

ITALIAN MIQUELET SPORT GUN

The miquelet lock introduced the combined striker and pan cover, but used an external mainspring (unlike the later true flintlock, in which the mainspring was internal). This miquelet lock musket is something of an oddity. It was manufactured in Naples by Pacifico around 1775, but has what is clearly an English-made barrel dating from around the time of the Battle of Waterloo (1815).

DATE	c.1775
ORIGIN	ITALY
WEIGHT	8¼ LB (3.75 KG)
BARREL	31½ IN (80 CM)
CALIBER	.75 IN

1500—1775

◄ 148–149 MATCHLOCK AND FLINTLOCK LONG GUNS   ◄ 150–151 WEAPON SHOWCASE: MATCHLOCK MUSKET   ► 260–261 INDIAN FIREARMS   ► 262–263 ASIAN FIREARMS

THE EARLY MODERN WORLD

ASIAN MATCHLOCKS

THE PORTUGUESE WERE THE FIRST EUROPEANS to reach the Indian subcontinent, in 1498, and 45 years later they arrived in Japan. They brought with them firearms in the shape of the matchlock musket. Accomplished armorers abounded in Asia, and indigenous craftsmen soon began to copy the weapons they saw, adapting them to their own needs. They also brought to firearms the same degree and style of decoration that they routinely applied to other weapons. This involved using precious metals and other valuable materials and, in the case of the Japanese, lacquerwork. Distinctive local styles soon evolved.

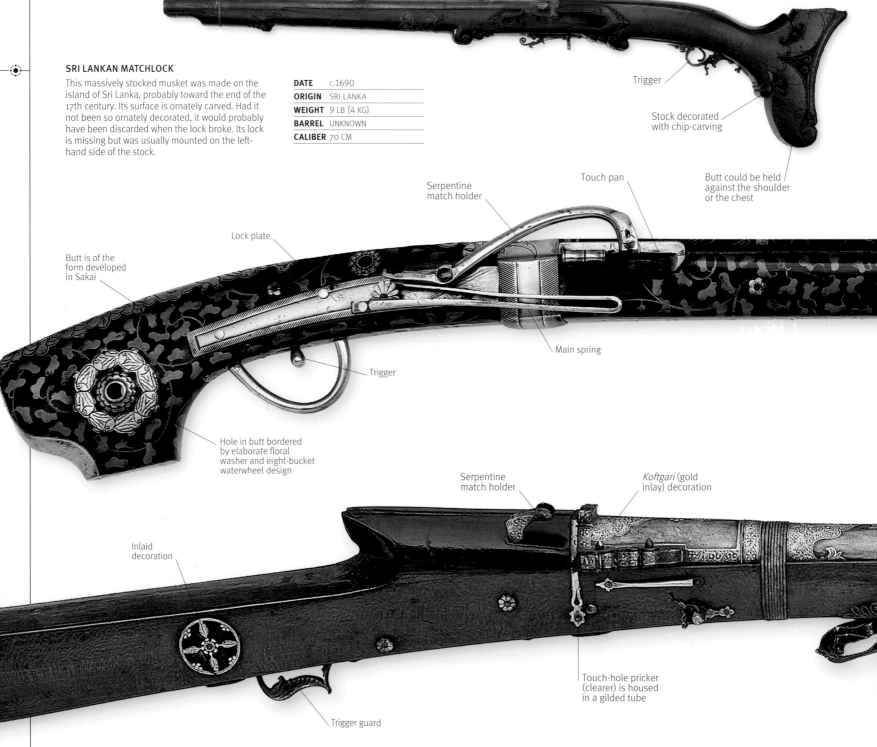

Fore sight

SRI LANKAN MATCHLOCK

This massively stocked musket was made on the island of Sri Lanka, probably toward the end of the 17th century. Its surface is ornately carved. Had it not been so ornately decorated, it would probably have been discarded when the lock broke. Its lock is missing but was usually mounted on the left-hand side of the stock.

DATE	c.1690
ORIGIN	SRI LANKA
WEIGHT	9 LB (4 KG)
BARREL	UNKNOWN
CALIBER	70 CM

Trigger

Stock decorated with chip-carving

Butt could be held against the shoulder or the chest

Serpentine match holder

Touch pan

Lock plate

Butt is of the form developed in Sakai

Main spring

Trigger

Hole in butt bordered by elaborate floral washer and eight-bucket waterwheel design

Inlaid decoration

Serpentine match holder

Koftgari (gold inlay) decoration

Touch-hole pricker (clearer) is housed in a gilded tube

Trigger guard

INDIAN CARNATIC TORADAR

The barrel of this matchlock from Mysore (in what is now Karnataka State, southern India) is exquisitely decorated with incised flowers and foliage, and entirely gilded. The incised side plates are made of iron, and on its trigger it has a tiger in *koftgari*—a method of inlaying gold into steel or iron.

DATE	18TH CENTURY
ORIGIN	SOUTHERN INDIA
WEIGHT	9 LB (4.05 KG)
BARREL	44½ IN (113 CM)
CALIBER	16 MM

Serpentine match holder

Gold inlay on muzzle

Barrel band

Pentagonal-section butt

Trigger

Iron side plates cover lock

JAPANESE MATCHLOCK

A rather less ornate weapon than that shown below, this matchlock is by Kunitomo Tobei Shigeyasu of Omo, on Japan's west coast. Its red-oak stock is in the style of the Sakai school. Decoration is limited to engraving on the octagonal barrel and some brass inlay; the lock and mainspring are also of brass.

DATE	EARLY 18TH CENTURY
ORIGIN	WESTERN JAPAN
WEIGHT	9¼ LB (4.14 KG)
BARREL	40½ IN (103 CM)
CALIBER	13.3 MM

Serpentine match holder

Rear sight

Octagonal barrel

Decorative inlay surrounds barrel pin

Barrel is retained by four pins

Shishi is brass inlay

JAPANESE TEPPO

This early 18th-century matchlock *teppo* is the work of the Enami family of Sakai, who are widely held to be among the finest Japanese gunmakers of the pre-industrial period. The stock is of red oak, decorated all over with *kara kusa* scrolls in gold lacquer, with additional inlays of brass and silver. The decoration may have been added at a later date.

DATE	c.1700
ORIGIN	JAPAN
WEIGHT	6 LB (2.77 KG)
BARREL	39½ IN (100 CM)
CALIBER	11.4 MM

Rear sight

Laquerwork *mon* is a pine tree in a circle

Octagonal barrel

Barrel band

Gold lacquering over red oak

FULL VIEW

INDIAN MATCHLOCK TORADAR

This 19th-century toradar has a stock of polished red wood with circular pierced medallions on either side of the butt of iron with gilding and *koftgari* applied over red velvet. The barrel has an elaborate arabesque decoration in gold *koftgari* at the breech, and the muzzle is fashioned into the shape of a tiger's head.

DATE	19TH CENTURY
ORIGIN	CENTRAL INDIA (NARWAR)
WEIGHT	10¾ LB (4.9 KG)
BARREL	49¾ IN (126.2 CM)
CALIBER	14 MM

Barrel bands of leather thongs

Sling

FULL VIEW

Tiger's-head muzzle

1500—1775

◀ 136–137 EUROPEAN ONE-HANDED STAFF WEAPONS   ◀ 140–141 EUROPEAN TWO-HANDED STAFF WEAPONS   ◀ 148–149 MATCHLOCK AND FLINTLOCK LONG GUNS   ▶ 196–197 INDIAN STAFF WEAPONS

THE EARLY MODERN WORLD

COMBINATION WEAPONS

GERMAN AND ITALIAN ARMORERS of the 16th century were particularly adept at incorporating firearms into other blunt and edged weapons. Many of the examples that survive were probably intended to be showpieces, since they frequently display the most ornate decoration, and it is not clear whether they were ever meant for martial use. The tradition continued—a rifle or pistol equipped with a bayonet can be said to be a combination weapon—and spread to other countries, notably to India, where more practical examples were produced during the late Mughal period.

Squared shaft takes the key that winds the action

Cock

Serrated striking wheel

Barrel

Point of flange is solid

Ramrod

Fork bayonet

Beak

Trigger

WAR HAMMER WHEELLOCK

This long-shafted war hammer (only the beak remains; the balancing hammer head is missing) incorporates a wheellock pistol. Equipped with a gunmaker's "standard" pistol lock and barrel, this weapon seems to have been produced for practical rather than ceremonial purposes.

DATE	c.1590
ORIGIN	GERMANY
WEIGHT	1.70 KG (3¾ LB)
LENGTH	24¼ IN (61.6 CM)
CALIBER	.35 IN

FULL VIEW

Hinged pomel

Cock

Wheellock

Mace head composed of six pierced flanges

MACE WHEELLOCK

The barrel of this wheellock pistol forms the shaft of a mace, the head of which has six pointed flanges, each pierced with a trefoil shape. The lock incorporates a simple safety catch that engages with the sear. The hollow lower section of the shaft contains a compartment that can be accessed by opening the hinged pommel. The entire weapon is engraved and selectively gilded.

DATE	UNKNOWN
ORIGIN	UNKNOWN
WEIGHT	3¾ LB (1.72 KG)
LENGTH	23 IN (58.5 CM)
CALIBER	.31 IN

Balancing fluke

Ax blade

Trophy of arms

FULL VIEW

HALBERD DOUBLE-BARRELED WHEELLOCK

A hunting halberd fitted with a double-barreled wheellock pistol. The pistol barrels are octagonal and mounted on either side of the leaf-shaped blade. The whole is etched and partly gilt with strap and scroll-work, the ax and fluke of the head having additional trophies of arms.

DATE	c.1590
ORIGIN	GERMANY
WEIGHT	7 LB (3.25 KG)
LENGTH	27¼ IN (69.1 CM)
CALIBER	.33 IN

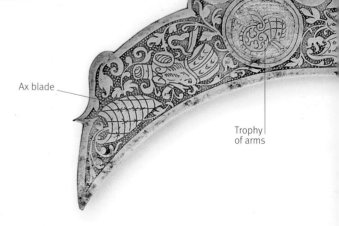

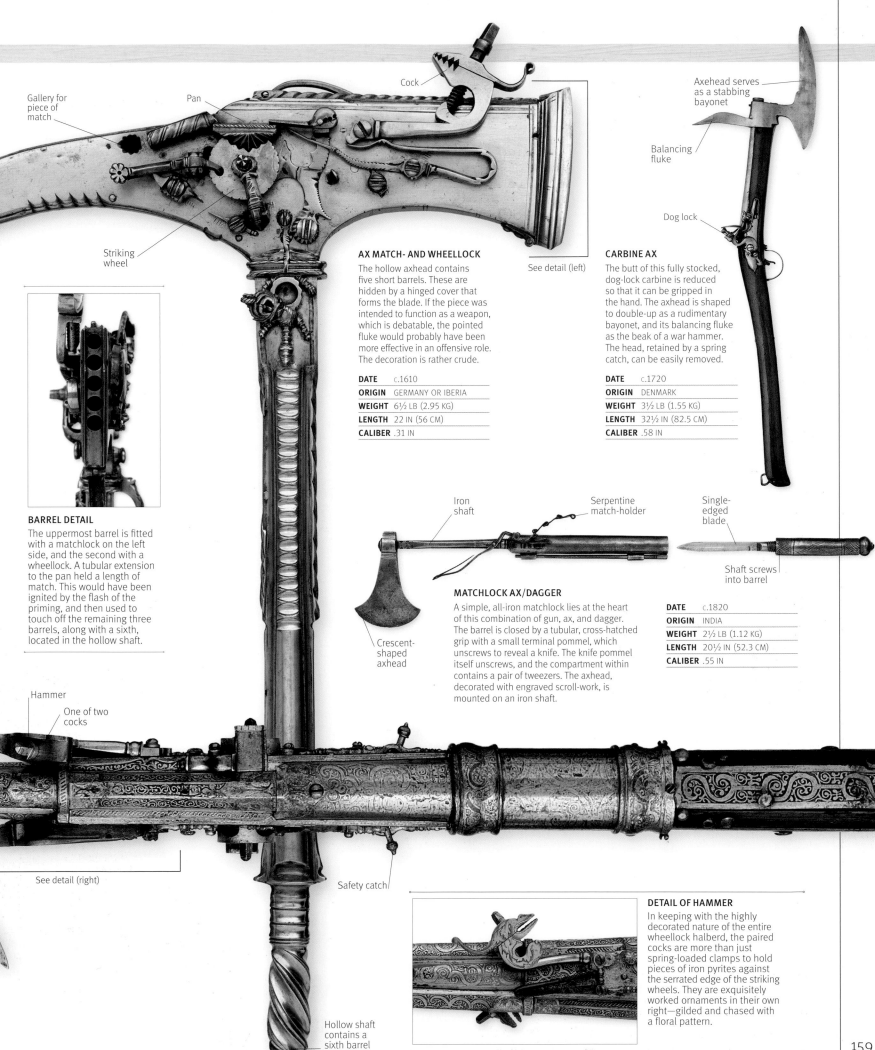

Cock

Pan

Gallery for piece of match

Striking wheel

Axehead serves as a stabbing bayonet

Balancing fluke

Dog lock

See detail (left)

BARREL DETAIL
The uppermost barrel is fitted with a matchlock on the left side, and the second with a wheellock. A tubular extension to the pan held a length of match. This would have been ignited by the flash of the priming, and then used to touch off the remaining three barrels, along with a sixth, located in the hollow shaft.

AX MATCH- AND WHEELLOCK
The hollow axhead contains five short barrels. These are hidden by a hinged cover that forms the blade. If the piece was intended to function as a weapon, which is debatable, the pointed fluke would probably have been more effective in an offensive role. The decoration is rather crude.

DATE	c.1610
ORIGIN	GERMANY OR IBERIA
WEIGHT	6½ LB (2.95 KG)
LENGTH	22 IN (56 CM)
CALIBER	.31 IN

CARBINE AX
The butt of this fully stocked, dog-lock carbine is reduced so that it can be gripped in the hand. The axhead is shaped to double-up as a rudimentary bayonet, and its balancing fluke as the beak of a war hammer. The head, retained by a spring catch, can be easily removed.

DATE	c.1720
ORIGIN	DENMARK
WEIGHT	3½ LB (1.55 KG)
LENGTH	32½ IN (82.5 CM)
CALIBER	.58 IN

Iron shaft

Serpentine match-holder

Single-edged blade

MATCHLOCK AX/DAGGER
A simple, all-iron matchlock lies at the heart of this combination of gun, ax, and dagger. The barrel is closed by a tubular, cross-hatched grip with a small terminal pommel, which unscrews to reveal a knife. The knife pommel itself unscrews, and the compartment within contains a pair of tweezers. The axhead, decorated with engraved scroll-work, is mounted on an iron shaft.

Crescent-shaped axhead

Shaft screws into barrel

DATE	c.1820
ORIGIN	INDIA
WEIGHT	2½ LB (1.12 KG)
LENGTH	20½ IN (52.3 CM)
CALIBER	.55 IN

Hammer

One of two cocks

See detail (right)

Safety catch

Hollow shaft contains a sixth barrel

DETAIL OF HAMMER
In keeping with the highly decorated nature of the entire wheellock halberd, the paired cocks are more than just spring-loaded clamps to hold pieces of iron pyrites against the serrated edge of the striking wheels. They are exquisitely worked ornaments in their own right—gilded and chased with a floral pattern.

THE EARLY MODERN WORLD

EUROPEAN PISTOLS 1500–1700

PRIOR TO THE INTRODUCTION of the wheellock—the first mechanical means of igniting a gun's powder charge—pistols were rare, since one could not pocket or holster a matchlock. The invention of the wheellock (perhaps by Leonardo da Vinci) late in the 15th century made it possible to carry a gun and still have one's hands free. Wheellocks were expensive, complicated, and prone to breakage—and usually only repairable by the man who had made the gun. By about 1650, they had been replaced by the less complex snaphaunce (which struck sparks with a spring-loaded flint). This then evolved into the even simpler "true" flintlock.

Serrated wheel strikes sparks from flint

Pan

"Flint" is really iron pyrites

Cock

Lock plate

Ramrod

Ramrod-retaining thimble

Spring holds cock in place

WHEELLOCK PISTOL

In northern Europe, pistols were known as dags (the origins of the name are obscure) until the late 16th century. The ball pommel, a common feature of dags, was designed to make the pistol easier to retrieve from a pocket or bag, rather than to be used as a bludgeon.

DATE	1590
ORIGIN	GERMANY
WEIGHT	4 LB (1.77 KG)
BARREL	12 IN (30.2 CM)
CALIBER	0.5 IN

Decorative ball pommel is attached to butt by a dowel

Jaw-clamp screw

Striking steel attached to pan cover

Flint wrapped in leather patch to improve jaw's grip

Plain lock plate

Stag-horn inlay

Pan

Feather spring flicks cover up when released, revealing pan

Trigger

FULL VIEW

Jaw-clamp screw

Pan cover

Cock

Lock plate

SILESIAN FLINTLOCK PISTOL

This large, sophisticated holster pistol was made in the principality of Teschen (now divided between the Czech Republic and Poland), but shows considerable German influence. The nature and quality of the decoration —the inlays are of stag horn—indicate that it was made as a presentation piece.

DATE	c.1680
ORIGIN	SILESIA
WEIGHT	2½ LB (1.1 KG)
BARREL	14 IN (35.5 CM)
CALIBER	29-BORE

Metal-bound butt

Feather spring

Rounded butt

Trigger guard

Cock

Striker for upper barrel

Barrel release

Striker for lower barrel

Flattened pommel

DUTCH DOUBLE-BARRELED FLINTLOCK

Early multiple-shot handguns normally had a lock for each barrel. However, by mounting a pair of barrels on an axial pin and providing each with a striker and pan with a secure cover, it was possible to present each in turn to a single lock, reducing the cost considerably.

DATE	c.1650
ORIGIN	NETHERLANDS
WEIGHT	2½ LB (1.2 KG)
BARREL	19¾ IN (50.3 CM)
CALIBER	36-BORE

Striking steel attached to pan cover

Cock

Round barrel

Steel mountings are selectively gilded

Feather spring

Trigger

Gilded steel decoration

AUSTRIAN FLINTLOCK

Made in Vienna by Lamarre, this ornate holster pistol, though certainly atypical in the level and high quality of its decoration, represents the state of the gunmaker's art as it was in the last decades of the 17th century.

DATE	c.1690
ORIGIN	AUSTRIA
WEIGHT	2½ LB (1.2 KG)
BARREL	14 IN (35.3 CM)
CALIBER	17-BORE

Round barrel

Ramrod-retaining thimble

Escutchion plate

Fore sight

Metal-bound butt

Incised decoration

FLEMISH FLINTLOCK PISTOL

Even everyday 17th- and 18th-century firearms frequently received some embellishment in the shape of carving. Some were even given silver mountings, as can be seen here on this piece by the Flemish gunmaker Guillaume Henoul.

DATE	c.1700
ORIGIN	NETHERLANDS
WEIGHT	2¼ LB (1 KG)
BARREL	10½ IN (26 CM)
CALIBER	25-BORE

Barrel is hexagonal toward the breech

Barrel becomes round toward the muzzle

Forestock cap

Ramrod-retaining thimble

ENGLISH FLINTLOCK PISTOL

English gunmakers did not come into their own until the end of the 18th century. In the middle of the 17th century, when this holster pistol was made, they were still taking their lead from continental colleagues, and the maker of this piece, which has a French-style lock, was no exception.

DATE	c.1650
ORIGIN	ENGLAND
WEIGHT	2¼ LB (1 KG)
BARREL	14¼ IN (34.2 CM)
CALIBER	25-BORE

1500—1775

◄ 148–149 MATCHLOCK AND FLINTLOCK LONG GUNS   ◄ 160–161 EUROPEAN PISTOLS 1500–1700   ► 212–213 FLINTLOCK PISTOLS FROM 1775   ► 214–215 FLINTLOCK PISTOLS TO 1850

THE EARLY MODERN WORLD

EUROPEAN PISTOLS 1700-1775

THE FRENCH COURT GUNMAKER Marin le Bourgeoys invented the true flintlock around 1610, when he combined the striker and pan cover of the miquelet lock with the internal mechanism of the snaphaunce, and modifed the sear, which "connected" cock and trigger, to act vertically instead of horizontally. While snaphaunces and miquelets were still produced for a long time after—as, for a while, were wheellocks and matchlocks—they were technically obsolete. Over the next 200 years, until the development of the percussion lock, only minor improvements were necessary, though the introduction of the enclosed box lock was a distinct step forward.

Cock has lost upper jaw to flint clamp

Steel striker is missing

Butt has incised decoration

Engraved box lock

Trigger

Tap

DOUBLE-BARRELED TAP-ACTION PISTOL

The tap is a rod that fits tightly into a cylinder below the pan. The tap is bored through; the bore is filled with powder, the tap is turned through 90°, and the pan is then primed in the normal way. After firing the upper barrel, the tap is turned again; the powder in the bore then primes the lower barrel.

DATE	1763
ORIGIN	ENGLAND
WEIGHT	6 OZ (170 G)
BARREL	2 IN (5.08 CM)
CALIBER	.22 IN

Striking steel

Cock

Lock plate

Silver medallion set into butt

Trigger has lost its finial ball

SCOTTISH PISTOL

It was the fashion in Scotland during the 18th century to make pistols entirely of brass or iron, with their entire surface covered by intricate engraving. Typically, they lacked trigger guards. Most were snaphaunces; this example is unusual, in that it is a flintlock. It was made by Thomas Cadell of Doune, who made some of the best iron pistols.

DATE	c.1750
ORIGIN	SCOTLAND
WEIGHT	1¾ LB (0.79 KG)
BARREL	9 IN (22.85 CM)
CALIBER	.57 IN

Fore sight

Plain, unadorned barrel

Pommel unscrews and is equipped with a touch-hole pricker

Ram's horn finial

Ramrod

Ramrod-retaining thimble

Screws retain lock

ENGLISH PISTOL

A pistol such as this would have been carried in a holster on the saddle of a horse (gun holsters worn by people were later inventions). Holster pistols were heavy, with long barrels, and after being discharged they were often used as bludgeons—hence the metal butt cap.

DATE	c.1720
ORIGIN	ENGLAND
WEIGHT	2 LB (0.88 KG)
BARREL	10 IN (25.4 CM)
CALIBER	.64 IN

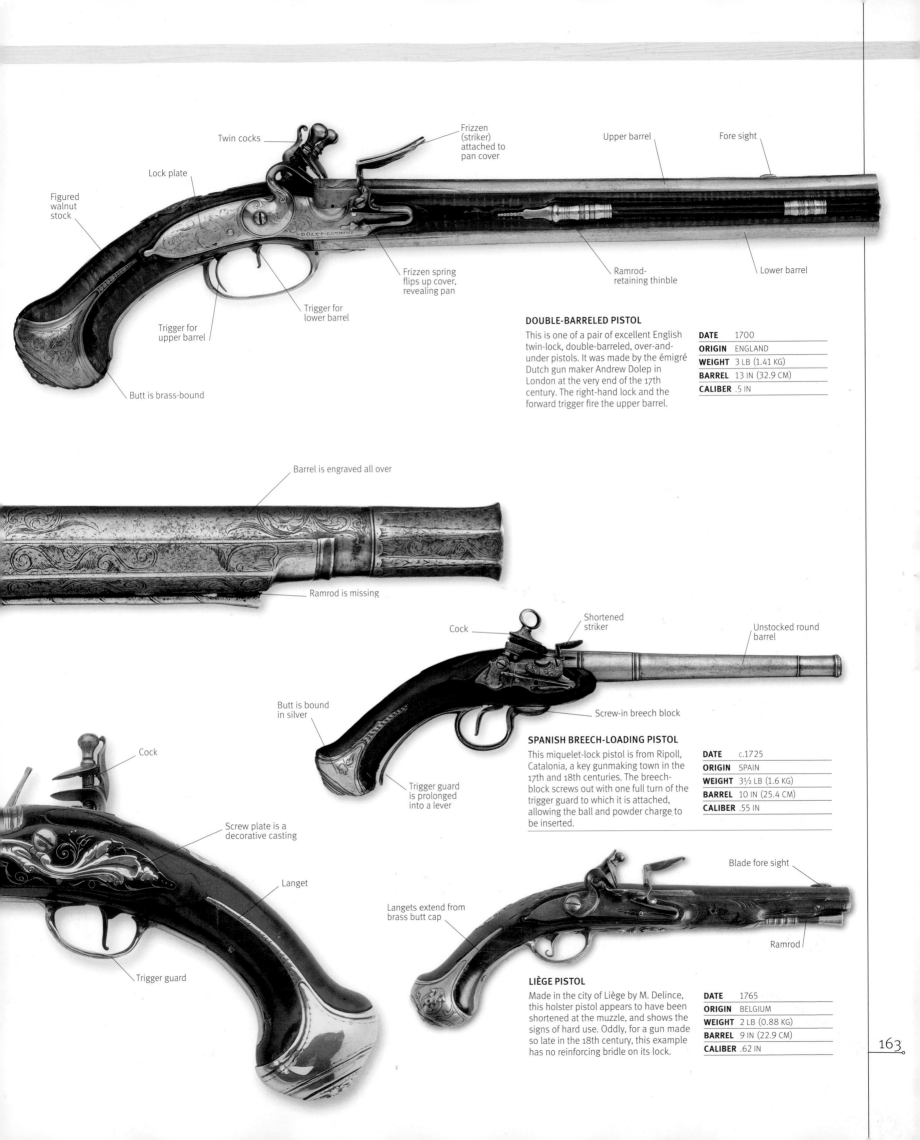

Twin cocks

Frizzen (striker) attached to pan cover

Upper barrel

Fore sight

Lock plate

Figured walnut stock

D OLEP·LONDINI

Frizzen spring flips up cover, revealing pan

Ramrod-retaining thinble

Lower barrel

Trigger for lower barrel

Trigger for upper barrel

Butt is brass-bound

DOUBLE-BARRELED PISTOL

This is one of a pair of excellent English twin-lock, double-barreled, over-and-under pistols. It was made by the émigré Dutch gun maker Andrew Dolep in London at the very end of the 17th century. The right-hand lock and the forward trigger fire the upper barrel.

DATE	1700
ORIGIN	ENGLAND
WEIGHT	3 LB (1.41 KG)
BARREL	13 IN (32.9 CM)
CALIBER	.5 IN

Barrel is engraved all over

Ramrod is missing

Cock

Shortened striker

Unstocked round barrel

Butt is bound in silver

Screw-in breech block

SPANISH BREECH-LOADING PISTOL

This miquelet-lock pistol is from Ripoll, Catalonia, a key gunmaking town in the 17th and 18th centuries. The breech-block screws out with one full turn of the trigger guard to which it is attached, allowing the ball and powder charge to be inserted.

DATE	c.1725
ORIGIN	SPAIN
WEIGHT	3½ LB (1.6 KG)
BARREL	10 IN (25.4 CM)
CALIBER	.55 IN

Cock

Trigger guard is prolonged into a lever

Screw plate is a decorative casting

Langet

Langets extend from brass butt cap

Blade fore sight

Trigger guard

Ramrod

LIÈGE PISTOL

Made in the city of Liège by M. Delince, this holster pistol appears to have been shortened at the muzzle, and shows the signs of hard use. Oddly, for a gun made so late in the 18th century, this example has no reinforcing bridle on its lock.

DATE	1765
ORIGIN	BELGIUM
WEIGHT	2 LB (0.88 KG)
BARREL	9 IN (22.9 CM)
CALIBER	.62 IN

THIRTY YEARS WAR
In 1620, the Battle of White
Mountain marked the start of the
Thirty Years War, which left few regions
of central and western Europe untouched.
Here, the Bohemian protestants are defeated by
the Christian Imperial army using pikes and muskets.

1500—1775

◄ 86–87 EUROPEAN HELMS AND BASINETS   ◄ 88–89 EUROPEAN JOUSTING HELMS, BARBUTES, AND SALLETS   ◄ 94–95 EUROPEAN PLATE ARMOR   ► 168–169 EUROPEAN TOURNAMENT HELMETS

EUROPEAN TOURNAMENT ARMOR

DURING THE 15TH century, specialist armor began to be developed for tournaments, a trend that reached its highest expression in the following century. Not only was additional armor introduced for specific events—such as strengthening the vulnerable left side for jousting—but the armor became increasingly ornate, with enormous attention being paid to the most exquisite decoration. Indeed, so great was the quality of this work that some items of armor became too precious to use in combat and were used for display as parade armor. Certain types of parade armor became increasingly fantastical, with armorers mimicking current styles of civilian dress and devising "grotesque" helmets in the shape of animals.

FOOT COMBAT ARMOR

In foot combat, two contestants wearing special suits of armor fought in the lists (the arena) with poleaxes, spears, maces, swords, and daggers. Foot combat as practiced in the 15th and 16th centuries historically derived from "judicial duels"—officially sanctioned fights, often to the death, to resolve legal disputes. Foot combat was the most dangerous of all the tournament competitions, and required an armor that gave head-to-toe protection to the wearer.

DATE	1580
ORIGIN	GERMANY

Ventilation holes pierced on right side, away from vulnerable left side that would face opponent's lance

Close helm with pivoted upper bevor and visor

FULL VIEW

Gorget (collar guard)

Breastplate constructed in "doublet" style

Rerebrace (upper arm guard)

Right pauldron (shoulder guard) reduced in depth to hold lance

One-piece visor pierced with multiple horizontal slits for ventilation

Detachable haut piece (upright guard)

Left pauldron

Couter (elbow guard) with detachable plates

Fauld (steel hoop) of three lames (connecting plates)

Mitten gauntlets

Long tasset (steel plate) of six lames

Greaves (plate guards for lower leg)

A KING'S ARMOR

Made for King Henry VIII of England in 1540, this harness of armor from the Italian-influenced Greenwich armories reflects the increasingly stout figure of the monarch. Intended for both field and tournament use, the decoration on this armor has been attributed to a Florentine, Giovanni de Maiano, with assistance from the painter Hans Holbein.

DATE	1540
ORIGIN	ENGLAND
WEIGHT	78 LB (35.33 KG)
HEIGHT	77¾ IN (187.5 CM)

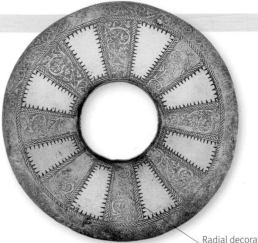

Radial decoration etched in gilt

DECORATED VAMPLATE

The vamplate was a funnel-shaped, circular guard fixed to the lance to protect the hand. The first vamplates appeared in the 14th century as a tournament feature. By the 16th century, they had evolved into large and finely decorated conical shapes.

DATE	16TH CENTURY
ORIGIN	ITALY
WEIGHT	c.1¼ LB (0.6 KG)
LENGTH	c.10 IN (25 CM)

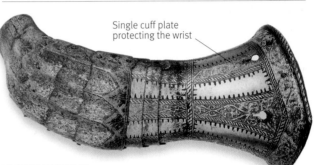

Single cuff plate protecting the wrist

LOCKING GAUNTLET

One of the dangers faced by a heavily armored knight was his sword dropping or being knocked from his hand. A gauntlet such as this prevented it by locking the sword into the steel mitten until unlocked after combat.

DATE	16TH CENTURY
ORIGIN	ITALY
WEIGHT	c.2½ LB (1.14 KG)
LENGTH	c.6 IN (40 CM)

Leather connecting straps to backplate

Lance rest

BREASTPLATE

Made in Italy, this light yet strong breastplate is a superb example of the armorer's art; its shape imitates the bulge of the close-fitting doublet of the period. The breastplate is decorated with engraved and gilded heavenly figures.

DATE	16TH CENTURY
ORIGIN	ITALY
WEIGHT	c.6¼ LB (2.80 KG)
HEIGHT	c.19 IN (48 CM)

1500—1775

◄ 86–87 EUROPEAN HELMS AND BASINETS ◄ 88–89 EUROPEAN JOUSTING HELMS, BARBUTES, AND SALLETS ◄ 166–167 EUROPEAN TOURNAMENT ARMOR ► 350–351 HELMETS FROM 1900

THE EARLY MODERN WORLD

EUROPEAN TOURNAMENT HELMETS

THE EVOLUTION OF parade and ceremonial helmets in the 16th century very much matched that of armor intended for use on the battlefield. In the case of tilting helmets, effective protection was of very practical use to stave off potentially fatal head injuries inflicted by jousting lances. Open-faced helmets, such as the burgonet, were less suitable for this purpose and it was in close helmets of the later 16th century that parade helmets reached the height of their magnificence—the greater protective surface areas of such helms also provided more space for the armorer to add decorative engravings and ornaments.

Rope comb

Cherub's head decoration

Hole to attach crest

Visor pivots at the same point as the rest of the faceguard

Peg for lifting visor

Two sections of skull plate join at the comb

Sleeping lion decoration

Upper bevor with figures in Roman armor

EMBOSSED CLOSE HELMET

The entire surface of this close helmet is of bright steel embossed with scenes of equestrian combat, figures in classical armor, trophies, lions, and cherub heads in low relief. A piece of such high quality, originally gilded, was clearly designed for parade purposes. The visor has flanges to fit into the bevor, a feature typical of the close helmet.

DATE	c.1575
ORIGIN	FRANCE
WEIGHT	5¾ LB (2.6 KG)

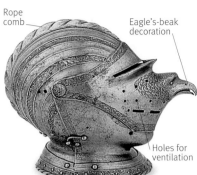

EAGLE'S-HEAD CLOSE HELMET

This close helmet is boldly shaped below the eyepiece into the form of an eagle's head. The plumage of the bird's head is represented by feathers etched into the metal. The skull has a low comb with rope decorations, on either side of which are seven rows of fluting, partly decorated with elegant bands of stylized foliage.

Rope comb
Eagle's-beak decoration
Holes for ventilation

DATE	c.1540
ORIGIN	GERMANY
WEIGHT	7 LB (3 KG)

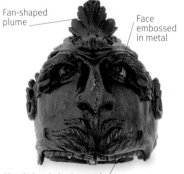

PARADE CASQUE

This ornate casque helmet forms part of a tradition of "grotesque" helmets intended for parades or masques, particularly popular in the 16th century. With its striking embossed man's face with staring eyes, and its extravagant plumelike comb, this piece may well have formed part of a whole suit of "costume" armor.

Fan-shaped plume
Face embossed in metal
Metal plate imitating teeth

DATE	c.1530
ORIGIN	ITALY
WEIGHT	5 LB (2.2 KG)

OPEN-FACE BURGONET

The burgonet has a characteristic low and rounded skull, turned outward to just below the ears, with the cheeks left unprotected. A dolphin mask in front of the skull has its skin and fins embossed in gold. On either side of the central mask are the tails of the dolphin, attached by turning points.

Dolphin mask
Blued, etched, and gilt wings

DATE	c.1520
ORIGIN	GERMANY
WEIGHT	5 LB (2.2 KG)

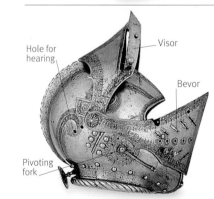

ARMET

The armet was an improved form of close helmet. It offered good protection, with large cheek pieces secured below the visor pivot, the opening at the back often protected by a round plate. The protruding stalk at the back was to connect a "wrapper"—a tall plate in front of the visor on the left side, the point at which a jousting lance might strike.

Hole for hearing
Visor
Bevor
Pivoting fork

DATE	c.1535
ORIGIN	GERMANY
WEIGHT	5 LB (2.2 KG)

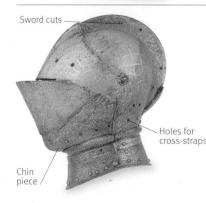

GILDED CLOSE HELMET

The whole of this tilting helmet is gilt, with decoration consisting of interlaced strapwork and scrolls deeply etched into the surface, with ornaments of foliage, winged heads, and grotesque animals. The other side of the visor is pierced by ten slots for breathing. The top of the comb is marked with sword cuts, which show that the helmet saw violent action. It formed part of a suit originally made for Emperor Ferdinand I.

Sword cuts
Holes for cross-straps
Chin piece

DATE	c.1555
ORIGIN	GERMANY
WEIGHT	5 LB (2.2 KG)

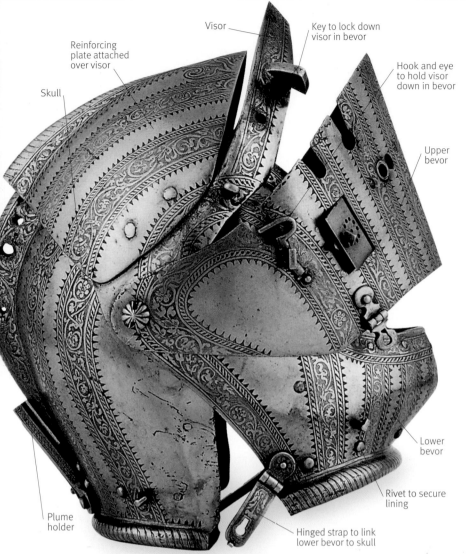

Reinforcing plate attached over visor
Visor
Key to lock down visor in bevor
Hook and eye to hold visor down in bevor
Skull
Upper bevor
Lower bevor
Rivet to secure lining
Plume holder
Hinged strap to link lower bevor to skull

ETCHED AND GILDED CLOSE HELMET

The surface of this close helmet is etched and gilded with vertical bands of flowing scrolls. Extra protection is added by a solid reinforcing plate that extends over the front of the skull. The lower edge of the helmet finishes in a hollowed roping, into which fitted the top plate of the gorget (neck armor).

DATE	c.1570
ORIGIN	ITALY
WEIGHT	6¼ LB (2.8 KG)

DEATH OF HENRI II AT JOUSTING TOURNAMENT, 1559

King Henry II of France was an avid hunter and participant in jousting tournaments. However, on July 1, 1559, he was killed by the lance of Gabriel Montgomery, captain of the King's Scottish Guard. His death was due to the Achilles heel of the close helmets of the day; his opponent's lance shattered and a fragment glanced down between the king's visor and bevor, piercing his eye and penetrating his brain.

THE EARLY MODERN WORLD

ASIAN ARMOR AND HELMETS

BETWEEN THE 16TH AND 18TH CENTURIES, broadly similar weapons and armor were used by armies from the Middle East to India and Central Asia. These included mail-and-plate body armor and a type of round shield, made of leather or steel, that was called a *dhal* in India and a *sipar* in Persia. China and Korea, while culturally distinct, were also influenced by these essentially Islamic styles. Even though firearms were widely used in Asia, armor and shields remained in use for longer than in Europe.

Spike socket

Plume holder

Sliding nasal bar

Mail aventail

INDIAN TOP

This style of helmet, which is known as a *top* in India, probably originated in Central Asia. The helmet's most striking feature is the mail aventail that guards the neck, shoulders, and part of the face. There would have been a spike on top of the helmet and plumes on either side of the skull.

DATE	c.18TH CENTURY
ORIGIN	INDIA

FULL VIEW

INDIAN MAIL-AND-PLATE COAT

This style of mail-and-plate armor, with four large plates at the front, two smaller ones at the sides, and further plates at the back, was favored by Mughal emperors, including Aurangzeb (reigned 1658–1707). It did not offer absolute protection: missiles and stabbing weapons could potentially penetrate the areas of riveted mail.

DATE	EARLY 17TH CENTURY
ORIGIN	INDIA

Lining of red silk

Column of small plates

Mail strip

INDIAN MAIL-AND-PLATE JACKET

Known in India as a *zereh bagtar*, this jacket combines both plate and mail armor. Mail-and-plate combinations were in general use across the Islamic world from the Ottoman Empire to Central Asia by the 15th century, and they were the predominant armor of Mughal India. This example has columns of 60 to 65 small metal plates and a mix of welded and riveted mail.

DATE	EARLY 18TH CENTURY
ORIGIN	INDIA
WEIGHT	17¾ LB (8.1 KG)
LENGTH	27¼ IN (69.5 CM)

Short mail sleeve

Large steel plates

Riveted mail covers waist

Silver cap

Iron helmet frame

Lacquered rawhide

Brass plate

Mail collar reinforced by plates

KOREAN HELMET

This lacquered leather helmet would have been worn by a wealthy Korean warrior, evidenced by the decorative silverwork on the cap and peak. Three fabric flaps containing internal iron plates protect the neck and cheeks. The tube at the apex of the helmet would have carried a plume.

DATE	LATE 16TH CENTURY
ORIGIN	KOREA
WEIGHT	2¼ LB (2.4 KG)
HEIGHT	13 IN (33 CM)

Riveted mail coat with long sleeves

Cheek guard with brass-headed rivets retaining internal iron plates

Gilt plume-holder

Coral and turquoise decoration

Riveted seam joins two halves of skull

Gilt band around base of skull

CHINESE ZHOU

This helmet, or *zhou*, is from Ming dynasty China. The skull of the helmet is made in two pieces joined by a riveted seam. This is a luxury item, elaborately decorated with precious stones and corals, and with a gilt holder at the apex into which a plume would have been inserted. Traces of blue silk remain at the base of the skull—probably all that is left of a neck guard.

DATE	16TH CENTURY
ORIGIN	CHINA
HEIGHT	13¾ IN (35 CM)

INDIAN DHAL

This Indian round shield, or *dhal*, is made of watered steel. It was held by passing an arm through two handles on the back. The handles are fastened by ring bolts, which are riveted to the four bosses on the shield's face. Shields gave Indian craftsmen an irresistible opportunity to indulge their passion for chiseled and gilded decoration.

DATE	c.1800
ORIGIN	INDIA
WEIGHT	8½ LB (3.8 KG)
WIDTH	24 IN (60 CM)

Boss covers attachment of handle

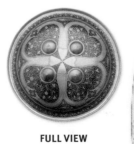

FULL VIEW

Gilded decoration

SAMURAI ARMOR

JAPANESE SAMURAI ARMOR, which evolved from the Asiatic tradition of lamellar (scaled) armor, consists of lacquered plates of metal or leather bound together by leather or silk lacing. This flexible armor gave adequate protection while permitting the free and rapid movement needed by a sword-fighter. Samurai armor increased in complexity over time, achieving its pinnacle in the *tosei gusoku* (modern armor) style from the 16th century onward. Armor and helmets were intended for display as well as combat. At their most ornate in the Edo period, after the pacification of Japan, the samurai had then ceased to be active warriors.

Shikoro (neck protection)

Sode (shoulder defence)

SODE (SHOULDER DEFENSE)

Suigyu-no-wakidate (gilt-wood buffalo horn ornament)

KABUTO (HELMET)

KOTE (ARM DEFENSE)

Leather-covered *fukigayeshi* (sweepback)

Gold lacquered browplate

Tekko (hand defense)

Skirts protect thighs

Suneate (greaves)

Cords attach mask to the head here

Ressei men ("Furious power") face mask

Tying bands

Yodare-kake (throat defense)

MEMPO (FACE DEFENSE)

SUNEATE (GREAVES)

TOSEI GUSOKU (MODERN ARMOR)

This fine quality *tosei gusoku* armor is twinned with a helmet spectacularly topped by imitation buffalo-horn *wakidate*, or side crests (antlers were also popular as *wakidate*). The black lacquered half-mask, or *mempo*, has wrinkles and teeth but lacks one frequently found feature: a moustache. The mask protected the lower face, helped hold the helmet on the warrior's head, and made the wearer look more frightening. Other details, such as the eyebrows embossed on the browplate, also helped to create an intimidating effect. An aesthetically pleasing color scheme is achieved through the use of gold lacquer and red silk.

DATE	19TH CENTURY
ORIGIN	JAPAN
WEIGHT	HELMET 6 LB (2.75 KG)

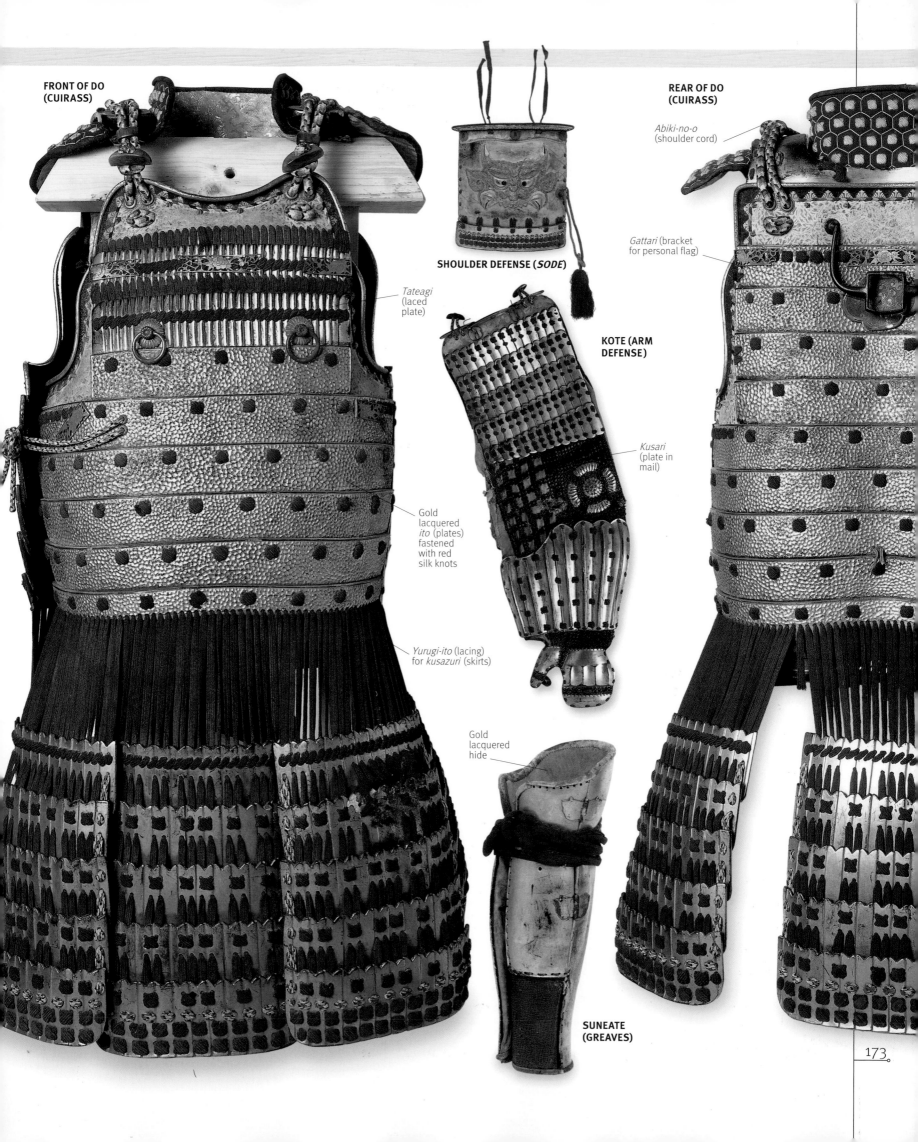

**FRONT OF DO
(CUIRASS)**

SHOULDER DEFENSE (*SODE*)

**REAR OF DO
(CUIRASS)**

Abiki-no-o
(shoulder cord)

Tateagi
(laced
plate)

**KOTE (ARM
DEFENSE)**

Gattari (bracket
for personal flag)

Kusari
(plate in
mail)

Gold
lacquered
ito (plates)
fastened
with red
silk knots

Yurugi-ito (lacing)
for *kusazuri* (skirts)

Gold
lacquered
hide

**SUNEATE
(GREAVES)**

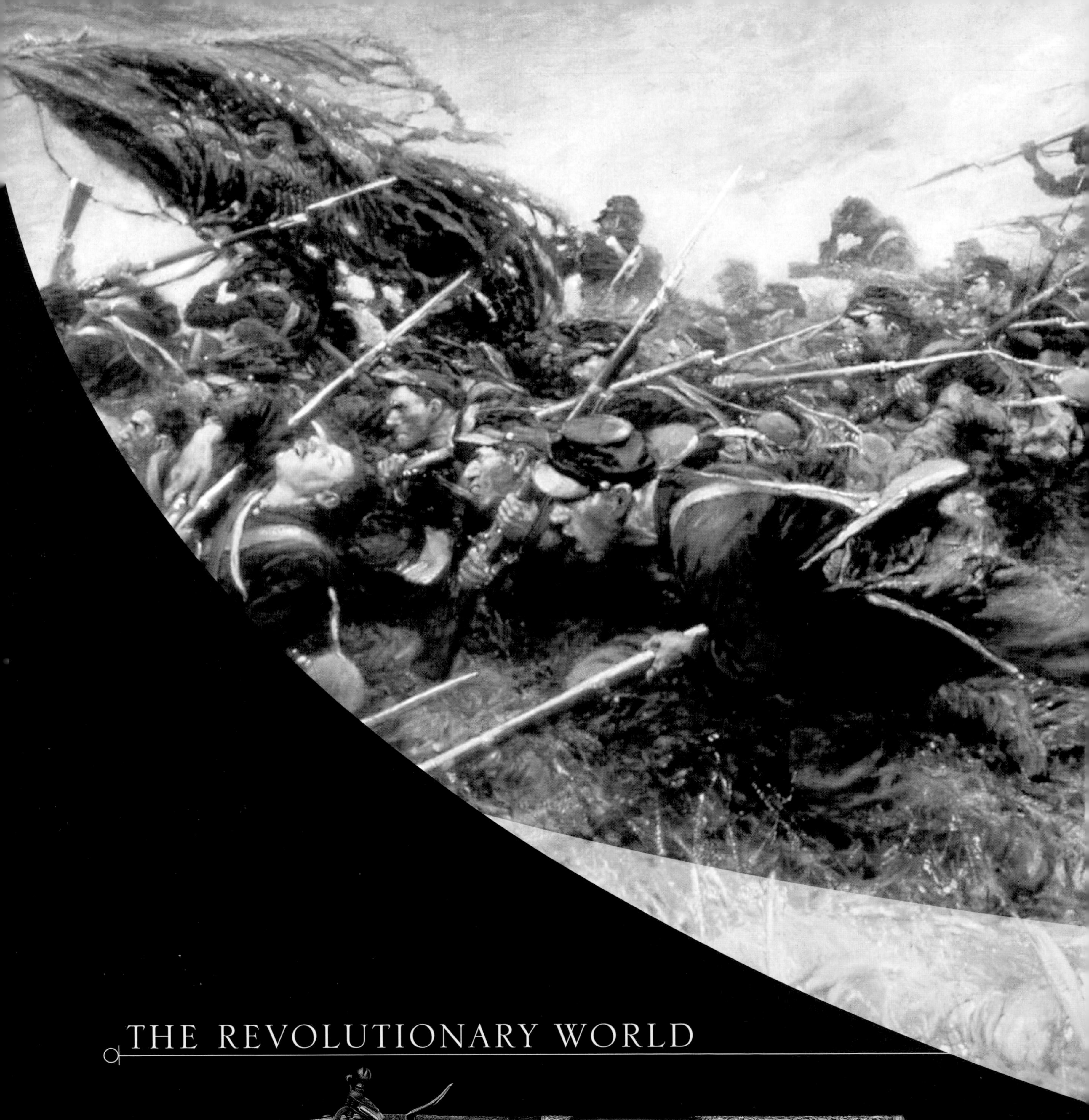

THE REVOLUTIONARY WORLD

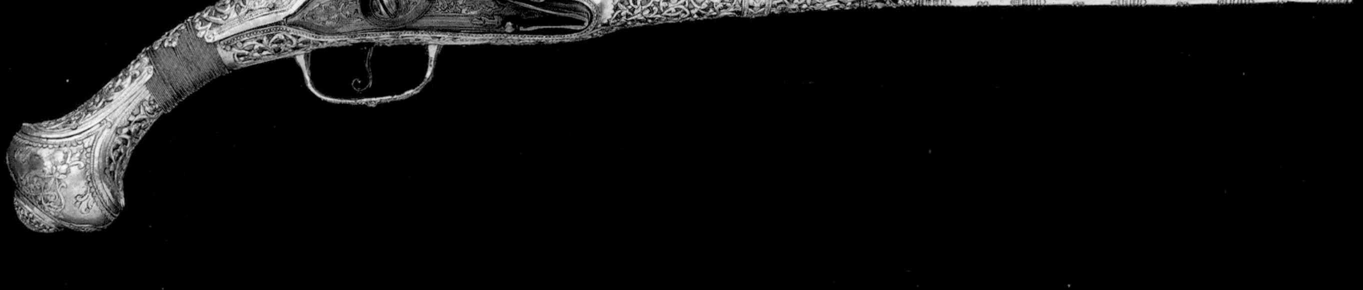

In 1770, Europe was ruled largely by dynastic sovereigns, who continued to conduct politics and fight wars much as they had done 200 years before. Yet over the next century, revolutions—both political and industrial—transformed the face of warfare, as new technologies, ideas of nationalism and democracy, and efficient bureaucracies gave ever more power to those who possessed them and reduced to political ciphers or colonies those who did not.

IRREGULAR WARFARE
The British underestimated the ability of their enemy's colonial militias during the American Revolution (1775–83). Here, Benedict Arnold—lying wounded—directs the assault on Bemis Heights in October 1777, with swords, rifles, and bayonets, which forced the British regulars to withdraw.

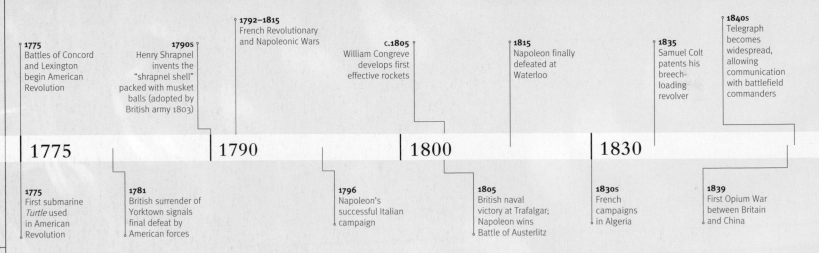

1775
Battles of Concord and Lexington begin American Revolution

1790s
Henry Shrapnel invents the "shrapnel shell" packed with musket balls (adopted by British army 1803)

1792–1815
French Revolutionary and Napoleonic Wars

c.1805
William Congreve develops first effective rockets

1815
Napoleon finally defeated at Waterloo

1835
Samuel Colt patents his breech-loading revolver

1840s
Telegraph becomes widespread, allowing communication with battlefield commanders

1775   1790   1800   1830

1775
First submarine *Turtle* used in American Revolution

1781
British surrender of Yorktown signals final defeat by American forces

1796
Napoleon's successful Italian campaign

1805
British naval victory at Trafalgar; Napoleon wins Battle of Austerlitz

1830s
French campaigns in Algeria

1839
First Opium War between Britain and China

BEGINNING WITH THE American Revolution, the traditional order was challenged, overthrown, and then, reconstituted. Britain fought a bitter war from 1775 to 1783 to retain its North American colonies, which demanded some share in their governance. George Washington, the commander of the rebel army, knew that he could not match the British in open battle. But the British depended on supplies reaching them by sea, and when French intervention in the war in 1778 hurt this, their control over North America became tenuous. The Americans became a fighting army with the help of Augustus von Steuben, a Prussian army officer, who devised a simplified drill for Washington's soldiers. The result was a humiliation for Britain and the loss of most of its North American colonies.

THE FRENCH REVOLUTIONARY WARS

Revolution broke out in France in 1789, in part provoked by anger at unemployment and high levels of taxation needed to fund the army, and Louis XVI's inability to do anything to remedy these problems. Most army officers fled the country, or at least resigned their commissions. By that time France was at war with Austria and so fewer experienced officers were available. Their replacements came from the middle and lower classes, so that by 1794, only one in 25 officers was a nobleman. A mass conscription in 1793 in effect, militarized France, as all men of military age were deemed to be in service. The new army adopted modified tactics—from 1792 skirmishers or sharpshooters were introduced into infantry battalions. These *tirailleurs* would harass enemy formations and screen the maneuvers of their parent battalions. A string of French Republican victories, most notably those of Napoleon Bonaparte in Italy from 1796, exhibited the new army's ability to use these revised combinations of line, column, and skirmishing tactics to great effect.

In the 1790s, the French army pioneered the use of the division, a self-contained unit of several regiments combining infantry, cavalry, and artillery. Napoleon took this further, establishing a system of army corps, each made up of several divisions. The corps system meant that parts of the French army, which "lived off the land" instead of relying on fixed supplies, could take separate routes to their objective, reducing the risk of exhausting the ability of the areas they marched through to support them. This flexibility and the speed of the French armies left Napoleon's enemies often seeming sluggish.

Napoleon also expanded the French artillery, and by 1805 the army had 4,500 heavy guns and 7,300 medium and light. A string of victories, most notably Marengo (1800) and Austerlitz (1805), left the successive coalitions formed against him reeling. Napoleon also realized the destruction of the enemy's field armies should be his main objective, rather than allowing himself to be delayed by protracted sieges.

Yet the strain on France's resources began to show. An estimated 20 percent of Frenchmen born between 1790 and 1795 died in the wars. Increasingly, Napoleon's soldiers were foreign, less well-trained and less motivated than the French. After 1808, divisions were standardized to two brigades, and the numbers of companies per battalion reduced to make command easier. The result was a less flexible force, and Napoleon's later battles tended to be elephantine affairs, with large masses of men hurled headlong against the enemy, and far fewer flashes of sheer brilliance. At Borodino, in the Russian

BATTLE OF THE NATIONS
French cuirassiers charge at the Battle of Leipzig in 1813. The sheer size of the force opposing him—at 365,000 men —was too much even for Napoleon. The situation was made worse by the fact that his army sorely missed the veterans who had perished in Russia the year before.

campaign of 1812, some 250,000 men fought on a narrow front just 5 miles (8 km) wide, leading to heavy losses on both sides.

ENGLISH TACTICS AGAINST NAPOLEON

During this period Napoleon's enemies, too, had learned and adapted their armies. The British experimented with light infantry from the 1790s, and in 1800 an experimental corps was set up armed with new rifled muskets, more accurate than the prevailing smooth-bores. The British favored line over column tactics and also paid more attention to logistics, not relying so consistently on foraging, which, in the guerrilla-infested hills of Spain, had badly failed the French forces. In 1813 the Prussians created regiments of Jäger, volunteer riflemen, as a riposte to the French *tirailleurs*. Attrition, the exhaustion of French resources, British naval superiority—most notably demonstrated at Trafalgar (1805)—and Napoleon's strategic greed led to his downfall in 1814, and his return from exile for the "Hundred Days" ended similarly in defeat at Waterloo in 1815.

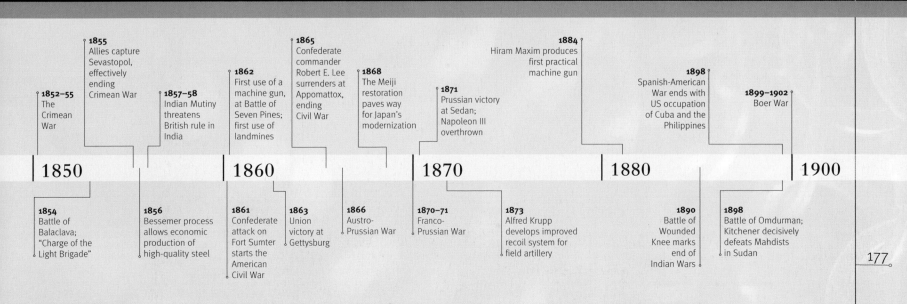

1852–55
The Crimean War

1854
Battle of Balaclava; "Charge of the Light Brigade"

1855
Allies capture Sevastopol, effectively ending Crimean War

1856
Bessemer process allows economic production of high-quality steel

1857–58
Indian Mutiny threatens British rule in India

1862
First use of a machine gun, at Battle of Seven Pines; first use of landmines

1861
Confederate attack on Fort Sumter starts the American Civil War

1865
Confederate commander Robert E. Lee surrenders at Appomattox, ending Civil War

1863
Union victory at Gettysburg

1868
The Meiji restoration paves way for Japan's modernization

1866
Austro-Prussian War

1871
Prussian victory at Sedan; Napoleon III overthrown

1870–71
Franco-Prussian War

1884
Hiram Maxim produces first practical machine gun

1873
Alfred Krupp develops improved recoil system for field artillery

1898
Spanish-American War ends with US occupation of Cuba and the Philippines

1890
Battle of Wounded Knee marks end of Indian Wars

1899–1902
Boer War

1898
Battle of Omdurman; Kitchener decisively defeats Mahdists in Sudan

1850   **1860**   **1870**   **1880**   **1900**

TRENCH WARFARE
The final stages of the American Civil War degenerated into a dogged campaign of entrenchment and siege. Here, Union soldiers wait in the trenches in front of the Confederate stronghold of Petersburg, Virginia.

TECHNICAL ADVANCES

The Congress of Vienna (1815) ensured no repetition of the revolutionary wars for several decades, and Europe relapsed into a sort of strategic slumber. Napoleonic drill and tactics were largely retained, but there were important technical advances, including the invention of the cylindro-conic bullet, which expanded on firing, gripping the rifling of the barrel more tightly, and doubled the effective range of firearms to around 440–650 yards (400–600 m). Adapted by Claude-Étienne Minié in 1849, the new rifles became the mainstays of European armies. The increasing firepower of troops, and the capacity of technologically advanced powers to produce large quantities of weapons that could be used even by raw conscripts, led to an increasing industrialization of warfare, in which it was the output of factories, the laying down of railroads, and strategic planning, rather than élan or tactical brilliance that delivered

victories. The new technology saw its first real test in the Crimean War (1853–55), in which Britain and France invaded Russia to prevent the tsar from picking bare the bones of the decrepit Ottoman empire. At Inkerman in 1854, British Enfield rifled muskets slaughtered the Russians, who suffered 12,000 casualties to the allies' 3,000. Yet the British neglected logistics this time—their supply base at Balaclava turned out to have a quayside of only 33 yards (30 m), and it was a 9-mile (15-km) journey to the front line. The campaign became bogged down in a bludgeoning siege of the fortress-city of Sevastopol, whose defensive trench networks presaged those of World War I.

THE AMERICAN CIVIL WAR

The American Civil War (1861–66) saw the full flowering of industrialized warfare. It was the North, which had over 70 percent of the undivided pre-war Union's population and almost all its industry—93 percent of pig-iron and 97 percent of firearms production—that possessed critical advantages from the outset. The South had brilliant generals, such as Robert E. Lee, and an army motivated by the desire to defend its way of life. Yet victories such as Bull Run (1861), and Fredericksburg (1862), and a near-run thing at Gettysburg (1863), amounted in the end to nothing. The Union commander Ulysses S. Grant realized that by cutting the Confederacy in two and destroying its fledgling industries and railroad system, its capacity to resist—no matter battlefield heroics—would be strangled. American Civil War soldiers could fire at a rate of five to six rounds per minute and extended lines proved more effective than the massed columns of Napoleonic warfare. Temporary earthwork entrenchments such as breastworks and rifle pits became more important, while the withering fire of Springfield rifled muskets meant that where infantry advanced unsupported in the open, as in "Pickett's Charge" at Gettysburg, they were simply mown down.

THE PRUSSIAN ARMY

In Europe, meanwhile, Prussia, under von Moltke—Chief of General Staff from 1858 —implemented a system of uniform education for all staff officers, and service in the army was extended to five years, so that by the late 1850s, the army had 504,000 troops (including reserves). The Prussians also invested heavily in railroads, laying down nearly 19,000 miles (30,000 km) by 1860. Their soldiers, moreover, were equipped with the Dreyse needle gun, a breech-loader which could be shot from a prone position, and which fired up to five times faster than muzzle-loaders. Although it was prone to misfire, the Dreyse gave the Prussians the edge on the battlefield and this, along with their superior planning, enabled them to win a crushing victory over the Austrians at Königgrätz in 1866, which freed Bismarck, the German Chancellor, to pursue his goal of a united German state.

The attempts by French emperor Napoleon III to interfere with Bismarck's ambitions led to the Franco-Prussian War (1870–71). The French were armed with the Chassepot rifle, a more reliable version of the Dreyse. The Prussians exploited their superior staff numbers to the full, and were able to deliver 380,000 men—in large part by train—rapidly to the frontier. They also possessed steel breech-loading cannons designed by Alfred Krupp, which had a range of up to 7,600 yards (7,000 m) and could devastate French formations as they formed up far from the battlefield. The French were outmaneuvered at a strategic level, and when their last operational field army was surrounded at Sedan (1871), its surrender spelled the end of Napoleon III's rule and any effective opposition to Bismarck's plans for Germany.

THE GROWTH OF EUROPEAN IMPERIALISM

Once Bismarck had forged a united country after 1871, he turned to acquiring an overseas empire, beginning with modern Namibia, Togo, and Tanzania in the 1880s. The late

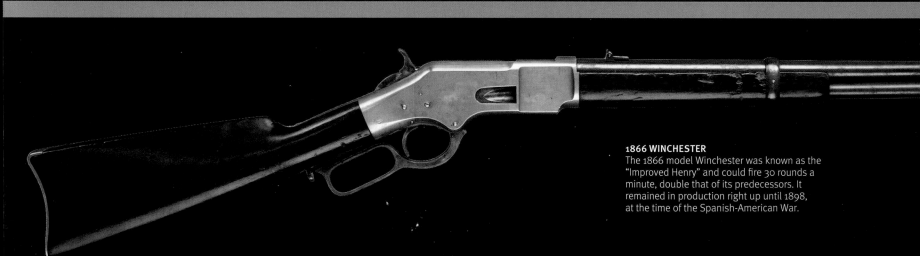

1866 WINCHESTER
The 1866 model Winchester was known as the "Improved Henry" and could fire 30 rounds a minute, double that of its predecessors. It remained in production right up until 1898, at the time of the Spanish-American War.

19th century was the high-point of European imperialism, which developed a momentum of its own far beyond the need to protect trading posts or suppress native opposition. Many of the wars fought in the last half of the century were imperial, in which Western technological superiority and organization normally proved decisive. At Omdurman in the Sudan in 1898, Kitchener, the British commander, simply deployed his 25,000 men in tight formation, and when the opposing Mahdists charged, they were scythed down by his Maxim machine guns: the Sudanese lost up to 30,000 men for the loss of only 50 of the Anglo-Egyptian force.

Non-European armies did, occasionally, emerge victorious. In 1896 the Italians were defeated at Adowa by an Ethiopian army armed with 100,000 rifles that the French governor of Somaliland had obligingly sold to them. Where native armies adopted guerrilla warfare, such as Samori Touré in West Africa in the 1880s and 1890s, European tactics struggled to overcome them. Eventually, however, even stubborn resistance was not enough. The Europeans or Americans had superior industrial and demographic resources, and could weather defeats their opponents could not.

Germany's victories in 1866 and 1870 led German statesmen and generals to believe that rapid deployment and the exploitation of technology should override all other concerns. At the end of the 19th century, European countries became embroiled in an arms race that was ruinously expensive and contributed to a chilling climate of mistrust in international diplomacy. The rapid growth of the German economy, unaccompanied by a corresponding increase in political sophistication, led to a dangerous alliance of economic power, nationalist agitation, and technological prowess, which, when a spark set it alight, would lead to the appalling carnage of World War I.

NATIONALISM

The French Revolution unleashed a political virus in Europe, with the notion that states should constitute the whole of a people or "nation." Hence, France was the nation of the French and should include all of them. Multiethnic empires, such as those of the Austrian Habsburgs or the Ottoman Turks, were threatened with extinction as this idea found political and military expression. In 1848, a wave of nationalist revolts burst across Europe, sweeping a revolutionary government to power in Hungary and threatening to overturn the Prussian and French regimes. In 1861 nationalism contributed to the unification of Italy—with Garibaldi (pictured here) playing a flamboyant role, and Germany in 1867. Similarly, nationalist feelings contributed to the decay of the Ottoman Empire, from the Greek declaration of independence in 1821. All these movements appealed to a national ideal, inspiring a fervor that loyalty to a dynasty, or remote imperial power, had almost never been able to do.

INSURRECTION IN 1861 AT PALERMO WHICH LED TO THE UNIFICATION OF ITALY

BOER PICKET
It cost the British two years, the despatch of 450,000 men, and 22,000 dead to win the Boer War (1899–1902). The Boers, armed with lethally effective Mausers, won a series of victories such as Spion Kop (1900). Even when their field armies were finally defeated, it took unconventional British tactics such as the use of concentration camps to force the last groups of guerrillas to surrender.

1775—1900

◄ 62–65 EUROPEAN SWORDS ◄ 104–107 EUROPEAN INFANTRY AND CAVALRY SWORDS ◄ 110–111 EUROPEAN RAPIERS ◄ 112–113 EUROPEAN SMALLSWORDS

THE REVOLUTIONARY WORLD

EUROPEAN SWORDS

BY THE TIME of the French Revolutionary (1789-1799) and Napoleonic Wars (1799-1815), cavalry edged weapons had evolved into the long, straight, thrusting sword of the heavy cavalry, and the light cavalry's curved saber that was designed for cutting and slicing. For the infantry, swords were already well on their way to becoming ceremonial weapons, but such was their status that they continued to be used as symbols of rank, carried by officers and senior NCOs. Having lost their practical function, infantry swords became increasingly decorative, some even harking back to weapons of the classical era.

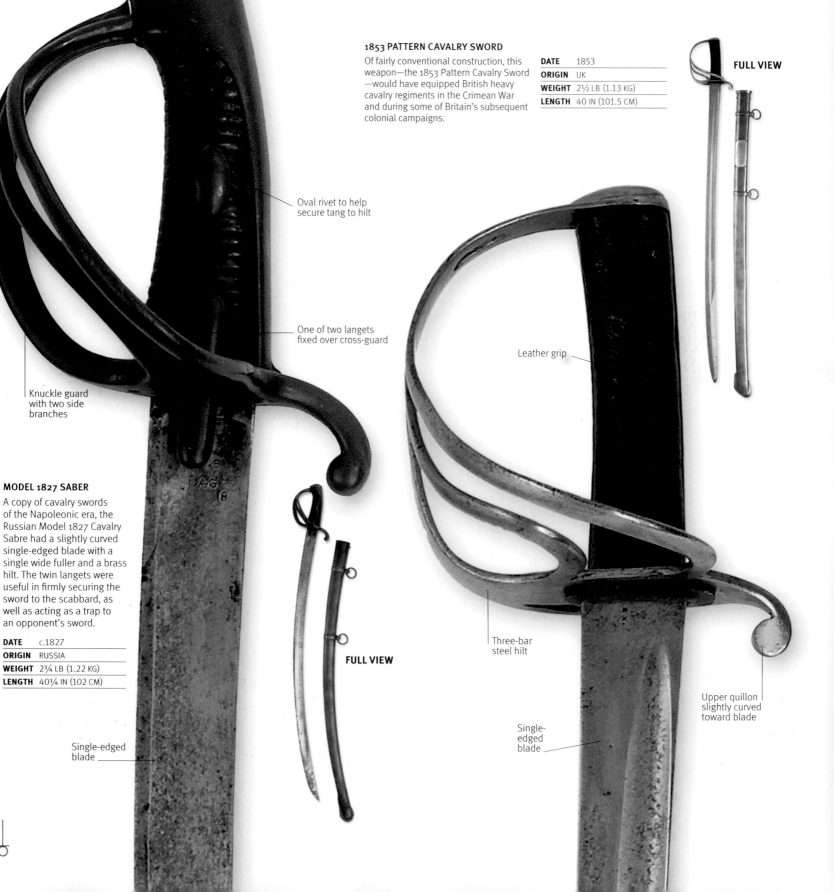

Brass pommel and back piece

Oval rivet to help secure tang to hilt

One of two langets fixed over cross-guard

Knuckle guard with two side branches

1853 PATTERN CAVALRY SWORD

Of fairly conventional construction, this weapon—the 1853 Pattern Cavalry Sword—would have equipped British heavy cavalry regiments in the Crimean War and during some of Britain's subsequent colonial campaigns.

DATE	1853
ORIGIN	UK
WEIGHT	2½ LB (1.13 KG)
LENGTH	40 IN (101.5 CM)

FULL VIEW

Leather grip

MODEL 1827 SABER

A copy of cavalry swords of the Napoleonic era, the Russian Model 1827 Cavalry Sabre had a slightly curved single-edged blade with a single wide fuller and a brass hilt. The twin langets were useful in firmly securing the sword to the scabbard, as well as acting as a trap to an opponent's sword.

DATE	c.1827
ORIGIN	RUSSIA
WEIGHT	2¾ LB (1.22 KG)
LENGTH	40¼ IN (102 CM)

FULL VIEW

Three-bar steel hilt

Single-edged blade

Upper quillon slightly curved toward blade

Single-edged blade

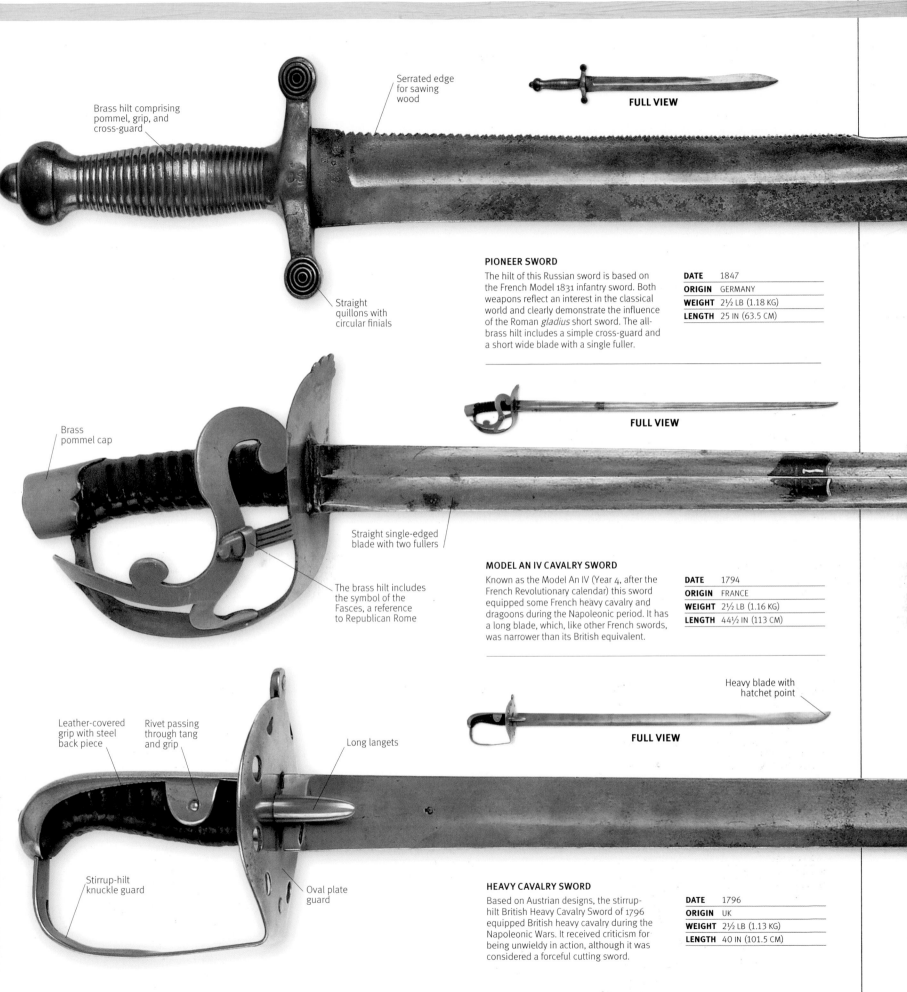

Brass hilt comprising pommel, grip, and cross-guard

Serrated edge for sawing wood

FULL VIEW

Straight quillons with circular finials

PIONEER SWORD

The hilt of this Russian sword is based on the French Model 1831 infantry sword. Both weapons reflect an interest in the classical world and clearly demonstrate the influence of the Roman *gladius* short sword. The all-brass hilt includes a simple cross-guard and a short wide blade with a single fuller.

DATE	1847
ORIGIN	GERMANY
WEIGHT	2½ LB (1.18 KG)
LENGTH	25 IN (63.5 CM)

Brass pommel cap

FULL VIEW

Straight single-edged blade with two fullers

The brass hilt includes the symbol of the Fasces, a reference to Republican Rome

MODEL AN IV CAVALRY SWORD

Known as the Model An IV (Year 4, after the French Revolutionary calendar) this sword equipped some French heavy cavalry and dragoons during the Napoleonic period. It has a long blade, which, like other French swords, was narrower than its British equivalent.

DATE	1794
ORIGIN	FRANCE
WEIGHT	2½ LB (1.16 KG)
LENGTH	44½ IN (113 CM)

Heavy blade with hatchet point

Leather-covered grip with steel back piece

Rivet passing through tang and grip

Long langets

FULL VIEW

Stirrup-hilt knuckle guard

Oval plate guard

HEAVY CAVALRY SWORD

Based on Austrian designs, the stirrup-hilt British Heavy Cavalry Sword of 1796 equipped British heavy cavalry during the Napoleonic Wars. It received criticism for being unwieldy in action, although it was considered a forceful cutting sword.

DATE	1796
ORIGIN	UK
WEIGHT	2½ LB (1.13 KG)
LENGTH	40 IN (101.5 CM)

EUROPEAN SWORDS

1796 LIGHT CAVALRY SWORD

Considered to be among the finest of cutting swords, the 1796 Light Cavalry Sword was developed in tandem with the Heavy Cavalry Sword. The broadening of the blade near the tip gave greater power at the point of impact.

DATE	1796
ORIGIN	UK
WEIGHT	2¼ LB (1 KG)
LENGTH	38 IN (96.5 CM)

D-shaped langets

Curved blade thicker at tip than hilt

Stirrup hilt

Wood-lined steel scabbard

NAPOLEONIC INFANTRY SWORD

Carried by the ordinary foot soldier during the Napoleonic Wars, this infantry hanger, known as a "briquet," has a simple, one-piece brass hilt and a curved steel blade. It was also issued to sailors.

DATE	EARLY 19TH CENTURY
ORIGIN	FRANCE
WEIGHT	2 LB (0.9 KG)
LENGTH	29 IN (74 CM)

Forward-facing quillon flowing from knuckle guard

Brass hilt

Curved steel blade

MODEL 1804 NAVAL CUTLASS

The British Model 1804 cutlass—issued a year before Trafalgar—is a utilitarian, straight-bladed weapon with a double disc guard and a serrated iron handle, painted black to protect against corrosion.

DATE	c.1804
ORIGIN	UK
WEIGHT	3 LB (1.32 KG)
LENGTH	33½ IN (85.5 CM)

Guard consisting of twin discs of thin iron, sometimes known as a "figure-of-eight" guard

Integrated cross-guard grip and pommel cast in bronze

Langet with Phrygian cap emblem—symbol of liberty in Revolutionary France

Decorative knuckle guard

Counter-guard quillon (too fragile to be effective)

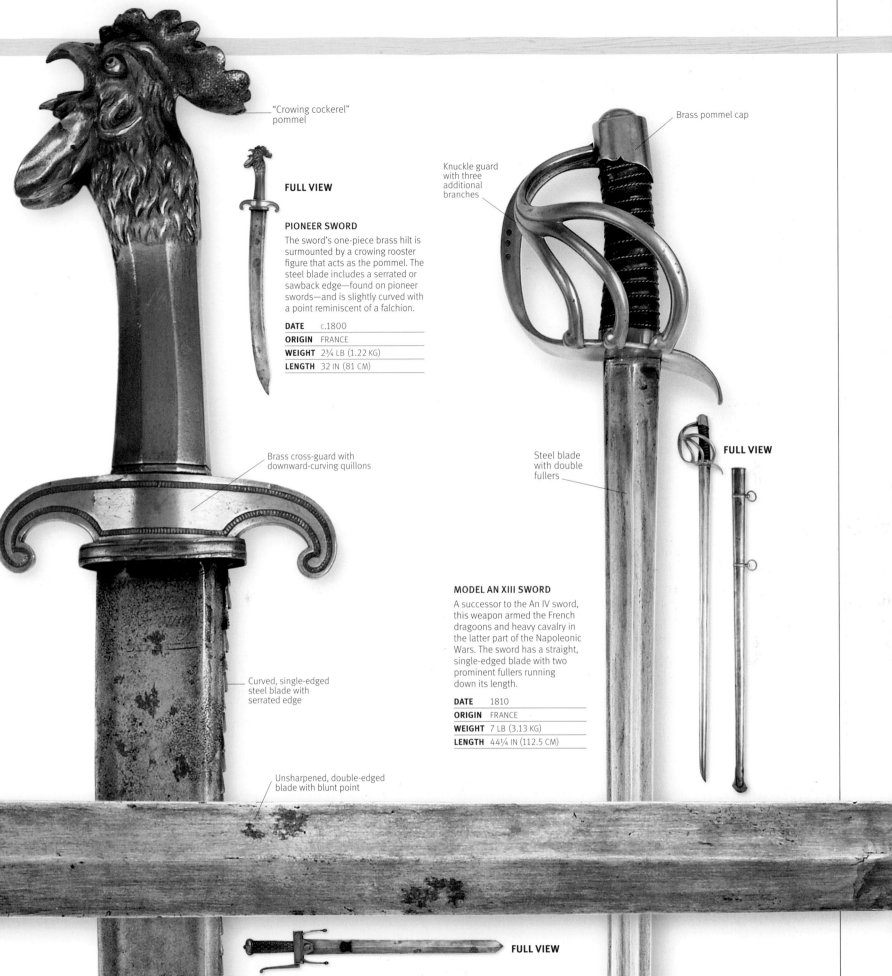

"Crowing cockerel" pommel

FULL VIEW

PIONEER SWORD

The sword's one-piece brass hilt is surmounted by a crowing rooster figure that acts as the pommel. The steel blade includes a serrated or sawback edge—found on pioneer swords—and is slightly curved with a point reminiscent of a falchion.

DATE	c.1800
ORIGIN	FRANCE
WEIGHT	2¾ LB (1.22 KG)
LENGTH	32 IN (81 CM)

Brass cross-guard with downward-curving quillons

Curved, single-edged steel blade with serrated edge

Unsharpened, double-edged blade with blunt point

Brass pommel cap

Knuckle guard with three additional branches

Steel blade with double fullers

FULL VIEW

MODEL AN XIII SWORD

A successor to the An IV sword, this weapon armed the French dragoons and heavy cavalry in the latter part of the Napoleonic Wars. The sword has a straight, single-edged blade with two prominent fullers running down its length.

DATE	1810
ORIGIN	FRANCE
WEIGHT	7 LB (3.13 KG)
LENGTH	44¼ IN (112.5 CM)

CEREMONIAL CADET SWORD

This ceremonial sword, designed by artist Jacques Louis David, followed the classical Roman model popular at the time, and was issued to students of the French military academy.

FULL VIEW

DATE	1794
ORIGIN	FRANCE
WEIGHT	2 LB (0.90 KG)
LENGTH	26½ IN (67 CM)

AMERICAN CIVIL WAR SWORDS

THE ARMORERS OF the new US Republic followed patterns for swordmaking from a mixture of German, French, and British sources. But from the 1840s onward, US swords were based almost exclusively on French designs, and it was these swords that armed the soldiers of the American Civil War (1861–65). While the forces of the Union North were well supplied with arms and equipment, the Confederate armies of the South were short of weapons of all kinds, including swords. They were forced to rely on captured Union stocks, foreign sources, and their own home-produced weapons.

Knuckle guard

Leather grip wrapped in twisted brass wire

Guard branches

Guard with the upper quillon swept forward

Leather grip wrapped in twisted brass wire

Engraved detail on brass hilt

Ricasso (unsharpened upper part of the sword)

MODEL 1850 "FOOT" OFFICER'S SWORD

This sword would have equipped officers on both sides during the Civil War, and was very similar to the Model 1850 "Mounted" Field and Staff Officer's Sword. Influenced by French patterns, this sword has a brass hilt and a grip made either from leather or the skin of a ray or shark—material which gave a very good grip. The single-edged blade is slightly curved.

DATE	c.1850
ORIGIN	US
WEIGHT	2 LB (1.13 KG)
LENGTH	31 IN (78.75 CM)

FULL VIEW

MODEL 1860 LIGHT CAVALRY SABER

The Model 1840 Light Cavalry Saber was a heavy, powerful sword whose weight made it unpopular with the troopers, who nicknamed it "Old Wrist Breaker." Its replacement, the Model 1860 Light Cavalry Saber, was not considered much of an improvement, although it was an effective thrusting and hacking weapon.

DATE	c.1860
ORIGIN	US
WEIGHT	3 LB (1.36 KG)
LENGTH	35 IN (90 CM)

FULL VIEW

MODEL 1850 INFANTRY SWORD

Edged weapons like this Model 1850 "Foot" Officer's Sword equipped the majority of infantry officers on the Union side. By the time of the American Civil War, officers would rarely have used a sword in actual combat, but such was its potency that it continued to be worn throughout the 19th century as a symbol of rank.

DATE	c.1850
ORIGIN	US
WEIGHT	2 LB (1.13 KG)
LENGTH	30 IN (76.8 CM)

FULL VIEW

Single-edged blade with sharpened "false edge"

"False edge"

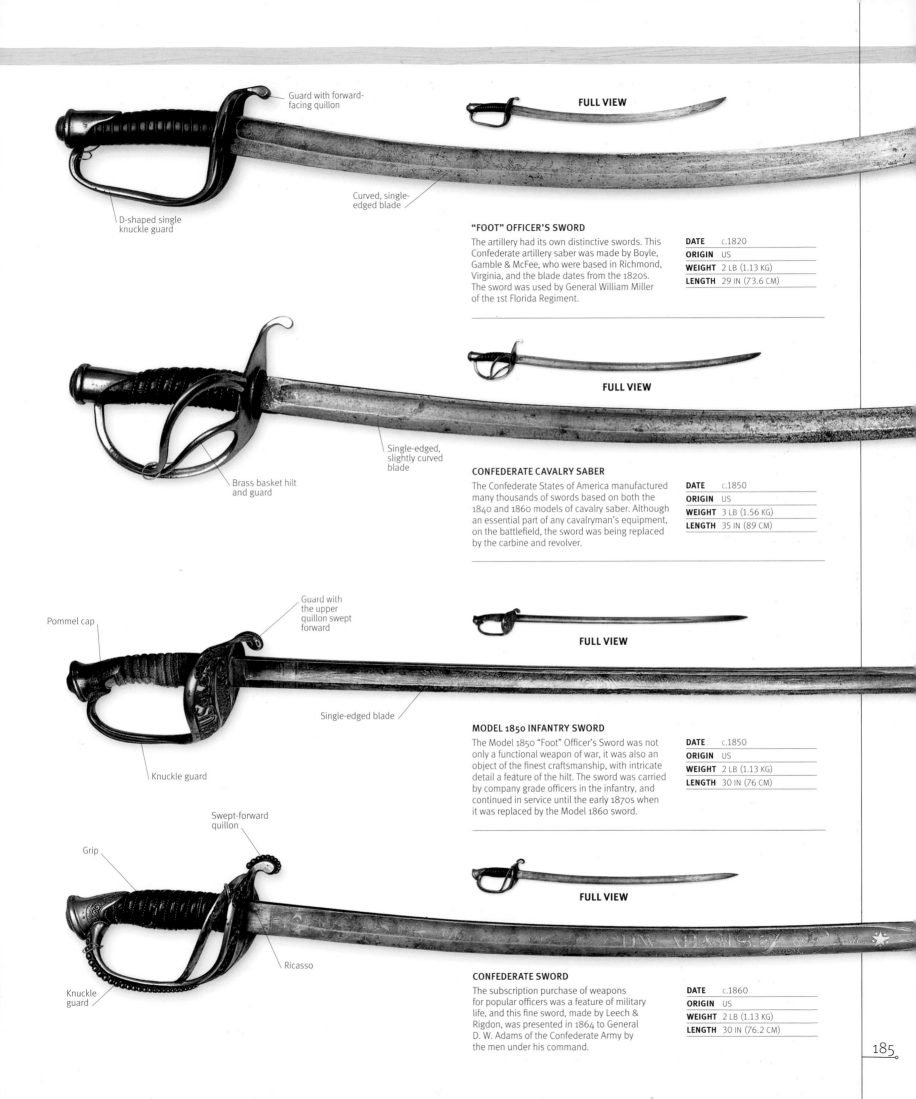

FULL VIEW

Guard with forward-
facing quillon

Curved, single-
edged blade

D-shaped single
knuckle guard

"FOOT" OFFICER'S SWORD

The artillery had its own distinctive swords. This
Confederate artillery saber was made by Boyle,
Gamble & McFee, who were based in Richmond,
Virginia, and the blade dates from the 1820s.
The sword was used by General William Miller
of the 1st Florida Regiment.

DATE	c.1820
ORIGIN	US
WEIGHT	2 LB (1.13 KG)
LENGTH	29 IN (73.6 CM)

FULL VIEW

Single-edged,
slightly curved
blade

Brass basket hilt
and guard

CONFEDERATE CAVALRY SABER

The Confederate States of America manufactured
many thousands of swords based on both the
1840 and 1860 models of cavalry saber. Although
an essential part of any cavalryman's equipment,
on the battlefield, the sword was being replaced
by the carbine and revolver.

DATE	c.1850
ORIGIN	US
WEIGHT	3 LB (1.56 KG)
LENGTH	35 IN (89 CM)

Pommel cap

Guard with
the upper
quillon swept
forward

FULL VIEW

Single-edged blade

Knuckle guard

MODEL 1850 INFANTRY SWORD

The Model 1850 "Foot" Officer's Sword was not
only a functional weapon of war, it was also an
object of the finest craftsmanship, with intricate
detail a feature of the hilt. The sword was carried
by company grade officers in the infantry, and
continued in service until the early 1870s when
it was replaced by the Model 1860 sword.

DATE	c.1850
ORIGIN	US
WEIGHT	2 LB (1.13 KG)
LENGTH	30 IN (76 CM)

Swept-forward
quillon

Grip

FULL VIEW

Ricasso

Knuckle
guard

CONFEDERATE SWORD

The subscription purchase of weapons
for popular officers was a feature of military
life, and this fine sword, made by Leech &
Rigdon, was presented in 1864 to General
D. W. Adams of the Confederate Army by
the men under his command.

DATE	c.1860
ORIGIN	US
WEIGHT	2 LB (1.13 KG)
LENGTH	30 IN (76.2 CM)

185

OTTOMAN EMPIRE SWORDS

THE OTTOMAN EMPIRE, at its height from the 15th to the 17th century, was founded by Turks who migrated to Anatolia from central Asia. Their curved swords reflect these origins, being derived from the central Asian Turko-Mongolian saber of the 13th century. Europeans encountered these curved blades in wars with the Ottomans, and collectively termed them "scimitars." Many of the swords shown here date from the 19th century, but they are typical of the Ottoman Empire at its peak. Similar weapons were used across the Islamic world, from North Africa to Persia and India.

Pistol-style hilt

Cross-guard terminates in finial

Grip decorated with precious stones

Intricate decoration at top of blade

Langet helps to attach blade to hilt more securely

PERSIAN KILIJ

Persian craftsmen were acknowledged masters of sword making. The *kilij* was first used in the Ottoman Empire in the 15th century. Over time, its blade showed many variations. This example has a deep curve cut away along its back edge, and flares into a *yelman* toward the point.

DATE	EARLY 19TH CENTURY
ORIGIN	PERSIA
WEIGHT	1¼ LB (0.6 KG)
LENGTH	32 IN (81 CM)

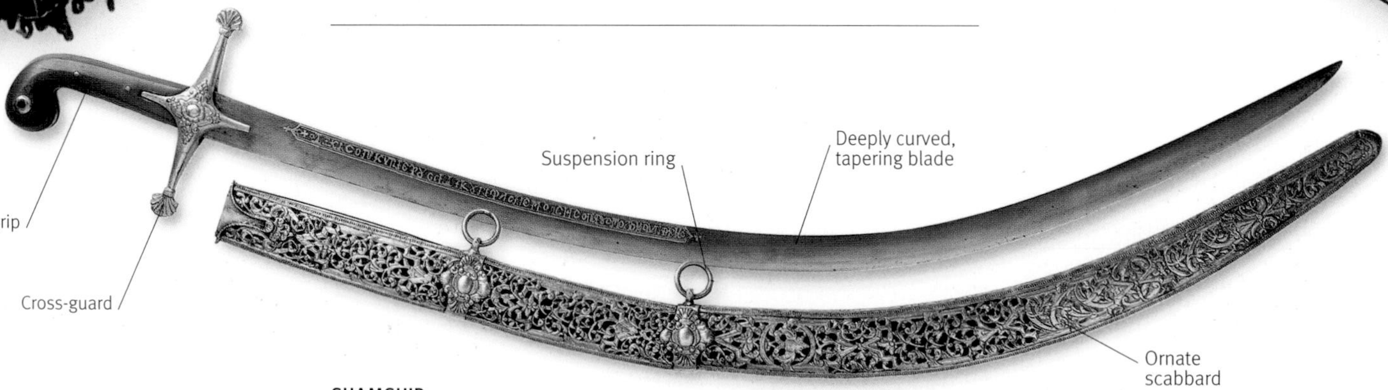

Pistol-style grip

Cross-guard

Suspension ring

Deeply curved, tapering blade

Ornate scabbard

SHAMSHIR

The form of saber known as a *shamshir* spread from Persia in the 16th century. Its blade had the curve of a *kilij*, but tapered to a point. It was a fearsome slashing weapon, whether used on foot or horseback. A horseman could also use the point to run an enemy foot soldier through.

DATE	EARLY 19TH CENTURY
ORIGIN	ARMENIA
WEIGHT	1½ LB (0.71 KG)
LENGTH	37 IN (94 CM)

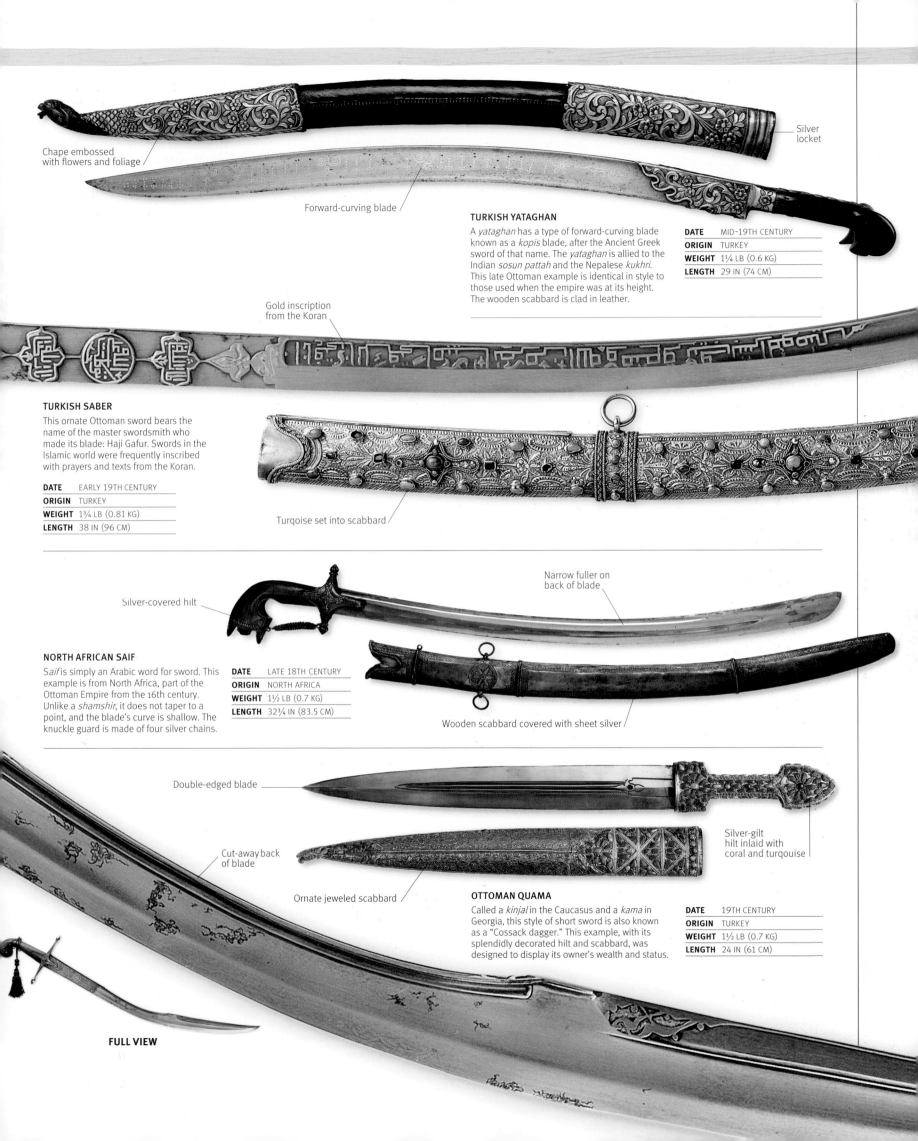

Chape embossed
with flowers and foliage

Silver
locket

Forward-curving blade

TURKISH YATAGHAN

A *yataghan* has a type of forward-curving blade
known as a *kopis* blade, after the Ancient Greek
sword of that name. The *yataghan* is allied to the
Indian *sosun pattah* and the Nepalese *kukhri*.
This late Ottoman example is identical in style to
those used when the empire was at its height.
The wooden scabbard is clad in leather.

DATE	MID-19TH CENTURY
ORIGIN	TURKEY
WEIGHT	1¼ LB (0.6 KG)
LENGTH	29 IN (74 CM)

Gold inscription
from the Koran

TURKISH SABER

This ornate Ottoman sword bears the
name of the master swordsmith who
made its blade: Haji Gafur. Swords in the
Islamic world were frequently inscribed
with prayers and texts from the Koran.

DATE	EARLY 19TH CENTURY
ORIGIN	TURKEY
WEIGHT	1¾ LB (0.81 KG)
LENGTH	38 IN (96 CM)

Turqoise set into scabbard

Narrow fuller on
back of blade

Silver-covered hilt

NORTH AFRICAN SAIF

Saif is simply an Arabic word for sword. This
example is from North Africa, part of the
Ottoman Empire from the 16th century.
Unlike a *shamshir*, it does not taper to a
point, and the blade's curve is shallow. The
knuckle guard is made of four silver chains.

DATE	LATE 18TH CENTURY
ORIGIN	NORTH AFRICA
WEIGHT	1½ LB (0.7 KG)
LENGTH	32¾ IN (83.5 CM)

Wooden scabbard covered with sheet silver

Double-edged blade

Cut-away back
of blade

Silver-gilt
hilt inlaid with
coral and turquoise

Ornate jeweled scabbard

OTTOMAN QUAMA

Called a *kinjal* in the Caucasus and a *kama* in
Georgia, this style of short sword is also known
as a "Cossack dagger." This example, with its
splendidly decorated hilt and scabbard, was
designed to display its owner's wealth and status.

DATE	19TH CENTURY
ORIGIN	TURKEY
WEIGHT	1½ LB (0.7 KG)
LENGTH	24 IN (61 CM)

FULL VIEW

1775—1900

◀ 66–67 JAPANESE AND CHINESE SWORDS ◀ 120–123 JAPANESE SAMURAI SWORDS ◀ 128–129 INDIAN AND SRI LANKAN SWORDS ▶ 190–191 INDIAN SWORDS

THE REVOLUTIONARY WORLD

CHINESE AND TIBETAN SWORDS

FOR THE CHINESE, the four major weapons of a fighting man were the staff, the spear, and two swords: the single-edged *dao* and the double-edged *jian*. While the straight-bladed *jian* was the more prestigious of the two sword types, the curved *dao* was more practical and easier to use. As in Europe, by the 19th century swords in China were becoming primarily ceremonial items. The military tradition of Tibet is often forgotten, but the Tibetans fought many wars and developed their own significant tradition of sword manufacture, which was loosely related to Chinese models.

Ring pommel

Guards with quillons

One- or two-handed grip

CHINESE DAO

Dating from the last century of the Ming dynasty, the single-edged, curved blade of this *dao* shows its affinity with Indian *talwars* and *shamshirs*, and with European sabers. The blade is of the form known as *liuyedao* (willow-leaf knife), with a longer, deeper curve than the *yanmaodao* (goose-quill knife), which can be seen below.

DATE	1572–1620
ORIGIN	CHINA
WEIGHT	3 LB (1.35 KG)
LENGTH	41½ IN (105.7 CM)

Curved hilt

Disc-shaped guard

Softer-steel back of blade

CHINESE DAO

This short *dao* has a near-straight *yanmaodao* blade. Primarily a cavalry weapon, its single edge was used for slashing, and its point for running through. The blade was layered, in a similar fashion to Japanese swords. The core of hard steel, which was exposed at the cutting edge, was sandwiched between layers of softer steel.

DATE	17TH CENTURY
ORIGIN	CHINA
WEIGHT	1¼ LB (0.52 KG)
LENGTH	25¼ IN (64 CM)

Pommel attached to tang of blade

Ivory grip

Lobed quillon block

Blade has diamond section, peaking at a ridge on each face

Gilded collar

Lacquered scabbard

FULL VIEW

CHINESE JIAN

With its straight, double-edged blade, the *jian* was the weapon chosen by Chinese swordsmen to show off their skills. It was also worn by high officials and officers as part of their ceremonial regalia. This *jian* sword dates from the reign of emperor Qianlong, of the Manchu Qing dynasty.

DATE	1736–95
ORIGIN	CHINA
WEIGHT	2¾ LB (1.25 KG)
LENGTH	42¼ IN (107.1 CM)

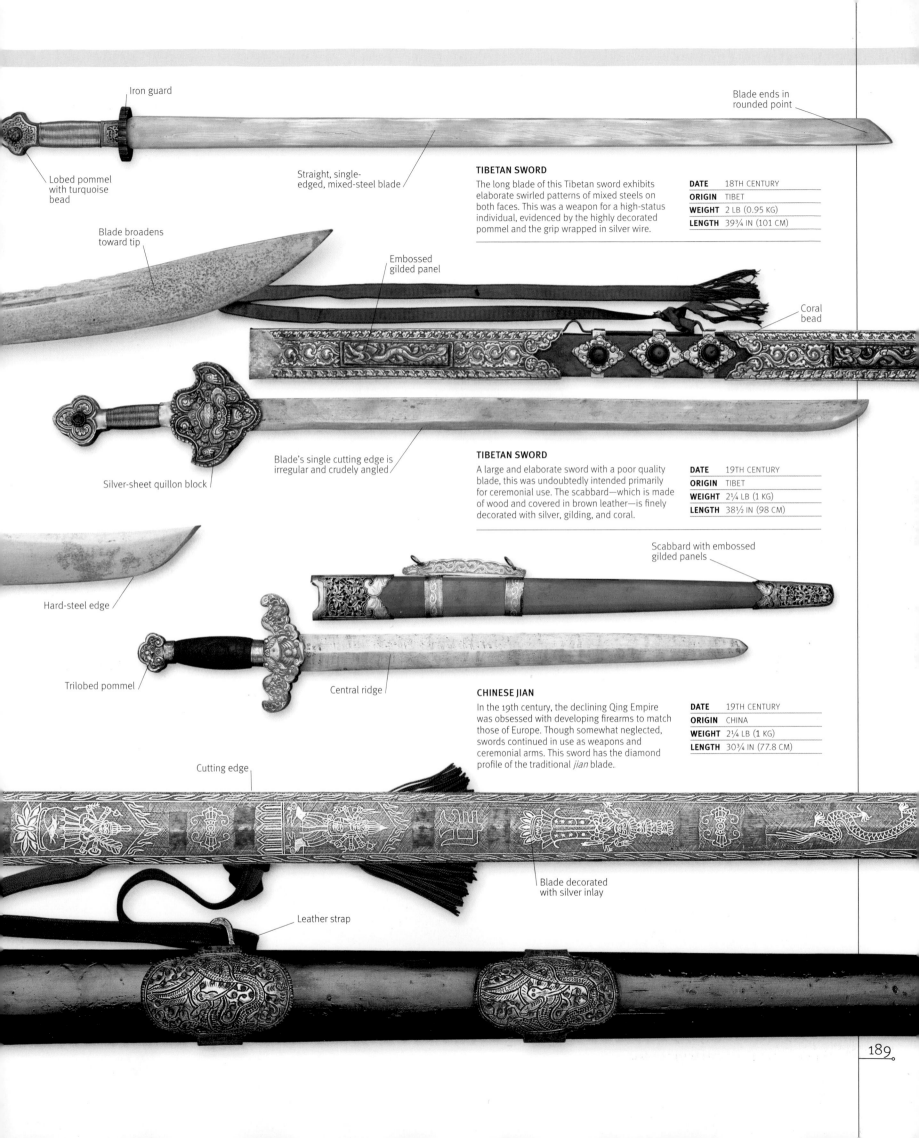

Iron guard

Blade ends in rounded point

Lobed pommel with turquoise bead

Straight, single-edged, mixed-steel blade

TIBETAN SWORD

The long blade of this Tibetan sword exhibits elaborate swirled patterns of mixed steels on both faces. This was a weapon for a high-status individual, evidenced by the highly decorated pommel and the grip wrapped in silver wire.

DATE	18TH CENTURY
ORIGIN	TIBET
WEIGHT	2 LB (0.95 KG)
LENGTH	39¾ IN (101 CM)

Blade broadens toward tip

Embossed gilded panel

Coral bead

Silver-sheet quillon block

Blade's single cutting edge is irregular and crudely angled

TIBETAN SWORD

A large and elaborate sword with a poor quality blade, this was undoubtedly intended primarily for ceremonial use. The scabbard—which is made of wood and covered in brown leather—is finely decorated with silver, gilding, and coral.

DATE	19TH CENTURY
ORIGIN	TIBET
WEIGHT	2¼ LB (1 KG)
LENGTH	38½ IN (98 CM)

Hard-steel edge

Scabbard with embossed gilded panels

Trilobed pommel

Central ridge

CHINESE JIAN

In the 19th century, the declining Qing Empire was obsessed with developing firearms to match those of Europe. Though somewhat neglected, swords continued in use as weapons and ceremonial arms. This sword has the diamond profile of the traditional *jian* blade.

DATE	19TH CENTURY
ORIGIN	CHINA
WEIGHT	2¼ LB (1 KG)
LENGTH	30¾ IN (77.8 CM)

Cutting edge

Blade decorated with silver inlay

Leather strap

1775—1900

◄ 120–123 JAPANESE SAMURAI SWORDS ◄ 128–129 INDIAN AND SRI LANKAN SWORDS ◄ 186–187 OTTOMAN EMPIRE SWORDS ◄ 188–189 CHINESE AND TIBETAN SWORDS

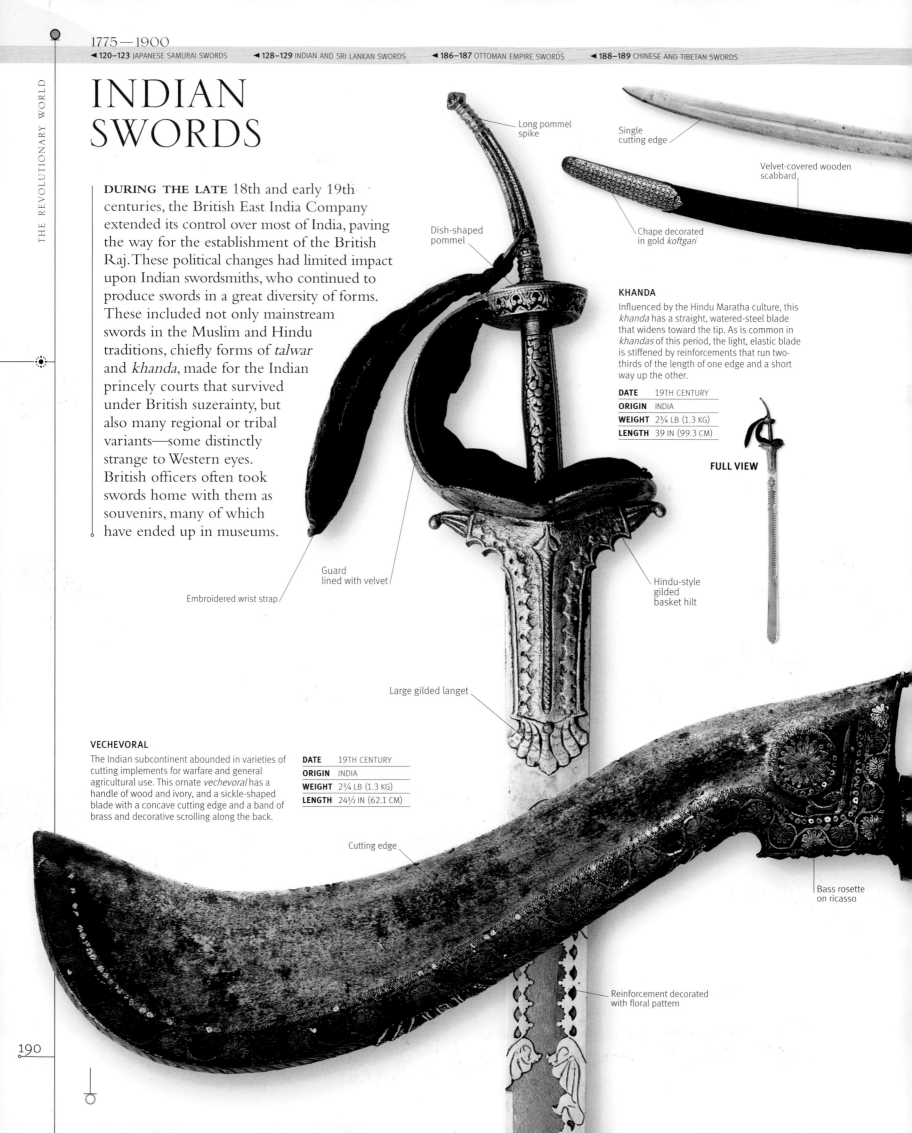

INDIAN SWORDS

DURING THE LATE 18th and early 19th centuries, the British East India Company extended its control over most of India, paving the way for the establishment of the British Raj. These political changes had limited impact upon Indian swordsmiths, who continued to produce swords in a great diversity of forms. These included not only mainstream swords in the Muslim and Hindu traditions, chiefly forms of *talwar* and *khanda*, made for the Indian princely courts that survived under British suzerainty, but also many regional or tribal variants—some distinctly strange to Western eyes. British officers often took swords home with them as souvenirs, many of which have ended up in museums.

Long pommel spike

Single cutting edge

Velvet-covered wooden scabbard

Dish-shaped pommel

Chape decorated in gold *koftgari*

KHANDA

Influenced by the Hindu Maratha culture, this *khanda* has a straight, watered-steel blade that widens toward the tip. As is common in *khandas* of this period, the light, elastic blade is stiffened by reinforcements that run two-thirds of the length of one edge and a short way up the other.

DATE	19TH CENTURY
ORIGIN	INDIA
WEIGHT	2¾ LB (1.3 KG)
LENGTH	39 IN (99.3 CM)

FULL VIEW

Guard lined with velvet

Embroidered wrist strap

Hindu-style gilded basket hilt

Large gilded langet

VECHEVORAL

The Indian subcontinent abounded in varieties of cutting implements for warfare and general agricultural use. This ornate *vechevoral* has a handle of wood and ivory, and a sickle-shaped blade with a concave cutting edge and a band of brass and decorative scrolling along the back.

DATE	19TH CENTURY
ORIGIN	INDIA
WEIGHT	2¾ LB (1.3 KG)
LENGTH	24½ IN (62.1 CM)

Cutting edge

Bass rosette on ricasso

Reinforcement decorated with floral pattern

THE REVOLUTIONARY WORLD

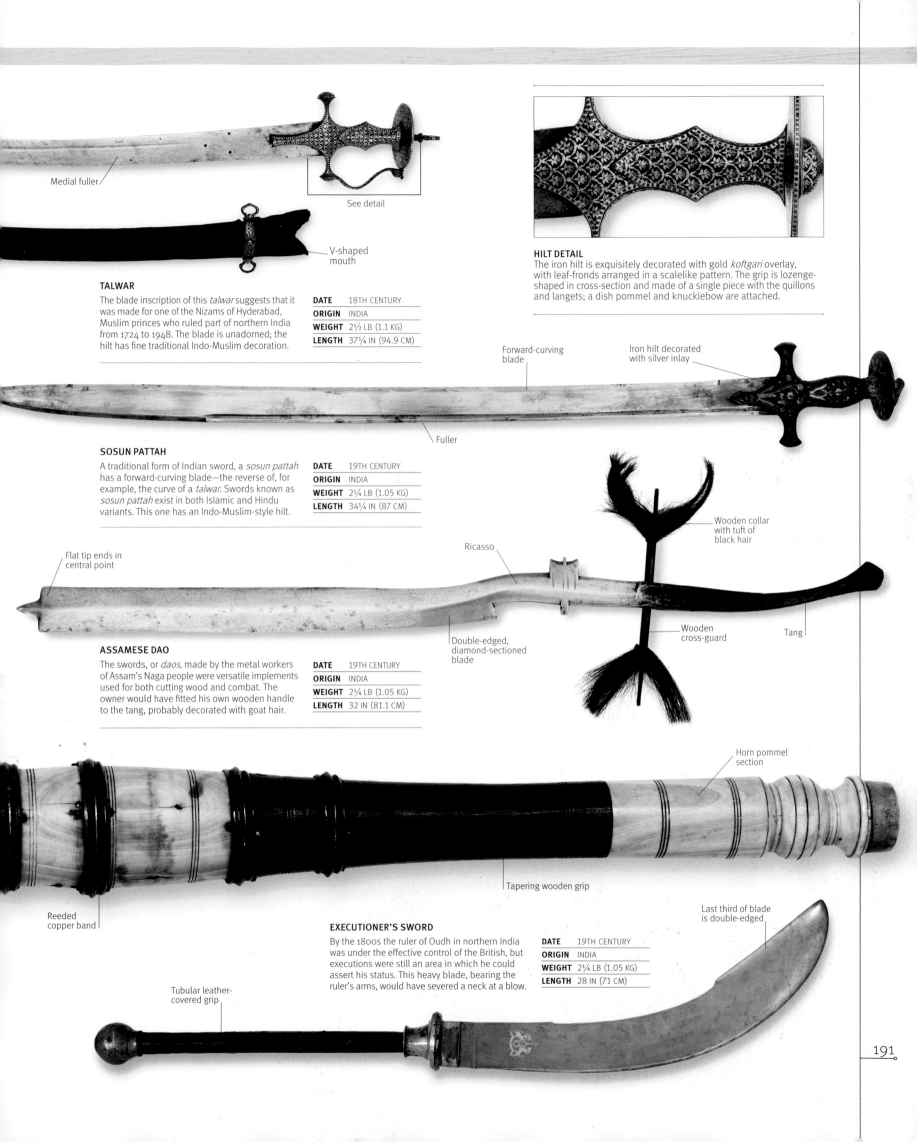

Medial fuller

See detail

V-shaped
mouth

TALWAR

The blade inscription of this *talwar* suggests that it
was made for one of the Nizams of Hyderabad,
Muslim princes who ruled part of northern India
from 1724 to 1948. The blade is unadorned; the
hilt has fine traditional Indo-Muslim decoration.

DATE	18TH CENTURY
ORIGIN	INDIA
WEIGHT	2½ LB (1.1 KG)
LENGTH	37¼ IN (94.9 CM)

HILT DETAIL

The iron hilt is exquisitely decorated with gold *koftgari* overlay,
with leaf-fronds arranged in a scalelike pattern. The grip is lozenge-
shaped in cross-section and made of a single piece with the quillons
and langets; a dish pommel and knucklebow are attached.

Forward-curving
blade

Iron hilt decorated
with silver inlay

Fuller

SOSUN PATTAH

A traditional form of Indian sword, a *sosun pattah*
has a forward-curving blade—the reverse of, for
example, the curve of a *talwar*. Swords known as
sosun pattah exist in both Islamic and Hindu
variants. This one has an Indo-Muslim-style hilt.

DATE	19TH CENTURY
ORIGIN	INDIA
WEIGHT	2¼ LB (1.05 KG)
LENGTH	34¼ IN (87 CM)

Wooden collar
with tuft of
black hair

Flat tip ends in
central point

Ricasso

Wooden
cross-guard

Tang

Double-edged,
diamond-sectioned
blade

ASSAMESE DAO

The swords, or *daos*, made by the metal workers
of Assam's Naga people were versatile implements
used for both cutting wood and combat. The
owner would have fitted his own wooden handle
to the tang, probably decorated with goat hair.

DATE	19TH CENTURY
ORIGIN	INDIA
WEIGHT	2¼ LB (1.05 KG)
LENGTH	32 IN (81.1 CM)

Horn pommel
section

Tapering wooden grip

Reeded
copper band

Last third of blade
is double-edged

EXECUTIONER'S SWORD

By the 1800s the ruler of Oudh in northern India
was under the effective control of the British, but
executions were still an area in which he could
assert his status. This heavy blade, bearing the
ruler's arms, would have severed a neck at a blow.

DATE	19TH CENTURY
ORIGIN	INDIA
WEIGHT	2¼ LB (1.05 KG)
LENGTH	28 IN (71 CM)

Tubular leather-
covered grip

INDIAN AND NEPALESE DAGGERS

THE INDIAN SUBCONTINENT is the source of some of the world's most effective and original melee weapons. These include a range of fearsome sharp-pointed knives with double-curved blades and various forms of fist dagger, which allowed the user to deliver a stabbing blow to an enemy with a punching movement. Parrying sticks were a feature that Indian armies had in common with African tribal forces. Nepal made its contribution with the very effective *kukri*, an implement with many practical non-military uses, as well its role as the weapon carried by all Nepalese Gurkhas.

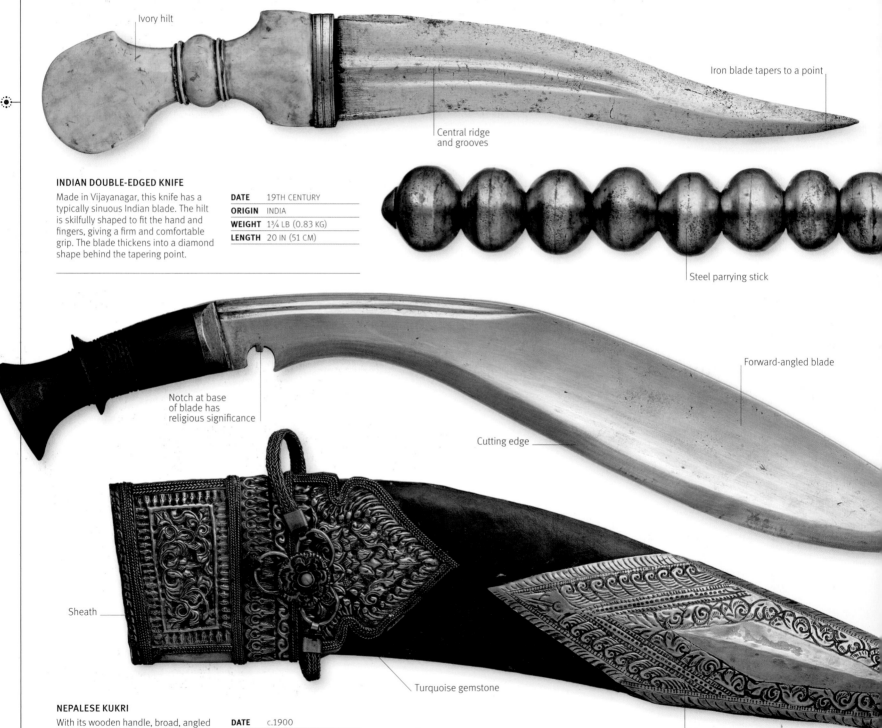

Ivory hilt

Iron blade tapers to a point

Central ridge and grooves

INDIAN DOUBLE-EDGED KNIFE

Made in Vijayanagar, this knife has a typically sinuous Indian blade. The hilt is skilfully shaped to fit the hand and fingers, giving a firm and comfortable grip. The blade thickens into a diamond shape behind the tapering point.

DATE	19TH CENTURY
ORIGIN	INDIA
WEIGHT	1¾ LB (0.83 KG)
LENGTH	20 IN (51 CM)

Steel parrying stick

Notch at base of blade has religious significance

Forward-angled blade

Cutting edge

Sheath

Turquoise gemstone

Silver decoration

NEPALESE KUKRI

With its wooden handle, broad, angled blade, and notch or *cho*, this is a typical example of the Nepalese Gurkhas' *kukri*. The *cho* has religious significance as the symbol of the destructive Hindu god Shiva. The quality of the sheath suggests this was the property of a wealthy man.

DATE	c.1900
ORIGIN	NEPAL
WEIGHT	1 LB (0.48 KG)
LENGTH	17½ IN (44.5 CM)

Double-curved
steel blade

Diamond
cross-section
at point

INDIAN BICH'HWA

The name of this dagger derives from
bichwa—a scorpion—whose deadly sting
the blade is presumed to resemble. The
four *bagh nakh* or tiger's claws, attached
to the steel rings on the handle, offer an
alternative mode of attack.

DATE	c.1900
ORIGIN	INDIA
WEIGHT	½ LB (0.3 KG)
LENGTH	12 IN (30.5 CM)

Steel ring
with claw

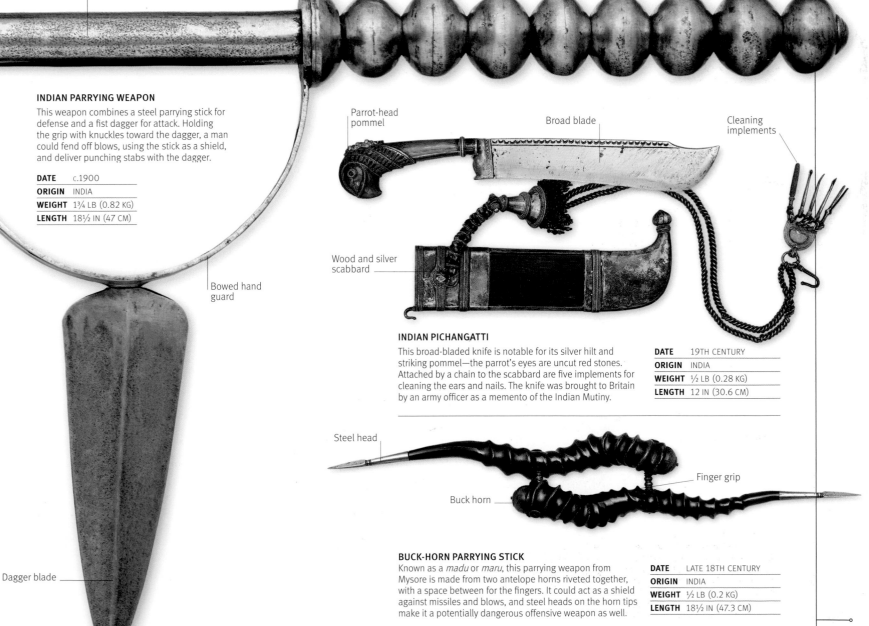

Central grip

INDIAN PARRYING WEAPON

This weapon combines a steel parrying stick for
defense and a fist dagger for attack. Holding
the grip with knuckles toward the dagger, a man
could fend off blows, using the stick as a shield,
and deliver punching stabs with the dagger.

DATE	c.1900
ORIGIN	INDIA
WEIGHT	1¾ LB (0.82 KG)
LENGTH	18½ IN (47 CM)

Bowed hand
guard

Dagger blade

Parrot-head
pommel

Broad blade

Cleaning
implements

Wood and silver
scabbard

INDIAN PICHANGATTI

This broad-bladed knife is notable for its silver hilt and
striking pommel—the parrot's eyes are uncut red stones.
Attached by a chain to the scabbard are five implements for
cleaning the ears and nails. The knife was brought to Britain
by an army officer as a memento of the Indian Mutiny.

DATE	19TH CENTURY
ORIGIN	INDIA
WEIGHT	½ LB (0.28 KG)
LENGTH	12 IN (30.6 CM)

Steel head

Finger grip

Buck horn

BUCK-HORN PARRYING STICK

Known as a *madu* or *maru*, this parrying weapon from
Mysore is made from two antelope horns riveted together,
with a space between for the fingers. It could act as a shield
against missiles and blows, and steel heads on the horn tips
make it a potentially dangerous offensive weapon as well.

DATE	LATE 18TH CENTURY
ORIGIN	INDIA
WEIGHT	½ LB (0.2 KG)
LENGTH	18½ IN (47.3 CM)

EUROPEAN AND AMERICAN BAYONETS

THE SWORD BAYONET with its long blade, became increasingly popular in the 19th century, replacing the hanger sword and socket bayonet of the ordinary infantryman. But the 19th century also saw the development of mass-produced, long-range firepower that rendered the bayonet irrelevant as a military weapon. Despite this, armies continued to place great emphasis on the bayonet, not least because it was believed to encourage an aggressive, offensive spirit among the infantry. It was this attitude that, in part, led to the mass slaughters of 1914, where soldiers, with bayonets fixed, were pitted against quick-firing artillery and machine guns.

Leather grip — Straight quillon

Knuckle guard — Muzzle ring with fore sight slot

VOLUNTEER INFANTRY SWORD BAYONET

During the Napoleonic Wars, the regular British Army was equipped with the Baker rifle and its sword bayonet; volunteer units, however, had to draw upon other sources for their rifles and bayonets. This sword bayonet was made for the London gunmaker Staudenmayer and features a gilded hilt and straight steel blade. Its use of the knuckle grip to lock the rifle to the bayonet proved less effective than the mortise slot and muzzle ring of the Baker rifle/bayonet, and it was this latter system that continued to set the pattern for most bayonet attachments.

DATE	1810
ORIGIN	UK
WEIGHT	1¾ LB (0.50 KG)
LENGTH	30½ IN (77.5 CM)

Brass pommel with press stud — Muzzle ring — Twin fullers

Hilt comprising D-ring and two branches

SWORD BAYONET

This French sword bayonet is unusual in having a basket hilt that was usually associated with a cavalry sword. The long, narrow blade has twin fullers running down the length of the blade to strengthen it.

DATE	MID 19TH CENTURY
ORIGIN	FRANCE
WEIGHT	1¾ LB (0.79 KG)
LENGTH	45½ IN (115.5 CM)

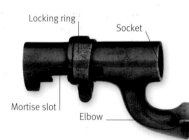

Locking ring

Socket

Mortise slot

Elbow

Brass handle

Locking-bolt spring — Tang stud — Muzzle ring with locking screw

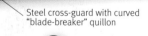

Steel cross-guard with curved "blade-breaker" quillon

CHASSEPOT BAYONET

This bayonet was designed for the famous Chassepot breech-loading rifle that armed the French during the Franco-Prussian War of 1870–71, and which continued in service until the arrival of the 1874 model. The distinctive "Yataghan" recurved blade influenced designs throughout Europe and the United States.

DATE	1866–74
ORIGIN	FRANCE
WEIGHT	1¾ LB (0.76 KG)
LENGTH	27½ IN (70 CM)

BAYONET CHARGE

Prussian troops (left) attack French lines during a battle in the Napoleonic Wars, August 27, 1813. The bayonet charge was much beloved of military painters of the 19th century, although they were rare occurrences in practice.

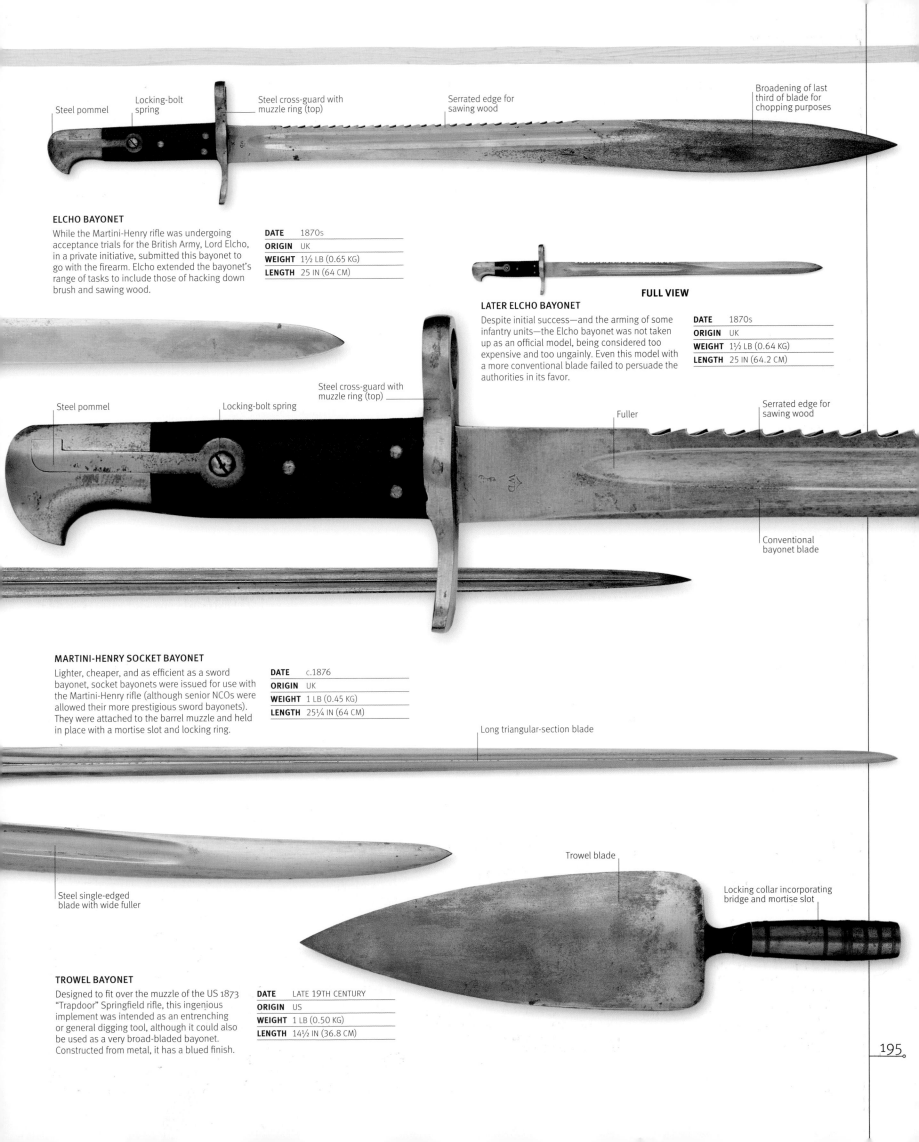

ELCHO BAYONET

While the Martini-Henry rifle was undergoing acceptance trials for the British Army, Lord Elcho, in a private initiative, submitted this bayonet to go with the firearm. Elcho extended the bayonet's range of tasks to include those of hacking down brush and sawing wood.

DATE	1870s
ORIGIN	UK
WEIGHT	1½ LB (0.65 KG)
LENGTH	25 IN (64 CM)

Steel pommel

Locking-bolt spring

Steel cross-guard with muzzle ring (top)

Serrated edge for sawing wood

Broadening of last third of blade for chopping purposes

FULL VIEW

LATER ELCHO BAYONET

Despite initial success—and the arming of some infantry units—the Elcho bayonet was not taken up as an official model, being considered too expensive and too ungainly. Even this model with a more conventional blade failed to persuade the authorities in its favor.

DATE	1870s
ORIGIN	UK
WEIGHT	1½ LB (0.64 KG)
LENGTH	25 IN (64.2 CM)

Steel pommel

Locking-bolt spring

Steel cross-guard with muzzle ring (top)

Fuller

Serrated edge for sawing wood

Conventional bayonet blade

MARTINI-HENRY SOCKET BAYONET

Lighter, cheaper, and as efficient as a sword bayonet, socket bayonets were issued for use with the Martini-Henry rifle (although senior NCOs were allowed their more prestigious sword bayonets). They were attached to the barrel muzzle and held in place with a mortise slot and locking ring.

DATE	c.1876
ORIGIN	UK
WEIGHT	1 LB (0.45 KG)
LENGTH	25¼ IN (64 CM)

Long triangular-section blade

Steel single-edged blade with wide fuller

Trowel blade

Locking collar incorporating bridge and mortise slot

TROWEL BAYONET

Designed to fit over the muzzle of the US 1873 "Trapdoor" Springfield rifle, this ingenious implement was intended as an entrenching or general digging tool, although it could also be used as a very broad-bladed bayonet. Constructed from metal, it has a blued finish.

DATE	LATE 19TH CENTURY
ORIGIN	US
WEIGHT	1 LB (0.50 KG)
LENGTH	14½ IN (36.8 CM)

INDIAN STAFF WEAPONS

THE DOMINATION OF INDIA by British forces in the late 18th and 19th centuries, armed at first with muskets and later with rifles, rendered staff weapons increasingly obsolete on the subcontinent. To be effective, Indian armies had to deploy artillery and firearms. Traditional varieties of battle-ax and mace continued to be found in the armouries of Hindu and Muslim princes, and among the weaponry of tribal peoples. Many of these weapons were more ceremonial than practical, their elaborate decoration being an indicator of their owner's wealth and status. They also proved attractive to European collectors of exotic weaponry.

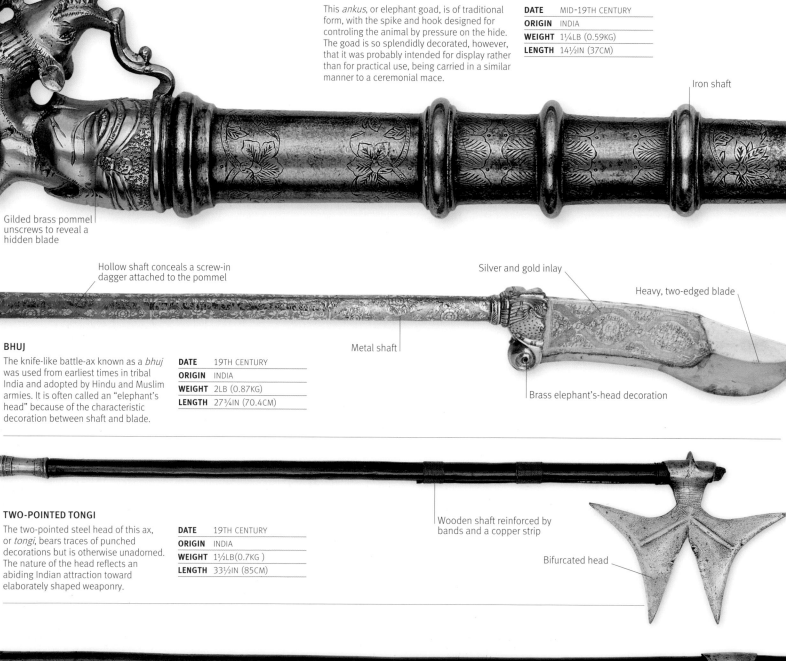

Decoration shows long-tongued beast emerging from tiger's mouth

Gilded brass pommel unscrews to reveal a hidden blade

Hollow shaft conceals a screw-in dagger attached to the pommel

Iron shaft

Silver and gold inlay

Heavy, two-edged blade

Metal shaft

Brass elephant's-head decoration

Wooden shaft reinforced by bands and a copper strip

Bifurcated head

Shaft of polished wood

Four-pointed blade

ANKUS

This *ankus*, or elephant goad, is of traditional form, with the spike and hook designed for controling the animal by pressure on the hide. The goad is so splendidly decorated, however, that it was probably intended for display rather than for practical use, being carried in a similar manner to a ceremonial mace.

DATE	MID-19TH CENTURY
ORIGIN	INDIA
WEIGHT	1¼LB (0.59KG)
LENGTH	14½IN (37CM)

BHUJ

The knife-like battle-ax known as a *bhuj* was used from earliest times in tribal India and adopted by Hindu and Muslim armies. It is often called an "elephant's head" because of the characteristic decoration between shaft and blade.

DATE	19TH CENTURY
ORIGIN	INDIA
WEIGHT	2LB (0.87KG)
LENGTH	27¾IN (70.4CM)

TWO-POINTED TONGI

The two-pointed steel head of this ax, or *tongi*, bears traces of punched decorations but is otherwise unadorned. The nature of the head reflects an abiding Indian attraction toward elaborately shaped weaponry.

DATE	19TH CENTURY
ORIGIN	INDIA
WEIGHT	1½LB(0.7KG)
LENGTH	33½IN (85CM)

FOUR-POINTED TONGI

Broadly similar to the two-pointed axe above, this *tongi* has a steel head that diverges into four points. This is a basic and functional weapon, possibly used by a member of the Dravidian Khond tribes.

DATE	19TH CENTURY
ORIGIN	INDIA
WEIGHT	0.5KG (1LB)
LENGTH	95CM (37½IN)

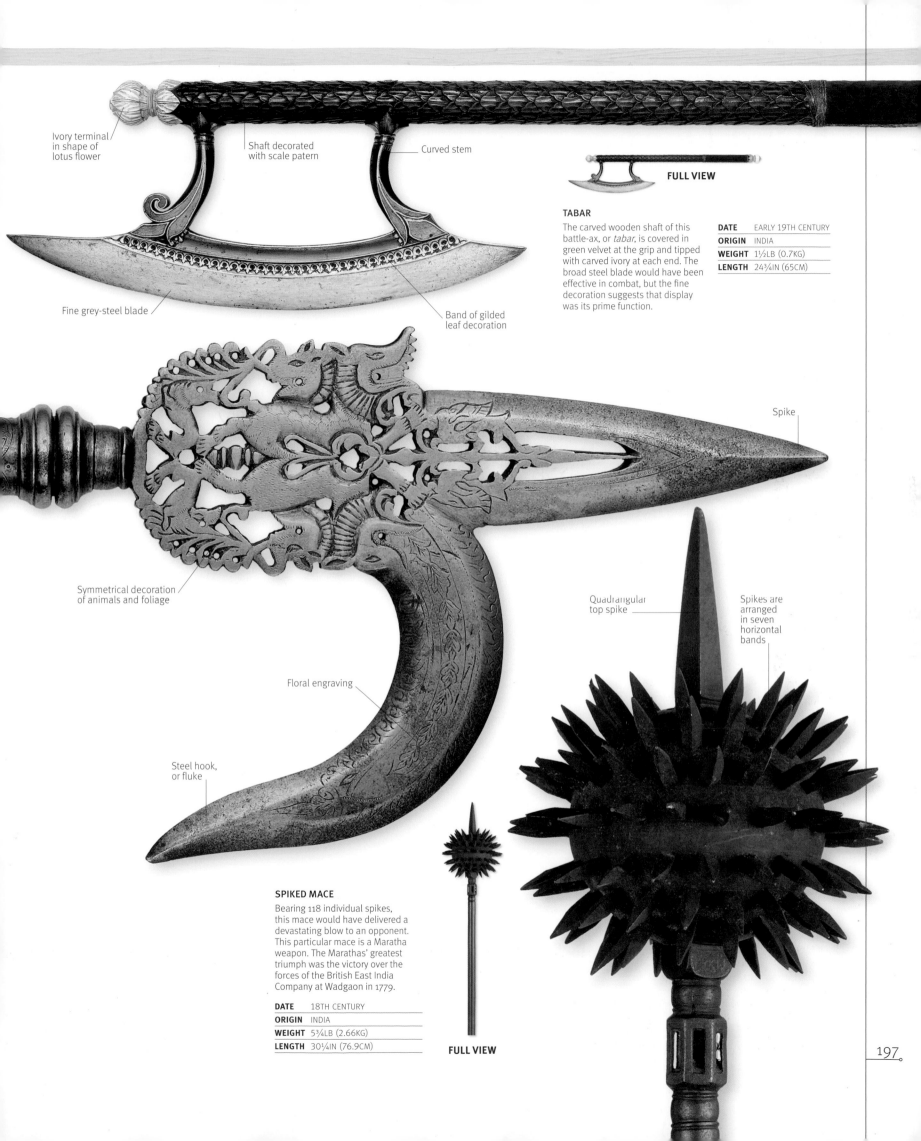

Ivory terminal in shape of lotus flower

Shaft decorated with scale patern

Curved stem

FULL VIEW

TABAR

The carved wooden shaft of this battle-ax, or *tabar*, is covered in green velvet at the grip and tipped with carved ivory at each end. The broad steel blade would have been effective in combat, but the fine decoration suggests that display was its prime function.

DATE	EARLY 19TH CENTURY
ORIGIN	INDIA
WEIGHT	1½LB (0.7KG)
LENGTH	24¾IN (65CM)

Fine grey-steel blade

Band of gilded leaf decoration

Spike

Symmetrical decoration of animals and foliage

Floral engraving

Steel hook, or fluke

Quadrangular top spike

Spikes are arranged in seven horizontal bands

SPIKED MACE

Bearing 118 individual spikes, this mace would have delivered a devastating blow to an opponent. This particular mace is a Maratha weapon. The Marathas' greatest triumph was the victory over the forces of the British East India Company at Wadgaon in 1779.

DATE	18TH CENTURY
ORIGIN	INDIA
WEIGHT	5¾LB (2.66KG)
LENGTH	30¼IN (76.9CM)

FULL VIEW

AFRICAN EDGED WEAPONS

AT THE END OF THE 18TH CENTURY Europeans were an influence only at the coastal margins of Africa. African states and tribal societies carried on traditional forms of warfare, despite the presence of imported firearms. By 1900 European colonial powers had carved up the continent between them, but even then most Africans were still largely unaffected by European ideas and technology. Traditional forms of weaponry were being made well into the 20th century, with African metalworkers displaying their skills in the forging of blades and heads for missile weapons.

RIVAL TRIBES IN ETHIOPIA
This European engraver's impression of tribes at war in southern Ethiopia was not based on any first-hand knowledge of their weaponry or fighting techniques. The sword has the look of an Islamic scimitar.

Copper-sheathed handle

Openwork iron blade

CONGOLESE AX
This is a ceremonial ax of a kind often carried by chiefs of the Songye people of southeastern Congo. The axes were made by the Nsapo subgroup, who were skilled at working iron and copper.

DATE	c.1900
ORIGIN	DEM. REP. OF CONGO
WEIGHT	3 LB (1.35 KG)
LENGTH	16¾ IN (42.8 CM)

Shaped metal eye

Metal collar

Patterned metal blade

Club head in form of animal head

Lizard-skin grip

Wooden handle

Iron barb

Iron binding

Multi-barbed arrowhead

Cane shaft

SUDANESE ARROWS

Tribal warfare in Sudan consisted of rushing forward to discharge arrows at the enemy from some 165 ft (50 m) range, then retreating to avoid arrows fired in reply. The multiple barbs on the arrowheads made them very difficult to extract from a wound.

DATE	TOP: c.1900	**DATE**	BOTTOM: c.1900
ORIGIN	SUDAN	**ORIGIN**	SUDAN
WEIGHT	1 OZ (28 G)	**WEIGHT**	1 OZ (28 G)
LENGTH	24 IN (61 CM)	**LENGTH**	26 IN (66 CM)

Covering of hide

Leaf-shaped blade

Tapering copper spearhead

Shaft wrapped in woven wire

FULL VIEW

FIGHTING PICK

This unusual fighting pick from West Africa has a barbed metal point with a tang inserted into a wooden shaft. The roughened skin of a monitor lizard has been used to improve the grip on the handle.

DATE	c. 1900
ORIGIN	GHANA
WEIGHT	1½ LB (0.65 KG)
LENGTH	20 IN (51 CM)

Barbed metal point

AFRICAN SPEARS

In tribal warfare, spears were almost always used as missile weapons, thrown in skirmishes where warriors avoided close combat. They might serve to finish off enemies wounded by arrows and unable to flee.

DATE	TOP: c.1900	**DATE**	BOTTOM: c.1900
ORIGIN	SUDAN	**ORIGIN**	AFRICA
WEIGHT	2½ LB (1.15 KG)	**WEIGHT**	1 LB (0.45 KG)
LENGTH	105 IN (267 CM)	**LENGTH**	48 IN (122 CM)

Polished wooden handle

AX CLUB

This decorative, highly-polished ax club was probably made in the West African kingdom of Dahomey. The weapon's metal blade is blunt, perhaps because it was for ceremonial use. A powerful slave-trading state during the 18th and 19th centuries, Dahomey was conquered by France in the 1890s.

DATE	c.1900
ORIGIN	DAHOMEY
WEIGHT	¾ LB (0.39 KG)
LENGTH	17¾ IN (45 CM)

BROAD-BLADED STABBING SPEAR

ZULU WARRIOR

THE ZULU OF SOUTHERN AFRICA, were transformed into a formidable military force under paramount chief Shaka from 1816 to 1828. Victories over neighboring peoples created an extensive Zulu empire that came into conflict with European settlers. Defeat by the British in 1879 brought Zulu ascendancy to an end, but not before allowing the Zulu warriors to display their fighting qualities against a modern European army.

DISCIPLINED FIGHTERS

The Zulu military system was based on the close bonding of unmarried men grouped by age. Brought together in a barracks when around 18 to 20 years old, they developed a strong identity as a "regiment" marked by a distinctive color of shield and details of ceremonial furs and feathers. They remained in service until the age of 40, when they were allowed to retire and marry. The Zulu warrior's main equipment was the heavy stabbing spear and large cowhide shield. Zulu also carried throwing spears, clubs, and latterly firearms—although these they used poorly.

Moving barefoot across country without supplies, foraging for food, their army was preceded by scouts and skirmishers who provided intelligence and masked their movements. Their attack formation consisted of an encircling movement from both flanks—the "horns"—a "chest" directly confronting the enemy center, and a reserve force in the rear, the "loins." Warriors advanced toward the enemy in loose order at a steady jog, taking full advantage of any cover. Once within range, they would loose their throwing spears or a volley from their firearms and then make a last rapid dash upon the enemy position, armed with stabbing spear and shield. If successful, they always sought to slaughter their enemy to the last man, taking no prisoners. Despite the use of magic potions to guarantee their safety, the Zulu were unable for long to sustain the heavy losses inflicted by British breech-loading rifles.

PHYSICAL PROWESS
Young Zulu warriors were extremely fit and hardy. When at war, they were expected to travel barefoot at around 20 miles (32 km) a day, twice the speed achieved by the British Army at that time.

Iziku necklaces —the Zulu equivalent of war medals

Each regiment had its own unique identifying feature —either headress or jewelry

Heavy broad-bladed stabbing spear

Range of clubs

BRITISH OFFICERS MEETING WITH CHIEFS UNDER SHAKA IN 1824

SHAKA

Paramount chief Shaka (1787–1828) transformed Zulu warriors into a potent military machine. Before his day, warfare was conducted through the largely ineffectual use of throwing spears and ritual combat between individual warriors. Shaka initiated war to the death. In ten years, through a series of exterminatory campaigns known as the *mfecane* ("crushing"), he created a large empire, killing possibly as many as 2 million in the process. His cruelty was also turned upon his own people, with thousands killed in mass executions. Shaka was assassinated by his half-brothers in 1828, but the empire he had created lasted another half century.

DRESSED TO KILL
A Zulu warrior's war dress was a stripped-down version of the full regalia worn for tribal ceremonies, but could still make elaborate use of cow's tails and feathers. This warrior carries a selection of throwing spears as well as his principal weapon, the large-bladed stabbing spear.

BATTLE OF ISANDHLWANA
The Zulus' most impressive victory over the British occurred at Isandhlwana in January 1879. The British force, over 1,600 strong, was overtaken by a surprise Zulu attack at 8 a.m., although the Zulu also suffered heavy losses. Six whole companies of the British 24th Foot Regiment totaling 602 men, later known as the South Wales Borderers, were wiped out to a man.

"WE KILLED EVERY WHITE MAN LEFT IN THE CAMP AND THE HORSES AND CATTLE TOO."

ZULU WARRIOR GUMPEGA KWABE ON MASSACRE OF BRITISH AT NTOMBE RIVER, MARCH 1879

TOOLS OF COMBAT

COWHIDE SHIELD

DECORATED CLUB

STABBING SPEAR

OCEANIAN CLUBS AND DAGGERS

THE POLYNESIANS AND other peoples who occupied the islands of the Pacific before the arrival of Europeans in the 17th century, were much given to warfare. They engaged in forms of combat ranging from revenge raids and ritualized skirmishing, to wars of conquest and extermination. Their weaponry was limited, consisting largely of wooden clubs, cleavers, daggers, and spears, sometimes edged with sharpened bone, shell, coral, stone, or obsidian. Weapons were intricately decorated, and often held as objects of religious significance and valued as heirlooms.

Patterned handle

Carved geometric design

Head of club broadens into diamond shape

TONGAN CLUB

This heavy club from Tonga is carved along its length with geometric patterns, human figures, animals, and fish. Holding the handle with both hands, a warrior could bring the diamond-shaped head down on an enemy's skull in a crushing blow. The sharp corners would have been very effective on focusing the mass of the weapon at its point of impact.

DATE	19TH CENTURY
ORIGIN	TONGA
WEIGHT	2¾ LB (1.3 KG)
LENGTH	32¼ IN (82 CM)

FULL VIEW

Cylindrical handle

MELANESIAN CLUB

This highly polished wooden club comes from one of the islands of Vanuatu. It has a stylized human face carved on each side of the head, a form of decoration that is quite frequently found on clubs in various parts of Oceania. The eyes are picked out with red beads and white shells. The club's cylindrical handle, ending in a circular butt, is quite long, but overall the club is relatively light in weight.

DATE	19TH CENTURY
ORIGIN	VANUATU
WEIGHT	1¼ LB (0.6 KG)
LENGTH	32 IN (82 CM)

FULL VIEW

Plain wooden handle

POLYNESIAN "CUTLASS"

The shape of this weapon, either a club or a cleaver, is most unusual, perhaps modeled on the cutlasses that were carried by European sailors. The Polynesian craftsman has blended that exotic shape with intricate indigenous carving—triangular sections and geometric motifs—that covers the head of the weapon.

DATE	19TH CENTURY
ORIGIN	POLYNESIA
WEIGHT	3¼ LB (1.5 KG)
LENGTH	30½ IN (77.5 CM)

Club swells to spatula shape

Pommel carved with human faces

DAGGER WITH OBSIDIAN BLADE

This dagger is from the Admiralty Islands, off New Guinea, where the volcanic glass obsidian occurs naturally. The Melanesians discovered how to flake obsidian to a razor-sharp edge. The blade of this dagger is flat on one side and raised to a ridge on the other. The pointed wooden handle is decorated with designs characteristic of this region.

DATE	c.1900
ORIGIN	PAPUA NEW GUINEA
WEIGHT	2 OZ (60 G)
LENGTH	11 IN (28 CM)

Handle painted
with red ocher

Obsidian blade
flaked to a point

Central ridge on
obsidian spearhead

Carved human figure

Remains of
wooden shaft

Characteristic
local design

Red bead and shell

OBSIDIAN SPEARHEAD

Like the dagger above, this spear was made by the Melanesian people of the Admiralty Islands. The obsidian has been flaked to make a spearhead with sharp edges and a point. The head is flat on one side and ridged on the other. Only part of the ocher-painted, decorated wooden shaft remains. It is fixed to the obsidian head with resin.

DATE	c.1900
ORIGIN	PAPUA NEW GUINEA
WEIGHT	½ LB (0.22 KG)
LENGTH	15 IN (38 CM)

Face carved
into head of club

Haliotis shell

Decorative carving

Head carved with
geometric motifs

MAORI PATUKI

The Maori, Polynesians who colonized New Zealand around 1000 BCE, were among the most warlike of Pacific peoples. This two-edged club, known as a *patuki*, comes from New Zealand's North Island and may have been taken as plunder by the British after their victory in the Maori War of 1860–69. It is decorated with iridescent haliotis shells, as well as elaborate carvings.

DATE	c.1860
ORIGIN	NEW ZEALAND
WEIGHT	¾ LB (0.31 KG)
LENGTH	14½ IN (37 CM)

NORTH AMERICAN KNIVES AND CLUBS

ALTHOUGH WOOD AND stone implements remained in use, by the late 18th century Native Americans were employing edged weapons with metal blades or heads. They were major purchasers of European and Euro-American manufactured edged tools and weapons, which they often customized with decorative motifs. Most of the items shown here were not primarily designed for combat, having a range of practical or symbolic uses.

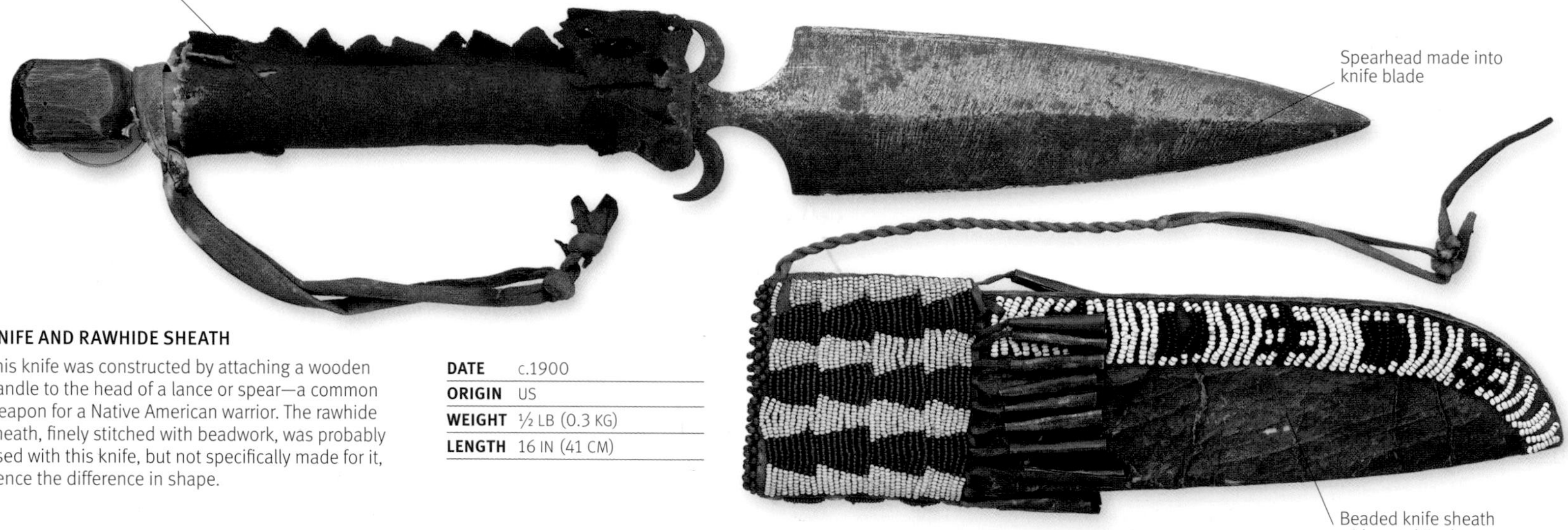

Wooden handle covered with red cloth

Spearhead made into knife blade

KNIFE AND RAWHIDE SHEATH

This knife was constructed by attaching a wooden handle to the head of a lance or spear—a common weapon for a Native American warrior. The rawhide sheath, finely stitched with beadwork, was probably used with this knife, but not specifically made for it, hence the difference in shape.

DATE	c.1900
ORIGIN	US
WEIGHT	½ LB (0.3 KG)
LENGTH	16 IN (41 CM)

Beaded knife sheath with metal jingles

Single-edged iron blade

Handle of animal horn

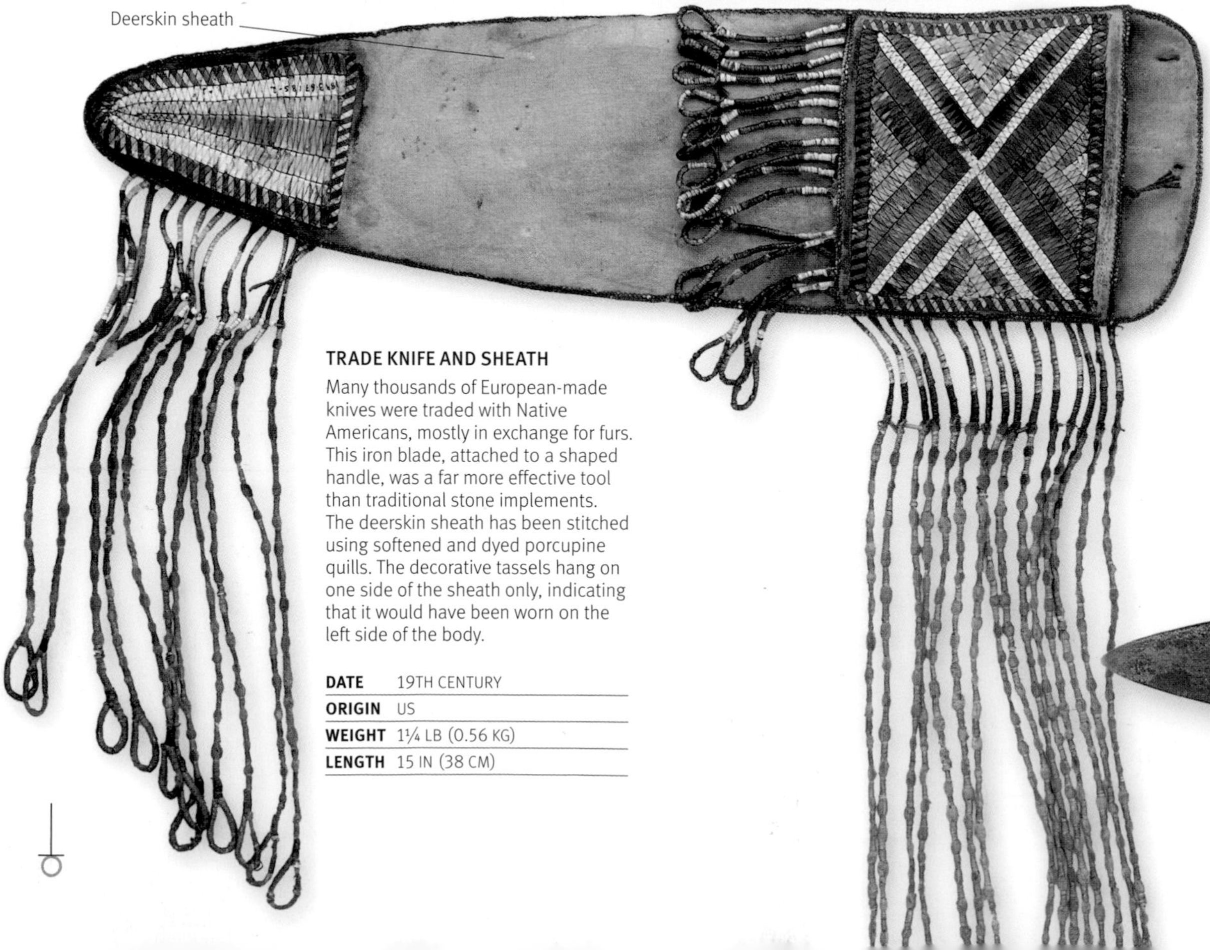

Deerskin sheath

TLINGIT FIGHTING KNIFE

The Tlingit people of the northwest Pacific coast were skilled metalworkers, producing good-quality copper and iron blades. The handle of this knife is wrapped in leather and topped with a fine totem carving, which is inlaid with abalone shell. Fighting in close combat, the Tlingit warrior would wrap the loose leather strap around his wrist to ensure a secure hold upon the weapon.

TRADE KNIFE AND SHEATH

Many thousands of European-made knives were traded with Native Americans, mostly in exchange for furs. This iron blade, attached to a shaped handle, was a far more effective tool than traditional stone implements. The deerskin sheath has been stitched using softened and dyed porcupine quills. The decorative tassels hang on one side of the sheath only, indicating that it would have been worn on the left side of the body.

DATE	19TH CENTURY
ORIGIN	US
WEIGHT	1¼ LB (0.56 KG)
LENGTH	15 IN (38 CM)

DATE	19TH CENTURY
ORIGIN	US
WEIGHT	1 LB (0.5 KG)
LENGTH	19½ IN (50 CM)

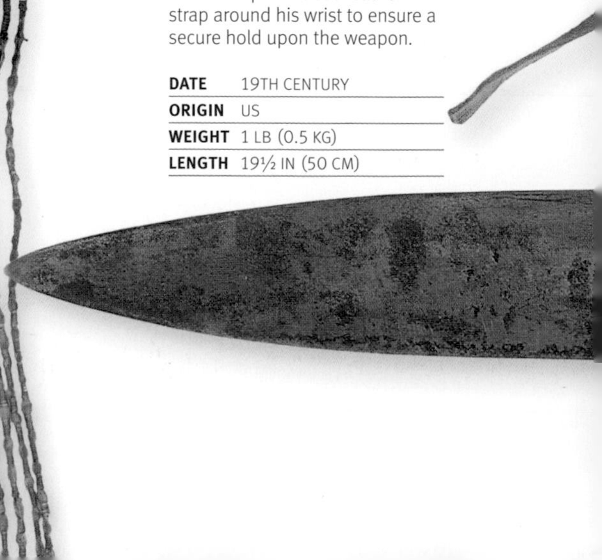

Stylized fish carving

Iron tobacco bowl

Cutting edge of blade

PIPE TOMAHAWK

The idea of combining a peace pipe and a war axe was dreamed up by Euro-American traders, but taken on by Native Americans with enthusiasm. They bought large numbers, making them a part of their culture. Pipe tomahawks were carried by Native American chiefs as symbols of prestige, and exchanged as diplomatic gifts.

DATE	c.1890
ORIGIN	US

Carved wooden shaft

HAIDA CLUB

Living on islands off the northwest coast of North America, the Haida people fished from canoes. This wooden club, showing a stylized fish, would have been used in halibut fishing. Halibut weighing around 400 lb (180 kg) were caught by setting hooks close to the ocean bed. Once hauled to the surface, they had to be stunned immediately with clubs, before their struggles upset the canoe.

DATE	19TH CENTURY
ORIGIN	US

Shaped rock forms club head

Rock is lashed to the handle

Club handle

PENOBSCOT STONE CLUB

The Penobscot Indian nation lives in Maine. Speaking an Algonquin language, they sided with the American rebels against the British and the Algonquins' traditional enemies, the Iroquois, in the Revolutionary War of 1775–83. This stone club would typically have been used to finish off a wounded moose or deer, which had been brought down by an arrow or spear.

DATE	19TH CENTURY
ORIGIN	US

Leather strap lashes handle to wrist in combat

Heavy iron blade

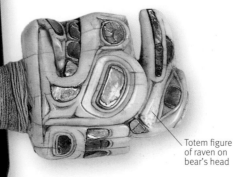

Totem figure of raven on bear's head

LITTLE BIGHORN
Both bows and arrows
and firearms (traded
with the English) were
used by the Native Americans in
battle. Amos Bad Heart Buffalo (1869–
1913), the artist who painted this picture,
was a Native American warrior who joined the
US army and made over 400 illustrations of his people.

NORTH AMERICAN HUNTING BOWS

BOWS WERE AMONG the most important weapons of the native peoples of North America, for hunting, warfare, and ceremonial use. They were "backed bows"—simple bows reinforced with sinew on the side facing away from the archer. The basic material was wood, although in some parts, horn or bone predominated. Arrows often had detachable foreshafts, which would stay embedded in the prey when the hunter pulled the shaft away. Unlike the longbowmen of Agincourt, who drew their bows with fingers on either side of the arrow, skilled North American Indian hunters used two fingers beneath the arrow to pull the string.

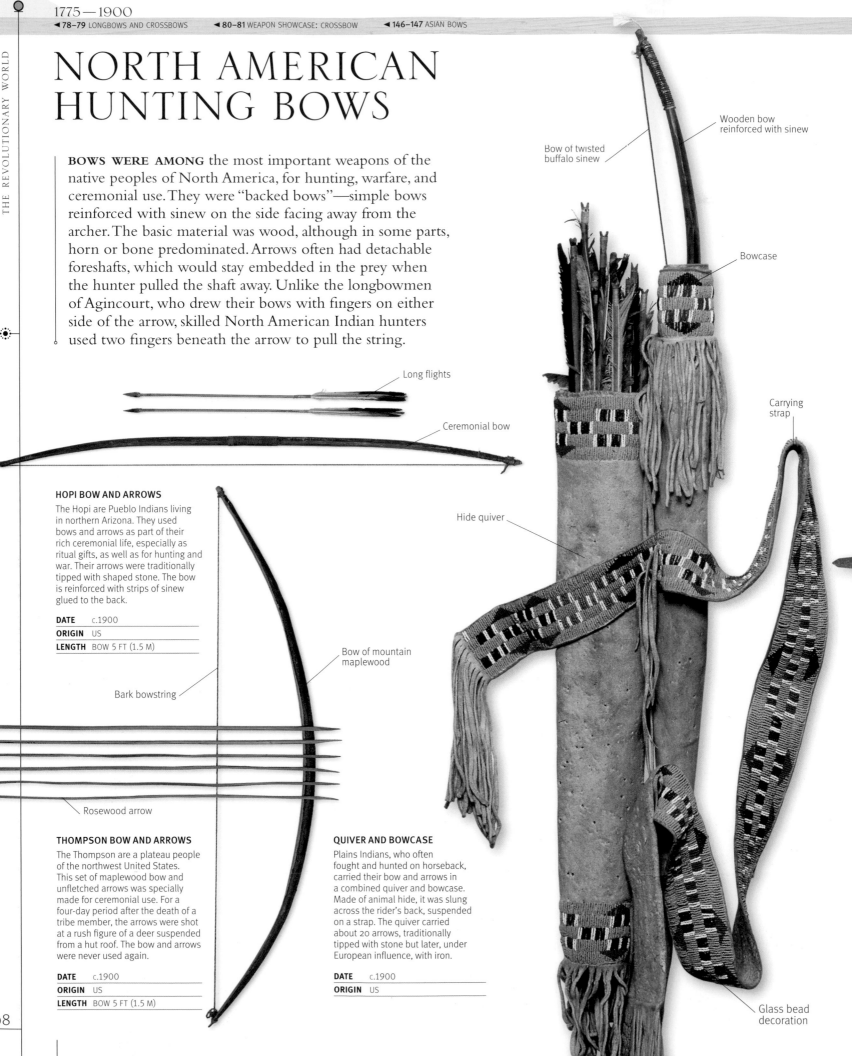

Bow of twisted buffalo sinew

Wooden bow reinforced with sinew

Bowcase

Carrying strap

Long flights

Ceremonial bow

Hide quiver

HOPI BOW AND ARROWS

The Hopi are Pueblo Indians living in northern Arizona. They used bows and arrows as part of their rich ceremonial life, especially as ritual gifts, as well as for hunting and war. Their arrows were traditionally tipped with shaped stone. The bow is reinforced with strips of sinew glued to the back.

DATE	c.1900
ORIGIN	US
LENGTH	BOW 5 FT (1.5 M)

Bow of mountain maplewood

Bark bowstring

Rosewood arrow

THOMPSON BOW AND ARROWS

The Thompson are a plateau people of the northwest United States. This set of maplewood bow and unfletched arrows was specially made for ceremonial use. For a four-day period after the death of a tribe member, the arrows were shot at a rush figure of a deer suspended from a hut roof. The bow and arrows were never used again.

DATE	c.1900
ORIGIN	US
LENGTH	BOW 5 FT (1.5 M)

QUIVER AND BOWCASE

Plains Indians, who often fought and hunted on horseback, carried their bow and arrows in a combined quiver and bowcase. Made of animal hide, it was slung across the rider's back, suspended on a strap. The quiver carried about 20 arrows, traditionally tipped with stone but later, under European influence, with iron.

DATE	c.1900
ORIGIN	US

Glass bead decoration

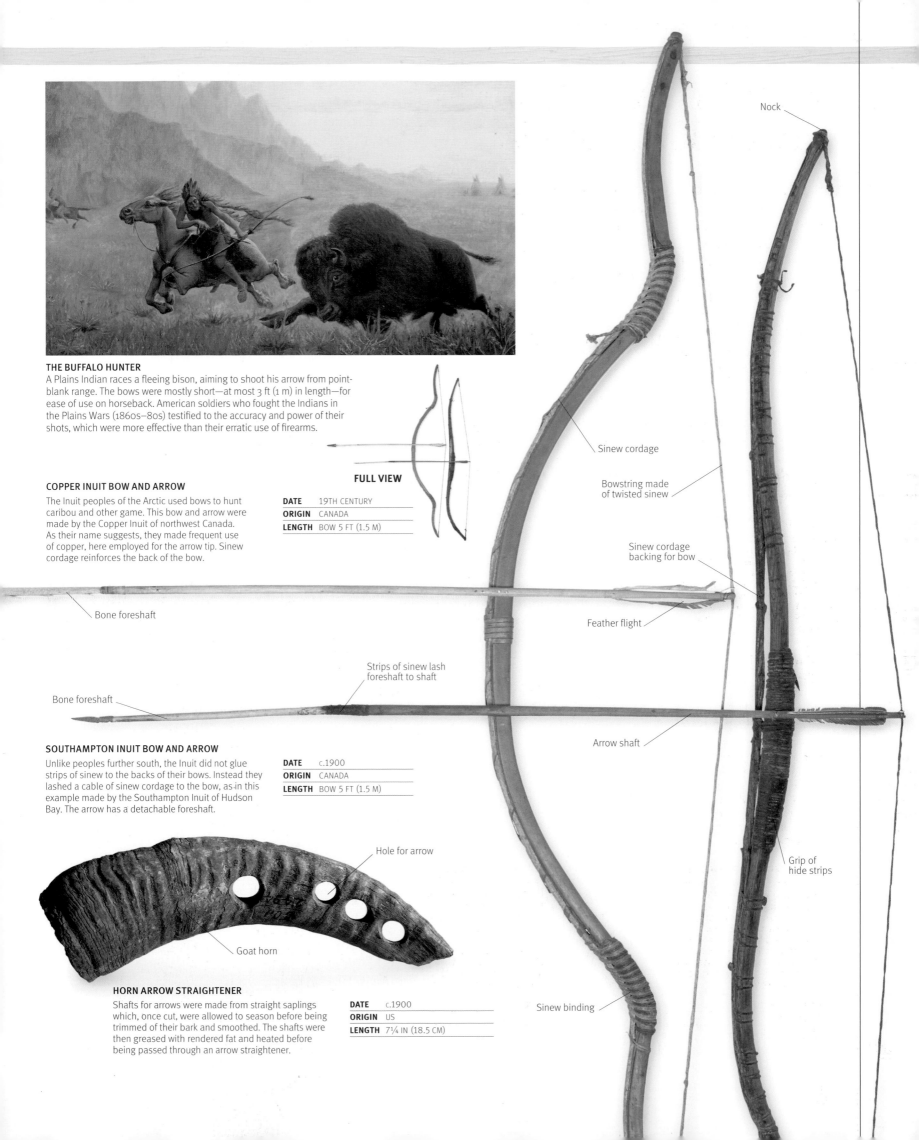

THE BUFFALO HUNTER

A Plains Indian races a fleeing bison, aiming to shoot his arrow from point-blank range. The bows were mostly short—at most 3 ft (1 m) in length—for ease of use on horseback. American soldiers who fought the Indians in the Plains Wars (1860s–80s) testified to the accuracy and power of their shots, which were more effective than their erratic use of firearms.

COPPER INUIT BOW AND ARROW

The Inuit peoples of the Arctic used bows to hunt caribou and other game. This bow and arrow were made by the Copper Inuit of northwest Canada. As their name suggests, they made frequent use of copper, here employed for the arrow tip. Sinew cordage reinforces the back of the bow.

FULL VIEW

DATE	19TH CENTURY
ORIGIN	CANADA
LENGTH	BOW 5 FT (1.5 M)

Bone foreshaft

SOUTHAMPTON INUIT BOW AND ARROW

Unlike peoples further south, the Inuit did not glue strips of sinew to the backs of their bows. Instead they lashed a cable of sinew cordage to the bow, as in this example made by the Southampton Inuit of Hudson Bay. The arrow has a detachable foreshaft.

DATE	c.1900
ORIGIN	CANADA
LENGTH	BOW 5 FT (1.5 M)

Bone foreshaft

Strips of sinew lash foreshaft to shaft

Hole for arrow

Goat horn

HORN ARROW STRAIGHTENER

Shafts for arrows were made from straight saplings which, once cut, were allowed to season before being trimmed of their bark and smoothed. The shafts were then greased with rendered fat and heated before being passed through an arrow straightener.

DATE	c.1900
ORIGIN	US
LENGTH	7¼ IN (18.5 CM)

Nock

Sinew cordage

Bowstring made of twisted sinew

Sinew cordage backing for bow

Feather flight

Arrow shaft

Grip of hide strips

Sinew binding

AUSTRALIAN BOOMERANGS AND SHIELDS

ALTHOUGH BOOMERANGS ARE not unique to Australia, they are most associated with its indigenous peoples. A mix of aerodynamic and gyroscopic effects determines their curving flight. Aborigines used boomerangs, throwing sticks, spears, and stone axes for hunting and in skirmishes. Battles consisting of an exchange of missiles warded off by shields caused limited casualties. Once European settlers arrived with firearms, Aboriginal weaponry was redundant for warfare.

INDIGENOUS AUSTRALIAN
In the 1870s, Australian photographer John William Lindt made studio portraits of Aborigines from Clarence Valley, New South Wales. Intending to document a vanishing way of life, he posed them with their artefacts, including here a boomerang and shield.

Hooked end of boomerang

Carved fluted design

Wood stained with red pigment

FULL VIEW

HOOKED BOOMERANG
This mulga-wood boomerang, similar to many used in the 19th century, was carved from the junction between a tree root and a trunk, exploiting the natural curve of the wood to create a strong hook. When the boomerang was used for fighting, the hook might catch on an enemy's shield or club and swing round to strike him on the face or body.

DATE	20TH CENTURY
ORIGIN	NORTHERN CENTRAL AUSTRALIA
WEIGHT	1 LB (0.41 KG)
LENGTH	28¾ IN (73.1 CM)

Incisions on inner edge

Fine grooves on surface

Decoration in ocher and pipe clay

Longer arm shaped to the point

CONVEX BOOMERANG
This boomerang from Queensland has a convex surface on both sides—some are convex on one side and flat on the other. Incisions on its curved inner edge show that it has been used for cutting or sawing, as well as for throwing. The surface has been finely grooved to enhance the natural grain of the wood.

DATE	LATE 19TH CENTURY
ORIGIN	QUEENSLAND, AUSTRALIA
WEIGHT	¾ LB (0.32 KG)
LENGTH	28½ IN (72.4 CM)

SHARP-ANGLED BOOMERANG
This boomerang or club has been finely carved to form a sharp angle. It is decorated on both sides with a design in red ocher and white pipe clay. Abstract designs of this kind are often connected with the Aboriginal "dreamtime" myths that link the clan or tribe to its ancestors and its local territory.

DATE	19TH CENTURY
ORIGIN	QUEENSLAND, AUSTRALIA
WEIGHT	1¼ LB (0.57 KG)
LENGTH	29½ IN (75 CM)

Ridged light wood
face of shield

Boss in center
of shield

Rounded end,
roughly shaped

Ridges picked
out in red ocher

PARRYING SHIELD

Despite its elongated shape, a parrying shield of this kind
was an effective defense against hostile missiles such
as throwing sticks or boomerangs, if used deftly by an
alert warrior to ward them off. The design of longitudinal
and diagonal lines, picked out in red and white ochers, is
typical of indigenous peoples in this area.

DATE	19TH CENTURY
ORIGIN	WESTERN AUSTRALIA
WEIGHT	1 LB (0.49 KG)
LENGTH	28 IN (73 CM)

Band of red ocher

Shield tapers to the point

BANDED SHIELD

This parrying shield is decorated with bands of red ocher
and an intricate pattern of finely engraved lines. The
markings at the ends may represent clan affiliations. Held
by a grip at the back made of solid wood, the shield was
robust enough to deflect a boomerang or other missile
even if thrown with considerable force.

DATE	19TH CENTURY
ORIGIN	AUSTRALIA
WEIGHT	2½ LB (1.19 KG)
LENGTH	32½ IN (83 CM)

Bold painted
design

CARVED SHIELD

This shield, known as a *gidyar*, originates from the Cairns
District, and is similar to types used in the 19th century.
It has been carved out of wood and painted in a bold
design. Although it may have found multiple other uses,
the shield was almost certainly employed primarily for
purposes of display in ceremonial dances.

DATE	20TH CENTURY
ORIGIN	QUEENSLAND, AUSTRALIA
LENGTH	26 IN (66 CM)

RIDGED SHIELD

This shield from northern Queensland is made out of
light ridged wood attached to a solid-wood handle
at the back. It is a decorative work as well as a piece
of defensive equipment. The meaning of the colorful
design on the shield is uncertain, but it may refer to the
achievements and status of the warrior who owned it.

DATE	c.1900
ORIGIN	QUEENSLAND, AUSTRALIA
LENGTH	38¼ IN (97 CM)

FLINTLOCK PISTOLS FROM 1775

BY THE LAST QUARTER of the 18th century, before police forces were widely established, pistols were commonplace in the homes of the wealthy, and pocket models were often carried by gentlemen and villains alike. Several types of pistol designed for specific purposes had been developed, including the dueling, or target, pistol and the blunderbuss pistol. The flintlock pistol was virtually ubiquitous, more often than not in the semi-enclosed box-lock form. Only in Spain did the less efficient miquelet style of lock still occur with any regularity.

Rectangular box enclosing lock mechanism

Jaw clamp screw

Striking steel

Bell mouth ensures wide spread of shot at close range

Brass barrel

Spring-loaded bayonet

Rear "trigger" releases bayonet

Trigger

BLUNDERBUSS PISTOL

The blunderbuss (from the Dutch *donderbus*, or "thunder gun") was a close-range weapon, its bell mouth aiding the loading and dispersal of the shot. This box-lock model was the work of John Waters of Birmingham, who held a patent on the pistol bayonet. Officers of the British Royal Navy often used such pistols during boarding operations.

DATE	1785
ORIGIN	UK
WEIGHT	2LB (0.95KG)
BARREL	7½IN (19CM)
CALIBRE	1IN AT MUZZLE

Prawl

Smooth-bore barrel

Fore stock extends to muzzle

Bead fore sight

Barrels unscrew for loading

Hair trigger

Feather spring

Ramrod

Steadying spur of trigger guard

Double barrels set side by side

MIQUELET DUELLING PISTOL

Pistols specifically designed for dueling made their first appearance in Britain after 1780. They were invariably sold as a matched pair, cased, with all the accessories necessary for their use. "Saw handle" butts with pronounced prawls and steadying spurs on the trigger guard were later additions, as was the custom of stocking the pistols fully, to the muzzle.

DATE	1815
ORIGIN	UK
WEIGHT	2¼LB (1KG)
BARREL	9IN (23CM)
CALIBRE	34-BORE

Cock

Cock

Striking steel

Safety catch locks pan cover in closed position

Internal box-lock

Ramrod

Cylinder loaded via muzzle, chamber by chamber

FLINTLOCK REVOLVER

Around 1680, John Dafte of London designed a pistol with a revolving, multichambered cylinder that was indexed (rotated) by the cocking action. Elisha Collier of Boston gained a British patent for an improved version in 1814; it was produced in London by John Evans in 1819. The indexing mechanism was unreliable, and the cylinder was usually turned by hand.

DATE	c.1820
ORIGIN	UK
WEIGHT	1½LB (0.68KG)
BARREL	5IN (12.4CM)
CALIBRE	.45IN

Trigger guard retains bayonet in closed position

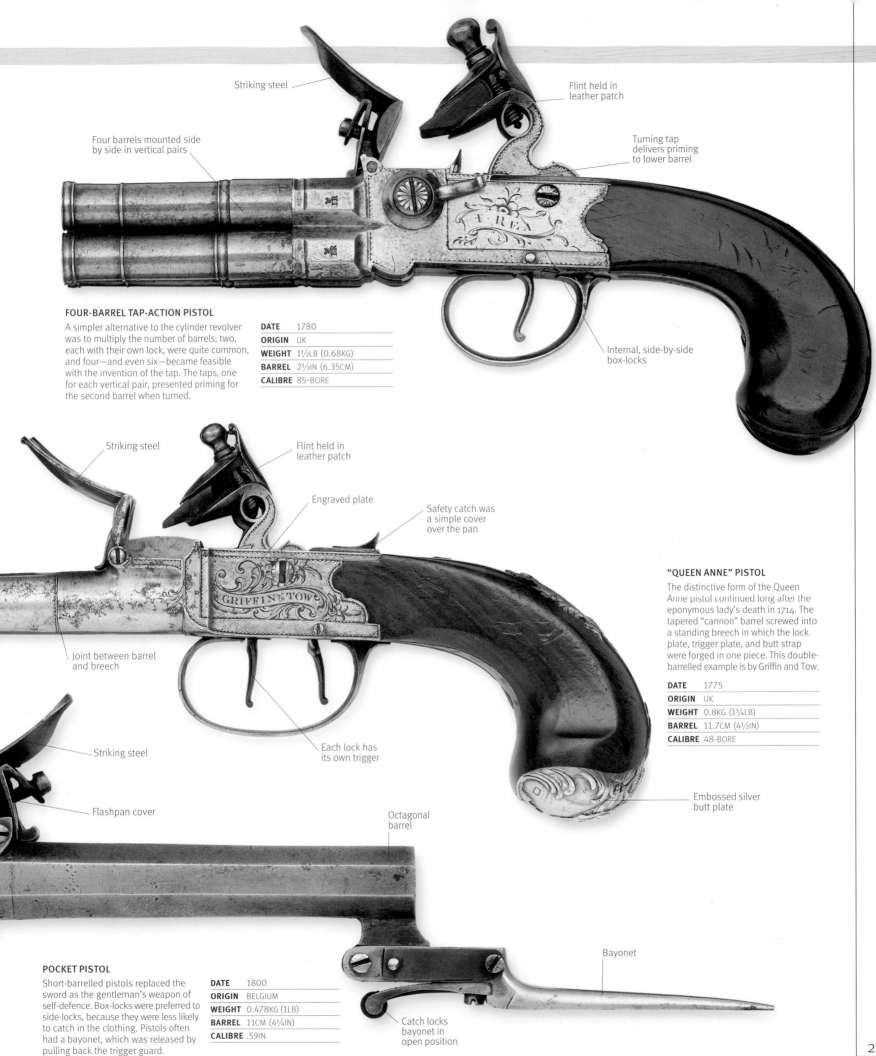

Striking steel

Flint held in
leather patch

Four barrels mounted side
by side in vertical pairs

Turning tap
delivers priming
to lower barrel

T. REA

FOUR-BARREL TAP-ACTION PISTOL

A simpler alternative to the cylinder revolver
was to multiply the number of barrels; two,
each with their own lock, were quite common,
and four—and even six—became feasible
with the invention of the tap. The taps, one
for each vertical pair, presented priming
for the second barrel when turned.

DATE	1780
ORIGIN	UK
WEIGHT	1½LB (0.68KG)
BARREL	2½IN (6.35CM)
CALIBRE	85-BORE

Internal, side-by-side
box-locks

Striking steel

Flint held in
leather patch

Engraved plate

Safety catch was
a simple cover
over the pan

GRIFFIN & TOW

"QUEEN ANNE" PISTOL

The distinctive form of the Queen
Anne pistol continued long after the
eponymous lady's death in 1714. The
tapered "cannon" barrel screwed into
a standing breech in which the lock
plate, trigger plate, and butt strap
were forged in one piece. This double-
barrelled example is by Griffin and Tow.

DATE	1775
ORIGIN	UK
WEIGHT	0.8KG (1¾LB)
BARREL	11.7CM (4½IN)
CALIBRE	48-BORE

Joint between barrel
and breech

Each lock has
its own trigger

Embossed silver
butt plate

Striking steel

Flashpan cover

Octagonal
barrel

Bayonet

POCKET PISTOL

Short-barrelled pistols replaced the
sword as the gentleman's weapon of
self-defence. Box-locks were preferred to
side-locks, because they were less likely
to catch in the clothing. Pistols often
had a bayonet, which was released by
pulling back the trigger guard.

DATE	1800
ORIGIN	BELGIUM
WEIGHT	0.478KG (1LB)
BARREL	11CM (4¼IN)
CALIBRE	.59IN

Catch locks
bayonet in
open position

1775—1900

◄ 148–149 MATCHLOCK AND FLINTLOCK LONG GUNS   ◄ 160–163 EUROPEAN PISTOLS 1500–1775   ◄ 212–213 FLINTLOCK PISTOLS FROM 1775   ► 232–233 FLINTLOCK MUSKETS ANND RIFLES

THE REVOLUTIONARY WORLD

FLINTLOCK PISTOLS TO 1850

MASS PRODUCTION WAS UNKNOWN before the 19th century. Until then, firearms had no interchangeable parts, because each element was made by hand for each individual weapon. Even relatively unsophisticated pistols were expensive, both to buy and to repair, despite the fact that demand was high and increasing. The decoration that had graced many earlier weapons was sacrificed to save money. Ultimately, quality too became a casualty—except at the top end of the market, where cost was no object.

Jaw-clamp screw

Heavy brass butt plate

Brass trigger guard

HARPER'S FERRY PISTOL

The Model 1805 was the first pistol manufactured at the newly-established Federal Arsenal at Harper's Ferry, in what is now West Virginia. Like all martial handguns of the period, it was robust enough to be reversed and used as a club, should the need arise.

DATE	1806
ORIGIN	US
WEIGHT	2 LB (0.9 KG)
BARREL	10 IN (25.4 CM)
CALIBER	.54 IN

Safety catch locks pan closed

Flashpan

Striking steel

Octagonal barrel

One-piece stock made of seasoned walnut

Pulling trigger guard releases bayonet

Spring-loaded bayonet

FLEMISH POCKET PISTOL

This simple box-lock pocket pistol has an integral spring-loaded bayonet, operated by pulling back on the trigger guard. There is some engraving on the lock plates and the butt is finely carved. It is the work of A. Juliard, a Flemish gunmaker of some repute.

Curved walnut butt

DATE	1805
ORIGIN	NETHERLANDS
WEIGHT	1 LB (.5 KG)
BARREL	4¼ IN (10.9 CM)
CALIBER	33-BORE

Internal box lock

Flint

Striking steel

Round brass barrel

Ramrod thimble

Wooden ramrod with brass cap

Brass-bound butt

ITALIAN POCKET PISTOL

Gunmaking flourished in post-Renaissance Italy (the English word "pistol" probably derives from Pistoia, a city famous for gun manufacture). Although the industry was in decline by the 19th century, craftsmen like Lamberti, creator of this pistol, still thrived.

DATE	1810
ORIGIN	ITALY
WEIGHT	1½ LB (0.62 KG)
BARREL	4¾ IN (12.3 CM)
CALIBER	.85 IN

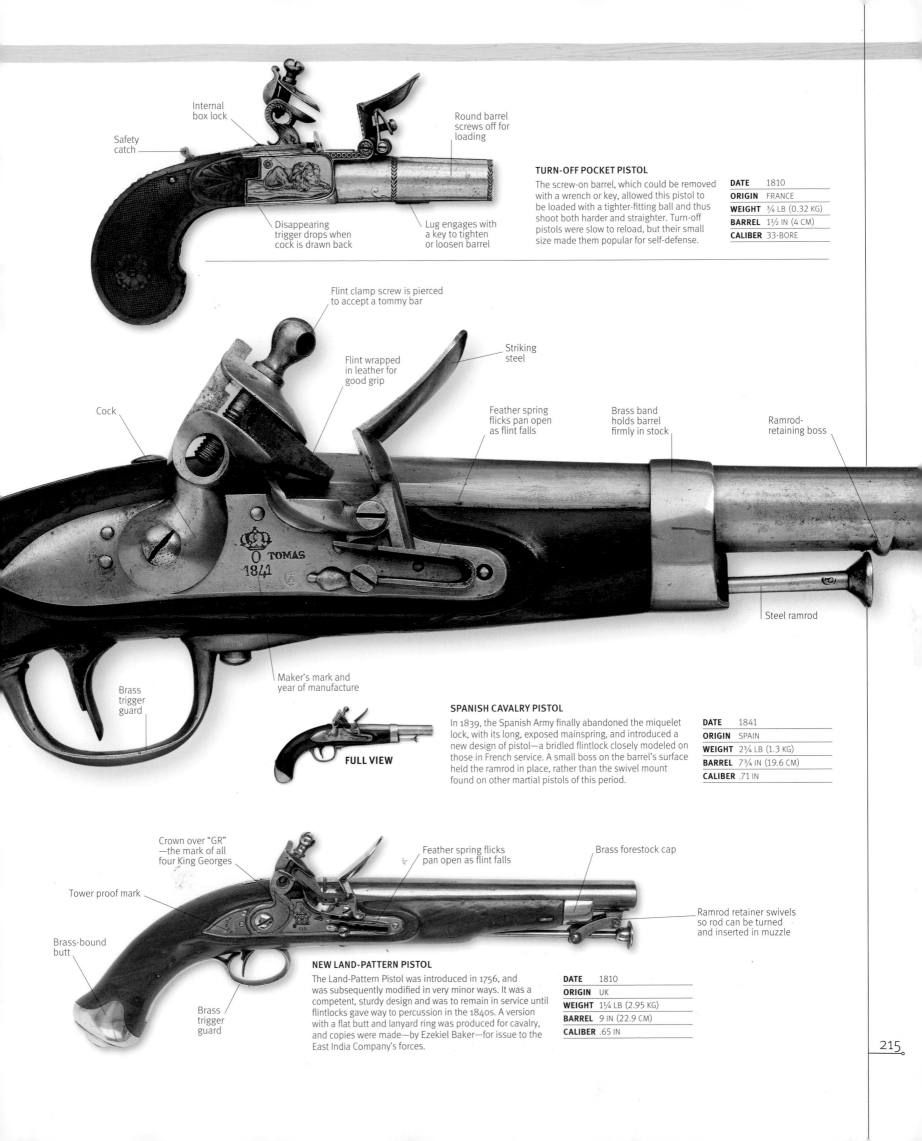

Internal
box lock

Safety
catch

Round barrel
screws off for
loading

Disappearing
trigger drops when
cock is drawn back

Lug engages with
a key to tighten
or loosen barrel

TURN-OFF POCKET PISTOL

The screw-on barrel, which could be removed
with a wrench or key, allowed this pistol to
be loaded with a tighter-fitting ball and thus
shoot both harder and straighter. Turn-off
pistols were slow to reload, but their small
size made them popular for self-defense.

DATE	1810
ORIGIN	FRANCE
WEIGHT	¾ LB (0.32 KG)
BARREL	1½ IN (4 CM)
CALIBER	33-BORE

Flint clamp screw is pierced
to accept a tommy bar

Flint wrapped
in leather for
good grip

Striking
steel

Cock

Feather spring
flicks pan open
as flint falls

Brass band
holds barrel
firmly in stock

Ramrod-
retaining boss

O TOMAS
1841

Steel ramrod

Brass
trigger
guard

Maker's mark and
year of manufacture

SPANISH CAVALRY PISTOL

FULL VIEW

In 1839, the Spanish Army finally abandoned the miquelet
lock, with its long, exposed mainspring, and introduced a
new design of pistol—a bridled flintlock closely modeled on
those in French service. A small boss on the barrel's surface
held the ramrod in place, rather than the swivel mount
found on other martial pistols of this period.

DATE	1841
ORIGIN	SPAIN
WEIGHT	2¾ LB (1.3 KG)
BARREL	7¾ IN (19.6 CM)
CALIBER	.71 IN

Crown over "GR"
—the mark of all
four King Georges

Feather spring flicks
pan open as flint falls

Brass forestock cap

Tower proof mark

Ramrod retainer swivels
so rod can be turned
and inserted in muzzle

Brass-bound
butt

Brass
trigger
guard

NEW LAND-PATTERN PISTOL

The Land-Pattern Pistol was introduced in 1756, and
was subsequently modified in very minor ways. It was a
competent, sturdy design and was to remain in service until
flintlocks gave way to percussion in the 1840s. A version
with a flat butt and lanyard ring was produced for cavalry,
and copies were made—by Ezekiel Baker—for issue to the
East India Company's forces.

DATE	1810
ORIGIN	UK
WEIGHT	1¼ LB (2.95 KG)
BARREL	9 IN (22.9 CM)
CALIBER	.65 IN

THE REVOLUTIONARY WORLD

PERCUSSION CAP PISTOLS

FULMINATE OF MERCURY was first used to ignite gunpowder in a gun barrel by Scotsman Alexander Forsyth, who took out a patent in 1807. It took some time to find a successful way of presenting the fulminate charge, or primer, to the breech. The solution, called the cap, consisted of primer sandwiched between two copper-foil sheets. The cap was shaped to fit over a pierced nipple set in what had been the touch-hole. It was struck by a hammer, rather than a cock and flint. Pistols using this system appeared around 1820.

Hammer

Cap fits over nipple

Fore sight

Incised chequering on butt

L. FOLVILLE À LIÈGE

Octagonal barrel

Maker's name

Slide secures barrel in lock

Steadying spur

Butt finishes in a pommel

BELGIAN DUELING/TARGET PISTOL

Percussion-cap pistols were more reliable than even the best flintlocks, and one of their earliest uses was as dueling pistols. This half-stocked pistol by Folville, one of a matched and boxed pair, is typical of those produced in Liège, in what is now Belgium.

DATE	1830
ORIGIN	BELGIUM
WEIGHT	2 LB (0.88 KG)
BARREL	9¼ IN (23.8 CM)
CALIBER	8 MM

Animal decoration on hammer

Rear sight

Incised chequering on butt

Trigger

Steadying spur

ENGLISH DUELING/TARGET PISTOL

Despite their lack of overt decoration, dueling pistols were usually produced without regard to cost. This example, one of a pair, was the work of Isaac Riviere of London. Riviere had considerable influence over the design of percussion pistols, and patented his own lock in 1825.

DATE	c.1830
ORIGIN	UK
WEIGHT	2½ LB (1.15 KG)
BARREL	9½ IN (24.1 CM)
CALIBER	44-BORE

Ornate octagonal barrel

Animal decoration

Barrel-retaining slide

Hammer

Engraved lock plate

Butt has incised decoration

Trigger is pre-set to a very light pull

FRENCH DUELING/TARGET PISTOL

Technically, there is little difference between dueling pistols and those used for shooting at paper targets. However, the latter, such as this example by the renowned Parisian gunmaker Gastinne-Renette, were often beautifully decorated.

DATE	1839
ORIGIN	FRANCE
WEIGHT	2 LB (0.95 KG)
BARREL	11¼ IN (28.3 CM)
CALIBER	12 MM

COOPER UNDER-HAMMER PISTOL

Joseph Rock Cooper was a prolific English firearms inventor. One of his patents was for this pistol, which has an under-hammer by a Belgian named Mariette. In effect it is a "double-action" pistol: pulling the trigger lifts and then releases the hammer.

DATE	1849
ORIGIN	UK
WEIGHT	½ LB (0.27 KG)
BARREL	4 IN (10 CM)
CALIBER	.45 IN

Butt is planed flat on the sides

Ring trigger is characteristic of Cooper's pistols

Round barrel

Combined main spring and hammer

Hammer

Nipple

Fore sight

Plain walnut stock

Lanyard ring

Lock plate

Ramrod retainer swivels to allow captive rod to be inserted in barrel

PATTERN 1842 COASTGUARD PISTOL

British pistols used by the coastguard, police, and other security agencies were similar in style to the Land- and Sea-Pattern pistols of the army and navy, but usually lighter and smaller. Revolvers replaced Pattern 1842 pistols in the 1850s.

DATE	1842
ORIGIN	UK
WEIGHT	2½ LB (1.05 KG)
BARREL	6 IN (15 CM)
CALIBER	24-BORE

Octagonal barrel

Fore sight

Ramrod thimble

Ramrod

Bar hammer acts vertically

Barrels rotate on axial pin

Checkering on butt

Nipples set horizontally

BAR-HAMMER "PEPPERBOX" PISTOL

Pepperbox pistols offered the advantage of multi-shot cylinder revolvers without their principle drawback—the leakage of propellant gas between chamber and barrel. Unfortunately, the type was generally inaccurate, except at point-blank range.

DATE	1849
ORIGIN	UK
WEIGHT	2¼ LB (1.01 KG)
BARREL	3½ IN (9.1 CM)
CALIBER	.55 IN

Side-mounted hammer

Breech lever

Fore sight

SHARPS BREECH-LOADING PISTOL

Christian Sharps was famous for his breech-loading rifles and carbines for military and sporting use. He also made pistols based on the same principles as his early rifles. The falling breech cut off the rear of the linen cartridge when it was returned to battery.

DATE	c.1860
ORIGIN	US
WEIGHT	2 LB (0.96 KG)
BARREL	5 IN (12.7 CM)
CALIBER	.34 IN

Trigger

1775—1900

◄ 216–217 PERCUSSION CAP PISTOLS   ► 222–223 BRITISH PERCUSSION CAP REVOLVERS   ► 296–297 REVOLVERS 1900–1950   ► 298–299 REVOLVERS FROM 1950

THE REVOLUTIONARY WORLD

AMERICAN PERCUSSION CAP REVOLVERS

SAMUEL COLT CLAIMED that the design of his cylinder revolver, patented in 1835, was inspired by the locking mechanism of a sailing ship's steering wheel. A pawl linked to the hammer breast engaged with a ratchet machined into the cylinder's rear face. As the hammer was pulled back, the pawl indexed the ratchet by one stop, bringing a fresh chamber into line with the barrel and its percussion cap under the hammer. The cylinder was locked in place at the moment of firing by a vertical bolt driven upward by the action of the trigger.

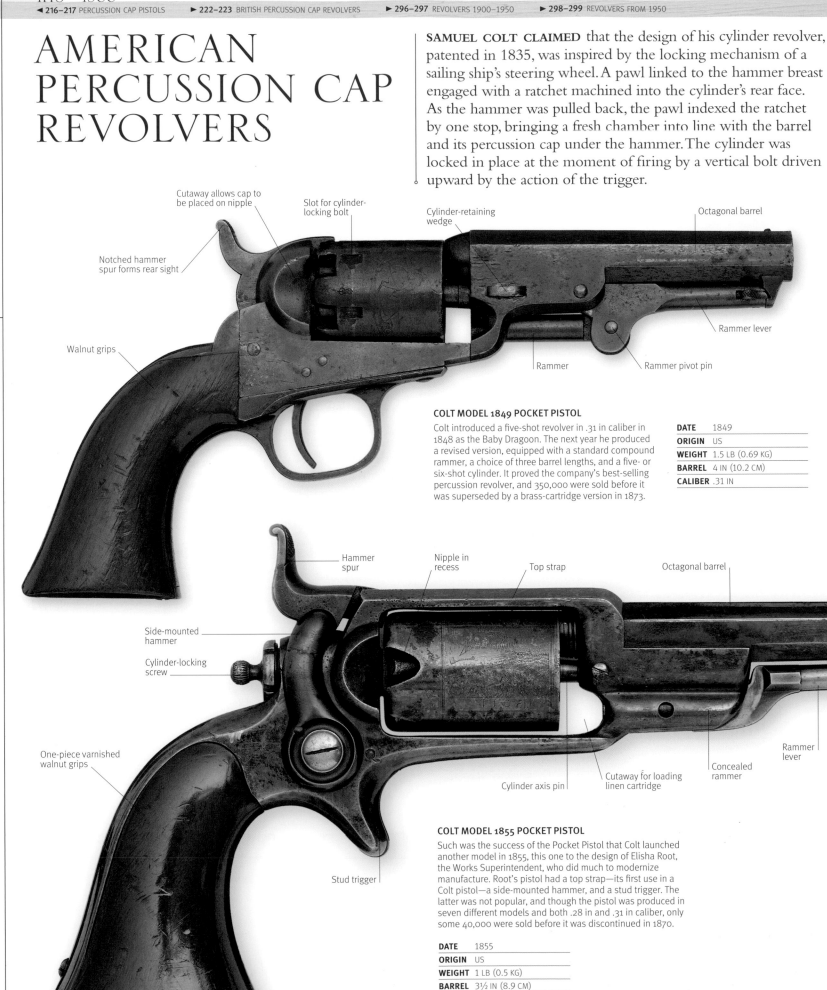

Cutaway allows cap to be placed on nipple

Slot for cylinder-locking bolt

Cylinder-retaining wedge

Octagonal barrel

Notched hammer spur forms rear sight

Rammer lever

Walnut grips

Rammer

Rammer pivot pin

COLT MODEL 1849 POCKET PISTOL

Colt introduced a five-shot revolver in .31 in caliber in 1848 as the Baby Dragoon. The next year he produced a revised version, equipped with a standard compound rammer, a choice of three barrel lengths, and a five- or six-shot cylinder. It proved the company's best-selling percussion revolver, and 350,000 were sold before it was superseded by a brass-cartridge version in 1873.

DATE	1849
ORIGIN	US
WEIGHT	1.5 LB (0.69 KG)
BARREL	4 IN (10.2 CM)
CALIBER	.31 IN

Hammer spur

Nipple in recess

Top strap

Octagonal barrel

Side-mounted hammer

Cylinder-locking screw

One-piece varnished walnut grips

Cylinder axis pin

Cutaway for loading linen cartridge

Concealed rammer

Rammer lever

Stud trigger

COLT MODEL 1855 POCKET PISTOL

Such was the success of the Pocket Pistol that Colt launched another model in 1855, this one to the design of Elisha Root, the Works Superintendent, who did much to modernize manufacture. Root's pistol had a top strap—its first use in a Colt pistol—a side-mounted hammer, and a stud trigger. The latter was not popular, and though the pistol was produced in seven different models and both .28 in and .31 in caliber, only some 40,000 were sold before it was discontinued in 1870.

DATE	1855
ORIGIN	US
WEIGHT	1 LB (0.5 KG)
BARREL	3½ IN (8.9 CM)
CALIBER	.28 IN

Notched hammer spur forms rear sight

Cutaway to facilitate placing of cap

Bead fore sight

Rammer lever

Octagonal barrel

Rammer pivot pin

Cylinder-retaining wedge passes through axis pin

Hole for locking bar in armory rack

COLT NAVY MODEL 1851

In 1851, Colt introduced a lighter pistol, the Navy Model, in .36 in rather than .44 in caliber. That same year, he traveled to London to show at the Great Exhibition, and obtained an order from the British government. The example shown here is one of the pistols produced at the factory the company established in London in 1853. Its cylinder is engraved with a naval scene.

DATE	1851
ORIGIN	US
WEIGHT	2¾ LB (1.2 KG)
BARREL	7½ IN (19 CM)
CALIBER	.36 IN

Nipple in recess

Slot for cylinder-locking bolt

Engraved cylinder

Cylinder axis pin

Cylinder-retaining wedge

Round barrel

Brass back strap

Rammer pivot pin

Rammer lever

Rammer

Walnut grips

Brass trigger guard

COLT SECOND MODEL DRAGOON PISTOL

Colt's mainstay during the first decade and a half of the percussion era was the Dragoon Pistol, so called because it was intended as a side-arm for cavalrymen. It first went into limited production at Whitneyville in 1847. Later that same year, Colt established a new factory at Hartford, expressly to produce the Dragoon Pistol to fulfil an army contract.

DATE	1849
ORIGIN	US
WEIGHT	4 LB (1.93 KG)
BARREL	7½ IN (19 CM)
CALIBER	.44 IN

Hammer nose extension

Top strap

Locking screw

Smooth-bore barrel acts as cylinder axis pin

Rifled barrel and cylinder screw onto smooth-bore barrel

Round barrel

Cylinder-locking slot

LE MAT PISTOL

Jean-Alexandre Le Mat's revolver design was produced in both pistol and rifle form. The nine-chambered cylinder revolved around not a pin but a second, unrifled barrel, which was charged from the muzzle with pellets. The hammer had a hinged extension to its nose, which could be angled up or down to fire either barrel.

DATE	1864
ORIGIN	US
WEIGHT	3½ LB (1.64 KG)
BARREL	LOWER 5 IN (12.7 CM)
CALIBER	.3 IN AND 16-BORE

STARR SINGLE-ACTION ARMY MODEL

Nathan Starr was a pioneer of the break-open pistol, in which the barrel, top strap, and cylinder were hinged at the front of the frame before the trigger guard. The forked top strap passed over the hammer and was retained by a knurled screw. When broken open, the cylinder could be removed for reloading.

DATE	1864
ORIGIN	US
WEIGHT	3 LB (1.35 KG)
BARREL	7½ IN (19.2 CM)
CALIBER	.44 IN

US CIVIL WAR INFANTRYMAN

.40 CALIBER LE MAT REVOLVER

THE ELECTION AS US PRESIDENT OF ABRAHAM LINCOLN, who opposed the spread of slavery, in 1860 led 11 southern states to secede from the Union and form the Confederacy. A bloody civil war ensued. Initially, hundreds of thousands volunteered to fight. Later, conscription was successfully introduced in the Confederate South; it was less effective in the Union states of the North, where the wealthy often evaded service by paying others to fight in their place. Both Confederate and Union troops were hard-bitten characters unused to obedience, but they showed tenacity, sticking to the fight when casualties were high and conditions awful.

INFANTRY FIGHTING

From April 1861 to April 1865, 3 million men joined the forces of the Union and the Confederacy. Most were infantrymen who walked or marched everywhere, carrying equipment, ammunition, personal items, and a field pack. The main weapon was the muzzle-loaded rifle-musket, firing Minié bullets. Although an advance over the flintlock musket, it still required infantry to fire in volleys from a standing position. On the offensive, infantry had to advance steadily across open ground in the face of withering fire from rifle-muskets and artillery that decimated their ranks. Both sides used the same basic weaponry, but the North was far more successful in equipping its armies. Union infantrymen were well supplied with standard uniform, boots of the right size, bullets, and powder, while the Southern infantry were short of everything but courage. Around 620,000 soldiers lost their lives, more through disease than combat.

BATTLE OF BULL RUN
The first major battle, First Bull Run was a chaotic affair. Confederate Jeb Stuart led the war's only significant cavalry charge. Exotic Zouave uniforms were worn by some volunteers on both sides, adding to the confusion.

"THE MAN WHO DOES NOT DREAD TO DIE OR TO BE MUTILATED IS A LUNATIC."

CIVIL WAR VETERAN

VOLUNTEER SOLDIERS

A Union infantry lieutenant, on the right, and two enlisted men during the first year of the war. Such early volunteers—motivated by enthusiasm for the cause or by a naive thirst for adventure—mostly elected their own officers, and tended to obey orders only when they saw fit.

FIGHTING FOR FREEDOM

At the start of the Civil War, African Americans were excluded from combat by both sides. During 1862 Union officers advanced from using escaped slaves as laborers to arming them. The first regiments of black volunteers were officially raised in the North in 1863. Around 180,000 ex-slaves and free black men served in the Union forces, in segregated regiments and mostly under white officers. Many distinguished themselves in combat, the 54th Massachusetts regiment, for example, performed outstandingly in the storming of Fort Wagner in 1863. The black troops' contribution to victory helped win Union support for the abolition of slavery.

A UNION SOLDIER OF THE 54TH MASSACHUSETTS INFANTRY, c.1863

UNIFORM OF A CONFEDERATE SOLDIER

Few Confederate soldiers managed to wear the regulation gray coat, gray forage cap, and blue trousers. Short jackets were more common, as were varieties of "butternut" brown or beige clothing.

Kepi

Short jacket

Beige trousers

UNIFORM OF A UNION SOLDIER

This is the winter uniform of a infantryman in the New York Volunteers. The Hardee felt hat, although regulation dress, was rarely worn, most soldiers preferring a lighter kepi or slouch hat.

Infantry cap badge—gold embroidered bugle

Hardee dress hat

Elbow-length cape

Box for percussion caps

Winter greatcoat

Jefferson boot

TOOLS OF COMBAT

ENFIELD BAYONET

ENFIELD RIFLE-MUSKET

UNION SOLDIER'S METAL CANTEEN

LEATHER KNAPSACK

G.L.P.
CO. E.
44TH M.V.M.

1775—1900

◄ 216–217 PERCUSSION CAP PISTOLS ◄ 218–219 AMERICAN PERCUSSION CAP PISTOLS ► 296–297 REVOLVERS 1900–1950 ► 298–299 REVOLVERS FROM 1950

THE REVOLUTIONARY WORLD

BRITISH PERCUSSION CAP REVOLVERS

ALTHOUGH LONDON GUNMAKERS, notably Robert Adams, were making revolvers by the mid-19th century, it was Samuel Colt's display at the Great Exhibition of 1851 that ignited interest in such pistols. For some years, Colt had the British market almost to himself, but by the decade's end, domestic gunmakers' revolvers had overtaken American Colts in popularity. Adams' pistols had double-action ("self-cocking") locks—a characteristic of British revolvers from the outset. Later models could also function in single-action mode.

Side-mounted hammer

Recessed nipple

Five-chambered cylinder

Octagonal barrel

Fore sight

Cylinder axis pin

Rammer lever

Grip retaining pin

Lock cover plate

KERR DOUBLE-ACTION REVOLVER

To address doubts about the reliability of the revolver, James Kerr fitted his with a simple box-lock and a side-mounted hammer. The lock was retained by two screws, and could be easily removed. Should a component—the spring, for example—break, any gunsmith would have been able to repair it. Kerr's five-chambered pistols came in either 54-bore or 90-bore caliber. They were manufactured until the mid-1870s.

DATE	1856
ORIGIN	UK
WEIGHT	2½ LB (1.2 KG)
BARREL	5¾ IN (14.7 CM)
CALIBER	54-BORE

Notched ridge forms rear sight

Cylinder-locking wedge

Octagonal barrel

Engraved plate covers double-action lock

Rammer

Chequered walnut grips

Flash shield

Fluted cylinder

Cylinder axis pin

JOSEPH LANG TRANSITIONAL REVOLVER

Open-framed "transitional" pistols combined elements of both the pepperbox pistols they superseded and the true revolvers. They continued to be produced, mostly in Europe, even after much more sophisticated designs had appeared. This example is of the type produced by one of the best known proponents, Joseph Lang of London. Lang was more successful than most gunmakers of the time in solving the problem of propellant gas leaking between chamber and barrel.

DATE	1855
ORIGIN	UK
WEIGHT	3 LB (1.36 KG)
BARREL	6 IN (15.2 CM)
CALIBER	54-BORE

Engraved plate covers double-action lock

Bar hammer

Cylinder

Octagonal barrel

Screw secures barrel to frame

Flash guard

TRANSITIONAL REVOLVER

By the late 1850s, there was considerable demand in Britain for cylinder revolvers, but the best of them, by Colt, Deane, or Adams, were very expensive. Cheaper designs such as this example, with a bar hammer derived from a pepperbox revolver, were less satisfactory, with a tendency to discharge two cylinders at once because of the lack of partitions between the nipples.

DATE	c.1855
ORIGIN	UK
WEIGHT	1¾ LB (0.81 KG)
BARREL	5¼ IN (13.5 CM)
CALIBER	.4 IN

Octagonal barrel

Fore sight

Nipple

Spurless hammer

Safety catch

Cylinder axis pin

Fore sight

ADAMS DOUBLE-ACTION REVOLVER MODEL 1851

This revolver—Robert Adams' first—is also called the Deane, Adams & Deane Model (he was in partnership at the time). The entire frame, barrel, and butt were forged out of a single iron billet, making it extremely strong. Adams' lock was later replaced by a superior design by a young army officer, F.B.E. Beaumont. The Beaumont-Adams was adopted by the British Army in 1855.

DATE	1851
ORIGIN	UK
WEIGHT	2¾ LB (1.27 KG)
BARREL	7½ IN (19 CM)
CALIBER	40-BORE

Rammer lever

Cylinder

Octagonal barrrel

Prawl prevents pistol from slipping through hand

Rammer lever

Checkered walnut grip

Trigger guard

DEANE-HARDING ARMY MODEL

When Adams broke with his partners in 1853, the elder Deane, John, set up his own business. Later he began manufacturing a revolver designed by William Harding with a new, simpler type of double-action lock—the forerunner of modern actions. The two-piece frame could be dismantled by removing the pin located in the top strap in front of the hammer nose. Considered unreliable, the pistol never achieved lasting popularity.

DATE	1858
ORIGIN	UK
WEIGHT	2½ LB (1.15 KG)
BARREL	5¼ IN (13.5 CM)
CALIBER	40-BORE

THE REVOLUTIONARY WORLD

BRASS-CARTRIDGE PISTOLS

SMITH & WESSON ACQUIRED the patent for a revolver with a bored-through cylinder to accept brass cartridges in 1856, from Rollin White. By the time their protection expired in 1869, the center-fire cartridge (with the primer located in the center, rather than in the rim, as in earlier examples) had been devised, and the world's gunmakers were poised to begin manufacturing what would prove to be the cylinder revolver in its final form. Later refinements made it possible to charge and empty the chambers more rapidly.

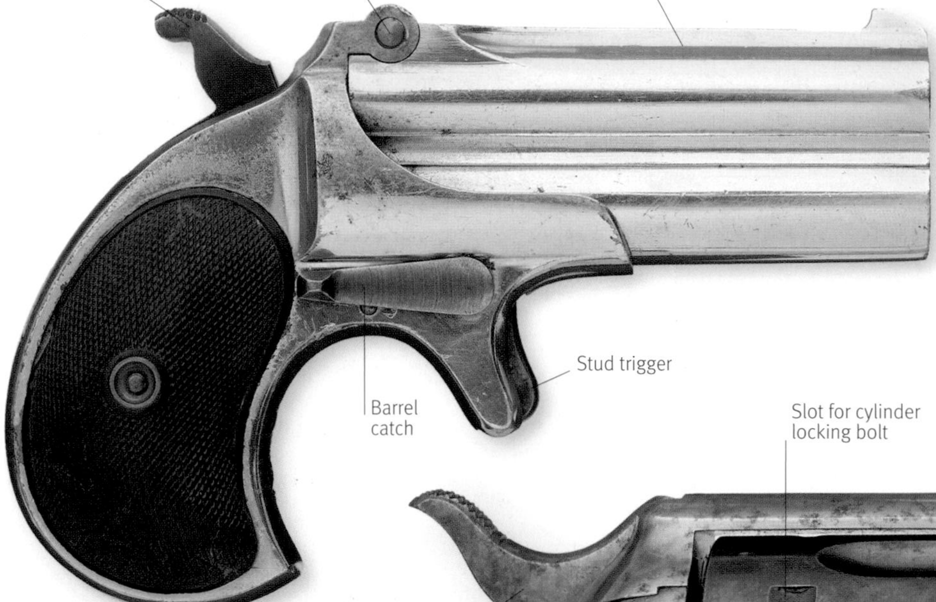

Hammer

Hinge

Barrels positioned one above the other

REMINGTON DOUBLE DERRINGER

Henry Deringer was a Philadelphia gun maker who specialized in pocket pistols; his name was ascribed—with the mysterious addition of a second "r"—to a genre of such weapons. The best known of them was the rimfire Remington Double Derringer, a top-hinged, tip-up, over-and-under design that was to remain in production until 1935.

DATE	1865
ORIGIN	US
WEIGHT	¾ LB (0.34 KG)
BARREL	3 IN (7.6 CM)
CALIBER	.41 IN

Stud trigger

Barrel catch

Slot for cylinder locking bolt

Barrel screws into frame

Notched hammer acts as rear sight

Loading/ejection gate swings down

COLT MODEL 1873 SINGLE-ACTION ARMY

The Colt SAA married the single-action lock of the old Dragoon model to a bored-through cylinder in a solid frame, into which the barrel was screwed. It was loaded, and the spent case ejected, by way of the gate on the right of the frame, and a spring-loaded ejector was fitted. This is the long-barreled Cavalry model.

DATE	1873
ORIGIN	US
WEIGHT	2½ LB (1.1 KG)
BARREL	7½ IN (19 CM)
CALIBER	.45 IN

Hard rubber-composition grips

Six-chambered cylinder

Single-action trigger is forced forward when hammer is cocked

Prawl prevents pistol slipping through hand under recoil

Lanyard ring

COLT NAVY CONVERSION

Colt replaced its angular 1851 Navy revolver with a new, streamlined version ten years later. This example has been converted to accept brass cartridges after the fashion of the Single-Action Army; many percussion revolvers were adapted in this way.

DATE	1861
ORIGIN	US
WEIGHT	2¾ LB (1.25 KG)
BARREL	7½ IN (19 CM)
CALIBER	.36 IN

Loading/ejection gate
Round barrel
Extractor-rod housing
Extractor rod
Plain walnut grip

LEFAUCHEUX PIN-FIRE REVOLVER

Casimir Lefaucheux invented the pin-fire cartridge in the mid-1830s, and his son Eugène later produced a six-shot, double-action revolver for it in 12 mm caliber. This is a Cavalry model of 1853. An Army model, without a steadying spur, was also produced.

DATE	1853
ORIGIN	FRANCE
WEIGHT	2¼ LB (0.95 KG)
BARREL	5¼ IN (13.5 CM)
CALIBER	12 MM

Loading/ejection gate
Round barrel
Ejector rod
Trigger guard with steadying spur

Fore sight
Extractor-rod housing

WEBLEY-PRYSE POCKET PISTOL

In 1876, Charles Pryse designed a tip-down, break-open revolver with a rebounding-hammer action and simultaneous extraction of spent cartridges. This Fourth Model Webley-Pryse, recognizable by its fluted cylinder, was made in calibers ranging from .32 in to .577 in.

DATE	1877
ORIGIN	UK
WEIGHT	2¾ LB (1.3 KG)
BARREL	6¼ IN (16 CM)
CALIBER	.45 IN

Frame catch
Rib reinforces barrel
Hammer
Rubber-composition grips
Cylinder axis pin
Frame pivot
Lanyard ring

SMITH & WESSON NO. 3, RUSSIAN MODEL

Smith & Wesson's early designs had been top-hinged, tip-up revolvers, but for the No. 3 revolver it utilized a single-action, bottom-hinged design with an automatic simultaneous extractor. It soon won a contract to supply the Russian Army with 20,000 of these pistols, chambered for a special cartridge (the second version is shown above). They were the most accurate revolvers of their day.

DATE	1871
ORIGIN	US
WEIGHT	2¾ LB (1.25 KG)
BARREL	8 IN (20.3 CM)
CALIBER	.44 IN

Frame locking catch
Rear sight
Barrel rib
Fore sight
Frame hinge
Trigger guard with steadying spur

FULL VIEW

THE REVOLUTIONARY WORLD

COLT NAVY PISTOLS

BY 1861, his patent protection a thing of the past, Samuel Colt had to rely on the quality of his products to outsell his competitors at a time (during the American Civil War) when the demand for firearms in the United States was running at an all-time high. His Hartford factory was in full production, under the superintendence of Elisha King Root, and that year, he introduced a new, streamlined version of his .36-caliber Navy revolver, which had appeared a decade earlier. Some 38,843 examples of the Model 1861 Navy were produced before it was discontinued in 1873.

AMMUNITION

The powder and projectile were made into simple cartridges with combustible cases made of fabric, rendered waterproof and rigid by an application of varnish. These were crushed when seated home in the chamber by the action of the compound rammer.

PERCUSSION CAPS

Percussion caps, so called because of their shape, were made of two layers of copper foil with a minute quantity of fulminate of mercury, oxidizer, and a sustaining agent sandwiched between them. They were first introduced in this form in about 1822.

Blade fore sight

Rammer lever

COLT NAVY MODEL 1861

Colt was a firm believer in standardization in manufacture. One of the factors that made Colt's pistols so sought-after was the interchangeablility of their components, which meant that replacements for broken parts could be bought off the shelf, and that improvements could be easily incorporated.

DATE	1861
ORIGIN	US
WEIGHT	2½ LB (1.2 KG)
BARREL	5½ IN (19.1 CM)
CALIBER	.36 IN

Cutaway allows caps to be placed on nipple

Nipple

Cylinder engraved with naval scene

Wedge passes through cylinder axis pin, retaining cylinder in frame

Compound rammer

Two bullets can be cast at once

Excess lead sheared by blade when bullet set

LEAD BULLETS

By 1861 the cylindro-ogival form had replaced the ball to become the standard shape for both rifle and pistol bullets. They were still being made from pure lead, without the addition of a hardening agent such as antimony.

BULLET MOLD

Even though calibers had by now become standardized, it was still almost unheard-of to buy loose bullets. Instead, one bought a bar of lead and made one's own bullets, using the mold supplied with the pistol.

LOADING THE REVOLVER

The procedure for loading a percussion revolver was straightforward. A cartridge was placed into the chamber as far as it would go, in the six o'clock position, via the cutaway in the front of the frame. Alternatively, loose powder (from a flask with an angled spout) and a loose bullet could be inserted. The lever of the compound rammer was then lowered, pushing the rammer proper against the nose of the bullet and forcing it into the chamber, where the fragile casing of the cartridge was broken open. When all six chambers were loaded, a percussion cap was placed on each nipple in turn by way of the cutaway at the rear of the cylinder.

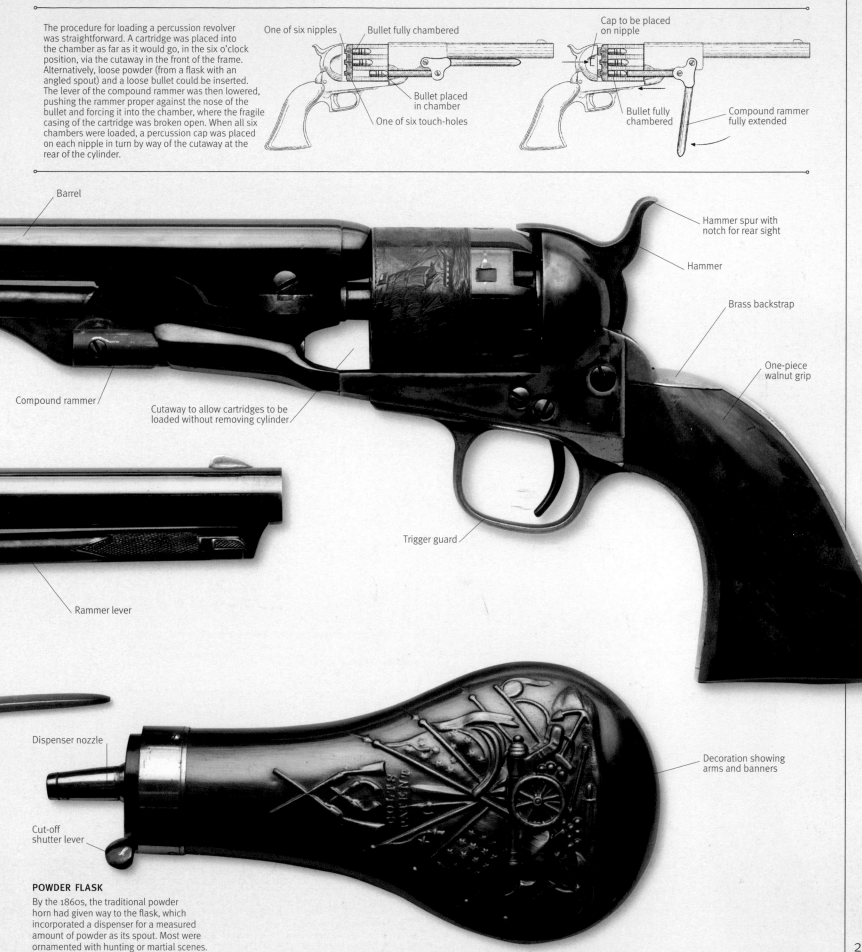

One of six nipples

Bullet fully chambered

Cap to be placed on nipple

Bullet placed in chamber

One of six touch-holes

Bullet fully chambered

Compound rammer fully extended

Barrel

Hammer spur with notch for rear sight

Hammer

Brass backstrap

Compound rammer

Cutaway to allow cartridges to be loaded without removing cylinder

One-piece walnut grip

Trigger guard

Rammer lever

Dispenser nozzle

Decoration showing arms and banners

Cut-off shutter lever

POWDER FLASK

By the 1860s, the traditional powder horn had given way to the flask, which incorporated a dispenser for a measured amount of powder as its spout. Most were ornamented with hunting or martial scenes.

1775 — 1900

► **290–291** SELF-LOADING PISTOLS 1900–1920   ► **292–293** SELF-LOADING PISTOLS 1920–1950   ► **294–295** SELF-LOADING PISTOLS FROM 1950

THE REVOLUTIONARY WORLD

SELF-LOADING PISTOLS

THE GERMAN GUN MAKER AND ENGINEER Hugo Borchardt emigrated, in 1860, to the US, where he worked for Colt, Winchester, and other gun manufacturers. When he returned to his native Germany in 1892 to work for Waffenfabrik Loewe, the company was already producing Maxim guns, and that motivated him to experiment with a self-loading pistol. By 1893 he had produced a satisfactory if somewhat cumbersome design, and that in turn inspired others. By the end of the century, there were a dozen self-loading pistols on the market, all of which were designed and produced in Europe.

Detachable stock

Leather holster

BORCHARDT C/93

In Borchardt's pioneering design, a toggle joint locks the bolt in place. Recoil forces the toggle to break upward, the bolt travels to the rear against a coil spring, and the spent case is ejected. Rebounding, the bolt picks up a fresh round, chambers it, and leaves the action cocked for the next shot. The gun was a commercial failure; only 3,000 were produced, and it was discontinued in 1898 due to the competition from Mauser.

DATE	1894
ORIGIN	GERMANY
WEIGHT	3¾LB (1.66KG)
BARREL	6½IN (16.5CM)
CALIBRE	7.63MM

Hammer   Tangent rear sight

Loading/ejection port

Blade fore sight

Fixed ten-round box magazine

MAUSER C/96

Although complicated and slow to load due to its fixed magazine, the "Broomhandle" Mauser Selbstladepistole soon became popular in military circles thanks to its very powerful ammunition. It remained in manufacture until 1937, and was copied the world over. It was usually supplied with a holster-cum-shoulder stock. Fully automatic versions were also produced.

DATE	1896
ORIGIN	GERMANY
WEIGHT	2½LB (1.15KG)
BARREL	5½IN (14CM)
CALIBRE	7.65MM

MAUSER ON FILM

British Prime Minister Winston Churchill carried a Mauser C/96 during the battle of Omdurman in 1898, a shoulder injury preventing him from using a saber. Here, Simon Ward plays the title role in the 1972 film *Young Winston*.

Rear sight

Toggle joint doubles as cocking piece

Ejection port

Fore sight

SYSTEM BORCHARDT. PATENT.

Recoil spring housing

Butt houses removable eight-round magazine

Recoil spring housing

Steadying grip

Rear sight

Cocking grip for pulling slide to rear

Fore sight

Rear sight

Recoil spring housing

Cocking grip

Safety catch

Butt houses removable seven-round magazine

Butt houses removable seven-round magazine

BROWNING MODEL 1900

John Moses Browning, probably the most prolific gun designer ever, moved to Belgium from his native USA in 1895. Here he produced an improved version of his first semi-automatic pistol – a simple, unlocked-breech, blowback design – that became known as the Model 1900. Small and light, it was hugely popular, and over 700,000 were sold before production ceased in 1911.

DATE	1900
ORIGIN	BELGIUM
WEIGHT	0.63KG (1½LB)
BARREL	10.2CM (4IN)
CALIBRE	7.65MM

Magazine release

GABBETT-FAIRFAX "MARS"

Perhaps inspired by the Mauser's success, Hugh Gabbett-Fairfax wanted to produce a super-powerful pistol; the result was the Mars. Described by users as "a nightmare," it was complex, awkward, and unwieldy, with a vicious recoil.

DATE	1898
ORIGIN	UK
WEIGHT	3½LB (1.55KG)
BARREL	11½IN (26.5CM)
CALIBRE	.45IN

Blade fore sight

Exposed hammer

Cylinder-indexing grooves

BERGMANN NO.3

Theodore Bergmann's No.3 pistol was rather simplistic in design. The pistol was held in battery by a coiled spring, and the spent cartridge case was blown out of the breech by gas pressure.

DATE	1896
ORIGIN	GERMANY
WEIGHT	0.88KG (2LB)
BARREL	11.2CM (4½IN)
CALIBRE	6.5MM

Recoil spring housing

Cover for five-round magazine

WEBLEY-FOSBERY

In 1899, Colonel George Fosbery designed a self-cocking revolver in which recoil propelled the barrel and cylinder backwards within a slide, indexing the cylinder. It proved too fragile for battlefield conditions.

DATE	1900
ORIGIN	UK
WEIGHT	2½LB (1.1KG)
BARREL	7½IN (19CM)
CALIBRE	.455IN

Slide

Cylinder-retaining wedge

Manual cocking lever

NAPOLEONIC WARS
Swords, bayonets, pistols,
and muskets were widely used in
the early 19th century for close fighting,
with artillery and long-range rifles used to
great effect over longer distances. The artillery caused
most damage, with cannonballs being fired, and canisters
and shells exploding near to, or amongst, the enemy's ranks.

1775—1900

◀ 148–149 MATCHLOCK AND FLINTLOCK LONG GUNS   ◀ 212–215 FLINTLOCK PISTOLS 1775–1850   ▶ 234–235 WEAPON SHOWCASE: BAKER RIFLE

THE REVOLUTIONARY WORLD

FLINTLOCK MUSKETS AND RIFLES

BY THE START OF THE 18TH CENTURY, the flintlock mechanism, simple and robust, had almost reached its final form. It lacked only roller bearings and reinforcing bridles—metal straps holding interdependent parts in alignment—that virtually eliminated misfiring. It is a tribute to the flintlock's reliability that individual weapons such as the British Land Service Musket and the French Charleville were to be made in their hundreds of thousands, and remain in service for almost a century with only minor modifications.

Grip extension

Flint clamping screw

Flashpan and touch-hole

Flint

Cock

Feather spring flicks steel and pan cover forward as cock falls

Barrel band secures the barrel to the stock

Rear sling attachment

Trigger guard

Pan

Flint clamp

Steel

Barrel band securing spring

Barrel band

Cock

Clamping screw

Clamp upper jaw

Cock

Rear sling swivel

Trigger

Proof mark

Comb of the stock

Small of the stock

Feather spring

Flashpan and touch-hole

Official mark

Barrel band

Fore sight

Forward sling swivel

Fore end cap
and barrel band

Cleaning rod

HALL RIFLE

John Hancock Hall's rifle, designed in 1811 and
introduced into service in 1819, was the first regulation
American rifle to incorporate an opening breech; hinged
at the front, it tipped up at a 30-degree angle for loading.
Hall rifles and carbines were eventually produced in
percussion form, too, when the entire breech unit could
be removed and used as a pistol.

DATE	1819
ORIGIN	US
WEIGHT	10½ LB (4.68 KG)
BARREL	32½ IN (82.5 CM)
CALIBER	.54 IN

Breech-block is hinged
at the forward end and
tips up through 30° for
loading

Breech block
release catch

Lock cover

Flash guard

Cock

Striker steel

Butt plate

Barrel band

Trigger

PRUSSIAN 1809-PATTERN MUSKET

The Prussian equivalent of the British Brown Bess or the
French Charleville, the 1809-Pattern musket was made at
the Potsdam Armoury in Berlin. Unlike its competitors it
was furnished with a (brass) flash guard around the pan
as standard, but in other respects it was similar. The
majority of these flintlocks were converted to percussion.

DATE	1809
ORIGIN	GERMANY
WEIGHT	8¾ LB (4 KG)
BARREL	41 IN (104.5 CM)
CALIBER	.75 IN

Forward sling swivel

Fore end cap
and barrel band

Ramrod

Retaining notch

Bayonet
mounting
tube

Triangular
stabbing blade

AUSTRIAN MODEL 1798 MUSKET

When Emperor Leopold of Austria and King Frederick
William of Prussia declared their intention to restore
Louis XVI of France to his throne in 1791, Austria found
itself quite literally outgunned by the French. As a result
a new musket, a copy of the French Model 1777, was
commissioned, but with some improvements, notably in
the way the ramrod was housed.

DATE	1798
ORIGIN	AUSTRIA
WEIGHT	9 LB (4.2 KG)
BARREL	45 IN (114.3 CM)
CALIBER	.65 IN

Fore sight

Bayonet
securing
pin

Forward
sling swivel

Bayonet
retaining
notch

Fore end cap
and barrel band

CHARLEVILLE MUSKET

The Charleville muskets were introduced in 1754 and,
modified a number of times, remained in service until the
1840s. Large numbers of Modèle 1776 guns found their
way to the US when a revised pattern was introduced the
following year; they were the main armament of the
Continental Army that defeated the British.

DATE	1776
ORIGIN	FRANCE
WEIGHT	9¼ LB (4.2 KG)
BARREL	44 IN (113.5 CM)
CALIBER	.65 IN

Barrel-securing pin

FULL VIEW

INDIA-PATTERN MUSKET

The Brown Bess in its final form differed from earlier
models in the length of the barrel. It was reduced from
46 in (117 cm) to 42 in (106.5 cm) in the 1760s and finally
to 39 in (99 cm). This modification was made for the
East India Company and later adopted by the British
Army which kept it in service until the 1840s.

DATE	1797 ONWARD
ORIGIN	UK
WEIGHT	9 LB (4.1 KG)
BARREL	39 IN (99 CM)
CALIBER	.75 IN

BAKER RIFLE

IN FEBRUARY 1800, the Baker rifle won a competition organized by the Army's Board of Ordnance and became the first rifle officially adopted by the British Army. It was similar to weapons in use in Germany, and its novel feature lay in its barrel. With shallow or "slow" rifling—just a quarter-turn in the length of the barrel—it stayed clean, and thus usable, for longer. It was issued to select men at first, and was superseded in 1838.

Brass
butt plate

Fixed fore sight

Lug for
attaching
bayonet

Protective
cover for cock
and steel

Ramrod
doubled as a
cleaning rod

Box for patches
and tools

Sling was also
used to steady
the aim

RIFLE

Ezekiel Baker's rifle was a robust weapon, designed to keep on working even under the most difficult conditions, and several modifications to the original design reflected that. With its short barrel (30 inches instead of the more customary 39) it was not particularly accurate, but was still a great improvement over the smooth-bore musket then in general use.

DATE	1802–37
ORIGIN	ENGLAND
WEIGHT	9 LB (4 KG)
BARREL	30 IN (76 CM)
CALIBER	.625 IN

Jaw
screw

Steel

Flint

Cock

Pan

Feather
spring

Standard Land-
Pattern lock

Armory mark

Brass cheek plate

Trigger

Leather
sling

Brass
trigger guard

RIFLEMAN OF THE 95TH REGIMENT

British rifle companies existed before the Baker was adopted, but a new regiment, the 95th (Rifle) Regiment, was raised specifically to exploit it. Dressed in green coats with black facings (and later known as the Green Jackets) they first saw action as marine infantry during the Battle of Copenhagen in 1801, but really came into their own during the Peninsular War of 1808–14.

Rolled
cowhide
head

Beechwood
shaft

MALLET

To begin with, small mallets were issued with Baker rifles, but were soon found to be unnecessary. Hand pressure alone was sufficient to ram down the ball.

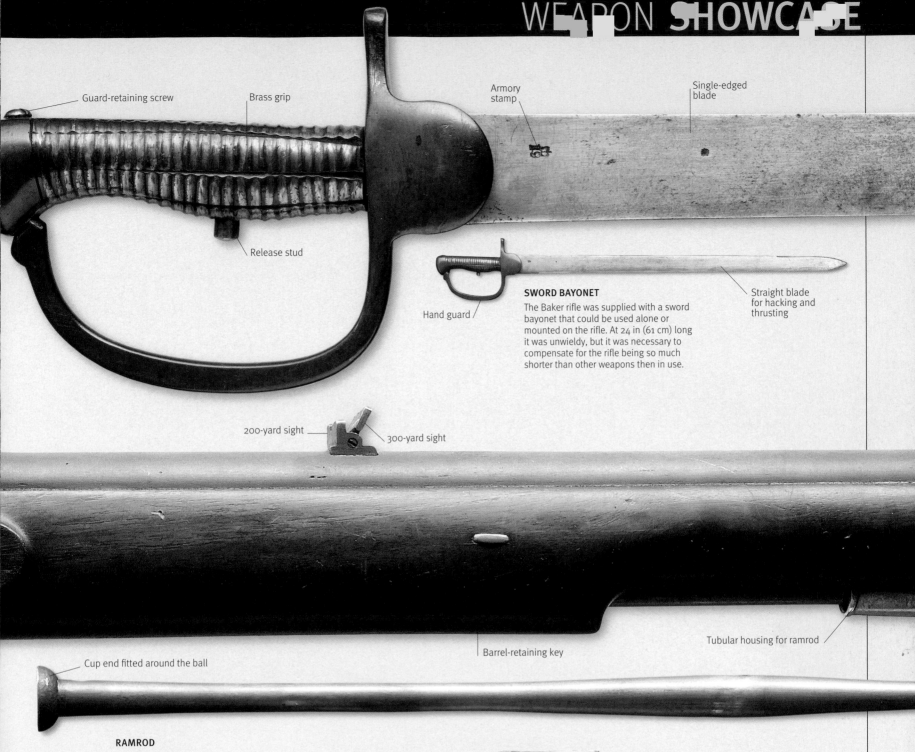

Guard-retaining screw

Brass grip

Armory stamp

Single-edged blade

Release stud

SWORD BAYONET
The Baker rifle was supplied with a sword bayonet that could be used alone or mounted on the rifle. At 24 in (61 cm) long it was unwieldy, but it was necessary to compensate for the rifle being so much shorter than other weapons then in use.

Hand guard

Straight blade for hacking and thrusting

200-yard sight

300-yard sight

Barrel-retaining key

Tubular housing for ramrod

Cup end fitted around the ball

RAMROD
The steel rod was used to ram the charge and projectile into the barrel.

Gunpowder wrapped in paper

Lead ball wrapped in paper

PAPER-WRAPPED CARTRIDGE
These contained a charge of powder and the ball. They were torn open with the teeth, with the ball held in the mouth. A small portion of the charge was poured into the pan and the rest down the muzzle. The paper would then be rammed down to form a wad, and the ball, wrapped in a patch taken from the patchbox, rammed down on top.

1775—1900

◄ 216–217 PERCUSSION-CAP PISTOLS   ◄ 218–219 AMERICAN PERCUSSION-CAP REVOLVERS   ◄ 222–223 BRITISH PERCUSSION-CAP REVOLVERS   ► 240–241 PERCUSSION CAP BREECH LOADERS

THE REVOLUTIONARY WORLD

PERCUSSION-CAP MUSKETS AND RIFLES

THE INVENTION, IN APPROXIMATELY 1820, of the fulminate of mercury percussion cap, revolutionized firearms, making them both simpler and more reliable. By the mid-19th century, all the world's armies had switched to the system, and were adopting the expanding bullet—developed by Norton and brought to its final form by James Burton—which allowed a muzzle-loading rifle to be charged as rapidly as a musket.

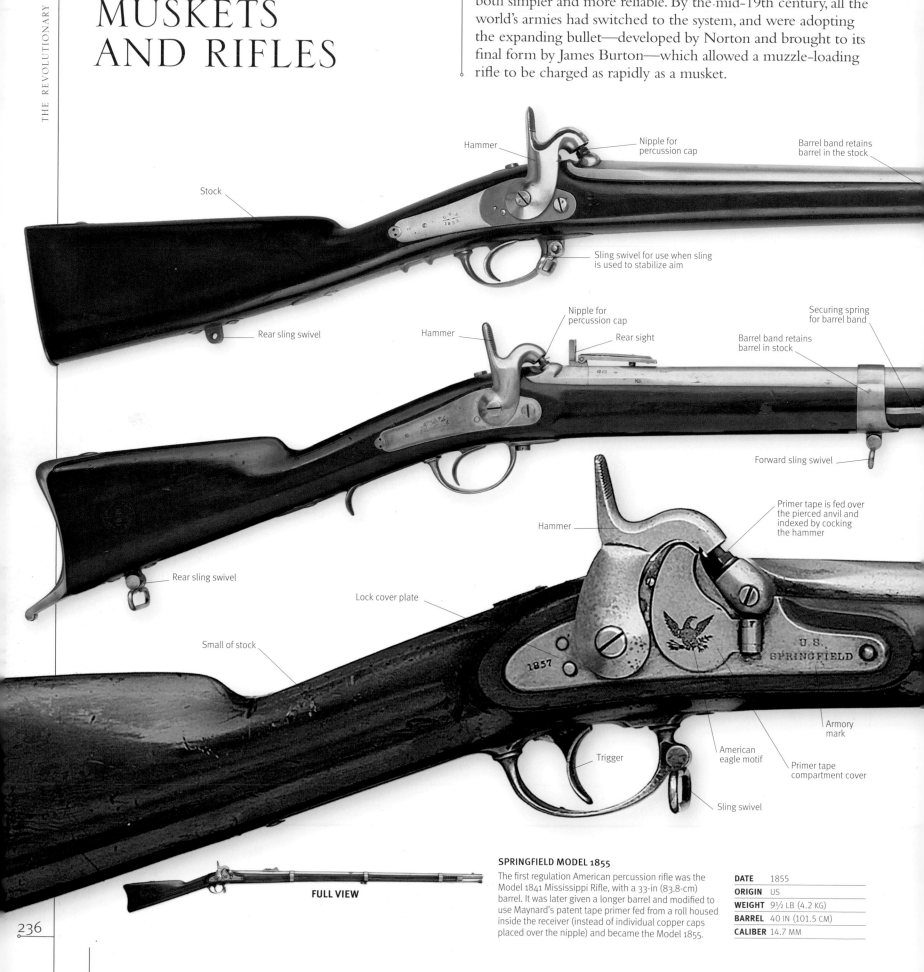

Hammer

Nipple for percussion cap

Barrel band retains barrel in the stock

Stock

Sling swivel for use when sling is used to stabilize aim

Rear sling swivel

Nipple for percussion cap

Hammer

Rear sight

Securing spring for barrel band

Barrel band retains barrel in stock

Forward sling swivel

Rear sling swivel

Hammer

Primer tape is fed over the pierced anvil and indexed by cocking the hammer

Lock cover plate

Small of stock

Trigger

American eagle motif

Primer tape compartment cover

Armory mark

Sling swivel

FULL VIEW

SPRINGFIELD MODEL 1855

The first regulation American percussion rifle was the Model 1841 Mississippi Rifle, with a 33-in (83.8-cm) barrel. It was later given a longer barrel and modified to use Maynard's patent tape primer fed from a roll housed inside the receiver (instead of individual copper caps placed over the nipple) and became the Model 1855.

DATE	1855
ORIGIN	US
WEIGHT	9½ LB (4.2 KG)
BARREL	40 IN (101.5 CM)
CALIBER	14.7 MM

SPRINGFIELD MODEL 1863 TYPE II

The Springfield M1855, with its tape primer system, was unsatisfactory and replaced by the M1861, which was itself not entirely free of faults; notably in the hammer and nipple. The Model 1863 saw the problems cured and other refinements made. The Type II was the last muzzle-loading weapon issued to the United States army.

DATE	1863
ORIGIN	US
WEIGHT	9½ LB (4.3 KG)
BARREL	40 IN (101.5 CM)
CALIBER	.58 IN

Nipple for percussion cap
Rear sight
Barrel band retains barrel in stock
Fore sight doubles as bayonet lug
Hammer
Securing spring for barrel band
Forward sling swivel
Forestock cap
Cleaning rod
American eagle motif
Rear sling swivel

FUSIL REGLEMENTAIRE MLE 1853

By the 1840s, steel had come to replace iron in the production of gun barrels. It was found to rust more easily, and a surface treatment known as blueing was introduced. Proof (i.e. prototype) weapons, like this one and the Modèle 1842, not intended for issue to troops, were often left unblued, and are said to be "in the bright."

DATE	1853
ORIGIN	FRANCE
WEIGHT	9¼ LB (4.25 KG)
BARREL	40½ IN (103 CM)
CALIBER	18 MM

Securing spring for barrel band
Forestock cap incorporates a third barrel band
Bayonet locking slot
Bayonet mounting tube
Forward sling swivel

MOUSQUETON D'ARTILLERIE MLE 1842

First issued to the French Army 20 years earlier and subsequently modified to percussion ignition, the Modèle 1842 received improved rifling and detail changes to the design of the hammer and nipple. It was produced in a variety of forms, but those for issue to artillerymen were 34 in (86 cm), with two barrel bands.

DATE	1843
ORIGIN	FRANCE
WEIGHT	10 LB (4.6 KG)
BARREL	34 IN (86 CM)
CALIBER	18 MM

Fore sight
Cleaning rod
Forestock cap incorporates a second barrel band
Rear sight
Barrel band secures barrel in stock
Retaining spring for barrel band

WHITWORTH RIFLE

Sir Joseph Whitworth (who was best known for standardizing screw threads) produced a rifle for a British Army trial, with an hexagonal bore, which fired an hexagonal bullet. It proved to be accurate to well over 1,500 yards (1.4 km), but it was four times the price of an Enfield Model 1853, and never adopted by the army.

DATE	1856
ORIGIN	UK
WEIGHT	10 LB (4.55 KG)
BARREL	36 IN (91.45 CM)
CALIBER	.45 IN

Hammer
Nipple for percussion cap
Rear sight
Barrel band
Hexagonal-bored barrel
Fore sight
Low comb to butt stock
Armory mark
Cleaning rod
Rear sling swivel

LE PAGE SPORT GUN

PIERRE LE PAGE set up in business as *arquebusier* in Paris, perhaps as early as 1716, and was later appointed gun maker to the king. He was succeeded by his nephew Jean in 1782, who was retained by the Emperor Napoleon to refurbish weapons from the royal gun-room for his own use. Jean's son Henri took over the firm in 1822, by which time Napoleon had died in exile on St. Helena. This sport gun was made to commemorate the return of his ashes to France in 1840.

"Worm" fixed here

FULL VIEW

Sling attachment point

Engraved hammers

"N" for Napoleon, surmounted by a serpent

Sling attachment point

LE PAGE SPORT GUN

While the technical quality of the gun is excellent, its appeal lies in its decoration. The scrollwork on the small of the stock is enhanced with steel wire, while the metalwork is engraved with scenes from Napoleon's life and the names of some of his battles.

DATE	1840
ORIGIN	FRANCE
WEIGHT	11LB (5KG)
BARREL	31½IN (80CM)
CALIBRE	8-BORE

Scrollwork on butt inlaid with wire

Front trigger fires right barrel

Rear trigger fires left barrel

Cutters for removing flashing from moulded bullet

Trigger guard engraved with date of the return of Napoleon's ashes

BULLET MOULD

A percussion sport gun could be loaded with pellets, for use against birds and wildfowl, but also with balls for use against large game. This mold was used to make such balls.

WAD PUNCH

Wadding, usually made of paper, was rammed into the barrels after the powder but before the bullets. As it was essential that the wads precisely fitted the barrels, a wad cutter was included with the gun's tools.

HAMMER HEAD

Clenched in the hand, this was applied to the ramrod to assist with seating the balls in the barrels.

RAMROD
The gun's ramrod doubled as a cleaning rod, and could be fitted with a "worm" to allow a dud charge to be drawn.

Hooks engage with a bar at the standing breech to secure barrels into stock

Nipple for percussion cap

Rib engraved with Le Page's name and those of Napoleon's battles

TOP VIEW OF BARREL

Forestock cap

Lock plate engraved with depiction of the Battle of the Pyramids

Barrel retained by pin

Cut-off shutter lever

POWDER HORN
It was customary to use animal horn to hold the powder, it being light and strong. The nozzle was fitted with a measuring device.

Nozzle dispenses measured amount of powder

Sling attachment point

PERCUSSION CAP DISPENSER
This dispenser was designed to present percussion caps direct to the nipples of the gun. The alternative (using a tin of loose caps) was both awkward and time-consuming.

Sling attachment point

PERCUSSION CAP BREECH LOADERS

19TH-CENTURY GUNMAKERS used ingenious methods to solve the problem of obturation—making an opening breech gas-tight. Though obturation would not be reliably achieved until the advent of the brass cartridge, some makers were successful enough that their guns found a sizeable market. Carbines were particularly popular among horsemen, because they were easier to manage, and breech loaders—in theory —could be reloaded in the saddle.

SHARPS CARBINE

Christian Sharps devised his breech-loading system in 1848. Pulling the trigger guard down and forward opened the breech, and the breech-block sheared off the rear portion of the linen cartridge as it closed. During the American Civil War, the Union Army bought over 80,000 Sharps' carbines for its cavalry regiments. This rare slant-breech version from 1852 uses a Maynard tape primer.

DATE	1848
ORIGIN	US
WEIGHT	7¾ LB (3.5 KG)
BARREL	18 IN (45.5 CM)
CALIBER	.52 IN

Hammer

Patchbox

Tape primer compartment

Sliding breech-block

Breech-opening lever

Rear sling swivel

Rear sight

Fore sight

Hammer

Bolt receiver; bolt handle turns down to the left

Rear sight

Rear sling attachment

Hammer

Primer tape compartment

Royal cypher

Trigger

Forward trigger advances primer tape

Breech-block

Steel butt plate

Patchbox

Rear sling swivel

TERRY BOLT-ACTION CARBINE

The Terry carbine was the first bolt-action weapon adopted by the British Army. Its paper cartridge included a greased felt wad, which remained in the breech after firing and was pushed into the barrel by the insertion of the next round, lubricating and cleaning the bore when it was fired. In a trial, one carbine fired 1,800 rounds without requiring additional cleaning.

DATE	1861
ORIGIN	UK
WEIGHT	7 LB (3.21 KG)
BARREL	20.13 IN (51.2 CM)
CALIBER	.54 IN

Bolt

Hammer

Nipple for percussion cap

Rear sight

Barrel band

Trigger

Lock cover

WESTLEY RICHARDS "MONKEY TAIL" CARBINE

Eminent Birmingham gunmakers, Westley Richards & Co. produced two types of carbine for the British Army. One had a falling-block action, the other (illustrated) had a front-hinged tilting breech with a long, curved actuating lever, which gave the weapon its nickname. Westley Richards' carbines required the percussion cap to be located at the mid-point of the cartridge.

DATE	1866
ORIGIN	UK
WEIGHT	6½ LB (3 KG)
BARREL	19 IN (45.5 CM)
CALIBER	.45 IN

Hammer

"Monkey Tail" breech lever

Cleaning rod

Lock plate

CHASSEPOT PERCUSSION CARBINE

In the mid-1850s, gunmakers at the French Imperial Armories began experimenting with bolt-action, percussion cap breech loaders. Alphonse Chassepot produced a design using a rubber washer to seal the breech. He subsequently replaced the hammer with a needle striker within the bolt, which was accepted for use by the French Army as the Modèle 1866.

DATE	1858
ORIGIN	FRANCE
WEIGHT	6¾ LB (3.03 KG)
BARREL	28 IN (72 CM)
CALIBER	13.5 MM

Barrel band retaining spring

Combined fore stock cap and barrel band

Cleaning rod

Fore sight

Staged barrel

GREENE CARBINE

The Greene carbine, produced in small numbers for the British Army during the Crimean War, lost out to its rivals due to its cumbersome mechanism. The barrel had to be rotated through a quarter-turn: this unlocked the breech, which was then free to swing out so that a new cartridge could be introduced. The carbine used Maynard's tape primer system, rather than individual percussion caps.

DATE	1855
ORIGIN	US
WEIGHT	3½ LB (3.4 KG)
BARREL	56 CM (22 IN)
CALIBER	.54 IN

CUSTER'S LAST STAND

First used in the Civil War and then in the Indian Wars, the Sharps carbine was favored by US cavalrymen. However, its use at Little Bighorn against the Sioux and Cheyenne Indians could not prevent the defeat of the Seventh Cavalry.

SWORD BAYONET

BRITISH REDCOAT

IN THE ERA OF musket-and-bayonet warfare, red-coated infantry formed the core of the British regular army. Recruited from the poor, landless, and unemployed, they took the "king's shilling" after being plied with drink, or tempted by the glamour of army life, or even as an alternative to imprisonment for petty crime. Yet these "scum of the earth," as the Duke of Wellington called them, were turned into resolute fighters who won many victories, notably over the French in the Napoleonic Wars.

DRILL AND DISCIPLINE

The Redcoat infantry were trained to fight as a unit, giving unhesitating obedience to orders and suppressing individual initiative. This was achieved through relentless drill, brutal discipline—with extensive use of flogging—and the cultivation of loyalty to the soldier's regiment and his colleagues. The emphasis on drill and discipline was essential given the weapons and tactics of the period. The key British infantry arm, the Brown Bess musket, was wildly inaccurate and thus effective only if infantry were trained to fire in volleys. They had to learn to form lines or squares on the battlefield—the latter to resist cavalry—to advance unarmored into musket fire, or stand firm under artillery bombardment. Holding steady was the surest way to avoid casualties, presenting an unbroken line of bayonets as the last line of defense. The bright red coat made sense on battlefields where men had to identify friend and foe through the thick smoke of gunpowder.

BATTLE OF WATERLOO
British infantry squares fight off French cavalry in the last battle of the Napoleonic Wars at Waterloo in June 1815. Ably led by the Duke of Wellington, British soldiers proved a match for Napoleon's forces throughout the later stages of the war, showing discipline and steadiness under fire.

"THEY WERE COMPLETELY BEATEN…BUT THEY DID NOT KNOW IT AND WOULD NOT RUN."

MARSHAL SOULT AFTER BATTLE OF ALBUERA, MAY 1811

SWORD BAYONET FOR BAKER RIFLE

BATTLE OF YORKTOWN
A 19th-century painting shows British infantry engaging the American rebels at bayonet-point in the outer redoubts of Yorktown in 1781. Surrender to the Americans and their French allies at Yorktown brought the American War of Independence to a humiliating conclusion for British forces.

PAPER-WRAPPED BAKER RIFLE CARTRIDGE

BAYONET FOR BROWN BESS MUSKET

BROWN BESS MUSKET

BAKER RIFLE

REDCOAT UNIFORM
This British infantryman wears early 19th-century uniform. The shako replaced the tricorne hat in 1801–02. By 1815 breeches and gaiters had been replaced by trousers and the "stovepipe" hat had given way to the "Belgic" shako with false front.

"Stovepipe" shako with brass plate

Red coat with short skirts at back

Buff leather cross-belts whitened with pipe clay

White breeches

Long buttoned gaiters

LEXINGTON AND CONCORD

At the outset of the American War of Independence, in Massachusetts in April 1775, British Redcoats were sent from Boston and Charleston to seize the arms and gunpowder of rebel Minutemen militia at Concord. There was an initial confrontation with militia at Lexington, in which eight Minutemen were killed. When the British reached Concord, they met stiff resistance. Obliged to retreat, the Redcoats were harassed by American snipers with rifles, using guerrilla tactics for which the British were unprepared. British losses numbered 273, compared with 95 on the Massachusetts rebel side. The encounter showed Redcoats at their worst. Trained to fight standing up in the open against European armies employing identical tactics, they were wrong-footed by opponents who used trees for cover and fired aimed shots instead of volleys.

BRITISH TROOPS MARCH ON CONCORD

SPORT GUNS

THE 19TH CENTURY WAS CHARACTERIZED by innovation and invention in many fields, and the gunmaker's trade was no exception. At the start of the period, even the most ordinary of guns had to be handcrafted from scratch, making them very expensive, not just to produce, but also to repair. Long before the end of the century, however, the majority of guns were being produced *en masse*, which not only made them more affordable, but brought to them the quality and reliability previously found only in the most prestigious guns.

Pellet dispenser

Nipple

Hammer

Forestock cap

Ramrod thimble

Bead fore sight

Barrel- securing pin

Trigger

Grip

Ramrod

ENGLISH PELLET-LOCK PERCUSSION GUN

Before the invention of the percussion cap, in 1822, the detonating material was made up in a variety of ways. One involved binding it with gum or varnish, and the pellets thus formed were contained in a rotating drum attached to the cock. Each revolution of the drum dispensed a single pellet to the anvil/nipple, where it was detonated by the hammer.

DATE	1820
ORIGIN	UK
WEIGHT	5¼ LB (2.39 KG)
BARREL	32¼ IN (82.2 CM)
CALIBER	12-BORE

Figured burr walnut stock

Hammer acts near-vertically on the primer pin

Forward sling attachment

Breech locking lever

Lock cover

Breech pivot pin

Rear sling attachment

FRENCH PIN-FIRE SHOTGUN

Casimir Lefaucheux invented a breech-loading gun with a break-open action, locked by a turning lever in front of the trigger guard. He also invented a cartridge, incorporating a short metal pin protruding from the case that detonated a fulminate charge placed within the cartridge. This shotgun incorporated both developments.

DATE	1833
ORIGIN	FRANCE
WEIGHT	7 LB (3.15 KG)
BARREL	25½ IN (65 CM)
CALIBER	16-BORE

GERMAN BREAK-OPEN DOUBLE RIFLE

Even after the perfection of the bolt-action magazine rifle, there were those who refused to embrace the new technology. Hunters, particularly of big and dangerous game, preferred to trust the simplicity of a break-open double-barreled design.

DATE	1880
ORIGIN	GERMANY
WEIGHT	7½ LB (3.43 KG)
BARREL	25½ IN (65 CM)
CALIBER	0.45 IN

FULL VIEW

Hammer

Nipple is recessed

Breech-locking lever

Gold-inlayed engraving

'Button' for adjusting the set trigger

Paired triggers

GERMAN BOLT-ACTION SPORTER

Receiver — Bolt — Rear sight

Safety catch

Fore sight ramp

Blade fore sight

Turned-down bolt handle

Five-round integral magazine

Incised checkering on semi-pistol grip

Rear sling attachment

Waffenfabrik Mauser came to dominate the world market for bolt-action rifles for both civilian and military applications, and its hunting rifles set the standard for the type. This rifle employs the action of the Model 1888 infantry rifle as modified for the carbine, with the flattened, turned-down bolt handle. The five-round magazine is of the pattern developed by Mannlicher.

DATE	1890
ORIGIN	GERMANY
WEIGHT	7 LB (3.2 KG)
BARREL	25 IN (63.5 CM)
CALIBER	7.9 MM x 57

COLT PATTERSON REVOLVING RIFLE

Rear sight

Recessed nipple for percussion cap

Cylinder-retaining wedge passes through the axis pin

Plain unfluted cylinder has eight chambers

Cocking ring

Samuel Colt was awarded his first patent, for a six-shot revolver pistol, in London in October 1835, and set up his first factory, in Patterson, New Jersey. As well as pistols, he began turning out revolver rifles, but his facilities were limited and he soon went bankrupt. Patterson-built Colts, such as this first-pattern concealed-hammer eight-shot rifle, are extremely rare.

DATE	1837
ORIGIN	US
WEIGHT	8½ LB (3.9 KG)
BARREL	32 IN (81.3 CM)
CALIBER	0.36 IN

ENGLISH ROOK AND RABBIT RIFLE

Hammer — Rear sight — Barrel band

Bead fore sight

Trigger

Breech-locking lever

Though unfashionable today, pies made from the common rook were often found on the Victorian cottage dinner table, and the type of simple small-bore rifle used to shoot both rooks and rabbits took their name as its own. This example is a break-open design, the breech locked by the lever in front of the trigger guard using a method patented by Frederick Prince in 1855.

DATE	1860
ORIGIN	UK
WEIGHT	3½ LB (1.63 KG)
BARREL	25 IN (63.5 CM)
CALIBER	0.37 IN

Incised checkering on the fore stock to improve grip

Rear sight

Forestock cap shaped to fit the hand

Barrel pivot pin

Abbreviated forestock

Barrel-securing pin

Hammer

Lock cover

ENGLISH PIN-FIRE SHOTGUN

Breech-locking catch

Paired triggers

Casimir Lefaucheux's pin-fire system remained popular with shotgun-armed hunters (particularly in Britain and France) long after it had been outmoded by Joshua Shaw's percussion caps. This example, with back-action locks and side-mounted breech-locking lever, is finely finished, but with little in the way of decoration. It was the work of Samuel and Charles Smith of London.

DATE	c.1860
ORIGIN	UK
WEIGHT	6¾ LB (3.07 KG)
LENGTH	30 IN (76.2 CM)
CALIBER	12-BORE

THE REVOLUTIONARY WORLD

OTTOMAN EMPIRE FIREARMS

BY THE END OF THE 17TH CENTURY, the Ottoman Empire stretched from Constantinople (Istanbul), its capital, through the Balkans to modern-day Austria, across North Africa almost to the Straits of Gibraltar, north into Russia, east almost to the Straits of Hormuz, and south to the Sudan. Conquering and controlling such a vast area required military acumen and also the most modern weapons, so Ottoman gunmaking flourished from an early date. Many of the surviving pieces are, broadly speaking, sumptuously decorated copies of European designs, although some Ottoman *tüfenk* (muskets) resemble Indian designs.

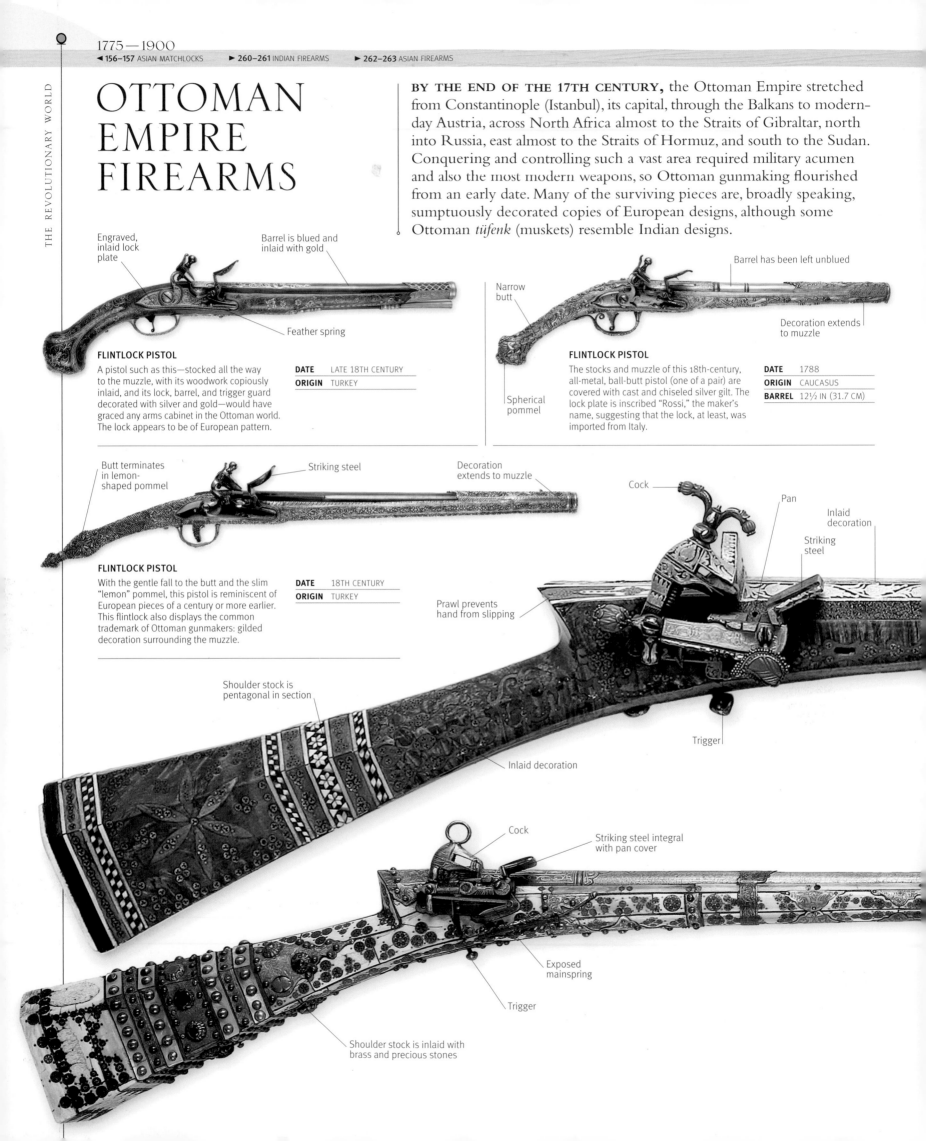

Engraved, inlaid lock plate

Barrel is blued and inlaid with gold

Feather spring

FLINTLOCK PISTOL

A pistol such as this—stocked all the way to the muzzle, with its woodwork copiously inlaid, and its lock, barrel, and trigger guard decorated with silver and gold—would have graced any arms cabinet in the Ottoman world. The lock appears to be of European pattern.

DATE	LATE 18TH CENTURY
ORIGIN	TURKEY

Barrel has been left unblued

Narrow butt

Decoration extends to muzzle

Spherical pommel

FLINTLOCK PISTOL

The stocks and muzzle of this 18th-century, all-metal, ball-butt pistol (one of a pair) are covered with cast and chiseled silver gilt. The lock plate is inscribed "Rossi," the maker's name, suggesting that the lock, at least, was imported from Italy.

DATE	1788
ORIGIN	CAUCASUS
BARREL	12½ IN (31.7 CM)

Butt terminates in lemon-shaped pommel

Striking steel

Decoration extends to muzzle

FLINTLOCK PISTOL

With the gentle fall to the butt and the slim "lemon" pommel, this pistol is reminiscent of European pieces of a century or more earlier. This flintlock also displays the common trademark of Ottoman gunmakers: gilded decoration surrounding the muzzle.

DATE	18TH CENTURY
ORIGIN	TURKEY

Cock

Pan

Inlaid decoration

Striking steel

Prawl prevents hand from slipping

Trigger

Shoulder stock is pentagonal in section

Inlaid decoration

Cock

Striking steel integral with pan cover

Exposed mainspring

Trigger

Shoulder stock is inlaid with brass and precious stones

Silver inlay

Decorated lock plate

Gilt appliqué

Barrel is left unblued

Flared muzzle

Suspension ring

Saddle bar

Incised checkering on grip

Carved walnut stock

FLINTLOCK CARBINE

Despite its being furnished with a shoulder stock that is incised, carved, and inlaid with silver, this blunderbuss is actually a large horse pistol. The work of "the Dervish Amrullah," according to an engraved inscription, it was clearly made for use by a cavalryman, as it has a bar and ring for suspension from a saddle.

DATE	EARLY 18TH CENTURY
ORIGIN	TURKEY
BARREL	13½ IN (34.3 CM)

Cast and chiseled decoration on stock

Lock plate

Cock

Pan

Striking steel

Muzzle flares to spread shot and facilitate loading

Trigger guard

Saddle bar

FLINTLOCK CARBINE

Even more ornate than the example above, this silver-gilt blunderbuss carbine was most likely made as a presentation piece. Upon its lock plate is the inscription "London warranted," which suggests that it is a copy of an English lock.

DATE	LATE 18TH CENTURY
ORIGIN	TURKEY

Octagonal barrel

Barrel bands made of twine

SNAPHAUNCE TÜFENK

This smooth-bore musket, or *tüfenk*, is very similar both in overall form and the manner of its decoration to muskets produced in northern India. The pentagonal-section butt stock terminates at the breech in a pronounced prawl. The barrel is octagonal in section, and the lock is a snaphaunce, which had become obsolete in the west by the early 17th century.

DATE	LATE 18TH CENTURY
ORIGIN	TURKEY
BARREL	28½ IN (72.4 CM)

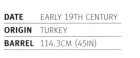

FULL VIEW

Barrel bands

Entire stock is covered in engraved and decorated ivory

Ramrod

BALKAN MIQUELET TÜFENK

Like the snaphaunce *tüfenk* above, this early 19th-century piece is reminiscent of Indian muskets. The stock is entirely covered in ivory and further embellished with inlays of precious stones and brass. The miquelet lock, common in Spain and Italy, is thought to have made its way to the Ottoman Empire via North Africa.

DATE	EARLY 19TH CENTURY
ORIGIN	TURKEY
BARREL	114.3CM (45IN)

SINGLE-SHOT BREECH-LOADING RIFLES

AFTER THE INTRODUCTION of unitary cartridges, which could be loaded by way of the breech, the challenge to gun makers was to develop a gas-tight seal. In the event, the bolt action—as pioneered by von Dreyse and Antoine Chassepot and perfected by the Mauser brothers—was to win out, but in the interim, a variety of other solutions was trialed, some of them conversions, others, such as the Martini-Henry and the Remington Rolling Block, purpose-designed.

Bolt handle

Rear sling swivel

Rear sight is graduated to 1 mile (1.6 km)

Bolt handle

Rear sight

"Trapdoor" breech cover incorporates firing pin

Rear sight

Hammer

Breech cover hinge

Falling breech-block

Rear sight

Action cocked/ uncocked indicator

Rear sling swivel (for steadiness while shooting)

Cocking lever

Rolling breech-block

Rear sight

Hammer

Trigger guard

THE BATTLE OF KÖNIGGRÄTZ

At the battle of Königgrätz (Sadowa), on July 3, 1866, thanks largely to the superior firepower of its Dreyse needle guns over the muzzle-loaders of the rival Austrians, Prussia was victorious, and went on to become the dominant force in Central Europe.

Fore sight

Cleaning rod

Front sling swivel

MAUSER M/71

Waffenfabrik Mauser began modifying Dreyse guns to accept brass cartridges, but Peter Paul Mauser produced a new design, strong enough to handle much more powerful ammunition and effective out to a range of 0.5 miles (800 m). The Infanteriegewehr M/71 established Mauser's pre-eminence among suppliers of military rifles.

DATE	1872 ONWARD
ORIGIN	GERMANY
WEIGHT	10 LB (4.5 KG)
BARREL	32 IN (83 CM)
CALIBER	11 MM

Barrel band retaining springs

DREYSE NEEDLE GUN, MODEL 1841

Dreyse produced a rifle with a simple turn-down bolt, terminating in a needle that penetrated the length of a (linen) cartridge to detonate a percussion cap in the base of a Minié bullet. The advent of the brass cartridge made the rifle obsolete, but still the Prussians used it to defeat the French in the Franco-German War in 1871.

DATE	1841
ORIGIN	PRUSSIA
WEIGHT	10 LB (4.5 KG)
BARREL	27 IN (70 CM)
CALIBER	13.6 MM

SPRINGFIELD TRAPDOOR

The perfection of the unitary cartridge left the world's armies with a dilemma: what to do with their millions of redundant muzzle-loaders. The US Army modified their rifled muskets by milling out the top of the barrel, creating a chamber for the cartridge, and installing a front-hinged breech cover incorporating a firing pin.

DATE	1874
ORIGIN	US
WEIGHT	10 LB (4.5 KG)
BARREL	32 IN (82.5 CM)
CALIBER	.45 IN

Barrel band anchoring the barrel in the stock

MARTINI-HENRY MK 1

The British Army's first purpose-designed breech-loading rifle, the Martini-Henry, incorporated a falling breech-block; lowering the under-lever opened the breech, and returning it both closed it and cocked the action. A skilled man could fire 20 aimed shots per minute.

DATE	1871
ORIGIN	UK
WEIGHT	10 LB (4.5 KG)
BARREL	33 IN (85 CM)
CALIBER	.45 MARTINI

Front sling swivel

REMINGTON ROLLING BLOCK

Remington's purpose-designed breech-loader struggled to find a market at home, despite having been declared the best rifle in the world at the 1868 Imperial Exposition in Paris. The rifle's rolling-block action, first introduced in 1863, was not as smooth in use as the falling breech-block of the Martini-Henry.

DATE	c.1890
ORIGIN	EGYPT
WEIGHT	9 LB (4 KG)
BARREL	35 IN (89.6 CM)
CALIBER	.45 IN

THE REVOLUTIONARY WORLD

ENFIELD RIFLE-MUSKET

WITH THE PERFECTION of the expanding bullet, it became possible to issue rifles to all troops, not just to sharpshooters, for they could now be loaded as fast as a musket. The British Army adopted one such rifle in 1851, but it proved unsatisfactory; its replacement, produced by the Ordnance Factory at Enfield, was adopted in 1853. It remained in service until 1867, when work began on converting the rifles to breech-loaders, using the method devised by Jacob Snider of America. For all its apparent simplicity, the Pattern 1853 Rifle-Musket has a total of 56 parts.

Packet of ten cartridges

Rifle Musket /53
577.Bore
2½.Drs F.G.
WOOD PLUG
BALL
1856

FULL VIEW

Hammer

AMMUNITION
The Pattern 1853 Rifle-Musket was loaded with 2½ drams (4.43g) of black powder and a 530-grain (34.35g) bullet of .568in caliber, which expanded to take the rifling of the barrel, which was .577in in diameter. Charge and ball were packed into cartridges and issued in packets of ten, with a dozen percussion caps.

Lock cover plate bears maker's name and insignia

Nipple pierced to allow flash from cap to enter breech

Small of stock fits hand

Attachment point for sling

PATTERN 1853 RIFLE-MUSKET
The rifle-musket was a highly successful weapon. In the hands of a competent infantryman it was effective beyond its sighted distance (820m/2,700ft), and at 90m (300ft) the bullet could pass through a dozen 1.5cm (½in) planks. A soldier was expected to maintain a firing rate of three to four rounds per minute.

Trigger

DATE	1853
ORIGIN	UK
WEIGHT	4.05KG (9LB)
BARREL	83.8CM (33IN)
CALIBRE	.577IN

Socket fits over muzzle

BAYONET
The socket bayonet, with its triangular-section blade, protruded almost 46cm (18in) beyond the muzzle. It alone required 44 separate manufacturing operations.

Triangular-section blade

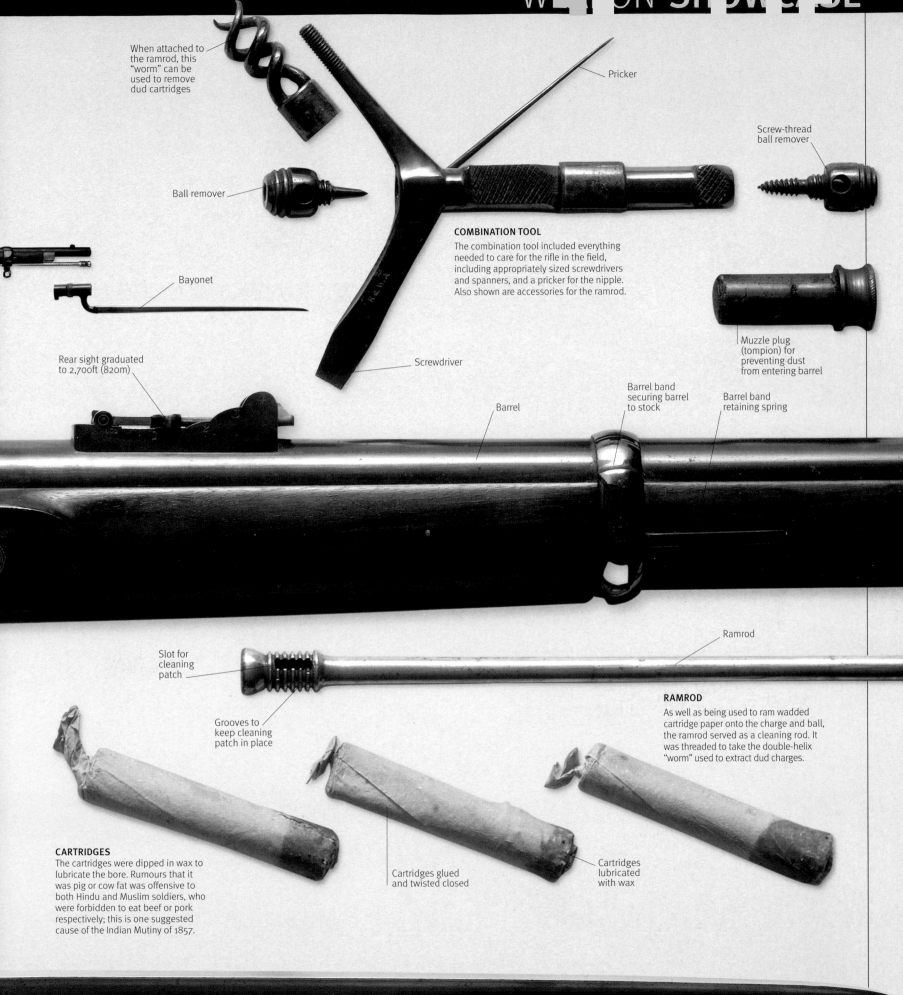

When attached to the ramrod, this "worm" can be used to remove dud cartridges

Pricker

Screw-thread ball remover

Ball remover

COMBINATION TOOL

The combination tool included everything needed to care for the rifle in the field, including appropriately sized screwdrivers and spanners, and a pricker for the nipple. Also shown are accessories for the ramrod.

Bayonet

Muzzle plug (tompion) for preventing dust from entering barrel

Rear sight graduated to 2,700ft (820m)

Screwdriver

Barrel

Barrel band securing barrel to stock

Barrel band retaining spring

Ramrod

Slot for cleaning patch

RAMROD

As well as being used to ram wadded cartridge paper onto the charge and ball, the ramrod served as a cleaning rod. It was threaded to take the double-helix "worm" used to extract dud charges.

Grooves to keep cleaning patch in place

CARTRIDGES

The cartridges were dipped in wax to lubricate the bore. Rumours that it was pig or cow fat was offensive to both Hindu and Muslim soldiers, who were forbidden to eat beef or pork respectively; this is one suggested cause of the Indian Mutiny of 1857.

Cartridges glued and twisted closed

Cartridges lubricated with wax

1775—1900

► 256–257 MANUALLY LOADED REPEATER RIFLES 1881–1891   ► 258–259 MANUALLY LOADED REPEATER RIFLES 1892–1898   ► 300–301 MANUALLY LOADED REPEATER RIFLES 1900–2000

THE REVOLUTIONARY WORLD

MANUALLY LOADED REPEATER RIFLES 1855–1880

THERE HAD BEEN ATTEMPTS to produce repeater rifles and muskets as early as the 16th century. Notwithstanding the success enjoyed by the "cap-and-ball" revolvers of Colt and others, it took the unitary cartridge containing priming, charge, and projectile in one package to make the repeater rifle a satisfactory reality. The breakthrough came midway through the 19th century, and within a decade repeating rifles had become commonplace. Contained in magazines, their ammunition was fed to the breech as part of the single action that cleared the chamber of a spent cartridge case, cocked the action, and readied the gun for firing.

Hammer

Cylinder has five chambers

Rear sight

Cylinder axis rod

Side-mounted hammer

Barrel band

Fore sight

Hammer

Magazine follower

847

Locking catch for cocking lever

Trigger guard and cocking lever

Butt contains tubular magazine, holding seven rounds

Lock plate

Hammer

Rear sight

Barrel band

Trigger guard and breech-operating lever

Rear sling swivel

COLT REVOLVING RIFLE

The third model of Colt's revolving rifles made a considerable impact, even though the loading procedure was cumbersome. The cylinder was removed, powder packed into the five chambers, a bullet packed on top, and the chambers sealed with wax. The cylinder was then covered with grease in order to protect against the possibility of loose powder igniting all the chambers at once.

DATE	1855
ORIGIN	US
WEIGHT	7½ LB (3.45 KG)
BARREL	27 IN (68.2 KG)
CALIBER	.56 IN

WINCHESTER MODEL 1866 CARBINE

The principle shortcoming of Benjamin Tyler Henry's underlever rifle lay in the way its tubular magazine was charged. In 1866, Nelson King, Henry's successor, introduced an improvement that allowed reloading, even of a part-full magazine, via a port on the receiver. This doubled the rifle's rate of fire to 30 rounds a minute.

DATE	1866
ORIGIN	US
WEIGHT	9¼ LB (4.2 KG)
BARREL	23 IN (58½ CM)
CALIBER	.44 RIMFIRE

Labels: Hammer, Loading port, Rear sight, Forestock, Barrel band, Fore sight, Tubular magazine holds 12 rounds, Spent cartridge case is ejected downward, Trigger, Trigger guard and cocking lever

LE MAT REVOLVER RIFLE

Based on a similar pistol, the Le Mat Revolver Rifle was an oddity. It boasted two barrels; the lower, charged with shot, acted as the axis pin for the nine-chambered cylinder, which was charged with ball cartridges. It was equipped with a loading/ejection gate and rod, similar to those found on Colt's early brass-cartridge pistols.

DATE:	1872
ORIGIN	FRANCE/US
WEIGHT	5 LB (2.2 KG)
BARREL	24¾ IN (62.8 CM)
CALIBER	.44 IN AND 6-BORE

Labels: Cylinder with nine chambers, .44 in caliber rifle barrel, Hammer, Cylinder-retaining catch, Small of the stock, Comb, 16-bore smooth barrel, Ejector rod, Ejector port, Trigger

HENRY MODEL 1860

When Oliver Winchester set up the New Haven Arms Co., he brought in Tyler Henry to run it. Henry's first act was to design a repeating rifle worked by an underlever that ejected the spent round, chambered a new one, and left the action cocked. To lock the action, he used a two-piece bolt joined by a toggle-joint. This same method was later used by Maxim in his machine gun, and by Borchardt and Luger in their pistols.

DATE	1862
ORIGIN	US
WEIGHT	9 LB (4 KG)
BARREL	20 IN (51 CM)
CALIBER	.44 IN RIMFIRE

Labels: Rear sight, Magazine holds 15 rounds, Brass-bound butt, **FULL VIEW**

SPENCER RIFLE

Christopher Spencer developed this rifle in his spare time, and it was to become the world's first practical military repeater. Its tubular magazine, which held seven rounds, was located in the butt stock; a lever that formed the trigger guard opened the rolling breech and extracted the spent cartridge. Closing the breech pushed a fresh round into the chamber. The hammer was cocked by hand.

DATE	1863
ORIGIN	US
WEIGHT	10 LB (4.55 KG)
BARREL	28¼ IN (72 CM)
CALIBER	.52 IN

Labels: Fore sight, Forward sling swivel, Forestock cap, Bayonet lug

BEST OF BOTH WORLDS

The Non-Commissioned Officer (NCO) of the Union Army had one foot in the past and the other in the future. He carried a sword into battle, but also a carbine, the shortened form of the magazine repeater rifle Christopher Spencer patented in 1860.

THE BOER WAR
The technological advances
of the early 20th century—
smokeless gunpowder, automatic
handguns, machine-fed rifles, and machine
guns—had an impact on the conflict between
the British and the two Boer republics (1899–1902).
Earlier weaponry, such as the bayonet, was also still in use.

1775—1900

◄ **252–253** MANUALLY LOADED REPEATER RIFLES 1855–1880   ► **258–259** MANUALLY LOADED REPEATER RIFLES 1892–1898   ► **300–301** MANUALLY LOADED REPEATER RIFLES 1900–2006

THE REVOLUTIONARY WORLD

MANUALLY LOADED REPEATER RIFLES 1881–1891

THE FIRST GENERATION OF REPEATER rifles were mostly American underlever designs. Having been introduced to the bolt action by Von Dreyse and seduced into accepting it by Peter Paul Mauser and others in the single shot rifles of the 1870s, European users believed it to have clear advantages over the American rifles. Not only was the bolt action more secure—because it locked its action by means of lugs, which engaged with others in the receiver when the bolt was turned—but it was more practical when shooting from the prone position.

Cocking piece

Bolt handle

Rear sight

Barrel band

Fore sight

Bayonet lug

Cleaning rod

Detachable 12-round box magazine

Rear sling attachment

SCHMIDT-RUBIN M1889

In 1889 Colonel Rudolf Schmidt of the Swiss Army developed a straight-pull bolt-action rifle with a 12-round box magazine. It was accepted as the regulation rifle, and remained in service, only slightly modified, until 1931, when its bolt action was rejigged to operate in half the length. The modified version was only discarded in the late 1950s, and a sniper's version was in use until 1987.

DATE	1889
ORIGIN	SWITZERLAND
WEIGHT	9.8 LB (4.45 KG)
BARREL	30.75 IN (78 CM)
CALIBER	7.5 MM

Bolt cover

Cocking piece

Bolt handle

Trigger

Magazine release catch

Ten-round detachable box magazine

Bolt is locked at the rear

Bolt handle

Rear sight

Straight-through stock

Barrel band securing spring

MAUSER MODEL 71/84

Peter Paul Mauser made many attempts to turn the single-shot bolt-action M1871 rifle into a repeater. Although obsolete almost immediately, the result was not superseded until 1888, even though its weaknesses in the design of its magazine, and its tendency to pull to the right, were well known.

DATE	1884
ORIGIN	GERMANY
WEIGHT	10 LB (4.6 KG)
BARREL	32 IN (83 CM)
CALIBER	11 MM

INFANTERIEGEWEHR M1888

When it came to replacing the M71/84 the German Army set up a specification commission but the characteristics of new 7.92 mm ammunition had been misunderstood, leading to many burst barrels. In addition, the box magazine was a poor design; it was never rectified.

DATE	1888
ORIGIN	GERMANY
WEIGHT	8 LB (3.82 KG)
BARREL	29 IN (74 CM)
CALIBER	7.92 MM x 57 M88

KRAG-JØRGENSEN M1888

Many held that the M1888 was obsolete before it was adopted by the Danish Army, because its five-round magazine had to be hand-loaded, one round at a time, and its bolt's single locking-lug limited it to low-velocity ammunition. It came as a surprise, even to its inventors, that it was also adopted by both the US and Norwegian Armies.

DATE	1888
ORIGIN	NORWAY
WEIGHT	9 LB (4.05 KG)
BARREL	30 IN (76.2 CM)
CALIBER	6.5 MM x 55

LEE-METFORD

FULL VIEW

The British Army opened a competition to find a replacement for the single-shot Martini-Henry rifle in 1879; 11 years later, it adopted the .303 in rifle, Magazine, Mark I (the name was changed in 1891 to include those of its designers). It had an enclosed bolt action and a box magazine, the work of James Lee, and had anti-fouling rifling developed by William Metford.

DATE	1888
ORIGIN	UK
WEIGHT	9 LB (4.05 KG)
BARREL	30 IN (76.2 CM)
CALIBER	.303 IN

CAVALRY CARBINE MODELLO 1891 TS

Often known as the Mannlicher-Carcano, it used a modified version of the bolt-action Mauser developed for the M1889. It continued, in modified form, in Italian service until after World War II, and many were sold to dealers in the US; one found its way to Lee Harvey Oswald, who probably used it to kill President John F. Kennedy in 1963.

DATE	1891
ORIGIN	ITALY
WEIGHT	6 LB (3 KG)
BARREL	17 IN (45 CM)
CALIBER	6.5 MM x 52

1775—1900

◄ 252–253 MANUALLY LOADED REPEATER RIFLES 1855–1880   ◄ 256–257 MANUALLY LOADED REPEATER RIFLES 1881–1891   ► 300–301 MANUALLY LOADED REPEATER RIFLES 1900–2006

MANUALLY LOADED REPEATER RIFLES 1892–1898

BY THE START OF THE LAST DECADE of the 1800s—a century that had seen firearms technology revolutionized, the world's armies were finally accepting that repeater rifles were reliable enough to be safely adopted for general use. In fact, the genre had almost reached its final form by this time; once the box magazine had been taken up, remaining modifications were often little more than cosmetic, to reduce weight or to allow cheaper manufacturing methods to be used.

Cocking piece · Bolt handle · Bolt · Rear sight

Wooden butt

Integral five-round box magazine

"3-LINE" RIFLE M1891

The M1891 is usually known as the Mosin-Nagant, after its designers. It was Imperial Russia's first repeater rifle, and its first in a "modern" caliber (a "line" was a measure approximating to one-tenth of an inch, and refers to its caliber). It was issued in a variety of forms, including a semi-carbine and a true carbine, and was still in service as a sniper rifle with the Red Army until the 1960s.

DATE	1891
ORIGIN	RUSSIA
WEIGHT	9¾ LB (4.43 KG)
BARREL	31½ IN (80.2 CM)
CALIBER	7.62 MM x 54R

Cocking piece · Bolt handle · Rear sight

Trigger

Eight-round tubular magazine within the stock below the barrel

Bolt handle · Rear sight · Bayonet lug

Semi-pistol grip · Five-round integral box magazine

Rear sling attachment

MANNLICHER M1895

The straight-pull bolt-action M1895 was the work of Ferdinand von Mannlicher, and used a rotating locking lug turned in a camming (spiraled) groove. Ammunition was fed from a fixed box magazine that Mannlicher also designed. It was used widely throughout the Austro-Hungarian empire.

DATE	1895
ORIGIN	AUSTRIA
WEIGHT	8½ LB (3.78 KG)
BARREL	30 IN (76.5 CM)
CALIBER	8 MM x 50R

MAUSER M1896

Waffenfabrik Mauser began exporting rifles, to China, in 1875; then came the Mauser-Koka, for Serbia, the Belgian M1889, the Turkish M1890, the Argentine M1891, and the Spanish M1893. The world's armies seemed to be beating a path to Mauser's door, and in 1895 it was Sweden's turn. The design it adopted had a number of modifications, some of which found their way into later types.

DATE	1896
ORIGIN	GERMANY
WEIGHT	8¾ LB (3.97 KG)
BARREL	29 IN (74 CM)
CALIBER	6.5 MM x 55

Leaf-type rear sight

Bolt handle

Bayonet lug

Cleaning rod

Integral five-round box magazine

ARISAKA MEIJI 30

At the conclusion of its war with China in 1895, the Japanese Army decided to adopt a modern weapon in a small caliber. This gun, designed by Arisaka, chambered for a 6.5 mm semi-rimmed round, with an enclosed five-round box magazine, was adopted. It used a turning bolt of the Mauser pattern with forward-locking lugs. It came into service in the 30th year of the Emperor Meiji.

DATE	1897
ORIGIN	JAPAN
WEIGHT	9½ LB (4.3 KG)
BARREL	31½ IN (80 CM)
CALIBER	6.5 MM x 50SR

Fore sight

Forestock cap

Cleaning rod

Forward sling attachment

Rear sight

Barrel band secures the barrel in the stock

Bolt handle

Semi-pistol grip

Integral five-round magazine

Bayonet lug

LEBEL MLE 1886/93

In 1885 Boulanger was appointed to the Ministry of War in Paris. One of his first priorities was to introduce a modern rifle. The result was the first rifle firing a small-caliber, jacketed bullet propelled by smokeless powder (invented by Meille in 1884/5); despite being mechanically unsophisticated, it rendered every other rifle in the world obsolete. This modified version followed in 1893.

DATE	1893
ORIGIN	FRANCE
WEIGHT	9½ LB (4.3 KG)
BARREL	31½ IN (80 CM)
CALIBER	8 MM x 50R

Barrel-band-securing spring

FULL VIEW

MAUSER INFANTERIEGEWEHR 98

By the time of the Gew98, Mauser had solved virtually every problem known to beset the bolt-action magazine rifle. It added a third rear-locking lug to reinforce the two forward-mounted lugs, as well as improving gas sealing and refining the magazine. If the rifle had a fault, it lay in the design of its bolt handle.

DATE	1898
ORIGIN	GERMANY
WEIGHT	9¼ LB (4.15 KG)
BARREL	29¼ IN (74 CM)
CALIBER	7.92 MM x 57

Bolt handle protrudes horizontally

Leaf-type rear sight

Regimental identification plate

Semi-pistol grip

Sling

Bayonet lug

INDIAN FIREARMS

FIREARMS WERE INTRODUCED to India from central Asia and Europe at the end of the 15th century. Well into the 19th century, indigenous craftsmen were still making matchlocks, rather than the more complicated wheellocks and flintlocks, because they were easier and cheaper to produce. However, Indian gunmakers were no strangers to intricate decoration, and produced some very ornate pieces using ivory, bone, and precious metals as inlays.

Pentagonal-section butt

Ivory decoration

Enclosed serpentine match holder

Pan

Decorated lock plate

Trigger

Serpentine slow-match holder

Decorative brass banding

Bone inlay

Trigger

Touch-holes

Enclosed serpentine match holder

Gilded barrel band

Gilded butt

Trigger

Overlayed lock plate

Pricker

Velvet sling

Serpentine

Pan

Steel barrel

Painted decoration

Ring for pricker chain

Trigger

Pricker holder

Ring for belt hook

Ramrod

Checkered grip

MATCHLOCK PISTOL

Matchlock pistols were a rarity in Europe, but were manufactured in small numbers in Asia. This example, from the end of the 18th century, was produced in northern India. The items below the pan are a holder for the prickers and a ring to which its chain was attached.

DATE	c.1800
ORIGIN	NORTHERN INDIA
WEIGHT	1¾ LB (0.75 KG)
BARREL	9¾ IN (24.5 CM)
CALIBER	18-BORE

Wire barrel band
Leather barrel band
Forward sling attachment
Fore sight
Rear sling attachment

INDORE TORADOR

This simple matchlock shows some features commonly found on firearms of this period, notably the pentagonal cross-section of the butt stock and its pronounced recurve. The side plates at the lock are iron with crudely incised decoration that continues down the barrel; there are four leather thongs serving as barrel bands, but that closest to the breech is wire.

DATE	c.1800
ORIGIN	INDORE, INDIA
WEIGHT	7½ LB (3.4 KG)
BARREL	44 IN (112 CM)
CALIBER	.55 IN

Ramrod
Revolving cylinder with six chambers
Chamber vents

MATCHLOCK REVOLVING MUSKET

Made near the start of the 19th century in the Indore region of northern India, this matchlock revolving musket is an ambitious attempt to marry the technologies of two periods using local materials and fabrication techniques. The cylinder is indexed manually; the vents in the barrel are there in case the charge in a chamber not aligned with the barrel is ignited by flash-over—a real possibility.

DATE	c.1800
ORIGIN	INDORE, INDIA
WEIGHT	13 LB (5.9 KG)
BARREL	24½ IN (62 CM)
CALIBER	.6 IN

Overlayed barrel
Fore sight
Ramrod

BUNDUKH TORADOR

Probably made in Gwalior at the beginning of the 19th century, this extremely ornate matchlock was almost certainly a presentation piece. Like all matchlocks, it was supplied with a touch-hole pricker, though since this, too, is gilded, it can hardly be considered to be entirely functional. Guns of this type were normally held beneath the arm, not against the shoulder.

DATE	c.1800
ORIGIN	GWALIOR, INDIA
WEIGHT	6½ LB (3 KG)
BARREL	45¼ IN (115 CM)
CALIBER	.55 IN

Flint clamp screw
Cock
Striking steel
Feather spring
Pan
English-style lock plate
Trigger guard
Trigger
Ramrod pipe
Ramrod

PUNJABI FLINTLOCK PISTOL

This is one of a pair of superbly decorated pistols made in Lahore (now part of Pakistan) early in the 19th century. By this time, Sikh gunmakers were well able to fashion the components of a flintlock, though most of their energies were devoted to somewhat more workaday muskets known as *jazails*. This pistol has a "damascened" barrel, formed by coiling strips of steel around a mandrel and then heating and beating them to weld them together.

DATE	c.1800
ORIGIN	LAHORE, INDIA
WEIGHT	1.9 LB (0.86 KG)
BARREL	8.5 IN (21.5 CM)
CALIBER	28-BORE

ASIAN FIREARMS

PORTUGUESE TRADERS INTRODUCED firearms to Japan when they first arrived there in 1543 CE, and indigenous craftsmen soon began to copy the new weapons. Less than a century later, all foreigners were expelled and the country was cut off from Western influences by imperial decree. As a result, later types of firearm were largely unknown in Japan, and Japanese gunsmiths almost exclusively produced matchlocks until the mid–19th century, using methods that were unlike those seen elsewhere.

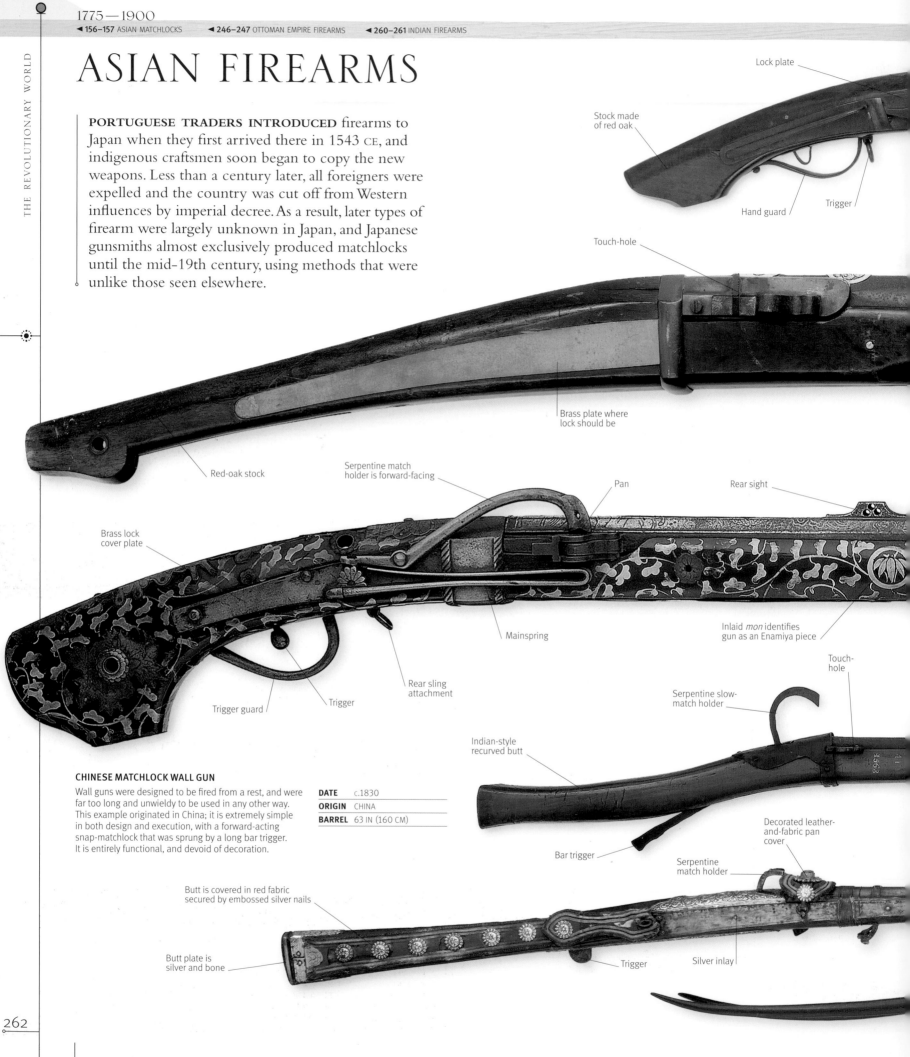

Lock plate

Stock made of red oak

Hand guard

Trigger

Touch-hole

Brass plate where lock should be

Red-oak stock

Serpentine match holder is forward-facing

Pan

Rear sight

Brass lock cover plate

Mainspring

Inlaid *mon* identifies gun as an Enamiya piece

Rear sling attachment

Trigger guard

Trigger

Touch-hole

Serpentine slow-match holder

Indian-style recurved butt

CHINESE MATCHLOCK WALL GUN

Wall guns were designed to be fired from a rest, and were far too long and unwieldy to be used in any other way. This example originated in China; it is extremely simple in both design and execution, with a forward-acting snap-matchlock that was sprung by a long bar trigger. It is entirely functional, and devoid of decoration.

DATE	c.1830
ORIGIN	CHINA
BARREL	63 IN (160 CM)

Bar trigger

Decorated leather-and-fabric pan cover

Serpentine match holder

Butt is covered in red fabric secured by embossed silver nails

Butt plate is silver and bone

Trigger

Silver inlay

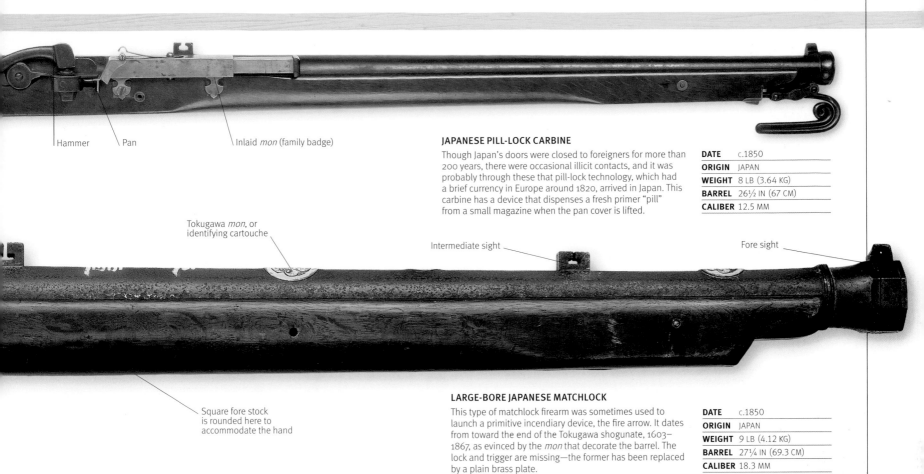

Hammer | Pan | Inlaid *mon* (family badge)

JAPANESE PILL-LOCK CARBINE

Though Japan's doors were closed to foreigners for more than 200 years, there were occasional illicit contacts, and it was probably through these that pill-lock technology, which had a brief currency in Europe around 1820, arrived in Japan. This carbine has a device that dispenses a fresh primer "pill" from a small magazine when the pan cover is lifted.

DATE	c.1850
ORIGIN	JAPAN
WEIGHT	8 LB (3.64 KG)
BARREL	26½ IN (67 CM)
CALIBER	12.5 MM

Tokugawa *mon*, or identifying cartouche

Intermediate sight

Fore sight

Square fore stock is rounded here to accommodate the hand

LARGE-BORE JAPANESE MATCHLOCK

This type of matchlock firearm was sometimes used to launch a primitive incendiary device, the fire arrow. It dates from toward the end of the Tokugawa shogunate, 1603–1867, as evinced by the *mon* that decorate the barrel. The lock and trigger are missing—the former has been replaced by a plain brass plate.

DATE	c.1850
ORIGIN	JAPAN
WEIGHT	9 LB (4.12 KG)
BARREL	27¼ IN (69.3 CM)
CALIBER	18.3 MM

Inlaid *kara kusa*

FULL VIEW

JAPANESE TEPPO

Produced by Sakai's eminent Enamiya family, gunmakers since 1560, this *teppo* displays their trademark features: the brass shapes inlaid into the stock, and the characteristic muzzle shape. It is decorated with *kara kusa* (vine motifs) and *mon* (family badges); the lacquerwork is probably a later addition. Its furniture is of brass, and the upper three flats of the octagonal barrel are decorated in silver, brass, and copper.

DATE	c.1800
ORIGIN	JAPAN
WEIGHT	6 LB (2.77 KG)
BARREL	39¼ IN (100 CM)
CALIBER	1.142 IN

Damascened barrel

Rest terminates in forked antelope horn

Ramrod is a modern replacement

TIBETAN MEDA

While Tibet, like Japan, was largely isolated from the rest of the world until the mid-19th century, it was for geographic rather than political reasons. Trade did occur, however, with India and China, and this matchlock, or *meda*, shows considerable Chinese influence in both form and decoration. Attached to the fore stock is a rest, an unusual feature.

DATE	c.1780
ORIGIN	TIBET
WEIGHT	9¼ LB (4.15 KG)
BARREL	43.75 LB (111 CM)
CALIBER	17 MM

1775—1900

◄ **218–219** AMERICAN PERCUSSION CAP REVOLVERS   ◄ **248–249** SINGLE-SHOT BREECH-LOADING RIFLES   ◄ **252–253** MANUALLY LOADED REPEATER RIFLES 1855–1880

THE REVOLUTIONARY WORLD

MULTI-SHOT FIREARMS

THE MAIN SHORTCOMING OF THE MUZZLE-LOADER was the time it took to reload. As a result, gunmakers the world over endeavored to produce weapons that could fire more than a single shot. The typical approach was to use multiple barrels, but guns with more than two barrels tended to be so heavy as to render them impractical. It was not until the 1830s that the young Samuel Colt developed his revolver—the first successful multi-shot, single-barreled firearm. Colt obtained a patent to protect his invention until 1857, but many sought ways to evade it. Most produced firearms that, at best, were only marginally effective.

Stock is made of walnut

Small of stock has incised checkering

Rear sight

Trigger   Hammer

Disc is bored with seven radial chambers

Nipple for a percussion cap

Cock   Striking steel   Revolving chambers

Stock inlaid with silver

Striking steel

Fore sight

Cleaning rod

Forward sling swivel

FLINTLOCK REVOLVING RIFLE

French gunmakers produced some of the finest sport guns of the 17th century. This example has three revolving chambers, each fitted with its own striker and spring. This type of multi-shot weapon risked a dangerous chain reaction, in which firing one chamber set off all of the others.

DATE	c.1670
ORIGIN	FRANCE
WEIGHT	7½ LB (3.37 KG)
BARREL	31¼ IN (79.5 CM)
CALIBER	22-BORE

See detail

Barrel-retaining pin

Maker's name

Cocking levers

Dual triggers

FLINTLOCK DOUBLE-BARRELED GUN

This double-barreled sport gun bears the name of its maker, Bouillet of Paris. The firing mechanism, including the flint, is concealed in a box. The two levers in front of the trigger guard cocked the piece ready for discharging the barrels.

DATE	c.1760
ORIGIN	FRANCE
WEIGHT	7¼ LB (3.25 KG)
BARREL	32 IN (81.3 CM)
CALIBER	22-BORE

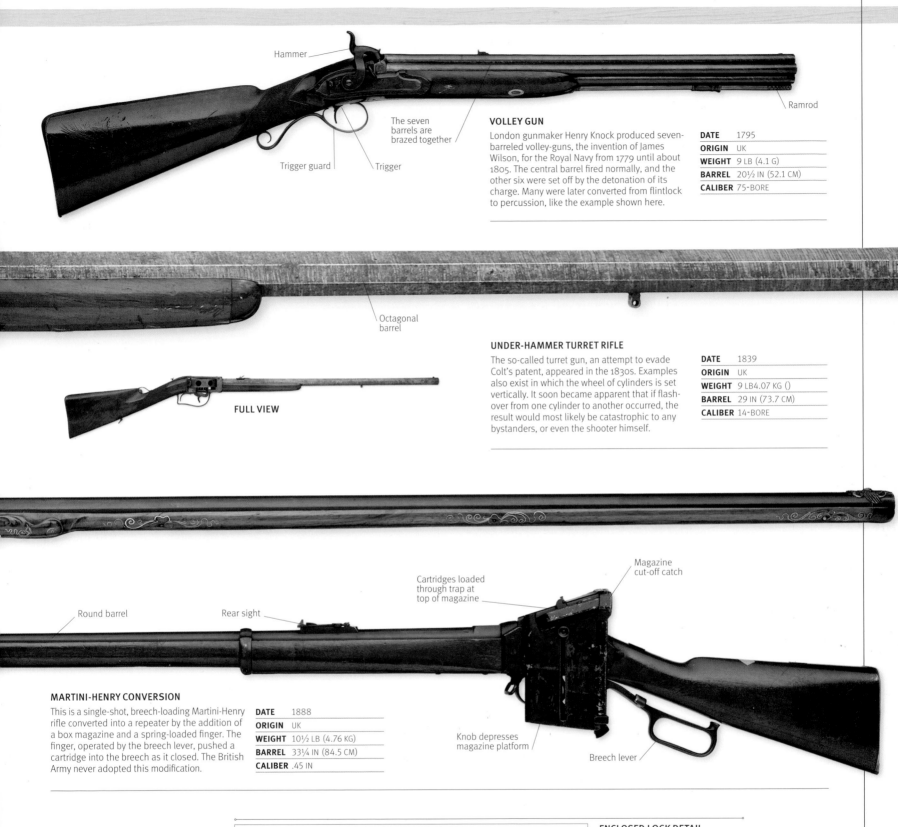

Hammer

The seven
barrels are
brazed together

Trigger guard

Trigger

Ramrod

VOLLEY GUN

London gunmaker Henry Knock produced seven-barreled volley-guns, the invention of James Wilson, for the Royal Navy from 1779 until about 1805. The central barrel fired normally, and the other six were set off by the detonation of its charge. Many were later converted from flintlock to percussion, like the example shown here.

DATE	1795
ORIGIN	UK
WEIGHT	9 LB (4.1 G)
BARREL	20½ IN (52.1 CM)
CALIBER	75-BORE

Octagonal
barrel

FULL VIEW

UNDER-HAMMER TURRET RIFLE

The so-called turret gun, an attempt to evade Colt's patent, appeared in the 1830s. Examples also exist in which the wheel of cylinders is set vertically. It soon became apparent that if flash-over from one cylinder to another occurred, the result would most likely be catastrophic to any bystanders, or even the shooter himself.

DATE	1839
ORIGIN	UK
WEIGHT	9 LB 4.07 KG ()
BARREL	29 IN (73.7 CM)
CALIBER	14-BORE

Magazine
cut-off catch

Cartridges loaded
through trap at
top of magazine

Round barrel

Rear sight

MARTINI-HENRY CONVERSION

This is a single-shot, breech-loading Martini-Henry rifle converted into a repeater by the addition of a box magazine and a spring-loaded finger. The finger, operated by the breech lever, pushed a cartridge into the breech as it closed. The British Army never adopted this modification.

DATE	1888
ORIGIN	UK
WEIGHT	10½ LB (4.76 KG)
BARREL	33¼ IN (84.5 CM)
CALIBER	.45 IN

Knob depresses
magazine platform

Breech lever

Metal-bound butt

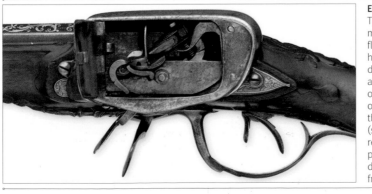

ENCLOSED LOCK DETAIL

The flintlock sport gun often misfired, either because the flint had broken or the primer had become damp. When it did fire successfully, the flash and smoke from the pan could obscure the target from view or frighten the game. Enclosing the firing mechanism in a box (seen here with the cover removed), solved two of these problems, keeping the powder dry and minimizing disruption from the flash and smoke.

AMMUNITION PRE-1900

A GUN IS nothing without a bullet. In early times, bullets were often made of iron, and could pierce armor, but later, lead was adopted because it was easier to mold. The bullet-shaped projectile was developed only in the 19th century, and so too was the cartridge.

The powder-and-ball era

To achieve any sort of accuracy, the ball fired from a smooth-bore gun had to be spherical and of an exact size. Rifling improved matters, but made the weapon slow to load; the problem was solved by the expanding bullet.

Rifle belt

MUSKET/RIFLE BALLS
The size of the ball was expressed in "bore," being the number of balls of a set size that could be cast from 0.45 kg (1 lb) of lead.

BELTED BALLS
To improve accuracy, barrels were "rifled" with pairs of grooves into which the belt on the ball fitted.

Skirt

Lubrication grooves

EXPANDING BULLETS
These bullets had a hollow base. The force of the powder detonating caused the bullets' skirts to expand and take the rifling.

LUBRICATION
The grooves around the bullet were greased to lubricate the barrel and make it easier to clean.

Cap

PERCUSSION CAPS
Fulminate, which explodes when struck, is sandwiched between two layers of thin copper foil, shaped to fit over a pierced nipple.

PAPER-WRAPPED CARTRIDGES
The first cartridges were nothing more than paper packages containing a measured charge of powder and a ball.

Transitional cartridges

Nineteenth-century gunmakers experimented with cartridges containing both propellant and projectile, which could be loaded whole. Wrapped in paper, skin, or fabric, they posed a problem for breech-loading guns, whose breeches had to be sealed. The solution was to switch to cartridge cases made of brass, into which the primer was integrated. This meant that the empty case had to be removed, but that was a small price to pay for perfect obturation (breech-sealing).

TEAT-FIRE CARTRIDGE
These were produced as a way around Smith & Wesson's monopoly of the bored-through cylinder. The bullet is entirely contained.

Small pin-fire cartridge

PIN-FIRE CARTRIDGE
The gun's hammer falls vertically on the pin, driving it into the primer that is contained in the base of the cartridge case.

SHARPS' CARTRIDGE
This case is made of linen. Its base was cut off by the edge of the breech-block when the action was closed.

BURNSIDE CARTRIDGE
Burnside's breech-loading carbine incorporated a drop-down breech, loaded from the front. It was chambered for this unique tapering cartridge.

WESTLEY RICHARDS "MONKEY TAIL" CARTRIDGE
This paper-wrapped carbine cartridge incorporated a greased felt wad at the rear, which remained in the breech until expelled ahead of the following round.

SNIDER-ENFIELD CARTRIDGE
The cartridge developed by Colonel Boxer for the Snider-Enfield rifle had a perforated iron base and walls built up from coiled brass strips.

Rifle cartridges

For a rifle to fire accurately, its ammunition must be properly formulated. Bullet weight and caliber must be matched accurately with the weight of the propellant charge.

.450 MARTINI-HENRY
The Martini-Henry rifle's cartridge was loaded with 85 grains (5.5 g) of black powder. The bullet weighed 480 grains (31 g).

.45-70 SPRINGFIELD
The cartridge devised for the Springfield rifle was loaded with 70 grains (4.53 g) of powder and a 405-grain (26.25 g) bullet.

.30-30 WINCHESTER
The .30-30 Winchester cartridge was the first "civilian" round to be charged with smokeless powder; it had 30 grains (1.94 g) of it.

.303 MK V
Until the 1890s, rifle bullets were blunt-nosed. The British Army's Lee-Metfords and Lee-Enfields were chambered for the one shown.

.56-50 SPENCER
This is the rimfire black-powder round for which the Civil War-era Spencer carbine, the first effective repeater rifle, was chambered.

11MM CHASSEPOT
After the Franco-Prussian War, the cartridge developed for the Mauser M/71 rifle was adapted for the Chassepot rifle, which was converted to take it.

5.2MM X 68 MONDRAGON
This early attempt at producing a high-velocity round in a miniature caliber was designed in Switzerland for the Mexican Mondragon rifle.

Pistol cartridges

In all cartridges, dimensional accuracy is essential. Cases that are even minutely undersize may split on firing, making them difficult to extract. This is easily rectified in a revolver, but less so with a self-loading pistol.

.44 HENRY
This rimfire round had primer arranged around the base of its case. It was soon superseded by the center-fire cartridge.

.44 ALLEN & WHEELOCK
Allen & Wheelock revolvers were chambered for "lip-fire" cartridges (similar to rimfire), chiefly in small calibers.

.45 COLT (BÉNÉT)
Colonel S.V. Bénét's 1865 version of the center-fire cartridge formed the basis for Berdan's later version.

.45 COLT (THUER)
Alexander Thuer developed a method of converting Colt "cap-and-ball" revolvers to fire this tapering brass cartridge.

.44 SMITH & WESSON AMERICAN
This first .44 in Smith & Wesson was unsatisfactory, as the projectile was "heel seated," rather than crimped in the case.

.44 SMITH & WESSON RUSSIAN
The revolvers Smith & Wesson supplied to the Russian Army were chambered for a cartridge of different dimensions.

.577 WEBLEY
Many small-caliber bullets lacked the power to stop a man. Webley addressed this with a .577 in caliber revolver.

.476 WEBLEY
The .577 in revolver was unwieldy and a replacement in .476 in caliber was adopted instead. It, too, was short-lived.

.455 WEBLEY
Webley's first smokeless powder cartridge was more powerful than earlier types, allowing a further reduction in bullet weight.

10.4 MM BODEO
The cartridge for the 10.4 mm Bodeo revolver, used by the Italian Army from 1891, gave a muzzle velocity of 837 ft (255 m) per second.

7.63 MM BERGMANN
The rimless, grooveless cartridge for which the Bergmann No 3 pistol was originally chambered was extracted by pressure alone.

Shotgun cartridges

Only the very largest shotgun cartridges were made entirely of brass. Others had cardboard bodies.

WILDFOWL CARTRIDGE
Large cartridges such as this were loaded with up to ¾ oz (20 g) of black powder and 3½ oz (100 g) of shot.

10-BORE PIN-FIRE
Pin-fire shotguns were still common long after other such guns had disappeared.

INDIAN ARMOR AND SHIELDS

SEVERAL INDIAN STATES put up serious resistance to the British forces that were extending their rule over the subcontinent during the 18th and 19th centuries. They included the kingdom of Mysore, which held out from 1766 to 1799, and the Sikhs in the Punjab, who lost two wars against the British (1846–47 and 1848-49) but each time imposed heavy casualties. Indian armies used European muskets and artillery alongside traditional edged weapons and armor. As the disciplined use of firepower grew increasingly dominant in warfare, armor and shields were gradually relegated to a purely decorative role on the battlefield.

HELMET DETAIL
The upper finial of the helmet's sliding nasal bar is decorated with an image of the elephant-headed Hindu god Ganesh.

Egret feathers mounted in plume tube

Sliding nasal bar

See detail

Mail shirt

Cuirass plate

Arm defenses (*dastana*)

Low-skulled cap

Skull and crossed bones

Plume holders

Quilted fabric cuirass

Aventail of iron and brass mail

PETI AND CAP
Indian warriors often wore a *peti*, a girdlelike cuirass made of padded leather or cloth. This example is from the arsenal of Tipu Sultan in Mysore. Like the low-skulled cap, it would have offered only limited protection in battle.

DATE	LATE 18TH CENTURY
ORIGIN	MYSORE, INDIA
WEIGHT	PETI 3 LB (1.4 KG)
LENGTH	PETI 8¾IN (22CM)

TOP
This helmet, or *top*, is of a type worn by warriors across much of Asia from late medieval times onward. Characteristic features are the mail aventail and the spike and plume holders. The decoration includes a skull-and crossed-bones motif, possibly a sign of European influence.

DATE	LATE 18TH CENTURY
ORIGIN	GWALIOR, INDIA
WEIGHT	2¾ LB (1.3 KG)
HEIGHT	35½ IN (90 CM)

SIKH ARMOR
A Sikh warrior would have looked impressive in this mail shirt, plate cuirass, and plumed *top* (helmet). However, the iron-and-brass mail is "butted"—meaning that the rings are pressed against one another, rather than riveted or welded—so it could have been pierced by stabbing weapons and arrows.

DATE	18TH CENTURY
ORIGIN	INDIA

FULL VIEW

SIKH DHAL

This round shield, or *dhal*, dates from the wars between the Sikhs and the British East India Company. The intricate decoration in gold damascene includes Persian inscriptions, so perhaps the shield was not the work of an Indian craftsman.

DATE	1847
ORIGIN	INDIA
WEIGHT	8½ LB (3.8 KG)
WIDTH	22¼ IN (59 CM)

Persian inscriptions

Conical cane cap wrapped in silk pagri

SIKH QUOIT TURBAN

The sharp-edged quoit, or *chakram*, is a weapon particularly associated with the Sikhs. This tall turban carries six quoits of different sizes, ready to be lifted off and thrown at enemies. There are also three small knives in the turban armory.

DATE	18TH CENTURY
ORIGIN	INDIA
WEIGHT	2½ LB (1.2 KG)
HEIGHT	18½ IN (47 CM)

HOLY WARRIORS

The Sikh Akali sect combined religious asceticism with fearless fighting spirit. The *chakram* was the Akalis' favored weapon, launched either by whirling around the forefinger or held between thumb and forefinger and thrown underarm. The position of the quoits on an Akali's turban showed his spiritual status in the sect.

Shield of black lacquered hide

Steel quoit

Pistol hidden in boss

PISTOL SHIELD

This shield has a hidden offensive capacity. Each of the four golden bosses has a hinged flap that opens to reveal the short barrel of a small percussion pistol. The pistols, firing mechanisms, and hinged bosses have been fitted to a pre-existing conventional lacquered shield.

DATE	MID-19TH CENTURY
ORIGIN	RAJASTHAN, INDIA
WEIGHT	7½ LB (3.4 KG)
WIDTH	21¾ IN (55.5 CM)

GUN MECHANISM DETAIL

On the back of the pistol shield, there is a single central grip, which is attached to the mechanisms of the four pistols. Each pistol can be cocked individually, but they are all fired by a single trigger, operated by the fingers of the hand holding the shield grip.

THE REVOLUTIONARY WORLD

AFRICAN SHIELDS

IN TRADITIONAL AFRICAN SOCIETIES, where body armor was not used, shields were the sole protection in warfare, aside from charms and amulets. Shields also played a prominent part in ceremonies and were decorated to show status or allegiance. Wood, animal hide, woven wicker, or cane made suitable materials for a shield to ward off arrows or blows from throwing knives, clubs, or spears. Shields could also be used offensively; for example, the sharpened lower tip of a Zulu shield stick might stab an opponent's foot or ankle.

Top end of shield stick

ZULU WAR SHIELD

The Zulu warrior's oval shield was made of cowhide that had been prepared by scraping, cleaning, and several days' burial in soil or manure. The shield face was bound to the shield stick by two rows of hide strips that ran vertically from top to bottom of the shield. When advancing to attack, warriors would sometimes beat their shields with the butts of their spears.

DATE	19TH CENTURY
ORIGIN	SOUTH AFRICA
LENGTH	48 IN (122 CM)

FULL VIEW

Shield of closely woven wickerwork

Leather shield

Outer frame

Slits cut in shield with strips of hide threaded through

Scraped and cleaned cowhide

Central staff

Two rods stiffen and strengthen shield

Color of shield indicates regiment to which warrior belongs, and his status

RECTANGULAR SUDANESE SHIELD

Peoples of southern Sudan and northern Kenya—such as the Turkana, Larim, and Pokot—traditionally made symmetrical rectangular shields from animal hides, including buffalo, giraffe, rhinoceros, and hippopotamus. The central wooden shaft doubles as a grip.

DATE	LATE 19TH/EARLY 20TH CENTURY
ORIGIN	SUDAN
LENGTH	32½ IN (82.5 CM)

WICKERWORK SHIELD

Craftsmen of the Zande people of north central Africa made lightweight wickerwork shields into the early 20th century. A Zande warrior carried the shield in his left hand, along with any spare weapons, while holding his spear or throwing knife in his right hand.

DATE	c.1900
ORIGIN	DEM. REP. OF CONGO
LENGTH	51 IN (130 CM)

KIKUYU CEREMONIAL SHIELD

This wooden dance shield, or *ndome*, is of a type made by the Kikuyu people of Kenya. It was worn on the upper left arm by young warriors during elaborate Kikuyu initiation rights. The serrated design on the inside of the shield was always the same, but the outer design varied to indicate the age group and local origin of the warrior.

Serrated design

Shield carved from single block of wood

DATE	19TH CENTURY
ORIGIN	KENYA
LENGTH	23½ IN (60 CM)

Cotton-covered concentric cane hoops

Iron reinforcing bars

Central boss

Iron boss

ORNATE ETHIOPIAN SHIELD

Shields were still in military use in the kingdom of Ethiopia in the early 20th century. They were typically round, made of animal hide, and mounted in silver clasps. As well as serving him in combat, an Ethiopian warrior's shield announced his status. Shields were often decorated with the mane, tail, or paw of a lion, all symbols of Ethiopian royalty.

Silver clasps

DATE	19TH CENTURY
ORIGIN	ETHIOPIA
WIDTH	19¾ IN (50 CM)

FULL VIEW

ROUND SUDANESE SHIELD

This round shield from Sudan is constructed of concentric cane hoops covered in colored cotton, with an iron outer frame, boss, and reinforcing bars. On the other side of the shield, there are hand grips of braided leather.

DATE	19TH CENTURY
ORIGIN	SUDAN
WIDTH	36.9CM (14½IN)

271

OCEANIAN SHIELDS

WARFARE WAS COMMON among the peoples of New Guinea and Melanesia, until largely stopped by colonial authorities during the 20th century. Wooden or wicker shields provided defense against weapons such as bone- or bamboo-tipped arrows, wooden spears, stone axes, and bone knives. The shields varied in size from large planks that could shelter the warrior's whole body to smaller parrying shields and breastplates. Many of the shields shown here date from the 20th century, but are identical to those in use before.

Head section

ASMAT WAR SHIELD

Warfare was central to the lives of the Asmat people, living on the south coast of the island of New Guinea. Their shields were not only a means of defense, but also psychological weapons, their decorative designs calculated to inspire terror. The flying fox fruit bat, represented on this shield, was symbolically associated with headhunting, since it took fruit from trees as a headhunter took a head from a body.

DATE	POST-1950
ORIGIN	IRIAN JAYA
LENGTH	51 IN (129 CM)

FULL VIEW

Stylized representation of flying fox fruit bat

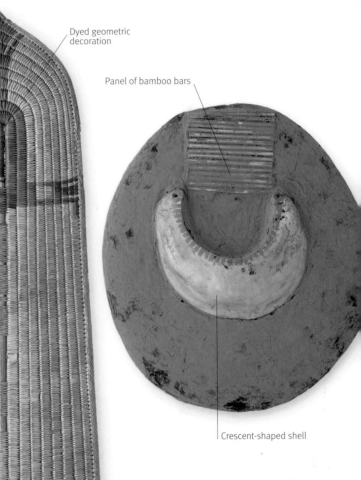

Dyed geometric decoration

Panel of bamboo bars

Crescent-shaped shell

MELPA CHEST-PLATE

This chest-plate shield, or *moka kina*, was made by the Melpa people of the Upper Sepik region of Papua New Guinea. Worn as body armor, it has shell and bamboo decoration.

DATE	c.1950
ORIGIN	PAPUA NEW GUINEA
LENGTH	15 IN (38 IN)

Woven coiled-cane wicker

BASKET-WEAVE WAR SHIELD

This elegant elliptical shield is typical of those used on headhunting raids in the Solomon Islands until the late 19th century. Its closely woven coiled-cane wicker was an effective block, even against spears. Too small for passive defensive tactics, it was manipulated actively to parry blows and missiles.

DATE	19TH CENTURY
ORIGIN	NEW GEORGIA
LENGTH	32½ IN (83 CM)

Ancestor figure

A tree kangaroo-tail design

ASMAT WAR SHIELD

Each Asmat shield was named after an ancestor and this, along with the design motif, gave the warrior spiritual power and protection. Shields were made of wood and carved with stone, bone, or shell tools. The colors used in the decoration had symbolic significance, red representing power and beauty.

DATE 19TH CENTURY
ORIGIN IRIAN JAYA
LENGTH 78¼ IN (199 CM)

MENDI WAR SHIELD

This Mendi shield is made of hardwood and decorated with a bold geometric pattern of opposing triangles known as a "butterfly wing" design. Unusually, highland shields were not used in ceremonies, but were purely for warfare. In combat, the shield was supported on a rope shoulder sling.

DATE POST-1950
ORIGIN PAPUA NEW GUINEA
LENGTH 48 IN (122 CM)

Hardwood shield with geometric decoration

Cane binding holds wood panels together

Panel containing zigzag motifs

ARAWE WAR SHIELD

This shield, from the Kandrian area of New Britain, is typical of those produced by the Arawe people. Made of three oval-section, vertical planks of wood joined with split cane strips, it is incised with distinctive zigzag and coiled motifs. Natural black, white, and red ochers are the only colors used.

DATE POST-1950
ORIGIN PAPUA NEW GUINEA
LENGTH 49¼ IN (125 CM)

BIWAT WAR SHIELD

This shield is from Biwat village on the Yuat River in Papua New Guinea. Although narrow, it is a tall shield that would have offered full body protection. It is boldly decorated with a central panel and geometric shapes around the edge.

DATE POST-1950
ORIGIN PAPUA NEW GUINEA
LENGTH 67¼ IN (171 CM)

Bold geometric edging

Turtle-like motif

THE MODERN WORLD

The 20th century saw the outbreak of warfare on a truly global scale. Two world wars caused mass casualties and economic dislocation, as armies bigger than ever before fought continent-wide campaigns. New weapons systems ushered in an age of mechanized warfare, with tanks, aircrafts, and missiles replacing infantry as the arbiters of victory. The invention of nuclear weapons, moreover, complicated strategists' calculations with a destructive power that, for the superpowers, made their possession essential, and their use unimaginable.

AT THE START OF THE 20TH CENTURY,

Europe lay in a state of uneasy calm, as countries shifted alliances in an attempt to gain advantage in the coming war, a conflict made ever more likely by their maneuvers. All had learned the lessons of Prussia's victories in the 1860s and 1870s, and by 1914, Europe's leaders had their fingers on a hair-trigger, believing that slowness to mobilize would lead to disaster. In the event, it was the very speed of their reaction to the assassination of Archduke Franz Ferdinand by Serbian nationalists in June 1914 that precipitated catastrophe.

Once Russia, fearful of Austrian plans, mobilized, the Austrians did so too, followed within a week by the Germans and French. Germany, desperate to knock France out of the war quickly, embarked on the Schlieffen Plan, which envisaged hooking its army around through Belgium and enveloping Paris from the north. The German General Staff, which throughout the war displayed great tactical ability, but strategic myopia, failed to realize the infringement of Belgian neutrality would bring Britain into the war. Even so, the German knock-out blow almost worked, as the French barely succeeded in halting the invaders in August at the Battle of the Marne.

The war stabilized into a confrontation along a 500-mile (800-km) front stretching from Switzerland to the Channel ports, a line from which it was barely to shift in four years of bitter and bloody fighting. Dug into trench-lines, each side's infantry forces proved almost impossible to dislodge, as machine guns, such as the air-cooled Hotchkiss, which fired 400–600 rounds per minute, made any attempt at assault a form of mass suicide.

ARTILLERY BOMBARDMENTS

Both sides struggled to find a means to break the deadlock. At Verdun in 1916, the Germans sought to bleed the French army dry by sucking it into holding a position where their artillery would inflict heavy casualties. The French defended Verdun tenaciously and did,

RUSSO-JAPANESE WAR
In February 1904, Japanese torpedo boats attacked the Russian fleet at anchor in Port Arthur. Outside observers drew the lessons that firepower would dominate any future conflict in Europe, and that the strategic imperative should be to strike fast, and hard.

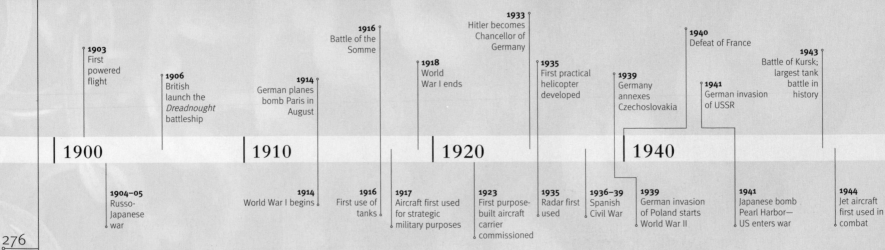

1903 First powered flight

1906 British launch the *Dreadnought* battleship

1914 German planes bomb Paris in August

1916 Battle of the Somme

1918 World War I ends

1933 Hitler becomes Chancellor of Germany

1935 First practical helicopter developed

1939 Germany annexes Czechoslovakia

1940 Defeat of France

1941 German invasion of USSR

1943 Battle of Kursk; largest tank battle in history

1900

1910

1920

1940

1904–05 Russo-Japanese war

1914 World War I begins

1916 First use of tanks

1917 Aircraft first used for strategic military purposes

1923 First purpose-built aircraft carrier commissioned

1935 Radar first used

1936–39 Spanish Civil War

1939 German invasion of Poland starts World War II

1941 Japanese bomb Pearl Harbor— US enters war

1944 Jet aircraft first used in combat

indeed, lose 120,000 men, but the German effort cost an equally damaging 100,000 dead. The use of artillery bombardments to precede assaults often turned the terrain into a morass —notably at Passchendaele in 1917—where forward progress was next to impossible and the floundering infantry made enticing targets for machine gun nests.

GAS AND TANKS

New weaponry was adopted to try to end the stalemate. Poison gas was first used on a large scale at Ypres in April 1915, and although the Germans then punched a 4-mile (6-km) hole in the French line, their advance was as much hindered as assisted by their fear of the chlorine gas's effect. Similarly, tanks first appeared at the Somme in September 1916, but did not really play a major operational role until Cambrai a few months later. Planes were at first used for reconnaissance, and from 1915, Zeppelin airships and then Gotha bombers made raids on British cities, but to little real strategic effect. At sea, the German U-boat submarine fleet threatened for a while to throttle British trade, but the introduction of the convoy system in 1917 stifled the losses.

Despite a temporary German breakthrough in spring 1918, their resources were overstretched, their manpower dwindling, and industry struggling to keep up with the army's demands. When the Allies pushed back, it was against an open door, and, on the point of military, economic, and social collapse, Germany accepted an armistice in November.

German nationalist leaders felt betrayed by the armistice, which they portrayed as a political rather than a military capitulation. The economic crisis of the Great Depression, and helped boosted the rise of Fascism in Italy and Germany and cemented the rule of Communism in the new Soviet Union. Throughout the late 1930s, Hitler rearmed Germany, intimidated or annexed his weaker neighbors, and cowed France and Britain into acceptance. Hitler's failure to perceive

that Britain was not fully acquiescent led to a strategic blunder—the invasion of Poland in 1939—which precipitated World War II. During 1940, German armies smashed through the Low Countries, Scandinavia, and France in a form of combat dubbed "Blitzkrieg." Armored formations moved far ahead of the infantry in France, wrong-footing the French high command who had expected the Germans to revisit the Schlieffen Plan from the previous war.

AERIAL BATTLE

Hitler's army, having outstripped their supplies, allowed the bulk of British forces to escape from Dunkirk. Hitler thus committed himself to the world's first purely aerial campaign, the Battle of Britain, in the summer of 1940,

MACHINE GUN NEST
The widespread deployment of machine guns in World War I helped change the balance of advantage from attackers to defenders. The unit depicted here fought in the Battle of the Somme in July 1916, during which 20,000 British soldiers died in the first day of the attack alone, many of them falling victim to machine gun fire.

attempting to defeat the Royal Air Force and so clear the way for the invasion of the British Isles. The British had, however, developed radar to detect attacking aircraft, and the German Luftwaffe, already depleted in the campaign for France, suffered irreplaceable losses to a new generation of British fighter aircraft such as the Spitfire. Stretched to the limit, the Germans switched to night-bombing of cities from

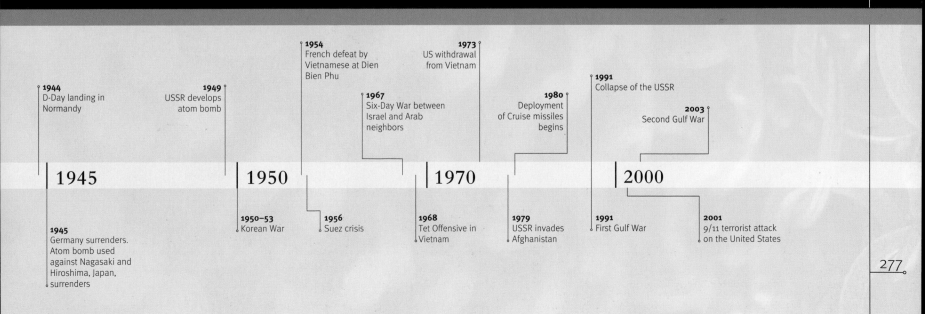

1944
D-Day landing in Normandy

1949
USSR develops atom bomb

1954
French defeat by Vietnamese at Dien Bien Phu

1973
US withdrawal from Vietnam

1967
Six-Day War between Israel and Arab neighbors

1980
Deployment of Cruise missiles begins

1991
Collapse of the USSR

2003
Second Gulf War

1945   1950   1970   2000

1945
Germany surrenders. Atom bomb used against Nagasaki and Hiroshima, Japan, surrenders

1950–53
Korean War

1956
Suez crisis

1968
Tet Offensive in Vietnam

1979
USSR invades Afghanistan

1991
First Gulf War

2001
9/11 terrorist attack on the United States

September and the invasion was indefinitely postponed. Strategic bombing was later employed by the British against Germany on a massive scale in an effort to destroy strategic industries, and—controversially—to undermine the enemy's morale. Dresden was virtually destroyed in February 1945 in a firestorm that engulfed it after an Allied bombing attack.

German troops were well-equipped, mostly with versions of the Mauser Gewehr 98 bolt-action rifle, and ably led by Europe's most professional officer corps. But at a higher level, strategic greed and overstretch bedevilled Germany's war. The invasion of the Soviet Union in June 1941 showed Hitler had not learned the lessons of Napoleon's 1812 campaign—Russia's vast size meant it could absorb huge losses of territory and manpower. Although the Germans reached the outskirts of Moscow in December 1941, their tanks could not operate in the cold, their infantry was not equipped for the freezing conditions,

and they had no manpower in reserve, while the Russians had fresh divisions from the Siberian hinterland.

Germany was short of oil, too, which played a part in Hitler's decision to push southward to the oil fields of the Caucasus. At Stalingrad in 1942, the Germans were sucked into a bitter house-by-house struggle, the first real example of modern urban warfare. The Soviet counterstroke that November trapped more than 200,000 troops in the city, a loss from which the German army never really recovered.

In the West, Allied armies made the largest amphibious landing in history in Normandy in 1944 and then thrust toward the German border. Germany developed a series of innovative weapons in a bid to turn the tide, including jet fighters (the V-2 rockets) and long-range missile systems, but could not prevent the fall of Berlin in May 1945.

NAVAL CAMPAIGN IN JAPAN

In the Pacific, the United States and its allies fought a parallel war against Japan from 1941. Precipitated by the unprovoked attack on Pearl Harbor in 1941, the war saw Japanese forces sweep through the Malay Peninsula, the Philippines, and a string of Pacific islands. The United States fought a naval-based campaign that left Japan's acquisitions isolated. At Midway in June 1942, the Japanese lost four aircraft carriers—a blow from which they never really recovered. Although Japanese resistance was tenacious, and the conquest of Okinawa alone in 1945 cost 65,000 American lives, the question became whether the United States had the stomach to invade Japan itself. America's response came with the first use

of nuclear weapons on Hiroshima and Nagasaki in August 1945, which forced Japan's surrender and transformed the calculations of military strategists. For the next 45 years, the world experienced a "Cold War" where a balance of terror kept the peace. The United States established the NATO alliance in 1949 to confront the Soviet Union in Europe, and the Soviets responded with the formation of the Warsaw Pact in 1955. NATO never had sufficient ground forces in western Europe to hold back a serious Soviet land offensive. Paradoxically, this weakness helped keep the peace, as any such attack would have unleashed a nuclear strike against the Soviet Union.

CONFLICT IN KOREA AND VIETNAM

Potentially dangerous confrontations between the superpowers did emerge, most especially in Asia. In Korea from 1950–53, the United States fought a war to prevent the peninsula falling into communist hands, part of a strategy of containment that also led it into a fatal entanglement in Vietnam in the 1960s. Fearful of communist movement into South Vietnam, the United States was sucked into the provision, first of military aid and advisers, and then hundreds of thousands of ground troops. The war saw the first large-scale use of helicopters in a military role, and strategic bombing on a massive scale, but the United States was consistently wrong-footed in what was essentially a guerrilla war. With the pullout of American combat forces in 1973, the South Vietnamese army were soon defeated.

MODERN WARFARE

The Middle East was historically an area of chronic tension, with a series of wars between Israel and its Arab neighbors (in 1948, 1967, and 1973). The superpowers did not become directly involved in conflicts in the region, except for funding proxies or diplomatic

AK47
The Kalashnikov assault rifle (or AK47) was first developed by the Soviet Union in 1947. Simple and inexpensive to manufacture, yet durable, it became a mainstay of guerrilla and liberation movements worldwide. This version, from around 1980, is of Chinese manufacture.

saber-rattling, until the 1990s. It was the oppressive Iraqi regime of Saddam Hussein, with ambitions for regional dominance and —it was claimed—to develop nuclear weapons —that precipitated two American-led campaigns in 1991 and 2003. The first war saw the first combat use of cruise missiles and "smart" bombs, which, with laser-guidance, were less likely to fall off-target.

The 2003 Iraq campaign, which caused the fall of Saddam Hussein, featured a similar array of advanced weaponry. Yet American ground forces still had to fight their way to Baghdad, a task that proved that for all the advances in aircraft, missile, and communications technology, it still took troops on the ground to command a battlefield. Similarly, the United States' failure to deal with a growing insurgency movement in Iraq showed that the possession of nearly unlimited logistical support, battlefield weaponry of a power almost unimaginable a century earlier, and an arsenal of nuclear missiles, meant little where this power could not be brought to bear. Terrorism, religious fanaticism, failed states, and genocidal civil wars were the new challenges, with death as often dealt by the machete as the M16. As throughout history, the possession of the most advanced weapons was never enough by itself to shape the political landscape.

GUERRILLA WARFARE

Although guerrilla tactics are almost as old as warfare itself—the Bar Kochba revolt of the Jews against Rome (132–35 CE) is but one example—in the 20th century, they have become identified with national liberation and revolutionary movements. When the Soviet Union invaded Afghanistan in 1979, it rapidly overran the cities, but found itself facing a disparate coalition of Afghan mujahidin guerrillas who dominated most of the countryside and received military aid, including Stinger anti-aircraft missiles, from the West. Eventually, the Soviets moved away from conventional armored tactics and mounted combined helicopter-infantry sweeps of the mujahidin's mountain strongholds. But, as with many guerrilla wars, they found it difficult to differentiate civilians from combatants and could not prevent the guerrillas from reinfiltrating areas they had just been driven from. Guerrilla warfare's aim is to undermine the political will of an occupier to remain by inflicting unacceptable losses. Finding itself at the wrong side of this equation, the USSR withdrew its forces from Afghanistan in 1989.

AFGHAN GUERRILLA FIGHTERS

GULF WARRIORS
An American Apache attack helicopter flies over a US tank formation in the Kuwaiti desert shortly before the assault on Iraq in 2003. Close air support of land formations played a key role in the American victory.

AFRICAN EDGED WEAPONS

THE TRADITIONAL WEAPONRY found in Africa reflects the continent's ethnic and cultural diversity. North of the Sahara and along the East African coast, under Arab and Ottoman Turkish influence, weapons broadly resembled those found across the Islamic world. South of the Sahara the prevailing traditions produced edged weapons such as throwing knives, fighting bracelets, and "execution" knives that were often highly original in design. Many of these were in use long after the European colonial powers took over parts of Africa.

Peacock tail pommel

Two-edged blade

Silver overlay on scabbard

Attachment for baldric (sash)

WOODEN-HILTED DAGGER

The "peacock" style of this dagger's pommel is functional as well as decorative, providing protection for the back of the hand. The pommel is typical of a Moroccan *koummya* knife. The elaborate sheath, overlaid with silver on one side, would have hung from a baldric (silk or leather sash) by its wearer's left hip.

DATE	19TH CENTURY
ORIGIN	NORTH AFRICA
WEIGHT	½ LB (0.23 KG)
LENGTH	14¾ IN (37.5 CM)

Carved wooden handle

Metal binding

Brass sheeting covers hilt

Straight back of blade

Triangular pattern decoration

Broad heel of blade

Cutting edge

FLYSSA

Although the origin of this knife is uncertain, in shape and decoration it resembles the *flyssa* saber used by the Kabyle Berbers of northeastern Algeria. The octagonal grip is covered in decoratively incised brass sheeting, which suggests this is a cut-down *flyssa*.

DATE	19TH/20TH CENTURY
ORIGIN	NORTH AFRICA
WEIGHT	¼ LB (0.16 KG)
LENGTH	14½ IN (37 CM)

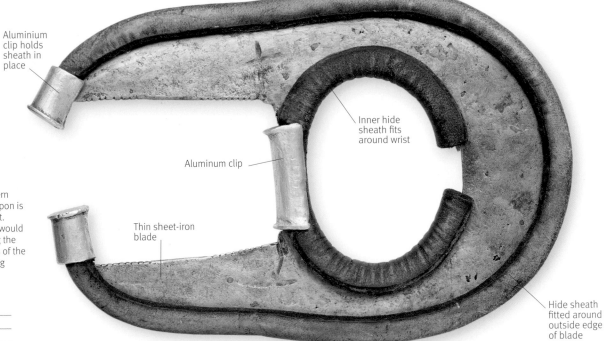

LARIM FIGHTING BRACELET

Known to the Larim people of southern
Sudan as a *nyepel*, this unusual weapon is
a two-pointed knife worn on the wrist.
Before entering a fight, a Larim man would
remove the outer sheath, uncovering the
sharp edge and slightly rounded tips of the
hammered iron blade. Similar fighting
bracelets and sheaths were used by
other Sudanese peoples.

DATE	20TH CENTURY
ORIGIN	SUDAN
WEIGHT	2½ OZ (70 G)
LENGTH	5½ IN (14 CM)

Aluminium
clip holds
sheath in
place

Aluminum clip

Inner hide
sheath fits
around wrist

Thin sheet-iron
blade

Hide sheath
fitted around
outside edge
of blade

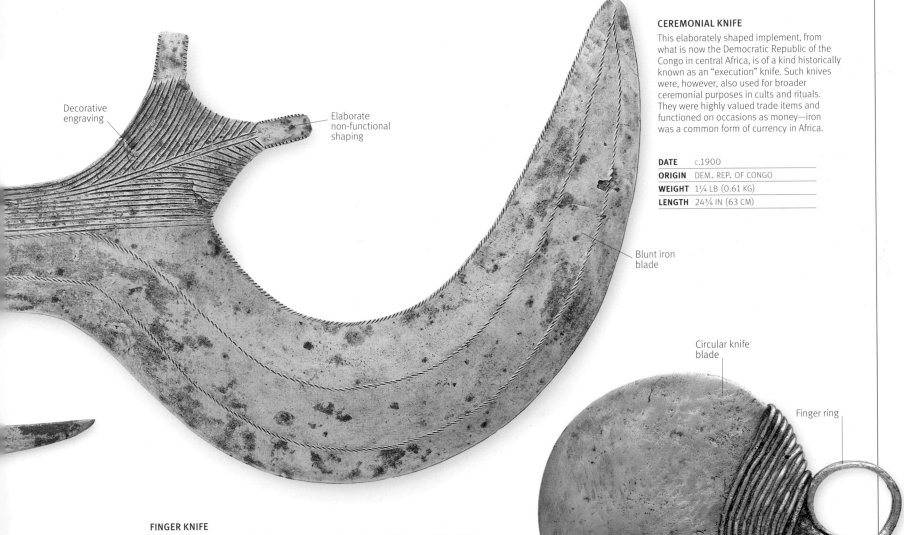

CEREMONIAL KNIFE

This elaborately shaped implement, from
what is now the Democratic Republic of the
Congo in central Africa, is of a kind historically
known as an "execution" knife. Such knives
were, however, also used for broader
ceremonial purposes in cults and rituals.
They were highly valued trade items and
functioned on occasions as money—iron
was a common form of currency in Africa.

DATE	c.1900
ORIGIN	DEM. REP. OF CONGO
WEIGHT	1¼ LB (0.61 KG)
LENGTH	24¾ IN (63 CM)

Decorative
engraving

Elaborate
non-functional
shaping

Blunt iron
blade

Circular knife
blade

Finger ring

FINGER KNIFE

This small, broad-bladed knife probably comes from the
Labwor people of northeastern Uganda. Made of iron, it
was worn on a finger, and could be used for everyday
purposes such as cutting meat, as well as for fighting.
Its advantage as a weapon was that, because of its
diminutive size, it could be concealed in the hand.

DATE	c.1890–1950
ORIGIN	UGANDA
WEIGHT	1¾ OZ (50 G)
LENGTH	3¾ IN (9.5 CM)

281

AFRICAN EDGED WEAPONS

Brass and
iron strips

Tang of blade

Polished-
wood handle
knob

CURVED SUDANESE KNIFE

Made by the Zande of southern Sudan, this "sickle knife"—so-called because of its curved blade—may have been used in war as a throwing knife, but could equally have served as a tool, or been carried as an emblem of power.

DATE	EARLY 20TH CENTURY
ORIGIN	SUDAN
WEIGHT	1¼LB (0.55KG)
LENGTH	18¼IN (46.5CM)

Decorated hilt

Copper blade

KASAI COPPER DAGGER

Originating from the Kasai region of what is now the Democratic Republic of Congo, the distinctive style of this copper-bladed dagger seems potentially influenced by models from the Islamic world. The hilt is well shaped to form a comfortable grip.

DATE	c.1900
ORIGIN	DR CONGO

Terminal brass ring

Carved ivory hilt

BENIN CEREMONIAL SWORD

Known as an *eben*, this sword is from the West African kingdom of Benin. Traditionally made of iron by Benin's blacksmiths' guilds, *eben* were carried by the Oba, the state's sacred ruler, and by his chief warriors.

DATE	c.1900
ORIGIN	BENIN
LENGTH	17¾IN (45CM)

Design of
punched holes

Wooden balls
covered in gold

ORNATE CEREMONIAL SWORD

This sword belonged to Kofi Karikari, ruler of the West African Asante kingdom from 1867 to 1874. It was an object of prestige rather than a weapon—its iron blade is unsharpened. The golden balls, representing seeds, are symbols of wealth and fertility.

DATE	c.1870
ORIGIN	ASHANTI

Broad ridge

Curved
iron blade
sharpened on
both edges

BENIN CHIEF WITH EBEN
The kingdom of Benin flourished
from the 15th to the 19th century.
This bronze panel, produced by Benin
craftsmen, shows a chief with an
eben, the ceremonial sword raised in
his right hand, which is a gesture of
allegiance to the authority of the Oba,
or king. The Oba himself carried an
eben in ceremonial dances honoring
his ancestors, touching it to the
ground in front of his father's tomb.
Eben continued to be made into the
20th century.

Curved metal
blade

Twin-pointed
blade

Leaf-shaped
blade

Ridged handle

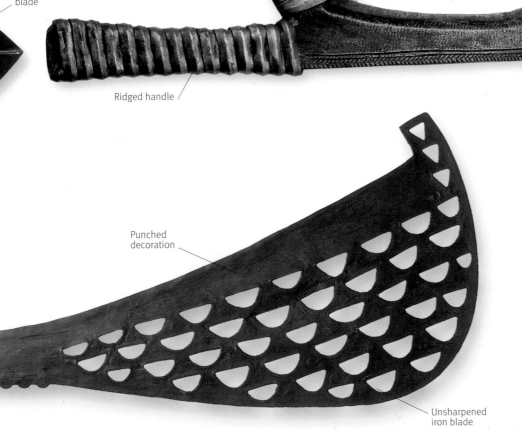

Punched
decoration

Straight
tapering blade

THROWING KNIFE
Eccentrically shaped multi-bladed throwing
knives are found in many parts of Africa.
This example is from the Congo. When the
knife is thrown it turns about its center of
gravity, making the blades scythe dangerously
through the air. It will inflict a wound on an
opponent whatever its point of impact.

DATE	LATE 19TH/EARLY 20TH CENTURY
ORIGIN	DEM REP CONGO

Unsharpened
iron blade

1900—2006

◀ 194–195 EUROPEAN AND AMERICAN BAYONETS   ◀ 234–235 WEAPON SHOWCASE: BAKER RIFLE   ◀ 250–251 WEAPON SHOWCASE: ENFIELD RIFLE MUSKET

THE MODERN WORLD

BAYONETS AND KNIVES 1914–1945

EUROPEAN ARMIES ENTERED World War I with faith in the bayonet charge as the key to victory in infantry combat. Reality proved different: troops advancing with bayonets fixed were mown down by machine guns and rifle fire. Soldiers cynically claimed that bayonets were more use for opening cans than for combat. However, bayonets have remained in use since, typically with shorter blades. Fighting knives, which proved their worth in the trenches in 1914–18, were used by special forces in World War II, and as a close-combat arm for infantry lacking bayonets.

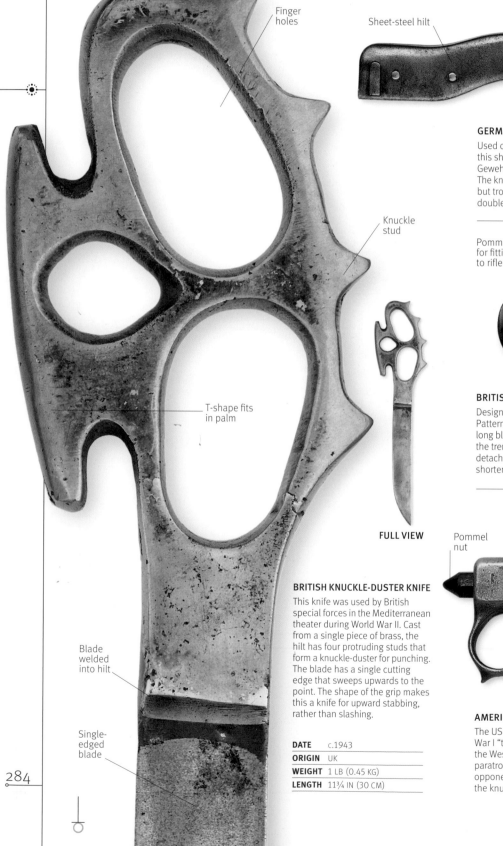

Finger holes

Knuckle stud

T-shape fits in palm

FULL VIEW

Blade welded into hilt

Single-edged blade

BRITISH KNUCKLE-DUSTER KNIFE

This knife was used by British special forces in the Mediterranean theater during World War II. Cast from a single piece of brass, the hilt has four protruding studs that form a knuckle-duster for punching. The blade has a single cutting edge that sweeps upwards to the point. The shape of the grip makes this a knife for upward stabbing, rather than slashing.

DATE	c.1943
ORIGIN	UK
WEIGHT	1 LB (0.45 KG)
LENGTH	11¾ IN (30 CM)

Cross-guard

Sheet-steel hilt

Double-edged blade

GERMAN KNIFE BAYONET

Used on the Western Front toward the end of World War I, this short, double-edged bayonet was fitted to the Mauser Gewehr 1898 rifle, attaching to the barrel by a press stud. The knife bayonet was not official German army equipment, but troops were permitted to buy it. Many did, since it also doubled as a highly effective trench knife.

DATE	1914–18
ORIGIN	GERMANY
WEIGHT	½ LB (0.22 KG)
LENGTH	10¼ IN (26.1 CM)

Pommel has slot for fitting bayonet to rifle

Muzzle ring

BRITISH 1907-PATTERN SWORD BAYONET,

Designed for the Short Magazine Lee-Enfield rifle, the 1907-Pattern was based on the Japanese Arisaka bayonet. Its long blade was meant to give a soldier extra reach, but in the trench warfare of 1914–18 it proved unusable when detached as a sword, and less apt as a bayonet than shorter blades.

DATE	1914–18
ORIGIN	UK
WEIGHT	1¼ LB (0.51 KG)
LENGTH	22 IN (56 CM)

Pommel nut

Maker's initials

Stabbing blade

U.S. 1918
L.F&C-1918

Brass knuckle-duster grip

AMERICAN KNUCKLE-DUSTER TRENCH KNIFE

The US Mark 1 1918 knuckle knife was intended as a World War I "trench-clearing tool," but arrived too late for use on the Western Front. Winning fame as a World War II paratroop weapon, it had three attack modes: striking an opponent's skull with the pommel nut, punching him with the knuckle-duster, and stabbing upward with the blade.

DATE	1940s
ORIGIN	US
WEIGHT	1¼ LB (0.5 KG)
LENGTH	22 IN (56 CM)

One-piece,
all-steel hilt
and blade

Grooved
plastic grip

Bayonet
release catch

Pressed-steel
throat

Single-edged
blade

US M1 KNIFE BAYONET

In April 1943, the US Army decided to adopt a
shorter bayonet for the M1 Garand rifle. Thus the
M1 knife bayonet, with its 10 in (25.4 cm) blade,
replaced the 16 in (40.6 cm) blade M1905 and
M1942 models. The bayonet's M7 scabbard was
manufactured by Victory Plastics.

DATE	1944
ORIGIN	US
WEIGHT	1 LB (0.43 KG)
LENGTH	14½ IN (36.8 CM)

Plastic
scabbard

Wooden hilt

Steel flash guard on top of hilt

Deep fuller

Short blade

GERMAN S84/98 BAYONET

This bayonet was introduced in 1915 as a cheap
and sturdy attachment for the Mauser Gewehr
1898 rifle. It has no muzzle ring, being held to the
rifle solely by a long groove in the pommel.
S84/98's continued to be produced up to World
War II, which is when this example was made.

DATE	1940s
ORIGIN	GERMANY
WEIGHT	1 LB (0.42 KG)
LENGTH	15 IN (38.2 CM)

Single-edged
blade

Deep fuller

Leather washers form grip

Diamond-section blade

AMERICAN MK 3 FIGHTING KNIFE

In 1943 the US Army introduced the Mk 3 knife for
hand-to-hand fighting. It was rapidly put into mass
production, with 2.5 million manufactured by 1944.
The hilt and blade were influenced by the British
Fairbairn-Sykes fighting knife (below). The US
Marines instead adopted the Ka-Bar combat knife.

DATE	c.1950
ORIGIN	US
WEIGHT	½ LB (0.24 KG)
LENGTH	11 IN (29.5 CM)

Recurved
quillons

Cylindrical grip

Double-edged blade

FAIRBAIRN-SYKES FIGHTING KNIFE

Modeled on daggers used by Chinese gangsters,
this knife was developed in the 1930s by Shanghai
police chief William Fairbairn and his colleague Eric
Sykes. In World War II, it was used by Allied special
forces such as Commandos, who were also trained
by Fairbairn and Sykes in hand-to-hand combat.

DATE	1941–45
ORIGIN	UK
WEIGHT	½ LB (0.23 KG)
LENGTH	12 IN (30 CM)

Slender blade slips between ribs,
but is also ideal for slashing

WORLD WAR I
The opposing lines on the
Western Front during World War I
stretched from the Swiss border to the
North Sea. These troops from the Kriegsmarine
(German navy), armed with Mauser Gew98 rifles,
occupied defensive positions at its northern extremity.

FRENCH WWI INFANTRYMAN

THE FRENCH CONSCRIPT infantryman who fought on the Western Front in World War I (1914–18) was a citizen-soldier, taught to regard service in the army as his duty to the republic and a source of patriotic pride. Despite immense losses and the demoralizing attrition of trench warfare, which reduced parts of the French army to mutiny in 1917, the "*poilu*" (French slang for "hairy one") held firm in the great battles of the Marne and Verdun.

CITIZEN ARMY

Before the war, every young Frenchman was obliged to undertake national service lasting two years (raised to three in 1913), after which he passed into the reserve for the rest of his adult life. As a result, France could theoretically regard all of its male population as trained soldiers. More than 8 million served at some time in the war with, at the peak, 1.5 million Frenchmen in service. The French army began the war with an antiquated rifle, inadequate machine guns, little heavy artillery, and bright uniforms that made perfect targets. Thus equipped, soldiers were committed to the offensive against overwhelming German firepower. Approximately 1 million French casualties were suffered in the first three months of the war, although the defeat of the Germans at the First Battle of the Marne ensured France's survival. Trench warfare followed, a natural consequence of the defensive superiority that rapid-fire rifles and machine guns gave to entrenched troops. French infantry suffered even worse conditions than their British allies, subjected to artillery bombardment and poison gas in generally poor quality trenches. Morale survived the slaughter at Verdun, but futile offensives in early 1917 brought widespread unrest. The authorities were forced to improve food and leave, and be less wasteful of men's lives. Morale recovered sufficiently for the French infantry to make a major contribution to victory in 1918.

FRENCH INFANTRYMEN FIGHTING AT VERDUN
In February 1916 the Germans attacked the fortified city of Verdun, aiming to "bleed the French army white." Pounded by German heavy artillery, French infantry held the front through months of desperate defensive fighting at a cost of around 400,000 casualties.

Adrian
helmet

Haversack with
personal items

MACHINE GUN CREW
French infantry operate a Hotchkiss machine gun in 1915. France's guns were generally of inferior performance—this Hotchkiss is being fed with 25-round strips of ammunition, rather than having a more efficient belt feed.

TRENCH UNIFORM
The French infantry's original blue overcoats, bright red pants, and cloth kepis were replaced in 1915 by this more discreet blue-gray uniform and steel helmet.

Pale blue-gray
greatcoat

COST OF THE WAR

Out of 8.3 million French soldiers who served in the Great War, almost 1.4 million were killed. Another 3 million were wounded, around three-quarters of a million suffering permanent or long-term disability. More than one in five of all Frenchmen was a casualty and the percentage of men between 18 and 35 who died was high enough to justify talk of a "lost generation." The terrible losses at Verdun were memorialized by the Ossuary at Douaumont, which contains the remains of hundreds of thousands of unidentified French and German soldiers.

**OSSUARY
AT DOUAUMONT**

Puttees from
ankle to knee

TOOLS OF COMBAT

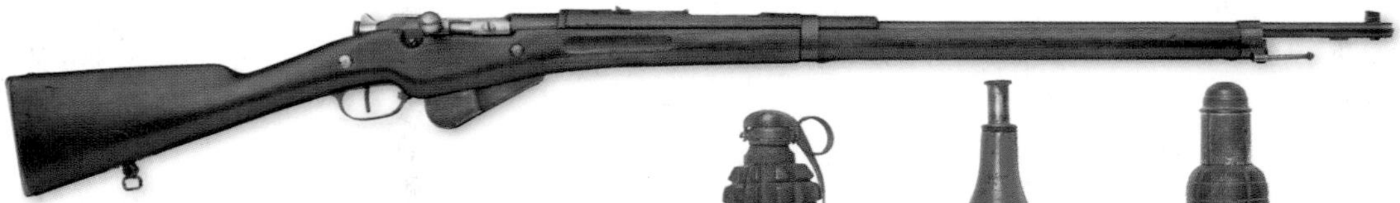

MANNLICHER-BERTHIER RIFLE

F1 GRENADE

P1 GRENADE

CITRON FOUG GRENADE

HOTCHKISS MACHINE GUN

"HUMANITY IS MAD! WHAT SCENES OF HORROR AND CARNAGE! HELL CANNOT BE SO TERRIBLE. MEN ARE MAD!"

SECOND LIEUTENANT ALFRED JOUBERT, DIARY ENTRY MAY 23, 1916, VERDUN

1900—2006

◄ 228–229 SELF-LOADING PISTOLS 1775–1900   ► 292–293 SELF-LOADING PISTOLS 1920–1950   ► 294–295 SELF-LOADING PISTOLS FROM 1950

THE MODERN WORLD

SELF-LOADING PISTOLS 1900–1920

THE BORCHARDT AND THE MAUSER C/96 demonstrated that self-loading pistols worked reliably; however, they were expensive to produce and rather unwieldy. The next generation of such guns became simpler, and thus cheaper to manufacture. The best of the weapons from the early years of the 20th century, such as John Moses Browning's Colt M1911 and Georg Luger's P'08, are still in demand, while originals are eagerly sought by collectors.

Fore sight

Lever holds slide back for stripping

Rear sight

Hammer

Safety catch

Recoil spring housing

Patent data

Grip safety

COLT M1911A1

Browning designed the Colt M1911 (the year it was accepted as the US Army's official side-arm) in response to a demand by soldiers fighting Moro rebels in the Philippines for a pistol firing the heavy .45 round in place of the less-effective .38-caliber revolvers with which they were issued. The example shown here is a later M1911A1.

DATE	1909 ONWARD
ORIGIN	US
WEIGHT	2 LB (1.1 KG)
BARREL	5 IN (12.7 CM)
CALIBER	.45 IN ACP

Magazine catch

Butt houses seven-round removable magazine

COLT M1902

As well as the Model 1900 pocket pistol, Browning designed a series of military self-loading pistols in .38 ACP caliber, with an unsatisfactory double-link locking system that produced a jerky action. That, and the light rounds they fired, disqualified them in the eyes of the US Army.

DATE	1902
ORIGIN	US
WEIGHT	2¼ LB (1.02 KG)
BARREL	6 IN (15.2 CM)
CALIBER	.38 IN ACP

Butt houses seven-round removable magazine

Hold-open catch holds the slide back

Removable butt stock

Tangent rear sight

Loading/ejector port

Hammer

Rate-of-fire selector

Lanyard eye

ASTRA M901

A direct copy of the Schnellfeuer ("Rapidfire") version of the Mauser C/96, the Astra was produced in Spain. It has an automatic-fire capability, but is impossible to control in that mode.

DATE	1920s
ORIGIN	SPAIN
WEIGHT	4 LB (2.1 KG)
BARREL	6¼ IN (16 CM)
CALIBER	7.63 MM MAUSER

20-round fixed magazine

Fore sight

4 in (10 cm) barrel, the longest permitted in Germany after World War I

Hold-open lever

Ejector port

Toggle doubles up as cocking grip

Ramp breaks toggle joint upward

Safety catch

Magazine catch

STEYR "HAHN" M1911

Barrel locking lug

Ejector port

Loading port

Hammer (or "hahn")

Safety catch

Butt houses eight-round fixed magazine

Werndl tried for many years to produce a successful military pistol, and succeeded with the M1911. It was similar in concept to the Colt, except that its barrel rotates, rather than tips, to unlock it from the slide.

DATE	1911
ORIGIN	AUSTRIA
WEIGHT	2¼ LB (0.9 KG)
BARREL	9 IN (12.7 CM)
CALIBER	7.63 MM

LUGER P'08

Butt houses ten-round removable magazine

Magazine grip

One of the best-known guns in the world, with almost iconic status, the Pistole '08 was designed by Georg Luger in 1900. He copied many features of Borchardt's gun of seven years earlier, but adopted a leaf recoil spring and moved it into the butt, improving the overall balance considerably. Luger also produced improved ammunition for his pistol, the "Parabellum" round, which was to become the world standard.

DATE	1908
ORIGIN	GERMANY
WEIGHT	2 LB (0.8 KG)
BARREL	4 IN (10 CM)
CALIBER	9 MM PARABELLUM

WEBLEY MODEL 1910

Fore sight

Concealed hammer

Hold-open lever

Butt houses seven-round removable magazine

Webley of Birmingham produced a range of locked-breech self-loading pistols from about 1904. They were all designed by J.H. Whiting, who collaborated with Hugh Gabbett-Fairfax on the Mars, and were taken up by some police forces.

DATE	1910
ORIGIN	UNITED KINGDOM
WEIGHT	2¼ LB (0.9 KG)
BARREL	5 IN (12.7 CM)
CALIBER	9 MM SHORT

STEYR-MANNLICHER M1905

Fore sight

Loading/ejector port

Hammer

Butt houses ten-round fixed magazine

Produced by Werndl at Steyr, the M1905 was the last in a series of designs executed by Ferdinand von Mannlicher, who was better known for his rifles. It was complicated and expensive to manufacture, and as a consequence, was short-lived.

DATE	1905
ORIGIN	AUSTRIA-HUNGARY
WEIGHT	2¼ LB (0.9 KG)
BARREL	6 IN (16 CM)
CALIBER	7.63 MM MANNLICHER

NAMBU TAISHO 14

Ejector port

Cocking grip

Fore sight

Safety catch

Magazine catch

Butt houses eight-round removable magazine

The first Nambu pistols appeared in 1909. Though they were clearly influenced by the Luger P'08, they have nothing in common with it internally, the unlocking of the bolt from the barrel being achieved by the rotation of a linking block.

DATE	1925
ORIGIN	JAPAN
WEIGHT	2¼ LB (0.9 KG)
BARREL	4 IN (12 CM)
CALIBER	8 MM NAMBU

1900—2006

◀ **228–229** SELF-LOADING PISTOLS 1775–1900   ◀ **290–291** SELF-LOADING PISTOLS 1900–1920   ▶ **294–295** SELF-LOADING PISTOLS FROM 1950

THE MODERN WORLD

SELF-LOADING PISTOLS 1920–1950

IF THERE WERE ANY LINGERING DOUBTS as to the reliability of the self-loading pistol, they were largely dispelled during World War I, when officers of four of the major participating armies (Austria-Hungary, Germany, Turkey, and the United States) all carried them. Poorly designed models were still being produced, but few of these found their way into military service (the Japanese Type 94 was an exception). The new types generally proved to be worthy successors to masterpieces like the Luger and the Colt M1911.

Fore sight

Data engraved on slide

Hold-open notch

Milled cocking grip

Rear sight

Hammer

Recoil spring housing

Hold-open lever retains slide to rear

Magazine release catch

Safety catch

Butt houses 13-round removable magazine

BROWNING GP35

The High Power (*Grand Puissance*) model, the last Browning design, was taken up by the Belgian Army, and during World War II, plans for it were smuggled to Britain, and it was put into production in Canada. Its basic principle was the same swinging link at the rear of the barrel seen in the M1911, but detailed changes made manufacture cheaper and maintenance easier. It was the first self-loading pistol adopted by the British Army, in 1954.

DATE	1935
ORIGIN	BELGIUM
WEIGHT	2 LB (0.99 KG)
BARREL	4 IN (11.8 CM)
CALIBER	9 MM PARABELLUM

STAR MODEL M

Manufactured by Echeverria in Eibar, the Star was one of the best of many copies of the Colt M1911, though it lacked the grip safety that the Colt had acquired by the mid-1920s. It was produced in a variety of models and calibers until the mid-1980s.

Fore sight

Safety catch   Hammer

Recoil spring housing

Hold-open lever holds slide back

Butt houses eight-round removable magazine

Lanyard eye

DATE	1932
ORIGIN	SPAIN
WEIGHT	2 LB (1.07 KG)
BARREL	5 IN (12.5 CM)
CALIBER	9 MM LARGO

TOKAREV TT MODEL 1933

The Tokarev TT was the first self-loading pistol on general issue to the Red Army. In design, it was similar to the Browning GP35, with a single swinging-link locking system. It was simple and could be field-stripped without tools. It lacked a safety catch, but could be put at half-cock.

DATE	1933
ORIGIN	USSR
WEIGHT	1¾ LB (0.85 KG)
BARREL	4 IN (11.6 CM)
CALIBER	7.62 MM SOVIET AUTO

Semi-shrouded hammer

Butt houses eight-round removable magazine

RADOM M1935

Wilneiwczyc and Skrzypinski's design for the Radom factory, executed in the early 1930s, was similar in concept to the Browning High Power, but it was more compact and had extra security features. These included a grip safety, plus a device that dropped the hammer and retracted the firing pin, allowing the pistol to be fired safely with one hand.

DATE	1935
ORIGIN	POLAND
WEIGHT	2 LB (1.05 KG)
BARREL	4 IN (11.5 CM)
CALIBER	9 MM PARABELLUM

Fore sight
Polish eagle proof mark
Data engraved on slide
Decocking lever
Rear sight
Hammer
Hold-open lever
Safety Catch
Grip safety

BERETTA MODEL 1934

Pietro Beretta SpA is one of the world's longest-established gunmakers, with a history spanning four centuries, and a tradition of supplying its nation's army with weapons. Its M1934 was to become the official Italian officer's side-arm during World War II. The design evolved from one executed two decades earlier. Blowback-operated and without any form of locking mechanism, it was restricted to firing a reduced-power round, originally in 7.65 mm caliber.

DATE	1934
ORIGIN	ITALY
WEIGHT	1 LB (0.65 KG)
BARREL	6 IN (15.2 CM)
CALIBER	9 MM SHORT

Fore sight
Data engraved on slide
Grip for pulling slide to rear
Hammer
Recoil spring housing
Safety catch and hold-open lever
Butt houses removable nine-round magazine
Magazine release catch

STECHKIN APS

The Stechkin was an unsuccessful attempt to produce a fully-automatic pistol for use by security forces. Like the Makarov, it was an unlocked blowback design based on the American Walther PP. In automatic mode it was practically uncontrollable.

DATE	1960s
ORIGIN	USSR
WEIGHT	2 LB (1.03 KG)
BARREL	5 IN (12.7 CM)
CALIBER	9 MM MAKAROV

Muzzle brake
Hold-open lever retains slide to rear
Combined safety and rate-of-fire selector
20-round double-column magazine in butt

MAKAROV PM

The Tokarev's replacement as the standard Red Army side-arm was a copy of the American Walther PP, with double-action and a two-stage safety device. Its ammunition was about as powerful as could safely be used in a blowback design at that time.

DATE	1950s
ORIGIN	USSR
WEIGHT	1 LB (0.7 KG)
BARREL	3 IN (9.7 CM)
CALIBER	9 MM MAKAROV

Safety catch
Hammer
Hold-open lever retains slide to rear
Butt houses removable eight-round magazine

1900—2006

◄ **228–229** SELF-LOADING PISTOLS 1775–1900   ◄ **290–291** SELF-LOADING PISTOLS 1900–1920   ◄ **292–293** SELF-LOADING PISTOLS 1920–1950

SELF-LOADING PISTOLS FROM 1950

THE DUKE OF WELLINGTON questioned the value of the pistol as a weapon of war as long ago as the early 19th century, and as soon as we entered an era of mechanized warfare, the answer became clear: it was of little value except as personal protection and therefore, perhaps, for bolstering morale. Where pistols did prove to be of lasting value, however, was in the field of security and police operations, and a new generation was developed with these applications in mind.

Enclosed hammer

Burst-fire selector

Push-button safety catch

Butt houses 18-round magazine

Telescopic sight

HECKLER & KOCH VP70M

The VP70M, the first pistol to make extensive use of plastic, was another attempt to produce a fully automatic handgun, this time limited to firing three-round bursts. The mechanism that controlled this was housed in the detachable butt stock; when it was removed, the pistol reverted to normal semi-automatic operation.

Fiber-reinforced polymer shoulder stock

DATE	1970s
ORIGIN	GERMANY
WEIGHT	3 LB (1.55 KG) INCLUDING STOCK
BARREL	4 IN (11.6 CM)
CALIBER	9 MM PARABELLUM

Interchangeable barrel

Muzzle brake

Fore sight

Milled cocking grip facilitates pulling back slide

Rear sight

Hammer

Slide-mounted safety catch

BERETTA MODEL 92FS

Chosen as the US Military's official side-arm to replace the Colt M1911A1 in the 1980s, the Beretta 92 was a conventional short-recoil design, its frame forged from aluminum to reduce weight. The slide top was cut away to allow single rounds to be loaded manually, should the magazine be lost or damaged.

Recurved trigger guard to facilitate two-handed grip

Hold-open lever holds slide to rear

Magazine release catch

DATE	1976
ORIGIN	ITALY
WEIGHT	2 LB (0.98 KG)
BARREL	4 IN (10.9 CM)
CALIBER	9 MM PARABELLUM

Butt houses 13-round magazine

GLOCK 17

The Glock 17's frame was fabricated entirely from plastic, with four steel rails to act as guides for the metal reciprocating parts. Uniquely, its rifling was hexagonal: a series of six flats linked by small arcs. It used Browning's single swinging-link/tipping-barrel locking system.

DATE	1982
ORIGIN	AUSTRIA
WEIGHT	1 LB (0.6 KG)
BARREL	4 IN (11.4 CM)
CALIBER	9 MM PARABELLUM

Recoil spring and laser target indicator housing

Enlarged trigger guard for gloved hands

Butt houses 17-round magazine

HECKLER & KOCH USP

The Universal Service Pistol was Heckler & Koch's answer to the Glock, and it, too, was largely made of plastic and employed the tried-and-tested Browning locking system. The USP was designed to facilitate modification, and could be configured in nine different ways.

DATE	1993
ORIGIN	GERMANY
WEIGHT	1 LB (0.75 KG)
BARREL	4 IN (10.7 CM)
CALIBER	9 MM PARABELLUM

Frame-mounted safety catch

Enlarged trigger guard

Butt houses ten-round magazine

Elevation adjustment

2X-6X REDFIELD

Adjustable eyepiece

Milled cocking grip

Hammer

Identification data

Safety catch

DESERT EAGLE

As befitting a pistol capable of handling the most powerful ammunition, everything about the Desert Eagle was made on a massive scale. Unlike almost all other self-loading pistols, it was gas operated, and of modular design. Its standard frame was able to accept sets of components for different ammunition, from .357 Magnum to .5 Action Express, and barrels of different lengths.

DATE	1983
ORIGIN	ISRAEL
WEIGHT	5 LB (2.66 KG)
BARREL	10 IN (24.5 CM)
CALIBER	.44 MAGNUM

Recurved trigger guard to facilitate two-handed grip

Butt houses nine-round removable magazine

295

THE MODERN WORLD

REVOLVERS 1900–1950

MOST OF THE DEVELOPMENT WORK on the revolver had been completed by the 1890s, and all that remained was for the design to be refined. There was little to be done to improve the reliability of such a simple design, but there were potential economies to be achieved in the production process, and this meant lower prices for the end user. In a very competitive marketplace, this often meant the difference between success and failure.

Fore sight

Cylinder-retaining key

Retaining stirrup locks barrel and cylinder assembly to frame

Cylinder contains six .455-caliber rounds

Recess for cylinder-locking bolt

WEBLEY & SCOTT MK VI

The last in a long line of service revolvers produced by the famous Birmingham partnership, the Mark VI was introduced early in World War I. It retained many of the features of its predecessors, and was renowned for its sturdy reliability.

DATE	1915
ORIGIN	UK
WEIGHT	2 LB (1.05 KG)
BARREL	6 IN (15.2 CM)
CALIBER	.455 ELEY

Fore sight

Fore sight

Cylinder holds six rounds of ammunition

Cylinder-retaining catch

Cylinder gate pivot pin

SMITH & WESSON MILITARY AND POLICE

Having championed the hinged-frame revolver, Smith & Wesson, with the advent of more powerful ammunition, was obliged to switch to a solid frame with a swing-out cylinder for its Military and Police pistol. This was chambered for the long .38 Special round.

DATE	1900
ORIGIN	US
WEIGHT	1 LB (0.85 KG)
BARREL	5 IN (12.7 CM)
CALIBER	.38 SPECIAL

Grip retaining screw

Cylinder axis and ejector rod

Cylinder-retaining catch

Lanyard eye for attaching strap

COLT POLICE POSITIVE

In 1905 Colt modified its Official Police revolver, fitting the Positive lock with an intercepting safety device. In various forms, the Police Positive stayed in production for well over half a century.

DATE	1905
ORIGIN	US
WEIGHT	1 LB (0.6 KG)
BARREL	4 IN (10.2 CM)
CALIBER	.38IN

ENFIELD NO.2 MK 1

After World War I, the British Army decided to adopt a lighter caliber for its service side-arm. The revolver it chose was almost a copy of the Webley Mark VI. The version shown was issued to tank crews, and lacks a hammer spur.

Spurless hammer

Cylinder holds six .38-caliber rounds

DATE	1938
ORIGIN	UK
WEIGHT	1 LB (0.76 KG)
BARREL	5 IN (12.7 CM)
CALIBER	.38 IN

SMITH & WESSON M1917

During World War I, Smith & Wesson was commissioned to produce a revolver that chambered the rimless .45 ACP round. The model was a success, but had extraction problems unless flat half-moon clips, each carrying three rounds, were used.

Pivot pin for cylinder gate

Cylinder holds six .45 ACP-caliber rounds

DATE	1917
ORIGIN	US
WEIGHT	2 LB (0.96 KG)
BARREL	5 IN (14.4 CM)
CALIBER	.45 ACP

Type and caliber stamped into barrel

Top strap

Cylinder bolt locking recess

Cylinder release catch

Maker's mark

Cylinder axis and ejector rod

Cylinder holds six rounds

Pivot pin for cylinder gate

THE ICONIC REVOLVER

From the earliest Hollywood westerns to the latest TV cop shows, the revolver has become an icon of civilian law enforcement.

COLT NEW SERVICE

The Colt New Service was the last standard-issue service revolver produced by Colt for the US Army. Unbreakable under normal conditions, it had a solid-frame design with a swing-out cylinder. The British Army also bought them in great numbers, chambered, like this example, for the .455 Eley round.

DATE	1907
ORIGIN	US
WEIGHT	2 LB (1.15 KG)
BARREL	5 IN (14.4 CM)
CALIBER	.455 ELEY

THE MODERN WORLD

REVOLVERS FROM 1950

BY THE 1950S it was widely accepted that the self-loading pistol, with its ease of operation and much greater capacity, had finally rendered the revolver obsolete. Around the same time, however, new and much more powerful ammunition types (the so-called Magnum rounds) were being produced. The trouble was that the Magnum used almost twice the energy of a traditional round, and this was far more than a self-loading pistol could handle safely. For this reason, the revolver was given a new lease on life.

MAGNUM PISTOLS
Pistols chambered for Magnum rounds are widely used among police forces. From here they have made their way into popular culture via such movies as *Magnum Force* (1973).

Ventilated barrel rib

Fore sight

Heavy N-Type frame

SMITH & WESSON

SMITH & WESSON MODEL 27

Smith & Wesson produced a huge variety of pistols chambered for the various Magnum calibers—.357 and .44 are only the most common—on light, intermediate, and heavy frames. The heavy Model 27, in .357 caliber, was the most popular model, and was produced with 4 in (10.2 cm), 6 in (15.2 cm), and 8 in (21.3 cm) barrels. The Model 29, in .44 caliber, was almost identical, but was produced with a 10 in (27 cm) barrel.

DATE	1938 ONWARD
ORIGIN	US
WEIGHT	3 LB (1.4 KG)
BARREL	11 IN (30 CM)
CALIBER	.357 MAGNUM

Cylinder holds five rounds of ammunition

Hammer shrouded, so it doesn't catch on clothes

Cylinder release catch

Cylinder axis rod

Grip safety

SMITH & WESSON AIRWEIGHT

As well as the giant Magnums, most gunmakers produced "pocket" revolvers. These were lighter in weight than semi-automatic pistols chambered for the same ammunition, and were easier to conceal. Smith & Wesson's Centennial range, which included the Airweight, carried five rounds and had shrouded hammers.

DATE	1952 ONWARD
ORIGIN	US
WEIGHT	84 LB (38 KG)
BARREL	2 IN (5 CM)
CALIBER	.38 SPECIAL

COLT PYTHON

Colt lost no time in producing its own Magnum pistols, based on the tried-and-tested New Service and Single-Action Army models, but it was the 1950s before it produced an all-new purpose-designed Magnum revolver; the Python. Other Magnum "snakes" (the Cobra, the King Cobra, and the Anaconda, the latter in .44 caliber) were to follow, and all have been kept up to date. The ventilated barrel rib has become a feature of these heavy revolvers.

DATE	1953 ONWARD
ORIGIN	US
WEIGHT	3 LB (1.4 KG)
BARREL	8 IN (20.3 CM)
CALIBER	.357 MAGNUM

Adjustable rear sight

Cylinder rotates clockwise

Cylinder axis rod

Six-chambered cylinder revolves counterclockwise

Recess for cylinder-locking bolt

Cylinder release catch

Maker's medallion

Six-round cylinder rotates counterclockwise

Adjustable rear sight

Cylinder-locking bolt recess

RUGER GP-100

Sturm, Ruger & Co. was a latecomer to the world of gun manufacture, opening for business in 1949. Initially, the company produced a range of traditional single-action revolvers, but later added designs incorporating the full range of modern ergonomic and safety features.

DATE	1987
ORIGIN	US
WEIGHT	2 LB (1.05 KG)
BARREL	4 IN (10.2 CM)
CALIBER	.357 MAGNUM

Cylinder axis rod

Cylinder release catch

Cylinder holds five rounds of ammunition

CHARTER ARMS UNDERCOVER

Charter Arms began trading in 1964, and the Undercover was its first product. It was intended to be easily concealed, and being chambered for .38 Special ammunition it had plenty of stopping power.

DATE	1964
ORIGIN	US
WEIGHT	1 LB (.45 KG)
BARREL	2 IN (5 CM)
CALIBER	.38 SPECIAL

Five-chambered cylinder revolves clockwise

CHARTER ARMS POLICE BULLDOG

Built on a heavier frame than the Undercover, the Police Bulldog was also available with a 2 in (6.5 cm) barrel, chambered for .357 Magnum or .44 Special ammunition. The molded rubber grips helped reduce the "felt" recoil.

DATE	1971
ORIGIN	US
WEIGHT	1 LB (0.6 KG)
BARREL	4 IN (10.1 CM)
CALIBER	.357 MAGNUM

Ergonomically designed molded-rubber grips

1900—2006

◄ 252–253 MANUALLY LOADED REPEATER RIFLES 1855–1880   ◄ 256–257 MANUALLY LOADED REPEATER RIFLES 1881–1891   ◄ 258–259 MANUALLY LOADED REPEATER RIFLES 1892–1898

THE MODERN WORLD

MANUALLY LOADED REPEATER RIFLES

THE MAIN DIFFERENCE between the rifles used during the Boer War and those used in World War I lay in the length of their barrels. At the turn of the century, the barrels of infantry rifles were 29½ in (75 cm) long. By 1914, some had been shortened by 4 in (10 cm), and the rest were soon to follow. The exception was France, where the barrel of the Berthier rifle, introduced into service in 1916, had actually increased in length.

Receiver   Bolt

Cocking piece

Bolt handle turned down

Rear sight

Experimental 25-round removable box magazine

Two-part sling

SPRINGFIELD M1903

Impressed by the Mauser rifles US troops encountered during the war against Spain, the United States Ordnance Department looked to replace its Krag rifles. Negotiating a license to build a Mauser design of its own, the result was the .30 in Rifle, Magazine, M1903. The example shown here has an experimental 25-round magazine.

DATE	1903
ORIGIN	US
WEIGHT	8½ LB (4 KG)
BARREL	24 IN (61 CM)
CALIBER	.30-03 (LATER .30-06)

Barrel band

Fore sight is mounted between protective blades

Bayonet lug

PATTERN 1914

At the start of World War I, manufacturing problems with the new Pattern 1913 rifle resulted in a change of caliber from 0.276 in to the standard 0.303 in chambering, and the weapon's redesignation as the Pattern 1914. The Model 1917, a 0.30 in-caliber version of the Pattern 1914, was later adopted by the US Army.

DATE	1914
ORIGIN	UK
WEIGHT	8½ LB (4 KG)
BARREL	26 IN (66 CM)
CALIBER	7 MM MAUSER (.30-06)

Experimental 20-round removable box magazine

Rear sling attachment

Rear sight   Receiver

Cocking piece

Bolt handle turned down

Magazine release catch

Ten-round detachable box magazine

Cocking piece

Fore sight

Cleaning rod

Rear sling attachment

Integral five-round box magazine

BERTHIER MLE 1916

The shortcomings of the Lebel rifle led to a revised design being issued to French colonial troops in 1902. Though it continued to use the bolt action of the Lebel, and was outmoded in appearance (due to the length of its barrel), its only serious defect lay in its magazine capacity—just three rounds. A modified version with a five-round magazine was issued from 1916.

DATE	1916
ORIGIN	FRANCE
WEIGHT	9 LB (4.15 KG)
BARREL	31¼ IN (79.8 CM)
CALIBER	8 MM x 50R

Bolt handle protrudes horizontally

Cocking piece

Foresight in protective shroud

Folding cruciform bayonet

Integral five-round magazine

Sling attached through a slit in the butt stock

MOSIN-NAGANT CARBINE M1944

In 1910, the 3-line Mosin-Nagant rifle was modified to produce a carbine by shortening its barrel. In 1938 it was revamped, largely to make it cheaper to manufacture, and in 1944 it attained its final form with the addition of a folding cruciform bayonet. Though it was obsolete by that time, the People's Republic of China began manufacturing copies in 1953.

DATE	1944
ORIGIN	USSR
WEIGHT	8½ LB (3.9 KG)
BARREL	20¼ IN (51.7 CM)
CALIBER	7.62 MM x 54R

Regimental identifying plate

Rear sling attachment

Fore stock cap

Integral five-round magazine

Steel-bound butt

MAUSER KAR98K

The "Karabiner" 98K embodied improvements to the Mauser Gewehr 98 rifle, and became the standard German service rifle of World War II. More than 14 million were manufactured between 1935 and 1945. A number of variations were produced, including those for mountain troops, paratroops, and snipers. During the war, the original design was simplified to speed up production.

DATE	1935
ORIGIN	GERMANY
WEIGHT	8½ LB (3.9 KG)
BARREL	23½ IN (60 CM)
CALIBER	7.92 MM x 57

FULL VIEW

LEE-ENFIELD RIFLE NUMBER 4 MARK 1

The new Lee-Enfield, which appeared late in 1939, differed very little from the model it replaced. The bolt and receiver were modified; the rear sight was a new design, and was placed on the receiver; the fore stock was shortened, exposing the muzzle, and its cap was redesigned. The Number 4 remained in service until 1954.

DATE	1939
ORIGIN	UK
WEIGHT	9 LB (4.1 KG)
LENGTH	25 IN (64 CM)
CALIBER	.303 IN

RED ARMY INFANTRYMAN

**TT TOKAREV
1933 PISTOL**

WHEN THEY INVADED the Soviet Union in June 1941, the Germans planned for a swift victory—completely underrating the endurance and resilience of the Soviet conscript soldier. The Soviet way of making war was immensely wasteful of men's lives, thrown away in ill-considered offensives or committed to "no retreat" when on the defensive. Yet the Red Army infantryman remained firmly committed to the struggle, either as a dedicated communist or as a patriot fighting in defense of the homeland.

HARSH DISCIPLINE

The Red Army infantryman was subject to harsh discipline by his officers, who themselves were under surveillance by political commissars and Soviet dictator Joseph Stalin's secret police, the NKVD. Officers and men alike were subject to arbitrary arrest. Men accused of political dissent or cowardice were put in the forefront of battle in suicide squads.

The Red Army suffered an average of 8,000 casualties a day through nearly four years of war —heavier losses per day than the Russian Empire had experienced in World War I. Yet after the initial disasters of 1941, morale never seriously wavered. The scale of early losses meant that the Red Army became largely a mix of the young, arriving at military age from 1941 onward, and those initially considered too old for service. But they held firm in front of Moscow in the bitterly cold winter of 1941–42 and, after further costly defeats, carried off the victory at Stalingrad that turned the tide. In the later stages of the war, better equipped and well led, the Soviet infantry showed initiative in mobile offensives, rolling the Germans all the way back to Berlin.

INFANTRY ACTION
Soviet infantry advance as one of their number loads a mortar. Early in the war, Red Army soldiers were frequently ordered forward with bayonets fixed in the face of machine gun or artillery fire that made attack suicidal. From 1943 better equipment and more sensible leadership cut losses sharply.

TOOLS OF COMBAT

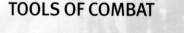

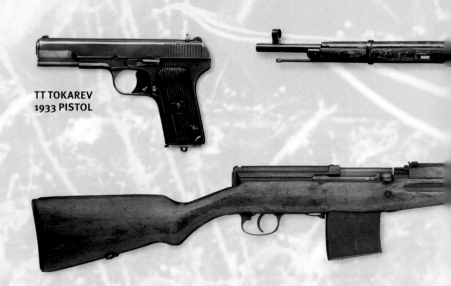

**TT TOKAREV
1933 PISTOL**

BATTLE OF STALINGRAD

The epic struggle for the Soviet city of Stalingrad was one of the turning points of World War II. From September 1942, heavily outnumbered Red Army soldiers resisted the German capture of the city, fighting house by house and street by street, until a counter-offensive in late November left the German forces encircled. After two agonizing, bitterly cold winter months under siege by the Red Army, the German commander finally surrendered on January 30, 1943.

SOVIET SOLDIERS AT STALINGRAD

"OUR AIM IS TO DEFEND SOMETHING GREATER THAN MILLIONS OF LIVES... THE MOTHERLAND."

SOVIET SOLDIER, DIARY ENTRY, JULY 1941

SOVIET SNIPER
A young Red Army marksman peers through the sight of his 7.62 mm Mosin-Nagant M91/30 sniper rifle. This was simply the Soviets' standard bolt-action rifle accuratized and fitted with a telescopic sight. The Red Army made extensive use of snipers during World War II and "top guns" such as Vasili Zaitsev—credited with killing more than 149 German soldiers —were lauded as Soviet heroes.

SOVIET UNIFORM
Like all World War II infantry uniforms, Red Army outfits were drab for camouflage purposes and distinguished Soviet soldiers from others only by an accumulation of details. Soviet infantry helmets, for example, broadly resembled the American M1 helmet in shape.

Ssch-40 steel helmet

Red Guard badge

PPSH submachine gun

Overhanging shirt secured by belt

MOSIN-NAGANT 1891/30 RIFLE

TOKAREV SVT40 RIFLE

THE MODERN WORLD

SELF-LOADING RIFLES 1914–1950

THE FIRST SUCCESSFUL self-loading rifle was developed by a Mexican, Manuel Mondragon, as early as 1890. Taken up by the Mexican Army in 1908, it proved too fragile for general use. Next, in 1918, came John Browning's Automatic Rifle, but this came to be used as a light machine gun instead because of its excessive weight. It was not until 1936 that a truly practical self-loading rifle, the M1, was adopted by the US Army. Further breakthroughs in self-loading rifles came in World War II. The best of these was the Sturmgewehr G44, but it was some time before the "intermediate" ammunition round, its most important design aspect, achieved universal acceptance.

Receiver

Cocking handle

Perforated sheet-steel hand guard

Muzzle compensator

TOKAREV SVT40

Fedor Tokarev designed a self-loading rifle with a tilting bolt locking into the floor of the receiver, and had it accepted by the Red Army in 1938. Two years later, he produced a more robust weapon that was cheaper and quicker to manufacture. The Samozaryadnaya Vintovka Tokarev 40 was issued to non-commissioned officers, though some were employed as sniper rifles.

DATE	1940
ORIGIN	USSR
WEIGHT	8 LB (3.9 KG)
BARREL	25 IN (61 CM)
CALIBER	7.62 MM x 54R

Ten-round detachable box magazine

Rear sight

Cocking handle

Bottom plate of internal eight-round magazine

Rear sight

Welded pressed-steel receiver

Rate-of-fire selector

Pistol grip

30-round detachable box magazine

M1 CARBINE

Designed as a replacement for the pistol and rifle, the M1 was issued from 1942. It was chambered for an intermediate round developed by Winchester, and had an action similar to that of the Garand, except it had a short-stroke gas piston. It was also produced with a folding butt, for issue to paratroopers.

Rear sight

Cocking handle

Fore sight in a protective shroud

Bayonet attachment

15-round detachable box magazine

DATE	1942
ORIGIN	US
WEIGHT	9 LB (4.35 KG)
LENGTH	20 IN (55.8 CM)
CALIBER	.30 IN

GEWEHR 43

Soon after the start of World War II, the German army began demanding a self-loading rifle. Walther's original design employed a cup at the muzzle that unlocked the bolt and cycled the action. In 1943 a modified version, using the same action but with a conventional gas cylinder and piston mounted above the barrel, was introduced as the Gewehr 43.

Fore sight

Rear sight

Cocking handle

Safety catch

Ten-round detachable box magazine

Semi-pistol grip

DATE	1943
ORIGIN	GERMANY
WEIGHT	9 LB (4.35 KG)
BARREL	20 IN (55.8 CM)
CALIBER	7.92 MM x 57

Barrel

Fore sight between protective blades

Gas cylinder

Forward sling swivel

Bayonet attachment

M1 GARAND RIFLE

John Garand opted for a rotating bolt design for his self-loading rifle. The piston in a cylinder below the barrel has a camming (spiraled) groove on its rear end, in which is located a stud on the bolt. As the piston is driven back, it causes the bolt to rotate and then drives it back against a spring that returns and relocks it, having picked up a fresh round from the magazine on the way.

DATE	1932
ORIGIN	US
WEIGHT	9 LB (4.35 KG)
LENGTH	24 IN (61 CM)
CALIBER	.30-06 IN

Fore sight

Gas cylinder cap

Perforated pressed-steel forestock

Forward sling attachment

STURMGEWEHR 44

In 1940 work began on a selective-fire rifle chambered for a new intermediate 7.92 mm x 33 round. The result was a gas-operated weapon with a tipping bolt, which was put into production as the Maschinen Pistole 43 and later renamed the Sturmgewehr 44. Small numbers were fitted with the Krummlauf, a barrel extension that turned the bullet through 30°, for use by tank crews against infantry.

DATE	1943
ORIGIN	GERMANY
WEIGHT	11 LB (5.1 KG)
LENGTH	16 IN (41.8 CM)
CALIBER	7.92 MM x 33

FULL VIEW

THE MODERN WORLD

AK47 ASSAULT RIFLE

DESIGNED BY MIKHAIL KALASHNIKOV, a young tank commander with little formal training, the assault rifle that bears his name was to achieve iconic status due to its rugged simplicity. Kalashnikov's first successful design, the AK47 was simple, handled well, and operated satisfactorily under virtually any conditions. It was adopted by the Soviet Army in 1949, and since then, between 50 and 70 million Kalashnikov-type rifles and light machine guns have been manufactured all over the world.

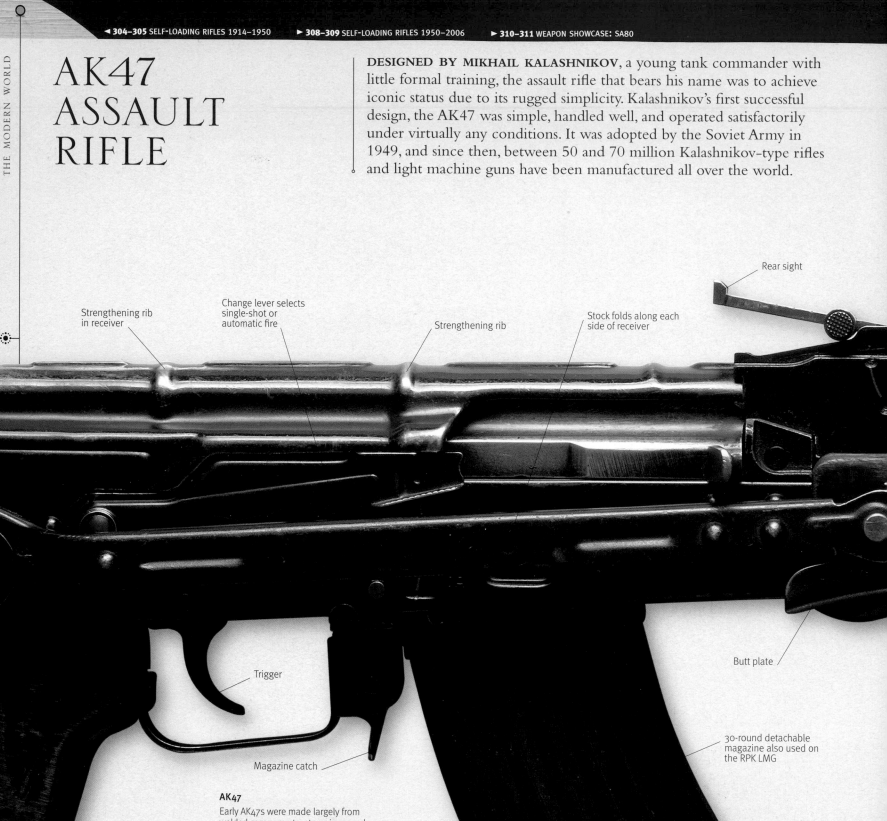

Rear sight

Strengthening rib in receiver

Change lever selects single-shot or automatic fire

Strengthening rib

Stock folds along each side of receiver

Butt plate

Trigger

30-round detachable magazine also used on the RPK LMG

Magazine catch

Pistol grip

AK47

Early AK47s were made largely from welded components, stampings, and pressed metal parts. However, problems arose, and from 1951, sturdier receivers machined from forged steel billets were introduced. The modified AKM was not only much lighter than the original AK47, but it also had a reduced cyclic rate of full automatic fire, which improved its accuracy. The AKM can be distinguished from the AK47 by the strengthening ribs in the top surface of the receiver.

DATE	1951
ORIGIN	USSR
WEIGHT	9½ LB (4.3 KG)
BARREL	16¼ IN (41.5 CM)
CALIBER	7.62 MM x 39

FULL VIEW

Fore sight

Folding stock

Hand guard
(upper part)

Gas cylinder

Gas vent

Gas tapped off
from barrel here

Cleaning rod

Barrel

Hand guard
(lower part)

AMMUNITION

It is generally believed that the design for the 7.62 mm x 39 cartridge was based on an examination of the ammunition used by the German MP43/MP44 in World War II. But Soviet designers had also been looking into the problems of producing their own intermediate cartridge to increase the combat efficiency of their submachine guns. The result was the 7.72 mm x 39 M43, a rimless, bottle-necked cartridge with a copper-washed steel case that remains practically unchanged in use around the world today.

MUJAHIDEEN WARRIOR

Now mass-produced on a global scale, the AK47 has become the most popular gun in the world. Here it is seen in the hands of a Mujahideen warrior in Afghanistan.

THE MODERN WORLD

SELF-LOADING RIFLES 1950-2006

ONE VITAL TACTICAL LESSON learned during World War II was the importance of firepower in the final phase of an assault. As a result, bolt-action weapons soon fell out of use, except as a sniper's arm, and the self-loading rifle became ubiquitous. Following the lead of the Sturmgewehr 44, introduced in 1943, the new weapons of the post-war era were capable of fully-automatic fire. The Sturmgewehr 44 also embodied another key development: the use of lighter, smaller, "intermediate" ammunition rounds, which eventually replaced those that had been in use since the start of the 20th century.

Rear sight — Cocking handle — Fore sight

Forward sling attachment — Gas cylinder — Gas regulator — Muzzle compensator — Bayonet lug

Magazine catch — 20-round detachable magazine

Rear sling swivel

M14

In 1953, the North Atlantic Treaty Organization's (NATO) armies adopted a new full-power rifle cartridge, in 7.62 mm caliber. To accommodate it, the US developed a version of Garand's 20-year-old M1, endowed with a fully automatic fire capability and a larger magazine.

DATE	1957
ORIGIN	US
WEIGHT	8½ LB (3.9 KG)
BARREL	22 IN (55.8 CM)
CALIBER	7.62 MM x 51 NATO

Rear sight — Ejector port

Carrying handle

20-round detachable box magazine

L1A1

The L1A1 was introduced in 1954, and was the standard British service rifle until its replacement by the L85A1 in 1988. It was adapted from the Belgian FN FAL, but with minor changes to the specifications to facilitate manufacture in the UK.

DATE	1954
ORIGIN	UK
WEIGHT	9½ LB (4.3 KG)
BARREL	21 IN (53.3 CM)
CALIBER	7.62 MM x 51 NATO

Carrying handle — Ejection port

Cocking handle

Bolt closing device

High-impact plastic butt stock

30-round detachable box magazine

Cocking handle | Gas regulator | Bipod mounting point

35-round detachable box magazine

Tubular butt stock folds to the left

Magazine catch

GALIL ASSAULT RIFLE

After the 1967 war, Israeli Military Industries was ordered to produce something similar to the AK47. It chose a design by Israel Galil, a near-copy of the Finnish Valmet M62, itself an AK47 derivative, but opted for the American 5.56 mm x 45 round.

DATE	1974
ORIGIN	ISRAEL
WEIGHT	9½ LB (4.35 KG)
BARREL	18 IN (46 CM)
CALIBER	5.56 MM x 45 NATO

Muzzle compensator

Rear sling attachment

HECKLER & KOCH G41

The G41 was an updated version of the G3, and shared its roller-delayed blowback action. The modifications were necessary to accommodate the 5.56 mm round, and other standard NATO features such as the universal sight mounting and magazine.

Carrying handle

30-round detachable box magazine

High-impact plastic butt stock

DATE	1987
ORIGIN	GERMANY
WEIGHT	4 KG (9 LB)
BARREL	45 CM (17½ IN)
CALIBER	5.56 MM x 45 NATO

Wooden forestock

Gas regulator

Muzzle compensator

Gas cylinder

Shrouded rear sight

STONER M63

This M63 by Eugene Stoner is a modular design, and its 15 basic sub-assemblies can be put together in six different ways to produce a submachine gun, a carbine, an assault rifle (shown here), an automatic rifle, a light machine gun, and a general-purpose machine gun.

30-round detachable box magazine

Cocking handle

DATE	1962
ORIGIN	US
WEIGHT	7¾ LB (3.52 KG)
BARREL	20 IN (50.8 CM)
CALIBER	5.56 MM x 45 NATO

High-impact plastic forestock

Fore sight

Flash hider

Gas regulator

FULL VIEW

STONER M16A1

Stoner's Armalite AR-15 was accepted by the US Air Force in the early 1960s, and subsequently taken into service as the M16. The M16A1 was fitted with a bolt-closing device and a revised flash hider. The later M16A2 acquired a three-round burst, and a heavier barrel with modified rifling better suited to the SS109 5.56 mm round, instead of the M193 for which it was designed.

DATE	1982
ORIGIN	US
WEIGHT	8 LB (3.6 KG)
BARREL	20 IN (50.8 CM)
CALIBER	5.56 MM x 45 NATO

Eyepiece with
protective rubber
shroud

SUSAT sight gives four-
power magnification and
has low-light capability

Cocking
handle

L85A1

The L85A1 was the last weapon
system to be developed and
produced at the Royal Smallarms
Factory, Enfield, UK, before it
closed in 1988. It was dogged with
problems during the development
stage, and trials continued even
after its adoption in 1985. It was
designed from the start to use an
optical sight. The body and many
other parts are steel samplings. All
the furniture is high-impact plastic.

DATE	1985
ORIGIN	UK
WEIGHT	11LB (4.98KG)
BARREL	20½IN (51.8CM)
CALIBRZ	5.56MM x 45 NATO

Pistol grip with
high-impact
plastic molding

30-round detachable
magazine compatible with
other NATO weapons

SA80 ASSAULT RIFLE

DURING THE LAST QUARTER of the 20th century, a new type of assault rifle, the "bullpup," began to enter service with the world's armies. The bullpup configuration places the action in the butt, with the magazine behind the trigger, allowing a full-length barrel to be accommodated in a much shorter weapon. Three bullpup rifles have been adopted so far: the French FAMAS, the Austrian AUG, and the British L85 Individual Weapon (shown here), part of the SA80 weapon family, which also includes the L86 Light Support Weapon and the L98 Cadet Rifle.

Flash hider

FULL VIEW

Gas regulator

RIFLE 5·56ᴹᴹ   L85AI   1005-99-966-6470

High-impact plastic fore stock

Large trigger guard for gloved hand

AMMUNITION

The SA80 weapon family was designed around the NATO-standard SS109 5.56mm round, which has a steel-tipped projectile weighing 61.7 grains (4g) and achieves a muzzle velocity of 3,085 feet per second (940m/s).

BAYONET

The bayonet supplied with the LA85 is unusual in that its shaft fits over the flash-hider at the muzzle. A lug on its scabbard fits the slot in the blade and the ensemble becomes a pair of wire cutters, an idea borrowed from the Soviet AKM.

Bayonet shaft fits over muzzle flash hider

Slot accepts tang on bayonet scabbard

Matt black blade

Fuller, or "blood groove," lightens blade

Wire-cutting blade

311

THE MODERN WORLD

SPORT GUNS

BY THE LAST DECADE of the 19th century, most of the technology found in modern firearms was already present. Later developments addressed concerns over safety (particularly in respect to the more powerful ammunition made possible by new formulations of propellant) and economy of manufacture. There was another, and this time quite new, element coming into consideration: during the previous century, little thought had been given to the ergonomic design of firearms, but this was now being addressed in some quarters, particularly in the design of sport guns.

Exposed hammer shows if the rifle is cocked

Rear sight

Barrel band

Fore sight in protective shroud

Loading gate

Ejection port

Actuating lever

Ten-round tubular magazine

WINCHESTER MODEL 1894

A young gunmaker named John Browning began working for Winchester in 1883. His first task was to revamp the action of the company's under-lever rifle to allow it to use new types of ammunition, and he supplemented Tyler Henry's toggle-jointed bolt with additional vertical locking bars. The system was perfected in the Model 1894.

DATE	1894
ORIGIN	US
WEIGHT	7 LB (3.18 KG)
BARREL	20 IN (50.8 CM)
CALIBER	.30-30

Breech-locking lever

Walnut stock

Engraved lock cover

Single trigger

Incised chequering on the straight-through grip

WESTLEY RICHARDS HAMMERLESS EJECTOR GUN

Master gunmakers Westley Richards produced various notable and highly innovative sporting guns and rifles. This example of a double-barreled hammerless ejector gun has a patent one-striker mechanism and locks that can be detached by hand. A press-button mechanism enables each barrel to be fired independently. Available in a choice of finishes, the gun could be tailored to suit the individual tastes of purchasers.

DATE	c.1930
ORIGIN	UK
WEIGHT	6 LB (2.76 KG)
LENGTH	26 IN (67.5 CM)
CALIBER	12-BORE

Decorated checkering on the semi-pistol grip

Press-button safety catch

Trigger

RIGBY MAUSER RIFLE

Rigby's began making guns in Dublin, Ireland, in the 18th century. In 1900, now in London, the company was appointed Mauser's UK agent, and began producing bolt-action rifles to its design in a variety of calibers. John Rigby, the company's head, oversaw the design of the British Army's bolt-action rifles.

DATE	1925
ORIGIN	UK
WEIGHT	6 LB (2.8 KG)
BARREL	27½ IN (70 CM)
CALIBER	.375 IN H&H MAGNUM

Incised checkering on the semi-pistol grip · Safety catch · Bolt handle · Bolt · Rear sight · Forward sling attachment · Internal five-round box magazine · Rear sling attachment

DARNE ROTARY-BREECH DOUBLE-BARREL SHOTGUN

Made by Darne, this shotgun has a patented breech action. Freed by means of the lever on top of the butt stock behind the breech, the entire lock rotates through a quarter turn to expose the chambers. Returning it to battery cocks the gun. The lever on the side of the breech-block is a cross-bolt safety.

DATE	1965
ORIGIN	FRANCE
WEIGHT	5 LB (2.4 KG)
BARREL	25 IN (65 CM)
CALIBER	16-BORE

Breech and lock, including triggers, rotate through 90° · Abbreviated forestock · Twin triggers · Safety catch · Checkered straight-through grip

BERETTA DOUBLE-BARREL SHOTGUN

Pietro Beretta is the longest-established gun maker in the world, having been in business since 1526. Its over-and-under double-barreled shotguns, like this Model S-686, have been the most popular configuration for both hunting and trapshooting. Over-and-under guns have the advantage of a single sight line. Most are fitted with single-trigger locks.

DATE	1982
ORIGIN	ITALY
WEIGHT	6 LB (3.08 KG)
BARREL	28 IN (71 CM)
CALIBER	12-BORE

Abbreviated forestock · Breech-locking lever · Barrel pivot pin · Ventilated barrel rib · Fore sight · Single trigger · Incised checkering on the semi-pistol grip

Ejector port · Cocking handle · Ventilated barrel rib · Loading port · Four-round tubular magazine located in the forestock · Magazine cap

FULL VIEW

REMINGTON 1100 AUTOMATIC SHOTGUN

John Browning produced the first design for a gas-operated, self-loading shotgun while working for Winchester, but it was not put into production. Modern automatics can be either gas- or recoil-operated. This Remington 1100 is gas-operated, and was produced in a variety of barrel lengths and calibers.

DATE	1985
ORIGIN	US
WEIGHT	8 LB (3.6 KG)
BARREL	28 IN (71 CM)
CALIBER	12-BORE

THE MODERN WORLD

SHOTGUNS

THE SHOTGUN HAS ALWAYS BEEN an effective close-quarters weapon, and its value was recognized by infantrymen in World War I. As well as sport guns, usually with their barrels cut down, they used purpose-built guns like Winchester's six-shot pump-action Model 1897, which became known as the "trench sweeper." More recently, developments centered on increasing the capacity of the magazine and on new types of ammunition for both military and civilian security operations.

Section folds down to become a shoulder piece

Stock folds upward through 180°

Cocking handle (gas operation)

Ejector port

Rear sight

Cocking slide

Fore sight

Safety catch

Loading port

Tubular eight-round magazine

FRANCHI SPAS 12

Developed as a close-combat weapon for both police and military use, the SPAS (Special-Purpose Automatic Shotgun) is gas-operated by an annular piston around the under-barrel magazine tube, acting on a tilting bolt. It can be switched over to pump action when required. They were expensive to manufacture, but reliable.

DATE	1978
ORIGIN	ITALY
WEIGHT	9 LB (4.4 KG)
BARREL	21 IN (54.5 CM)
CALIBER	12-BORE

Rear sight

M16-style carrying handle

Pressed-steel barrel shroud

USAS-12
12GA. 2¾ INCH

Rate-of-fire selector safety catch

Ejector port

20-round drum magazine

Decocking lever **Loading port** **Rear sight** **Fore sight**

**Cocked/
uncocked
indicator**

**Cocking
lever**

Bayonet lug

Rear sling attachment

GREENER-MARTINI POLICE SHOTGUN
Developed after World War I for use by British colonial
police forces, this gun was unconventional in that it had
a Martini falling-block action. Furthermore, it accepted
only cartridges of an unusual form, to prevent stolen
guns from being used by civilians.

DATE	1920
ORIGIN	UK
WEIGHT	8 LB (3.68 KG)
BARREL	2 IN (6.3 CM)
CALIBER	14-BORE

Shrouded hammer

**Abbreviated wooden
fore stock**

**Tubular four-round
magazine**

Trigger guard

Actuating lever **Fore sight**

WINCHESTER MODEL 1887
Another action unique in a shotgun is the lever-action
rolling block of the Winchester Model 1887, designed
by John Browning. Produced in 10-bore and 12-bore
chamberings (and a very few to accommodate .70 in
bulleted cartridges), the lever action proved unsuitable
for shotgun cartridges, and was discontinued in favor
of pump-action guns.

DATE	1887
ORIGIN	US
WEIGHT	8 LB (3.76 KG)
BARREL	19 IN (50 CM)
CALIBER	12-BORE

Gas cylinder cap

USAS-12
Designed in the United States, and manufactured in
South Korea by Daewoo, the USAS-12 is unusual in two
respects. Firstly, it is a selective-fire weapon, with the
option for single-shot or automatic operation; secondly,
it can be set up for either right- or left-handed operation.

FULL VIEW

DATE	1992
ORIGIN	US/SOUTH KOREA
WEIGHT	12 LB (5.5 KG)
BARREL	18 IN (46 CM)
CALIBER	12-BORE

**Exposed hammer shows
if the weapon is cocked**

Ejector port

**Perforated barrel
shroud**

Loading gate

Trigger

Semi-pistol stock

Six-round tubular magazine **Cocking slide**

**Bayonet
attachment**

WINCHESTER MODEL 1897
Browning's first pump-action gun for Winchester, the
Model 1893, was a rare failure. Browning strengthened
and modified the action, and the Model 1897 proved to
be everything that its predecessor was not, and remained
in production until the 1950s. The military version, shown
here, was produced up to 1945.

DATE	1897
ORIGIN	US
BARREL	20 IN (51 CM)
CALIBER	12-BORE

VIETNAM WAR
Australian forces fought
alongside the US army and
Marine Corps in Vietnam. The men
of this patrol, disembarking from a CH-47
Chinook helicopter, are armed with the self-loading
FN FAL rifle, which was also issued to British troops at the
time, and the American M60 general-purpose machine gun.

THE MODERN WORLD

SNIPER RIFLES 1914–1985

BY THE TIME OF THE CIVIL WAR in the United States, weapons technology had progressed to the point where it was possible to shoot an identified individual at very long ranges. By World War I, the sniper had already become a very important figure on the battlefield, but it was only in World War II that he (and often, particularly in the Red Army, she) really made his or her mark. At that time, sniping was perhaps best described as a 'black art', but more recently, technological advances have turned it into more of a science.

Busch Visar telescope sight

Elevation adjustment

Objective

Eyepiece

Leaf sight

Safety catch

Bolt

Bolt handle

Combined forestock cap and barrel band

Cleaning rod

MAUSER GEW 98
Specially selected examples of the Mauser Infanteriegewehr 98, the German Army's standard rifle of World War I, continued to be used as snipers' weapons throughout World War II. The rifles were fitted initially with a 2.75x telescopic sight produced commercially as the Visar by Emil Busch AG. The sight was graduated from 100 to 1,000 m, and matched to a particular rifle.

DATE	1900 ONWARD
ORIGIN	GERMANY
WEIGHT	9¼ LB (4.15 KG)
BARREL	21¼ IN (75 CM)
CALIBER	7.92 MM

PSO-1 telescopic sight

Battery compartment

Cheek pad

Skeleton wooden butt stock

Safety catch

Shrouded blade fore sight

Type PU sight

Fixed-focus eyepiece

Windage screw

Integral five-round box magazine

Stock selected for density and straightness of grain

MOSIN-NAGANT M1891/30PU

In the 1930s the Red Army began issuing specially selected Model 1891/30 Mosin-Nagant rifles, fitted with Type PE telescopic sights, to its most accomplished marksmen. The sight was replaced with the 3.5-power PU. Some 330,000 M1891/30PU sniper rifles were produced during World War II, and it was widely accepted to have been the most accurate in use.

DATE	1941
ORIGIN	USSR
WEIGHT	11¼ LB (5.15 KG)
BARREL	28¾ IN (73 CM)
CALIBER	7.62 MM x 54R

Hensoldt fixed-power telescopic sight

Elevation adjustment

Cheek pad

Polymer fore stock

Cold-forged barrel with hexagonal rifling "floats" in the forestock

Five-round detachable box magazine

Trigger is adjustable for weight of pull

Pommel locates the hand on the pistol grip

Pistol grip

Reticule lamp

HECKLER & KOCH PSG-1

Intended as a police sniper rifle, the PSG-1 was essentially a heavily modified G3, as issued to the German Army, with the same roller-delayed blowback action. The most significant differences lie in the cold-forged, hexagonally rifled barrel and the Hensoldt 6x42 fixed-power sight, which has an illuminated reticle.

DATE	1985
ORIGIN	GERMANY
WEIGHT	17¼ LB (8.1 KG)
BARREL	25½ IN (65 CM)
CALIBER	7.62 MM x 51 NATO

Rear sight

Cocking handle

Ejector port

Ten-round detachable box magazine

Gas cylinder

Gas regulator

FULL VIEW

Muzzle compensator and flash hider

DRAGUNOV SVD

The Snaiperskaya Vintovka Dragunova (chambered for the rimmed 7.62 mm round developed for the "3-line" Mosin-Nagant rifle in 1891) was adopted by the Soviet bloc armies in 1963. Its PSO-1 telescopic sight has a limited infrared capability.

DATE	1963 ONWARD
ORIGIN	USSR
WEIGHT	9½ LB (4.3 KG)
BARREL	24 IN (61 CM)
CALIBER	7.62 MM x 54R

319

THE MODERN WORLD

SNIPER RIFLES 1985–2006

UNTIL THE 1990S, SNIPER RIFLES used conventional ammunition. Some new models then adopted more powerful ammunition that gave both a flatter trajectory and increased the "point-blank" range to several hundred feet. It also allowed them to reach out to greater distances. Others changed their nature more substantially, adopting the "bullpup" configuration that allowed their overall size to be much reduced, while retaining the all-important long barrel.

WALTHER WA2000

Developed for police use, most were produced in .300 Winchester Magnum caliber. The example shown here is the experimental Series 1 version: the operational Series 2 had an upgraded gas system and an unfluted barrel, which improved accuracy. Both types were fitted with variable-power Schmidt & Bender telescopic sights.

DATE	1978–88
ORIGIN	GERMANY
WEIGHT	15 LB (6.95 KG)
BARREL	25½ IN (65 CM)
CALIBER	7.62 MM NATO

FULL VIEW

Magnification selector, 2.5–10x

Windage adjustment

Mounting clamp

Combined flash hider and muzzle compensator

Ejector port

Semi-shrouded trigger

Thumb hole

Magazine release catch

Six-round detachable box magazine

WA 2000
Carl Walther Waffenfabrik ULM/Do.
MADE IN GERMANY

WALTHER

Polymer stock

Fully floating
stainless-steel barrel

Attachment point for
steadying sling

Bipod in folded
position

Ten-round removable
box magazine

L96A1

The British Army's L96A1 sniper rifle,
in service since 1986, was the first to
be developed specifically for sniping:
earlier versions had been based on
various models of the Lee-Enfield. It
has an aluminum frame to which its
components are attached. Each rifle
is individually fitted with a Schmidt
& Bender 6x telescopic sight.

DATE	1986 ONWARD
ORIGIN	UK
WEIGHT	14 LB (6.5 KG)
BARREL	25¾ IN (65.5 CM)
CALIBER	7.62 MM NATO

Elevation adjustment

Mounting rail

Objective in its
shielded cover

Bipod in the
folded position

Safety catch

Cocking handle

Eyepiece

Elevation adjustment

Objective

Walnut fore stock

Ejector port

Folded bipod

BARRETT MOD.90

In 1982, 20-year-old Ronnie Barrett designed a .50-
caliber sniper rifle as a bet. The gas-operated Model 82
(adopted by the US Army as the M107) revolutionized the
field, and was followed by the lighter, bolt-action, bullpup
Model 90, and an upgraded version, the Model 95. The
heavy .50-caliber round makes the rifle an effective anti-
material weapon to a range of 5,900 ft (1,800 m).

Recoil pad

Bolt handle

Five-round
removable
box magazine

DATE	1990–95
ORIGIN	US
WEIGHT	22LB (10 KG) LESS OPTICS
BARREL	29 IN (73.7 CM)
CALIBER	.50 IN

THE MODERN WORLD

RECOIL-OPERATED MACHINE GUNS

UNTIL THE SECOND DECADE of the 20th century, Maxim's method of harnessing a gun's recoil was ubiquitous; the British Vickers, incorporating only minor modifications, was the only newcomer. Then John Moses Browning, who had previously gone to great lengths to disguise the fact that he had violated Maxim's patents in his Colt M1895, came up with a new way of harnessing the same force.

Vernier aperture sight (folded down)

Recoil enhancer

Condenser hose connection

Water jacket

Clamping band for auxiliary tripod

Ammunition belt feedway

"Five arch" sight bridge

Trigger bar

Trigger bar extension for use with Youlton Hyperscope

Sangster auxiliary tripod

Muzzle cap

Tripod extension pantograph

Traversing turntable

Traversing turntable clamp

Elevation screw

Elevation wheel

VICKERS MK 1 FOLDED DOWN

VICKERS MK 1

Adopted by the British Army as a replacement for the Maxim in November, 1912, the MK 1 differed from its predecessor in that its locking toggle-joint broke upward rather than downward, reducing the size of the receiver. Thanks to the use of steel throughout, it was 30 lb (13.6 kg) lighter than the Maxim. Its rate of fire was unchanged, at around 450 rounds per minute (rpm). It was declared obsolete only in April 1968.

DATE	1912
ORIGIN	UK
LENGTH	43¼ IN (110 CM)
CALIBER	.303 IN

Tripod leg

Tripod foot

Flash hider

Ventilated barrel shroud

21 in (53.3 cm) barrel

Recoil transmission bar

Recoil-actuated automatic traverse mechanism

Pistol grip

MG42

Germany was prohibited from developing new weapons by the Treaty of Versailles, but it did so in secret, abroad. In 1934 the Maschinengewehr 34 was officially adopted as the MG08's replacement. At just 26.6 lb (12 kg), it was light, yet robust enough to deliver sustained fire at up to 900 rpm, but it was expensive to produce, and was superseded by the MG42, far and away the best automatic weapon of its day, capable of 1,200 rpm.

DATE	1943
ORIGIN	GERMANY
LENGTH	48 IN (122 CM)
CALIBER	7.92 MM MAUSER

Pad for ease of carrying

Bracing bar

45 in (114 cm) barrel

Handle for barrel

Receiver

Ammunition belt

Trigger bar

Barrel shroud

Spade grips

BROWNING M2 HB

The US Army was pleased with Browning's M1917 (below), but wanted a heavier weapon too, and Browning obliged with the water-cooled M1921. Like the rifle-caliber gun, its water jacket was later removed, and it metamorphosed into the M2. The only important later modification was the provision of a heavy barrel. It remained in service into the 21st century, and formed the basis for other, more sophisticated weapons.

DATE	1936
ORIGIN	US
LENGTH	64½ IN (164 CM)
CALIBER	12¾ IN (12.7 MM)

Ammunition belt supporting box

Ammunition belt feedway

Water jacket

Fore sight

Rear sight

Pistol grip

BROWNING M1917

John Browning first produced a design for a machine gun in 1895, and when he had finished work on the M1911 pistol, he returned to the subject, and came up with a simpler method of locking breech-block and barrel than Maxim had used. His new gun was adopted by the US Army as the M1917. It soon lost its water jacket and became the air-cooled M1919, and remained in service in that form until the 1960s.

DATE	1912
ORIGIN	US
LENGTH	38½ IN (58 CM)
CALIBER	.30-06 IN

FULL VIEW

THE MODERN WORLD

GAS-OPERATED MACHINE GUNS

WHEN MAXIM BUILT HIS FIRST machine gun, there was no question of using propellant gases to cycle the action because they carried too much particulate residue, but by the 1890s, the introduction of smokeless propellants had changed that. In 1893 an Austrian cavalryman, Odkolek von Augezd, sold a design for just such a gun to the Hotchkiss company in Paris. Since then, gas operation has become commonplace.

Fore sight

Flash hider

Gas port

Gas cylinder

Cooling fins

Ammunition belt feedway

Shoulder brace

26.7 in (67.8 cm) barrel

Combined pistol grip and cocking handle

ZB 53 (VZ/37 OR BESA)
Machine gun designer Vaclav Holek was one of the stars of the 1930s. He used similar locking methods on both the Bren gun and the ZB 53. The latter was known as the VZ/37 by the Czechs and Besa by the British, who used it in their tanks.

DATE	1937
ORIGIN	CZECHOSLOVAKIA
BARREL	26¾ IN (67.8 CM)
CALIBER	7.92 MM MAUSER

Ammunition belt feedway

Fore sight

Trigger bar

Gas port

Flash hider

Carrying handle

GORYUNOV SGM
The Red Army used its Maxims well into World War II, but by 1942, it desperately needed a cheaper replacement. Goryunov mated elements of an earlier unsuccessful design with Holek's locking system. His original SG43 underwent modification, post-war, and became the SGM.

DATE	1943
ORIGIN	USSR
LENGTH	44 IN (112 CM)
CALIBER	7.62 MM x 54

Gas cylinder

Rear sight

FN MAG (GPMG)
The MAG (Mitrailleuse à Gaz), produced by FN, used a modified form of the locking system developed by John Browning for his Automatic Rifle; this was mated to the feed mechanism of the MG42. The gun was adopted by the British Army as the General-Purpose Machine Gun.

Pistol grip

DATE	1958
ORIGIN	BELGIUM
LENGTH	40½ IN (104 CM)
CALIBER	7.62 MM NATO

Ammunition belt

Ammunition box

Optical sight

Cooling fins

Rear sight

Ammunition
strip feedway

Steadying grip

Elevation
gear

Trigger

Pistol grip

HOTCHKISS MLE 1914

The original design Baron von Augezd sold to
Hotchkiss in 1893 was robust and simple, the bolt
being locked against the barrel by means of a pivoting
flap until pushed aside by gas tapped off the barrel
at its mid-point. Its major weakness was a tendency
to overheat. Between 1897 and 1914, it underwent
a series of modifications aimed at correcting this
fault, and also to make it cheaper to produce and
to improve its feed mechanism, which employed
metallic strips holding 24 rounds, rather than fabric
belts. The M1914 remained in use until World War II.

DATE	1914
ORIGIN	FRANCE
LENGTH	50 IN (127 CM)
CALIBER	8 MM LEBEL

Elevation wheel

Traversing turntable

Gunner's seat

Ammunition
belt feedway

Heat shield

22 in (56 cm) barrel

Feed cover

Flash
eliminator

Bipod (folded)

M60

The US Army replaced its Browning M1917 derivatives
with a new, gas-operated, general-purpose machine gun
in the early 1960s. The M60 used the feed system of the
MG42 and the locking system of the German FG42 assault
rifle. It was unsatisfactory to begin with, but a series of
modifications over two decades corrected most of its faults.

DATE	1963
ORIGIN	US
LENGTH	43½ IN (110 CM)
CALIBER	7.62 MM NATO

THE MODERN WORLD

MG43 MACHINE GUN

HECKLER & KOCH'S ANSWER to FN's Minimi Squad Automatic Weapon, the MG43 is a conventional gas-operated light machine gun with an action based on a rotating, rather than the roller-locked, bolt employed in H&K's other contemporary weapons. It is simpler in design than the Minimi, being belt-fed only, and is consequently cheaper to manufacture. Like virtually all modern firearms, it makes use of molded glass-reinforced polymers wherever possible. It has an integral bipod, plus mounting points for the M2 tripod, as well as a Picatinny rail (named after a US Army Research and Development establishment) on the receiver that will accept all NATO-standard optical sighting units as well as a basic aperture rear sight.

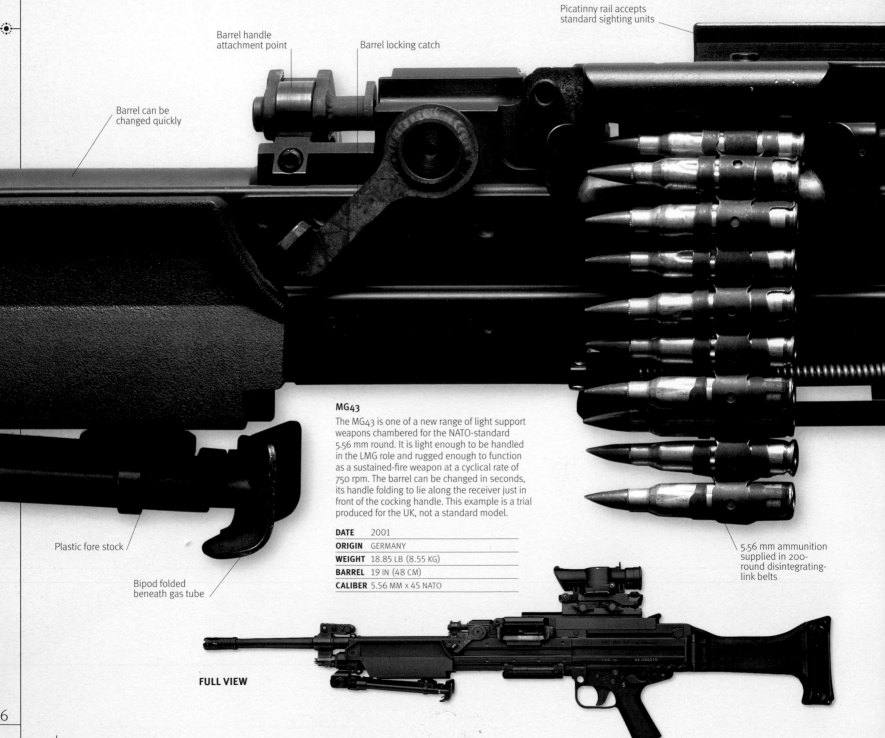

Picatinny rail accepts standard sighting units

Barrel handle attachment point

Barrel locking catch

Barrel can be changed quickly

Plastic fore stock

Bipod folded beneath gas tube

5.56 mm ammunition supplied in 200-round disintegrating-link belts

MG43

The MG43 is one of a new range of light support weapons chambered for the NATO-standard 5.56 mm round. It is light enough to be handled in the LMG role and rugged enough to function as a sustained-fire weapon at a cyclical rate of 750 rpm. The barrel can be changed in seconds, its handle folding to lie along the receiver just in front of the cocking handle. This example is a trial produced for the UK, not a standard model.

DATE	2001
ORIGIN	GERMANY
WEIGHT	18.85 LB (8.55 KG)
BARREL	19 IN (48 CM)
CALIBER	5.56 MM x 45 NATO

FULL VIEW

SUSAT sight with four-power magnification and low-light capability

Plastic butt stock hinged here to fold to left

HK MG 43   Kal. 5,56mm×45

AC 96-000015

Safety catch with provision for fully automatic fire only

Molded plastic pistol grip

Trigger

1900—2006

◀ **322–323** RECOIL-OPERATED MACHINE GUNS ◀ **324–325** GAS-OPERATED MACHINE GUNS ▶ **330–331** LIGHT MACHINE GUNS SINCE 1945

THE MODERN WORLD

LIGHT MACHINE GUNS 1914–1945

THE FIRST GENERATION of machine guns were too cumbersome to be used in anything but fixed positions, so there was also a need for a lighter, portable weapon capable of putting down sustained fire. The barrels of early light machine guns tended to overheat. This problem was solved by the development of systems that enabled the barrels to be changed quickly and easily, even under combat conditions.

Ejector port

Barrel

Gas tube

Trigger guard with security lock in place

Shoulder support (hinged down)

20-round detachable box magazine

BROWNING AUTOMATIC RIFLE

John Browning set out to design a self-loading rifle, but it was soon obvious that the weapon he produced was better suited to the role of light support weapon. Though it had a fixed barrel and poor magazine capacity, it remained in front-line service with the US Army and Marine Corps until the mid-1950s.

DATE	1918
ORIGIN	US
WEIGHT	16 LB (7.3 KG)
BARREL	24 IN (61 CM)
CALIBER	.30-60

Stoppage indicator

Cooling jacket holds 7½ pt (4 l) of water

Wooden butt stock

Pistol grip

Ammunition belt feedway

Flash hider

MG08/15

Germany's first, hurried attempt to produce a light machine gun saw the Maxim MG08 fitted with a butt stock, a pistol grip, and a conventional trigger. It also had an integral bipod, with a shortened ammunition belt contained in a drumlike container. It was far too heavy, but around 130,000 were produced, and it became the principle support weapon for the Reichswehr's stormtroopers.

DATE	1917
ORIGIN	GERMANY
WEIGHT	48½ LB (22 KG)
BARREL	28¼ IN (72 CM)
CALIBER	7.92 MM x 57

Bipod

Rear sight

Pan magazine holds 47 rounds

Gunner's left hand grips stock here

Trigger

Ejector port

Cocking handle

Cooling fins continue inside barrel shroud

DEGTYAREV RP46

The Red Army adopted the Degtyarev DP in 1928. It was modified in 1945, and the following year, it received a heavier barrel and was adapted to take belts as well as drum magazines. The RP46 was still not entirely satisfactory, however, and was soon replaced by the RPD.

DATE	1946
ORIGIN	USSR
WEIGHT	28¾ LB (13 KG)
BARREL	23¾ IN (60.5 CM)
CALIBER	7.62 MM x 54R

Laminated wooden butt stock

Recoil spring housing

Ammunition belt feedway

Barrel

Ejector port

Gas tube

Flash hider

Bipod

Rate-of-fire selector and safety catch

BREN

Developed at Brno and modified at Enfield (hence its name) the Bren gun was the British Army's principle light support weapon from its introduction until the 1970s, latterly in 7.62 mm NATO chambering. If it had a deficiency, it lay in its (rimmed) ammunition, not in the gun itself.

DATE	1937
ORIGIN	CZECHOSLOVAKIA/UK
WEIGHT	22½ LB (10.15 KG)
BARREL	25 IN (63.5 CM)
CALIBER	.303 IN

30-round detachable box magazine

Rear sight

Carrying handle

Fore sight

Body locking pin

Magazine port cover

Left-hand grip

Adjustable gas regulator

Cocking handle

Gas cylinder

Tripod attachment point

Barrel shroud and heat dissipator

LEWIS

The British Army adopted the air-cooled, gas-operated Lewis gun in 1915, and it remained its standard light support weapon until it was superseded by the Bren. The original design was the work of Samuel MacLean, but it was modified by Colonel Isaac Lewis of the US Army, who went on to market it aggressively. The US Army Air Corps adopted it as a flexibly mounted weapon.

DATE	1912
ORIGIN	US
WEIGHT	26 LB (11.8 KG)
BARREL	26¼ IN (66.5 CM)
CALIBER	.303 IN

FULL VIEW

Bipod attachment clamp

Bipod

1900—2006

◄ 310–311 WEAPON SHOWCASE: SA80 ASSAULT RIFLE   ◄ 322–323 RECOIL-OPERATED MACHINE GUNS   ◄ 324–325 GAS-OPERATED MACHINE GUNS   ◄ 328–329 LIGHT MACHINE GUNS

THE MODERN WORLD

LIGHT MACHINE GUNS SINCE 1945

DURING WORLD WAR II engagements took place at shorter ranges than previously. This had two consequences: the barrels of rifles and light machine guns became shorter, and the rounds they fired became lower-powered and lighter. For the individual soldier, this meant a welcome reduction in the load he had to carry. More recently, weapons became even lighter when plastic replaced wood and bullpup configurations were introduced.

Rear sight

Skeleton light-alloy butt stock

NEGEV

Israel Military Industries' Negev is one of the breed of lightweight automatic weapons that has blurred the distinction between LMG and GPMG. Chambered for the SS109 NATO round in 5.56 mm caliber, it can deliver automatic fire at 700 or 900 rounds per minute (rpm).

DATE	1988
ORIGIN	ISRAEL
WEIGHT	15¾ LB (7.2 KG)
BARREL	18 IN (46 CM)
CALIBER	5.56 MM X 45 NATO

Cocking handle

Bipod folded under gas cylinder

Carrying handle

Rear sight

Cocking handle

Ejector port

Rate-of-fire selector and safety catch

FULL VIEW

Ammunition belt container

FN MINIMI

FN's gas-operated, air-cooled Minimi accepts the NATO STANAG magazine or disintegrating-link belts, without modification. It was adopted by the US Army as its M249 Squad Automatic Weapon, and by the British Army as the L108A1.

DATE	1975
ORIGIN	BELGIUM
WEIGHT	15 LB (6.83 KG)
BARREL	18½ IN (46.5 CM)
CALIBER	5.56 MM X 45 NATO

Plastic butt stock

Cocking handle

Perforated barrel shroud

Fore sight (folded)

CETME AMELI

Similar to CETME's assault rifle, with its roller-locked delayed action, the Ameli has a cyclical rate of fire that is determined by the type of bolt fitted. A light bolt gives 1,200 rpm, while a heavy bolt gives 850 rpm. A lightweight version of this weapon was also developed.

DATE	1982
ORIGIN	SPAIN
WEIGHT	14 LB (6.35 KG)
BARREL	15¾ IN (40 CM)
CALIBER	5.56 MM x 45 NATO

Fore sight

Barrel

Muzzle compensator

Safety catch and selective fire lever

Optical sight

Gas tube

Gas regulator

Magazine release catch

30-round magazine box

Folded bipod

RPK74

The RPK74 was developed from the successful AKM assault rifle, and many parts are interchangeable with those of other Kalashnikov weapons. It entered service in the early 1960s, and replaced the RPD as the standard light machine gun of the Soviet infantry. However, the gun's fixed barrel meant that the rate of fire had to be kept below 75 rpm to prevent overheating.

DATE	1976
ORIGIN	USSR
WEIGHT	11 LB (5 KG)
BARREL	23¼ IN (59 CM)
CALIBER	5.45 MM x 39

Foresight

Muzzle compensator

SUSAT optical sight

Plastic forestock

Cocking handle

Barrel support

L86A1 LIGHT SUPPORT WEAPON

The introduction of the L85A1 Individual Weapon into British service meant that a new support weapon had to be developed with the same caliber ammunition. The result was the L86A1, which replaced the L484 Bren gun. It has a heavier and larger barrel than the L85A1, and a rear grip to aid sustained firing. There is no quick-change barrel, so the gun must be fired in short, controlled bursts to prevent overheating.

DATE	1986
ORIGIN	UK
WEIGHT	12 LB (5.4 KG)
BARREL	25½ IN (64.5 CM)
CALIBER	5.56 MM x 45 NATO

STANAG 30-round detachable magazine

THE MODERN WORLD

SUBMACHINE GUNS 1920–1945

EARLY ATTEMPTS TO PRODUCE a light, rapid-fire weapon centered on pistols, but it soon became obvious that these were difficult to control, and that something more akin to a carbine, but firing a reduced-power round suitable for a handgun, was more likely to be effective. It was not until World War II that it became clear that the butt stock was superfluous to a submachine gun (SMG) and could be eliminated without negative effects.

Magazine catch

Magazine port

Wooden butt stock

Front sling attachment

Barrel shroud

Ejection port

Cocking sleeve

Single-shot trigger

Burst-fire trigger

VILLAR PEROSA

The first SMG was manufactured in 1915 as a double gun, paired in a simple mounting and fitted with spade grips, a single trigger bar, and a bipod. Later, these were revamped as carbines, with butt stocks and conventional triggers.

DATE	1920s
ORIGIN	ITALY
WEIGHT	6 LB (3.06 KG)
BARREL	11 IN (28 CM)
CALIBER	9 MM GLISENTI

Fore sight

Cocking handle

MP40

In 1938, the German Army adopted a new, handier design for a SMG, but it was still uneconomical to produce. Two years later, it was re-engineered to replace expensive machining with pressed and welded construction. This later design set the trend for an entire generation of SMGs.

Skeleton butt stock (folded)

Pistol grip

DATE	1940
ORIGIN	GERMANY
WEIGHT	9 LB (4.03 KG)
BARREL	9 IN (24.8 CM)
CALIBER	9 MM PARABELLUM

32-round magazine

Cocking handle

Magazine port

Fore sight

Magazine release catch

Forward pistol grip

THOMPSON M1921

US General John Tagliaferro Thompson began by designing an unsatisfactory self-loading rifle in 1916, but by 1919, he had produced an early version of what would be known universally as the Tommy Gun. The M1921 was the first to come to the market, but it was not until 1928 that the US Government adopted it, in small numbers, for the Marine Corps.

50-round magazine drum

Winder for clockwork mechanism

DATE	1921
ORIGIN	US
WEIGHT	10 LB (4.88 KG)
BARREL	10 IN (26.7 CM)
CALIBER	.45 ACP

PPSH41

Shpagin's "Peh-Peh-Sheh," reliable and simple both to manufacture and to maintain, was to become the mainstay of the Red Army after it stopped the German advance into the Soviet Union. At least five million had been produced by 1945, and infantry tactics were modified to make the best use of them.

DATE	1944
ORIGIN	USSR
WEIGHT	7 LB (3.5 KG)
BARREL	10 IN (27 CM)
CALIBER	7.62 MM SOVIET

Compensator reduces muzzle lift

Body locking pin

Magazine port

Rate-of-fire selector

71-round drum

BERGMANN MP18/I

The Hugo Schmeisser-designed MP18/I can lay claim to being the first effective submachine gun. It was produced in response to a request from the German Army's storm troopers for a handier weapon than the heavy, cut-down MG08/15s they were using when assaulting defended positions.

DATE	1918
ORIGIN	GERMANY
WEIGHT	11 LB (5.25 KG)
BARREL	7 IN (19.6 CM)
CALIBER	9 MM PARABELLUM

Magazine port

Graduated rear sight

Perforated barrel shroud

32-round "snail" drum magazine

STEN MARK 2 (SILENCED)

The Sten cost less than a good pair of shoes to buy, but if one ignored its more obvious shortcomings, it was an effective way of putting devastating short-range firepower into the hands of inexperienced combatants. This version had an integrated noise- and flash-suppressor, and was produced only in small numbers.

DATE	1941
ORIGIN	UK
WEIGHT	7 LB (3.4 KG)
BARREL	35 IN (91 CM)
CALIBER	9 MM PARABELLUM

Noise/flash suppressor

Rear sight

Fore grip insulated against heat

Pressed and stamped steel body

Fixed skeleton butt

32-round magazine

Receiver machined from solid steel billet

Rear sight adjustable for windage and elevation

THOMPSON SUBMACHINE GUN.
CALIBRE 45 AUTOMATIC COLT CARTRIDGE
MANUFACTURED BY
COLT'S PATENT FIRE ARMS MFG. CO.
HARTFORD, CONN., U.S.A.

Wooden butt stock removable in some models

Rear sling attachment

Rate-of-fire selector

Safety catch

Rear pistol grip

GANGLAND FAVORITE

If the Thompson was slow to find favor with the US Army, it received a warm welcome from the criminal fraternity defying Prohibition Laws in the US during the Roaring Twenties. It soon became a firm favorite.

THE MODERN WORLD

MP5 SUBMACHINE-GUN

HECKLER & KOCH'S MP5 is the submachine-gun of choice for most of the Western world's police and special forces units. Mechanically it is very similar to the company's range of assault rifles, with a roller-locked delayed-blowback action. Firing from a closed bolt (most SMGs hold the bolt back when they are cocked) makes it considerably more accurate than others, and also improves controllability in the automatic mode, when it fires at a cyclical rate of 800 rpm. Laser target designators are often fitted, and a powerful torch can be mounted in place of the grenade launcher shown on this example.

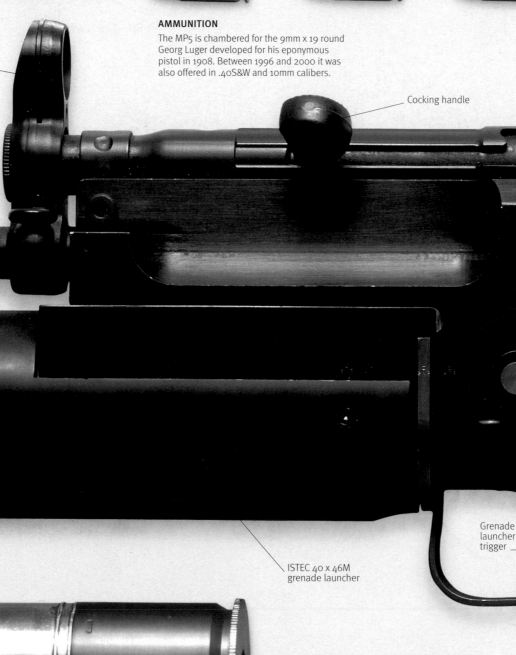

AMMUNITION
The MP5 is chambered for the 9mm x 19 round Georg Luger developed for his eponymous pistol in 1908. Between 1996 and 2000 it was also offered in .40S&W and 10mm calibers.

Fore sight in annular shroud

Cocking handle

Attachment lugs for barrel-mounted accessories, including silencer

ISTEC 40 x 46M grenade launcher

Grenade launcher trigger

Grenade launcher safety catch

GRENADE
Fitted with an under-barrel grenade launcher, the MP5 can fire the complete range of 40mm grenades, including lethal, non-lethal, and illuminating rounds, over distances of several hundred meters.

FULL VIEW

Stock retracted

MP5A5

The MP5 is also available with a rigid plastic stock. The trigger group (this example has safe/single/three-round/full-auto options) is also from the HK33, but it can be exchanged for one of a different configuration. A version with an integral silencer is also available, as is one with a short barrel.

DATE	1966
ORIGIN	GERMANY
WEIGHT	6¼LB (2.82KG)
BARREL	8¾IN (22.5CM)
CALIBRE	9MM PARABELLUM

Mounting for standard NATO sights

Rear sight

Recess for telescoping butt

Butt locking pin

Magazine release catch

Safety catch and rate-of-fire selector

Moulded plastic pistol grip

15-round magazine can be exchanged for one holding 30 rounds

Rate-of-fire icons: single-shot, three-round burst (above), and automatic (top)

1900—2006

◄ **328–329** LIGHT MACHINE GUNS 1914–1945   ◄ **330–331** LIGHT MACHINF GUNS SINCE 1945   ◄ **332–333** SUBMACHINE GUNS 1920–1945

THE MODERN WORLD

SUBMACHINE GUNS SINCE 1945

THE SECOND GENERATION of submachine guns, introduced during and just after World War II, were unsophisticated weapons, designed for mass–production. They produced devastating short–range firepower and a great deal of noise, but were notoriously inaccurate and difficult to control, and were of limited military value as a result. More recently, developments have concentrated on applications for security and police.

Fore sight in protective shroud

Cocking handle

Pressed-steel receiver

Barrel-locking nut

Replaceable barrel

Molded-plastic fore grip

Forward sling swivel

Rate-of-fire selector

UZI

The secret of the Uzi's legendary stability lies in its bolt being wrapped around its barrel; this brings the center of gravity forward, and helps to cure the tendency for the barrel to rise during automatic fire. Heavy moving parts keep its rate of fire to a manageable level.

DATE	1950s
ORIGIN	ISRAEL
WEIGHT	8 LB (3.6 KG)
BARREL	10 IN (260 MM)
CALIBER	9 MM PARABELLUM

Cocking-handle cover acts as safety catch

Cocking handle

Barrel locking nut

Retractable skeleton butt

Flash suppressor

Pistol grip

M3/M3A1 ("GREASE GUN")

The Grease Gun was cheap to produce and simple to strip, clean, and maintain. It fired the same heavy round as the Colt automatic pistol.

Carrying sling

30-round detachable box magazine

DATE	1940s
ORIGIN	US
WEIGHT	8.05 LB (3.66 KG)
BARREL	8 IN (203 MM)
CALIBER	.45 IN ACP

32-round detachable box magazine

Retractable skeleton butt

Rear sight

Ejector port

Barrel shroud

Fore sight shroud

MAT 49

The MAT 49's distinctive feature is its pivoting magazine housing; as well as making the weapon easier to conceal, it's a very positive safety device.

Rear pistol grip

Pivoting magazine housing doubles as fore grip

32-round detachable box magazine

DATE	1950s
ORIGIN	FRANCE
WEIGHT	7 LB (3.53 KG)
BARREL	9 IN (288 MM)
CALIBER	9 MM

Replaceable
barrel

Cocking
handle

Safety catch/rate-
of-fire selector

Retractable
skeleton stock

Rear sight in
protective
shroud

Pistol grip

VZ/68 SKORPION MOD 83

The Skorpion was designed as a
close-protection weapon that could be
carried in a holster and used with one
hand. Its unlocked blowback action
and lightweight moving parts would
give a very high rate of fire, but a clever
counterweight mechanism in the butt
reduces the rate.

20-round
detachable
box magazine

DATE	1960s
ORIGIN	CZECHOSLOVAKIA
WEIGHT	3 LB (1.34 KG)
BARREL	4 IN (115 MM)
CALIBER	9 MM PARABELLUM

Rigid wooden
butt stock

Rear sling
swivel

Optional noise/
flash suppressor

Cocking handle

Skeleton stock both
retracts and hinges to
lie over the receiver

Rubber
recoil pad

Wrist strap

INGRAM MAC-10

Combined pistol
grip and magazine
housing

A telescoping bolt and a magazine incorporated
into the pistol grip allowed Ingram to reduce the
overall size of the MAC-10 to little more than that of
an automatic pistol. With a cyclical rate of fire of well
over a thousand rounds per minute, it can empty
its 32-round magazine in little more than a second.

DATE	1970s
ORIGIN	US
WEIGHT	7 LB (3.4 KG)
BARREL	5 IN (146 MM)
CALIBER	9 MM PARABELLUM

Optical sight

Trigger

Transparent plastic 50-round
detachable box magazine

Injection-molded
plastic butt stock
contains receiver,
bolt, and lock

FN P90

The first attempt to produce an entirely new
compact automatic weapon, the P90 uses a
"miniature" caliber round designed with
damage limitation in mind. All its non-
mechanical components are molded from
plastic, and its unique horizontal ammunition
feed mechanism allows the magazine to be
incorporated into the receiver.

DATE	1990s
ORIGIN	BELGIUM
WEIGHT	6 LB (2.7 KG)
BARREL	11 IN (300 MM)
CALIBER	5.7 MM

AMMUNITION SINCE 1900

FOLLOWING THE DEVELOPMENT of the unitary brass cartridge, which combined all three essential elements (primer, propellant, and projectile) in one package, it only remained for the nature of those elements to be improved. Primers became more effective and bullets more aerodynamic, but the most important developments were in propellant. These took place in the last decade of the 19th century, first with the advent of smokeless powder and later of a nitroglycerine-based mixture generally known as cordite; this replaced gunpowder entirely.

Rifle cartridges

Rifle bullets acquired a sharply pointed nose and a taper toward the tail, which almost doubled their effective range and improved their accuracy. In these examples, both velocity (feet per second) and energy (foot-pounds) are measured at the muzzle.

.30-06 SPRINGFIELD
The .30-06 remained in US service from 1906 until 1954. Its 152-grain (9.85-g) bullet leaves the muzzle at 2,910 fps with 2,820 ft-lb of energy.

7.92 MM X 57 MAUSER
The SmK cartridge, as it was known, was loaded with a steel-jacketed 177-grain (11.5-g) boat-tailed bullet that left the muzzle at 2,745 fps.

.5/12.7 MM M2
Developed for the M2 machine gun and adopted as a rifle round, the M2 has a 710-grain (46-g) bullet and a muzzle velocity of 2,800 fps.

.470 NITRO EXPRESS
"Nitro" refers to the propellant, while "Express" refers to the bullet, which is hollow at the tip. Muzzle velocity is 2,150 fps, with 5,130 ft-lb of energy.

7.62 MM X 54R RUSSIAN
The "3-line" cartridge developed in 1891 was loaded with a 150-grain (9.65-g) bullet that left the muzzle at 2,855 fps.

.458 WINCHESTER MAGNUM
Developed in 1956 as a "big game" round, with a 500-grain (32.4-g) bullet, it give a muzzle velocity of 2,040 fps and 4,620 ft-lb of energy.

7.7 MM X 56R JAPANESE
The fully rimmed version of the round for which the Arisaka rifle was chambered had a 175-grain (11.35g) bullet and a muzzle velocity of 2,350 fps.

.416 REMINGTON MAGNUM
A development of a cartridge produced by Rigby in 1911, the .416 Remington produces a muzzle velocity of 2,400 fps and 5,115 ft-lb of energy.

7.7 MM X 56R ITALIAN
Almost identical to the above, the Italian 7.7 mm cartridge had a 173-grain (11.25-g) bullet and a smaller charge that produced 2,035 fps.

8 MM X 58 KRAG
This is an alternative chambering for the Norwegian Krag rifle, which the Danish Army adopted. A 195-grain (12.7-g) bullet left the muzzle at 2,525 fps.

.303 MKVII
This version of the Lee-Enfield cartridge, with a 180-grain (11.66-g) bullet, developed a muzzle velocity of 2,460 fps and 2,420 ft-lb of energy.

.338 WINCHESTER MAGNUM
Developed for large North American game, this cartridge can be loaded with a variety of projectiles from 175 to 300 grains (11.34g to 19.44 g) in weight.

7 MM REMINGTON MAGNUM
Loaded with 62 grains (4.02g) of propellant and a 150-grain (9.72-g) "spitzer" bullet, this produces a muzzle velocity of 3,100 fps and 3,220 ft-lb of energy.

.257 WEATHERBY MAGNUM
A "hot" round, loaded with an 87-grain (5.31-g) "varmint" bullet, this achieves a muzzle velocity of 3,825 fps and delivers 2,826 ft-lb of energy.

.243 WINCHESTER MAGNUM
This short-case round delivers less power than a normal cartridge: a 100-grain (6.48-g) bullet leaves the muzzle at 2,960 fps with 1,945 ft-lb of energy.

.22 HORNET
One of very few high-velocity miniature rounds, the .22 Hornet was developed in the 1920s. Its 45-grain (2.9-g) bullet leaves the muzzle at 2,690 fps.

.30 M1 CARBINE
This "intermediate" round developed for the US World War II-vintage M1 Carbine is loaded with a 110-grain (7.13-g) blunt-nosed bullet, good to 600 ft (180 m).

7.92 MM X 33 KURTZ
The first effective intermediate round, it was copied by the Soviet Union in slightly smaller dimensions. It was effective to around 1,950 ft (595 m).

SS109 5.56 MM
The NATO-standard SS109 5.56 mm round has a steel-tipped projectile weighing 61.7 grains (4 g) and achieves a muzzle velocity of 3,085 fps.

7.62 MM X 51 NATO
When NATO chose a new rifle and machine gun cartridge in the early 1950s it opted for one based on the .30-06.

5.45 MM X 40 SOVIET
This replaced the Red Army's 7.62 mm x 33 round for the AK74 family. It is similar to the 5.56 mm NATO round in performance.

Bullet is contained within charge

4.73 MM G11
The wheel turns full circle with the advent of the caseless round developed for Heckler & Koch's G11 assault rifle.

Pistol cartridges

The only significant change in the character of pistol ammunition after 1900 was the introduction of the high-performance Magnum load.

.45 MARS
This was the most powerful pistol ammunition in the world prior to the arrival of the .44 Magnum.

9 MM MARS
Severely bottlenecked cartridges are unusual in pistols, but the designer insisted on a heavy propellant load for the 9 mm Mars.

9 MM STEYR
There are many varieties of 9 mm revolver cartridge; this one was developed for a pistol designed by Mannlicher.

9 MM PARABELLUM
Also known as 9 mm Luger, this is the most common cartridge in the world. Countless firearms have been chambered for it.

.45 ACP
Another iconic pistol cartridge, the .45 Automatic Colt Pistol round was developed for the John Browning-designed M1911.

.32 LONG
Though a popular caliber for revolvers, the original .32 cartridge was low on power. A longer version was produced in 1896.

.38 S&W
This is the least powerful .38 cartridge; it gives the 145-grain (9.4-g) bullet a muzzle velocity of 685 fps and 150 ft-lb of energy.

.380 ENFIELD/WEBLEY
Made for the Enfield Mk 1 revolver, this 200-grain (12.96-g) bullet was almost as powerful as the .455 it replaced.

.32 AUTO
A popular caliber for small self-loading pistols, the .32 has a 60-grain (3.89-g) bullet and produces 125 ft-lb of energy.

8 MM NAMBU
The Japanese officer's pistols issued from 1909 onward were the only weapons ever made for this powerful round.

.357 MAGNUM
Developed in 1935, this has since been produced in many varieties. Average muzzle velocity is around 1,300 fps.

.44 MAGNUM
This round was developed in 1954. A 240-grain (15.55-g) bullet leaves the muzzle at 1,500 fps with 1,200 ft-lb of energy.

.5 ACTION EXPRESS
Developed for the Desert Eagle pistol, this 325-grain (21-g) bullet leaves the muzzle with 1,415 ft-lb of energy.

THE MODERN WORLD

MAN-PORTABLE ANTI-TANK WEAPONS

DURING WORLD WAR I, the only weapon capable of engaging a tank was a field artillery piece. Over the next two decades, dedicated anti-tank guns came into service, but there was a need for a lighter weapon that an infantryman could use, and anti-tank rifles were developed to meet it. These were of questionable effectiveness, and were soon abandoned, to be replaced by launchers for rocket-propelled bombs. The latter used a new technology, the shaped charge, which burned through armor like a blowtorch.

Pad absorbs some recoil

Box magazine holds five rounds

Fore sight

Bolt handle

Pistol grip

Monopod supports weight of rifle

Left hand grip

Flash hider

BOYS ANTI-TANK RIFLE

Birmingham Small Arms produced the Boys rifles in the mid-1930s. They were bolt-action weapons firing a heavy tungsten-steel round. Even though the barrel recoiled into the stock, the effect on the firer was fearsome. It was abandoned as ineffective in 1941 and replaced by the PIAT.

DATE	1936
ORIGIN	UK
WEIGHT	36 LB (16.3 KG)
BARREL	36 IN (91.5 CM)
CALIBER	.55 IN

Fore sight

Trough holds bomb before launch

Two fingers required to pull trigger

Shaped-charge warhead can penetrate 3 in (7.5 cm) of armor

Shrouded stabilizing fins

Propellant charge in body tube

Supporting monopod

PROJECTOR, INFANTRY, ANTI-TANK

The PIAT, like the Sten, was a wartime expedient design that put function before form. It was actually a spigot mortar, firing a bomb with a shape-charged warhead. The spigot's spring was very powerful and ignited the bomb's propellant charge after it had hurled it from the weapon.

DATE	1942
ORIGIN	UK
WEIGHT	32 LB (14.5 KG)
LENGTH	36 IN (91.4 CM)
PROJECTILE	3 LB (1.36 KG)

Gas regulator

Flash hider

Some propellent gas
bled off to act on piston
to cycle action

Rubber pad
absorbs
some recoil

SOLOTHURN S18-100 ANTI-TANK RIFLE

The Solothurn anti-tank rifle fired a base-fused
shell (an artillery round in miniature) that gave
acceptable results against light armor. An
upgraded version, the S18-1000, saw service
with the German Army as the PzB41.

DATE	1930
ORIGIN	SWITZERLAND
WEIGHT	99¼ LB (45 KG)
BARREL	35½ IN (90 CM)
CALIBER	20 MM

Fore sight

Barrel recoils
into receiver

Left hand pulls stock
tightly to shoulder

Rear sight
folds down

PTRD ANTI-TANK RIFLE

The PTRD was a more complicated
weapon than it appeared. It had a barrel
that recoiled into the stock and unlocked
the bolt in the process; this was held
back when the barrel returned to battery,
opening the breech and ejecting the spent
round. A fresh round was then introduced
and the bolt closed by hand.

DATE	1941
ORIGIN	USSR
WEIGHT	38¼ LB (17.3 KG)
BARREL	48¼ IN (122.7 CM)
CALIBER	14.5 MM

Tubular receiver contains
spigot and driving spring

Shoulder pad

Slings for
carrying on
back

Wooden shoulder
support

Rocket inserted
at rear

Trigger is the switch in a
battery-powered circuit

M1A1 "BAZOOKA"

The Bazooka was the forerunner of the German
Raketenpanzerbüchse and the Soviet RPG
rocket launchers. It was no more than a tube
from which a solid fuel rocket, with a shaped-
charge warhead, was launched. It was operated
by two men, one to fire, the other to load.

DATE	1942
ORIGIN	US
WEIGHT	13¼ LB (6 KG)
LENGTH	54 IN (137 CM)
PROJECTILE	3½ LB (1.54 KG)

THE MODERN WORLD

RIFLE-MOUNTED GRENADE LAUNCHERS

UNTIL THE DEVELOPMENT OF the percussion cap, which could also be used to detonate explosive devices, grenades had slow-match fuses, and were so unreliable that they went out of use during the 19th century. By 1915, however, William Mills had invented a safe, reliable, primer-detonated grenade, which the British Army adopted as the No. 36. Soon after, a device that allowed it to be launched from a standard infantry rifle was introduced.

Bolt · Receiver · Rear sight · Fore sight · Mills No. 36 grenade · Arming lever retaining ring

Ten-round magazine · Bayonet (broken)

SMLE WITH MILLS BOMB LAUNCHER

The Mills bomb was adapted for rifle-use by the addition of a rod to the base cap. The rifle itself was fitted with a ring or cup, mounted at the bayonet lug, to retain the grenade's arming lever. To fire the grenade, a specially formulated blank cartridge was used.

DATE	1915
ORIGIN	UK
GRENADE	ANTI-PERSONNEL
CALIBER	.303 IN
RANGE	490 FT (150 M)

Bolt handle · Grenade launcher fore sight · Stabilizing fins

Ten-round magazine · Marker capsule

NO. 4 RIFLE WITH AT-GRENADE LAUNCHER

With the introduction of the No. 4 Rifle, with its exposed muzzle, the British Army was able to develop a new style of tubular launcher. Mounted over the muzzle on the bayonet lugs, the No. 4 launched a fin-stabilized anti-tank grenade. Using an overpowered blank cartridge, it was fired with the butt of the rifle grounded. This example is fitted with a later model L1A1 practice grenade.

DATE	1940s
ORIGIN	UK
GRENADE	ANTI-TANK
CALIBER	.303 IN
RANGE	330 FT (100 M)

Folded rear sight for grenade launcher

Rifle cocking handle

Rifle trigger · Grenade trigger

Receiver   Cocking handle   Gas cylinder   Gas regulator   Grenade sight

Launcher tube

Folding bayonet

Ten-round magazine

Shaped-charge warhead

Stabilizing fins

SIMONOV GRENADE

M59/66 WITH AT-GRENADE LAUNCHER

This was the Red Army's standard anti-tank grenade launcher during the 1950s. Mounted on the self-loading M59/66 assault rifle, it employed an overpowered blank cartridge. While effective, it proved unpopular due to the disastrous effect of mistakenly chambering a regular live round.

DATE	1949
ORIGIN	USSR
GRENADE	ANTI-TANK
CALIBER	7.62 MM x 39
RANGE	330 FT (100 M)

Rear sight   Muzzle compensator

Rifle cocking handle

Gas cylinder

Rifle trigger

30-round magazine

Pistol grip

Grenade launcher trigger

Grenade launcher tube is rifled

40 mm anti-personnel grenade

GP25 GRENADE

AK74 WITH GP25

The barrel-mounted grenade launcher was slow to use. The answer was to fit the grenade with its own propellant charge. The Red Army adopted one with the charge in the body of the grenade. Nothing remained in the launcher's barrel after it had been discharged. This AK74 lacks the recoil pad that is normally fitted to grenade launcher rifles.

DATE	1978
ORIGIN	USSR
GRENADE	ANTI-PERSONNEL
CALIBER	40 MM
RANGE	490 FT (150 M)

Launcher fore sight in the folded position

Rifle fore sight

Launcher mounts onto forestock

Muzzle compensator

Loading/ejector slide

Rifled grenade launcher tube

M16A1 WITH M203

The US Army's version of the assault rifle-mounted grenade launcher, the M203, employs a grenade mated to a cartridge case containing the propellant charge. The empty case remains in the chamber after the round has been fired and needs to be ejected. The M203 was developed to replace the stand-alone M79 grenade launcher.

DATE	1972
ORIGIN	US
GRENADE	ANTI-PERSONNEL
CALIBER	40 MM
RANGE	490 FT (150 M)

STAND-ALONE GRENADE LAUNCHERS

THERE ARE TIMES WHEN a rifle-mounted launcher is not what is required; for example, non-lethal 40 mm grenades are available for riot control purposes, when rifles would not normally be issued. On the battlefield, rapid-fire launchers have come to supersede light mortars, since not only can they be used in the direct- and indirect-fire role (i.e. against visible and invisible targets, the latter on a compass bearing) they can also put down a greater weight of bombs.

Rifle barrel has cooling fins

Non-disintegrating belt emerges here

AGS-17 "PLAMYA"

The Soviet equivalent of the American 40 mm M19 that was first used in the Vietnam war. It is a belt-fed, blowback-operated launcher with a maximum range of 1 mile (1.61 km). Such weapons are commonly mounted in ground vehicles, boats, and hovercraft, and aboard helicopters and fixed-wing aircraft.

DATE	1975
ORIGIN	USSR
WEIGHT	48¼ LB (22 KG)
BARREL	11¾ IN (30 CM)
CALIBER	30 MM

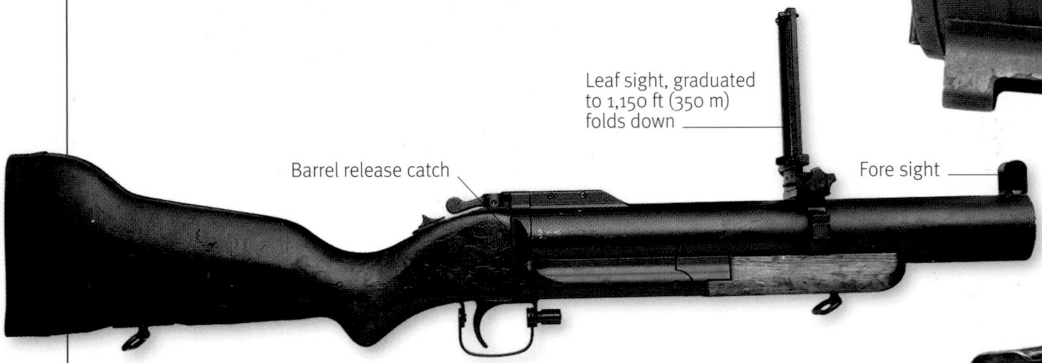

Drum contains 29 30 mm grenades in non-disintegrating belt

Elevating quadrant

Leaf sight, graduated to 1,150 ft (350 m) folds down

Fore sight

Barrel release catch

M79 "BLOOPER"

Developed as a stand-alone grenade launcher during the 1950s, the M79 became known as the Blooper to the troops issued with it. It is a simple break-open design, a bit like a giant shotgun. Opening the breech ejects the spent casing, a fresh round is loaded, and closing the breech cocks the action.

DATE	1960
ORIGIN	US
WEIGHT	6 LB (2.75 KG)
BARREL	12 IN (30.5 CM)
CALIBER	40 MM

M79 40MM GRENADE

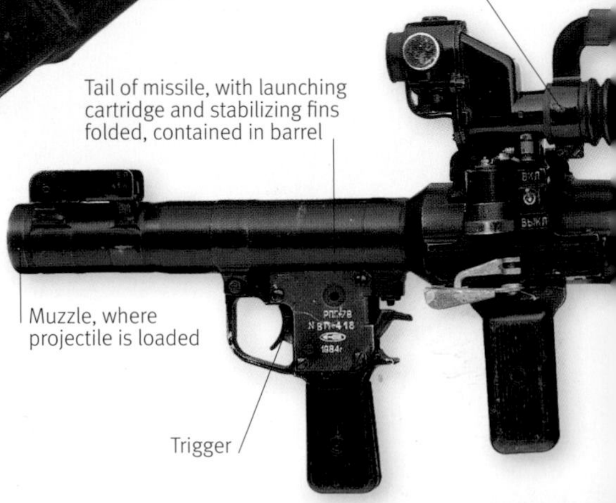

Optical sights graduated to 1,650 ft (500 m)

Tail of missile, with launching cartridge and stabilizing fins folded, contained in barrel

Muzzle, where projectile is loaded

Trigger

Laser designator

Fore grip can be
loosened to rotate
around barrel

Skeleton butt stock
can be folded forward

Optical sight
graduated to
1 mile (1.7 km)

Cocking handle has
toggle attached

Horizontal grips on
both sides of receiver

Cylinder holds six
40 mm grenades

FULL VIEW

MECHEM/MILKOR MGL MK 1

A scaled-up version of a shotgun of similar
design, the MGL MK 1 is a six-shot revolver
grenade launcher. Indexing is performed by a
spring, wound by rotating the cylinder manually
when it is swung out of the frame for loading.
Its maximum range is around 1,150 ft (350 m).

DATE	1990
ORIGIN	SOUTH AFRICA
WEIGHT	12 LB (5.6 KG)
BARREL	12 IN (30.5 CM)
CALIBER	40 MM

Elevation screw

Tripod leg
clamp

Wooden heat shield for
firer's shoulder

Exhaust gas
collector/diffuser

RPG-7V

The shoulder-launched RPG-7 is a much-
improved version of the RPG-2. Its projectiles
have a two-stage launcher/sustainer propellant
charge, and a range of up to 500 m (1640 ft). A
wide variety of grenades is available, including
anti-personnel, fuel-air explosive, and high-
explosive anti-tank projectiles.

DATE	1962
ORIGIN	USSR
WEIGHT	14 LB (6.3 KG)
BARREL	37¼ IN (95 CM)
CALIBER	40 MM

US NAVY SEAL

ESTABLISHED IN 1962, the US Navy SEAL (Sea-Air-Land) teams have built a reputation as the most impressive of American special operations forces. SEAL training is widely considered the most rigorous of any military force. It includes a strong emphasis on physical and mental fitness, including a week where students have less than four hours' sleep. Skills in which SEALs need to become proficient range from scuba diving and parachuting to close-quarters combat and demolition.

**M16 RIFLE
WITH GRENADE
LAUNCHER**

SPECIAL FORCES

The SEALs were created as part of President John F. Kennedy's drive to prepare US armed forces to meet the threat of guerrilla warfare. They were first sent into combat against communist forces in Vietnam in 1966, specializing in riverine operations. Since 1987 the SEALs have been grouped with all other American special forces under US Special Operations Command.

Deployed in landlocked Afghanistan after the American intervention in 2001, the SEALs fought in a role effectively indistinguishable from other special forces. Although the invasion of Iraq in 2003 gave SEALs a chance to exploit their waterborne role, for example capturing offshore oil terminals, once again their "Air-Land" element was much more prominent. SEALs led the way in the fast-moving campaign that destroyed the Iraqi army. US conventional forces were regularly called in to support them, rather than the other way around.

In 2006 the US Defense Department announced future war plans that envisaged a starring role for special forces in meeting the threat of global terrorist networks, described as "new and elusive foes." The Pentagon envisaged in particular that terrorists would be "found, fixed, and finished" by special forces calling in air strikes. If these plans are implemented, the future of the SEALs seems assured.

MULTI-TASKING
The many tasks potentially assigned to the 2,450 SEALs include recovering downed pilots, locating and freeing hostages, sabotage, reconnaissance, counterterrorism, and counter-drug operations. Such wide-ranging tasks require a wide variety of clothing, weapons, and equipment.

ARMED RIVER PATROL
Special Boat Units (SBUs) are, like the SEALs, a part of Special Naval Warfare Command. They are trained to carry out special operations in small surface craft, including river or sea patrols, and clandestine waterborne infiltration of commandos. SEAL seaborne or riverine operations are supported by teams of Special Warfare Combat-Craft Crewmen (SWCC).

"READY TO LEAD, READY TO FOLLOW, NEVER QUIT."

FROM THE SEAL CODE

FIGHTING IN AFGHANISTAN

In October 2001 the United States invaded Afghanistan, to overthrow the Taliban regime and destroy al-Qaeda terrorist bases. SEAL commandos participated as part of a Combined Joint Special Operation Task Force. Dropped by helicopter in hostile terrain, they searched caves and houses believed to be used by the enemy, located and directed air strikes against enemy fighters, and sought to capture or kill al-Qaeda leaders. A SEAL was among seven US special forces personnel killed at Takur Ghar in March 2002, when an attempt to establish a mountain-top reconnaissance post was resisted by guerrilla forces.

SEAL COMMANDO IN ACTION IN AFGHANISTAN

TOOLS OF COMBAT

SEAL PROTECTION
In action SEALs normally wear personal body armor, considered essential for survival in special operations. They often complement their standard-issue kit by purchasing high-quality specialist gear that is available on the market.

Protective goggles

Headset for communications

Body armor

Pouches strapped around chest and thighs to carry supplies

M16 AUTOMATIC RIFLE WITH M203 GRENADE LAUNCHER

H&K MP7 SUBMACHINE GUN

H&K MP5K SUBMACHINE GUN

1900—2006

◄ 294–295 SELF-LOADING PISTOLS FROM 1950 ◄ 300–301 MANUALLY LOADED REPEATER RIFLES 1900–2006 ◄ 332–333 SUBMACHINE GUNS 1920–1954

THE MODERN WORLD

IMPROVISED GUNS 1950–1980

WHEN AMMUNITION IS AT HAND, there is sometimes a temptation to fashion a weapon capable of firing it. In its simplest and crudest form, this need be no more than a piece of tubing of roughly the right diameter, a nail to act as a striker, and a means of propelling it with enough force to detonate the primer in the cartridge. Discharging such a device is likely to be at least as dangerous to the person holding the weapon as to the intended victim.

Trigger

Bolt handle

Barrel band and rear sight

Fore sight

Unrifled barrel

Stock reminiscent of a Lee-Enfield

Sling

MAU-MAU CARBINE

Somewhat more sophisticated than many of its type, this short-barreled, bolt-action, single shot carbine was made in Kenya during the time of the "Mau-Mau" insurrection against British rule in the 1950s. Most of the improvised weapons made by the rebels, the majority of whom were from the Kikuyu tribe, exploded when they were fired.

DATE	1950s
ORIGIN	KENYA
WEIGHT	3½ LB (1.6 KG)
BARREL	20¼ IN (51.2 CM)
CALIBER	.303 IN

Perforated barrel shroud serves as the fore grip

Cartridge case from 20 mm cannon shell serves as barrel

Hole used to ignite charge

Roughly carved wooden grip

EOKA PISTOL

This "gun" is so crudely fashioned that it barely qualifies for the name. The barrel is a spent 20 mm-caliber cartridge case, secured to the rough-hewn wooden frame by means of wire. For it to have been at all effective, the "muzzle" would have needed to be virtually in contact with the victim's body before the gun was discharged.

DATE	1950s
ORIGIN	CYPRUS
WEIGHT	½ LB (0.23 KG)
BARREL	4¼ IN (11 CM)
CALIBER	UNKNOWN

Wire wrapping secures barrel to stock

Barrel-retaining band

Hammer

SOUTH AFRICAN PISTOL

This homemade pistol, recovered in South Africa, is a bit more sophisticated than it appears at first sight. It boasts a simple, single-action lock linking trigger and hammer, perhaps derived from a child's toy pistol, and can thus be used single-handedly. It would have been so inaccurate as to render the rudimentary sights redundant.

DATE	1980s
ORIGIN	SOUTH AFRICA
WEIGHT	2¼ LB (1 KG)
BARREL	8¾ IN (22 CM)

Smooth-bore barrel

Retaining bolt

Trigger

EOKA SHOTPISTOL

EOKA (*Ethniki Organosis Kyprion Agoniston*—
National Organization of Cypriot Fighters) fought a
guerrilla campaign against British colonial rule on
the Mediterranean island of Cyprus from 1955 until
1959. During that time, small numbers of crude guns
were fashioned. This all-metal gun has a simple
break-open action. It fires a shotgun cartridge by
means of a spring-loaded plunger.

DATE	1950s
ORIGIN	CYPRUS
WEIGHT	2¾ LB (1.25 KG)
BARREL	4¼ IN (11 CM)
CALIBER	12-BORE

Fore sight

Rear sight

Trigger

Barrel
made from
gas pipe

Break-open
hinge

Cocking
handle

Pistol grip

Magazine port

Magazine release catch

Square-section
receiver

Safety catch

Trigger

Pistol grip

34-round box
magazine from
Sterling SMG

FULL VIEW

LOYALIST SUBMACHINE GUN

Modeled on the World War II-vintage Sten gun, this
homemade machine pistol was produced by loyalist
paramilitaries in Northern Ireland. The barrel shroud
and receiver have been fashioned from square-
framed tubing, while the magazine appears to be
that of an L2 Sterling SMG, as issued to British
troops stationed in Northern Ireland at that time.

DATE	1970s
ORIGIN	UK
WEIGHT	5¾ LB (2.6 KG)
BARREL	7¾ IN (20 CM)
CALIBER	9 MM

THE MODERN WORLD

HELMETS FROM 1900

HAVING BEEN LARGELY ABANDONED by European armies in the 1680s, metal helmets made a swift comeback amid the carnage of World War I. Although all combatants started that conflict wearing cloth or leather headgear, in 1915 they began adopting steel helmets to reduce casualties suffered through head wounds, especially from shrapnel. Broadly speaking, the same types of helmet developed during World War I served, with modifications, up to the 1980s, when all body armor was revolutionized by the introduction of synthetic Kevlar as a lightweight substitute for steel.

Helmet composed of leather plates

Plates riveted together

Leather strap secures plate to helmet

"Coal scuttle" shape protects neck

Visor protects against flying metal

Eye-slits allow only limited vision

WORLD WAR I TANK CREW HELMET

When the British introduced tanks to the battlefield in 1916, they quickly found that the vehicles' armor gave inadequate protection to the tank crew inside. When bullets struck the armor, shards of metal flew off the inside of the hull. After early casualties, tank crews were issued with helmets and visors to protect their heads and faces.

DATE	c.1916
ORIGIN	UK
WEIGHT	MASK ¾LB (0.29KG)

Mail mouth guard

Model 1916 helmet

Brow plate (*Stirnpanzer*)

Ventilation lug

Peak of helmet

GERMAN HELMET WITH BROW PLATE

Having entered World War I in spiked leather *Pickelhaube* helmets, the German army adopted the steel *Stahlhelm* in 1916. Soldiers believed to be at special risk, such as machine-gunners, were also issued with the *Stirnpanzer*, a 4mm (⅛in) thick steel plate to protect the front of the head. Since these plates weighed around 4kg (9lb), they were donned for short periods only.

DATE	1916
ORIGIN	GERMANY
WEIGHT	1.95KG (4¼LB)

UN SOLDIERS IN MOGADISHU, SOMALIA

United Nations peacekeeping forces are often referred to as the "blue helmets" because of their distinctively coloured headgear. These helmets thus perform a dual function, offering the soldier protection but also identifying him clearly as a peacekeeper.

"Soup bowl' shape

Wide brim

BRITISH BRODIE HELMET

Designed by John L. Brodie, the "tin hat" was first used by the British army in September 1915. Made of hardened manganese steel, it was cheap to produce but offered little protection for the neck or lower head. Brodie-pattern helmets continued in use with British and Commonwealth forces throughout World War II.

DATE	1939
ORIGIN	UK
WEIGHT	2½LB (1.6KG)

Steel skull plate covered with green cloth

Steel ear flap

US AIRCREW HELMET

Steel flak helmets were adopted by US bomber crews in response to heavy casualties sustained on daylight raids over Germany in World War II. Colonel Malcolm C. Grow developed this M4 helmet when the 1944-issue M3 proved too bulky to wear in the gun turrets of bombers. He also developed light body armor, called "flak suits."

DATE	c.1944
ORIGIN	USA
WEIGIIT	9½LB (4.28KG)

Helmet net

US M1 HELMET

The US Army's M1 helmet was first used in combat in 1942. It consisted of an outer steel shell with a flimsier liner inside. The shell could be separated from the liner to serve as anything from a shovel to a latrine. Evolved forms of the M1 remained in use with the US Army until the 1980s.

Narrow brim

DATE	1940s
ORIGIN	USA
WEIGHT	2¼LB (0.99KG)

NORTH VIETNAMESE HELMET

During the Vietnam War, the soldiers of the North Vietnamese Army wore varieties of headgear, including this kind of sun helmet, or pith helmet. Such helmets were made of pressed paper or, less often, of plastic. Not surprisingly, they offered no protection against the firepower of US and South Vietnamese weapons.

Helmet made of lightweight material

DATE	c.1970
ORIGIN	NORTH VIETNAM
WEIGHT	1LB (0.5KG)

Cotton DPM cover

BRITISH KEVLAR HELMET

Until the 1980s, British Army soldiers continued to wear Brodie-pattern steel helmets, similar in style to those worn in the two World Wars. These were replaced by helmets made of Kevlar – a synthetic material that, weight-for-weight, is stronger than steel, and is also heat-resistant. The shape of the new helmet also provides protection to more of the head. The helmet is often covered with DPM (Disruptive Pattern Material) for camouflage.

Chincup

DATE	1990
ORIGIN	UK
WEIGHT	3LB (1.36KG)

CROWD CONTROL
Bolivian riot policemen
shoot rubber bullets during a
strike in downtown La Paz, 2004.
These are often used to aid crowd control
because although they can pierce the skin, they do
not cause permanent injury unless fired at short range.

INDEX

Page numbers in **bold** indicate main references

3-Line rifle, 258
92FS Beretta pistol, 294

A

Acre, 59
Adams, Gen. DW, 185
Adams, Robert, 222
Admiralty Islands, 203
Adophus, Gustavus, 100
Adowa, Battle of, 179
Afghanistan, guerrilla warfare, 279, 307, 347
Afzal Khan, 100
AG36, grenade launcher, 334
Africa, edged weapons, 11, **198–9**, **280–3**
  North African *saif*, 187
  shields, **270–1**
Afzal Khan, 100
AG36, grenade launcher, 334
aikuchi (sword), 66
aircraft, fighter, 277
  jet, 276
airship, 277
AK47, grenade launcher, 343
  machine gun, 278, **306–7**, 331
AK74, machine gun, 331
Albuera, Battle of, 242
Alexander the Great, 12, 27, 28, 42
  at Pavia, 98, 138
Algeria, French campaigns in, 176
Alison of Dundee, 153
al-Qaeda, 347
Ameli machine gun, 331
American Civil War, 177, 178, **220–1**
  swords, **184–5**
American War of Independence, 107, 176–7, 205, 233, 243
ammunition, bullet lubrication, 266
  bullet shape, 226, 338–9
  cartridge, 16–7, 101, 235, 243, 250–1, **266–7**, 307, **338–9**
  invention, 17
  development of, 16–17
  expanding bullet, 236, 250, **266**
  hollow-point, 19
  jacketed bullet, 259
  Luger "Parabellum," 291
  Magnum, 298
  MP5 submachine gun, 334
  musket/rifle ball, 14, 150, **266**
  percussion cap, 226, 236, **266**
  primer, 19
  SS109, 311
amphibious craft, 278
Anaconda revolver, 299
Anglo-Boer war, 254
Anglo-Saxon, weapons and armor, **50–1**
angon (spear), 50
ankus, 143, 196
antitank weapons, **340–1**
Arab, dagger, 11
Arabia, rise of army, 29
Arawe (shield), 273
archery, glossary, 9

thumb ring, 147
Argive (shield), 27–8
Arisaka rifle, 259
  bullet, 338
armet (helmet), 23, 169
arming cap, 23
armor, Asian, **170–1**
  Assyrian scale, 33
  crocodile skin, 34
  Crusades, 59
  Egyptian, 34
  European plate, **94–5**
  European tournament, **166–9**
  Frankish, 9, **50–1**
  garniture, 166
  gauntlet, 23, 95, 167
  German, 22, 88, 89, 91
  glossary, 23
  Greek, **40–1**, 42
  Indian (Sikh), **268–9**
  Japanese, 22, 127, **172–3**
  Kevlar, 23, 351
  knightly, 91
  mail, 22, 52, 87, 91, **92–3**, 94, 170, 268
  Mongolian, 76
  Navy SEAL, 347
  overview, **22–3**
  pauldrons, 95
  Roman, 22, 28, 44, 46
  samurai, 22, 127, **172–3**
  Spanish, 84–5
  Viking, 22
army, drilling, 99
  size of, 99, 101
Arnold, Benedict, 176
arquebus, matchlock, 61, 108, **150–1**
  at Pavia, 98, 138
arrow, Aztec, 99
  flint, 31, 35
  head, 35, 79, 147
  Japanese, 8
  longbow, 79
  Sudanese, 199
  see also bow
artillery, development of, 98–9
  field, 101
  gunner's stiletto, 133
  horse, 99
  Napoleonic Wars, 230
  Redcoat training for, 242
  siege, 100
  World War I, 276–7
Asian, armies, 99
  armor, **170–1**
  bow and arrow, **146–7**
  helmet, 23
  musket, **156–7**
  rifles, 260, **262–3**
  staff weapons, **74–5**
Assam, sword-ax, 9
assassins, 131
assault rifles, **306–7**, **310–11**, 331
Assyria, archery, 8, 27, 33
  armor, 33
  rise and fall, 26–7
Astra pistol, 290
Athens, 42
Augsburg, Peace of, 98
Augustus, Emperor, 45
Aurangzeb, Emperor, 99, 170
Austerlitz, Battle of, 176, 177
Australia, boomerang, 9, 210
  shields, 211
Austria, flintlock, 161
  hunting sword, 105

musket design, 233
  pistol, 295
  repeater rifle, 258
Austrian Succession, War of the, 99
Austro-Prussian War, 177
automatic weapons, **308–9**, 313
  see also machine gun and submachine gun
aventail, mail, 23, 87, 93, 268
ax, African club, 199
  battle, 9, 26, 37, 59, 74, 196–7,
  Bronze Age, 9, 49
  carbine, 159
  ceremonial, 37
  combination weapon, 158
  Congolese, 198
  Egyptian, 9, 34
  Frankish, 51
  Indian, 74
  Iron Age, 49
  lochaber, 13
  long-handled, 73
  Mesopotamian, 26
  pole arms, 13, **72**
  saddle, 142
  short, 73
  stone, 30–1
  tabar, 197
  throwing, 9, 51
  tomahawk, 9, 205
  tongi, 196
  Viking, 52–3, 73
ayudha katti sword, 129
Aztec, Spanish defeat of, 84–5, 99
  weapons and shields, **82–3**

B

Baghdad, 279
Baker, Ezikiel, 215, 234
Baker rifle, **234–5**
Balaclava, Battle of, 177, 178
ball, musket/rifle, 14, 150, **266**
ballack dagger/knife, 69, 131
Baltic lock (rifle), 153
bandenhelm (helmet), 23
bandhelm (helmet), 23
Barbarossa, Frederick, 58
barbute, Corinthian, 89
bardiche, 12, 13, 72, 141
barding (horse armour), 23
barrel, cooling, 322, 328
  insulation, 333
Barrett, Ronnie, 321
Barrett sniper rifle, 321
baselard, 64, 68
basinet, European, 23, **86–7**, 93
Bayeux Tapestry, 59, 73
bayonet, 20th century, **284–5**, 311
  American, **194–5**
  Baker, 235, 243
  British 1907 pattern, 284
  Brown Bess, 243
  charge, 194
  Chassepot, 11
  Elcho, 195
  Enfield, 250, 284
  European, **194–5**
  German, 284, 285
  introduction of, 101
  musket, 233
  origin, 130
  plug, 101, 133
  socket developed, 99
  sword, 242, 243
  trowel, 195

Bazooka antitank rifle, 341
Beaumont, FBE, 223
Belgium, Browning pistol, 292
  dueling/target pistol, 216
  machine gun, 330
  pistol, 163, 292
  rifle production, 19, 308
  submachine gun, 337
Bemis Heights, assault on, 176
Bénét, Col. SV, 267
Benin, sword design, 282–3
Beretta, pistol, 293
  shotgun, 313
Bergmann, Theodore, 229
Bergmann submachine gun, 21, 333
Besa machine gun, 324
besagaw (shield), 91
Besserm process, 177
bevor, 23, 87, 94, 168
bhuj (axe), 196
Bhutan, dagger, 135
bich'hwa (dagger), 100, 135, 193
bill (staff weapon), 12, 140
Birmingham Small Arms, 340
Bismark, Chancellor, 178–9
Blenheim, Battle of, 99, 101
Blooper grenade launcher, 344
blowback, 15, 17
bluing, on rifle barrels, 237
blunderbuss, 15, 212, 247
Boer, Battle of, 177
Boer War, 179, 228, 254, 300
Bolivia, rubber bullet use, 352–3
bolt, crossbow, 78, 80
  bolt-action, mechanism, 19
  rifle, 245, 313
bomb, atomic, 277, 278
  Mills, 342
  nuclear, 278
  smart, 279
bombing raids, 277–8
boomerang, 9, 210
Borchardt, Hugo, 228, 253
Borchardt pistol, 19
Borodino, Battle of, 177
Boru, Brian, 58
Bourgeoys, Marin le, 162
Bouvines, Battle of, 93
bow, Asian, **146–7**
  Assyrian, 8, 33
  backed, 208
  bullet, 144
  Chinese, 146
  composite, 8, 26, 33, 35, 76, 146–7
  crossbow, 8, 59, **78–81**, 108, **144–5**, 146
  Egyptian, 35, 38–9
  fingering, 208
  from horseback, 26, 76
  Indian, 8
  Japanese, 146
  laminated, 146
  longbow, 8, **78–9**
  Mongol, 76
  North American, 27, **208–9**
  recurved, 76
  samurai, 8, 126
  shortbow, 59
  stone, 144
  thumb ring, 147
box-lock, 15
Boyle, Gamble & McFee, 185
Boys antitank rifle, 340
break-open rifle, 244
breastplate, 167

breech-loader rifle, **248–9**
breech-loading carbines, 240–1
Breitenfeld, Battle of, 100–1
Bren machine gun, 329
Britain, Battle of, 277
  Bronze Age weapons, **48–9**
  Royal Air Force, 277
  Tower of London Armoury, 149
  war with China, 176
British Army, 95th (Rifle)
  Regiment, 234
  in American War of Independence, 176
  antitank weapon, 21
  bayonets, 194–5, 284
  cavalry, 149, 181, 182
  concentration camps, 179
  Enfield rifle, 250
  fighting knife, 285
  grenade, 342
  Kevlar, 351
  machine gun, 20, 323, 324, 329, 331
  in Napoleonic Wars, 177
  pistol, 292
  Redcoat infantry, **242–3**
  revolver, 223, 297
  rifle, 234–5, 249, 257, 265, 300, 313, 321
  shrapnel shells, 176
  sniper rifle, 320
  submachine gun, 333
  World War I helmets, 350–1
  Zulu Wars, 200
British East India Company, 129, 190, 197, 215, 269
British Royal Navy, cutlass, 182
  volley gun, 265
broadsword, 104, 108
Brodie, John L, 351
Bronze Age, 26, **48–9**
Brown Bess (musket), 99, 149, 153, 233, 243
Browning, John Moses, 19, 229, 290, 304, 312, 313, 315, 323, 324, 328
Browning, Automatic Rifle, 304, 328
  machine gun, 20, 229, 323
Bull Run, Battle of, 178, 220
Bulldog revolver, 299
bullet, expanding, 178, 236, 250
  invention, 17
  jacketed, 259
  lubrication, 266
  Minié, 220
  mould, 226
  NATO standard, 311
  rubber, 352
  shape, 178, 226, 338–9
bullet gun, continuous, 100
bullpup, definition, 15
  rifles, 21, 311, 320, 330
  shotgun, 315
bunker buster, 21
Bureau, Jean, 61
burgonet (helmet), 169
Burton, James, 236
byrnie mail, 92
Byzantium, 29

C

C/93 Borchardt pistol, 19
C/96 Mauser pistol, 19, 228
Cadell, Thomas, 162

Cadet Rifle L98, 311
Cadet sword, 183
camouflage, helmet, 351
Cannae, 29
cannon, hand-, 14
　introduction of, 14, 61
　Portuguese, 100
caracole, cavalry tactic, 101
carbine, bayonet, 194
　blunderbuss, 247
　capping breech-loader, **240-5**
　Chassepot, 178, 194, 241, 267
　definition, 15
　dog-lock, 159
　flintlock, 148
　Greene, 241
　light dragon flintlock, 149
　M1 (Garand), 21, 285, 304-5
　Mau-Mau, 348
　Mauser KAR98K, 301
　Monkey Tail, 241, 266
　pill-lock, 263
　rifle, 301
　Sharps, 16, 240
　Terry, 241
cartridge ammunition, 16-7, 101,
　235, 243, 250-1, **266-7**, 307,
　338-9
Castillon, Battle of, 59, 61
　sword, 63
castle, Norman building, 59
catephract (Roman cavalry), 22
cavalry, armor, 22-3
　Assyrian, 27
　British Army, 149, 181, 182
　Celtic, 49
　charge, 60, 220, 230
　Chinese, 188
　Companions, 28
　defeated, 242
　Dragoon pistol, 219, 224
　flintlock use, 149
　halberd used against, 13
　hammer, 12, 136
　Lechfeld, Battle of, 58
　Light Brigade, 177
　Mongol, 59
　Persian, 27
　revolvers, 224-5
　sabres, 180-1
　Spanish pistol, 215
　sword, 11, **104-7**, 180-1
　tactics, 101
Celt, weapons and armor, 48-9
Ceresole, Battle of, 99
Cerignola, Battle of, 98
CETME Ameli machine gun,
　331
chakram, 269
chapeau de fer, 23
chariot, Celtic, 48
　Egyptian, 26, 34, 38-9
　Greek, 42
　Sumerian, 26, 32
Charlemagne, 29
Charles I, 107
Charles V, 99
Charles VIII of France, 59
Charles the Bold, 99
Charter Arms, 299
Chassepot, Alphonse, 241, 248
Chassepot, bayonet, 11
　carbine, 194, 241, 267
chimalli (shield), 83
China, armor, 171
　bow design, 8, 146
　continuous bullet gun, 100
　crossbow, 8
　firearms introduced, 61
　gunpowder invented, 58
　mace, 60, 74

China (cont.)
　matchlock wall gun, 262
　Opium War, 176
　rifle manufacture, 301
　swords, **66-7**, 77, 188-9
　terracotta army, 29
chivalry, code of, 90
Churchill, Winston, 228
citron foug grenade, 289
claymore, 102
cleaver, club, 9
　hunting, 118
Clontarf, Viking defeat, 58
club, Aztec, 83
　composite, 9
　goedendag, 13
　knobkerrie, 9
　Melanesian, 202
　North American, **204-5**
　Oceanian, 202
　patuki, 203
　throwing, 9, 210
　Tongan, 202
　whalebone, 9
　wood, 13
coastguard, pistol, 217
Cobra revolver, 299
coif, 92
Cold War, 278
Colt, Samuel, 16, 218, 222, 226,
　245, 264
Colt, pistols, 18, 290, 292
　revolvers, 16, 18-19, 218-19,
　224-5, **226-7**, 296-7, 299
　revolving rifles, 16, 245, **252-3**
combination weapons, **158-9**
Cominazzo, Lazarino, 152
commando, 346-7
communications, telegraph, 176
concealed weapon, 299
concentration camps, 179
Concord, Battle of, 176, 243
Congo, dagger/knife designs,
　282-3
Congreve, William, 176
conquistadors, 84
coolus (helmet), 23
Cooper, Joseph Rock, 217
Cooper brass cartridge pistol, 16
Copenhagen, Battle of, 234
corned powder, 59, 61
Cortés, 98
Courtrai, Battle of, 13, 59, 60, 72
cranequin, 8, 80
Crécy, Battle of, 8, 61, 78, 91
Crimean War, 154, 177, 178,
　180, 241
crossbow, 8, **78-81**, 108, **144-5**,
　146
　armour penetration, 22
　Battle of Hastings, 59
Crusades, 58-9, 62, 70
Cuba, US occupation, 177
cuirass, European, 23, 95
　Greek, 40
　Indian, 268
　Japanese, 172-3
Custer, Gen., 241
cutlass, 182, 202
Cyprus, improvised pistol, 348,
　349
Czechoslovakia, German invasion,
　276
　machine gun production, 324,
　329, 337

D

da Vinci, Leonardo, 160
Dacian Wars, 46
Dafte, John, 212

dag (pistol), **160-1**
dagger, African, 280
　Asian, **134-5**
　ballock, 69
　bich'hwa, 100, 135, 193
　Celtic, 48
　combination weapon, 158
　Cossack, 187
　dirk, 131
　dudgeon, 131
　Egyptian, 36
　European, **68-9**, **130-3**
　flint, 30-1
　gauche, 11
　gunner's stiletto, 133
　Highland dirk, 131
　Indian, 100, 192-3
　Iron Age, 49
　jambiya, 11
　Japanese, 127
　kard, 134
　Kasai, 282
　katar, 11, 134
　kris, 11
　maingauche, 130
　Medieval, 11
　Mesopotamian, 32
　Mongolian, 77
　Nepalese, 192-3
　Oceanean, 203
　piha kaetta, 135
　quillon, 68, 69, 91, 133
　rondel, 69
　stiletto, 131, 133
　Sumerian, 32
　sword, 131
　sword-breaker, 11, 132
Dahomey, axe design, 199
daisho, sword combination, 121
Damascus, sword manufacture, 11
Dame, 313
dao (sword), 9, 77, 188, 191
David, King of Scotland, 59
Deane, John, 223
Degtyarev machine-gun, 329
Deringer, Henry, 224
Derringer, pistol, 18
　Remington Double, 224
Desert Eagle pistol, 20, 295
Devolution, War of, 99
Dien Bien Phu, French defeat,
　277
Dinan, assault of, 58
dirk, 131
Dolep, Andrew, 153, 163
Dolstein, Paul, 109
Doppelhänder swords, 102
double barrel, flintlock, 264
　gun, 244
Dragunov SVD sniper rifle, 319
Dreadnought battleship, 276
Dresden, destruction, 278
Dreyse needle-gun, 178, 249
drilling, American War of
　　Independence, 177
　Greek games, 42
　musket, 100
　Napoleonic, 178
　Redcoat, 242
　Roman, 46
　see also training
dudgeon, 131
duelling, weapons, 212
Dunkirk, 277
Dürer, Albrecht, 102
Düsack, 105
Dutch combination long gun,
　149
DWM, 19

E

Echeverria, pistol manufacture,
　292
Ecuador, machete, 11
Edgehill, Battle of, 148
Edward I, 59
Egypt, armor, **34-5**
　arrows, 35
　axe, 9, 34, 37
　bow, 33, 38
　chariots, 26, 38
　dagger, 36
　mace, 12, 137
　shield, 35
　spear, 35
　sword, 36
　Tutankhamen, 35, 36, 38-9
Elcho, Lord, 195
elephant goad, 143, 196
Enfield, revolver, 339
　rifle, 237, 267, 300-1, 339
　Royal Ordnance Factory, 19
England, flintlock, 161
　holster pistol, 162-3
　matchlock, **150-1**
　Normans conquer, 58, 59
English Civil War, 99, 107, 148
English longbow, 79
EOKA pistol, 348, 349
estoc, 11
Ethiopia, defeats Italy, 179
　shield, 271
　tribal warfare, 198
European, bayonets, **194-5**
　dagger, **68-9**, **130-3**
　helms and basinets, **86-7**
　hunting guns, **152-5**
　imperialism, 179
　jousting armor, **88-9**
　mail armor, **92-3**
　pistols, **160-3**, **212-17**
　plate armor, **94-5**
　rapier, **110-11**
　staff weapons, **72-3**, **136-7**,
　　140-1
　sword, **48-51**, **62-5**, **102-7**,
　　110-13, **180-3**, **188-9**
　tournament armor, **166-9**
execution, knife, 281
　by sword, 102-3

F

Fabrique National of Herstal, 19
Fairburn, William, 285
Fairburn-Sykes fighting knife,
　285
falchion (sword), 116
Falkirk, 8, 60
Fascism, 277
Ferara, Andrea, 104
Ferdinand, Archduke Franz, 276
feudal armies, 58, 60
FG42 assault rifle, 325
fighting bracelet, 281
firearm, mass production, 214
　overview, **14-21**
　range improvements, 178
firanghi sword, 128
flail, with quoits, 143
flamberge, 109
Flanders, 101
flight, first powered, 276
flint, 10, 15, 35
flintlock, blunderbuss, 15
　box-lock, 15
　Brown Bess, 99, 149, 153, 233
　English, 153
　hunting guns, **154-5**
　invention, 15

flintlock, blunderbuss, (cont.)
　long gun, **148-9**
　mechanism, 15
　muskets, 101, 149, **232-3**
　pistols, **160-3**, **212-15**, 246,
　　261
　repeating, 153, 264
　shotgun, 155
　Swedish, 152
Flobert, Louis, 17
flyssa (knife), 280
FN, FAL rifle, 308
　Minimi machine gun, 330
　P90 submachine gun, 20, 337
Folville, 216
Forsyth, Alexander, 16, 216
fortification, 100
Fosbery, Col. George, 229
France, Algerian campaigns, 176
　artillery, 177
　bayonet, 101, 194
　Berthier rifle, 300-1
　carbine, 241
　cavalry, 72, 93
　civil war, 99
　conquers Dahomey, 199
　Franco-Prussian War, 177, 178
　German invasion, 277
　gunnery schools, 101
　hunting sword, 117
　knights, 138
　Landsknecht, 102, **108-9**, 114
　machine gun, 20, 325
　musket, 233
　pistol designs, 215, 216
　Revolution, 176, 177, 179, 180
　rifle designs, 237, 259, 300-1
　shotgun, 244
　submachine-gun, 336
　sword, 181, 182-3
　tournament helmets, 168-9
　WWI infantry, **288-9**
Franci SPAS shotgun, 314
francisca (axe), 9
François I, 98, 99, 108, 114, 138
Frankish, dagger, 11
　rise of kingdom, 29
　weapons and armor, 9, **50-1**
Frederick the Great, 99
Fredericksburg, Battle of, 178
French Revolution, 176, 177,
　179, 180
Friuli, siege of, 59
Fusil Reglementaire rifle, 237

G

G41 Heckler & Koch rifle, 309
Gabbett-Fairfax, Hugh, 229, 291
Gafur, Haji, 187
Gaillard, chateau, 59
Galili assault rifle, 309
Gallienus, 29
gambeson, 92
Garand, John, 304, 305
Garand rifle, 21, 285, 304-5
gas, poison, 277, 286
　propellant use of, 21
Gatling, Richard, 17
Gatling gun, 17, 179
Gaugamela, Battle of, 28
gauntlet, 23, 95
　locking, 167
Gempei Wars, 126
Genghis Khan, 58-9, 76
Germany, armor, 22, 88, 89, 91
　bandenhelm helmet, 23
　Bismarck, 178-9
　bolt action gun, 244
　break-open double rifle, 244
　broadsword, 108

Germany, armor (cont.)
Bronze Age sword, 48
cavalry sword, 107
combination weapons, **158–9**
crossbow, 80–1
double-handed swords, 102–3
halberd, 72, 141
hunting sword, 105, 117,
118–19
Luftwaffe, 277
M43 ammunition, 307
partisan (staff weapon), 13
pistol design, 294–5
repeater rifle, 257, 301, 305
staff weapons, 140
Treaty of Versailles, 323
tournament helmets, 169
wheellock, 14, 152
World War I bayonet, 284
World War I helmets, 23, 351
World War I rifles, 286
Gettysburg, 177, 178
GEW43 rifle, 305
GEW98 rifle, 318
gladiator, armor, 45
gladius (sword), 28, 45, 181
glaive (staff weapon), 12, 13, 140
global warfare, 101
Glock pistol, 295
goedendag (club), 13
gorget, 22, 87, 94
Goryunov SGM machine gun,
324
GP35 Browning pistol, 292
Grand Alliance, War of, 99
Grant, Ulysses S, 178
Grease Gun (submachine gun),
336
Great Northern War, 99
greaves, European, 23, 91, 95
Greek, 41
Japanese, 172–3
Roman, 28
Greece, armor, **40–1**, 42
cavalry, 27
chariot, 42
helmet, 41, 42, 43, 89
hoplite infantry, 10, 12, **42–3**
kopis sword, 129, 187
Marathon, Battle of, 26, 28, 42
pikes, 99
spear, 40
Greener Police shotgun, 315
grenade, AK47, 343
anti-tank, 342
launcher, rifle-mounted, 310,
334, **342–3**
stand-alone, **344–5**
Mills, 342
Simonov, 342
World War I French, 289
Griffin, Benjamin, 155
Grow, Col. Malcolm C, 351
guerrilla warfare, Afghanistan,
279, 307, 347
American War of
Independence, 243
Boer War, 179
combating, 347
tactics, 177
Vietnam, 278
West Africa, 179
Guiscard, Robert, 58
Gulf War, 277
gun, Gatling, 17, 179
improvised, **348–9**
invention, 14
pellet-lock, 244
sport, 238–9, **244–5**
sport long, **312–13**
gunnery schools, 101

gunpowder, invented, 14, 17,
58, 61
smokeless, 254
gurze (mace), 75

H

Hadley, flintlock shotgun, 15
Hadrian's Wall, 46
Haida people, club, 205
halberd, 9, 13, 59, 72, 141
combination weapon, 158
training required, 59
Hall, John Hancock, 233
hammer, cavalry, 12, 136
war, 13, 73, 137
hand-cannon, 14, 150
handgun, automatic, 254
introduction, 61
hanger sword, 117
Hannibal, 28
Harlech castle, 59
Harold II, King, 59
Hastings, Battle of, 58–9
Hattin, Battle of, 70–1
haubergeon (mail), 92
hauberk (mail), 23, 92, 93
Heckler & Koch, machine guns,
21, 326–7, 334–5, 347
pistol, 294–5
rifle, 309, 319
helicopter, in Iraq, 279
in Vietnam, 278, 316
helm, barbute, 89
close, 94
European, **86–7**, 94
frog-mouthed, 88
great, 23, 86, 88–9
jousting, 23, 88–9
sallet, 88, 89
helmet, Asian, 23
basinet, 23, 86–7, 93
burgonet, 169
Chinese *zhou*, 171
Coolus, 23, 45
Corinthian, 28, 42, 43
crocodile skin, 34
European tournament, 166–7,
168–9
Frankish, 51
gladiator's, 45
horned, 48
Indian, 23, 170, 268
Iron Age, 48
Korean, 171
pewter, 45
Red Army, 303
Roman, 23, 44, 45, 46
samurai, 23, 172
segmented, 23
spangenhelm, 50, 51, 86
Viking, 23, 53
wig, 32
World War I, **350–1**
Henoul, Guillaume, 161
Henri II, King of France, 169
Henry, Benjamin Tyler, 18, 253,
312
Henry VIII, 79, 167
Henry rifle, 253
Hideyoshi, Toyotomi, 120
Hiroshima, 277, 278
Hitler, Adolf, 276–8
HK33 assault rifle, 335
Holbein, Hans, 167
Holek, Vaclav, 324
holster, pistol, 162
Hopi people, bow and arrow, 208
hoplite infantry, 10, 12, **42–3**
horse, armor, 23

horse, armor (cont.)
artillery, 99
bow firing from, 26, 76
crossbow preparing, 80
Hotchkiss machine gun, 20,
324–5
Howard, Edward, 16
Huang Di, Emperor, 29
Hugo-Schmeisser, 333
Hundred Years War, 59, 60, 73
hunting, cleaver, 118
crossbow, 80–1, 144
guns, **152–5**
knife, 119
spear, 117
sword, 105, **116–19**
trousse, 118–19
Hussein, Saddam, 278–9
Hyksos, Egyptian warfare with,
34

I

Immortals (Persian corps), 27
Inca, Spanish defeat of, 99
incendiary launcher, matchlock,
263
India Mutiny, 177
armor, 170, **268–9**
bow and arrow, 8, 147
British East India Company,
129, 190, 197, 215, 269
British rule, 177
combination weapons, 158
dagger, 11, **134–5**, 192–3
early military treatise, 26
firearms, **260–1**
helmet, 23, 170, 268
mace, 75
Mughal conquest, 99
parrying weapon, 193
pichangatti, 193
staff weapons, 74–5, **142–3**,
196–7
swords, 10, 11, **128–9**, 186,
190–1
torador (matchlock), 157
tulwa (saber), 10, 11
Indian Mutiny, 251
Indian Plains, Battle of, 206
Indian Wars, 177, 184, 206, 241
infanteriegewehr rifle, 257
infantry, antitank projector, 340
hoplite, 10, 12, **42–3**
Japanese, 126–7
Napoleonic, 182
Redcoat, **242–3**
sword, **104–5**, 107
infra-red, sighting, 319
Ingram MAC-10 submachine
gun, 337
Inkerman, 178
Inuit, bow and arrow, 209
Investiture, Wars of, 58
Iraq, US campaign, 279, 346
Ireland, Rigby manufacturer, 313
Irian Jaya, shields, 273
iron, in Africa, 281
working methods, 10, 27
Iron Age, weapons and armor,
48–9
Isandhlwana, Battle of, 201
Islam, rise of, 70
Israel, Desert Eagle pistol, 20
Galili assault rifle, 309
machine gun, 330
pistol, 295
submachine gun, 336
walled city, 26
Issus, Battle of, 28
Italy, armor, 88, 89, 94–5

Italy, armor (cont.)
Beretta pistol, 293
cavalry carbine, 257
combination weapons, **158–9**
Italian Wars, 59
maingauche (dagger), 130
Monte Varino castle destroyed,
14
pocket pistol, 214
rapier, 10, 110, 111
stiletto, 131, 133
submachine gun, 332
sword, 10, 91, 116
tournament helmets, 169
wheellock, 152

J

Jäger (riflemen), 177
jambiya, 11
Japan, Arisaka rifle, 259
armor, 22, **172–3**
arrow, 8
atom bomb used against, 277,
278
bow design, 146
firearms, 262–3
helmet, 23
incendiary launcher, 263
magari yari, 13
matchlock musket, 14, 100
Meiji restoration, 177
Mongol invasion, 61
naginata (staff weapon), 13, 75
Onin Wars, 100
perfect *katana*, 59
pistol Type 94, 292
ritual suicide, 126
sode garami, 13
swords, 11, **66–7**, **120–5**
tactics, 100, 101
tanto (dagger), 11
teppo matchlock, 157
World War II, 278
javelin, Celtic, 49
Roman, 28
Jericho, 26
Jerusalem, in crusades, 58
jian (sword), 188, 189
John the Fearless, 61
John of Salisbury, 91
Joubert, Alfred, 289
jousting, 12, 13, 87, 88–9
armor, 23, 166
Juan, Don, 98
Juliard, A, 214

K

kabuto (helmet), 23
Kadesh, Battle of, 27
Kalashnikov, Mikhail, 306
Kalashnikov, assault rifle, 278,
306–7, 331
KAR98K Mauser rifle, 301
kard (dagger), 134
kastane (sword), 128
katana (sword), 10–11, 59, 66–7,
121, 122–3, 127
katar (dagger), 11, 134
Katsuie, Shibata, 120
Katsuyori, Takeda, 101
Kennedy, Pres. John F, 257, 346
Kenya, improvised carbine, 348
shield, 271
Kerr, James, 222
Kevlar, 23, 351
khanda sword, 190
Khwarazam, empire of, 76
kilic, 11
kilij, 11

King revolver, 299
kissaki, 11
Kitchener, Lord, 177, 179
knife, African, 11, 281, 283
American fighting, 285
Aztec, 82
ballack, 131
chalcedony, 83
finger, 281
flint, 30, 82
flyssa, 280
hunting, 119
Japanese *kogatana*, 125
knuckle, 11
knuckleduster, 284
Larim fighting bracelet, 281
North American, **204–5**
obsidian, 82
pichangatti, 193
Sudanese, 282
throwing, 11, 283
trench, 284
World War II, 284
knight, armor, **86–7**, 166–9
Crusades, 58–9, 62
jousting, 58
Knights Templar, 90
lance, 12, 61, 73, 90
overview, **90–1**
swords, 62–5, 90–1
knobkerrie, 9
Knock, Henry, 265
knuckleduster, 284
knuckle knife, 11
Königgrätz, Battle of, 178, 249
kopis (sword), 129
Korea, helmet, 171
shotgun manufacture, 315
Korean War, 277, 278
Kosovo Polje, Battle of, 59
Krag rifle, 18, 300
bullet, 338
Krag-Jørgensen rifle, 257
kris, 11
Krupps, Alfred, 178
kukri (dagger), 11, 192
Kürsk, Battle of, 276
Kurtz bullet, 339
Kwabe, Gumpega, 201

L

L1A1 practice grenade, 342
L85 Individual Weapon, 311
L86 Light Support Weapon, 311,
331
L96A1 sniper rifle, 321
L98 Cadet Rifle, 311
Lachish, 27
Lamberti, 214
lance, couched adopted, 58
jousting, 12, 61, 73
Mongol, 76
landmines, 177
Landsknecht, 102, **108–9**, 114
Lang, Joseph, 222
langet, 13
Larim fighting bracelet, 281
laser-guided bombs, 279
Lateran Council, 60
le Bourgeois, Marin, 15
Le Mat, Jean-Alexandre, 219
Le Mat rifle, 253
Le Page, Henri, 238
Le Page, Jean, 238
Le Page, Pierre, 238
Le Page sport gun, **238–9**
Lebel rifle, 259
Lechfeld, Battle of, 58
Lee, James Paris, 19, 257
Lee, Robert E., 177, 178

Lee-Enfield rifle, 18, 300-1
Lee-Metford rifle, 257
Lefaucheux, Casimir, 225, 244
Lefaucheux, Caspar, 245
Lefaucheux, Eugène, 225
Lefaucheux percussion-cap
  revolver, 16
Leipzig, Battle of, 177
Leopold, Emperor, 233
Lepanto, Battle of, 98
Leuthen, Battle of, 99, 101
Lewis, Col. Isaac, 329
Lewis machine-gun, 20, 329
Lexington, 176, 243
Loewe, Ludwig, 19
Lombard League, 58
long gun, Dutch combination,
  149
  matchlock and flintlock, 148-9
  sporting, 312-13
longbow, at Agincourt, 8, 59, 208
  development of, 8, 60, 78
  early use of, 59
  English, 78-9
Lorenzoni, Michele, 153
Louis XIV, 99, 101
Louis XVI, 177, 233
Luger, Georg, 19, 253, 290, 334
Luger, pistol, 19, 290, 339

M

M1 (Garand) carbine, 21, 285,
  304-5
M1 helmet, 23
M1A1 Bazooka anti-tank rifle,
  341
M2 machine-gun, 323
M3 submachine-gun, 336
M14 rifle, 308
M16 rifle, 309, 310, 347
M16A2 assault rifle, 21
  with grenade launcher, 343
M18/1 Bergmann submachine-
  gun, 333
M19 grenade launcher, 344
M60 Browning machine-gun,
  325
M63 Stoner rifle, 309
M71 Mauser rifle, 17, 18, 249
M79 Blooper grenade launcher,
  344
M91/30 Mosin-Nagant rifle, 303
M107 sniper rifle, 321
M203 grenade launcher, 343, 347
M901 Astra pistol, 290
M1863 Springfield rifle, 17
M1871 Mauser rifle, 256
M1888 rifle designs, 257
M1889 Schmidt-Rubin rifle, 256
M1891 Mosin-Nagant rifle, 258,
  319
M1895 Colt, 322
M1895 Mannlicher rifle, 258
M1896 Mauser rifle, 259
M1902 Colt pistol, 290
M1903 Springfield rifle, 18, 300
M1905 Steyr-Mannlicher pistol,
  291
M1911 Colt, 19, 290, 323, 339
M1911 Steyr 'Hahn', 291
M1914 Hotchkiss machine-gun,
  325
M1917 Browning designs, 323,
  325
M1917 Enfield rifle, 300
M1921 machine-gun, 323, 332
M1935 Radom pistol, 293
M1944 Carbine, 301
MAC-10 submachine-gun, 337
mace, Asian, 74-5

Chinese, 60, 74
European, 136-7
flanged, 12
foliate, 137
Indian, 142
Mongol, 76
Ottoman gurz, 75
spiked, 73, 142, 197
stone, 26
Turkish, 13
wheellock, 158
machete, 11
machine-gun, AK47, 306-7, 331,
  343
AK74, 331
ammunition, 338
Bergmann, 21
in Boer War, 254
definition, 17, 19
first use of, 177
gas-operated, 324-5
Gatling, 17, 179
heavy, 19
Hotchkiss, 20, 289, 324-5
light, 308, 328-31
Maxim, 19, 20, 177, 228, 322,
  323, 324, 328
MG43, 326-7
recoil-operated, 322-3
Russo-Japanese War, 276
Vickers, 20
World War I, 20, 276-7, 286,
  289, 328
World War II, 20, 21, 330, 336,
  349
MacLean, Samuel, 329
madu (parrying stick), 193
magari yari (trident), 13
magazine, design, 18
Magnum, 298, 339
Maiano, Giovanni, 167
mail, aventail, 23, 87, 93, 268
  failings of, 11, 170
  Indian, 170, 268
  Roman, 22
  shirt, 23, 52, 91, 92, 93
maingauche (dagger), 130
Makarov pistol, 293
Maldon, Battle of, 51
Malibar Coast sword, 129
Mannlicher rifle, 258
Mannlicher-Berthier rifle, 289
Mannlicher-Carcano rifle, 257
Maori War, 203
maquahuitl (club), 83
Marathon, Battle of, 26, 28, 42
Marengo, Battle of, 177
Marignano, Battle of, 114-5
Marlborough, Duke of, 99, 101
Marne, Battle of, 276, 288
Mars pistol, 229, 291, 339
Martini-Henry rifle, 17, 194,
  249, 265
Maschinen Pistole 43, 305
MAT 49 submachine-gun, 336
matchlock, arquebus, 61
British, 14, 149
Chinese, 262
English, 148
incendiary launcher, 263
Indian, 260-1
Japanese, 14
long gun, 148-9
mechanism, 14-15
pistol, 108, 150-1, 156-7, 160,
  260
revolving musket, 261
teppo, 263
wall gun, 262
Mau-Mau carbine, 348
Maurice of Nassau, 99

Mauser, Peter-Paul, 256
Mauser, bolt-action rifle, 245
breech-action rifle, 248-9
Broomhandle, 228
infanteriegewehr (Gewehr) 98
  rifle, 259, 278
KAR98K carbine, 301
M71 rifle, 17
pistols, 290
repeater rifle, 18, 256, 258-9
sniper rifle, 318
UK agent, 313
Maxim, Hiram, 20, 177
Maxim, machine-gun, 19, 20,
  177, 228, 322, 323, 324, 328
Maximilian I, Emperor, 108
Mechem/Milkor grenade
  launcher, 345
meda (matchlock rifle), 263
MEIJI 30 Arisaka rifle, 259
Melanesia, shields, 272
Melsa, Sir John, 87
mempo (mask), 23
mercenary fighters, hoplites, 42-3
  Landsknecht, 102, 108-9, 114
Mescalam-Dug, helmet, 32
Mesopotamia, 26-7, 32-3
Metford, William, 257
MG08 machine-gun, 20, 328
MG42 machine-gun, 323
MG43 machine-gun, 326-7
MGL Mk1 grenade launcher, 345
Middle East, modern warfare, 278-9
Midway, Battle of, 278
Miller, Gen. William, 185
millile, cruise, 277
Mills, William, 342
Mills bomb, 342
Minié, Claude-Étienne, 178
Minié (bullet), 178, 220
Minimi, FN machine-gun, 330
  Squad Automatic Weapon, 326
Minoa, swords, 10
miquelet lock, invention, 15
  musket, 155, 247
  pistol, 162, 163, 215
missile, cruise, 279
Mississippi rifle, 236
Miyamoto, Musashi, 127
MLE, 1842 Mousqueton
  D'Artillerie rifle, 237
  1853 Fusil Reglementaire rifle,
  237
  1886/93 Lebel rifle, 259
  1916 Berthier, 301
MOD.90 Barrett sniper rifle, 321
Modin-Nagant rifle, 258
Mondragon, Manuel, 304
Mongol, armour, 22
  bow, 8
  dagger, 77
  helmet, 23
  tactics and warfare, 59, 60-1
  warriors, 76-7
Monkey Tail (carbine), 241, 266
Monte Varino, castle of, 14
Montgomery, Gabriel, 169
Morgarten, Battle of, 72
morning star, 141, 142
mortar, 302
Moscow, 278
Mosin-Nagant rifle, 258, 301, 303
Mosin-Nogant sniper rifle, 319
Mototada, Torii, 127
Mousqueton D'Artillerie rifle,
  237
MP5 submachine-guns, 21, 334-
  5, 347
MP18/1 Bergmann machine-
  gun, 21
MP40 submachine-gun, 332

Mughal, armour, 22
mujahidin, 279, 307, 347
multi-shot weapons, 264-5
Murten, Battle of, 108
musket, Brown Bess, 149, 153,
  233, 243
  drill, 100
  English flintlock, 148
  English matchlock, 14, 153
  flintlock, 15, 101, 148, 149,
  232-3
  German, 14
  introduction of, 14, 98
  Japanese, 14, 100, 157
  long land-pattern flintlock,
  149
  matchlock, 14-15, 108, 150-1,
  153, 156-7
  miquelet lock, 155
  muzzle-loaded rifle-, 220
  Ottoman tüfenk, 247
  percussion-cap, 236-7
  revolving, 261
  rifling barrels, 99
  short land-pattern flintlock,
  149
  tactical use, 99
  teppo matchlock (Japanese), 157
Mycena, swords, 10

N O

Nadir Shah, 99
Naga people, club, 9
Nagasaki, 277, 278
Nagashino, Battle of, 100, 101,
  127
naginata (staff weapon), 13, 75
Nambu Taisho pistol, 219
Namibia, invaded, 178
Nancy, Battle of, 61, 108
Napoleon III (Bonaparte), 101,
  177, 178, 238
Napoleonic Wars, 107, 180, 181,
  182-3, 194, 230, 242
Narmer, Palette of, 12
NATO alliance, 278, 308
Navy SEAL, 347
needle-gun, Dreyse, 178, 249
Negev machine-gun, 330
Nepal, daggers, 192-3
Netherlands, civil war, 99
  pocket pistol, 215
New Britain, shields, 273
New Zealand, Maori, 203
Nicopolis, Battle of, 59
Nine Years' War, 101
Nitro Express bullet, 338
Nobunaga, Oda, 100, 101, 127
Norman Conquest, 58, 92
Normandy landings, 278
North America, bayonets, 194-5
  Harper's Ferry pistol, 214
  Indian War, 177, 206, 241
  knives and clubs, 204-5
  Massachusetts Indians, 99
  revolvers, 218-19
  War of Independence, 107,
  176-7, 233, 243
  see also USA
North Vietnam, helmet, 351
Northern Ireland, submachine-
  gun, 349
Norway, repeater rifle, 257
Novara, Battle of, 98
obsidian, edged weapons,
  10, 82, 203
Oceania, clubs and daggers,
  202-3
  shields, 272-3
Okinawa, 278

Omdurman, Battle of, 177, 179
Onin Wars, 100
Opium War, 176
Oswald, Lee Harvey, 257
Otto I, 58
Ottoman Empire, firearms, 246-7
  swords, 186-7
  tactics, 61, 99-100

P

P'08 Luger pistol, 19, 290-1
P90 submachine-gun, 337
Palestine, Knights Templar, 90
Panipat, Battle of, 98
Papua New Guinea, shields,
  272-3
parang, 11
parrying weapons, 193
partisan (staff weapon), 13
Passchendaele, 277
patuki (club), 203
pauldrons, 95
Pavia, Battle of, 98, 108, 138-9
Peacemaker, 18
Pearl Harbor, 278
pellet-lock gun, 244
Peloponnesian Wars, 42
Pembridge, Sir Richard, 86
Penobscot people, stone club, 205
pepperbox pistol, 16, 217
percussion-cap, mechanism, 16
  pistol, 216-17
  revolver, 218-19, 222-3
percussion lock, pistol, 162
Permjakov, Ivan, 154
Persia, Alexander defeats, 28
  cavalry, 27
  empire, 27-8
  mace, 75
  swords, 128, 186
Peru, civil war, 99
phalanx, 12, 28, 42-3
Philip II of Spain, 99
Philippines, Japanese invasion,
  278
  US occupation, 177
Phillipsburg, Siege of, 99, 101
pichangatti (knife), 193
pick, fighting, 199
Pickett's Charge, 178
Pietro Beretta SpA, 293
piha kaetta (dagger), 135
pike, demise of, 101
  Japanese, 101
  Landsknecht, 108, 109
  overview, 12, 13
  at Pavia, 98, 138
  sarissa, 12, 28
  spontoon, 13
  Swiss, 13, 114
  tactical use of, 98-9
pill-lock carbine, 263
pilum (spear), 8, 28, 47
pin-fire shotgun, 244, 245
pistol, ammunition, 16, 224-5,
  267
  Astra, 290
  Beretta, 293, 294
  Bergmann, 229, 267
  Borchardt, 19, 290
  brass cartridge, 224-5
  breech-loading, 163, 217
  Browning, 229, 292
  cavalry, 215, 219
  coastguard, 217
  Colt, 18, 290, 292
  Cooper brass cartridge, 16
  Desert Eagle, 20, 295
  Dragoon, 219
  duelling/target, 15, 17, 212, 216

pistol, (cont.)
European, 17, **160-3**, **212-17**
flintlock, 15, **212-15**, 246, 261
four-barrel tap-action, 213
Gabbett-Fairfax Mars, 229, 291
Glock, 295
Harper's Ferry, 214
Heckler & Koch, 294, 295
horse, 247
improvised, 348-9
Luger, 19, 290-1
Makarov, 293
matchlock, 108, **150-1**, **156-7**, 160, 260
Mauser designs, 290
Nambu Taisho, 219
Peacemaker, 18
pepperbox, 16, 217
percussion-cap, **17**, **216-17**
plastic manufacture, 294
pocket, 213, 214-15, 224
Queen Anne, 213
Radom, 293
self-loading, **228-9**, **290-5**
shield, 269
Star, 292
Stechkin, 293
Steyr "Hahn," 291
Steyr-Mannlicher, 291
under-hammer pistol, 217
Walther PP, 293
Webley, 267, 291
Webley-Fosbery, 229
see also revolver
Plains Indian, weapons, 208-9
Plamya grenade launcher, 344
plastic, in gun manufacture, 294, 330
Plataea, hoplites at, 42
Poitiers, Battle of, 60, 78
Poland, German invasion, 277
Radom pistol, 293
poleaxe, 13, 72, 140
police, revolvers, 296, 298-9
Polynesia, cleaver, 9
Port Arthur, 276
Portugal, introduces firearms to Japan, 262
matchlock, 156
powder, and ball weapons, 14
flask, 227
horn, 239
PPSH41 submachine gun, 333
prehistory, timeline, 26-7
weapons, **30-1**
primer, 19
Prince, Frederick, 245
projector, antitank, 340
Prussia, armed forces, 148, 178
bayonet charge, 194
Jäger (riflemen), 177
Potsdam musket, 233
Pryse, Charles, 225
PSG-1 Heckler & Koch sniper rifle, 319
PTRD antitank rifle, 341
Pu-Abi, Queen (Sumerian), 32
Python revolver, 299
PzB41 antitank rifle, 341

Q R

quarrel (crossbow bolt), 78
quarterstaff, 13
quillon, 11, 68, 69, 133
quiver, Indian Maratha, 147
Plains Indian, 208
radar, 276
Rameses II, Pharaoh, 27
rapier, 10-11, 112
footsoldier use, 105

Ravenna, Battle of, 98
recoil, **20**, 21
Red Army, **302-3**, 306
Redcoat (British Army), **242-3**
Reformation, 99
religion, Islam, 27, 29
wars, 58-60, 70, 99
Remington, automatic shotgun, 313
Double Derringer pistol, 224
Magnum bullet, 338, 339
pistol, 18
rolling block rifle, 249
Reno, Maj. Marcus, 206
repeating rifles, **252-3**, **256-9**, **300-1**, **304-5**, **308-9**
Revolutionary War, see American War of Independence
revolutions, 176-9
revolver, Allen & Wheelock, 267
alternative to, 213
Bodeo, 267
brass cartridge, **224-5**
break-open, 219
breech-loading, 176
Colt models, 18, 176, 218-19, 224-5, **226-7**, 295-6, 299
double-action, 222
Enfield, 297, 339
flintlock, 212
grenade launcher, 345
invention, 18
Lefaucheux, 16
Magnum, 298-9
musket, 261
pepperbox, 16, 217
percussion-cap, **218-19**, **222-3**
pocket, 298
post-1900, **296-9**
revolving rifle, 16, 245, 252-3
Smith & Wesson, 296-8
Webley & Scott, 296
Richard I, King, 58
ricochet, used in combat, 99
rifle, 3-Line, 258
anti-tank, **340-1**
Arisaka, 259
assault, 21, 309, **310-11**
automatic, 21, 347
Baker, **234-5**, 243
Berthier, 300-1
bluing, 237
bolt-action, 17, 19, 245
break-open, 244
breech-loader, 178, 194, **248-9**
Browning Automatic, 304
carbine M1944, 301
cartridges, **267**
Colt Patterson revolving, 245
Dreyse needle, 178, 249
Enfield, 178, 237, **250-1**, 267, 300-1
flintlock, 152-3, **232-3**, 264-5
folding butt, 305, 308
Galili, 309
GEW43, 305
Hall, 233
Heckler & Koch G41, 309
Henry, 253
improved range of, 178
infanteriegewehr, 257
Kalashnikov, 278, **306-7**, 331
Krag, 18, 300
Krag-Jørgensen, 257
Le Mat, 253
Lebel, 259
Lee-Enfield, 18, 221, 267, 284, 300-1
Lee-Metford, 257, 267
long guns, **312-13**
magazine, 300, 304, 308-9

rifle (cont.)
Mannlicher, 258
Mannlicher-Berthier, 289
Mannlicher-Carcano, 257
Martini-Henry, 17, 195, 249, 265, 267
Mauser designs, 17, 98, 245, 248-9, 256, 258-9, 278, 285, 318
Mosin-Nagant, 258, 301, 303
Mousqueton D'Artillerie, 237
multi-shot, **264-5**
percussion-cap, 17, 221, **236-7**
pits, 178
Remington rolling block, 249
repeater, manual-loading, 18, **252-3**, **256-9**, 289, **300-1**
self-loading, **304-5**, **308-9**
revolving, 19, 245, 252-3
rifling, 21
Rigby Mauser, 313
rook and rabbit, 245
Schmidt, 19
Schmidt-Rubin, 256
sight, 303, 310, 318, 320, 326
sniper, 21, 302-3, 304, **318-21**
Spencer, 253, 267
sport guns, **238-9**, **244-5**, **312-13**
Springfield designs, 17, 178, 236-7, 249, 267, 300
Sturmgewehr STG44, 305
Tokarev, 304
under-hammer turret, 267
Westley Richards, 312
Winchester, 178, 253, 267, 312
World War I German, 286
see also ammunition and bayonet and carbine and musket
rifle-musket, 220
Rigby, John, 313
Rigby Mauser rifle, 313
Rivera, Diego, 84
Riviere, Isaac, 216
rocket, invented, 176
V-2, 278
Rocroi, Battle of, 99
Roman, armor, 22, 23, **44-5**, 46, 181
auxiliaries, 46
edged weapons, 11, 27, **44-5**, 181
empire, 27, 28-9
gladius, 10, 28, 45, 46-7, 181
helmet, 23
legionaries, **46-7**
pikes, 99
pilum, 8, 28, 47
punishments, 46
Rome sacked, 48, 109
scutum, 28, 44, 46
spatha, 11, 27
rondel (dagger), 11, 69
rook and rabbit rifle, 245
rotary-breech action, 313
Royal Ordnance Factory, 19
RP46 Degtyarev machine gun, 329
RPG-7V grenade launcher, 345
RPK74 machine gun, 331
Rudolf IV, Hapsburg Duke of Austria, 93
Russia, AK47 Kalashnikov, 306-7, 331
bardiche, 141
cavalry saber, 180
Crimean War, 154, 177, 178, 180, 241
flintlock, 154
Infantry Code, 101
Japanese attack, 276

Russia (cont.)
Maxim guns, 20
Napoleonic front, 177
Pioneer sword, 181
repeater rifle, 258
revolvers used, 225
Russo-Japanese War, 276

S

S18-100 antitank rifle, 341
S-686 Beretta shotgun, 313
SA80 rifle, **310-11**, 331
sabre, 10, 11, 128, 182, 184-5, 191
Russian cavalry, 180, 186
Turkish, 187
Turko-Mongolian, 186
sacrifice, Aztec, 82, 83
Sadakatsu, Gassan, 123
saif (North African sword), 187
sainte (spear), 75
Saladin, 59, 70
sallet, 23, 88, 89
Samori Touré, 179
samurai, armor, 22, 127, **172-3**
helmet, 23
sword, **66-7**, **120-5**, 127
tanto (dagger), 11
warriors, 126-17
San Romano, Battle of, 61
Sargon of Agade, 26
sarissa, 12, 28
Saxon, dagger, 11
long-handled ax, 73
spear, 8
Scandinavia, ax, 9
German invasion, 277
staff weapons, 72, 73
Schmidt, Col. Rudolf, 19, 256
Schmidt-Rubin rifle, 256
Schnellfeuer pistol, 290
Schwarzlose machine gun, 20
scimitar, 128, 198
Scotland, broadsword, 106
cavalry charge, 230
claymore, 102
Falkirk defeat, 8
Highland dirk, 131
pistol, 162
snaphaunce, 153
Wark castle captured, 59
scramasax (dagger), 11, 50
scutum (shield), 28, 44, 46
scythe, 12
seax, 50
Sedan, Battle of, 178
serpentine, 14
Sevastopol, 177, 178
Seven Pines, Battle of, 177
Seven Years War, 99, 101, 149
SG43 machine gun, 324
SGM Goryunov machine gun, 324
Shaka (Zulu chief), 200
shamshir sword, 128
shaped charge, 340
Sharps, Christian, 217, 240
Sharps percussion-cap carbine, 16
Shaw, Joshua, 16, 245
shell, shrapnel, 176
shield, African, **270-1**
Argive, 27-8
Australian, 211
Aztec, 83
Celtic, 49
Egyptian ceremonial, 35
Indian dahl, 171, **269**
Oceanic, **272-3**
pistol, 269
scutum, 28, 44, 46

shield (cont.)
Viking, 52
Zulu war, 270
Shigeyasu, Kunitomo Tobei, 157
Shivaji, 100
shortbow, Battle of Hastings, 59
shotgun, automatic, 313
Beretta, 313
cartridge, **267**
flintlock, 15, 155
Franci SPAS, 314
Greener Police, 315
Hadley flintlock, 15
over-and-under, 313
pin-fire, 244, 245
pump-action, 19
rotary-breech, 313
self-loading, 19
USAS-12, 315
Winchester models, 315
shotpistol, improvised, 349
Shrapnel, Henry, 176
Sicilian Vespers, War of the, 59
siege, artillery, 100
Assyrian, 27
Sevastopol, 177, 178
warfare, 98-9
sight, optical, 345
telescopic, 303, 310, 318, 320, 326
Sikh Akali sect, 269
silencer, 21
Simonov, assault rifle, 343
SKS with grenade launcher, 343
Skoda machine gun, 20
Skorpion submachine gun, 337
slavery, 221
smallsword, 10, 11, **112**
Smith, Charles, 245
Smith, Horace, 18
Smith, Samuel, 245
Smith & Wesson, 18-19, 224, 225, 267, 296-8
SMLE rifle with grenade launcher, 342
snaphaunce, 15, 153, 160, 162, 247
Snider, Jacob, 250
sniper, American War of Independence, 243
rifles, 21, 302-3, 304, **318-21**
sode garami, 13
Solomon Islands, shield, 272
Solothurn antitank rifle, 341
Somme, Battle of the, 277
sosun pattah sword, 191
Soult, Marshal, 242
South Africa, club, 9
grenade launcher, 345
improvised pistol, 348
shotgun manufacture, 315
South Korea, shotgun manufacture, 315
US action in, 277, 278
Spain, Astra pistol, 290
cavalry pistol, 215
conquistadors, 84, 99
Granada falls, 59
machine gun, 331
miquelet lock, 15
pistol, 163, 292
Spanish-American War, 177, 178
tercio, 13, 99
War of Succession, 101
spangenhelm (helmet), 23, 50, 51, 86
Spanish-American War, 177, 178
Spanish War of Succession, 101
Sparta, 42

spatha (Roman sword), 11, 27
spear, African, 199
  angon, 50
  Aztec, 83
  boar, 13, 117
  Celtic, 49
  design, 45
  Egyptian, 34-5
  Greek, 40, 42-3
  North American, 204
  obsidian, 203
  prehistoric, 31
  Roman, 8, 28, 45, 47, 50
  saintie, 75
  samurai, 127
  Saxon, 8
  stabbing, 200
  Viking, 55
  Zulu, 200, 201
Special Boat Unit, 346
Spencer, Christopher, 18, 253
Spion Kop, 179
Spitfire, 277
spontoon, 13
sport guns, **238-9, 244-5, 312-13**
Springfield, rifles, 17, 236-7, 249, 267, 300, 339
Spurs, Battle of the, 98
Sri Lanka, dagger, 135
  matchlock, 156
  staff weapons, 142-3
  swords, **128-9**
staff weapons, Asian, **74-5**
  European, **72-3, 136-7, 140-1**
  glossary, 13
  Indian, **142-3, 196-7**
  overview, **12-13**
  Sri Lankan, **142-3**
Stalin, Joseph, 302
Stalingrad, Battle for, 278, 302-3
Starr, Nathan, 219
Stechkin pistol, 293
steel, manufacture, 27, 177
Sten submachine gun, 333, 349
Steyr "Hahn" pistol, 291
Steyr-Mannlicher pistol, 291, 339
STG44 rifle, 305, 308
stiletto, 11, 131, 133
stone, club, 205
Stoner, Eugene, 309
Stuart, Jeb, 220
Studenmayer, 194
Sturmgewehr STG44 rifle, 305
submachine gun, 21, 308, **332-7, 347**, 349
  improvised, 349
submarine, German U-boat, 277
  Turtle, 176
Sudan, fighting bracelet, 281
  knife, 282
  Mahdists defeated, 177, 179
  shield, 270, 271
Suez crisis, 277
Sumeria, organized warfare, 32
Sumpter, Fort, 177
SVT40 Tokarev rifle, 304
Sweden, cavalry sword, 105
Switzerland, antitank rifle, 341
  halberd, 72, 141
  pike, 13, 114
sword, African, 282-3
  aikuchi, 66
  American Civil War, **184-5**
  Baker rifle sword bayonet, 235
  baselard, 64
  bayonet, 194-5, 242, 243
  boar, 117
  broadsword, 104, 106, 108
  Bronze Age, 48
  cadet, 183

sword (cont.)
  cased, 113
  Castillon, 63
  cavalry, **104-7**, 180, 181, 182, 184-5, 189
  Chinese, 67, 77, 188-9
  colichemarde forte, 113
  crusader, 62
  cutlass, 182
  dao, 9, 77, 188, 191
  decorated, 112-13
  doppelhänder, 102
  double-edged, 54, 65
  dress, **112-13**
  Düsack, 105
  eben, 282, 283
  Egyptian, 36
  estoc, 11
  European, **48-51, 62-5, 102-5, 112-13, 180-3**
  execution, 102-3, 191
  falchion, 116
  firanghi, 128
  flame-edged, 102, 109
  French, 181, 182-3
  gladius, 28, 45, 181
  glossary, 11
  hand-and-a-half, 64, 91
  hanger, 106, 116, 117
  hunting, 105, **116-19**
  Indian, **128-9, 190-1**
  infantry, **104-7**, 184-5
  Italian, 10, 91, 116
  Japanese, **66-7, 120-5**
  jian, 189
  kastane, 128
  katana, 10, 11, 59, 66-7, 121, 122-3, 126, 127
  khanda, 190
  khepesh, 35
  knuckle guards, 112-13
  medieval, 63
  mortuary, 107
  North African *saif*, 187
  Ottoman designs, **186-7**
  parade, 102
  pioneer, 183
  rapier, 10, 107, **110-11**
  replaced, 11, 213
  riding, 63
  saber, 10, 11, 128, 180, 182, 184-5, 186, 187, 191
  Saxon, **50-1**
  schiavona, 106
  scimitar, 128, 198
  short, 10, 36, 65
  smallsword, 10, 11, **112**
  sosun pattah, 191
  spatha, 11, 27
  Sri Lankan, **128-9**
  sword-breaker dagger, 11, 132
  sword-broadsword, 104
  tachi, 67
  talwar, 128, 191
  Tibetan, 188-9
  transitional, 65
  two-handed, **102-3**, 109
  vechevoral, 190
  Viking, 54-5
  wakizashi, 67, 121, 122-3, **124-5**, 127
  war, 63
Sword-hunt Edict, 100

T

tabar (axe), 142, 197
tachi (sword), 67
talwar (saber), 10, 11, 128, 191
tank, antitank weapons, 21, **340-1**

tank (cont.)
  battle, 276
  crew helmet, 350
  revolver, 297
  rifles, 305
  World War I, 277, 286
Tannenberg, Battle of, 59
tanto (dagger), 11
Tanzania, invaded, 178
telegraph, 176
Templar knights, 90
Tenochtitlán, 98
teppo (matchlock rifle), 263
tercio formation, 13, 99
terrorism, 277, 347
Thebes, 42
Thirty Years War, 99, 100-1, 164
Thompson, Gen. John Tagliaferro, 332
Thompson people, bow and arrow, 208
Thuer, Alexander, 267
Tiberius, Emperor, 45
Tibet, matchlock musket, 262
  swords, 188-9
Tiglath-Pileser III, 27
Til-Tuba, Battle of, 33
timeline, 3000bce-1000ce, 26-7
  1000-1500, 58-9
  1500-1775, 98-9
  1775-1899, 176-7
  1901-2000, 276-7
Togo, invaded, 178
Tokarev, Fedor, 304
Tokarev weapons, 292, 304
tomahawk, 9, 205
Tommy Gun, 332
tongi ax, 196
top (helmet), 23
trace italienne, fortification, 100
Trafalgar, Battle of, 177
training, gunnery schools, 101
  knightly, 90
  see also drilling
Trajan's Column, 46
Treaty of Versailles, 323
trench warfare, 178, 276
trident, 12, 13
trigger, development, 14, 21
trousse, hunting, 118-19
Truce of God, 58
tüfenk (musket), 247
turban, Indian, 269
Turkey, armor, 22
  fortified village, 26
  helmet, 23
  mace, 13, 75
  swords, 10, 129
  yataghan (sword), 10
Turtle (submarine), 176
Tutankhamen, 35, 36, 38-9

U V W

U-boat, 277
Uganda, finger knife, 281
Uji, Battle of, 126
UK, antitank rifle, 340
Ulm, Napoleonic campaign, 177
under-hammer, pistol, 217
  turret rifle, 267
United Kingdom, coastguard pistol, 217
  dueling/target pistol, 216
  Lee-Enfield rifle, 18, 221, 267, 284, 300-1
  musket design, 233
  percussion cap revolver, **222-3**
  pocket pistol, 215
  rook and rabbit rifle, 245
  Whitworth rifle, 237

Ur, 26, 32
urban warfare, 278
USA, American Civil War, 177, 178, **220-1**
  antitank rifle, 341
  bayonet, 285
  fighting knife, 285
  grenade, 343
  grenade launcher, 344
  helmet, 23
  Indian Wars, 177, 206
  invades Afghanistan, 347
  Korean action, 278
  musket design, 233
  Navy SEAL, **346-7**
  Prohibition era, 333
  revolvers, 296-9
  rifles, 236-7, 300, 304-5, 308-9, 312
  submachine guns, 332-3, 337, 347
  terrorist attack, 277
  Vietnam War, 277, 278, 316, 345, 347
  World War I helmets, 351
  World War II, 278
  see also North America
USAS-12 shotgun, 315
USSR, invades Afghanistan, 279
  antitank rifle, 341
  collapse, 277
  Communism, 277
  German invasion, 278
  grenade, 343
  grenade launcher, 344-5, 347
  machine gun, 20, 331
  Makarov pistol, 293
  sniper rifles, 319
  Stechkin pistol, 293
  submachine gun, 333
  Tokarev weapons, 292, 304
Uzi submachine gun, 336
V-2 rocket, 278
vamplate, 167
vechevoral sword, 190
Verdun, Battle of, 276, 288
vervelle, 86
Vickers machine-gun, 20, 323
Vienna, Congress of, 178
  siege of, 100
Vietnam War, 277, 278
  grenade launcher, 345
  helicopter use, 316
  Navy SEAL, 347
Viking, armor, 22, 52-3
  ax, 9, 52-3, 73
  defeated at Clontarf, 58
  helmet, 23, 53
  rise of, 29
  spear, 55
  swords, 54-5
Villar Perosa submachine gun, 332
volley gun, flintlock, 265
von Augezd, Baron Odkolek, 324
Von Dreyse, 248, 256
von Mannlicher, Ferdinand, 19, 258, 291
von Moltke, 178
von Steuben, Augustus, 177
von Wallenstein, Albrecht, 101
VP70M Heckler & Koch pistol, 294
VZ/68 Skorpion submachine gun, 337
WA2000 Walther sniper gun, 320
Wadgaon, Battle of, 197
Waffenfabrik Loewe, 228
Waffenfabrik Mauser, 19
wakizashi (sword), 67, 121, 122-3, **124-15**, 127
Wales, longbow, 8, 78, 91

wall gun, 262
Walther, pistol, 293
  sniper gun, 21, 320
war hammer, 73
  wheellock, 158
warfare, beginning of organized, 32
  siege techniques, 32
Wark castle, 59
Warsaw Pact, 278
Washington, George, 177
Waterloo, Battle of, 177, 242
Waters, John, 212
Weatherby Magnum bullet, 339
Webley, pistol, 229, 267, 291
Webley & Scott revolver, 296
Wellington, Duke of, 242, 294
Werndl, 291
Wesson, Daniel, 17, 18
Westley Richards, guns, 241, 266, 312
Westphalia, Peace of, 99, 101
wheellock, dag, 160
  design, 14-15, 148
  muskets, 14, 152-3
  pistol, 14-15, 150, **158-9**, 160
White, Rollin, 224
White Mountain, Battle of, 164
Whiting, JH, 291
Whitney, Eli, 226
Whitworth, Sir Joseph, 237
William, King Frederick I, 148, 233
William, Norman duke, 59
William Louis of Nassau, 99
Wilson, James, 265
Winchester, Oliver, 253
Winchester, bullet, 338, 339
  rifles, 18, 178, 253, 267, 312
  shotguns, 315
windage, 21
World War I, bayonet, 284
  causes, 179
  cost of, 288
  French infantry, **288-9**
  gas, 286
  German weapons, 286-7
  grenades, 289
  helmets, 23, **350-1**
  machine guns, 20, 276-7, 286, 289, 328
  pistols, 292, 296
  rifles, 289, 300-1
  shotgun, 314, 315
  snipers, 318
  tanks, 286
  timeline, 276
  Treaty of Versailles, 323
World War II, bayonet, 285
  causes, 247
  machine guns, 20, 21, 330, 336, 349
  pistols, 293
  Red Army, **302-3**
  rifles, 308
  snipers, 302, 318
  timeline, 276-8
Wounded Knee, Battle of, 177

X Y Z

yataghan (sword), 10
Yorimasa, Minamoto, 126
Yorktown, surrender of, 176, 243
Yoshihira, Minamoto, 126
Ypres, 277
Zaitsev, Vasili, 303
ZB 53 machine gun, 324
Zeppelin airships, 277
Zulu, knobkerrie, 9
  war shield, 200, 270
  warrior, **200-1**

ACKNOWLEDGEMENTS

The publisher would like to thank the following for their kind permission to reproduce their photographs.

ABBREVIATIONS KEY:
Key: a = above, b = below, c = center, l=-left, r=-right, t=-top, f=-far, s =-sidebar

1 DK Images: By kind permission of the Trustees of the Wallace Collection (c). **2-3** Alamy Images: Danita Delimont . **8** DK Images: The Museum of London (tr); By kind permission of the Trustees of the Wallace Collection (tl). **10** DK Images: Museum of the Order of St John, London (b). **11** DK Images: Pitt Rivers Museum, University of Oxford (tr); By kind permission of the Trustees of the Wallace Collection (tc). **12** DK Images: By kind permission of the Trustees of the Wallace Collection (b). **13** DK Images: By kind permission of the Trustees of the Wallace Collection (cl) (b). **14** DK Images: By kind permission of the Trustees of the Wallace Collection (br). **16** DK Images: Courtesy of the Gettysburg National Military Park, PA (cla). **22** Ancient Art & Architecture Collection: (r). DK Images: Courtesy of David Edge (b). **23** DK Images: Universitets Oldsaksamling, Oslo (tl). **24-25** The Art Archive: Museo della Civiltà Romana, Rome / Dagli Orti . **26** Corbis: Pierre Colombel. **27** akg-images: Erich Lessing. **28** akg-images: Rabatti - Domingie (c). DK Images: British Museum (b). **29** Corbis: Keren Su (r). **32** akg-images: Iraq Museum (r). Ancient Art & Architecture Collection: (l). **33** The Art Archive: British Museum / Dagli Orti (bl). DK Images: British Museum (tl). **34** The Trustees of the British Museum: (l). DK Images: British Museum (cr). **35** Corbis: Sandro Vannini (r) (cb). DK Images: British Museum (tl) (cl) (b). **36** DK Images: British Museum (tl) (b). **36-37** DK Images: British Museum (ca). **37** DK Images: British Museum (tr). **38-39** The Art Archive: Egyptian Museum Cairo / Dagli Orti. **40** DK Images: British Museum (cr) Shefton Museum of Antiquities, University of Newcastle: (cl). **41** DK Images: British Museum (cr) (br) (bl). **42** akg-images: Nimatalla (bl). DK Images: British Museum (tl) (c) (cra) (crb). **42-43** Bridgeman Art Library: Louvre, Paris / Peter Willi (c). **43** The Art Archive: Archaeological Museum, Naples / Dagli Orti . Shefton Museum of Antiquities, University of Newcastle: (cla). **44** DK Images: British Museum (bc); Courtesy of the Ermine Street Guard (cla); Judith Miller / Cooper Owen (cr); University Museum of Newcastle (bl). **45** akg-images: Electa (br). DK Images: British Museum (c); Courtesy of the Ermine Street Guard (fclb/ lancea and pilum); Courtesy of the Ermine Street Guard (tr); University Museum of Newcastle (cr). **46** The Art Archive: National Museum Bucharest / Dagli Orti (A) (tr). Corbis: Patrick Ward (cb). DK Images: Courtesy of the Ermine Street Guard (cr); Judith Miller / Cooper Owen (tl); University Museum of Newcastle (crb). **47** Archivi Alinari: Museo della Civiltà Romana, Rome (b). DK Images: British Museum (tl); Courtesy of the Ermine Street Guard (tr/short sword and scabbard) (cla). **48** DK Images: British Museum (cr); The Museum of London (cl). **49** DK Images: British Museum (tl) (r) (crb) (t); The Museum of London (cl); The Museum of London (clb) (tc). **50** DK Images: The Museum of London (clb/short and long spears); The Museum of London (b). **51** Ancient Art & Architecture Collection: (br). **52** DK Images: Danish National Museum (crb/engraved iron axehead). **53** Ancient Art & Architecture Collection: (tl). DK Images: The Museum of London (bl); Universitets Oldsaksamling, Oslo (tr). **54** DK Images: Danish National Museum (c/double-edged swords). **54-55** DK Images: The Museum of London (ca). **56-57** The Art Archive: British Library . **58** Bridgeman Art Library: Musée de la Tapisserie, Bayeux, France, with special authorisation of the city of Bayeux. **59** Bridgeman Art Library: Bibliothèque Nationale, Paris. **60** The Art Archive: British Library (tl). Bridgeman Art Library: Courtesy of the Warden and Scholars of New College, Oxford (c). **61** Bridgeman Art Library: National Gallery, London. **63** DK Images: By kind permission of the Trustees of the Wallace Collection (t). **64-65** DK Images: By kind permission of the Trustees of the Wallace Collection (b). **65** DK Images: By kind permission of the Trustees of the Wallace Collection (double-edged sword). **72** DK Images: By kind permission of the Trustees of the Wallace Collection (tl/poleaxe) (clb/German halberd). **73** DK Images: British Museum (bl) (bc) (tr); Museum of London (br); By kind permission of the Trustees of the Wallace Collection (cl/war hammer). **74** DK Images: By kind permission of the Trustees of the Wallace Collection (clb). **76** The Art Archive: British Library (l). Bridgeman Art Library: National Palace Museum, Taipei, Taiwan (b). DK Images: British Museum (tl). **77** Bridgeman Art Library: Bibliothèque Nationale, Paris. DK Images: British Museum (cra/ Mongolian dagger and sheath). **78** DK Images: By kind permission of the Trustees of the Wallace Collection (br). **78-79** DK Images: By kind permission of the Trustees of the Wallace Collection (hunting crossbow and arrows). **79** The Art Archive: British Library (tr). DK Images: Robin Wigington, Arbour Antiques, Ltd., Stratford-upon-Avon (cr). **82** DK Images: INAH (cl) (cla) (tl) (cr). **82-83** DK Images: INAH (b). **83** DK Images: British Museum (tl); INAH (cr) (c) (bl). **84-85** Corbis: Charles & Josette Lenars. **86** DK Images: Courtesy of Warwick Castle, Warwick (tc). **87** DK Images: By kind permission of the Trustees of the Wallace Collection (c/hunskull basinet). **89** DK Images: By kind permission of the Trustees of the Wallace Collection (tl) (tr) (crb). **90** akg-images: VISIOARS (b). **90-91** The Art Archive: University Library Heidelberg / Dagli Orti (A) (c). **91** akg-images: British Library (c). **92** DK Images: Courtesy of Warwick Castle, Warwick (crb). **93** akg-images: British Library (tl). DK Images: By kind permission of the Trustees of the Wallace Collection (clb). **94** DK Images: Courtesy of Warwick Castle, Warwick (bl). **94-95** DK Images: Courtesy of Warwick Castle, Warwick (gorget) (breastplate). **95** DK Images: Courtesy of Warwick Castle, Warwick (tc) (cl) (cr) (tr) (clb) (crb) (bl) (br). **96-97** Werner Forman Archive: Boston Museum of Fine Arts. **98** The Art Archive: Museo di Capodimonte, Naples / Dagli Orti. **99** akg-images: Rabatti - Domingie. **100** The Art Archive: Private Collection / Marc Charmet (r). **101** Tokugawa Reimeikai: (r). **103** The Art Archive: University Library Geneva / Dagli Ort (tc). 106 Bridgeman Art Library: Royal Library, Stockholm, Sweden (tr). **107** DK Images: By kind permission of the Trustees of the Wallace Collection (b); Judith Miller / Wallis and Wallis (crb). **108** akg-images: (bl) (br). **108-109** The Art Archive: Château de Blois / Dagli Orti (c). **109** akg-images: (tr). **114-115** The Art Archive: Basilique Saint Denis, Paris / Dagli Orti. **116** DK Images: By kind permission of the Trustees of the Wallace Collection (l). **117** DK Images: Courtesy of Warwick Castle, Warwick (b). **120** Corbis: Asian Art & Archaeology, Inc (bl). **120-121** DK Images: Board of Trustees of the Royal Armouries (t). **122-123** DK Images: Pitt Rivers Museum, University of Oxford (t); By kind permission of the Trustees of the Wallace Collection (c). **126** Bridgeman Art Library: School of Oriental & African Studies Library, Uni. of London (bl). **126-127** Bridgeman Art Library: Private Collection (c). **127** akg-images: (r). Ancient Art & Architecture Collection: (tl). DK Images: Board of Trustees of the Royal Armouries (fcrb); By kind permission of the Trustees of the Wallace Collection (clb). **128** DK Images: Pitt Rivers Museum, University of Oxford (cr). **132** DK Images: By kind permission of the Trustees of the Wallace Collection (r) (l). **133** DK Images: By kind permission of the Trustees of the Wallace Collection (t) (cb) (b). **136-137 DK** Images: By kind permission of the Trustees of the Wallace Collection. 137 **DK** Images: By kind permission of the Trustees of the Wallace Collection (t). **138-139** The Art Archive: Museo di Capodimonte, Naples / Dagli Orti . **141** DK Images: History Museum, Moscow (cr); By kind permission of the Trustees of the Wallace Collection (r). **142-143** DK Images: By kind permission of the Trustees of the Wallace Collection. **162** DK Images: Courtesy of Ross Simms and the Winchcombe Folk and Police Museum (tl); Courtesy of Warwick Castle, Warwick (br). **163** DK Images: Judith Miller / Wallis and Wallis (br). **164-165** akg-images: Nimatallah. **166** DK Images: By kind permission of the Trustees of the Wallace Collection. **167** DK Images: By kind permission of the Trustees of the Wallace Collection (tr) (cr); Courtesy of Warwick Castle, Warwick (br). **168** DK Images: By kind permission of the Trustees of the Wallace Collection. **169** Corbis: Leonard de Selva (bl). DK Images: By kind permission of the Trustees of the Wallace Collection (tr) (cra) (cr) (crb) (br). **170** DK Images: Pitt Rivers Museum, University of Oxford (tl). **171** DK Images: Pitt Rivers Museum, University of Oxford (br). **172** DK Images: Board of Trustees of the Royal Armouries (l) (cb) (br) (tr). **173** DK Images: Board of Trustees of the Royal Armouries (bc) (tc) (r). **174-175** Corbis: Minnesota Historical Society. **176** Corbis: Bettmann. **177** akg-images. **178** The Art Archive: National Archives Washington DC (tl). **179** The Art Archive: Museo del Risorgimento Brescia / Dagli Orti (tr). Corbis: Hulton-Deutsch Collection (b). **184** DK Images: Courtesy of the Gettysburg National Military Park, PA (c) (r); US Army Military History Institute (l) (br). **185** DK Images: Confederate Memorial Hall, New Orleans (ca) (cra) (bc) (br) (tc) (tr); US Army Military History Institute (cb) (crb). **186-187** DK Images: By kind permission of the Trustees of the Wallace Collection. **194** akg-images: (br). **196** DK Images: Pitt Rivers Museum, University of Oxford (ca). **198** The Art Archive: Biblioteca Nazionale Marciana Venice / Dagli Orti (tl). **200** Mary Evans Picture Library: (bl) (bc). **200-201** Bridgeman Art Library: Stapleton Collection (c). **201** Bridgeman Art Library: Courtesy of the Council, National Army Museum, London (tr). **205** DK Images: The American Museum of Natural History (tl) (br) (bl). **206-207** Corbis: Stapleton Collection. **208** DK Images: The American Museum of Natural History (cla) (r). **209** American Museum Of Natural History: Division of Anthropology (bl). Corbis: Geoffrey Clements (tl). DK Images: The American Museum of Natural History (r). **210** Getty Images: Hulton Archive (tl). **219** DK Images: Courtesy of the Gettysburg National Military Park, PA (bl) (br). **220** Bridgeman Art Library: of the New-York Historical Society, USA (bl). DK Images: Courtesy of the Gettysburg National Military Park, PA (tl). **220-221** Corbis: Medford Historical Society Collection (c). **221** Bridgeman Art Library: Massachusetts Historical Society, Boston, MA (tr). DK Images: Courtesy of the C. Paul Loane Collection (br); Civil War Library and Museum, Philadelphia (cl); Civil War Library and Museum, Philadelphia (cr); Courtesy of the Gettysburg National Military Park, PA (crb); US Army Military History Institute (bl). **225** DK Images: Courtesy of the Gettysburg National Military Park, PA (tr). **228** The Kobal Collection: COLUMBIA (br). **230-231** Corbis: Fine Art Photographic Library. **241** Bridgeman Art Library: Private Collection / Peter Newark American Pictures (br). **242** akg-images: Victoria and Albert Museum (l). **242-243** Bridgeman Art Library: Delaware Art Museum, Wilmington, USA, Howard Pyle Collection (c). **243** The Art Archive: Laurie Platt Winfrey (br). Bridgeman Art Library: Private Collection (bc). **246-247** DK Images: By kind permission of the Trustees of the Wallace Collection. **249** akg-images: (t). **253** Corbis: Bettmann (br). **254-255** The Art Archive. **269** Sunita Gahir: (cl). **270** DK Images: Powell-Cotton Museum, Kent (l) (c). **271** DK Images: Exeter City Museums and Art Gallery, Royal Albert Memorial Museum (tl); Powell-Cotton Museum, Kent (bl). **272** DK Images: Judith Miller/Kevin Conru (c); Judith Miller/Kevin Conru (r); Judith Miller/JYP Tribal Art (l). **273** DK Images: Judith Miller / JYP Tribal Art (l) (clb) (cr) (r). **274-275** Corbis: The Military Picture Library. **276** akg-images. **278** Getty Images: Hulton Archive (tl). **279** Getty Images: Rabih Moghrabi/ AFP (b); Scott Peterson (t). **282** DK Images: Pitt Rivers Museum, University of Oxford (t); Pitt Rivers Museum, University of Oxford (ca); Pitt Rivers Museum, University of Oxford (c); By kind permission of the Trustees of the Wallace Collection (b). **283** Corbis: Bettmann (tr). DK Images: Pitt Rivers Museum, University of Oxford (cr). **284** DK Images: RAF Museum, Hendon (br). **285** DK Images: Imperial War Museum, London (b). **286-287** popperfoto.com. **288** akg-images: Jean-Pierre Verney (br). The Art Archive: Musée des deux Guerres Mondiales, Paris / Dagli Orti (tr). Corbis: Adam Woolfitt (bl). **289** Corbis: Hulton-Deutsch Collection (b). **297** Corbis: Seattle Post-Intelligencer Collection; Museum of History and Industry (bl). **298** The Kobal Collection: COLUMBIA / WARNER (tl). **302** akg-images: (bl). **302-303** Getty Images: Picture Post / Stringer (c). **303** Getty Images: Sergei Guneyev / Time Life Pictures (br); Georgi Zelma (tl). **307** Rex Features: Sipa Press (bc). **316-317** The Art Archive. **319** DK Images: Imperial War Museum, London (t); Courtesy of the Ministry of Defence Pattern Room, Nottingham (ca). **333** Corbis: John Springer Collection (br). **346** Corbis: Leif Skoogfors (bl). **346-347** Getty Images: Greg Mathieson / Mai / Time Life (c). **347** Getty Images: Greg Mathieson / Mai (bc); U.S. Navy (tr). **350** DK Images: Imperial War Museum, London. **351** Corbis: Chris Rainier. DK Images: Courtesy of Andrew L Chernack (crb). **352-353** Corbis: David Mercado/Reuters

All other images © Dorling Kindersley For further information see: www.dkimages.com

Dorling Kindersley would like to thank Philip Abbott at the Royal Armouries for all his hard work and advice; Stuart Ivinson at the Royal Armouries; the Pitt Rivers Museum; David Edge at the Wallace Collection; Simon Forty for additional text; Angus Konstam, Victoria Heyworth-Dunne and Tamsin Calitz for editorial work; Steve Knowlden, Ted Kinsey, and John Thompson for design work; Alex Turner and Sean Dwyer for design support; Myriam Megharbi for picture research support.